PRESENTED TO BRO. JAMES SHIELS
ON WINNING BOTH SINGLE + DOUBLES
AT PUTTING.
ST. ANDREWS HOUSE AYR JUNE 1971
9TH SHOP STEWARDS SUMMER SCHOOL.

J Barrie
Convener

Jim Sillars, M.P.

4.6.71.

THE SCOTTISH CARTER

THE SCOTTISH CARTER

THE HISTORY OF
THE SCOTTISH HORSE AND MOTORMEN'S
ASSOCIATION
1898–1964

by

ANGELA TUCKETT

FOREWORD BY
ALEXANDER H. KITSON, JP
General Secretary

Illustrated

London
GEORGE ALLEN AND UNWIN LTD
RUSKIN HOUSE · MUSEUM STREET

PRINTED IN GREAT BRITAIN
in 11 pt. Plantin type
BY C. TINLING AND CO. LTD.
LIVERPOOL, LONDON AND PRESCOT

FOREWORD

BY ALEXANDER H. KITSON, JP

General Secretary

This is the history of our Union from 1898 until 1964, when the new constitution changed the name to the Scottish Commercial Motormen's Union, and of its forerunners.

The book gives, firstly, a real human picture of the gallant struggle by the old carters to overcome the intolerable conditions and humiliations imposed upon them; of how they learned from bitter experience the need for a skilful and permanent organization and the need to fight for its recognition. We are made to appreciate the miserable treatment meted out by employers in our industry both in the days before the motorman appeared and after.

Decade by decade new and complex problems arose; yet the transport workers always found new ways of solving them finally. Reading their history, transport workers will not only realize the great debt they owe to each member who pioneered the Union, suffering hardship and painful and unexpected setbacks, often dejected but never defeated. They will also draw inspiration from what can be learned from their past in overcoming today's seemingly novel difficulties in changing circumstances.

Union histories all too often contain uninteresting information 'for the record' only, of mere alterations to rules, wage rates and lists of officials, only of fleeting concern and without lasting significance. That has been avoided in this history, which is a balanced narrative, set against the background of an epoch of unprecedented speed of change, in an industry which has been changing out of all recognition. The author's personal knowledge of the trade union movement has helped her to present our history in a way that enables active trade unionists to recognize their own problems and what is of lasting importance in their day-to-day affairs.

In my opinion, Angela Tuckett has put in a tremendous and successful effort to gather all the material, when all too often records have been missing, inadequate or faulty; being trained to sift evidence with legal acumen, she has submitted it to severe scrutiny and checking; and yet she has married it into a form that gives a vivid picture of human struggle, in which any trade unionist will recognize his own life.

Whilst in many instances she shows affection and respect for the pioneers and those who have built the union, this has never clouded any deficiencies, which she weighs where necessary with a due sense of proportion. Because the picture is painted in its true colours, appreciating what is bright and not avoiding what is dark, we are able to identify ourselves with the struggles of our fellow members over nearly seventy years.

I am sure that our members today and tomorrow will be proud to carry on the struggle that was so gallantly borne by their earlier comrades, and to be worthy of their history.

A. H. KITSON

CONTENTS

CONTENTS

CONTENTS

CONTENTS

ILLUSTRATIONS

ILLUSTRATIONS

15

ACKNOWLEDGEMENTS

It would have been impossible to write this history, especially since the records of the first thirty-five years are so scanty where they are not non-existent, without the great help given me by the members themselves. Without the patience and industry of the chief officials and head office staff, and particularly Mr Alex Kitson (General Secretary), Mr James Barrie (Assistant General Secretary) and Mrs Joyce Smith (Cashier) the labour would have been hard toil. I must also acknowledge gratefully the kindness and enthusiasm of past and present officials and members, such as, amongst many others, Mr Adam Anderson, Miss Kitty Brown, Mr John Carabine, Bailie William Cockburn, Messrs Dugald Connell, John Connell, John Cullen, Angus Cummings, Dan Duffy, William Frew, James Gormley, Peter Hamilton, Andrew Inglis, Alexander Irvine, John Kyle, Robert Lowe, John Lowry, George McCready, Peter McGroarty, Robert McIntyre, Norman MacPherson, John McQuade, Robert Morrison, John Murphy, James Revie, John Shand, John Steedman, Robert Stewart, David Strachan, Peter Talbot, Robert Taylor, Bailie Alexander Urquhart, Messrs John Welsh and James White.

January 15, 1967   A.T.

CHAPTER ONE

INTRODUCTION

I. THE ROAD AND THE LOAD

THIS book deals with the Scottish men who help to shift Britain's wealth by road; the changing nature of their work and problems; why they came to hold the views they do; and how they reached their decisions during the years between 1898 and 1964. It does not, of course, attempt to describe the industry,[1] nor to deal with the employers and their problems. But the briefest sketch of events and of the wider trade union movement from time to time is unavoidable to fill in the background. For the lives and fate of the men and women who produce the wealth in Scottish mines, shipyards, and factories are bound up with those of the men who transport it by road, rail, air, and sea. None of this wealth can begin to be realized until the road transport worker has started his engine to drive it through the gates. This great-grandson of the humble, downtrodden, and despised carter and horseman is today a man of power. His position in society is changed: his is a key industry. He does not stand alone; in Scotland there are 21,000 organized road transport drivers who share his outlook and have a common economic interest, and he knows it. It must be hard for him to understand how great is the difference in this respect between himself and his great-grandfather; and his own great-grandson has further yet to go.

There can be few industries where the workers have seen such vastly changed conditions this century as in road transport. In motive power, there has been the change from a one-horse lurry or lorry to immensely powerful diesel lorries and articulated vehicles and trailers 80 foot and more in length; and to load-carriers, heralded by an escorting fleet of police cars and motor-cycle outriders. The loads now carried are of a weight and bulk which would have been inconceivable to those who marvelled when a team of two dozen horses was needed to shift a new boiler in Dundee in the first year of this century. The length of hauls has greatly increased; once they comprised a few miles about town, with vans plodding round the district as far as a rate of five miles an hour in a twelve- or fourteen-hour day would take them. The old joke used to be: 'Why

[1] Transportation of all kinds is properly ranked as a 'service' and is so classified by Government Departments. But it has become the custom for commercial motormen who transport goods by road to refer to their work as 'the road transport industry'; this has been adopted throughout the book.

don't they put a roof over Glasgow to give the carters an indoor job?'
Today, long-haulage lorries run from John o' Groats not merely to the
south, but over the Channel Ferry to Brussels and far beyond. All this
would have been impossible without the development of the motor
vehicle and the internal combustion engine. Today, any further technological change in motor transport must depend upon the development
of the roads: in Scotland that means bringing them from the one-horse
cart and cattle-droving age into that of the mechanically-propelled vehicle.

If the roads on which they operate have changed little, the men have
changed a lot. They have changed from the carter, with his horse-sense
and skill in managing horses, to men with road-sense, skilled at keeping
the great giants of the road rolling, or the fast van running, in all weathers
and over great distances. Whatever the skills, driving is still not an
apprentice trade. However much the motorman may have changed since
the days of the horseman and carter, the outlook of the road transport
worker remains, on the whole, very different from that of the man who
works in factory, dock, or depot, whether craftsman or labourer, within
the view of the overseer and within hail of the intercom. The long-
distance driver is no longer tied to the stables, as the carter or lurryman
was. He has big responsibility and the illusion of independence, a feature
which has its attraction. Like his colleagues on the footplate, he is usually
on lodging-turns, away from home for several days in the week, which
presents special problems of organization and makes active participation
in union affairs difficult for him.

Since the advent of the petrol-driven internal combustion motor vehicle
there has been, of course, an immense expansion in road transport. There
has been a big increase in the number of employers, side by side with
great concentration of ownership into bigger and bigger units. There has
been the struggle for traffic, with varying fortune, between the expanding
private road haulage contractors and the declining private railway companies. There was the nationalization of road transport, never complete
and cut short in its earliest years. There was denationalization, and a new
phase of struggle for traffic by privately-owned road transport employers
against the publicly-owned railways. Transport being ancillary to production and dependent upon it, there is a tendency for the industrialist,
merchant and trader to exert pressure for an efficient system. Yet the
contradictory tendency also makes itself felt; so serious was the collapse
of the railways under private control that some industrialists began to turn
to establish their own private road transport network.

In any planned society the need for an integrated transport system would
be recognized as self-evident. Yet, in Britain, grass is growing on the
unused monopoly road of the publicly-owned railways, whilst motor
traffic is bringing transport of goods near the big centres to a standstill,
killing more and more people each day, and costing over £235,000,000

annually in accidents.[1] It is not surprising that the road transport workers showed themselves to be amongst the most far-sighted in campaigning for an integrated publicly-owned transport system. In this, the Scottish Horse and Motormen's Association has been, and remains, in the lead.

The industry falls into a number of fairly sharply distinguishable stages of development. Looking back from the eve of the twentieth century, when the Scottish Carters' Association was formed, one year after Queen Victoria's diamond jubilee, we note that during the sixty years of her reign the economy had developed immensely. Britain had gained, and was having to defend her position as 'the workshop of the world'. Yet inland transport, other than the railways, which had come into use only during Victoria's reign, was poorly developed. The railways, a technological advance, ousted the canals as bearers of the hugely increased heavy traffic, but left the roads and road traffic in a relatively primitive state. The railways killed the development of road-coaches driven by steam, which had begun to be introduced in the early thirties of the nineteenth century to replace the horse-drawn coaches. Because of the fast expansion and complete dominance of the railways, the decisive improvement of the roads was held back, and they were developed almost exclusively as 'feeders' to the railways, or as links with coastal shipping. There could be no serious competition from the steam wagons and locomotives, shifting heavier freight by road, with both legal and physical restrictions on their speed and weight of load. Thus it is that, up to the opening of the twentieth century, the typical picture is of carters short-hauling, mostly from the point of production to railhead or docks, the enterprise being carried on by local contractors on a city-wide scale, with the steam wagon and locomotive far more important on the road than the later petrol-driven internal combustion engine. Occasionally there were specialists reaching somewhat further. In Scotland, the railway companies owned their own lurries and horses. In addition there were the three railway contracting haulage firms of very long-standing: Wordie's, Mutter Howey's and Cowan's.

From 1901 to 1914 road transport follows the developments of industry as a whole, beginning with the dislocation arising from the demands of the Boer War (1899–1902) and the acute post-war depression in the years 1902 and 1903 and in 1908. The fundamental technological changes which

[1] *Basic Road Statistics, 1964,* published by the British Road Federation, quotes the estimate prepared by the Royal Society for the Prevention of Accidents of the cost of road accidents to the community during the fifties and sixties.

	1953	1958	1959	1960	1961	1962	1963
Compensation in £ million for personal injuries (loss of earnings, hospital treatment)	128	156	180	189	190	187	195
Damage to and repair of property	13	17	19	19	19	19	19
Administrative costs	14	14	20	21	21	21	22
	155	190	219	229	230	227	236

were later to revolutionize transport had mostly been opened up in the reign of Edward VII, from January 1901 to his death in the summer of 1910, at the time when Britain's world economic pre-eminence was beginning to disappear and the challenge from Germany, in particular, was moving towards the crisis proportions which culminated in the First World War of 1914–18. But, during the decade leading up to the war, whilst the dominance of the horse-drawn vehicle was being undermined by the motor vehicle in the transport of passengers, it was not decisively broken in goods traffic, much of which remained profitably horse-drawn for several decades. Examples of this were coal-carts, brewers' drays, and light delivery vans, such as bread-vans and milk-carts. These last were still in use in the sixties in Edinburgh, for example, where the milk-cart was still found to be more economic than the electrically-driven milkfloat.[1] The total number of goods vehicles in use throughout the whole of Great Britain which were petrol-driven during this decade is shown below:[2]

Year	Goods vehicles in use in Great Britain
1904	4,000
1905	9,000
1906	12,000
1907	14,000
1908	18,000
1909	22,000
1910	30,000
1911	40,000
1912	52,600
1913	63,600

But, although at first sight the speed of advance is notable and was not checked during years of trade depression, such as 1908, the numbers are insignificant when compared with the post-war years:

1923	173,363
1933	387,487
1943	449,400
1953	995,562
1963	1,529,100

The 1914–18 war had accelerated the big change.

[1] During the 1939–45 war the petrol shortage brought the electric float to the fore for the pooled milk deliveries—an odd reversion to the early 'electric carriage'. What a different Britain we should see today if the electrically-driven carriage had been universally developed instead of the oil-fuelled internal combustion engine. One result would have been an immense development of Britain's natural resources of hydro-electric power and coal, instead of the exploitation of oil, and of the people in whose lands it was discovered, by the biggest private trusts in the history of the world.

[2] Basic Road Statistics, 1964.

The needs of modern warfare called for huge numbers of motor vehicles. After the war many thousands of these surplus vehicles were sold off by the Government, whilst the products of the greatly expanded new motor industry poured on to the roads. Horse-drawn traffic stood still, in more senses than one; but the post-war glut of petrol-driven vehicles grew to such an extent that the traffic on the roads—quite undeveloped outside the main cities, some of them only recently macadamized[1]— became so much in need of regulation that the government of the day was forced finally to introduce some degree of public control. On August 4, 1928, the Government appointed a Royal Commission on Transport, which was the source of the complex road traffic legislation throughout the thirties. The Road Traffic Act of 1930 was the first legislation regulating road transport on any serious scale since the Motor Car Act of 1903. Public regulation was further developed under the Road and Rail Traffic Act, 1933, and finally by the Road Haulage Wages Act, 1938. These set the pattern for the new industry and the national negotiating machinery, with its statutory enforcement of wage awards upon the employers.

This decade, therefore, was an extremely important one for road transport organizations and their members. In the fast-developing new road transport industry the trend towards national negotiation came much later than in other industries. It took long and painful effort under the 1938 Act to erect the national negotiation machinery, the main architect of which was Ernest Bevin, then General Secretary of the powerful Transport and General Workers Union. Before this was fully complete, the Second World War began, bringing its own problems, with far-reaching political, social, and economic consequences, which transformed the whole outlook for transport. Once again, in the interests of efficiency and war economy, transport had to be controlled by the state. This laid the basis at last for the nationalization of the four railway companies and for the partial nationalization of road transport, spread over the years 1946 to 1949, under the first post-war Labour Government. In road transport, the measures, which coincided with a policy of wage restraint, were scarcely completed under the second short-lived Labour administration. Long before they had cleared their first trial run, the Conservative Government, elected in 1951, began to denationalize road transport. A new stage of competition for traffic opened between the road haulage contractors and the railways. For the next decade and a half each year brought greater chaos. The need for an integrated, publicly-owned service of rail, air, docks, and road transport of passengers and goods became ever more plain to the

[1] Glasgow was perhaps an exception, partly owing to the problems raised by the tramways which came under municipal ownership very early.

In March 1903, the Executive of the Scottish Carters' Association instructed their General Secretary to approach the Glasgow Town Council 'in support of the sett makers who were against the macadamizing of the streets'. (*Executive Minutes Book* March 3, 1903)

Association. Yet, during these years, the trend was in the opposite direction. At the same time, some of the problems and shortcomings of national machinery, and the difficult question of the impact upon it of governmental economic policies in a managed economy came to the fore.

That, very briefly indeed, is the broad picture of road transport and its load from the beginning of this century.

2. THE HORSEMAN AND THE MOTORMAN

At different stages different features had to be shown by an organization making good a claim to take care of the road transport workers' interests, present and future. The name of the Association changed with its membership. When it was founded in October 29, 1898, it was called the Scottish Carters' Association. By August 16, 1908, this was no longer sufficient, as it appeared to exclude the drivers of the emerging motor vehicles and the name was changed to the Scottish Horse & Motormen's Association. By the fifties, some were arguing that to leave the 'Horse' in the title at all was misleading; but there it remained until July 22, 1964. At that point, under a new constitution, the name was changed to the Scottish Commercial Motormen's Union. In this title, emphasis was laid on the fact that the union specialized in organizing the drivers of goods vehicles, not of passenger traffic, and a regretful farewell was paid to the old carter and horseman.

Upon occasion, big agglomerations and federations of transport workers of different types arose—transport and general, indeed. At times this was regarded as favouring the organization of the transport worker; but there also arose small specialist unions, which were seen, at different stages, to be a necessary advance. In Scotland, local conditions and history brought the road transport worker very close to the railway worker, later organized in the National Union of Railwaymen. At the same time he was close to the docker, the development of whose organization in Scotland was not identical with that of the dock workers of England. As the road haulage industry finally developed, it took with it features from the past which were peculiar to Scotland, or had survived from the old carting days in Scotland only.

Sporadic attempts by the carters to organize themselves go right back to the early days of the last century, when many carters and horsemen[1] were farm servants on half-yearly hiring agreements, usually employed by small employers and remote from other carters. It was far easier to wait for the next hiring-fair and find a new master than to seek protection by

---

[1] The distinction between the horseman and the carter in rural areas was that, when horses were used for work other than draught, the man in charge was called a horseman. A ploughman using a horse-drawn plough would be a horseman: a wagoner would be a carter. On farms, too small to encourage much division of labour, they might well be interchangeable and the distinction cease to have any importance.

organization. But when the farm servants as a whole began to make gains, it had an important bearing on the development of the carters, no less than the degree to which they were influenced by contact with the urban workers. In the last quarter of the nineteenth century and in the early years of the twentieth century most of the carters in Scotland were former farmworkers or crofters, forced by hard times to leave the land. Sometimes the new recruits to carting were unemployed or sick colliers from the mining villages, who migrated to towns like Aberdeen and Dundee, where the granite works, the jute mills, and other factories were busy. In the big cities the cab-drivers were a concentrated and cohesive group: this was perhaps why the earliest strand of organization as a bona fide trade union was the Edinburgh and Leith Cab-Drivers' Association, formed in 1885 and amalgamated with the Association in 1912. When the great movement amongst the general workers, labourers and unskilled, arose in the late eighties and early nineties, resulting in the formation of so many general unions, the carters' organizations again revived, but only on a local scale. With this 'New Unionism', there were big moves amongst town council employees, gas workers and, above all, the dockers, led by Ben Tillett and Tom Mann from London, affecting the docks in every part of Britain.

It is curious that Mr George Barnes, formerly Secretary of the Amalgamated Society of Engineers, who joined Lloyd George's Coalition administration in 1916–20, in his foreword to Hugh Lyon's book of memoirs,[1] showed himself to be under the impression that the carters, alone of the unskilled, stood aside from the surging movement of the 'New Unionism'. He does less than justice to the carter, and especially to the Scottish carter. For, in the key year of 1889, the Glasgow Carters' Society, which had been in existence for a number of years, was sufficiently strong to lead a strike of 3,000; they and their womenfolk marched demonstrating through the city. There was no apathy or lack of fervour and fight amongst

[1] In the new unionism of the 90s, other classes of labour were swept into the movement, but for the carters it seemed to have no message and no hope. There was one exception, I remember, in the London Carmen's Union, which made gallant efforts to establish itself, in spite of the prevailing apathy, but whether it survived and survives now, I am unable to say.

'In Scotland there was no sign. At all events, there was no sign observable to the naked eye. For the purposes of this foreword I have been looking up the records; I have been through the files of the *Labour Press* of 1890, edited by Shaw Maxwell, to the columns of the *Trade Unionist*, which, under the direction of Fred Maddison, had a brief career in 1899. But neither in the records of the revolutionary fervour of the earlier years, nor of those in the less strenuous latter days, have the carters a place.' (*The History of the Scottish Horse and Motormen's Association, 1898–1919* by Hugh Lyon, General Secretary. With an introduction by the Right Hon. George N. Barnes, MP, Glasgow Civic Press, 1919, 334 pp.)

He should have consulted the Glasgow United Trades Council *Minutes*, *Commonweal*, *Justice*, or the British Trades Union Congress *Annual Report* of 1892, which describes the carters and the horsemen leading the demonstration of welcome in Glasgow that year.

the Scottish carters; their problem was to find the way to maintain a permanent organization.

In these years the railwaymen, too, had been on the move against incredibly long hours, and, in the late nineties, attacks on their right to organize on the London and North-Western Railway had spread 'all along the line'; and a big 'all-grades' movement developed, which had much in common with the 'New Unionism' of the general workers. When the railwaymen's militancy carried them beyond the protection which a friendly-society type of union was capable of affording, and victimization followed, they found employment elsewhere and sought a spirited organization to defend their interests. Thus it was that, when a new organization of carters arose under the influence of the railwaymen's struggle and with the encouragement of Glasgow and Edinburgh Trades Councils, many former active railway trade unionists were amongst them. They elected as their secretary John Sampson, himself formerly a signalman; and several of the first branch secretaries were also railwaymen. Established on October 29, 1898, under its first name of the Scottish Carters' Association, it was registered on December 2, 1898.

How was it that this body survived, established itself, and became consolidated, when many others with more promising beginnings failed to maintain their independence? Little is known from its own records of its struggles during the first half-dozen years; only the admirably kept minute book survives of the Plantation Branch in Glasgow, the Secretary of which was another former signalman, Willie Lowden. Much was owed to these former railwaymen, experienced trade unionists, meticulous in attention to detail, not least to the care of funds, at a time when many attempts at organization had collapsed and become discredited through carelessness or inexperience in handling dues. These men succeeded in helping the youthful Association through its birth pangs and the crises that arose during the Boer War.

Although many of the problems of the industry were the same throughout Britain, there were differences in Scotland: and only in Scotland was a union established which survived and finally became consolidated to serve the special interests of commercial road transport workers, exclusively and continuously for over sixty-five years. The story of the Association shows unique features; it provides valuable lessons, both by example and by awful warning, of importance for trade unionists in any industry. In this new industry, where at some stages there were tempestuous changes, leaders were needed who were capable of sensing the need for change and quickly adapting to it. Different qualities were needed at different stages. The Association found the leaders, but sometimes almost too late. Men whose abilities were valuable in dealing with the problems of one period proved to be at a loss when they came suddenly to the next stage. Sometimes the delay in adapting to the needs of the time was dangerously long.

In 1898, men like the first General Secretary, John Sampson, and Willie Lowden, both men with experience in the railways and of the 'New Unionism', saw the need to organize the carters on an all-Scotland basis, by linking them up beyond the confines of an organization covering only a single town, and at the same time to defend wider interests than a friendly society could do.

But by 1902 the slump following the Boer War had brought new and great difficulties. That year John Sampson was ejected and replaced as General Secretary by a young iron-moulder from Falkirk, Hugh Lyon. The next ten years are a story of slow recruitment on a narrower basis and the patient organization of the carters to fight for the crucial needs of the day: for the acceptance of a standard working-day and the limitation of the shocking hours, for trade union recognition, for the right to payment for overtime, for the abolition of unpaid Sunday stable duties, and for improvement of wages, which had sunk below the level of 1889. In the next decade, ending with the outbreak of the First World War, the second General Secretary displayed those qualities which were needed to give the carters confidence to carry through a long struggle to wrest from local employers these demands which could lay the basis for substantial advance.

Hugh Lyon's pre-occupation with the funds led him to introduce methods of administration, such as the house-to-house collection of dues instead of stable collection, which were vital in ensuring the Association's survival at that stage. Whilst it must be noted that in doing so he abolished the first constitution, which was a model one and remarkably advanced for those days, and replaced it with one which greatly restricted the democratic powers of the branches, the Association nevertheless achieved substantial progress: that was the test. Under his leadership the carters gained confidence and status, and gradually moved forward, caught up in the great wave of 1910–12, when trade unionism was leaping ahead in every industry. At the end of a period of strikes and intense struggle amongst the workers by whom carters were most influenced—miners, dockers, and railwaymen—they themselves launched a big strike movement, especially in Glasgow and Leith, under the brilliant leadership of Hugh Lyon. Formidable campaigns planned for the autumn of 1914 were interrupted by the First World War, which left them in 1918 in no mood to give up without a struggle the shorter hours and increased wages which they had gained when Lyon had seen himself in a strong bargaining position in the conditions of war-time manpower shortages.

For nearly two decades the Association passed through an intensely difficult time of great changes. In this period, Hugh Lyon's leadership fell away, and so did the Association over which he had ruled unchallenged for a decade and a half, as a dominating but yet successful leader. Economic crises and mass unemployment coincided with the vast changes and expansion of the road transport industry; but the corresponding change in methods, outlook and leadership were not forthcoming. Motor vehicles began to pour on to the roads; overwhelmingly they dominated the industry. The main strength of the Association had been amongst the carters; organization of the motormen was delayed and neglected until mass unemployment doubled the difficulties. Wages were cut and hours lengthened.

At a time when the numbers of the unorganized and the unemployed were increasing every day, Lyon would not spend any money on organization. Instead, he welcomed the sliding-scale agreements on which he met the employers periodically to register the level to which wages should automatically rise or fall according to the prevailing cost-of-living index. It seemed to him to resemble the collective bargaining he had so long been seeking. He husbanded resources by insisting upon increasing the dues, not to provide the sinews of war to strengthen the organization, but to build it up in the manner of friendly benefit societies. The result was to swell the bank account whilst the membership sank to half its size. Lyon always insisted that the horse—and the financial strength of the union— would last his time.

Hugh Lyon followed a somewhat uncertain course in his relations with the broader labour movement. At times he brought the Association close to the policies of the Scottish Trades Union Congress, of which he was President in 1919; he was on the strike committee during the 1919 Clydeside Hours' Strike. During the General Strike of 1926, his Assistant General Secretary, Peter Webster, was President of the STUC and, therefore, the chairman of the strike committee for Scotland. But, on both these occasions, there were events which led to charges of blacklegging being brought against the Association. These left bitter feelings amongst Scottish Trade Unionists, which lasted many years, and which it often took only some trivial incident to revive. Indeed, it was not until the sixties that these feelings, based to some extent on misunderstanding, were eliminated once and for all, when the fifth General Secretary, Alexander Kitson, laid it down that no member should in any circumstances take any action which might impede a dispute in which members of another union were engaged. In this period of decline, members complained that Lyon's main preoccupation was to keep the union funds intact, whether from demands for strike pay or by commitment through affiliation, federation, or amalgamation to sympathetic action in defence of others. Militancy, expansion, moves towards a more democratic constitution and more vigorous activity by branch members, amalgamation, 'Reds'—all these became anathema to him in his later years. He had led the carters effectively and well in the early days, where work involved day-to-day confrontation with local employers. But, when the favourable conditions ended after the 1914–18 war and the motor vehicle opened up intense development of road transport and long distance haulage, he was at a loss. He left his Assistant General Secretary, Peter Webster, to master the complexities of the road traffic legislation, and the new problems which members encountered daily on the road. Above all, he would not undertake a drive to organize the motormen, and no other official was left free to handle it. Finally this was the basis for his ejection from office in 1936 after thirty-four years. For his first seventeen years he had been dealing with problems he understood and he played a creative part. Weaknesses in democratic practices in the Association made the break, when it came, painful and almost too late, after a long period of dissension and division in the Association.

He was replaced by Robert Taylor, who displayed marked gifts for administration. In the late thirties, when the national negotiating machinery was at last becoming a reality, much of the third General Secretary's efforts were concentrated upon working out the final terms in association with Ernest Bevin. Whilst that was in hand, he had with him John Brannigan, who was brought in as an organizer after Lyon's ejection had been followed by the dismissal of Peter Webster. Brannigan could provide the much needed skill as field organizer, so necessary at that time to support the techniques of more modern administration. When, in 1944, Robert Taylor left the Association, after seven years in office, to become Director and later President of the Scottish Co-operative Wholesale Society, he was succeeded by John Brannigan. The fourth General Secretary remained in office until his death in 1959, when conditions had changed greatly.

The Second World War broke up the familiar pattern and introduced yet another stage; the industry had indeed become unrecognizable from what it was in the early days of the Association. Now the union was part and parcel of the new set-up in road transport, with all the complex consequences of national negotiating machinery now to be tested in peace conditions. Once again a period of great change had set in and the decade, marked by nationalization in transport, opened up new opportunities and brought quite new problems. When Alexander Kitson was elected to office in July 1959 as fifth General Secretary, the future of national negotiation had been placed at issue by governmental policy on the regulation of incomes; the future of the organization of the industry itself, integrated or disintegrated, publicly owned or not, remained an open question; the Association needed to increase its strength, an essential need being for modern methods of organization allowing for close relationships and co-operation between leadership and membership. It was some years before the Association could produce from its own ranks a man who had spent his whole life in the industry as a driver of all types of vehicles; a man who must unite dynamic leadership and new initiative with constant consultation of the members, to meet the complex problems which the industry would have to face in the second half of the twentieth century.

Such is the picture presented by the briefest general survey of the Association during the span of a working-man's life—sixty-five years. These 'seven ages of man' we will now examine in detail. First we return to the years of infancy.

CHAPTER TWO

FORERUNNERS AND FOUNDERS

I. FIRST ATTEMPTS AT ORGANIZATION

IT is known that, as long ago as the first decade of the nineteenth century, Scottish carters achieved some form of organization; but it was not until the end of the century that they succeeded in setting up one permanent union throughout Scotland. That was at last established when the Scottish Horse & Motormen's Association, then called the Scottish Carters Association, was founded on October 29, 1898, by their first General Secretary, John Sampson and other founding members in Glasgow and Edinburgh, so many of whom had been active in other unions among railwaymen or horsemen, throughout the great wave of 'New Unionism' during the early nineties.

In the nineteenth century, organization of carters was either short-lived or undertaken by local bodies which could not for long extend their influence beyond the area in which they arose, and so had only a precarious existence. They were not always organized solely as carters. Sometimes they were recruited as farm servants, general labourers, railwaymen or tramway servants. Hard times and recurrent bouts of unemployment, or 'general distress' as the records of the Glasgow or Edinburgh Trades Councils often describe it in the second half of the nineteenth century, sent carters on the tramp throughout Scotland. As they moved on from croft, bothy, and mining village to the ports and great industrial centres, it was exceptionally difficult for carters to set up any permanent organization of their own, until such time as road transport developed into a separate industry. Yet, as they shifted, they were continually witnessing or sharing in the struggles of workers in a wide range of industries. Every carter must have seen organisations break down, with leaders victimized or funds vanished. As they learned the need for organization they could, at the same time, see the difficulties. The history of their attempts to build their own organization bears all the marks of these early experiences and influences, both for good and for ill. To understand to the full both the problems and the great achievement of those who established the Association, it is necessary to know something of the carters' conditions and of the forerunners of the founders who set them in the way of defending themselves. For the struggle to found the Association did not begin

29

with the landmark of its registration late in 1898; it was an arduous struggle, for well over a decade, by stubborn and courageous men whose very names rarely survive, except in the records of the proceedings of other bodies.

Generations before the cynic could say that any fool can drive a car and most fools do, men could come easily to carting from most other occupations. When crofters or farm servants were forced to leave the land and migrate to the towns, their skills were useless save one—their skill with horses. Miners who were unemployed or forced to work above ground through sickness could handle ponies. Men might be employed as carters by the railway companies, or by one of the three big Scottish firms of railway cartage contractors, Cowan's, Wordie's or Mutter Howey's. Apart from railway and docks work, there were general contracting firms and the cleansing departments of the municipalities. The co-operative societies, too, began to build up large transport departments. In Dundee, the busy jute mills provided plenty of heavy transport work for men who could drive horses; so did the stone industry in Aberdeen; while in many centres throughout Scotland the coal trade, the breweries and the fishing industry early maintained big stables.

Passenger transport developed fast, providing not only employment driving the cabs and hackney carriage or driving for general hiring, but also, from the seventies, working the horse-drawn omnibuses and tramways in the big cities. By the early eighties, the great private monopoly on the West coast, the Glasgow Tramway and Omnibus Company, known everywhere simply as 'The Company', owned some 2,000 horses, 233 tramcars, and twenty-four omnibuses. From the first, however, workers in passenger transport tended to be separately organized, although their fortunes were often closely linked with carters and lorrymen; and there are splendid examples of the support they rendered each other.

Even before the trade unions there were the friendly societies, the carters' amongst them.[1] In Chartist times a Labourers' Society was formed (1852) in Glasgow, with thousands of members; the body which, many years later, became known as the Glasgow Cab and Motormen's Friendly Society was established in 1853. It was a time of intense unemployment. Carters became organized as the United Carters and Storemen. When they had work, their wages were 16s, a week; they claimed an advance of 2s, and gave eight months' notice to strike. One of its leaders was Andrew Cumming, who became the first secretary of the Glasgow United Trades Council when it was formed in 1858, replacing an older 'united trades committee'. Under Andrew Cumming's leadership the trades council's policy at that time was that the government should promote 'a system of emigration, whereby the condition of the unemployed

---

[1] In Greenock articles and regulations, still extant, of a Society of Carmen or Carters were revised in the year 1813.

operatives in this country would be improved'; and a resolution in those terms was passed at a public meeting in September 1858, in the City Hall, which 'was crowded in every part by an audience composed almost entirely of working-men'.[1] There were other policies with regard to the unemployed. Six months earlier the first soirée[2] of carters ever held in Scotland had taken place in the same hall, with the Lord Provost present, at which the representative of Wordie & Co. had spoken on behalf of the master carters. It was thought that the gathering would 'have the effect of bringing the carters nearer to those on the platform'. The United Carters and Storemen's Union took over the soirées; but, as a separate organization of carters, was short-lived.

Yet, nearly twenty years later, in the seventies, the carters were again caught up in a great wave of trade unionism. After the railways had expanded, the railway carters were organized to some extent by the Amalgamated Society of Railway Servants. In the smaller towns and the countryside, they joined in with the agricultural workers. In Aberdeen, the Farm Servants Union of that day organized the carters; and although organization fell away, it revived in the last decade of the century, and twenty-five years later the Aberdonian carters were still closely linked with the agricultural workers. They shared delegates to the Aberdeen Trades Council and sent representatives to the second Scottish Trades Union Congress in 1898. With the growth of the railways in Glasgow, Edinburgh, and Dundee, the railway carters were working from fourteen to sixteen hours a day, whilst the average carter's working-week was eighty-four hours, for a wage of 24s. Following a prolonged crisis at the end of the seventies, the great upward turn of the next decade began, and separate organizations of carters, and cab-drivers, and horsemen appeared in the larger towns. Not all were registered as trade unions; but the first road transport workers' organization to become so was the Edinburgh and Leith Cab-Drivers Association. It was formed on April 21, 1885, and was registered on January 2, 1886, with headquarters at Buchanan's Hotel, 114 High Street, Edinburgh. It maintained its independent existence for twenty-seven years until it amalgamated with the Association in 1912.

This was the first of the many strands which went to make up the Association. The first Secretary and Treasurer was Francis Carruthers. He was replaced a year later by James Brown, who remained at its head for twenty-three crucial years, and was succeeded in 1909 by J. S. Greig, who became an official of the Association on amalgamation. The cab-drivers affiliated to the Edinburgh United Trades Council. These Scottish cab-drivers were thus firmly organized nine years before the London cab-drivers appear as a registered trade union, and three years before the London carmen. By 1886, the Amalgamated Carters' Society, whose

[1] *Glasgow Herald*, September 17, 1858.
[2] See Appendix A.

meeting place was 'The Hall', 17 Brunswick Street, were sending a delegate to the Glasgow United Trades Council. Carters were also organized in Greenock and in country towns. Early in the eighties there had been bitter resistance to clearances in Scotland, and the military were called out to force the crofters to go quietly. This led to a Royal Commission on crofting tenures in 1883, and to legislation in 1886, as well as to the development of the Scottish Land and Labour League. Yet another generation of Scottish crofters was being driven off the land to seek work in the growing towns. In Aberdeen in 1886, the newly-formed branch of the Scottish Farm Servants Union began enrolling carters and labourers: it is often referred to in the Aberdeen Trades Council records as the Scottish Farm Servants', Carters' and General Labourers' Union.

At the age of eighty-eight, a Dundee man,[1] formerly an official of the Association, gave a vivid picture of how a family would come into carting during the eighties:

'Mine was a typical country family, which came into Dundee to get work in the jute mills. Like many agricultural labourers and crofters driven by economic necessity off the land, the only adaptable skills of my father and brothers were with horses. So they became town carters. When my Dad went out carting, I was about 10 or 12; that would be about 1887 or 1889. He went out at 5 a.m. and I never saw him back till 8 at night. My brother Bill was 'on the beef'; he was a keen union lad.

'The carters were very close to the dockers and railway workers in Dundee, because they would always be driving loads to one or other, even if they weren't employed by one of the three companies of railway cartage contractors.

'Jute lurries with loads of two hundred-weight bales had two horses; later a motor truck could take four times as much. From Cox's jute mill two-horse and one-horse lurries went to the docks; the journey was to fill up with jute, and it was a mile and a half trip. When they took a big boiler out of Dundee it meant two dozen horses—impressive sight.'

Bob Stewart remarked on the effect on the carters in Dundee when there was ferment amongst dockers and railwaymen. As a boy he used to go to his brothers' stables:

'I liked polishing the harness for them. Amongst my early recollections were the decorated horse parade shows, in aid of the hospital or Life

[1] Bob Stewart was never himself a carter. He became full-time collector in Dundee before the First World War, replacing Harry Erskine. He was on the Dundee Trades Council, and from a very young man was a noted Socialist propagandist, both in the British Socialist Party and later, on its foundation in 1920, in the Communist Party. When he went to gaol in 1915 as a war resister, his wife took on his collector's round. Stewart said, in 1965: 'I paid up my card till I was seventy, to Bob Davison in Dundee; that is, until 1947.'

Boats. The first holiday I ever had was when I went to Leith with brother Bill, who was a grooming expert. I helped him; and he took first prize.'

In 1886 there had been severe unemployment all over the British Isles. In London there had been demonstrations of unemployed with processions through the district of the Pall Mall clubs. William Morris, writing to his friend and fellow member of the Socialist League, Dr John Glasse of Edinburgh, on February 10, 1886, describes the reaction of 'the upper classes':

'At any rate it is a glimpse for them of the bedrock of our present society, and I hope they like it. Yesterday they were gibbering with terror in spite of the sham calm heroics of the newspapers.'[1]

Throughout that decade and well into the next, William Morris was one of the many Socialist propagandists to visit the main Scottish cities. They included Eleanor Marx-Aveling, H. M. Hyndman, Cunninghame Graham, Bruce Glasier, Enid Stacy,[2] H. H. Campion, Tom Mann, and many others. These leaders of the many Socialist societies were closely connected with the fast developing 'New Unionism'. In Scotland many leading trade unionists were members of socialist societies, like George Carson, who was later secretary of the Glasgow Trades Council, and George Duncan, of the Scottish Ploughmen's and Labourers' Union in Aberdeen.

By the spring of 1889, the 'New Unionism' was taking hold in Scotland, not least amongst transport workers. 'The progress made by the Tramway Employees Society and the Edinburgh and Leith branches of the Horsemen encourage the Council in their work.'[3] Further north, late in 1888 the National Scottish Horsemen's Union was formed by George Farquhar in Dundee to demand a ten-hour day.

'A meeting of those interested was held and over 100 lorrymen and carters joined the Society. Mr Farquhar afterwards visited Greenock, Glasgow, Edinburgh, Leith, Coatbridge, and other commercial centres, with the result that the membership now amounts to 1400.'[4]

[1] *Unpublished Letters of William Morris:* Introduced by R. Page Arnot. Labour Monthly Pamphlet Series, 1951: No. 6. 16 pp.

[2] Enid Stacy (1868–1903), former Fabian, joined the I.L.P. when it was founded, and became the first lecturer on socialism under the Hutchinson Trust, spending most of her time in North Britain. Even at the height of Jingoism in the Boer War, she could always command attention at open air meetings by her dignity, sincerity and ability. Of socialist principles there was 'probably no clearer or more convincing exponent', said Bruce Glasier at her funeral; by 'her admirable grasp of political problems she did a great deal to further the advent of women into politics.' George Bernard Shaw wrote of her to her niece, Joan Tuckett, fifty years later: 'She was an extraordinarily vital and attractive woman.' William Gallacher said that with her deep melodious voice, she was one of the finest speakers he knew. Her father was a painter, Henry Stacy, whose Bristol studio was a centre for Socialists. Every gathering ended with music, folk singing, and dancing by her two sisters, the younger of whom was the author's mother.

[3] Edinburgh United Trades Council, *Annual Report*, 1889.

[4] Reprinted from the *Dundee Advertiser*. John Leng & Co. describing the Trades Union Congress Meeting in Dundee, September 1889.

The Union had a badge and a benefits club for sickness, funerals, and victimization; it was represented on the Glasgow, Dundee and Edinburgh Trades Councils; and, in 1890, it affiliated on a membership of 4,000 and sent delegates to the British Trades Union Congress. It grew greatly in numbers during the great Glasgow carters' strike of 1889.

2. THE GREAT CARTERS' STRIKE OF 1889

The storm broke in August 1889. By early summer there was already much unrest in passenger transport, particularly on the West coast, which took up much of the time of the Glasgow United Trades Council. Chisholm Robertson, the miners' leader, brought into the Council in May details of the shocking conditions imposed on the tramway servants by 'The Company'. They were working sixteen or seventeen hours a day for 20s a week; stablemen, strappers, and others received only 15s to 18s. When they held a meeting of protest, their whole twenty-one-man committee was dismissed. The Trades Council passed a resolution of protest in June 1889 and also demanded municipal ownership. From that time on, it became an important campaign for the Glasgow Trades Council—and, indeed, for the whole Scottish trade union and labour movement. Not only did it give great impetus for 'the trades' to assist in organizing the labourers, the semi-skilled and unskilled; it also provided a lever for building organization within both the public and private stables; it stimulated the campaign for a 'Fair Wages Clause' in sub-contracts from municipalities. All this had a far-reaching influence on local politics, and also strongly influenced the later development of the Association. The Glasgow United Trades Council planned a mass demonstration in support of the tramwaymen and for public ownership of passenger transport. But, meanwhile, the carters took the initiative, which led to the great Scottish carters' strike of that year.

In June 1889, the secretary of the Amalgamated Carters' Society sent to the masters a demand for 2s to increase wages to 26s, shorter hours and payment for overtime after 6 p.m. The Glasgow Cartage Contractors Association refused to recognize the union, or to meet any representatives; employers who received delegates from their own stables mostly replied that the state of trade 'did not warrant' meeting the claims. Some employers, however, paid an advance.

On Sunday, August 4th, a mass meeting of carters and railway lurrymen at the Albion Halls decided on strike action. Some 5,000 carters were organized in Glasgow; 2,000 were already receiving the advance, but the remaining 3,000 went on strike the following day. The strike lasted over a week. There were daily mass meetings of 2,000 and more, sometimes twice a day, mass picketing, parades and marches. A striking feature was that the strike was run as a united effort by the Horsemen's Union and the Carters'

Society, with the support of the Glasgow Trades Council and encouragement from Edinburgh and Leith, Ayr, Dundee, Greenock, Kilmarnock, Paisley, and Aberdeen. The chief leaders of the strike were John Campbell, president of the Amalgamated Carters' Society, and Robert Stevenson, secretary of the National Scottish Horsemen's Union. In Greenock pickets were out and no carter left town. Railway contractors' men were all on strike; and, when men were brought from Aberdeen and Edinburgh, the railway pickets sent them back. Bills were posted in Kilmarnock to prevent carters being brought from that town. The recently organized dock labourers stopped goods from being shifted.

Each day that week the Press described huge meetings of 2,000 and more held in the Albion Halls and the National Halls, or at Infirmary Square, at Nelson's Monument, at Townhead, sometimes 'enlivened by singing a number of songs'. Stevenson called for a mass picket and announced 'pecuniary support' promised from the Edinburgh and Leith Horsemen: 'They had £6,000 at their back', he remarked. A subsidiary strike swelled the numbers when Cleansing Department carters, who were not at that time organized, refused to work to the premises of a contractor whose men were on strike; and six were dismissed by Mr John Young of the Cleansing Department, who was later to be the first manager of the Glasgow tramways when the Corporation finally took them over from 'The Company'. When an appeal for help came before the Glasgow Trades Council, the miners' representative, Chisholm Robertson, said:

'He felt sure that if working men would pay attention to their minimum duties, they would not have the police sent to protect scabs and that even John Young would pause before paying off men for the reason assigned.'[1]

The same *Minutes* record support for the main strike: 'Mr John Campbell, President of the Carters Society, appeared and asked a deputation to be sent at once to a meeting in the National Halls.' The deputation, including typographical and millmen officials at once left the trades council to address a mass meeting of strikers. Next morning, the strikers 'assembled at the headquarters of The Carters' Society in Brunswick Street and marched in procession carrying a number of banners to Infirmary Square where a mass meeting was held.'[2]

Commonweal, the organ of the Socialist League, edited by William Morris, carried lively eyewitness accounts of the strike and the demonstrations on August 10th and 24th: 'While a meeting was being held on the Infirmary Square, the drivers of a number of lorries down the High Street were hooted, and in one or two cases attempts were made to loosen the harness.' *Commonweal* commented: 'It is sixteen years since

[1] Glasgow United Trades Council *Minutes*, August 7, 1889.
[2] *Glasgow Herald*, August 8, 1889.

the carters were last out on strike, and since then they have been organizing themselves, i.e. paying salaries to officials, etc.'

Another march along the Clyde to the Green was headed by the Blind Asylum Band. The strike began to weaken, some of the railwaymen began to go back to work, as new men were imported from a considerable distance. But the contractors' men stood firm, and on Saturday, August 10th, marched in procession, headed by a brass band, along the Broomielaw. There were clashes; a marcher was arrested when he ran out of the ranks to strike a Caledonian Railway carter who was standing by his lorry. He was lodged in the steamboat shed; but the strikers overpowered the police and rescued him, and, as the *Glasgow Herald* put it, 'then moved quietly off'.

Although the railway carters were defeated, some general contractors granted the men's demands, including payment for overtime. Twenty years later, as we shall see, Scottish carters would have been glad indeed to win such recognition to the right to overtime payment; it was a battle which the Association had to win again. By Tuesday, August 13, 1889, the main body of the strikers had returned to work.

The next day, August 14, 1889, there began in London the historic London dockers' strike, the success of which, together with that of the gasworkers a few months earlier, had such a massive influence on trade union organization throughout Britain. Thus, although the Scottish carters were defeated for the most part, the climate was such that morale remained at a very high point. A month later came the Glasgow United Trades Council's procession in support of the Tramway Servants and the demand for Glasgow Corporation to take over the transport services from 'The Company'. When the Committee was making arrangements for this historic procession, one week after the end of the strike, it was decided to give the carters pride of place in the procession: and the unity between the carters and the horsemen was again demonstrated at the next meeting: 'The carters reported that it had been arranged between them and the Horsemen's Union that they would be first in the procession.'[1] And so, on September 21, 1889, the carters, immediately followed by the horsemen, once again marched through the streets of Glasgow. But behind them now there marched 13,000 men of many trades.[2] This campaign for municipal ownership of passenger services, which was maintained for four years, played an important part in creating the public opinion to support the Corporation when it finally took them out of private hands in 1894.

[1] Glasgow United Trades Council *Minutes*, September 4, 1889.

[2] Following is the order of the procession: carters, ironmoulders, seamen, sailmakers, railwaymen, miners, lithographers, and calico engravers, labourers, tinplate workers, tailors, brushmakers, plumbers, glass and bottle makers, cabinet makers, horseshoers, printers, coopers, hammermen, blacksmiths, shoemakers, cotton operatives, steelworkers, upholsterers. (Glasgow United Trades Council *Minutes*, August 28, 1889.)

3. THE TRADE UNIONS GROW APACE

These events gave a great impetus to trade union organization, not least amongst the transport craftsmen. Scottish workers who were already organized with branches affiliated to the trades councils, gave much help throughout the next decade to help labourers and workers in the non-apprenticed trades to organize, whether at the height of enthusiasm, or to hold the line during the days of terrible trade depression later in the nineties, after a series of catastrophic defeats in strikes. The records of the Scottish trades councils at the time show new unions being formed, more branches of those already established, and frequent co-operation between them. Horsemen doubled their number of delegates in Edinburgh and Leith, where their secretary was Robert Thomson, who played an important part later when the Association was founded.

The Edinburgh cab-drivers went on strike and gained a 2s rise under the leadership of John Greig. In Glasgow, where the Trades Council refused to countenance any difference between 'what is called skilled and unskilled labour', many had been helped during the year, including cabmen, sailors, firemen, and dockers: the Scottish Hackney Carriage, Tramways and Omnibus Employees strengthened their position, and became registered officially as a trade union.

As yet there was still close harmony. When Robert Stevenson, of the Horsemen, and Hugh Johnstone, of the Dock Labourers, had addressed a meeting of the victimized carters from the Cleansing Department, they had urged them to join the Amalgamated Carters' Society, or, if they hesitated to do that, nevertheless to organize themselves in some way. The carters, horsemen, and dock labourers all increased the number of their branches and delegates. Unfortunately few of the unions' own records survive from this time; but a minute book from the Musselburgh and Fisherrow branch of the National Scottish Horsemen's Union, established in autumn of 1890, has been found. At that time the union had a number of branches and a badge of its own, with weekly dues of 2d. A quotation or two from the Musselburgh and Fisherrow Minute Book give a clear picture of a body of men at work, full of spirit, and quite accustomed to trade union practice.[1]

In December 1890, the private railway companies, taking action to check organization amongst the railwaymen, provoked a bitter strike in Lanarkshire, with wholesale evictions of railwaymen from company cottages. It was finally defeated when 'blacklegs' were imported from over the Border. A movement which had much in common with the 'New Unionism', began to develop amongst the railway employees, including the railway carters. This led to the formation of the General Railway Workers

[1] See Appendix B.

Union, branches of which later emerged in Scotland and were the immediate predecessors of the Association.

But the first impact of the railway strike was to encourage still further the development both of the National Scottish Horsemen's Union and of the Amalgamated Carters' Society. By 1891–2 they had joined forces and had become The Associated Carters' Society of Scotland. The carters' delegation from four branches to the Glasgow Trades Council included John Urquhart, prominent in the Association some years later, and two former Horsemen, Richard Russell and Robert Lemmon of Greenock. Lemmon was appointed delegate for the Associated Carters' Society of Scotland, affiiliating on 2,000 members, to the British Trades Union Congress, which met in September 1892 in Glasgow. The Glasgow Trades Council arranged a 'Grand Conversazione' of welcome in the municipal buildings, with 1,700 present, and a river trip for 600. But the main welcome was a trades demonstration and procession from the Green through the city on Saturday, September 10th, to Nelson's monument, where the speakers on four platforms included Ben Tillett, Chisholm Robertson, Henry Tait, and Keir Hardie. There were 15,000 taking part, from thirty-five societies. An English account describes the event, which much impressed the visiting delegates:

'The Carters' Associated Society led the van, and made a grand display, lurries filled with their wives and families, carrying large open frameworks covered with flowers and evergreens, and drawn by teams of four horses beautifully caprisoned and decorated from ear to tail with flowers, whilst horsemen wearing wide-spreading Kilmarnock bonnets, and otherwise got up in the style of Tam O'Shanter, lent additional picturesqueness to the show. One of the superstructures on the lurries bore on its top a young boy bestriding a hobby horse and wearing the inevitable Kilmarnock after the manner of his seniors.'[1,2]

But hard times followed. Trade depression grew; there was a bitter but unsuccessful four-month strike in the Scottish coalfield and another by the Clydeside engineers. Their success would have meant encouragement to the carters, whose organization might well have become consolidated four years sooner; defeat played a part in setting the carters' progress back for over fifteen years. Where the carters' organizations survived they dwindled in size and influence. The unity of the carters and horsemen

[1] British Trades Union Congress, *Annual Report*, 1892.
[2] On one lorry typographical workers were printing off leaflets showing which Glasgow newspapers were employing non-union labour; also song sheets, which were handed out. *A Song For The Time* declared:

'To Labour, a third of existence we'll give,
That we and our dear ones may honestly live;
And, stern and determined, each nerve we shall strain:
Eight hours we demand and eight hours we shall gain.'

broke up; all that was left on the West coast were two newly-grouped organizations: the Associated Horsemen in Greenock, led by Robert Lemmon, and the Glasgow Carters, which was reduced to little more than a friendly society. Both were registered as trade unions in 1894. In Edinburgh and Leith only the cab-drivers maintained their separate existence. Glasgow United Trades Council's Annual Report for 1894/5 stated that societies disaffiliated. There appeared for the first time a branch of the General Railway Workers' Union, which was to have such an intimate connection with the Association; and two years later in Edinburgh, after efforts by the Trades Council, a branch was also formed there, led by Robert Thomson, formerly the Leith Horsemen's secretary. Disharmony continued and the result was confusion;[1] but at last breaches began to be healed; and in the following year, although there were neither Glasgow carters' nor tramwaymens' delegates, three branches of the old Railway Servants had reaffiliated and the General Railway Workers Union returned to the trades council with two delegates. They were: John Sampson of 133 Allison Street, Crosshill, and George Martin, of 171 Kennedy Street, Townhead.[2]

Together with the secretary, William Smith, also of Townhead, all were founding members of the Association within a few months, with John Sampson as the first General Secretary. The General Railway Workers' Union in Glasgow was still in being in the spring of 1898, when it affiliated to the year-old Scottish Trades Union Congress, at 1,500 members on a fee of £1 15s, with John Sampson as delegate and secretary. That year, Robert Lemmon was a delegate to the Scottish Trades Union Congress from Greenock Trades Council, and the Aberdeen Carters were also affiliated.

Carters had been recruited in Aberdeen by the Scottish Ploughmen and General Labourers' Union, formed by amalgamation of the old Scottish Farm Servants Union with the Scottish Ploughmen's Federal Union in 1895. In 1896, under their Secretary George Duncan, they had rapidly recruited carters. When, in 1897, the Aberdeen Master Carters' Association refused to recognize their union, 700 carters went on strike. They won and also gained a wage increase, after clashes with the police and other animated scenes. The Scottish Ploughmen thereupon set up two separate branches in Aberdeen, one for general labourers and the other for carters.

In Edinburgh the carters had asked the trades council for help in organizing:

[1] 'Some trade societies, and worse still different branches of the same trade, have elected to fight out their quarrel at the Trades Council or before the Trade Disputes Committee, which, having given a decision in accordance with what it believed to be right, has been treated in an ill-deserved manner.' (Glasgow United Trades Council *Annual Report* 1895/6)

[2] Glasgow United Trades Council *Annual Report*, 1896/7.

'Mr Blaikie reported that the carters are making efforts in the direction of organizing and requesting that a deputation from the Council attend their first meeting. Agreed Messrs Blaikie, Blackburn and Harvey attend.'[1]

And again:

'Mr A. Paterson reported having along with others attended an organization meeting of the General Railway Workers' Union in St Mungo Hall. The meeting was small, though enthusiastic.'[2]

That year the General Railway Workers affiliated to the Edinburgh United Trades Council, with Robert Thomson as their delegate, and began to develop fast. 'A soirée of the General Railway Workers Union in Queen Street Hall on Saturday January 29th was a great success.'[3]

By the autumn of that year the decisive step was taken. John Sampson, together with others in Glasgow, prominent in the General Railway Workers' Union, decided to form a union exclusively of carters, disregarding by whom they were employed, at a meeting in central Glasgow on October 29, 1898. Those present decided to hold a mass meeting on Sunday, November 20th, in the Albion Halls, Glasgow, to launch the new society.

APPENDICES

A.

Early Carters' Soirées

The first soirée of the United Carters and Storemen was held on January 28, 1859, in the City Hall, 'which was crowded to excess'. The main speaker was Mr Robert Dalgleish, MP, who said:

'Such meetings as the present proved that the carters wished to raise themselves in the scale of civilization, and he could not conceive of any better uses to which they could apply their surplus funds than in founding a library in connection with their society, and with their permission he would subscribe 10 guineas towards that object.' (*Great applause.*)[1]

There was organ and piano music, singing and story-telling, followed by a ball.

They held their second annual soirée on December 16, 1859, at which the chairman was Mr John McGavin. The main address advocated education, thrift, kindness to horses, and the use of friendly societies, and congratulated the carters on their improved status:

[1] Edinburgh United Trades Council *Minutes*, April 13, 1897.
[2] Edinburgh United Trades Council *Minutes*, July 13, 1897.
[3] Edinburgh United Trades Council *Minutes*, February 8, 1898.
[4] *Glasgow Herald*, January 29, 1859.

'Some thought the good old times were better than this age of intellectual and social revolution, and that to reform is not always to improve. If any such objector be here, let him look round this vast hall and say that the United Carters and Storemen of Glasgow are not in a better position than they were twenty years ago.

'When he looks on such a gathering as this—the carters and storemen with their wives and children, their friends and sweethearts—he can doubt no longer that a great improvement has taken place.

'I can look back for upwards of twenty years in Glasgow, and I have no hesitation in stating that such a meeting as this would not then have been held.

'Your hours of work were then longer, your wages were less, and the depressing effect of these working their natural results.

'But the tide has turned—the wave has reached you and now you are higher up than you were then. Allow me to speak in your name; if we are not so well as we will be, not so elevated as we wish to be, but with our own earnest effort and God's help we will not only be, but deserve to be, better, higher, happier.

'It is in such true, manly, Christian spirit that all labour becomes dignified and every man a hero.'

The speaker went on to stress the importance of the carters in the growing economy of the country:

'To you, my friends, is committed a very important task, the carrying on of the products of our industry and those which we import from one part of the city to another. From our mills, our warehouses and stores, our railways, canals and river you have the distribution of these vast quantities of merchandise, and I need scarcely say, that to perform this duty rightly, all must be steady, sober men and scrupulously just.'[1]

B.

A Branch of a Carters' Union in Action in 1890–1
The first meeting of the Musselburgh and Fisherrow Branch of the National Scottish Horsemen's Union was held on October 27, 1890, in St John Hall, Musselburgh, and was presided over by Robert Thomson, who, after experience in the General Railway Workers' Union, finally became one of the early members of the Association in Leith.

'Mr Robert Thomson presiding on the Lodge and after address had been delivered by Mr Thomson, Samuel Anderson was elected president; vice-president, David Bruce and Peter Muir, and voted for Bruce and Muir to be vice-president. Election of secy: Mr Inglis was proposed and

---

[1] *Glasgow Herald*, December 17, 1859.

unanimously agreed. Also secy Archibald Tait (2). Mr Stobie voted for Treasurer. Election of check Bookkeep: Moffat, Rutherford 6 William Baxter 5 James Stephen 25. When then put to the meeting Mr James Stephen was duly elected. Election of Trustees: David Bruce, Will Young, Thomas Anstruther.'[1]

They held monthly and sometimes fortnightly meetings at first; and Robert Thomson, who was the Leith Secretary of the Union, was invited to attend 'a full meeting' of members at their third meeting on December 8, 1890. At their fifth meeting they elected their Treasurer, Mr Thomas Stobie, to go as their delegate to a conference at Greenock, and the minutes of their next meeting, February 2, 1891, gives the result:

'Meeting of the Members of National Scottish Horsemen's Union. The members hear the result of delegates Meeting at Greenock. The weekly payments are increased to 3d per week instead of 2d as before, after the night of the 2 Feb 2/2/91. I wrote to the general secretary Glasgow requesting him to write to Mr John Hickman, Carling, contractor, Fisherrow as regards an increase of pay to the extent of two shillings per week on and after Saturday the 6th Febr. The men will have to look for an answer on Saturday night at pay table.'

By their fortnightly meeting, six men were on strike, and the proceedings are recorded as follows:

'Mr John Hickman contractor received notice from the General Secy Glasgow. Mr John Hickman's reply to the men after taking a week to consider the matter; he offers one shilling of rise on condition the carter will take out an extra rake. This the men refuse to do. Six of the men came out on strike today. The result of meeting tonight, the men agree to go to work morrow Feby the 17.'

A fortnight later the men at another stables had won an advance: 'Mr McGregor's men came out on strike on the 2nd March and they went in to their work on the Wednesday the 4th with one shilling of advance.'

But the employer hit back. On March 16th they recorded: 'Two of Mr McGregor's men got their leave through the strike and received Thomas Moffat 10s, James McQueen £1.' Up to this point, the dues were in a remarkably good state, no less than two thirds of the members being fully paid up. But this victimization proved too severe a blow. After May 11, 1891, the records of this branch cease.

[1] National Scottish Horsemen's Union, Musselburgh and Fisherrow, *Minute Book*.

CHAPTER THREE

THE FIRST YEARS

I. THE ASSOCIATION IS FOUNDED

OFFICIAL records of the Scottish Carters' Association are lacking for the first four years. Reminiscences exist but they are not contemporary, and most appear to be based on the memoirs of Mr Hugh Lyon, the second General Secretary, who did not join the union until 1901, and did not publish his memoirs until 1919.[1] Fortunately, a minute book of the Plantation Branch survives from the first days, from which a more reliable and accurate account of the union's first seven years can be established than from Lyon's colourful sketch, dashed off seventeen years later. Indirect glimpses can also be gained in these years from the day-to-day records of organizations to which the Association was affiliated, such as the Scottish Trades Union Congress, the Glasgow Trades Council, and the Edinburgh Trades Council. All help to establish the reliability of the Plantation Minute Book.

The men who came together from the branches of the General Railway Workers' Union to form the Association were predominantly railway carters or railway cartage contractors' men; but they also included signalmen, engine drivers, and others who were dissatisfied with the railwaymen's organizations as the century's last decade ended. John Sampson was a signalman; so was William Lowden, who became the secretary of the Plantation Branch, Paisley Road, Glasgow. It was Lowden who kept the scrupulously correct minute book which is of such historic value to us today. In Glasgow they joined together with a number of carters, some of whom were members of the Glasgow Carters' Society, formed four years before (after the break-up of the militant organization) which had become little more than a friendly benefit society. Many maintained a dual membership in the Glasgow Carters' Society. Relations were not uncordial in the first years; it was necessary to present a common front against the sick benefit scheme which the railway companies provided in the stable societies in company-union style.

But the new Association was a genuine trade union and set out to organize the carters into a campaigning body. Sampson and his colleagues

[1] *The History of the Scottish Horse and Motormen's Association 1898–1919* by Hugh Lyon. Civic Press Ltd., Glasgow, 1919.

in the first few months travelled around both West Coast and East Coast, inaugurating branches, which began holding stable organizing meetings. In the opening years, the Association was led in a thoroughly democratic fashion by men fully experienced in trade union affairs. Branches elected the General Secretary and Executive Council members, as well as their own branch officials, under a model constitution. The first two meetings minuted in the Plantation Branch give the pattern, with references to the inaugural mass members' meeting and the election of John Sampson.[1] No other account or reference remains of the first meeting in the Albion Halls on November 20th, which endorsed the election of John Sampson as General Secretary and the election of the first Executive Council and trustees. Executive meetings took place quarterly, the minutes being circulated to branches and discussed at local branch quarterly meetings. Special committees were set up to deal with the problems of organizing carters in various classes of work. From November 1899 the young Association was fully launched.

Within two weeks of the mass meeting at the Albion Halls the Association was registered, on December 2, 1898, under the Trade Union Acts, 1871 and 1876. The application was signed on December 1st by seven members and two trustees. These were: Angus Macdonald, of South Side; George Martin, of Townhead, who had been a delegate to the Glasgow Trades Council from the General Railway Workers' Union; Niels Larsen, of Glasgow Central; Robert Henderson, of Glasgow; Alexander Miller; Thomas Findlay, of Glasgow Central; and John Sampson, as General Secretary. The two trustees were K. Robson, of Plantation Branch, and William Morrison, both of Glasgow. The office was Central Chambers, 93 Hope Street. The rules of the Scottish Carters' Association opened with the motto: 'Unity is Strength: All Men Are Brothers'. It was described as 'An Association of Carters, Lorrymen, Vanmen and Stablemen united to advance their Social Position'.

The rules of the Association put overriding control firmly in the hands of the membership; on this, the founding members, who were former railwaymen, had strong views based on some experience. Four years after the foundation, a severe difference of opinion on policy arose, and there was a prolonged struggle. The leadership at that time wished to abandon annual general meetings, to centralize all funds, and to exclude non-Glaswegians from office. But the original rules and constitution[2] dispose of any suggestion that the carters lacked ability or were inexperienced in trade union practice. After registration, the task of the Scottish Carters' Association was to live up to its name and organize carters all over Scotland. Before there could be much progress, carters had to be freed from the chains of the stable societies. These had been imposed by the bigger

[1] See Appendix A.
[2] See Appendix B.

44

employers to blunt the militancy which in 1889 and 1890 had gained recognition of payment for overtime and advanced some wages to 26s a week. Above all, carters had to be encouraged to raise themselves until they were no longer regarded as outcasts. The conditions of the carter at the turn of the century were indeed deplorable. As Hugh Lyon wrote years later in his memoirs:

'Everyone looked upon him as part of the harness of the horse. In fact, the employers demanded that the harness should be well kept, while the welfare of the man was a matter of indifference. Men could be got easily, harness had to be paid for.'

The late Sir Patrick Dollan wrote: 'The carters and stablemen were, in my boyhood, regarded as the outcasts of industry and treated much worse than the horses they looked after.'[1]

At the time when John Sampson was beginning his task, Sir Patrick Dollan had started work as a grocery apprentice and pony driver, delivering goods to villages near Baillieston, for which he 'received 3s 6d for a sixty-seven-hour week'. Asked how carters could live on the wages they got in general carting, a veteran replied: 'They couldn't. Some made it up by tips and thieving.' The hours commonly worked varied from fourteen to sixteen and upwards. There was no longer a recognized day, and no payment for overtime.

The custom was for a carter to be allotted by the employers a number of rakes, or journeys, when he started from the stables at 5.30 a.m. He went on working until these were completed, no matter what the conditions. This could mean waiting hours at dock gates or railhead for his turn to be unloaded. Traffic blocks, the closing of bridges and quays— none of this was taken into account. Even when he had finished his last rake, he had to bring his horse back to stables and see to it before he plodded his own way home, just as he had to groom his horse next morning before the weary day began. Not only did he work six days in the week, but every Sunday he had to come into the stables, without pay, to attend to the animals, on penalty of a fine if he did not do so. The earliest demand, as in the case of the old National Scottish Horsemen's Union in 1891, was not to reduce the hours, but to reduce the number of rakes, or to be paid overtime for rakes over and above a certain number.

There were three main classes of workers. The first group were the men who did the cartage work in connection with the railways. Some worked directly for the railway companies from company stables, such as the 'Caledonian men' or the 'Terminus men' in Glasgow.[2] The rest were employed by the three large firms of railway cartage contractors, who

---

[1] *The Highway*, February 1948.
[2] The three chief railway-companies were: The North British Railway Company; The Caledonian Railway Company; and the Glasgow and South Western Railway Company.

specialized in this work all over Scotland and were known as the 'Railway contractors'. Next, there were the Corporation men, employed by the local authorities, ranging from cleansing to passenger transport. There was also a vast number of haulage contractors, from small firms to large ones, known as the 'general contractors', some of whom specialized, for example in coal, flour, timber, brewery work, and jute. A section which became of increasing importance comprised the delivery services of the co-operative societies, from bakery and milk vans to hearses. At this time, wages varied from 19s to 21s a week for the railway carters, with certain extras; 26s for Corporation carters; from 17s to 25s for the general contractors' men; and for the co-operative societies' men between 24s and 27s.

To bring about any change the carters had first to build a basic organization—in Glasgow and Edinburgh, where very large numbers of carters were concentrated, then spreading along the coast and finally to the whole of Scotland. For it was essential to reach the other cities, and to maintain organization there, if any union was to be permanent. The carters of a single city, except perhaps one the size of Glasgow, could not for long make any headway against the employers. Hard times on the land in the highlands and islands and in the countryside were constantly forcing men into the ranks of the carters. There were also men driven over the water from Ireland by hunger and high rents, who found it hard to believe that when things were bad in Ulster they could possibly be worse on the Clyde. In any event, Glasgow was nearer home than the United States and Canada across the wide Atlantic. There were, besides, 'tramp carters', casual migrants, moving from place to place, working as carters when there was work, moving on, when the wind of trade changed, into the next town. These men were exceedingly difficult to organize; but, in any case, hard times make a bad recruiting sergeant for unionism. Hard times may lead to desperate affrays, but it is usually from the men who have something to lose that anger and stubbornness come, with an understanding of the need for organization on a permanent footing. But for a nucleus of such men to bring to the general body of carters the understanding of basic trade union principles, and the conviction that they could and must be put into practice, called for hard work, courage and patience of a high order. The pioneers who were arguing for trade unionism were themselves working the long hours, sometimes with great distances to walk after work. A carefully-timed dismissal by an employer and there would be yet another case reported to the branch: 'a new collector needed in our stable'; and a stable without a collector quickly lost its members. Again, few of these men were scholars, nor were they angels. They hauled the increasing wealth of the country about in immensely valuable loads on meagre wages which did not put a man's soul in his body—nor keep it there. They knew what could happen to breakages and losses, accidental or otherwise, especially in loads of foodstuffs, tobacco and liquor.

46

Carters were suspicious even of their fellows when it came to cash, ready to see betrayal where, often enough, inexperience and muddle alone were to blame. It was true that local societies had collapsed through money difficulties. The wonder was that so few had done so; but there had been enough, and enough propaganda about them, to make the ignorant fear that if he joined a union he would not only lose his livelihood but his union dues too. It was one of the main obstacles to success for the Association.

2. HOW THEY ORGANIZED

It was one thing to set up an organization, with offices and officers; it was another matter to get down to the formidable task of making it work, with only the former signalman, John Sampson, as a full-time official. Conditions varied in the different centres. In Glasgow, particularly, where the stable societies amongst the railway carters had a marked influence and where there were other very big concentrations of men, there was no alternative but to build organization in and around the stable. Elsewhere much could be done initially by propaganda meetings, 'soirées', or 'organizing-meetings', supported and sometimes sponsored by the local trades council, which would appoint delegates from the organized trades to attend.

Under the leadership of a number of members of the Socialist Societies, Edinburgh had a particularly striking record in this respect. Their zeal in pressing workers to join an organization without being too closely concerned as to which, produced results fast; even if it led to a certain number of jurisdictional disputes, these were settled without undue difficulty. The Annual Reports of the Edinburgh United Trades Council for 1897 to 1903 without exception declare that the council had been busy rendering assistance to new organizations and helping to strengthen others. Amongst the workers so organized were tramway servants, railway workers, dockers, and gasworkers, as well as carters.

In Edinburgh and Leith, the branches of the General Railway Workers' Union continued for a few months after the foundation of the Association. In November 1898, the Trades Council sent its Treasurer, Tom Blaikie, and two other delegates to assist one of the Association's organization meetings, and next month recorded their first help to the Association:

'Mr McManus reported that along with Mr Bell he had attended an organization meeting of the Scottish Carters' Association in the Moulders Hall on Sunday 11 December, which was very largely attended; and it was intimated that 15 members had joined the Society that day.'[1]

Two months later, there was further aid:

[1] Edinburgh United Trades Council *Minutes*, December 13, 1898.

'Mr Stewart reported having attended along with Messrs Greenhill & Mallinson an organization meeting of the SCA in the Moulders Hall on Sunday 19th which was a very successful meeting, and at the close 24 new members joined the society.'[1]

By May, Robert Thomson, ex-Horseman, and James Coull, who had both formerly represented the Leith branch of the General Railway Workers' Union, appear as delegates of 'the Scottish Carters'; and in May the credentials of Mr James Mark were accepted for the Scottish Carters' Association, Leith branch. Whilst the Association's affairs were progressing in this way in Edinburgh, there were two developments on the West Coast.

The Association began to play a bigger part in the Glasgow Trades Council. In 1898, only the Association's Central Branch had been affiliated, the secretary of which was Angus Macdonald and their delegates John Sampson and William Smith. By the following year, Cowcaddens branch was added, of which Will Laidlaw was secretary and delegate, together with Neil Murdoch; while Sampson and George Martin represented Central branch. Sampson had also been appointed to the Parliamentary Bills Committee, and was also a trustee, of the Glasgow Trades Council. It is recorded that the carters and the gasworkers were in dispute:

'A dispute between these two societies as to overlapping—the carters charged the gasworkers with taking members of the carting industry into their association—was referred to the Disputes Committee, the Societies having failed to agree on it themselves. The Disputes Committee, after an exhaustive consideration of the matter in dispute, representatives of both sides having been heard in the presence of each other by the Committee with several meetings, came to a unanimous finding on the subject.'[2]

The terms of the decision must have given considerable satisfaction to the ex-railwayman, John Sampson:

'They found that all persons employed as vanmen and lorrymen, carters and stablemen should be classed as belonging to the carting industry, and as such should be eligible for membership only in the Scottish Carters' Association; and that the Gasworkers' Union should not enrol members of this industry in its ranks. The two societies through their officials accepted this finding and the Council by a unanimous vote approved of it on the clear understanding that it should regulate all future disputes between the Societies on the matter of overlapping.'[3]

When John Sampson and his colleagues formed the Association in the closing months of 1898, they set up branches when and where membership

[1] Edinburgh United Trades Council *Minutes*, February 21, 1899.
[2] Glasgow United Trades Council *Annual Report*, 1898/9.
[3] Glasgow United Trades Council *Annual Report*, 1898/9.

and the prospects warranted it. The Plantation Branch was entrusted with the south side of Glasgow: when four months later one of their number 'said that some of the members wished to have a branch further along on the south side,' the General Secretary argued against over-enthusiasm:

'Mr Sampson said it would not be advisable in the interests of the Society to have any more branches at the present time, as the men themselves would not attend and the system that was being carried out with a collector in each stable allowed them to organize and know exactly what stables were organized and who were not, and how many men in each stable were in the Society; but after a time it might be advisable to have more branches opened.'[1]

Another important branch was Central Branch, Glasgow, delegates from which frequently attended Plantation meetings to discuss points of common interest, just as Plantation often sent delegates to Central. Paisley Branch also co-operated closely, and usually asked Plantation's delegate to represent them at general meetings of members. Other early Glasgow Branches included East End, Cowcaddens and Townhead. The difficulties that had to be surmounted in organizing the stables and the problems of holding stable meetings can be seen in the *Minutes* of the Plantation Branch, our only contemporary picture of the time. In his memoirs, Hugh Lyon describes his own experiences:

'I have seen two or three of us start out on a Sunday morning, say at 7 o'clock, and walk to Govan or Partick, returning home about 2 p.m., after gaining the questionable satisfaction of joining one new member for all our trouble. Three nights in the week I attended stables, my method being to go to the gate about 6 p.m., and, as they were coming out at 7 o'clock, advise them to join our union. Sometimes, by way of encouraging myself, I merely got their names, with the promise of payment the following Saturday. But promises are always easy to get. I found that paying of the bob was like drawing blood from a stone, and the means whereby payment of same was evaded proved that the carters were not altogether honourable in this matter. One night after holding a good meeting at R. D. Spittall's, Garngad Road, where nearly a hundred horses were employed, I got over 30 names and the promise of sure payment the Saturday following. I believed them to be, as they had stated to me themselves, most anxious to join the union. I had three other stables to attend that same Saturday, but agreed to be at Spittall's at 2 p.m. I stood there until 5 o'clock when I learned that the carters were all away home, having climbed over the wall at the back of the stable rather than face me.'

[1] Plantation Branch *Minutes*, March 19, 1899.

This was three years after John Sampson and his enthusiasts in the Glasgow branches had gained a considerable measure of success in their first efforts.

Week after week and month after month the Plantation Minutes record that branch members were appointed to attend at Glasgow stables 'to assist on Sunday morning' at recruiting meetings and discussions with the carters. After working seventy or eighty hours in the week this was no light matter; sometimes the flesh was weak:

'One of the delegates for Sunday meeting asked why some of those appointed had not turned up to meeting. It was explained that they were unable to attend. Mr Grier had been too late in getting up and Mr Mills, owing to family matters, had not been able to attend. It was then asked what was being done to get the men organized. It was explained that Mr Sampson had been at Spittals Stables, other stables had also been visited, and altogether there had been about 30 had given in their names.'[1]

Sampson frequently attended their Saturday night meetings during the first year, as well as going to stables on the Sunday mornings; but by the autumn of 1899 a new figure, Ross, makes his appearance on Saturday night and Sunday morning, for it had been decided that it was necessary to appoint a full-time Glasgow organizer. Sometimes assistance was given to other branches, as when Central Branch wrote asking Plantation:

'To elect a deputation to meet a few of their members on Sunday morning for organizing purposes at Gushetfaulds. A few members voluntarily agreed to attend.

'The Secretary then explained that we have had a good increase of members for this month, but full particulars would be given at the end of the quarters.'[2]

When their secretary, Willie Lowden, came to make his quarterly report to the Plantation Branch on April 18, 1899, at the end of their first half-year of existence, they had reason for satisfaction, but not complacency:

'The Report showed that 97 new members had joined in this quarter, making 148 clear on the books and 14 over three months in arrears. It was hoped that the members do their utmost so that we may be able to show a better increase for next quarter.'[3]

Some of the carters' more grievous complaints recur time and again during that first year. There was a question which angered those in railway cartage: although most of the contractors paid wages weekly, some did not; in particular, the men on the Caledonian railway system were paid

[1] Plantation Branch *Minutes*, March 11, 1899.
[2] Plantation Branch *Minutes*, March 18, 1899.
[3] Plantation Branch *Minutes*, April 8, 1899.

only every second week. The Plantation Branch were anxious 'that a petition be got up', and they asked 'that Mr Sampson get petitions ready and a committee be appointed to look after same and act as a deputation'. There was also bitter feeling about the long hours worked, which came up in a grievance particularly affecting those engaged on working to the railways. One result of the anarchy which reigned, when competing private railway companies were operating in Glasgow, was that the gates at the various stations were closed to goods traffic at different hours. Even when the companies finally agreed to close all gates at the same hour, the carters' troubles were not over:

'It was explained that the companies still closed the gates at 20 minutes to six and those outside after that time were short shipped. Mr Paterson then discussed the question at some length and advocated getting clear at six o'clock no matter whether loaded or empty, or be paid overtime after that hour at the rate of sixpence an hour.'[1]

This was the demand, partly won, which their predecessors had put forward during the great carters' strike of 1889. Members described how they had been kept for hours inside the gates before getting unloaded 'and they wished that something should be done to get clear after working a day's work of ten hours, or be paid overtime after that'. The branch went on to record that:

'So far as waiting through the day was concerned the Masters ought to look after that themselves and seek redress at the proper quarter, but as regards the men having to wait after hours it would be the duty of this Society to do all in its power to see that the men were paid overtime for it. It was then proposed that we have a meeting on Sunday next and instructions given to ask Mr Sampson if he could arrange for a meeting on that date.'[2]

Yet it was to be years before the Association was strong enough for the railway carters to get any satisfaction.

There was one question which affected every carter alike; this was the universal imposition of Sunday stable duty, by which men were forced to come back to stables on Sunday to care for the horses, without pay.

'Members explained that in the stable they were in everyone had to attend on Sunday, and failing to do so they were fined a shilling, which was paid to the man who had stable duty for that day. In some other stables it was explained that the shilling was kept off and handed over to the Stable Society. The whole system was condemned and the opinion of those present was that the men should be paid for six days and when they were

[1] Plantation Branch *Minutes*, January 14, 1899.
[2] Plantation Branch *Minutes*, February 25, 1899.

asked, or when their turn should come, they should be paid for that day by itself at a higher rate of wages than that paid on a week-day.'[1]

It can be seen that these 'company' Stable Societies were a cause of serious concern to the Association. Members who had been lured into contributing to these private sick benefit funds, from which they were entitled to 10s sick aliment, were reluctant to lose benefit. They were also reluctant to ask prospective new recruits to the Association to do so. Was it compatible with membership in the Association ? It was a question much discussed in consultation with Central Branch; and both came to the conclusion that they should 'allow members to do whatever they thought best themselves until they were in a better position to take some definite action'. Once again it was a question of how soon the Association would be strong enough to force improvements. Sampson's view of Sunday work was that they could not yet do away with it altogether, but that the Association should aim as soon as possible to try and get paid for Sunday labour at the rate of one shilling for each horse cared for; and instead of turning out every Sunday, to have a rota for Sunday duties. This demand was first put forward when Plantation Branch instructed their delegate to raise it at the second Executive Council meeting, held in April 1899:

'A motion was made that the question of Sunday work should be brought up. A motion by D. Marquis, that we be paid 3s, was lost, there being no seconder. A motion was then made by John Paterson that we be paid 1s for each horse, seconded by J. Muir. There being no amendment, the motion was declared carried unanimously.'[2]

The whole question was thoroughly discussed on the Executive at several meetings; but yet again it was a question which depended upon the strength of the Association.

3. THE FIRST BIG CAMPAIGN

Unable to make major gains in skirmishes on these battlefields, which had nevertheless aroused interest in the new organization amongst carters throughout the stables, John Sampson then marshalled the whole Association to concentrate on a frontal attack upon the employers on the central issue of wages. In the early months he had already sent in petitions for increased wages addressed to particular employers. In May 1899, he sent a notice to all contracting carters. This led to a variety of results. In some stables some of the men got an advance in pay and not others. In others the men went on strike and then sought support from the branch. Thus, at Plantation Branch, six weeks later, it was recorded:

[1] Plantation Branch *Minutes*, February 4, 1899.
[2] Plantation Branch *Minutes*, April 8, 1899.

'Two delegates who were present from Gunnulls stable, where a strike has been for this last ten days, and who wished to put the matter before this branch, were allowed to do so. Having explained the whole circumstances of the case a good deal of discussion took place thereon. It was ultimately agreed to do what we could for them until the strike was settled.'[1]

The response was uneven, but it led to stepping up the number of organizing gatherings on Saturday nights and Sunday mornings round the stables of Glasgow; and as members were recruited, collectors were appointed by the branch for each stable where there were members. A month later the Executive launched a further campaign asking for an increase of 2s a week in wages. Through summer and autumn there was intense activity round the stables in Glasgow; every week the organizer, Ross, or Sampson, or both, went to one stable after another, with members of the branch appointed 'as delegates to assist'. This was far from being a campaign merely in Glasgow and on the West Coast. In Falkirk, for example, the trades council answered an appeal for help to organize the carters by appointing their secretary to attend a meeting of carters. This was Hugh Lyon, a young ironmoulder. The chairman was a carter called Jamie McMurtrie, and John Sampson came from Glasgow to explain the wages campaign. Lyon later recalled this, his first meeting with John Sampson, and it was finally decided that the claim should be two shillings, 'as in making a demand for two, they might possibly receive one'.

In Edinburgh and Leith a considerable drive was made. The trades council gave every help:

'Mr Coull stated that the Scottish Carters' Association Edinburgh and Leith branches intended holding three organization meetings, the first upon the evening of Thursday June 15th at Fountainbridge at 8 o'clock and two on Sunday the 18th, the one on the Leith Links at 3 o'clock and the other in the meadows at 6.30, and asking the Council to appoint speakers to attend the various meetings. Mr Moffat moved and Mr McDougall seconded that we accede to the request. Agreed to unanimously.'[2]

They appointed five delegates to attend the three meetings. At the Thursday evening 'the attendance was very small but enthusiastic and several new members joined the society at the close of the meeting'. The Sunday meetings were 'very fairly attended'. At the Leith Links:

'addresses were delivered by the delegates and by Mr Sampson, Organizing Secretary of the Scottish Carters, bearing on the benefit of being members

[1] Plantation Branch *Minutes*, June 21, 1899.
[2] Edinburgh United Trades Council *Minutes*, June 6, 1899.

of a trade union. At the close of the meeting several new members joined the society.'[1]

The meetings continued through the summer. Trades council delegates were sent to another at Fountainbridge on Thursday, July 6th, 'which was largely attended and at the close of the meeting a large number joined the society'. By September the campaign for increased wages was well in hand. A Sunday meeting at the Queen Park on September 24th 'was very large and enthusiastic' and they 'adopted a resolution empowering their Secretary again to memorialize their employees in regard to the increase of 2s per week asked for some time ago.'[2]

At the July meeting of the Association's Executive, and again at the First Annual General Meeting, held on August 27, 1899, proposals had been put forward dealing with other grievances of the men, in particular the question of the Sunday duty and how to end the employers' stable societies. But the consensus of opinion was that all resources should be concentrated for the time being on the wages campaign. When the Plantation Branch delegate reported back at their next meeting, the question was raised,

'when it was explained that the Sunday question was still before the employers; but until the men were better organized there could not be much done so far as that was concerned, and the agitation for a rise of wages is expected to bring together such a number of men as would justify the Society in fighting this question.'[3]

Throughout October there was progress, not only in Glasgow but also in Edinburgh, where in Picardy Hall on October 29, 1899 'a very largely attended' meeting learned that 'several employers had granted an increase of 1s': and 'a great many joined the branch at the close of the meeting'. The Executive Council met, with representatives from Edinburgh and Leith, Falkirk, Paisley, and the Glasgow branches, followed by a mass meeting in the Albion Halls, with Chisholm Robertson, the miners' leader, in the chair. Sampson reported that many employers, including the railway companies, had offered 1s increase; and the meeting recommended this should be accepted. He had written all branches to give delegates instructions 'regarding what action should be taken to force the hands of the Masters on the hours and wages question' where the advance had not been conceded. What should be the next steps? Should the Association try to force fuller recognition, or could more be got by each group approaching their own employer? On this, there was a difference of opinion. Finally it was decided that Sampson should send a further circular to the

---

[1] Edinburgh United Trades Council *Minutes*, June 20, 1899.
[2] Edinburgh United Trades Council *Minutes*, October 3, 1899.
[3] Plantation Branch *Minutes*, September 13, 1899.

employers, and mass meetings should be held to discuss what action should be taken to enforce the demands. Amongst the speakers at this enthusiastic mass rally was George Carson, secretary of the Glasgow Trades Council. The secretary of the Falkirk Trades Council, Hugh Lyon, was also present. 'I left for Falkirk feeling a proud man', he recalled years later. 'My duty was to advise the Falkirk carters to accept the shilling, as they did that night.'

At the Plantation Branch, when Sampson attended on November 2, 1899, he was asked 'what action should be taken where they had not got the rise ?' Sampson replied that 'it would have to be carefully considered, but he had no doubt but the great majority of the Masters would give it; but in the event of any of them not doing so they should consider bringing out the places where the demands have not been conceded'. Gains were certainly made: the Caledonian Railways Company gave 1s rise, and some of the men had got it at Terminus. Others giving the increase included Shaws, McArthurs, Bows, Curries, Osbornes, Turnbulls, Clarks, Ritchies, and Haymans, whilst McLellan, Wordie & Co., and Cowan & Co., had conceded part. This was a considerable achievement and gave a basis for adding considerably to the Association's strength. As Plantation recorded on November 9, 1899: 'It was hoped that everything would be done to get these stables organized where they had had an increase of wages, but where they have not assisted in bringing it about; the stable referred to being Cowans, McLellans, Bows, G. & S.W., Wordies, and Camerons.'

But such gains had not been achieved without cost. In some stables a warning had been put up that all carters who were members of the Association would be given three days' notice. Employers had offered a rise, provided they would leave the Association. Apart from lock-outs, many men were out on strike for long periods. Individual members were sacked; frequently the branch was called upon to appoint new collectors at stables. Without a collector, members quickly lapsed. It had been an exhausting and long-drawn out struggle and finances became a serious problem. By the end of November 1899, the strikes were over and it was time to consolidate the gains.

4. OTHER ACTIVITIES

The Association's activities were not taken up by the wages and hours' struggle alone. Delegates were sent to trades councils, and to the West of Scotland Housing and Land Reform Conference.[1] Close attention was paid to the annual general meetings, for which their elected delegates were fully mandated, as were their members on the executive. During Sampson's time, branches were fully consulted by the General Office and enjoyed a great deal of autonomy; he was in constant touch with them.

[1] It was held on March 10, 1900.

At special meetings there were speakers on trade unionism in general. Social life was not overlooked. The West Coast branches organised soirées and balls, dinners, and outings for their members, as well as an annual concert to which they invited delegates from other branches.

It must have been a notable New Year's Day which greeted the opening of the twentieth century. The Leith branch held a social on January 10, 1900, which guests from the trades council described as 'a splendid gathering', adding that they had 'made splendid progress, having added upwards of 200 to their ranks within a year'. An Edinburgh social also was 'a grand success. It was intimated during the evening that they had added upwards of 400 to their membership.'

The last week of the old century and the first week of the new century passed without a Plantation branch meeting; at the next, on January 11, 1900, we detect a faint echo of the rejoicings which had taken place. 'Mr Thompson reported being to Strathearn's Stable and that some of the men were quite willing to join but asked to have it put off for another week until the New Year holidays were over.' But, the festivities over, the members had once again to return to the harsh realities which we have been considering. For, at the same first meeting of Plantation members in the twentieth century, John Sampson gave a report

'of how matters were getting along. He said the Association was getting along splendid. He said branches had been opened in different places and they were all doing well, and that he had a letter from Dundee asking him to come through and open a branch there which he said he was going to do at an early date. He said that Plantation had done fairly well but he saw no reason why they should not do a great deal better next year if the members would just show a little energy in the matter.'[1]

John Sampson was a busy man. There were the regular stable meetings in Glasgow, mass organizing meetings in Edinburgh and elsewhere. He went to Dundee and formed a branch there. He attended branches and their quarterly meetings, as well as the Executive Council meetings. In addition, he himself was a delegate both to the Glasgow Trades Council and to the Scottish Trades Union Congress, to which the Association in the year 1900 paid £2 15s od affiliation fees in respect of 2,500 members. He took part in the Congress debate on a resolution calling for the regulation of street traffic. He was also active in political affairs.

Scotland was in the lead in campaigning for independent labour representation in the House of Commons. On March 4, 1899, representatives of the Independent Labour Party and the Social Democratic Federation met the Parliamentary Committee of the Scottish Trades Union Congress and with them decided to call a Special Congress 'in view of the great necessity for direct representation in Parliament and on local bodies of

[1] Plantation Branch *Minutes*, January 11, 1900.

Labour interests'. The conference of 226 delegates met in the Free Gardeners' Hall, Edinburgh, on January 6, 1900. The Association was represented and John Sampson was elected as one of the five-man Standing Orders' Committee. Robert Smillie was in the chair and George Carson was secretary. The Standing Orders' Committee was kept busy with resolutions and amendments. The terms of the main resolution were finally agreed as follows:

'Recognizing that no real progress has been made with those important measures of social and industrial reform, which are absolutely necessary for the comfort and well-being of the working classes, and, further, recognizing that neither of the two political parties can or will give effect to these reforms, the Conference is of opinion that the only means by which such reforms can be obtained is by having Direct Independent Working-Class Representation in the House of Commons and on Local Administrative Bodies, and hereby pledges itself to secure that end as a logical sequence to the possession of political power by the working classes.'

The conference[1] then appointed a Joint Committee of twelve representatives from trade unionists, co-operators, ILP, and SDF, 'to be known as the Scottish Workers' Parliamentary Elections Committee'.

Thus the Scottish working-class had taken the decisive step one month before the Labour Representation Committee, the forerunner of the Labour Party, was set up in London. The conference passed a number of other resolutions[2] including a pledge 'not to support or appear on the platform of candidates belonging to either of the two political parties and to support independent action in the House of Commons'; and outlined a number of questions which should be concentrated upon. Some of these

[1] A full account of the conference is given in the Twenty-Fifth *Annual Report* of the Scottish Trades Union Congress, under the title: 'The Scottish Workers' Parliamentary Committee; How It Was Formed.' The delegates were drawn from the following organizations:

From 16 Trades Councils		29
From 69 Trades Unions		116
	Total	145
From 4 Co-operative Conference		7
From 14 Co-operative Societies		21
	Total	28
From 1 District Executive, ILP		2
From 16 Branches, ILP		32
	Total	34
From 1 District Executive, SDF		2
From 9 Branches, SDF		17
	Total	19

A grand total of 226 from the four organizations.

[2] See Appendix C.

were of particular importance to the Association and were soon to influence the tactics adopted by the leadership. They included: the legal eight-hour day; organization by imperial and local authorities of self-supporting industries, by which right-to-work would be secured to everyone, especially in times of trade depression; the fixing of a minimum wage by law, particularly in the sweated trades. An amendment 'to secure the nationalization of the means of production, distribution and exchange' was, however, defeated.

At this time, the Association's leadership had in mind that the time was ripe to get a strong organization going in the cleansing departments and amongst other employees of local authorities, and then to bring pressure to bear on the general cartage employers, either indirectly or, where possible, through getting 'fair wage clauses' inserted in sub-contracts from the municipalities. Edinburgh Trades Council had already held a deputation to the town council urging a 'Fair Wage Clause' in November 1899. In September 1901, following a strike in the Glasgow cleansing department the officials of the Glasgow Trades Council, of whom Sampson was one, led a deputation to Labour members on that town council to press for the clause in all contractors' agreements. The Association set up a Municipal Committee as a first step, and Sampson and Willie Lowden, of Plantation Branch, had responsibility for helping it.

5. TROUBLES BEGIN

The 1899 wages campaign was the first the Association had carried out; it was important for several reasons. It staked the claim for recognition from the employers, and, indeed, gained it from certain sections. This was an encouragement to those who worked in the stables against great odds and always at personal risk. Faint-hearts were helped to stand firm: the militant pioneers began to see results from their labours, and could demonstrate them to others. Moreover, in the darker days which were to come, carters could always be reminded that the possibility of recognition was once within a touch of being achieved, and that next time it could be a reality. This gave the Scottish carters in these early years of the new century a prospect which they had not had before. Nor had there been demonstrably in earlier years a serious possibility of organizing all the carters of Scotland into one body. But the 1899 campaign was taken up in every part, even when, as in Aberdeen, it was fought out under other auspices. There the Aberdeen carters' branch of the Scottish Ploughmen's and General Labourers' Union had an unsuccessful strike, and, as the union broke up, the branch joined the Gasworkers' union for a short time. The reason given was that this 'would be more effective if any dispute arose, than a local union'.[1]

[1] Aberdeen Trades Council Minutes, September 5, 1900.

This argument that an all-Scotland carters' union would be stronger than a purely local organization was an important point that the Association's wages campaign had demonstrated. This and the degree of success of the campaign led to expansion everywhere, and, at the same time, brought with it a serious problem. The problem was easy enough to understand but hard indeed to solve. Plantation Branch *Minutes* for November 16, 1899, record that collecting sheets were 'distributed to the different stables for the purpose of raising money to bring up the finances of the Society, owing to the heavy drain made upon it during this agitation, and the paying of so many men who are out on strike for the advance'. At the same time, the wages agitation had roused such widespread interest that branches began to spring up sporadically everywhere in Scotland. To put them on a firm footing and prevent them from falling away as rapidly as they had begun, meant greatly increased organizing work, which put a further heavy burden on the young Association's slender purse. Where was the concentration to be, both in expenditure and in organizing effort: to consolidate the main areas, or to spread the Association's network all over Scotland? Could both be attempted simultaneously?

Finances had to be strengthened. The Executive sought to effect this by two means; first by economies, such as the dismissal of the Glasgow organizer, Ross, whose value had been highly appreciated by Plantation in particular. The second step was to propose to raise the entrance fee from 1s to 2s 6d, and also to increase contributions, and to leave a smaller proportion than the original twenty-five per cent with the Branch. But both measures made it harder for the branches, on whose members the main burden inevitably fell, to recruit in the stables in their neighbourhood. With the trend towards centralizing the financial sinews of war went centralization of control; it made deep inroads into the 'primitive democracy' of the early days; branches became estranged from each other. There was an apparent conflict of interest. The Executive's policy sowed the seeds for a division of opinion, and deep rifts did develop later. In some cases there were breakaways; and, although the cause of these might have the superficial appearance of animosities and intrigues between ambitious men, at bottom the cause was the failure to resolve this one problem. Serious trouble emerged in Govan, Edinburgh, and Leith. Even a branch like Plantation, which was not led into a breakaway, came increasingly into conflict, as did Sampson himself, with the Executive. Once again the Plantation *Minutes* help to illustrate events.

After the objection to the dismissal of Ross in May 1900, the first phase can be seen in the Plantation minutes of July 3, 1900, when the branch discussed the agenda for the Annual General Meeting, and instructed their delegates to vote against proposed alteration of rules. There was far less activity around the stables that summer, with no organizer present to lead it and Sampson himself being able to attend far less often. By late autumn, however, he had tried to open the next round against the employers.

The new move was to win a reduction of hours. On this, Sampson campaigned hard, building up support for a recognized working-week of fifty-six hours and time and a quarter for all hours worked thereafter. Edinburgh Trades Council minutes record his making 'stirring addresses' on October 28, 1900, at the Moulders Hall in Edinburgh, and announcing a big demonstration the following month, when 'a large and enthusiastic meeting' demanded the reduction in hours on which carting contractors had been approached. But the regular meetings on the East Coast were left largely in the hands of the local officers: Jim Mark, Alexander Philip, William McQueen, and others. Back in Glasgow, the Plantation Branch Minutes for November 3, 1900, records:

'Mr Sampson who was present gave a lengthy speech dealing with the circular that is to be issued to the employers and urging all members to do all they can to raise the agitation at the present time.'

By the first few weeks of 1901 the Executive had decided on two measures, both of which were opposed by Plantation. They decided to appoint three organizers—for Glasgow, Dundee, and Edinburgh with Leith, and they asked branches to nominate candidates. Secondly there were proposals to rid the Association of the burden of its responsibility for its sick fund by coming to an arrangement to transfer the funds to the Glasgow Carters' Society and to build up a complicated system of death benefits. On the question of the organizers, Plantation Branch decided 'that we instruct our EC member to vote strongly against it at the next EC meeting'; and on the second point that 'we take nothing to do with the handing over of our sick fund members to the old Carters Society.'[1]

Nevertheless, the Executive went ahead with their plan. On May 1, 1901, they interviewed nine applicants for the three posts of organizer. They appointed William McQueen organizer for Edinburgh and Leith; and for Glasgow they appointed the secretary of Falkirk Trades Council, the ambitious young ironmoulder, Hugh Lyon. This is how Lyon described the scene:

'When my turn came, I found Geordie Martin, Townhead, Glasgow, in the chair while twelve or fifteen carters, with Mr John Sampson, General Secretary, made up the Executive Council. The Chairman stated the terms on which I would be engaged and also said they wished a man who would be able to organize the carters; and, in order to test the ability of the applicants, and find out who would be able for such, they had agreed that each candidate should suppose he were at a stable and the members of the Executive Council non-unionists, and address them

[1] February 16, 1901.

for 15 minutes on the need for becoming trade unionists. He then called on me to make a speech. For the life of me I could not, and instead burst out laughing. The Chairman seemed rather taken aback, so, to relieve his mind, I informed him that I had never been an actor in my life. My imagination could not carry me to make such a speech, but I would take up the fifteen minutes in telling them what I had endeavoured to do for trade unionism in Falkirk.

'The fact that I refused to play the clown that night (although the proposal was made by the Chairman with the best intention), I afterwards learned was the means of me being unanimously elected organizer of the Scottish Carters' Association.'

This colourful and characteristic self-portrait, drawn seventeen years later in his memoirs, may be compared with the sober contemporary impression he made on branch members. Here is the first glimpse of the man who was, in less than a year, to become General Secretary, and to remain in office for thirty-four years, when he first visited Plantation on June 8, 1901. Even in the formal language of the former railwayman, Willie Lowden, who minutes it, we get a hint of the style of the young man:

'The new organizer Mr Lyon being present and who was in a hurry to get away to Cowcaddens Branch was asked to address the meeting at this stage. He stated what he had been doing since taking up organizing duties and asked the assistance of the members in Plantation Branch to give him all the assistance in their power so that he would be able to do his work in a satisfactory manner. He also said he had a meeting in Cook Street G. & S.W. stables on Sunday morning and asked for a member of this branch to be present. Mr Mills agreed to be there.'

But the branch were not mollified: 'A discussion took place regarding the appointment of the organizer, when considerable dissatisfaction was expressed.'[1]

The new organizer did not attend the branch again for some months, and the membership dwindled to 102, with members over thirty weeks in arrears by September, when Lyon was sent to organize in their area for two weeks. He attended their meeting in October 1901 to report upon a housing reform conference to which the Branch had sent him; but that was the last time the branch were to see him in attendance as organizer.

6. THE GENERAL SECRETARY IS OUSTED

The Association was at an important turning-point. There was a great need for wise leadership, which, whilst never damping down the ardour of men who were roused, nevertheless took into account that simultaneous

[1] Plantation Branch *Minutes,* June 8, 1901.

work must be carried out amongst the less advanced in other towns or stables. It was inevitable that the work went ahead unevenly, depending partly upon local conditions, partly upon the energy and ability of the men who were leading on the spot. A prolonged struggle provoked in one town might have disastrous effects on the Association as a whole; this happened on more than one occasion. If there was a local defeat, the funds of the whole Association suffered a set-back. If a success, it sometimes gave rise to local branches' feeling that much more could be achieved when, in fact, this depended upon the Association's strength elsewhere. Such events led to frustration, separatism, and the emergence of strong local characters who deteriorated from leadership to petty chieftainship, and jealousy of headquarters, which was reciprocated and appeared to degenerate into personal animosities.

At all events, early successes frequently ended in breakaways or collapses. Some of these took place under the first General Secretary, John Sampson; they were endemic under Hugh Lyon and could still be found in later days. What experience has to teach all trade unionists—and the carters and motormen took long enough to learn it—is that there must be firm central leadership by men who have earned their members' trust on a forward-looking policy, combined with the greatest degree of local rank-and-file initiative and freedom in branch, stable, and garage. The combination of these two characteristics, which appear to an employer as hopelessly incompatible, is of course the heart of democracy in the working-class movement. Wherever it is lacking, danger lies, and an opportunity for the enemy to defeat the members.

Much had been going on behind the scenes. Tom O'Mally, the secretary of the Govan branch who, according to Lyon, in his memoirs, was disappointed at not being appointed a permanent official, had 'succeeded in getting his members to join the Amalgamated Union of Labourers, with the appointment of himself as organizer'. William McQueen, the newly-appointed Edinburgh and Leith organizer, started a breakaway union less than a year after his appointment. He had taken the members and their £30 local funds into it. Following upon this, the Executive proposed to appoint another organizer, which was far from pleasing to the Plantation Branch, who thought it 'a great mistake'.

'Minutes of Executive meetings were read when a good deal of discussion took place regarding the appointment of an organizer. The Secretary explained that he had opposed the appointment; the result was that it was put off for a fortnight and that branches were to be asked to nominate a candidate if they desired to do so.'[1]

The Branch, therefore, appointed their secretary, Willie Lowden, to be delegate to the Executive and he was 'instructed to oppose the appointment

[1] February 15, 1902.

of an organizer at the present time'. He came back with a full report of the proceedings, which showed that not only had the matter of the appointment gone against their wishes, but it had been decided to give up the office at Hope Street. Lowden's opposition was endorsed by the Branch.

But there were, in fact, other moves afoot. Lyon describes in his memoirs how he had had 'serious thought of giving up the job and returning to Falkirk'; but he was dissuaded by two close friends he had made in the Cowcaddens and East End Branches, Willie Laidlaw and Alexander ('Sanny') Macfarlane, both on the Executive, 'who were already determined to see me General Secretary'. Now that opportunity arrived; at a stormy meeting of the Executive in April 1902, John Sampson was ousted from office. Those nominated to succeed him were Angus Macdonald, of the Central Branch and a founder member, and Hugh Lyon; Lyon was declared elected.[1] At the next Executive meeting, with Lyon installed, John Sampson was present; and when an item of £6 16s 2d expenses, which he had incurred, was objected to, he refused to hand over the books. The Executive 'agreed that Mr Lyon go over the Books with Mr Sampson before paying'. The minutes[1] of this meeting, the earliest record of the Executive Council to survive, fail to tally in certain respects with Lyon's own account in his memoirs.

Whatever may have passed between Sampson and Lyon after this meeting, one thing is certain: Sampson's claim for what was owing to him was not paid. No records of his term of office are available, and the Association premises were transferred by Lyon to 17 Oswald Street where the Association rented a room from the Gas Workers' and Labourers' Union. Lyon stated that, when he took office, the coffers were empty and the Association was in debt to printers, hallkeepers, factors, and for taxes. He added that there were only '400 or 500 members, paying 3d per week and the majority never in benefit', the branches which had sprung up so thickly in 1899 and 1900 having died away. The year 1902 was one of unemployment and hard times as the Boer War ended. The total number of carters and tramway workers in Great Britain who were organized in trade unions stood at 31,280; it had fallen by 1,000 from the year before and was to fall further.[2] The Scottish Carters' Association looked as though it were about to pass into limbo, like the many others before it, despite the self-sacrificing efforts of its members in its three and a half years' existence.

[1] See Appendix D for the full minutes of this meeting.
[2] *Report on Trade Unions in 1908–1910 With Comparative Statistics for 1901–1910.* Board of Trade (Labour Department). Cd. 6109.

APPENDICES

A

The First Meetings of Plantation Branch, 1898

The first meeting took place two weeks after a handful of men in Central Glasgow had met and decided to form the Scottish Carters' Association:

> Scottish Carters Association,
> Gordon Halls, Paisley Road.
> Nov. 12, 1898

'The opening Meeting of Plantation branch of this Union was held on above date. Mr Sampson in the Chair. A good attendance of members being present. In opening the meeting the Chairman explained at length the reason for starting the new Association, and also explained the aims and objects of same. It was then proposed to elect office bearers. Nominations were asked for Chairman. Mr Miller proposed, seconded by Mr Wilson, that Mr Bryan be elected, which was carried unanimously; for Vice-Chairman Mr Caldwell was proposed by Mr Bryan seconded by Mr Marquis and agreed to: for Secretary, W. Lowden was proposed by Marquis, seconded by Bryan and agreed to. The following members of Committee were then elected, namely: Arch. McBeth, J. Graham, David Wilson, David Irvine, J. Armstrong. Trustees, Chas. Millar, John McCune. Auditors: J. McCann, J. McConnachie.

'Mr Sampson then explained that a mass meeting was to be held in the Albion Halls on Sunday, 20th November, and asking everyone present to do his best to make the meeting a success. Mr Ferguson, who was present, also addressed the meeting, wishing the new Movement every success. This being all the business the meeting closed about 9 p.m.

> (Sgd.) Wm Lowden.'

The meetings were held weekly, on Saturdays. The next week the Plantation minute book records:

> 'Nov. 19th, 1898

'The ordinary meeting of Plantation branch of above was held on above date, Mr Bryan in the Chair. A fair attendance of members being present. Minutes of previous meeting were read and adopted on the motion of Mr Irvine, seconded by Mr Aitken. No discussion taking place on the Minutes, the election of General Secretary then took place. Mr Irvine proposed Mr Sampson, Mr Robson seconded. No other nomination being made it was declared carried unanimously.'

1. The first solid-tyred lorry to be fitted with electric lamps, used by the Northern Co-operative Society. *From left to right:* John Shand and James Murison (junior).

James Murison (senior), who first started working for the Northern Co-operative Society in 1902, unloading his coal cart in Aberdeen on his last round.

A van for collecting waste paper, as used in 1903. Glasgow Corporation.

2. An uncovered two-wheeler for collecting night soil from dry closets in the last century. Outside St Rollox Stables. Glasgow Corporation.

Introduced about 1900, a covered four-wheeler van, carrying sealed galvanized pans in which fish gut from fishmongers and night soil was collected. Outside St Rollox Stables. Glasgow Corporation.

Daimler petrol-driven lorry, purchased 1903, loaded with feed for Glasgow Corporation stables. Outside the Granary in Graeme Street (now Bell Street) Glasgow.

B

The First Constitution of the Scottish Carters' Association, 1898

Registered on December 2, 1898, the rules were clear, detailed and explicit. The entrance fee was 1s; contributions were 3d weekly, and cards were 1d. Rule II, 3 declared: 'Every member of good standing to be eligible to hold office in the Association'. To be in good standing required that the member should not be more than thirteen weeks in arrear: over thirteen weeks excluded from benefit, and over twenty-six weeks from membership, (II, 4). Youths over sixteen were eligible for membership. Benefits included 15s for ten weeks and 7s 6d up to twenty weeks, for victimization after a report to the branch and thence to the general office; and a grant could be made up to £20, provided there was no conduct which justified dismissal. Unemployment benefit was 10s for ten weeks and 5s up to twenty weeks. Strike pay was payable if on strike 'at the demand and with the sanction' of the union, and there was provision for assistance in legal defence. The government of the Association was the Annual General Meeting which was to meet each August (VIII, 1) with power to alter rules, provided proposed alterations were 'agreed to by any branch in good standing and by the Executive', and were issued to branches (VIII, 2). A special general meeting could be summoned on one month's notice, by the Executive Committee or at the request of two thirds of branches (VIII, 5). The Executive had to meet at least each quarter in January, April, July and October, (IX, 5), with the chairman elected at each session (IX, 6) a prior agenda and quarterly report to be sent to all branches (IX, 10). The General Secretary was to be elected by ballot vote of membership, 'and to continue in office during the will and pleasure of the Members who, through the Executive Committee and Annual General Meeting, have power to call upon him to resign' (XIII, 1). Branches could be of twelve or more members; they were allowed to retain one-third of dues, (XVI 8), and entitled to spend twenty-five per cent of gross receipts for branch management. (XVI 9). A particularly important point, which came to be challenged when John Sampson was ejected and his successor, Hugh Lyon, began to change the rules, was that there should be no alteration of rules 'except by the Annual General Meeting as provided for in Rule VIII, 2' (XIX, 1).

C

The Resolutions passed at the Workers' Conference on Parliamentary and Local Representation, January 6, 1900.

Resolution 1
Recognizing that no real progress has been made with those important measures

of social and industrial reform, which are absolutely necessary for the comfort and well-being of the working-classes, and, further, recognizing that neither of the two political parties can or will give effect to these reforms, the Conference is of the opinion that the only means by which such reforms can be obtained is by having Direct Independent Working-Class Representation in the House of Commons, and on Local Administrative Bodies, and hereby pledges itself to secure that end as a logical sequence to the possession of political power by the working classes.

Resolution 2

To give effect to the foregoing resolution *re* Independent Working-Class Representation in Parliament and on Local Administrative Bodies, this Conference agrees to appoint a Joint Committee, such Committee to consist of four members from the Trade Unionists, four from the Co-operators, two from the ILP, and two from the SDF, and to be known as the Scottish Workers' Parliamentary Elections Committee.

Resolution 3

The duties of Joint Committee shall be to see that the principle and policy agreed to at the Conference are put into active operation; to raise funds by appeals, contributions, and otherwise, to enable them to carry on their work; to aid candidates when possible; to see that candidates who make application for their approval pledge themselves not to support or appear on the platform of candidates belonging to either of the two political parties, and to support independent action in the House of Commons; and that they subscribe to the principles and policy of the Joint Committee, as approved by Conference from time to time, and render assistance in the formation of Local Committees; and take such steps as may be deemed necessary to give effect to the decisions of the Conference; and should circumstances arise at any time which, in the opinion of the Joint Committee would call for the convening of a Special Conference, they shall have power to summon same.

Resolution 4

As indicating the questions upon which public attention might be concentrated by such a Party in Parliament, this Conference would name the following as of outstanding importance: A Legal Eight-Hour Day; Old Age Pensions and ample Provision for those Disabled; Accumulative Taxation of Land Values; and all other forms of Unearned Income, save on Investments made under the Industrial and Provident Societies' Acts; the Organization by Imperial and Local Authorities of Self-Supporting Industries by which right to work would be secured to everyone, especially in times of trade depression; the Fixing of a Minimum Wage by Law, particularly in the Sweated Trades, as has already been done in the Colony of Victoria. In addition to these there would always be the resolutions of the Trades Union Congress and special legislation affecting the interests of particular trades to be attended to, together with measures for increasing and extending the political power of the working classes.

Resolution 5
Each Affiliated Organization shall be responsible for the Election Expenses and maintenance of its candidates, but the Joint Committee shall endeavour to raise an Election Fund wherewith to assist in defraying the costs of such candidates as shall have obtained the endorsement of this Conference, or of the Joint Committee, issuing therefrom.

Resolution 6
This Conference, recognizing the very great importance of the work committed to the care of the Joint Committee, and believing that such work can only be carried to a successful issue by loyal and generous support from the various organizations represented, pledges itself to use every effort to have such generous financial support promptly accorded to every appeal issued by the Joint Committee.

D

The Earliest Surviving Minute of the Executive Council, 1902

'SCOTTISH CARTERS' ASSOCIATION

JOHN SAMPSON,   Chief Office,
General Secretary   Central Chambers, 93 Hope Street,
                              Glasgow.   May 3, 1902

'A meeting of the EC of the above Association was held here tonight. Mr Martin in the Chair. Present, Messrs Martin, Stewart, Macfarlane, Lowden, Laidlaw, Crombie, Cochrane, Sampson, and Lyon, Gen. Secy. The Minutes of the previous meeting were read and adopted on the motion of Mr Stewart, secd. by Mr Lowden. Mr Macfarlane drew attention to the Minutes which he held were only half reported. Mr Martin then inquired if Mr Sampson had made any arrangements regarding the office. Mr Sampson stated he had seen the factors and made arrangements to take over the office for the ensuing twelve months. He produced a letter to this effect which was handed over to Mr Martin. A discussion then took place in reference to Mr Sampson not sending circulars as instructed at last meeting to contractors in several Districts where a demand for an increase of wages had been made. Mr Sampson stated as an excuse that he thought it was bad policy to put out circulars. As a new Gen. Secy. would be appointed before the replies came in, he thought it would be better for Mr Lyon to take up this business. The question then dropped on the understanding that Mr Lyon would get out the circulars as soon as possible. The Finance Committee were then asked several questions. One in particular being the sum of £6 16s 2d claimed by Mr Sampson for visiting Govan 40 times. A lively discussion took place on this question, Messrs Crombie, Macfarlane and Martin condemning Mr Sampson for charging this expenditure. Another item of expense was brought forward by the Finance Committee in which it seemed that a Lawyer's account amounting to £4 10s 11d had been standing since the year 1900. Several items of expense was also taken exception to by the Executive. Mr Sampson was then asked if he was prepared to hand over the Books, Vouchers, furniture, etc., to the new Gen. Secy. This he refused to do unless paid the amount due him which amounted to £6 16s 2d. The Chairman then requested Mr Sampson to leave the office until the members discussed this question, this he refused to do. The Chairman then advised that the members retire from the office for the purpose of settling this question. Latterly it was agreed to come to a discussion in the presence of Mr Sampson. After some expressed themselves, Mr Macfarlane moved and Mr Stewart seconded to pay Mr Sampson. This was agreed to. Mr Sampson on again being asked to hand over the Books, etc., refused until the money was paid down. It was agreed that Mr Lyon go over the books with Mr Sampson before paying. That was all the business.'

CHAPTER FOUR

THE SINEWS OF WAR

I. THE NEW SECRETARY CHANGES THE RULES

FINANCES were low. The books were no longer available. The Govan and the Edinburgh and Leith Branches had defected. Nevertheless there remained branches in Airdrie, Alloa, Ayr, Bonnybridge, Coatbridge, Dundee, Paisley, and there were five in Glasgow: Central, Cowcaddens, East End, Plantation, and Townhead. All demanded immediate attention; most of them asked for the new General Secretary to attend their meetings at once and to help them strengthen their organizing efforts. But the branches had to face a most unusual situation: hardly had he taken office than the new General Secretary disappeared from the members' view.

Shortly after the May Executive meeting, a strike of carters began in Hugh Lyon's home town of Falkirk; it lasted nearly five months, and he spent almost all his time there. Meanwhile the fourth annual general meeting, which should have taken place in August, was not called. There was no all-Scottish campaign on hours about which the employers were to be circularized, nor any summer organizing meetings. Paisley, Glasgow Central, and Plantation branches began to protest, and to press their own needs. Six weeks after the Falkirk strike began, Willie Lowden minuted that the Plantation branch chairman, McInnis,

'complained that Mr Lyon had never put in an appearance. He also said that he had heard a strike was taking place in Falkirk and some other districts, and asked if there was any information to give regarding the dispute, and how it was brought about. The Secretary reported that no information of any kind had come from Mr Lyon since he became secretary, unless asking that all money be sent on to him.'[1]

Three weeks later, Lyon was in Glasgow for an Executive meeting, briefly minuted, of which the main item was his 'full explanation regarding the Falkirk strike'. The five men present on the Executive included Lyon's warm supporters, 'Sanny' Macfarlane (East End), who was chairman, and William Laidlaw (Cowcaddens); but the biggest branches, Central and Plantation, were not represented. The Executive resolved 'that branches

[1] Plantation Branch *Minutes*, June 21, 1902.

be requested to send fifty per cent of their branch funds to the General Secretary'.[1] Ten days later, the Plantation chairman stated that 'he thought it strange that the General Secretary had not been to this branch, neither had he sent any word regarding the affairs of the Association. He also advised the secretary to send on no money until such time as he gave a proper explanation',[2] If the figures Lyon gives in his memoirs of the total membership at that time of 'only 400 or 500, are correct, then Plantation Branch must have been as large as any, if not the largest, for its membership was over one hundred. From this time onward, the new General Secretary was at loggerheads with the branch throughout its active life. Certainly the interests of the big branches at this time ran contrary to the policy which he pursued in his first year of office.

During the months when Lyon was preoccupied with Falkirk affairs in the summer of 1902, the Glasgow Trades Council had organized a great housing protest demonstration, in which branches had taken part, supporting it with a horse parade. Now the branches asked for a grant towards expenses from the Executive, when it met, at long last, on September 6, 1902. On the grounds of expense, vehement opposition to the grant was put up by Laidlaw, Macfarlane, and Lyon. At the same time, Lyon also put forward new rules aimed at increasing the contributions; taking the funds out of the branches and centralizing them, thus changing the whole government of the Association. At the same meeting, the third after Hugh Lyon had become General Secretary, they decided 'to take steps to form a new EC'.

It was a total alteration of rules. They were registered on January 21, 1903. The application for registration was signed by one of the signatories to the original rules, Angus Macdonald. The others were Peter Crombie, of Townhead, John Murphy, A. Hendry, Alexander Macfarlane, of East End, Will Laidlaw, of Cowcaddens, and Hugh Lyon. The rules were declared to have been passed at a general meeting held in May 1902, the date being left blank. There is in fact no record of any general members' meeting having taken place then; the first mention of the intention to alter the rules appears in the Executive Minutes of September 1902.

The most fundamental change was that there was no provision for any general meetings of members for the government of the Association, for alteration of rules, or for the election of the Executive Council, which was left in ultimate control. The Executive was to consist of seven members, including President, Vice-President, and Trustees, all of whom had to reside 'not more than a seven-mile radius from the registered office'. Half their number was elected on branch nomination every six months, and were to hold office for twelve months; they themselves were

[1] Executive *Minutes*, July 8, 1902.
[2] Plantation Branch *Minutes*, July 19, 1902.

to elect the officers. Entrance fees and contributions were increased. All monies were to be handed over by branches, less twenty-five per cent for branch management.

Finances are the sinews of war. Hitherto the Association had depended upon strong branch organization and branch autonomy. The fact had not been faced that centralized policy and centralized finances would go together. But hitherto, except at the height of the general wages campaign, the young Association had not developed a comprehensive policy. Now branches were being called upon to provide the means while the end was still undefined.

As may well be imagined, Lyon's new rules had a very mixed reception amongst members. Lyon's keen supporters, Macfarlane and Laidlaw, won agreement in their branches. But other branches, with a strong nucleus of members and healthy branch finances, were against having their money appropriated and spent, they knew not how, in running disputes elsewhere, about the merits of which they were not informed, by a General Secretary, who had no time to do what they regarded as his prime duty—the key matter of organizing the stables. Those who, like Willie Lowden of Plantation, were also former railwaymen, had appreciated Sampson's careful ways, abiding by the Association's rules with the regularity of a signalman's or engine-driver's time-table. Sampson would never have moved to form a new Executive by nomination, instead of by due election by members at annual conferences. But this energetic young ex-ironmoulder who had been told—and remembered the phrase nineteen years later— that 'Falkirk is ower sma' for ye, Hughie'—had a very different approach. He knew money and time were short; he determined to build an organization which was strong financially. He kept the minimum of books, if any, especially in the first years; and even as late as 1936 he gave the impression to his successor of having small regard for normal methods of bookkeeping; a bank deposit receipt was enough for him. He earned a reputation for being careful almost to the point of eccentricity, and he would fly into a rage when it was proposed to spend money on organizing. An old member expressed the view: 'Hughie never got over how little cash there was when he started'. Lyon's policy of centralizing funds and control, his impatience of criticism, and his refusal to regard the Association's rules as of first importance combined to engender amongst older members not only misunderstanding but even suspicion. Their distrust must have been increased by the fact that a number who proved to be dishonest were attracted by the vigorous and resourceful young man. He made not a few appointments which turned out badly indeed; whilst those of strong personality, who disagreed with him, disappeared first from the Executive and then even from branch office.

In the opinion of several who knew him in the years before the First World War he need not have fallen out with a number of strong personali-

ties of whom Peter Gillespie,[1] of Dundee, was one. It took years before
unfortunate and unnecessary divisions and breakaways, as in Dundee and
Edinburgh and Leith, were mended. Lyon's great error in these first
months of office had not been in throwing himself so wholeheartedly into
the Falkirk strike, but in doing so to the exclusion of all attention to the
membership and in keeping members in ignorance of the situation. It was
no way to ensure winning a local strike nor to build the Association; in
fact it tended to encourage a sectional outlook which stood in the way of
the development of the Association.

Yet the Falkirk strike was a highly creditable and hard-fought battle.
It was a great achievement for a hundred downtrodden carters to hold out
for nineteen weeks. It raised the standing of carters not only in the eyes
of the trades in Falkirk but also in their own. Central Branch, Glasgow,
passed a resolution condemning Lyon for spending so much time on it;
when he attended their quarterly meeting and explained the strike and how
it was conducted, their criticism was silenced.

The Falkirk men, working for the railway cartage contractors Cowan &
Co. and Wordie, had been pressing for a 2s rise. When the employers
refused to concede it or to meet a deputation, the men met to consider
strike action. Two leading carters in Falkirk, James McMurtrie and Willie
Neil, sent for Hugh Lyon. He advised the men not to come out: 'They had
been led to believe that there was money in the funds, and I had to tell
them we were in debt.' Nevertheless, they decided to strike. With the
leaders, Lyon held open-air meetings every night all over town, at which
there were collecting-boxes, appealing for funds. The ironmoulders collected for them; and, by the end of the week, enough had been collected
to pay every striker 10s. The employers brought in 'blacklegs'; but no
lodgings could be found for them. Lyon relates in his memoirs: 'The
people of Falkirk, through our agitation, refused to house the blacklegs,
and the hotel-keepers refused also'. Collections continued; there were
subscription sales, to which the local shopkeepers contributed. 'Blacklegs'
and strikers came into conflict; a carter named Bill Haxton was arrested
and gaoled for a month. On the day he was to be freed a demonstration was
arranged and a lorry was decorated to meet him at the station; but Haxton
had been released early and arrived home beforehand.

'Immediately we heard this, we went to his home, had him disguised and
taken back to Grahamston Station. He and two other carters were sent to
Polmont and advised to take a certain train back in the afternoon. Only
three of us knew that he had already been home. But we were determined
the people of Falkirk should receive him as a martyr and that our demonstration should be a success.

[1] Later Bailie Gillespie, and a leading official of the Transport and General Workers'
Union.

'So on the Saturday afternoon our procession started to meet the train from Edinburgh and I am positive Grahamston Station has never seen such a crowd of people since. Falkirk, turned out in thousands to welcome our martyr.'

He was carried shoulder high through the streets while the band played 'See the Conquering Hero Comes,' and the strikers took a collection. Although the strikers did not win outright, theirs was a moral victory and they went back to work in good order after nineteen weeks, on receiving a promise that their wage demands would be considered.

But from May until October there had been no central campaign on the hours, nor on Sunday labour, nor on the many continuing grievances of the Association's members. All this time the general office in Oswald Street had been closed. Members were falling out of benefit; numbers were dropping. Lyon himself stated that 'there were only a few members left in Glasgow and about half a dozen in Paisley'. Now he had to return to the humdrum of the day-to-day struggle, and to meet the branches' reaction to the new rules, which insisted on centralizing funds.

2. THE BRANCHES OPPOSE THE GENERAL SECRETARY

The Central Branch, Glasgow, was in favour of increasing the contributions, but it was against centralizing the finances. Paisley was against both, and began to press for the General Secretary to set to work in Paisley, or, failing him, for the appointment of an organizer. Central and Paisley might find the new rules unacceptable, Plantation's secretary saw them in the blackest colours. An intense battle developed which seems to have taken up a large part of Lowden's energies. He minutes: 'The meeting was entirely opposed to the alterations contained in the letter.'[1]

The Branch appointed Lowden as its representative on the Executive. Direct personal contact by no means increased regard between Lowden and Lyon. Under Willie Lowden's leadership, the Plantation Branch were insisting that the Association's constitution declared that no rule should be altered 'except by the Annual General Meeting', with explicit provision for prior notice to, and discussion by, branches, within stipulated dates. There was no getting over the fact that the new rules were in breach of the constitution; whilst the dismissal of John Sampson might well be regarded as irregular until confirmed by an Annual General Meeting which was abolished under the new rules.

'Several members spoke very strongly on the matter and wished to know by whose authority they were being altered. Also why Mr Lyon had not sent a copy of Executive Minutes.'[2]

[1] Plantation Branch *Minutes*, September 13, 1902.
[2] *idem*, November 15, 1902.

Lyon hit back instantly, and hard:

'The Secretary reported that Mr Lyon wanted to have a Special Meeting so that he might advise them to get another branch Secretary. It was moved, seconded and agreed to, that Mr Lyon mind his own business. It was decided that no Special Meeting be held; and that Mr Lyon be asked to attend the next meeting and explain why no report of Executive meetings had been sent this branch; also that no Financial Statement had been made; and by whose authority the rules were being altered.'[1]

The atmosphere remained frigid at Plantation's quarterly meeting of members; some had clearly not forgotten his first appearance before them as organizer, twenty months before:

'On being called upon by the Chairman he said he had very little time to waste as he had to attend two other meetings. A good deal of discussion took place between several of the members, and the General Secretary, the Chairman remarking that he seemed to be always in a hurry when he came to Plantation. The General Secretary then made a number of statements but ignoring the main question why the Executive took it upon themselves to alter the Rules.

'The General Secretary said he had no time to discuss the matter, but, if we would elect a member to meet him some other night, he would be pleased to go into the whole matter. The branch then discussed the matter and agreed on the motion of Runcie seconded by McInnis that we elect a committee to meet the Secretary and have the whole matter discussed, and all present to attend. Mr Runcie moved that we adhere to the old Rules in the meantime. This was seconded by McPhee and agreed to.'[2]

Lyon gave way and did attend a special meeting of the Plantation branch, at which he 'explained the position at great length, saying the rules were altered by the Rules Committee and Executive to save expense in calling a General Meeting'. This did not convince Plantation, whose newly appointed Executive member, Alexander Runcie, was asked to pursue it on the Executive, but he had no success. The branch began to fall away. When this was raised, Lowden minuted that:

'The apathy had been caused by the members of the EC and Gen. Sec. In the first place they have taken it upon themselves to alter the rules of this society without the sanction of the members, whereby members are asked to pay 4d instead of 3d as formerly. The members objected to these men dictating to them what they are and what they are not to do. In short, they have failed to carry out the rules of this Society for which they

---

[1] *idem*, December 27, 1902.
[2] Plantation Branch *Minutes*, December 27, 1902.

are appointed, thereby causing discontent amongst the members. In the second place, the Gen. Sec. has done nothing in this district to try and get the men organized.'[1]

It was the second point which counted most with the members. Branch after branch, those on the West Coast, such as Paisley and East End, Glasgow, as well as Falkirk and Dundee, had written asking for the services of the General Secretary. Sometimes they moved on the Executive to censure him for not visiting them. Lyon had quite other ideas; in particular, he intended to concentrate upon the Co-operative Societies and local authorities, and to get from them facilities for organization by agreement. He did not propose to tackle the difficult general contractors nor the railway contractors, but aimed at those who he believed would be susceptible to public pressure. That required publicity. To achieve this he skilfully sought out opportunities for representing carters in court, writing to the press, and getting the Association talked about in every possible way.

This meant that not only did he not attend Glasgow districts for organizing meetings, but he was unconcerned about the fate of branches elsewhere, other than Falkirk. Branches which had sprung up in the last year of Sampson's office, when the big wages campaign had been carried on, needed a great deal of help if they were not to fall away in the bad old way from which carters had suffered for fifty years and more. Bonny-bridge and Alloa disappeared within a very short time. Lyon minuted that his Executive, when he had at last returned from the Falkirk strike, had decided as follows: 'Letters were read from Dundee, Coatbridge, Ayr and Airdrie, when it was agreed . . . to spend no more time on branches of this kind.'[2]

There was another difficulty. Lyon was in no position to know either what was the membership nor what was the financial position of distant branches who had no representatives on the Executive which had ejected John Sampson. The old ex-railwayman stubbornly refused to hand over the books until what he claimed as due to him was paid.

Lyon had been instructed to look over the books with Sampson and to settle the matter. Nothing came of this; but after letters had passed between Lyon and Sampson's lawyers, the Executive instructed Lyon to pay part of the money, and appointed a deputation of the Executive to meet with Sampson. When Sampson maintained his claim in full they refused to pay it. After a long discussion, Lyon minuted on November 1, 1902, that they decided that 'we trouble Mr Sampson no further but allow him to keep the books.'

So, for a matter of a few pounds the Association lost its books, and with

[1] Plantation Branch *Minutes*, February 28, 1903.
[2] Executive *Minutes*, November 1, 1902.

them their records of what was owed by branches. A fortnight later the General Secretary was setting out 'to investigate whether branches had funds left belonging to the sick section'. He wanted these centralized too, for all sorts of claims were coming in.

3. A STRUGGLE TO CONTROL BRANCH FUNDS

It was one thing for Lyon, without calling a general meeting of members, to get the new rules approved by a majority of the branches: it was another thing to get the cash out of the branch secretaries' hands. A protracted struggle began. Central Glagow wrote refusing to send their branch funds to the general office. Their representative on the Executive put it tactfully: 'Mr Johnstone explained that the Central thought the fund was as safe there as at the Head Office.'[1]

The Executive decided 'that the branches be instructed to return their balance'. Central remained hesitant; but this instruction was a complete non-starter with Willie Lowden of Plantation. His members 'expressed themselves as very dissatisfied. It was considered that the EC and General Secretary had usurped the whole powers to themselves'.[2]

When a Scot uses the word 'usurped', a rebellion is at hand. Members began to take a strong line:

'Mr Mackay thought that nothing should be left undone to have the rules altered, as he considered it detrimental to the best interests of the society to have the powers vested in two or three to alter or amend these to suit their own particular interests.'

They decided to work to get the rules reversed, decided that 'we have no confidence in the rules as at present constituted', and called on the EC to issue instructions to branches to send in amendments to rules 'with a view to calling a general meeting'. As to their own money, they decided that 'the funds remain in the branch meantime'. Lyon had tried to divert the opposition by offering an organizer, who should also be a branch secretary; but at this stage, Plantation were not to be blandished: they disapproved of the appointment of any organizer at that time 'until the funds were in a more flourishing condition'. Lyon and the Executive counter attacked and instructed the branch to call a special meeting in May 1903, which all Executive members living in Glasgow would attend. There was a struggle in the branch; but a number of members, led by John Hair, persuaded the branch to call the special meeting. Willie Lowden thereupon resigned from the branch secretaryship. In his stead, the branch appointed Hair, who was a great admirer of Lyon and later became his chief clerk and the Association's treasurer. But although Lyon had scored

---

[1] Executive *Minutes*, April 18, 1903.
[2] Plantation Branch *Minutes*, April 11, 1903.

by getting Lowden forced out, still the Branch funds remained in their hands.

Now he sought to persuade Plantation's new committee by a proposal for appointing an assistant organizer on the South Side, with 'a long statement of how it might be wrought for the advantage of the Association'. The branch still stood their ground. A general meeting of branch members was called for July 4, 1903, but 'it was considered that this Branch was quite capable of taking care of its own branch funds themselves'. They decided to keep the money 'in the meantime', and pressed for a general meeting of the Association 'to consider and discuss any grievance that may be brought forward'. Lyon offered to come to the South Side for a month to organize there; neither Central Branch nor Plantation would shift. When it was said that the Executive might 'prosecute' branches, Plantation told them 'to proceed with the case as we intend to hold by the rules of the Association'. On August 22nd, the branch called for a quarterly statement of all moneys.

At this stage Lyon strengthened his position by having himself appointed as secretary of the Central Branch. He began to arrange for contributions from stables, which were normally collected by Plantation, to be intercepted by Central Branch. This led to a special meeting, at which Hair minuted that Lyon 'gave many instances of the necessity of unity in all things and explained to the members very fully the working of the EC, how their business was conducted, and explained how the business of our branch meetings should be conducted'. Lyon was questioned closely by Lowden, whose remarks are not very fully minuted:

'He objected to the methods Mr Lyon had stated in regards to the way the rules had been passed. He asked Mr Lyon various questions regarding the rules and impressed upon the members to keep and use all powers in reference to the management of the business and not to invest all powers in the EC.'[1]

Runcie pressed once again for an annual general meeting for hearing and submitting resolutions, which would be 'the means of keeping in closer touch with one another'. A second member asked what would be the process under the new rules if a member had a grievance which the Executive would not take up. Lyon replied that if it was connected with the union it could be settled by arbitration; if it was 'outside the union he could go to law, the loser to pay'. When a motion was put 'that we centralize the funds of this branch', it was finally carried, despite opposition. The branch set up a committee to present a testimonial to Willie Lowden. But still the battle was not over. Lowden continued a rearguard action with a number of points, pressing for a regular report on Executive proceedings, for an annual meeting of members, and for three men from

[1] Plantation Branch *Minutes*, October 17, 1913.

a South Side stable to see the books and finally voting against a proposed rise in the General Secretary's salary until the branch had seen a balance sheet. On each of these issues, Lowden carried the branch; and a supporter of his was appointed to the Executive, where he was in continual dispute about the increasing erosion of branch autonomy, until his resignation was forced. Lyon reported to the Executive on January 9, 1904, that Lowden had refused to go with him to the bank to draw out the branch money which was in his name, as he believed it to be against the rules. Lyon found a way round this, and with the funds of Central Branch now handed over, the main opposition to Lyon and his new methods was at last broken.

Eighteen months after he became General Secretary, Lyon was fully in control. The new rules gave him wide powers, and the money to implement them was in his hands. Effective opposition from those branches which still hankered after autonomy was no longer possible; their only recourse would be to break away and join other organizations which were soon wooing the Scottish carters.

Lyon had a free hand and a free run; what use would he make of it? If he could show that, in the short run, he could produce results which would improve the conditions of the carters even if they failed to 'keep and use all powers', in Lowden's phrase, he would win their support. A measure of his success in this was that, six years later, the Association was the third largest union in Britain, catering for tramway servants, busmen, cabmen, and carters, and over six times the combined size of the three other surviving Scottish unions in this category.

In the first place, Lyon showed a useful ability at this time of his life to learn from his own mistakes; and he was quick and flexible, and adapted himself to circumstances. Never again did he absent himself for long from the centre of things to concentrate all his energies and resources on a limited issue in one locality. Indeed, for the next two or three years he was never far from Clydeside. He argued on the Executive that here was the big concentration and that it cost nothing to organize stables in Glasgow and its neighbourhood. But here he took up every kind of grievance, many of which were common to carters in all areas; and this served to keep the Association on the map even in those remoter areas where organization fell away. The task of strengthening the Association's influence and organization on Clydeside, to make a firm base from which to expand, took up most of the Association's energies between 1902 and 1907. Next, although he was adamant against calling annual general meetings until the requirements of the National Insurance Act made this obligatory ten years later, he had learnt the value of holding combined quarterly meetings of the membership of branches, at which the members' opinion could be tested. Sometimes a stubborn nucleus in one branch was counterbalanced by calling upon the mass of members from elsewhere.

In March 1904, he introduced combined quarterly meetings of the Glasgow branches. It had the excellent result of ensuring large regular meetings of rank and file members to discuss policy. It was a feature which shaped the development of the union.

He learned important practical lessons from the battle over the funds, in the course of which he had diverted stable collections from one branch to another. He learned, too, from the bitter memories of contributions which never reached head office at all, either because McQueen of Edinburgh, for example, had used them to start a breakaway union, it would have cost too much to stop, even if there had been a practicable way of doing so; or because of defalcations, in which even members of the Executive were concerned. His search for a quicker, safer, and surer way of getting the money and reducing the scale of loss led him to the method, characteristic of the Association, of house-to-house collection, with its important effects described in the next chapter. Finally, Lyon realized that unless organizers were appointed, even at some expenditure of the carefully hoarded funds, he would not be left free to do the work he had planned. By the end of 1902, his warm adherent, Will Laidlaw, permanent collector and secretary of Central Branch, was acting as assistant general secretary.

CHAPTER FIVE

POLICY, PUBLICITY AND RECOGNITION

I. THE COURT CASES

THIS long internal struggle for branch democracy and in defence of a democratic constitution was important in its long-term effects. Hugh Lyon was left with almost autocratic powers, uncorrected by the active participation of the membership, and with a weakened Executive. At times he exercised a one-man rule, and, if the ambitious young man should come to lose touch with changing needs and moods, collapse or upheaval would be inevitable. The seeds were sown in 1902 for disasters which happened decades later. But the question in these early stages was whether the Association could survive at all for, important though this struggle was, it was not calculated to recruit men to the Association. For that, what was important in the opening decade of the twentieth century for the Scottish carters was publicity and a policy.

In the art of publicity Lyon became most skilful. He was not only always ready with letters to the Press under his own name; he was a believer in saving the hard-working journalist's time by providing write-ups of events. Thus the moment Sampson had been ousted as General Secretary, the local Press was supplied with a news story about the appointment of the new secretary.[1] Indeed, in the introduction to his memoirs he described himself as 'moulder, trades council secretary and reporter'. Although this is not of course to be taken literally, it shows the importance he attached to the use of the Press. He soon had friends amongst the pressmen and was a strong pillar of the Civic Press Ltd. He did not hesitate to make full use of inspired Press reports of expected strikes, as a means of inducing an accommodating frame of mind in employers. But there can be no effective publicity unless there is news to report; from 1903 onwards, the Scottish carters were increasingly becoming 'news'.

At every meeting of the Executive court cases of considerable variety were reported, in some of which the carter was represented by the Association's then lawyer, Mr Walker, and, at a later date, by Mr J. J. Hunter. In other cases, Lyon himself got a hearing in the court or advised

---

[1] 'He is very fairminded, not an extremist in any views he holds, and possesses the quality of holding the balances equal as between master and man, a principle essential in a General Secretary.'

the man concerned. Early cases included accidents and charges of negligent driving, cruelty to horses,[1] drunkenness, and driving without lights. Another category was where the Association took or threatened, action against employers for illegal or unfair practices. Examples of such practices were the deduction from wages of fines imposed by employers, sometimes illegally, for broken harness, for example, for losses from the load, for not attending or for being late for Sunday stable duty. Occasionally the Association would claim that the carter, who had been found guilty of an offence under a by-law, should be entitled to recover the fine from the employer, on the ground that the fault was really his. Typical were cases of driving without a lamp when none was provided in the stable. A bitter grievance amongst carters was the practice of some employers of deducting from a man's pay a fine for going a rake too few. Carters would be allotted a certain number of rakes, or journeys, which they were to carry out during the day. If for any reason they did not go that number of rakes, the employer fined them, regardless of whether they had been delayed by weather, the state of traffic, the closing of gates or bridges, or any other circumstances.[2]

An early case, which gained the Association respect in stables throughout Glasgow, is a good illustration of the way Lyon went about things. Two carters employed by a contractor, David Murray of Maryhill, went a rake too few, for which deductions were made from their wages. Lyon wrote to their employer:

May 12, 1903

'D. Murray Esq.,
'Dear Sir,

'Complaint has been to us by two of our members in your employment, Messrs Martin and Gillon, that you have on the 9th of May deducted 2s from their wages. I have endeavoured to encourage harmony between employer and employee. I have no wish to cause trouble between you and your men, but I feel that on second thoughts you will recognize that it is illegal to make these deductions.

'I therefore trust to save further trouble this will have your earnest and earliest consideration.

'Yours respectfully,
'H. Lyon.
'Secretary.'

[1] Fifty years earlier such cases were frequent; they often proved to be cases of carters driving unfit animals. Employers were rarely charged; but one contractor was charged with 'torturing' a horse through overloading, as reported in the *Glasgow Herald*, February 24, 1858.

[2] Thus we have minuted:
'Messrs Bryce, McFail and Syme employed by Gillespie's. Had deducted from their wages 8s 9d each and refused to give Syme any wages. The Secretary intimated that he had settled these cases satisfactory to all by recovering the whole of Syme's wage and 6s 6d to Messrs Bryce and McFail. (Executive *Minutes*, June 6, 1903.)

The men's wage was 4s 4d, and they had worked from 5.15 a.m. to 6.40 p.m. The deduction left them with 2s 4d for working thirteen hours. The employer's response to Lyon's letter was to sack both men.

The Association took the case to court, where it was triumphantly won, and, when the employer locked out all men who failed to leave the union, there was a six weeks' strike.

Other cases followed; all sought the union's advice, whether members or not. But now the tone of Lyon's letters became more assured.[1]

The Association took many contractors to court on the issue; every case was won, and this practice of the employers was killed stone dead. It was a considerable victory.

Nothing enhanced the reputation of the Association more than the campaign in Glasgow during 1905 and 1906 to defend carters from fines, under new by-laws, for obstructing the tramcar rails. On May 6, 1905, 'It was agreed to hold an Indignation against the Tramway Department.' Six weeks later, the Town Clerk received a deputation from the Association, with whom he agreed that there should be no further prosecutions until the decision of the High Court on an appeal had been received; that plain-clothes men whose activities the carters had particularly objected to should be withdrawn; and that a copy of the by-laws should be sent to all stables. Three months later the Secretary reported:

'that something like 177 men had been booked. A long discussion on the question of the bylaws in which most of the members took part, when it was agreed to instruct the Secretary to arrange if suitable an Indignation meeting be held on Glasgow Green against the bylaws at 3.30 on October 1st.'[2]

At the next Glasgow combined Quarterly Meeting, on October 29, 1905, members were advised to tackle all candidates for the Town Council on the subject, and it was decided 'to defend all cases until we had a decision from the Corporation and that meantime the EC write the employers to approach the Town Council jointly. But if they refuse, that EC send a deputation themselves urging that the Byelaws be rescinded'. In the course

[1] He wrote to the Glasgow contractor, John Frew, on October 5, 1903,
'Dear Sir,
'A complaint has been made by a few of your men who are members of our Association to the effect that 3s was deducted from their wages on Saturday the 3rd inst because they did not go a certain amount of rakes while they at the same time had wrought the amount of hours stipulated as a day's work. If this statement is true you will recognize that it is illegal. I have endeavoured so far to encourage harmony between employer and employee and therefor write you with the expectation of preventing trouble and giving you an opportunity of putting your side of the question before us. Trusting that this will have your earliest consideration.

'Yours respectfully,
'pro H. Lyon.
W.L.'

[2] Executive *Minutes*, September 18, 1905.

of a year some 2,000 carters were taken to court on the information of plain-clothes men, regardless of the conditions of the streets which were long overdue for improvement.[1]

In his memoirs Lyon described the consequences of the campaign:

'In one year over 1,500 were summoned, and to have employed a lawyer to defend these cases would have taken the whole of our funds. Every morning I attended the courts, and I have seen as high as 50 carters in one court in a morning. The whole of the cases were taken at once, I appealing on their behalf, the carters usually being dismissed with an admonition. A meeting was then held outside, and I addressed them on the need for organizing, and as they generally had money with them in the expectation of being fined, I was able to make good capital out of the tramway by-law. In this way I advertised the union and, at the same time, joined hundreds of members.'

The campaign continued up to May 1906, with further deputations received by the Town Clerk or the Tramways Committee, until a satisfactory arrangement was finally reached.

Another method of obtaining publicity was by reviving in 1904 the Old Annual Horse Parade which had not been held in Glasgow for at least twenty years. For this colourful event, branch banners were prepared and there was an impressive turn-out. There were 300 horses and decorated lorries, with bands of music, as they processed through the streets, collecting for the infirmaries. Many must have remembered the great turn-out to welcome the British Trades Union Congress, twenty-two years before, when the carters led the procession. At the next quarterly meeting of Glasgow branches: 'The Chairman in opening the meeting made a few complimentary remarks anent the Horse Parade. The Secretary intimating that £120 7s 1¾d had been collected.'[2]

On the East coast the Leith Horse Parade had never been allowed to drop: it was the famous holiday, and drew thousands from many miles around. Annual soirées, balls, suppers, and concerts continued, together with the annual trip, for the first of which in 1903, to Aberdour, no less than 1,500 tickets were sold.

The Association was beginning to be heard of throughout the working-class movement in Scotland. Lyon was usually a delegate to the Scottish Trades Union Congress and took part in debates. In 1904 and 1906 he

[1] The men felt that the strict and, as they considered, unreasonable enforcement of the by-laws in these circumstances was due to the insistence of the forceful manager of the municipally-owned tramways, Mr James Dalrymple, who had just been appointed to replace the first manager, John Young. He was later to earn the reputation for being a martinet, constantly in dispute with staff. Twenty-two years later, after the 1926 General Strike, when he refused to reinstate large numbers of men, it became so important an issue that his resignation was forced. Lyon often said that the carters' thanks were due to Dalrymple, for his methods forced hundreds of them to join the Association.

[2] Executive *Minutes*, October 16, 1904.

moved resolutions on a practice, which was peculiar to Scottish carting, and appears over and over again at annual gatherings of the Association and of the Scottish Trades Union Congress. Some employers insisted upon their carters being in charge of two carts simultaneously, the second being used as a 'trailer' to the first. This frequently led to accidents over which the carter would have little control and yet must bear the responsibility; it was by no means a new grievance.[1] Lyon used every effort to bring such problems of the carters to the notice of other trade unions. A measure of the degree to which the Association began to be accepted as part of the broader movement was the number of appeals received from organizations to many of which the Executive responded with small grants.[2]

2. PRESSURE AND LOCAL POLITICS

An echo of a far-reaching and vital case is found in this minute:

'A circular was then read from the London Trades Council advising that trade unions send for pamphlet of cases lately decided affecting trade unions. After some discussion it was agreed to get a dozen. 9d.'[3]

This was the newly published pamphlet[4] written as part of the campaign to reverse the Taff Vale judgment, 1901. The decision in this case laid trade unions open to attack from employers, who could claim the right to recover damages from their funds on the ground that individual workmen had been induced to break their master-and-servant contract by going on strike. This brought home to many trade unionists, who had believed politics was outside the business of the unions, that industrial action alone would not save union funds; hence the increasing number of appeals from Workers' Representation Committees and Election Committees, and the Association's support for them. The Royal Commission, appointed in 1903 to inquire into the law affecting trade disputes, recommended that unions take full responsibility for their officials' actions when it reported in 1906; and only the Liberal-Labour landslide election which had thrown out the Conservative Government in January 1906 led to the shelving of its recommendations, and the passing of the Trade Disputes Act, 1906.

This was one of the factors which led the Association and its General Secretary as early as 1903 to start 'getting into politics', following the

[1] In January, 1856, a carter named Peter O'Hara pleaded guilty to culpable homicide at the Glasgow Winter Assizes. He had been charged with 'driving a cart along the Turnpike road leading from Strathaven in a reckless manner'. The facts were that he had been in charge of two carts: 'The second horse becoming restive, he left the first horse for a moment to attend to it.' The first horse bolted, knocking down and killing a child. He was admonished and the case dismissed, the *Glasgow Herald* records on January 11, 1856.

[2] See Appendix.

[3] Executive *Minutes*, February 21, 1903.

[4] *The Law on Strikes and Lockouts*, by Herman Cohen. London Trades Council. 1d.

general trend of the movement in Scotland. Glasgow Trades Council decided that their own Secretary, George Carson, should stand for the town council. 'A letter was read from the Trades Council advising that the General Secretary be allowed to act as Election Agent for Mr Carson in the Cowlairs ward.'[1]

Accordingly, 'after some discussion', it was agreed that Lyon should be allowed to act as Carson's election agent. Even where financial considerations decided the Executive not to support an appeal from a political organization, it never passed them by without careful deliberation.

Lyon was quick to seize any opportunity of going on a deputation to be received by the Corporation—on behalf of the sett-makers, or of the street cleaners, for example—before the Association itself won trade union recognition from the Glasgow Corporation in 1904. He spoke on May Day at the request of the Labour Day Committee in 1903, and the Association was asked 'that three lorries be sent to the Green on Sunday'. But, although to be even election agent was good, Lyon wanted to be the man who held the whip. He had some trouble in getting the Executive to see that it would be to the advantage of the Association if their secretary was busy in other spheres, such as local politics. They probably had in mind that the membership was already complaining of the organizer, Willie Laidlaw, secretary for Central Branch, who was thought to be allowing the Tenants Defence Committee, of which he was also secretary, to take up too much of his time. Lyon's first supporter was ignominiously dismissed for neglecting his work.[2] But the Executive certainly wanted to see their money's worth for the small salary they were paying the General Secretary; so, in the autumn of 1904, they refused to allow him to stand as candidate for the Town Council in Anderson ward, although they let him go forward for the Townhead Parish Council. It was not for some years that Lyon realized his ambition and became a town councillor in Townhead. Meanwhile he cultivated local contacts; and, the moment the Association had any funds to invest, they went into Glasgow Corporation and similar stock, or Civic Press and co-operative societies' shares. The Association's General Secretary patronized local enterprise; he expected—and got— dividends of more than one kind.

Of the four main categories of employers—municipalities, co-operative

---

[1] Executive *Minutes*, February 7, 1903.

[2] Questioned at a general meeting of members in Albion Halls Glasgow on January 29, 1905, the General Secretary said: 'He was sorry to have to inform them that Mr Laidlaw had become worse this year. He never attended his duties. He had been forced to suspend him and Cowcaddens had confirmed his action. The Executive Committee that were here tonight had agreed to leave it in the hands of this meeting. He believed drink had been the downfall of Mr Laidlaw.' This was unfortunately not an isolated case. A year before, the Executive had held a special meeting at which a resolution had been carried: 'That all members of the Executive Committee coming to the Executive Committee meeting the worse for drink be not allowed into the meeting, as it is impossible for anyone to be able to take part in the business rationally when they are intoxicated.' (December 13, 1903)

societies, railway company and railway cartage contractors, and general contractors—the first two were susceptible to the direct pressure of public opinion, if it were aroused. The lively and resourceful young Lyon was fully aware that for this it was necessary that the carters' conditions should be known and that the carters as a body should be respected. It was essential that there should be recognition of the Association by influential sections of employers. Carters employed by the local authorities were in the haulage services (other than those engaged in the passenger services) which consisted largely of the cleansing departments. The Association early had dealings with these departments, particularly in Glasgow, Govan, Springburn, and Paisley. In addition, there was the possibility of bringing pressure to bear to protect the carters of employers who depended upon the local authorities for contracts. As we have seen, the 'Fair Wage Clause' had been a treasured objective of the Scottish trade union movement since the great carters' strike of 1889. Lyon took pains to build connections with town councillors and others who were influential in local politics; he himself was on the Parliamentary Committee of the Scottish Trades Union Congress in 1902, and again in 1909.

The carters suffered under every kind of grievance, but Lyon was careful not to strain the resources of the Association. He did not allow the Executive to take on anything from which he thought no immediate result could be obtained. He went for short-term achievable objectives. He refused at this stage, for instance, to start a general all-out attack on the bitter grievance of Sunday labour, 'owing to the state of trade'. But he knew that it was an issue on which a response could be forced from local authorities. His tactic was to get a personal hearing from committees. Here is a characteristic letter to a town councillor:

'March 9, 1903

'Dear Sir,

'I regret that I am again forced to draw your attention to the fact that Mr McColl Super. of the Cleansing Department absolutely refused to give any satisfaction re the Cleansing Carter. I have wrote him several times to (meet) the men along with I. This he refuses.

'We feel confident if we could get an interview with Mr McColl or the committee we would be able to impress upon them the necessity of the three following questions. Two meal hours per day. The privilege of the Saturday half holiday by stopping at 1 p.m. Also payment of Sunday duty.

'I trust that you will allow me an interview with the Committee as I have endeavoured to prevent trouble so far with any of the employers, by this method. The fact of Mr McColl refusing to hear the men's grievance in itself causes dissention [sic].

'I therefore hope this will have your serious consideration.

'Yours respectfully,

'H. Lyon'.

He tackled Partick local authority on the issue: getting no satisfaction he wrote to a bailie:

'August 17, 1904

'I am taking the privilege of writing you in the expectation that you will support a demand that has been submitted to your Council some months ago by the Cleansing Carters and which we are confident is reasonable. At present our Carters turn out on a Sunday morning. Two of them are paid 3s 6d each for cleaning the Dumbarton Road while the other two attend the horse and get nothing. We believe that if your Council or Committee of that department would grant an interview to a deputation of the men and myself that this grievance could be easily rectified. The very fact of your Council refusing to recognize the men's position is causing great dissatisfaction.

'I have always endeavoured to encourage harmony and prevent friction between employer and employee. In conclusion I might point out that all Stable Bodies and many private employers pay their carters Sunday duty. I therefore trust this will have your earnest support. Thanking you in anticipation.

'Respectfully yours,
'pr. Hugh Lyon
'W.L.'

Amongst other authorities he approached was Govan, where he added the demand to stop work on a Saturday afternoon at 1 p.m. and to pay double time for every hour worked on Sunday. He kept the publicity going until the God-fearing Sabbatarian Glasgow Corporation were at last ready to pay 5s for Sunday duty, with an accepted system of a roster of duties. It was not abolition of the evil; but at least it was recognition, not only of the evil, but of the Association. This was the first trade union which Glasgow Corporation recognized. It was also the thin edge of the wedge with the other groups of employers.

Once the great Glasgow Corporation had recognized the right of payment for Sunday labour, it was a strong argument to use with other local authorities. Lyon would hold out the example and argue that the question affected the carters from a moral standpoint also. There had been a public outcry against running Clyde steamers on Sundays. At a mass meeting at Hamilton in 1907, to open a branch there, he made effective use of this, asking when the local ministers of religion had protested against carters being forced to work on Sundays. He argued that a hundred men were turning out on Sunday mornings in Hamilton 'when, if properly regulated, ten men could do the same work, giving the other ninety an opportunity of attending church'. Long hours, the practice of working late on Saturday afternoons and then having to wait until the last man came in before the employer began to pay out wages, as well as Sunday labour, were all grievances which affected carters everywhere. Anything towards a break away from unrestricted Sunday labour without pay was of vital importance to them.

It made a very great deal of difference in the lives of the carters, who enjoyed the victory, and also to their families, for the children now stood some chance of seeing their fathers occasionally. It gave more leisure, too, for organizing, and for strengthening the Association; the concert, the 'soirée and ball', trips and excursions, which they took pride in organizing, did much to raise their own standing. All this was in addition to the un-premeditated jollifications and 'songs with which members then obliged' which closed many a branch meeting.

Such campaigns gained much local publicity; it was noted by employers, public and private alike. It had also the most important effect of raising the self-respect of the carters, on which the drive to recruit at the stables depended. If successes in dealing with the Sunday labour question, though still restricted in scope, had a very important effect on the carters, there was another campaign which had even more far-reaching conse-quences. It centred on the West Coast in long drawn-out negotiations to induce the Glasgow Corporation to refuse contracts to firms who 'were dealing unfairly with their carters'. Here is an example of Lyon's methods at an early stage of the campaign. On January 30, 1903, he wrote to a firm of contractors demanding an increase of 1s a week:

'We have no intention of causing trouble and I am always prepared to endeavour to work in harmony with the employers of the men. But if forced to take other steps I shall endeavour to bring the matter before the Town Council with whom I believe you have certain contracts.'

When a response was forthcoming, he pressed the employers further,

March 13, 1903:
'I am instructed by the Carters in your employment to thank you for your kindness in granting an increase of wages, but would beg to point out that only a few of the men received this increase. While we are thankful for small mercies, we trust that to save further trouble you will endeavour to extend it to the rest of the men. I feel that you must recognize that the men are underpaid when we take into consideration the wages paid in other stables.'

He was not slow to form a special relationship with employers prepared to co-operate with him, as the following letter (October 2, 1902) shows:

'In reference to our talk this morning, I am pleased to inform you that I saw several of the Councillors and advised them how to act with the result that G——— was thrown out altogether, part of the work being divided between C——— and W——— and the rest I understand going to you which I trust will be satisfactory. If my present support at any future time will do you any good I shall always be pleased to help the employer whom I believe is doing his best to keep up the wages of the workers under the present system of competition.'

In later years, his emphasis on conceding favours to employers who were prepared to co-operate with the Association went very much further. On at least two major occasions, in 1919 and 1926, his use of this tactic crossed the danger line and laid him open to serious criticism. But, in the years 1903–7, the skilfully conducted struggle over the corporation contractors and for formal recognition of the Association went hand in hand.

At the time there was keen competition to get Glasgow Corporation contracts. The result was that a contractor might hire a horse and cart with driver to the Corporation for 7s a day, with the carter receiving 3s for ten hours' work. Could the Corporation be pressed to insist upon a minimum wage? It took many months of campaigning in many different ways. It was a notable event when the then Glasgow organizer, Peter Gillespie, could report in 1907 that the Corporation had received a deputation from the Association; and that the Town Clerk later asked the Association 'to pick from thirty-nine contractors the names of those we thought suitable to meet them re contracts. Twelve names were selected and agreed to'.

Nine contractors were interviewed by a special committee of the Corporation on November 27, 1907, and agreed to terms. It was decided to add the following conditions:

'Provided that in all contracts for cartage work the contractors should be bound to employ competent workmen only for the work to be performed under their contracts, and to pay such workmen a minimum wage of 24s per week.'

Although they did not succeed in getting the minimum raised above 24s, they got the principle accepted that no new contracts would be offered by the Corporation to contractors who paid less than the minimum. Thus, although the wage was low and they were tied to it, the seed of a 'Fair Wage Clause' had been planted in a sphere where intense competition for tenders had forced carters' wages to a very low level. Other contractors were quick to take note. An example was an East End employer, with thirty carters receiving 22s per week. The Association objected to his receiving Corporation contracts. He approached Lyon, asked him to visit the stables, to recruit the men. He would dismiss those who would not join; and he would then raise wages to 24s. Lyon wrote in his memoirs:

'I went up to the first man and asked him if he were a member of the union. For answer I was told: 'No, and I have no intention of joining it.' 'Well,' I said, 'This is Friday, and if you don't join tomorrow, don't come back on Monday, look for another job.' And so I went through the whole stable, and on the Saturday most of them joined the Society while the others were dismissed, and it was my duty to fill the places they had vacated with members of the union.'

Public pressure had been roused sufficiently to produce some surprising results.

The second group of employers on whom public opinion might be expected to have a strong influence were the co-operative societies. Whilst they were to be found all over Scotland from Cowlairs to St Cuthberts, from Aberdeen to Ayr, they varied in size and strength and in the closeness of their relations with the Association. There was a wide variety of work; their carters and drivers managed all sorts of vehicles, including bakers' vans, hearses, and coal-wagons. There was a marked difference of outlook amongst most categories of carters in those days. There was the lorryman employed by the railway companies; the driver who was also a salesman, as, for example, the baker's roundsman or the driver employed by aerated water companies; the vanman; and the common carter. Sometimes there was distrust between them. The vanmen tended to hold aloof, more especially the United Co-operative Baking Society men. In March 1905, Lyon invested £500 in the funds of this Society. He applied for permission to hold meetings in their stables and in local societies. Usually he got it, but it took two years before he made headway in those co-operative stables where men thought of themselves as a class apart. Under pressure from the trade union movement, the directors of the United Co-operative Baking Society decided that all their employees must join some trade union. The bakers' vanmen still held off from the Association; they were hard to convince that they had need of a union which catered for all groups of carters. They formed a union of their own, which failed; they joined the Glasgow Cabmen's union or the Co-operative Employees' Union. Finally the difference was resolved:

'A letter was read from the Directors of the United Co-operative (Baking) Society stating that the New Starts had been told to join our Society.'[1]

It was impossible in those early days to achieve anything like uniform wages, hours, and conditions from the co-operative societies; but at least there was a substantial degree of recognition. For two years the Association had studied the position with a number of co-operative societies, looking for a favourable moment to win improvement from amongst those who ought to be the best of employers. Many societies, however, were themselves suffering from hard times. The Cowlairs Co-operative Society, for example, could not find the 2s increase which the carters asked for; instead they offered 1s 6d for every extra rake above ten. This was an

---

[1] Executive *Minutes*, September 11, 1907.

approach to the conception of a fixed day's work and, therefore, to the possibility of overtime payments. Lyon became a director of that society; he saw it as a vantage point from which to gain improvements for carters in other societies too.

3. THE HUNGRY YEAR OF 1908

The third main category of employers were the railways and the three firms on contract to the railways, the railway contractors, Wordie & Company, Cowan & Company, and Mutter Howey. They operated in all the main railway centres of Scotland. Up to the years just before the First World War, the Caledonian Railway Company, for example, used some hundreds of horses; in addition, however, they had to employ the railway contractors because they had insufficient horses to do all their work. The same applied to the North British Railway Company. There was a Railway Contractors' Association, which was a tough nut to crack.

The closing years of the Association's first decade were not a favourable time to make an onslaught upon the contractors. Prolonged and bitter unemployment in 1907 and 1908 put this class of employer in a strong position. All over Scotland thousands were near starvation point. The carters were not the least hardest hit. An interesting book,[1] describing what openings were available for juveniles in four main centres in Scotland in 1908, gives these numbers of men employed in carting and van-driving:

	Male	Female
Glasgow	10,747	11
Dundee	1,787	—
Edinburgh	3,090	1
and Leith	1,384	2
Aberdeen	1,810	—
	18,818	14

The Edinburgh United Trades Council's Annual Report for 1908 gives the wages and usual hours of members of societies affiliated to it. Amongst them are included cab-drivers, 18s and eighty hours; co-operative carters, 28s and fifty-four hours; municipal carters, 24s and fifty-six hours. Mass unemployment in all trades brought great pressure to bear on the carters. In London a Right-to-Work Conference was held on December 5, 1908. There were big demonstrations in George Square in Glasgow; thousands had to be fed there each day.[2]

[1] *A Handbook of Employments*, by Mrs Ogilvie Gordon (Hon. corresponding secretary of the International Council of Women, Vice-President of the National Union of Women Workers). The Rosemount Press, 1908.

[2] Lyon described in his memoirs what happened to one Association member: 'One day

Trade had been bad year after year. This crushing slump came on top of years of low wages and long hours. Appalling as were the conditions in railway cartage, employment was steadier than in other classes of work. Many men worked from 4 and 5 a.m. till 8 and 9 p.m., without any meal hours; on Saturday it was generally 4 or 5 p.m. before they finished. They were kept standing in the stations till 7 and 9 p.m. in all weathers. Their wages ranged between 19s and 25s per week, on condition that they turned out again at 8 a.m. on Sunday morning to feed and clean their horses, failing which 1s was deducted from their already low wages. The men worked an average of seventy-five hours per week for a wage of 23s, and were responsible for all breakage of material and loss of goods from the lorry. There were cases of men paying up claims of £50 at 2s 6d per week for goods that were stolen from their lorries. If summoned to the court for any street irregularity, the carter had to pay all fines and for loss of time. Only a very big movement could succeed in making a breakthrough to protect the men on railway cartage. That was to come when all the railway-men themselves moved, in the turbulent days of industrial strife in 1910 onwards. But, for the time being, little progress could be made by the Association in this sector.

There remained the immensely varied group of employers, the general contractors. For the most part they did not deal with light deliveries or parcels, which were handled direct by the railway companies' light lorries and vans. The general contractors used drays and heavy horse-drawn vehicles. Typical loads would be bricks, wood, pig-iron, flour, jute, brewage, and other heavy materials to the docks and elsewhere. They were badly organized, and, like tramp carters, largely unorganizable. The workers in this sector were the first to feel the effects of mass unemployment.

In the demonstrations and conferences called by Glasgow Trades Council or sponsored by the Scottish TUC about unemployment, and in support of the great Belfast strike of that time, the Association played its part. But the number of unemployed, as well as the number of the tramp carters on the move, made the Executive hesitant to start a campaign for a general 2s increase, which they finally decided upon. They embarked on it step by step. After the Clydebank coal carters had been given 26s a week, with 1s for vanmen and 6d per horse payment for Sunday duty,

---

a member came to me for sick aliment. From his appearance I thought he had been drinking, and made inquiries at his house, when I found that he had been a total abstainer for years, but had been out of work for some weeks. Next day he called again. I gave him some money. He rushed to the first butcher's shop, bought some beef, hurried home to his wife and told her to feed the bairns. This man had been slowly losing his reason through watching his children starving. The day following he was taken to the asylum, where he died.'

'It was also agreed to organize the stables which were not paying 26s per week and if necessary bring them out on strike until they got it.'[1]

It was some six weeks later that they proceeded to the next step after having

'reports submitted by all members of the EC regarding the agitation for an increase of wages which went to show that a large number of contractors were favourable to an increase of 1s. After a general discussion which lasted over an hour, it was decided to bill a meeting for Sunday April 14, 1907, and get further reports and also getting the feeling of the men.'[2]

With the purpose of encouraging a conciliatory spirit in the employers, Lyon planted an inspired report in the Glasgow Press that 10,000 Glasgow carters were coming out on strike. At the mass meeting in the Albion Halls, it was announced amid great enthusiasm that more than forty contractors had already agreed to an increase of 1s, whilst Lyon read aloud letters which he had written to employers who had refused. The railwaymen also had decided to petition for an increase. Whether the contractors believed what they read in the papers, we cannot tell; but it is certain that the carters did. For to Lyon's embarrassment and dismay many stables began coming out on strike on the strength of the story which had appeared, unionists and non-unionists alike. He tried to order stable after stable back to work, but the non-unionists did not recognize his authority. In his memoirs, Lyon says that the planting of the Press story which induced the men to strike 'taught us a lesson to be more careful'. But he was always a great believer in the efficacy of frightening the employer with Press threats of strikes, and he was continually doing it. He did not like strikes, but he regarded the threat of strikes as legitimate and skilful practice.

At the end of 1907, when the railway carters were claiming an increase from the three railway contractors, he inserted inspired strike threat stories in the Glasgow Press once more. Similarly, the next year, when starting a wage campaign in Dundee, he used the *Dundee Advertiser* in the same way. In May 1908, when the Glasgow Cabmen's Union dissolved and joined the Association, one of their employers who was a town councillor threatened to dismiss them. Lyon put an inspired report in the Press that he himself was contesting the employer's ward, where many cabmen and their families lived; the employer gave in at once. If Lyon was unpredictable, domineering, and apt to shout the members down, there was a large number amongst the rank and file who did not at all resent it. As an old member put it admiringly: 'That was how he treated the employers, too, you see!'

[1] Executive *Minutes*, February 20, 1907.
[2] Executive *Minutes*, April 10, 1907.

Most of those who remember Lyon's early organizing efforts from 1902 to 1914 remark upon his skill, energy, resourcefulness, and mental agility. An Aberdeen veteran, John Shand, stressed that 'Lyon's organizing campaigns gave the carter self-respect. When he first came here he spoke very sharply to the men: "You'll buy a yard of ribbon for your horse's mane, but you don't buy a ribbon for your little girl." And that was true!' Some of the carters had suffered so long that it seemed inevitable and part of the natural order of things. Lyon describes the reaction of an old member in the Glasgow cleansing department when it was first proposed that payment should be demanded for Sunday duty. This man rose up and said: 'Well, Lyon, I hae often heard you speak but I never heard you blethering such nonsense before. He's a gey funny carter that drives a horse six days in the week and canna gang and feed and water him on the Sunday.'

Before the members had learnt the self-confidence and self-respect which can only come finally from a knowledge of their own strength proved in battle, it is not surprising if they looked for champions rather than leaders. At least they felt that Lyon was bringing their case before the public, and they began to see themselves with changed eyes as the public began to take notice.[1]

Slowly the seeds of the organizing campaigns began to grow. Old branches began to revive or become re-established and new ones were

---

[1] Their slowly changing attitude is well expressed by the following verses, written in 1906:

'Dear freen', in reading o'er this screed
I hope tae it ye wull pey heed,
An' if ye think that we are richt
Come help us mak the burden licht.

Noo, cairter chaps are pushed gey sair,
Their pay, ye ken, is ocht but fair,
Their hours are lang the hale week roun',
Nae men wark langer in the toon.

Anither pint that we maun mark,
Is getting nocht for Sunday wark,
For tranship rakes the pey is sma'
In fac', it widna feed a craw.

Although we wark wi' micht and main,
In sunshine, hail, an' sna', an' rain,
Oor maisters for us dinna care
Supposin' auld age made us puir.

The maisters lang ha' kicked the ba',
Noo, let us cheenge it, yince for a',
An' things wull alter if ilka man
Wull dae what's richt an' jine the van.

Maist every Union chap can tell
That jining the Union helps yoursel',
Sae dinna bide back, 'list the noo,
An' if ye'll help us, we'll help you.

set up. Several permanent collectors were appointed, such as Peter Gillespie, 'Sanny' Macfarlane, and Bob McAulay, usually from amongst Executive members. In the autumn of 1906, former members in Edinburgh and Leith applied to rejoin the Association. A deputation of Harry Erskine and George Malcolm came from Leith to a Glasgow Quarterly meeting, and negotiations began. It was agreed to accept them all, provided William McQueen, who had led the breakaway in 1902, was not admitted. Other moving spirits were Archie and Jim Mark, John Imrie, and John Williamson. In December 1906, Lyon and Tom Manuel, an Executive Council member, went to Leith and addressed a meeting in Kirkgate, Leith, at which forty joined. Branches opened up in Hamilton, Barrhead, Wishaw, Cambuslang, and Motherwell, while Townhead branch began to recruit heavily amongst the railway carters. In March 1907, the Dundee Trades Council, as part of its efforts to assist in organizing there, offered to organize a meeting of carters to be addressed by Lyon. Organization in Dundee had sadly fallen away and their conditions were deeply depressed; wages were as low as from 16s to £1, with no payment for Sunday duty and no regulation of hours. It took a number of meetings and a week of organizing effort before a strong branch was formed in the early summer of 1907. One of the biggest obstacles was the collapse of earlier union organization. But they campaigned for a 23s minimum; and, after the usual Press stories that a strike was imminent, gained substantial advances from a number of contractors. By the autumn of 1908 the branch was strong enough to justify the appointment of a permanent collector, and Harry Erskine moved there from Leith. A few years later, he was succeeded by Bob Stewart, whose elder brother had been a founder member of the branch when it was first formed by Sampson in 1902.

Although the bulk of the Association's membership were horsemen, motor vehicles were beginning to come into use all over Scotland. The younger carters were learning to drive motors, and it was finally decided that the name should be changed from Scottish Carters' Association. After a series of meetings an application was made for a change of name, which was registered on June 11, 1908. It read:

'The following is a copy of a resolution passed by the consent of two-thirds of the total number of members of the trade union: "That the time has arrived when we should alter our name to the Scottish Horse & Motormen's Association".'

It was signed by Richard Russell, Hugh Heslin, John Hair, Robert Carson, Thomas Manuel, John Forsyth, Peter Johnstone, and Hugh Lyon. At a meeting in the Albion Halls on August 16, 1908 a banner inscribed with the new name was unfurled. Formerly it had been the banner of the Edinburgh & Leith carters. The Association had been in existence for a decade, all but two months.

Not the least important factor enabling the Association to survive its first decade had been a change in the organization of the finances. This was a change from collecting dues through stable and branch to having collectors call at the men's homes instead. As a veteran collector remarked: 'Without developing this method, the Association could not have lasted out its first twenty years, but would have gone under like all the others before it.' If a stable collector were victimized, the branch would find it hard to find a replacement; arrears mounted and were not collected. The branch itself fell away. Stable collectors also sometimes became defaulters. Sometimes, when money was handed over weekly to the branch for delivery to the central office each month, after deduction of branch expenses, it would go astray at that level. Slackness in collecting dues and allowing arrears to mount, together with muddled accounts and occasional downright defalcation, had a seriously demoralizing effect. This came to a head in 1905, when one of Willie Lowden's opponents in Plantation Branch was charged by Coplawhill Stable 'with not acting honestly as collector'. Peter Gillespie was appointed to replace him and go into his books, where a deficiency was found. After discussing this for some weeks, Plantation recommended to the Executive that collectors should be appointed 'to work on the same method as the Assurance Societies'. This was supported on the Executive by Lyon and by those who saw in it a further step towards centralization, both of funds and of control. They thought that this would remove the need of a branch committee, believing that all a secretary should do was to collect dues and hand them over to head office. The proposal was opposed at first not only by the Paisley branch but also by the committee of the Glasgow Combined branches. But Lyon had written to England to consult the Amalgamated Carters, Lurrymen and Motormen whose headquarters was in Bolton; they had experience of a similar method. He reported that he had heard 'from the English Association stating that the success of their Association depended on house-to-house collecting'.[1]

It was decided to send Lyon and 'Sanny' Macfarlane to England 'to find out about conditions and wages and how their Association was conducted'. When they reported back, 'Gillespie moved that we recommend the Quarterly Meeting to centralize the whole of the branches and to establish at once the method of house-to-house collecting.'[2] Collectors were to be paid ten per cent, and 3d for all new members. Paisley was the only branch at this stage to object. But at the next quarterly meeting 'it was agreed to centralize the whole of the branches and close the halls as early as possible'. This method of collection and the system of Quarterly Meetings became the characteristic pattern of the Association.

An important side effect was that it brought the carters' womenfolk

[1] Executive *Minutes*, March 25, 1905.
[2] Executive *Minutes*, June 17, 1905.

3. A horse-drawn rotary sweeping brush. Road-sweeping vehicles were used in 1869 in Glasgow; this later model dates from the turn of the century. The driver is John Smith, a carter and later a stableman at St Rollox.

'Water butts' were used as early as 1873 by Glasgow Corporation; this model dates from the turn of the century.

4. An incident during the carters' strike at Leith, 1912. (pp. 114–6).

The Glasgow Carters' Strike of January/February 1913. Mounted police protecting a master's house at Marghill, outside which carters burnt his effigy. (pp. 119–24).

directly in touch with the Association. The housewife paid the dues and was kept up to date with news of wages and hours and the campaigns of the Association. A collector with many years' experience said: 'Once they knew what was going on, the wives were often as good and better union members than the menfolk.' No longer did the members fall into arrears or get out of touch when they moved from stable to stable. Three years later, in June 1908, the funds stood at £4,000 and the membership had crept up to 3,000.

In these years, between 1904 and 1907, there was another development characteristic of the Association and of the times. It was on November 15, 1903, that a special meeting of the Executive 'decided to recommend to the members the advisability of forming a sick fund'. This had been attempted from the first, but it had been hampered by the continued existence of the old Glasgow Carters' Society and the schemes of the employers' Stable Societies, together with the weakness of the young Association's own finances. Now the fund was to be compulsory; contributions were to be raised to 6d; but older carters were required to pay more and no carter over fifty years of age was allowed to join without the special permission of the Executive, to make sure that he was healthy enough not to be likely to claim too heavily. There was a 2s fee for new members, and no sick aliment was paid for six months, when it was 10s a week for the first six weeks, 5s for the next six weeks, and thereafter no more within the next year.

For some months, following a general meeting of Glasgow members, there was argument and discussion, both as to the scheme and its rules. One contentious rule was that, to help to finance the fund it was decided to reduce to fifteen per cent from twenty-five per cent the percentage of contributions which a branch was entitled to devote to its own needs, to reduce collector's commission from ten per cent to seven per cent, and to cut back from seven per cent to five per cent the branch secretary's commission on the dues collected weekly from the stable collectors. As far as the Glasgow membership went—and that was decisive—the scheme was in essence accepted by the change to the house-to-house collection of dues. Paisley's opposition did not count, and, by the end of 1903, Plantation's spirit had already been broken.

A general meeting in the Albion Halls on November 22, 1903, with 120 attending, approved the necessary change of rules, which were registered in December 1903. The fund came into force on January 1, 1904, and first payments were made in July 1905. But, for a very long time to come, each Executive, and most Quarterly Meetings, went through much discussion about the treatment of exceptional cases. Throughout, Lyon took an unwavering line on this subject, which he expressed most forcibly on the Executive a year after the scheme was proposed. It was a stormy meeting, notable for more than one fierce row between Lyon and his last remaining chief supporter, 'Sanny' Macfarlane, who remarked at one point that 'he had been longer connected with the Union than Mr Lyon, who thought he knew everything, but had a great deal to learn yet'. The Executive discussed whether to pay benefit in some exceptional cases, where doctor's lines were late. Sometimes a branch representative pleaded for consideration on the ground that 'this was one of his best members'. The General Secretary said:

'He would take the whole of these cases to the Quarterly meeting and show that the EC were breaking the rules as none of the men were entitled to aliment; and if rules were to be carried out, members should be learnt to take an interest in them. So far as he could see it seemed the EC were simply following the footsteps of the old unions and paying money to anybody. This had been their ruin and he for one refused to be a party to it while he was Gen. Sec.'[1]

He got his way on that occasion. Some members had entertained hopes that the Sick Fund would help break the grip of the 'company' Stable Societies, that its main purpose was to be, in today's parlance, a 'fringe benefit', which would prove an easy means of recruiting to the Association, but that was not Lyon's idea. He saw the Sick Fund as the main source of revenue, and so it proved to be; he watched benignly every shilling that came into it, but he scrutinized closely every penny that went out. In reading over the decisions on the payment of sick aliment of those years, 1904 to 1907, it is difficult not to be shocked by the very high proportion of claims for the death of children. The infant mortality rate was significantly high in those days in Glasgow amongst the carters' families.

It is a sidelight on the dreadful conditions, out of which the Scottish carters still had to raise themselves, that the second combined quarterly meeting on July 3, 1904, could be told of a stable where men were working nineteen hours a day—longer in those post-Boer War, Edwardian days than during the Crimean War and the Indian Mutiny, in 'the Old Queen's time'. When they put aside the mourning weeds and the fantastic trappings of the old Queen's funeral, the prospect presented by Parliamentarians, publicists, and leaders in every walk of life was that they were to move into a new century of modern times, of peace and prosperity, with Edward the Peacemaker. At the end of the Association's first decade, the carters might well have learnt that there was to be no peace and prosperity handed to them on a dish, but great misery from unemployment, and, for those in work, continuing long hours and low pay.

---

[1] Executive *Minutes*, September 3, 1904.

APPENDIX

Organizations appealing for support, 1902-6

Organizations which appealed for funds, membership, representation, or support of some kind during early years included the following:

**Workers' Representation Committee, inviting delegates to Dundee, of January 1903 (November 15, 1902)

*Glasgow Trades Council for Housing Demonstration Committee. (November 6, 1902)

**Free Ferries Committee. (November 6, 1902)

**Glasgow Workers' Election Committee. (November 6, 1902)

**Paisley Election Committee. (November 6, 1902)

**Glass Workers' Strike Committee. (December 6, 1902)

**Edinburgh Trades Council, about a compensation test case. (January 10, 1903)

**Shaw Maxwell's Election Fund ('As we took no action in the election we take no action in the question of finance'). (February 7, 1903)

*Scottish TUC, AGM (February 7, 1903)

*Glasgow Trades Council, asking that Lyon be permitted to act as Carson's Election Agent. (February 7, 1903)

*London Trades Council, about a pamphlet on the Taff Vale case (February 21, 1903)

*Ballachulish Quarrymen Disaster Fund. (April 18, 1903)

**Falkirk Workers' Election Committee. (April 18, 1903)

*Labour Day Committee, asking for delegates. (April 18, 1903)

**Scottish Workers' Representation Committee. (June 6, 1903)

*Tenants' Defence Committee, asking for members. (June 6, 1903)

*Glasgow Municipal Workers' Election Committee's annual meeting on August 14, 1903. (August 1, 1903)

*Glasgow Trades Council, asking for delegates to a meeting in support of Tailors on strike. (September 5, 1903)

*Paisley Workers' Election Committee, asking for branch support. (September 5, 1903)

*Workers' Representation Committee, inviting delegates to Annual Conference. (November 7, 1903)

**Chinese Labour Committee ('Decided to give nothing since we are not taking part in the demonstration'). (June 4, 1904)

*Workers' Election Committee Conference. (August 6, 1904)

**Keir Hardie, MP, Testimonial Committee. (September 3, 1904)

*Scottish Workers' Election Committee Conference, delegates appointed. (November 5, 1904)

*Pipeclay Workers' Strike Committee. (January 29, 1905)

** No action
* Supported

*Glasgow Labour Party Unemployed demonstration. (February 4, 1905)

*Labour Literary Society. (April 1, 1905)

**Edinburgh Conference on Land Values. (April 1, 1905)

*Glasgow Trades Council Committee, for opening Art Galleries on Sunday. (April 1, 1905)

*Glasgow Trades Council Conference on Unemployment. (June 17, 1905)

*Hemsworth Miners, Yorkshire, on strike. (October 2, 1905)

*Partick Liberal Association asked for members to act on their committee; decided to allow members to do so. (December 25, 1905)

*Welsh miners on strike. (February 5, 1906)

*Scottish Women's League. (July 29, 1906)

** No action
* Supported

CHAPTER SIX

THE CARTER'S DAY'S DARG

I. CONSOLIDATING LOCAL SUCCESSES

As it entered its second decade in 1909, the Association was growing in numbers, even in the bad times of miserable trade. It is difficult to get an exact picture of the membership in the first dozen years of the life of the Association. Lyon did not give detailed figures until 1911. We know, for example, that, at three combined quarterly meetings during 1903, it was claimed that a total of 1,588 new members had been booked, but there is no record of how many lapsed, and we do not, therefore, know the total membership. A government publication[1] gives the Association's membership in 1906 as 2,500 and in 1910 as 5,000; in the 1911 Annual Report, Lyon gives the current total as 7,266, and claims that 3,485 were added during the year, again without stating the figure for those who lapsed. The numbers of those organized amongst tramway servants, busmen, cabmen, and carters, whilst fluctuating through the years from 1901 to 1910, ended with a ten per cent rise:

Year	Railway Servants	Tramway Servants, Carters, etc.	Seamen	Dock & Canal Workers etc.	Total
1901	76,207	32,156	22,234	48,831	179,428
1902	74,727	32,280	17,070	45,450	168,527
1903	74,895	30,862	15,950	44,994	166,701
1904	86,999	32,866	17,800	43,707	171,372
1905	72,605	32,582	16,859	43,871	175,917
1906	102,085	34,988	16,625	46,754	200,452
1907	138,887	38,490	17,874	53,655	248,906
1908	118,713	37,237	18,767	55,025	229,742
1909	112,130	38,535	20,820	51,309	222,794
1910	116,214	42,420	24,377	59,259	242,270

In 1906 there were twenty-five in this category of trade unions: no less than eleven had ceased to exist five years later. Of the road transport

---

[1] *Report on Trade Unions in 1908–1910*. With Comparative Statistics for 1901–1910. Board of Trade (Labour Department).

unions whose numbers ran into four figures, the Association rose from fifth to third place:

Name	1906	1907	1908	1909	1910
Amalgamated Tramway & Vehicle Workers	13,011	15,010	14,833	15,391	17,076
London Carmen	6,531	6,051	5,065	4,942	5,690
Amalgamated Carters, Lurrymen & Motormen	3,300	3,880	4,050	3,695	3,995
London Cab Drivers	2,885	2,421	1,632	2,426	3,309
Scottish Horse & Motormen's Association	2,500	3,024	3,352	4,302	5,000
National Amalgamated Coal Porters	2,143	1,914	1,505	1,540	1,535
United Carters of England	2,073	2,465	2,564	2,754	2,839

To take the Scottish organizations only, the number of unions had fallen from eight to four by 1911, and the Association was six and a half times the size of the other three put together:

Name	Year Founded	1906	1907	1908	1909	1910
Edinburgh & Leith Cab-Drivers	1885	216	213	213	210	212
Scottish Hackney Carriage, Tramway & Omnibus Employees (Glasgow)	1890	126	*(Ceased to exist about the end of 1907)*			
Associated Horsemen (Greenock)	1894	310	310	320	310	315
Glasgow Carters	1894	360	350	320	300	260
Scottish Horse & Motormen	1898	2,500	3,024	3,352	4,302	5,000
Scottish Hackney Carriage & Tramway Employees	1899	86	64	74	85	22
			(Dissolved 1911)			
Edinburgh Carters & General Workers	1901	250	135	*(Joined the Association in 1908)*		
Inverness Cabmen	1906	45	35	35	15	
			(Dissolved 1910)			

How was all this achieved during the first dozen years? In part, of course, it was in line with the general trend, and particularly with the growth of transport and communication as a whole, responding to the needs of the expansion of industry, similar to the still developing basic industries of coal-mining and iron and steel. The growth of organization of dockers and general labourers and the all-grades movement amongst the railworkers could not be held back. The days of hard times, when in all the Minutes there is some reference to 'the present state of trade', were followed by great strike struggles and mounting industrial unrest, and class clashes on a very big scale all over Britain. The introduction of the national insurance scheme by the National Insurance Act of 1911 did not stop it. The underpaid, the underdog, was on the move; and the strikes of the miners, dockers, and railwaymen brought them into full confrontation with the Government itself in 1911, 1912, and, indeed, right up to the outbreak of war in August 1914.

With this strong spirit of militant struggle went the organization of masses of those hitherto unorganized, and a tendency to look for allies in amalgamations and federations. These in their turn stimulated further organization. One example, parallel to the building of the National Union of Railwaymen as an all-grade, new type of industrial union, occurred amongst the transport workers, where Robert Williams had formed the National Transport Workers Federation, in November 1910, out of a mass of local and fragmentary unions all over the British Isles. The Association's relations with this Federation fluctuated. On occasion, the Association affiliated; at other times Lyon was on terms which could scarcely be described as less than abusive. But in the early stages he saw it, whatever its other merits or demerits, as a means of bringing pressure to bear on some of the rival Scottish organizations, which, in addition to the Greenock Horsemen, included by 1912 a notable breakaway from the Association in Dundee, led by Peter Gillespie. The moves towards and away from amalgamation and federation we shall discuss in Chapters Seven and Eight.

By the end of the first decade, the Association had had a measure of success with its campaigns. In the main centres of Scotland, the principle of payment for Sunday labour was fairly well established. A number of local authorities, especially on the West Coast, had conceded that contractors on corporation contracts must afford their carters fair wages and conditions. In the public sector the Association had gained a certain degree of recognition as a negotiating body. During 1909 and the first half of 1910, these gains were slowly consolidated town by town. A minimum was achieved in Paisley; Leith Corporation agreed not to give contracts where the employers were paying as little as £1 a week; contractors to Dundee Corporation were required to pay a minimum of 23s, which made it easier to bring pressure upon those undertaking general carting work; Falkirk town council agreed to payment for Sunday work. In Edinburgh the Association began a campaign in the courts against employers who imposed illegal fines; the first employer taken to court being D. Y.

Abbey, who had made deductions from the pay of men who went too few rakes.

Organization began to look up. In Edinburgh it improved, and the first combined quarterly meeting was held with Leith; more branches were opened, or revived, as in Motherwell and Kilmarnock. But organization efforts failed in Perth; there was little success at first in Aberdeen, where wages had fallen as low as 19s, with a foreman receiving only 21s, following the collapse of the carters' organization at the turn of the century. The gains were still local successes, but the Association's influence was spreading. But before any considerable progress throughout Scotland could be made, two major problems had to be tackled. First and foremost it was necessary to gain a recognized working-day, or standardized working-week. Secondly, a minimum wage had to be established. Only on the sure foundation of these principles could a fruitful campaign be launched to cut down the appalling hours in carting and to raise the general standard of wages from the depths to which they had dropped.

2. THE HOURS' MOVEMENT BEGINS

Towards the end of 1909, the movement on hours began in Glasgow. At first it was only a propaganda campaign; circulars were sent to all employers demanding a week of fifty-six hours. Meetings were held all over Glasgow. The employers as a whole did not move; but the all-grades movement in the railways, with its demand for the eight-hour day, had a big influence on the railway carters. This, together with the publicity that was given to the fact that railway carters were working seventy-five hours in the week, brought some response from the railway companies. They received deputations of carters from the stables and made a tentative agreement to pay overtime before 6 a.m. and after 6 p.m. In Dundee, the railway employees, after prolonged agitation and threats of a strike, got a wage increase of 2s. But when the year 1910 opened, which was to see many industrial battles and a rising ferment amongst miners and transport workers of all kinds throughout Britain, there was still no normal working-day for the carters in Scotland.

Speaking of thirty years later, when even the most arbitrary of the road haulage employers had been brought not only to accept but indeed to rely upon collective bargaining, a prominent Association negotiator said of their leaders: 'It was always the hours and overtime they stuck on'. In the first decade of the century they would not even hear of discussing the possibility of a regular number of hours in the carter's normal day, let alone limiting it or conceding overtime. The employers fixed the number of rakes, or journeys, which made up the day's darg, or stint, of the carter; when he had done these, and had tended his horse and harness in the stable, he was perfectly at liberty to go home, so far as the employers were concerned. Now, with the death of Edward VII in 1910 and the accession of George V, the Association was to develop a massive campaign on hours.

Hours and conditions in the railway stables, the biggest single concentration, were particularly bad in Glasgow. There were no fixed hours when work began, because of the special conditions of railway haulage; carters who started at four and five o'clock in the morning to tend their horses were still at work at eight and nine in the evening, with no allowance for meal times; on Saturday they finished at four or five in the afternoon.

Lyon sought opportunities for a test case to strengthen an agitation for a fixed working-week. An occasion soon presented itself. King Edward VII died on May 6, 1910; and for many weeks there were funeral ceremonies and royal visitations all over Britain, including Scotland. In Glasgow, a carter named J. Duncan was employed for seventeen hours continuously in carting timber for the crush barriers along the route of the funeral procession on May 20th. He claimed 3s overtime from his employer, James Frew, a contractor of Townhead, who refused to pay it. The Association took the case to the Glasgow Sheriff's Court on July 14, 1910. 'Mr J. Jeffrey Hunter argued for the pursuer that the Motormen's and Carters' Union had taken up this case on principle, as many of their members complained of long hours without overtime.'[1] Frew called on other employers to prove that there was no general custom in the trade to pay overtime; they argued that there was no fixed or standard day. If there were no standard day, no claim for overtime could succeed. 'The Sheriff said no clear custom had been proved. Carting was an irregular trade, where the long hours of one day were compensated for by the short hours of another.'

Such was the state of affairs in the city where, twenty-one years earlier, the carters had struck to advance their wages from 24s to 26s and for the payment of overtime after 6 p.m. Some of the employers in 1889 had conceded the claims; yet, in 1910, the carters had no fixed hours, no entitlement to overtime, and wages well below those of their fathers. The case which the Press described as 'The Carter's Day's Darg', attracted a great deal of attention. Industrial unrest all over Britain was mounting fast; the time was ripe for a big campaign. A meeting of carters on September 10, 1910 at the Tinplate Workers' Hall was so crowded that it had to be adjourned to Glasgow Green, where the following resolution was passed:

'That this meeting of horsemen is of opinion that the time has arrived when all horsemen should have a regulated week's work. We, therefore, instruct our Executive Council to request a ten hours' day, with 6 hours on Saturdays making a 56 hours' week; and further, payment for Sunday duty.'

[1] *Glasgow Herald*, July 15, 1910.

Lyon said that they were not to strike, but that the EC would advise them on one declared day not to start work until 6 a.m. and to stop at 6 p.m.

On September 13th, all Glasgow employers were circularized with the demand for a 56-hour week. But once more no response was forthcoming. There were persistent demands for a strike. A ballot was taken, the result of which was overwhelmingly in favour of strike action. The day was fixed. Then at the eleventh hour the railway companies offered terms.[1] They recognized that a normal working-week should be sixty hours, and conceded the right to overtime. This was a major victory for the railway carters in Glasgow and for others as well.

November 1910, had been a stirring month. Lyon had heavily defeated a leading contractor who stood against him in the local elections. Big meetings had been held everywhere, and carters were flocking to join the Association. In the bitterly fought strike of the Welsh miners, troops had been sent to Tonypandy. Everywhere the mood was to take the offensive. Each struggle had repercussions elsewhere. So had the victory of the railway carters in Glasgow. For example, the railway companies warned that merchants who kept carters waiting for loads, so that overtime was incurred, would be charged with it. This altered the complacency with which the railway contractors had regarded the fact that their carters were kept waiting to load and unload at the docks; hitherto the men had had to wait in their own time. Now it would be in the time of the railway contractors, and *their* time was money. Loads began to move faster; more motor vehicles were introduced for the lighter deliveries.

With the general contractors, however, there were protracted negotiations. A strike ballot was taken and the carters showed in no uncertain fashion their willingness to support action. Some general contractors were willing to come to terms, but feared undercutting from competitors; an employers' association was forced upon them by the circumstances. Lyon was as anxious as the employers, on this occasion, to avoid a strike and had to face a stormy eve-of-strike meeting, when he counselled a week's delay. Meanwhile Lyon came to a private arrangement with a big general contractor, who co-operated with him to force a last-minute agreement upon the newly-formed Glasgow employers' association. They conceded a 62½-hour week and payment for overtime and Sunday

[1] It is hereby intimated that the following conditions of service, as affecting the Companies' carters in Glasgow, will come into operation on Thursday, December 1, 1910, viz:

Hours of Duty: 60 hours per week shall constitute the standard hours of work, inclusive of stable duty on week-days, but exclusive of meal hours.

Overtime: Overtime at ordinary rate shall be paid in respect of hours worked on week-days in excess of the standard weekly hours, viz. 60 hours.

Sunday Duty at Stables: In cases where carters are not relieved of Sunday stable duty, such duty shall be paid for at the rate of 5s per day, not exceeding 10 hours, exclusive of meal times.

duties.[1] But it was touch and go. The spirits of the carters were raised high; and this was to bear fruit two years later when they entered a bigger clash still. Where Glasgow led the way, the employers in other Scottish cities one by one were forced to follow suit.

In Paisley, the general contractors held out, and in February 1911 a bitterly fought two-week strike of 350 carters took place there, under the leadership of John Elliott, to win the hours and overtime agreement. In the course of picketing, several Association members were charged with assault, obstruction, and abusive language; but the Paisley employers finally had to fall into line when Glasgow contractors began to take over their work. Noting this, the railway companies granted sixty hours, payment for overtime and Sunday duty in Paisley. In fact, under the impetus of the whole movement, there was a tendency for the carters in different towns outside Glasgow to take independent action, according to the strength of the men and the forcefulness of the leadership, especially since rates and conditions varied from one place to another. Some felt that the attack should first be centred on wages rather than hours; others were dissatisfied with the terms reached by Lyon with the general contractors, and believed that better terms could have been got if the strike had not been called off. Indeed, in Edinburgh and Leith, they extracted better terms than in Glasgow from the general contractors, getting from them and the railway companies alike sixty hours, and payment for overtime and Sunday duty. In Dundee, where Peter Gillespie had recently been transferred as organizer from South Side, increases of between 1s and 2s were won, and a branch of 900 sprang up.

Gillespie and Lyon came into violent collision. Gillespie had been a very popular man in Glasgow and a chairman of the Executive. He was a forceful figure; some said 'a better man than Lyon'. In May 1911 Gillespie led the Dundee members out of the Association and formed the Northern Horse & Motormen's Association. This was a shock to the members; Lyon referred to it in his Annual Report for the year in these terms: 'Mr Gillespie was the means of advising a section of the men to form a local union—merely because he did not get his own way in our Association.' In his memoirs, Lyon says Gillespie was expelled on May 2,

---

[1] Agreement between the Glasgow Contractors' and Horse-owners' Association and the Scottish Horse & Motormen's Association, December 15, 1910.
'That on and after 1st January 1911 subject to the latitude after-mentioned, the working hours on ordinary days be 5.30 a.m. to 6.30 p.m., with an hour for breakfast and an hour for dinner; and on Saturday, 5.30 a.m. to 2 p.m., with an hour for breakfast; provided that where business of any Contractor makes a variation on these terms desirable, mutual arrangements allowing the necessary latitude will be made:
'That as regards Sunday duty, Contractors can arrange for it as they like, and the men can if their employer please, be relieved of it altogether, but if men are brought out on Sunday, they are to be paid at the rate of 5/- a day for the time employed; that the above terms will hold good for twelve months from 1st January next, at the end of which time Deputations will again meet to consider the question.'

1911, 'for wanting to be the general secretary'; if he did, he certainly was not without precedent. The Association sent Harry Erskine to Dundee to collect such dues as he could. The breach widened considerably when the Dundee dockers struck towards the end of the year, and Gillespie's Northern Horse & Motormen came out in support of them; but Lyon records that the Association's members 'took no part in this strike'. On his advice they 'took up a passive position', with Lyon paying them strike aliment when there was no work available for them.

A former official of those days told the author that in his opinion Hugh Lyon was seen at his best in the movement for shorter hours. 'He was young, energetic and resourceful at that time. He did well for the carters then. It was a fight he understood.' He became deeply concerned over the finances of the Association; over £450 had been spent in 1911 on strike aliment. Now came the National Insurance Act, 1911. He believed the best way to build up the resources was to take the fullest advantage of the new Act, which was to come into force in July 1912. The new Insurance Department of which B. H. Shaw, later the leader of the Scottish Labour Party, was clerk during the years 1912 to 1913, was to become a very important part of the work when the Association became an Approved Society. Lyon looked forward to the possibility that 'every carter will become Approved in our Association, as it is the only hope of getting the best out of the Act'. This was the view he expressed in the first Financial Report and Balance Sheet, published in accordance with the requirement of the Act.

By the end of 1911, in addition to the four Glasgow branches, there were nineteen in other towns, Aberdeen, Dumbarton, and Bellshill having been added during the year. In the Report he remarked: 'Let us trust that the general unrest that permeates the industrial world at present will lead to the workers getting a fairer return for their labour.' Reckoning that the Association's members had had some £40,000 added to their wages in the past year, he added in characteristic style, which must have expressed what the members were feeling at that time:

'In fact the Carter is only now beginning to recognize that he is a Man as well as a Carter, and has a right to some measure of justice. We have also issued badges for our members to wear, which I trust will be the means of bringing or forcing those who are prepared to share the victories of our Members within the pale of our Union. So that we may be able in the near future to see every Carter earning at least Thirty Shillings per week.'[1]

The total membership was shown as 7,266, and he claimed to have enrolled 3,485 members during the year. There was a total balance of £9,282 18s 7d, with investments in seven Corporations besides the United Co-operative Baking Society and the Civic Press. There were grants to

[1] *Financial Report*, 1911.

eight trades councils and to two Labour Representation Committees and a grant of £10 to the Welsh miners who were locked in the historic struggle with the Cambrian Combine. Lyon himself had become a town councillor.

Their success in winning the standard day and the principle of payment for overtime and Sunday duty set the carters up in spirits. The man with the heavy load felt that he was ceasing to be the most downtrodden of all. If Charles J. Kirk, the author of *The Car Conductor*, is to be taken seriously —and the people's songs rarely lie in that regard—there were even people to be found who actually envied them:

> 'Och, I'd rayther be a cairter wi' a horse and coal briquettes,
> Or an interfering polis catching bookies making bets,
> Than to staun' a' day collectin' maiks and gettin' tons o' lup
> Frae auld wives and cheeky weemen—Man, it fairly feeds me up.'[1]

They had need of raised spirits, for they had only acted out the prologue to the play. The hours' agreement had to be implemented, and this led almost automatically to disputes about pay. There were strikes in consequence in many towns in Scotland, some resulting in negotiation or voluntary arbitration with important results; strikes sharp and short or long and embittered, which went on through 1911 and 1912, and finally culminated in a great general strike of Scottish carters in Glasgow, with 3,500 out for six weeks in January 1913. The aftermath, together with a separate struggle with a number of co-operative societies, ran on well into the spring of 1914.

3. MAN, BOY AND HALF A BOY

When the standardized week of 60 to 62½ hours had been largely conceded the question of increasing wages became urgent. These varied widely from as little as 22s, with some general contractors, upwards to 35s for vanmen in some co-operative societies; but they also differed by as much 6s or 7s for carters in the same stable. Except with certain corporation work, there was no general standard wage. In those years, a minimum wage had been much canvassed in the larger trade union movement, amongst miners, railwaymen, engineers, dockers, and transport workers and labourers generally.

After their victory over hours, the Glasgow carters and motormen, who were appearing in ever-increasing numbers, were pressing for a strike for better wages. In his memoirs, Lyon says:

'The men were thirsting for a strike, while some felt there was too much money in the funds, and questions were thrown at me wherever meetings were held, such as: "You are afraid of a strike: what are you going to do with all the money?"'

[1] *Glasgow University Verses.*

In December 1911, the Association began to press a demand for a 3s a week increase. Lyon was doubtful whether the railway companies and the general contractors could be taken on simultaneously, but the railway carters would stand for no further delay. They were in a special position. They received between 19s and 25s, the variation being due to a long outdated anomaly.

For, as long ago as the eighties of the nineteenth century it had been found necessary in Glasgow for the railway companies to use boys to guard the parcel vans whilst the drivers were delivering; it was never necessary in the Scottish countryside. The companies therefore used to allow a man 4s for a boy, assuming that his wage was 23s a week. He could employ that boy or do without him; but he still continued to get the 4s. If any goods were lost from the lorry, however, he was held responsible, and had to pay it back at so much per week. It was easy to get a boy at 4s a week, because at that time a boy could leave school at ten or eleven years of age, if he had 'got in his attendances' at school; there was no age limit. In hard times boys would work for 4s a week. Their hours were even worse than the men; for they were often at the stable before the men in the morning and finished after them. A vivid description of the conditions of these lads was given by Hugh Lyon before a Departmental Committee[1] at which he gave evidence on June 21, 1912:

'MR CYRIL JACKSON: 'You say that the boys come earlier in the morning and stay later at night. How much earlier in the morning would they come?'
MR. HUGH LYON: 'Possibly they would come half an hour earlier and stay half an hour later at night. At the same time I should not say there was any great need for them being there either behind or before the men. It is merely a case of my working along with a man whom I regard as master and wanting to do my best for him, and therefore I arrive early in the morning to save him the trouble and I get the harness all ready and put it on the horse. Then at night I should take the harness off and attend to the horse. I should probably do the harness for my master while he was cleaning the horse.'

By 1912 very few railway van-boys were actually employed, although the allowance was still made to the drivers. This was because the drivers could no longer get a boy for 4s a week for some sixty hours' work. As the railway companies engaged new men, they dropped the allowance; but at that time there were still some ten per cent of the railway carters who were allowed 4s on top of their ordinary wage for a boy, but were taking the responsibility themselves. Some were even paid 2s for 'half

[1] *Report of the Departmental Committee on the Hours and Conditions of Employment of Van Boys and Warehouse Boys.* 1913. Cmd. 6886.

a boy', and had been claiming 'half a boy' for fifteen or twenty years. As far as the railway companies were concerned, they had finished with the van-boy. But they employed other juveniles directly, at the same long hours as the men; there were 'trace' boys, for instance, some ten to every hundred carters. They stood at the foot of a hill with a spare horse, which they put on to each lorry as it came, to help pull the load up, and then returned to the bottom ready for the next. In 1912 a 'trace' boy was paid 6s to 8s a week; they were generally between fourteen and seventeen years of age. Lyon explained:

'There is a habit that a boy goes to a trace-horse until he is 16 years of age, and then his father puts him to a trade. But I would say that 70 per cent of them drift into the horse line. Then if they continue to keep in the horse line, if the railway company has a light lorry and a light horse, or a light van, such as you see in the case of the passenger parcel vans of the railway companies, when the boy arrives at possibly 17 or 18 years of age, they put him on to those, and his wages are possibly raised to 15s. As he gets older they gradually put him on to heavier work, and his wages rise accordingly.'

Even worse hours were to be found outside the railway companies, worked by the aerated water salesmen, the laundry delivery vans, and the bakery and biscuit vans—dreadful hours, which were shared by the boys. There were about a dozen manufacturers of aerated water and lemonade in Glasgow, some employing 150 salesmen driving horses, accompanied by boys. In the summer-time the men were paid 'fairly good wages' and commission; but they started at four or five in the morning and did not get home until ten or eleven at night. The boys were employed 'anything from twelve to sixteen hours a day in the summer', and were at the stable before the men in the morning, getting the harness cleaned and the horse ready. At night they cleaned the harness again and helped the men lay it by. For this they got 7s to 9s a week in all. The laundrymen and their boys worked from twelve to sixteen hours, summer and winter as well. Even after the great struggle in 1910 to win a standard day, no settlement could be reached for the aerated water salesmen, nor for the laundrymen and bakers' delivery vanmen. There were then still about 3,500 van-boys in Glasgow. When the Committee asked Lyon about the possibility of education, facts were elicited which cast more light on hours and conditions.[1]

Another factor which led to the railway carters showing a marked degree of impatience was the great railway strike, which had been taking place in the high summer of 1911. A special meeting of railway carters was called in Glasgow at the St Mungo Halls on the eve of a strike in support of their demand for a 3s increase. Lyon, of course, was a member of the

[1] See Appendix.

town council; in that capacity he was approached on the day of the meeting by the Lord Provost, Sir D. M. Stevenson, and shown a draft offer which he had negotiated with the railway companies. The Lord Provost urged Lyon to persuade the men to continue at work pending confirmation that the offer would be made. Lyon describes the scene in his memoirs:

'When I got to the St Mungo Halls I found thousands of men inside and outside who all seemed to have come with their minds made up not to work the next day. Immediately I got up to speak and suggested they continue at work, I was howled down, hissed, called traitor, and every other kind of name. For three solid hours I stood on the platform and endeavoured to address them but failed, while all the time I had news in my pocket that would have pleased them, but in their own interests I dare not tell it, as the Lord Provost was still to meet the railway representatives the following day, and this, of course, had all been done privately.'

Late that night, when he adjourned the meeting for three days, fighting broke out, inside and outside the hall, among the disappointed railway carters. They had certainly shown the mood they were in. The following day the offer was made and endorsed at the adjourned mass meeting. They received advances which established a minimum of 24s, whilst those already receiving more also gained an increase of 1s.

4. THE GLASGOW CONTRACTORS ARBITRATE

The Association next approached the general contractors in Glasgow. Refusing an offer of 1s, the Association agreed to go to arbitration, the first case of which their members had had experience. The Association was represented by George Irvine, James Stewart, J. Forsyth, and Hugh Lyon, who led evidence on February 7, 1912. Chief spokesman for the Glasgow Carting Contractors and Horse Owners' Association was their president, Mr David Murray; the arbitrator was John Craigie, KC, Sheriff Substitute of Lanarkshire.

Lyon said that it was nearly twenty years since the general contracting carters of Glasgow had had an increase; that their wages ranged between 22s and 26s; and that prices of the 'necessaries and commodities of life' had gone up. The carter was a semi-skilled man; and the wages of other semi-skilled workers' were rising everywhere. He referred to the great strikes in 1911, particularly the dockers:

'I do not need to mention the dock labourers. I am pleased to say that we have avoided their position by having you here, sir, but even the dock labourers last summer were able to get their wages increased. The wages of the ordinary labourer run on an average at 6d per hour, and he is a very low-paid labourer who has 5½d an hour. . . . Our men are merely earning something on an average of 4½d per hour. We do not think we are asking too much when we ask 3s of an increase, which is practically 6d per day.'

The arbitrator sought to contrast the unskilled dock labourer with the carter:

ARBITER: 'Would you say the work of a carter was as hard as that of a dock labourer?
LYON: 'I would not say that; that is to say, if the dock labourer wrought continuously alongside the carter I would say that the dock labourer had harder work than the carter, but he would have more wages by a long way; but to put alongside of that, the carter has got the responsibility on the street, which is nerve-shattering to some extent.'
ARBITER: 'And then of course a carter must be a man of fairly good conduct: he cannot get drunk, like a dock labourer, and keep his situation.'
LYON: 'No, but I will be quite honest and admit, of course, that the carters are not all teetotallers.'
ARBITER: 'It would be very difficult to convince me of that but at the same time I suppose it is the case that a carter must be a fairly sober man in order to keep his situation.'
LYON: 'You can recognize that for yourself, because it would never do to have carters going about drunk on the streets of Glasgow; they are liable to not only lose their places, but they are liable to prosecution and to be severely fined.'[1]

For the Glasgow contractors it was argued that the rates paid 'to competent carters' were higher than elsewhere[2] and that they had to face competition from contractors in adjoining towns and from the railway companies and railway contractors.

Murray laid considerable stress on the consequences of the agreement to limit hours to 62½, which had 'entailed a very considerable additional oncost to employers and . . . put contractors in a very unfortunate position'.

[1] *Report of Proceedings in Arbitration between The Glasgow Carting Contractors and Horse Owners' Association and the Scottish Horse and Motormen's Association. 1912.*
[2] He cited wages paid in the following places:

Place	Wages	Place	Wages
Aberdeen	20s–22s 6d	Kilmarnock	22s
Ayr	21s	Liverpool	27s (67½ hours)
Bradford	20s–23s	Leeds	22s
Bristol	23s 6d	London	27s (72 hours)
Birmingham	21s	Manchester	25s (65 hours)
Barrhead	20s	Montrose	22s
Coatbridge	24s	Perth	21s
Dundee	23s	Paisley	23s
Edinburgh	20s–23s	Sheffield	24s
Glasgow	26s	Stirling	21s
Hamilton	24s	Sunderland	24s
Hawick	22s		

Now that the waiting was in the employers' time, they took this 'detention' very seriously:

'While the employers suffer through this serious difficulty the men on no occasion suffer, although they stand five, or six, or seven hours, or even as long as eight hours . . . it entails a very large outlay.'

In Glasgow also there was 'the matter of cross-over communication. Detention occurs there, often for half an hour or an hour'. Lyon retorted:

'Is the fact that the carter has to stand, say, half an hour at the dock before he can get across and possibly the same before he can get back, a reason why he should have to work for less wages than he is able to keep body and soul together?'

Murray replied that carters were not so detained in Edinburgh, Aberdeen, and Dundee, where wages rates were lower, because there was not the volume of traffic. Both agreed that Glasgow traffic was congested beyond what roads and bridges could bear; and that the Glasgow carter had to be a better driver than a man in any other city.

The outcome of the members' first taste of arbitration was that the arbitrator awarded an increase of 2s to carters receiving 23s or under, and 1s to those with 24s or over. Lyon commented: 'It goes without saying that Sheriff Craigie let us down badly; still, we had established a minimum of 25s per week. We decided, however, that when we demanded the next increase, no Sheriff would decide the question for us!'

5. LEITH MILITANT

Achieving a minimum wage in Glasgow (25s for general contractors' men and 24s for railway carters) gave a marked impetus to the struggle for wages in other towns. Advances were forced in Paisley, Aberdeen, Barrhead, and Kilmarnock. In Kirkcaldy, a strike early in 1912 won the carters a 1s increase; in November 1912, they struck again for over a week and won a further 2s. The fiercest struggles developed in the autumn in Edinburgh and in Leith, where there was a general strike of carters. The demand had been for the 3s increase for which the Association had been pressing throughout the year. The Edinburgh contractors formed an association, and in September finally offered 1s, with a further 2s to be paid in May 1913. The Edinburgh men accepted this. But the Leith men were in militant mood. When they rejected the 1s down, the Leith contractors tried to go to arbitration. The men refused and a strike began on October 15, 1912, after a morning meeting on Leith Links had been addressed by Lyon. Pickets went into action; they stopped lorries from a flour mill, unloaded them and unyoked the horses. When police were brought out to escort lorries, all the carters in the town went on strike.

On Leith Links the strikers caught a provision lorry, belonging to an Edinburgh contractor who had failed to sign the Edinburgh agreement; it was overturned.

On October 17th, there took place in Leith Walk what the *Edinburgh Evening News* described as 'one of the most novel scenes of the strike'. An attempt to stop a lorry failed when the driver whipped up his horse to a good speed:

'One man held the horse's bridle and was practically pulled along for a considerable distance. Police arriving, he was knocked off by one of them, but made his escape among the crowd. Great crowds were attracted to the spot by the accident.'

At that point an Edinburgh brewer's lorry appeared; it was waylaid; the horse was taken out of the shafts and the lorry overturned:

'There being few police left on the scene, the driver thought it better to go away with his horse, and there was left a load of beer and a large crowd, which probably included many who were already thirsty after the exertions of the morning. One after another bungs were removed, and the thirsty ones made use of what devices suggested themselves to convey the liquor to their mouths or put their lips to the bungs. Beer was seen running in the street. In a little while the shafts were thrown off the top of the lorry and several casks followed them and here and there might be seen a barrel of beer being rolled stealthily but quickly along the street and so by some side street to a hiding place.'[1]

So wrote a thirsty journalist at the time.[2]

The Lord Provost of Leith and other dignitaries tried to bring both sides together. A tentative agreement was made of 1s advance immediately, the parties to go to arbitration and the strike to be called off pending the result. John Williamson, the Edinburgh secretary, and Archie Mark, the Leith Secretary called in Hugh Lyon. But at a mass meeting in the Assembly Rooms, Leith carters showed that they would have nothing to do with arbitration. Nor would they accept the next move: an offer of the Edinburgh agreement of 1s at once and 2s in six months' time. Finally the employers conceded 2s immediately and a further 1s in May. This put

---

[1] *Edinburgh Evening News*, October 17, 1912.

[2] There was a huge crowd at the court next day to hear the charges against the men who had stopped and overturned the McEwan's brewery lorry. One of the accused had been stopped by pickets the day before when driving to the docks; and had decided to join the pickets. Asked for an explanation of his conduct, the accused said that the day before he passed down the Walk and his lorry was stopped. He had either to be a brave man and go on to the docks and be struck with a baton or a brick, or go home. If his bread was to be deprived from him, he could not see why McEwan's man should be allowed to earn his.

Bailie Dresner: 'You have no right to take the law into your own hands. I am determined to put an end to these riots I saw yesterday. You are fined 30s or 15 days.'

the Leith contractors' men is ahead of Edinburgh and on level terms with Glasgow. At a mass meeting, a local press account relates:

'. . . there was much jubiliation amongst them. Councillor Lyon was not allowed to leave the meeting until he sang 'The Red, White and Blue', the carters joining lustily in the chorus.'

The mood at the time throughout Britain was all against arbitration and all in favour of vigorous industrial action.

It was immediately following these stirring events that the old Edinburgh & Leith Cabdrivers, now led by John Greig decided to join the Association, in their thirty-seventh year. On November 28, 1912 the oldest road transport union in Britain gave notice of amalgamation with the largest in Scotland. It was registered on December 4, 1912. Seven members of each body signed, all the signatories for the Association being Executive Council members or officials.[1] They joined 140 members at the rate of £1 17s 6d per member. John Greig was appointed full-time collector; he resigned a year later.

The year 1912 had been an important one. The standard week of 60 and 62½ hours had been won. The sum of £666 4s 3d had been expended in strike pay, but a local minimum wage had been established in the key centres: Glasgow contractors, 25s; Leith, 25s; Edinburgh, 24s; Aberdeen, 23s; Dundee 23s. The time had now come to force up the miserably inadequate scale of wages everywhere.

An Annual General Meeting took place in Glasgow just after the amalgamation, at which the rules were modified; executive representation was opened to all districts elected at annual conference; officials were no longer to be eligible for the Executive; henceforth annual meetings were to be held. Two Glasgow members moved that 'this conference recommend agitation for better wages and conditions should be general instead of sectional.' This was agreed to, after Lyon, who took the chair had supported it:

'He pointed out, also, the difficulties caused in sectional strikes by the railways transferring canvassers, foremen etc, to take the place of men in dispute. The railway could spend £1,000 for every £100 of ours. We could only beat them by striking as a whole. It would be a year before anything effective could be done. He suggested that the EC should seriously consider the question of a general as against a sectional strike. This was agreed to.'[2]

---

[1] For the Edinburgh & Leith Cabdrivers: Thomas Anderson, George Hoy, John H. Dagger, William Reid, James Ovenstone, William Day, James Finlay, and John S. Greig (Secretary). For the Scottish Horse & Motormen's Association: Robert Carson (President), William Smith, James Stewart, William Laidlaw, J. Stewart, James Donald, Thomas Manuel, and Hugh Lyon (Secretary).

[2] Annual Conference *Minutes*, November 23, 1912.

In less than two months a general strike of Glasgow carters took place. When the Glasgow carters had struck in 1889, their wages were 24s, and they were claiming a 2s increase to raise the figure to 26s, and some achieved this. Now, in 1913, some twenty-four years later, the general contractors' carters with a wage of 25s, were claiming 3s to reach 28s. But, during those years, food prices had advanced greatly, and the sovereign had fallen in value by nearly a quarter; they would have, in 1913, to reach 31s 6d to get back to the 1889 standard.[1] They had a long way to go.

APPENDIX

Conditions of Van-boys in 1912

This is a passage from the evidence given by Hugh Lyon and published in the *Report of the Departmental Committee on the Hours and Conditions of Employment of Van Boys and Warehouse Boys*. 1913. (Cmd. 6886). He was questioned by Mr Cyril Jackson.

QUESTION: 'The length of time a man is out depends on all sorts of accidents. He might be longer on one day than on another?'
ANSWER: 'Yes.'
Q. 'That would tend to prevent boys going to any night school, because they will be uncertain as to when they can get there?'
A. 'It is impossible for the boys at present time to go to the school.'
Q. 'They are always uncertain and could not attend regularly?'
A. 'It would be utterly impossible.'
Q. 'Even if you said they were going to get off at 6 o'clock?'
A. 'Might I tell you that in connection with our Association we never attempt to hold a meeting of the men on week-days. If we desire to meet them we have to call a meeting for Sunday, or we could not get the men to attend.'
Q. 'Because of the uncertainty of the time at which they come in?'
A. 'Yes; we have tried it over and over again. We have always had to hold our meetings on Sundays, unless we have merely wanted to hold such a thing as a business meeting.'
Q. 'Has the Act which made compulsory evening classes had any effect on the van boys in Scotland?'
A. 'Not to my knowledge.'

[1] In 1913 the Board of Trade gave figures for the changing in the value of the sovereign as follows:

1895	20s	1901	18s 4d	1907	17s 7d
1896	20s	1902	18s 3d	1908	17s 2d
1897	19s 3d	1903	17s 11d	1909	17s 3d
1898	18s 6d	1904	18s	1910	16s 11d
1899	19s 4d	1905	17s 11d	1911	17s
1900	18s 5d	1906	18s	1912	16s 3d

During the 1914–18 war, with steeply rising food prices, the value of the sovereign fell much more sharply.

Q. 'I think under the Act of last year an employer was bound to allow a boy to go to evening classes?'

A. 'Well, if so, I have never heard tell of it.'

Q. 'I understand that the Act really says the employer must let the boy go, but not that the boy must go, and that therefore the Act is really a dead letter?'

A. 'That is quite possible.'

CHAPTER SEVEN

THE 1913 STRIKE AND AFTER

I. DISUNITY AMONGST THE MASTERS

TEN months after arbitration had provided Glasgow contractors' carters with a 25s minimum, the men were itching for a new showdown. It rankled that their standard week of 62½ hours was still two and a half hours longer than the railway carters'. None were satisfied with the establishment of a minimum wage if it was to be pegged as low as 25s. They had seen what dockers, railwaymen, and miners were ready to do. There was no holding them back; a demand was put forward for a 3s increase, which would raise the minimum to 28s. All over Glasgow meetings of contractors' men were demanding strike action; a ballot was practically unanimous for it. On January 20, 1913, just on twelve months after the Craigie arbitration, the 3,500 contractors' men in Glasgow came out on strike. Every veteran member of the Association who was in Glasgow in those days has vivid recollections of that strike.

The masters were determined to resist. It was clear that a long struggle lay ahead. From the first, Lyon planned not only to keep the men from the different stables and garages together, but also to keep their womenfolk in touch with events. In every district, strike committees were formed and strike committee-rooms rented, where strike aliment was paid weekly. Each Tuesday men marched from their committee-rooms, sometimes headed by pipers, to the Panopticon Music Hall in Trongate. Here entertainment was provided, with film shows and the like. Lyon would give a progress report on the strike. He was keenly alive to the influence the womenfolk would have in a long drawn out struggle. Every Thursday the carters' wives were guests at the Panopticon, to which they also marched through the street; they too heard an address from Lyon. A Press account shows Lyon in characteristic form:

'The wives of the strikers crowded the Panopticon this forenoon at a meeting addressed by Cllr. Lyon. The proceedings were novel in that it was the first gathering of a like character that had been held in Scotland in connection with a labour dispute. The proceedings were most enthusiastic and the women followed the speech of the General Secretary for the men's union with deep interest. . . .

'His object in asking them to attend was to gain their confidence in the dispute, as he recognized that the wife was a very important factor in the strike, she being the party who had to make all the sacrifices. However, he wished to remind them of the many sacrifices they had made in the past owing to the low wages and long hours that their husbands were compelled to labour under.

'The present fight, which could not last long, (*applause*) was being waged for the purpose of trying to give the carters' wives the same opportunities as the other women—to be able to give the bairns the necessary comforts in life, which they had never been in the habit of getting in the past (*applause*). . . . He also wanted to remind them of their happy courting days (*laughter*) when many promises were made by their husbands of how well they would take care of them (*laughter*).

'They should also bear in mind the fact that their husbands were just as anxious today to keep their promises, but the system under which they worked prevented them from doing so (*applause*). Therefore, they were fighting to try to alter that so that their husbands might be able to carry out some of their promises (*laughter and applause*).

'The cause of half of their troubles and worries at home was the fact that their husbands could not provide them with the wherewithal to make life what it ought to be—happy and bright! (*applause*).'[1]

But Lyon did not feed the womenfolk with words only. In addition to the 10s strike aliment to which the men were entitled and which they received each Saturday, each married member had his aliment increased by a further 5s, which was paid out directly to the wives themselves each Wednesday. This shrewd stroke of paying strike aliment directly to the women also got over what might have been an awkward problem. Non-unionists were on strike and received aliment; there were many tramp carters with no settled homes and with casual women to whom they were not permanently allied. While assisting every striker, member or non-unionist alike, Lyon found this way of not falling out with the people from whom the regular union dues were collected, the members' wives. Another popular move was that the officials asked the Executive Council to put them on strike benefit too, 'not because of the few shillings that would be saved, but to prove their sincerity in trying to help on the cause'. Again, from the start, Lyon urged the members and their wives to see that whilst the strike lasted the children should be fed at school; he was not a town councillor for nothing. He insisted that the 'children had as much right to demand their food from the School Board' as members to demand strike aliment.

It proved to be a long strike, lasting just over five weeks and three days. It was solid throughout. The Glasgow dock labourers, who had themselves been on strike the previous year, refused to handle goods. The sheds for

[1] *The Evening Times*, January 30, 1913.

incoming cargoes at the harbour became congested, while ships had to sail short-shipped or without their cargoes, and coasting sailings were cancelled. The railways carters, too, co-operated fully, without retort from the railway companies, which were none too anxious to provoke their own men, strongly influenced by the militancy amongst both their brother railwaymen and their brother carters. The police were restrained and there were virtually no disturbances.

One exception was on the first day, when a Port Dundas contractor decided to drive one of his own lorries. Pickets stopped him, took out the wheel pin and the lorry collapsed in the street with the owner on top of it. A disturbance of a different kind occurred when a contractor's son was taking cases of alarm clocks to the docks; one case fell off and set all the alarms going. An eyewitness remarked 'It created the greatest hullabaloo that was heard on the docks for some time'. The carters employed by the railway companies, the Corporation, and the co-operative societies undertook a voluntary levy of 2s 6d. Lyon remarked: 'Never was a strike so popular with everyone but the contractors.'

An important factor which favoured the carters was the state of the industry, as it was coming to be recognized at that time. Motor traction for commercial work was still in its early youth. Whereas the manufacturers of Glasgow faced competition from the rest of Scotland, from England, and from yet further afield, this was still not so with the carting contractor. No rival from Edinburgh or Manchester, far less from London, could break into his line of business. On the other hand, it did not need much capital for a contractor to set up in carting, even for the larger employers with some 150 to 200 horses, like Hamilton's or Roberts & Lyle of Govan, who later had a great deal to do with the formation of the Scottish Federation of Haulage Employers. There were therefore many small contractors; and this led to undercutting and intense competition upon which the larger employers had been frowning severely but unsuccessfully.

Two factors, apart from skilful publicity and organization in conducting it, made this great strike successful. Firstly, the militancy of the men, after they had seen how limited were the achievements gained by arbitration and how effective the strike weapon had proved elsewhere; this resulted in a high degree of unity amongst them. Secondly, there was no such unity amongst the employers at that moment of the development of the industry, the big contractors being at variance with the smaller. Many small contractors signed the agreement to pay 3s. This in itself strengthened the Association's case that the employers were able to pay the wages demanded. If a contractor with six horses could give the carters 29s and a sixty-hour week and yet make a profit, surely the contractor with 200 horses could do better. Although pressure was brought upon the smaller contractors to withdraw their signatures, nevertheless some eighty employers came to terms. Again, as the strike wore on, traders and manufacturers, who for years had employed contracting firms, began to buy horses and plant and to cart their own goods, one example being the Carron Iron Company.

An incident, which *Forward* reports, gives a measure of the division amongst the contractors and the special position in which Lyon found himself. A firm of contractors, which supplied coal to a Glasgow hospital, unable to find a carter ready to work for them, appealed to the manager of the Infirmary to get them a permit. The manager asked a magistrate to approach Lyon:

MAGISTRATE: 'I say, Mr Lyon, could you not instruct your men to allow coals to be carted to the Victoria Infirmary without interference?'
MR LYON: 'Who's the contractor?'
MAGISTRATE: 'Mr So-and-So.'
MR LYON: 'He has refused our terms. There is another contractor in the same district who has conceded our demands. Engage him to cart the coals.'
MAGISTRATE: 'But that wouldn't be fair to Mr So-and-So.'
MR LYON: 'Perhaps not. But it's fair to us. If you don't care to engage the fair-wage contractor you can't get the permit.'
MAGISTRATE: 'Come, come! You chaps are trying it on too much!'
MR LYON: 'We are not going to be bluffed this time. Either you engage the contractor I mentioned or do without the permit.'
MAGISTRATE: 'Oh, very well.'[1]

Incidents of this kind show Lyon in his element. To play one Glasgow contractor off against another was a tactic he understood. The hours' campaign, followed by this Glasgow strike, was his finest hour. He was eager to use the same tactics in very different circumstances and seasons. Indeed, it was his practice in issuing permits to employers whom he favoured, during the General Strike, which brought him and the Association into collision with the rest of the trade union movement. But in the year 1913, pulling strings amongst the small Glasgow contractors, who were soon to disappear from the scene as the industry was transformed and private monopoly developed, was right up Councillor Lyon's street.

The Glasgow Carting Contractors and Horseowners' Association, whose chairman was Mr David Murray and whose secretary was Mr Donald Mackay, had been formed only just two years before, when it felt the pinch from the Association's historic hours' campaign. Now it was in disarray, as contractors broke away and signed independently. Moves were set on foot to bring the strike to an end. Sheriff Craigie came forward to suggest submitting the case to arbitration. He was perhaps an unfortunate choice; the men would have none of it from him. The Chamber of

[1] *Forward*, January 25, 1913.

Commerce made another effort; the Board of Trade was called in; Glasgow's Lord Provost intervened. The carters, however, were determined to let their own strength decide the outcome.

Nearly five weeks had elapsed. The ranks of the contractors were thinning; some were ruined. But those who dominated the masters' organization would not shift. Finally, two fellow members of the town council asked Lyon to meet privately three of the big contractors who desperately wanted an end. Lyon brought out a compromise plan for a 2s advance which would raise the minimum to 27s, and proposed that they should put it as their own proposal at a meeting of the masters' organization. He was waiting for them when they came out of that meeting, angry men, for they had been shouted down. The moment was timely; Lyon persuaded them to sign his agreement. This was on the eve of a joint meeting between the two organizations arranged by the Lord Provost, who pressed the parties to come to terms. The employers offered 1s. Lyon wrote in his memoirs:

'I thought the time had come for my surprise. The Lord Provost was prevailing on me the acceptance of the 1s, when I told him I could not accept it, as three of the largest contractors had last night granted me what I was now asking. Mr Murray denied this, so I pulled out the agreement with the three signatures, and Mr Murray collapsed. The representatives of the Contractors' Association then agreed to our terms. Mr David Murray, always the gentleman, then shook hands and complimented me on the fight.'

The strike was won.[1] It was a remarkable victory. Nor was it only a victory for the Glasgow carters and their wives; every town in Scotland soon reaped the benefit and got a similar increase, although the minimum was still not standard. Over £7,000 had been paid out in strike aliment, but even the careful Lyon thought it worth it, and remarked of the strike, 'It was the making of our society all over the country'.

Lyon had been in his element. He knew every trick—local politics, local publicity, playing off one employer against another, pulling strings, coming to private arrangements with this employer, overreaching that, cajoling the strikers' wives. When negotiations were on a local scale and subject to local influences, Lyon knew very well what to do. In such circumstances he was close to his members and carried them with him. But these con-

---

[1] Agreement between the Glasgow Carting Contractors and Horseowners' Association and the Scottish Horse & Motormens' Association: 'That men under 25s get 2s of an increase, and that those with 26s per week and over get 1s of an increase. Hours to be same as in Agreement. In the case of youths and old men the terms to be subject to such moderation as may be agreed upon between the employer and employee.' (March 5, 1913)

Both parties agreed to meet as soon as would be practicable to adjust a graduation scheme of wages and conditions. The Parties also agreed to meet within three months to adjust the former Agreement.

ditions in the industry, when Lyon was at his best and fully at home, were fast vanishing. The First World War, which was only eighteen months away, was to change all that. But meanwhile, as the late Sir Patrick Dollan[1] said: 'In the period 1900–14, he was a man of power in the Clydeside trade unions.'

The Press noted it. Soon after the 1913 strike had ended, the *Bailie* printed a satire. It pictured an imaginary invasion by the German Fleet, with nothing to stop them. A large force is landed at the Broomielaw 'to seize the City Chambers, the Gas Works, Buchanan Street Station and other places of prehistoric importance'; but a despatch is thrust into the hands of the German Commander, who turns pale and sounds the retreat:

'A great psalm of triumph arises from the Subway, where the inhabitants of Glasgow have sought shelter. For their city is saved. Their Great Dictator, their Mighty Man, has spoken. In other words, Councillor Lyon has refused to grant the German Commander a permit for his troopers and gun-carriages to pass through the town.'[2]

Amongst the places where the general contractors at once granted increases, following Glasgow's victory, were Paisley, Barrhead, Motherwell, Dumbarton, Ayr, and Kirkcaldy. The employers began to organize themselves into bodies, similar to the Glasgow masters' association, in Dundee, Edinburgh, Kirkcaldy, Leith, Paisley, and Rothesay. In some cases the masters agreed to employ none but Association members. Branches were opened or re-opened in Alloa, Ayr, Irvine, Helensburgh, Dunfermline, and Rothesay; the Lanarkshire Tramwaymen dissolved their union and joined the Association.

2. FEDERATION: FOR OR AGAINST?

On April 13, 1913, the total change of rules was registered, made necessary by the National Insurance Act, which carried out the decisions of the only annual delegate conference since John Sampson's day, which had been held in Glasgow the previous November. The fifth annual delegate conference in the Association's history was held six months later on October 27, 1913, in Edinburgh. Delegates were still in militant spirit. The main topic for debate was the tactics to be adopted in getting higher

[1] In a message on the occasion of the Golden Jubilee of the Association in 1948, Sir Patrick Dollan wrote:

'Hugh Lyon, as General Secretary of the Association, was an enthusiast for the unions "minding their own business". He was more of a Radical than a Socialist, but wanted the workers to develop their own industries and trades; during his membership of the Glasgow Town Council he was known as a "stalwart" rather than a man with a red flag.

'He was a canny man who thought three or four times before he spoke once. In the period 1900–14 he was a man of power in the Clydeside trade unions.'

(*The Highway*, February, 1948)

[2] The *Bailie*, February 12, 1913.

wages for railway carters. Should they restrict their opening offensive to the railway cartage contractors, or take on the railway companies as well? It was finally carried 'that we stop the whole of the railway companies'. During the year 1913, some 2,669 new members were won; and, though 1,023 lapsed, the net numbers on the books were 9,311, nearly double the membership in 1910. Despite heavy expenditure on strike aliment, their funds stood at £7,458 13s 11d.[1]

But all was not well in Dundee, where there were two competing organizations for carters: the small remnant of the Association's members, led by Harry Erskine, who had been sent there as collector, and Peter Gillespie's Northern Horse & Motormen's Association. Yet the whole trend of the times was towards amalgamation and federation. In November 1910, the National Transport Workers' Federation had been formed, with Robert Williams as Secretary, which was intended to strengthen the links between dockers, seamen and road transport workers all over the United Kingdom. It played a large part in the strike movements of these groups of workers throughout 1911 and 1912. The Association's balance sheet for the year 1911 records the payment of an affiliation fee of £1; but this was not repeated for some years. A further big impetus towards the principle of amalgamation was the formation of the National Union of Railwaymen in 1913. The hitting power of the big battalions became clearer as each month passed, as the feeling grew that a great class showdown was at hand. In September 1913, it was announced that British employers were forming a huge guarantee fund of £50,000,000. If the employers could make common cause, trade unionists felt that in the big industries they too needed a common policy on strike action and mutual aid. By the summer of 1914, the Miners' Federation of Great Britain, the National Union of Railwaymen, and the National Transport Workers' Federation (which by then had upwards of 200,000 members), formed the Triple Industrial Alliance. But closer linking in a federation was one thing and all-out amalgamation, to which federation might later lead, was another. Leaders of some organizations which were expanding were ready for the protection offered by federation, provided it did not lead to amalgamation.

Lyon's union was one of those which was expanding. It had just taken in the Edinburgh & Leith cabdrivers and the Lanarkshire tramwaymen; the remaining carters' unions in Scotland of any significance were the

[1] The Financial Reports for the years 1911–13 show a wide range of causes which the Association had championed. They included: Sailors' and Firemen's Union (£5); Greenock Carters (£20); Welsh Miners on strike (£5); The Blind Asylum (£1 10s 0d); the Glasgow Right-to-Work Conference (5s); the Bristol Blind (£1); the Furnishing Trade strike (£2); the Great Dublin Transport strike (£10); the Seafarers' Union (£1); the Edinburgh Free Speech Committee (5s); the Falkirk Labourers' strike (£3); the Kilbirnie Girls' strike (£2); grants to the Labour Representation Committees of Anderston and Camlachie; and grants or fees to the following trades councils: Glasgow, Edinburgh, Aberdeen, Dundee, Hamilton, Govan, Falkirk, Kirkcaldy, Paisley, and Motherwell.

old Greenock Horsemen, led by the veteran Bailie Lemmon, and the newly formed Northern Horse & Motormen's Association. When, in September 1913, an invitation was received to a conference of carters' unions in Manchester, to discuss the merits of closer linking and their attitude towards Robert Williams's National Transport Workers' Federation, the Executive Council of the Association decided to send representatives. Thomas Manuel and Hugh Lyon attended; but they were not impressed. In his memoirs, the reason Lyon gave for 'nothing coming of it' was that there were a hundred and one English carters' unions, 'and the officials are all jealous of each other'. The Scots saw no advantage in linking up with them. The carting industry, Lyon remarked, had no competition outside its own town. What far-off days those must sound to the long-distance haulage men of fifty years later, perhaps having to lodge away in Inverness one night and in Southampton the next. Another factor might have been Lyon's doubt whether the Association would be able to keep its financial autonomy and uncertainty as to what policy demands might be made upon it.

But although at this time Lyon was cool towards federation over the Border, he had nothing against amalgamation of carters within Scotland. The Scottish Trades Union Congress made efforts to bring the Association and Gillespie's organization together. Under the auspices of the Parliamentary Committee of the STUC, Lyon made an offer on November 29, 1913, to the Northern Horse & Motormen's Association for amalgamation, with assurances to Gillespie and his fellow officials of security. The terms were put in writing on January 10, 1914, but Gillespie stood off. The problem remained until, as we shall see, new efforts were made by the STUC in 1916, with Robert Williams as intermediary. Meanwhile the division continued.

3. ARBITRATION WITH A CO-OPERATIVE SOCIETY

Although the Association had achieved successes with the many corporations, with general contractors, and with the railway companies and contractors, another class of employer presented difficulties. These were the co-operative societies, which Lyon claimed were the most difficult. This was not perhaps true of all; flexible tactics were necessary. The opening months of 1914 saw two important cases of arbitration with co-operative societies. First the Association took to arbitration the leading society in the east of Scotland. St Cuthbert's Co-operative Association of Edinburgh. The evidence was led by Hugh Lyon on January 12, 1914, before Bailie James Ross. The claim was for an advance for the vanmen and motormen of 2s with a minimum wage of 22s for all men at the age of twenty-one.

The Association had been negotiating with the society for six months, and it had been fifteen years since there had last been a general increase. There were no fixed hours; wages ranged from 18s to 31s, the average being 25s 9d. The value of the goods carried by a single van might amount to as much as £100, and the vanman was also responsible for collecting the money. Lyon argued strongly that a co-operative concern was expected to set an example to private enterprise. The main case for the society was expressed by the manager:

'We feel that when a body of workmen employ another body of workmen and pay the highest wages with the best conditions to be found in the occupation, it is all that can be expected.'[1]

He claimed that, although there was not a stipulated working-week, the hours were not in fact long, and quoted fifty-two, fifty-four, and fifty-six hours as examples. They got commission on sales which could amount to 7s 6d a week; and van-boys were employed, which made the work easier. At this point a vanman present interjected: 'with regard to commission, the vanmen had to pay a part of this to the van-boys, usually about 2s a week.' Lyon replied that comparison of wages could be made only with other co-operative societies, and that the standard wage of the Leith Provident Society was 29s a week. They did not have to contend with the competition that other employers had: 'The co-operative society makes its members buy from it.' The society's spokesman said that van-boys had to be found employment, if they were not to be left in a blind-alley job; they therefore began as spare drivers at 14s, rising to 18s when they became regular drivers. Fewer would be kept on if they had to be paid more. Lyon seized on this to good effect:

'A boy, say, of twenty years of age, driving a van for several weeks, is paid 14s a week, while the man whose place he is filling had 29s per week; boys with 8s, 14s, and 18s filling positions of men. You say that if you have to pay the wage demanded you will have to dispense with some of the boys. It is better that you should do so. Pay the man who is doing the work a fair wage.'

The arbitrator awarded a minimum of 22s 'to any man of 21 years of age or over who is capable of taking full charge of a horse and van'; and general increases to others.[2] It was a move in the right direction, where improvement was long overdue.

They were less successful in arbitration with the Scottish Co-operative Wholesale Society a month later, when the award went against them. The SCWS satisfied the arbitrator that their wages and conditions were better

[1] Report of Arbitration Meeting, January 12, 1914.

[2] (a) To the men in their first year of service a rise of 1s per week. (b) To the men of over one year's service (up to and including those at present receiving 26s per week) a rise of 2s per week. (c) To the men at present receiving 27s per week or over a rise of 1s per week.

than those of other carting contractors in Glasgow, and that hours were being reduced to sixty, with payment for overtime. But the cases showed that the Association was moving towards full recognition in sector after sector.

The co-operative arbitration cases were also an important assertion of the principle that co-operative societies should be model employers, which the Association has always stressed. In these years, headway had been made in a number of occupations covered by co-operative activity. Under the influence of the Women's Suffrage Movement and the application of the Trade Board Acts, co-operative societies had recognized the right of women to a living wage and were paying a minimum wage of 17s at the age of twenty. It might well be compared favourably with the state of affairs which caused 30,000 metal-workers in Birmingham to go on strike in 1913 for a minimum wage of 23s a week for men and 12s a week for women.

The whole mood of those months as society moved towards the First World War was one of inevitable impending change, however much the privileged and the powerful would have wished to ignore it. A popular year-book[1] of the time presented articles on 'The Six Questions of the Year'.[2] The dominating question was described as 'The Strike Fever'.

'All our life and the lives of all seem in these days to be passed in the shadow of some strike, actual or prospective. Perhaps in the near future some enterprising novelist will give us a picture of an industrial period in the forgotten past when strikes were practically unknown; and, reading his pages, we shall rub our eyes and wonder if such "good old times" ever existed.'

After marshalling facts and statistics and examining the trends, including 'the prevalence on the part of the men to go on strike in defiance of the advice of their leaders', which 'tendency has been vigorously denounced by one or two of the Labour leaders, notably by Mr J. H. Thomas, MP', the author went on to state the causes. It was not trade depression: in the last few years there had been marked trade prosperity. It was that 'the majority of the people of this country are still miserably poor'. The cost of living had gone up ten per cent in the previous seven years. Three-fifths

---

[1] *Nelson's Year Book, 1913–1914.*

[2] The first was 'The Balkan War' which that year had 'bathed the Balkans in blood'; secondly, was 'The March of Science,' which praised the progress made 'with the task of establishing long-distance speech with out wires', and had a special section on 'The New Locomotion: Flying'. Third came 'The Land Question', which deplored the growing depopulation of rural areas, where an official inquiry had established that the average earnings in England and Wales were 17s 6d a week. Fourthly, 'The Home Rule Question', in Ireland, with the threat of armed uprising in opposition to it in Ulster, led by Sir Edward Carson. Fifthly there was 'The German Question: Is There a German Peril?' in which it was argued that a strong British Navy would prevent the German Empire from declaring war.

of old people were receiving the new pension, payable only to those whose annual income was less than £31 10s. But there was another cause cited in the article, written three years before the beginning of the world's first socialist revolution:

'It may be an unpleasant fact to many, but there is no doubt whatever that the working man is beginning to realize his power. For a long time voters of this class have been in a big majority, but today they *know* they are in a majority, and those who imagine that they will use this power to enrich others are living in a fool's paradise. Like other classes in the past, they will use it to benefit themselves.'[1]

This was the background to the campaign for a general advance in road transport wages in Scotland which the Association planned to launch. The opening shots in the campaign were timed for August 1914. But the shot which assassinated the Austrian Archduke at Sarajevo precipitated the First World War. On August 4th, Britain declared war.

---

[1] op. cit., 'The Strike Fever'.

CHAPTER EIGHT

WAR'S PROBLEMS AND OPPORTUNITIES

I. THE ATTITUDE TO THE WAR

It is a sobering thought that, even after these years of success in their struggle, pay was so low and hours so arduous that from the moment war was declared the younger carters flocked into the forces. Some told collectors frankly that they would be better off. Some did not live to be better off. Others returned at the end of the war to conditions which were 'a Paradise compared with 1914'.

When the war broke out there were 11,045 members and £10,700 in the funds. In all, 6,000 members joined the forces, 1,700 in the first weeks. Association members agreed to a levy of 1s a month to keep clear the books of those away on service. Five years later, there were 9,334 members and the balance was no less than £34,200. Wages had more than doubled in money value, going up by an average of 30s. The Glasgow minimum was 57s; the Corporation was paying 60s, the co-operative societies up to 70s. More important still, whilst the wages were going up the hours were coming down; they fell from 62½ and sixty a week to fifty-four and forty-eight.

Throughout the war emergency, carters and motormen were at a premium; there was an enormous increase in all transport, including road transport. The need for more and more transport workers raised issues which no one in the Association had ever dreamt of. These not only included the question of boys' wages, with any lad employed as a carter finally winning man's pay at eighteen; the shortage reached the stage when to the amazement and, indeed, shock of the older carters and officials, women had to be accepted as drivers, both of horses and motors. Hugh Lyon felt it necessary to steady the members by this passage in his 1916 Report:

'We have at last had females introduced into our ranks, owing to the scarcity of labour, and there may have been a feeling in some quarters that protest ought to have been made against such, but your Executive feel that there is no cause for anxiety. While women play many parts in life, we feel quite confident that when the war is finished, there is one part that she will not play, and that is driving a horse.'

Lyon is reported to have believed not only that women had not come to stay, but also that the motor vehicle itself was merely a passing phase. The Hamilton and Motherwell District had taken up the cause of the women. The Lanarkshire Tramway Company and some of the town councils started employing women in 1915, and the Association's district official, James Jackson, thought it a duty to organize them and to see that they were paid the same rate as the men who had gone to war. In a few weeks they had enrolled one hundred new members; considerable wage increases were gained for motormen and for motorwomen. Motherwell therefore sponsored a resolution at the Falkirk Annual Conference that year, which was seconded from Aberdeen by J. M. Fraser. After delegates from Glasgow and Edinburgh had moved the previous question, the admission of women members was agreed to by eighteen votes to two.

As we shall see, there were many major changes in the carters' conditions and in the position of the Association during those five years; not least was a changing general attitude towards the war itself, apart from the well-known difference between those who supported it and those who, as Socialists, resisted it, and looked to international working-class action to bring it to an end.

Exactly a month after the declaration of war the Association held a one-day Annual Conference, the first of which there is a printed account, incorporated in the Financial Report for the year. It was held at Hamilton on September 5, 1914, with twenty-seven delegates; the General Secretary and Peter Webster, who had been put in charge of the Insurance Department six months before, were also in attendance. Delegates came from Aberdeen, Alloa, Ayr, Dundee, Dunfermline, Edinburgh, Falkirk, Glasgow, Hamilton, Irvine, Kirkcaldy, Leith, Motherwell, and Paisley. Jack Elliott of Paisley presided. There was, however, only slight reflection of the outbreak of the war in the proceedings; they sent a letter of sympathy to the wife of the Falkirk branch secretary, who had already been sent to the Front and wounded, and they made a grant of £100 to the National War Relief Fund. The other issues were: a discussion about raising the fees, which was deferred for a year; a resolution to ballot on joining the Labour Party (but this was, in the event, to be put off from year to year); a resolution calling on 'the Government to nationalize the Infirmaries and Hospitals'; and the item which was always cropping up, the protest against one man being obliged to drive two horses and vehicles.

In the Financial Report for that year, Hugh Lyon pointed out that in the spring of the year they had decided to have a wage-increasing campaign; but, when the war broke out and 'the world seemed on fire', it was decided 'to withhold our hand so far as strife with employers was concerned, and to join loyally in support of our country's cause'. But late in the year, 'it began to slowly dawn on most people that while giving our best in flesh and blood to fight the foreign enemy, we were face to face with the same old enemy at home, namely, the Profit-Monger.' Prices of foodstuffs had risen steeply, owing to 'the anxiety of a few individuals to make profit, with the result that as the year closes, we find our members forced to ask for increased wages, not to make profit, but that they may live'. He went on to his recurring theme throughout the war:

'When the war on the Continent ends, there will be war at home, and the only way to prevent or shorten such a war will be to have a strong and intelligent membership.'

He explained the basic fact that was to make such a difference to them. Already, by the end of 1914, there was a shortage of carters; this was not only because so many had gone into the army, but also because 'many of our members have found better jobs owing to the large amount of other workers who have also joined the army'. But he foresaw—and it was increasingly to colour his actions and policy—that when the men returned there would be 'a general upheaval'.

'When this greatest of wars is over, the same old war will still remain between Capital and Labour. There is a general feeling of unity at present, because we are anxious to prevent injury to the island we all love so well. But will the same unity exist when we are again forced to fight for the right to live? We should be fools to believe such.'

From this dilemma he drew the conclusion that 'the trade that is well organized and financially equipped will play a more important part in the future in bringing about peace and justice throughout the world'. In the meantime, the fact was that although 'the war had disastrous effects on our agitation for increased wages', in the words of J. M. Fraser, the Aberdeen secretary, the shortage of labour greatly increased their bargaining power.

This was not at all what some had expected. James Jackson, in his report from Motherwell, said:

'It was generally thought at the beginning of the war that we would suffer from a dislocation of business and a great amount of unemployment. Fortunately these evils may be said to be non-existent, so far as this district is concerned. On the other hand, trade has been good and men are scarce.'

John Elliott from Paisley noted the effect that many changes had had on dues payments: 'Good members are now so unsettled about the war that they no longer worry about working conditions. Their patriotism makes them forget their immediate interests, and they fail to realize that the employers are there all the time, just as eager, greedy and remorseless as before, and they will not hesitate to take advantages of any weakening of our organization.' But the carter, for the time being, had the whip hand;

the most 'greedy and remorseless' of employers could not drive his own carts, lorries, and motors. The year 1914 ended with an advance gained as a war bonus of 3s for railway carters and some contractors and corporation men, and 2s almost universally for co-operative society drivers. It was the first war bonus to be won; each year led to a battle for an addition to meet the rising cost of living.

In his 1915 Report, Lyon said frankly that the year had been 'a record of records'; he felt it was their duty to safeguard not only their own interests but the interests of those who were 'fighting the country's cause'. What the war had proved so far was that: 'Never in the history of the carting industry has the carter proved more indispensable to the welfare of the general community'. He remarked: 'If the carter is so valuable today, then it will be his fault if the same standard is not retained in peace-time.'

They were recruiting heavily; their membership was 12,031, with 2,848 already in the forces; and their balance had risen to £14,732. At their Annual Conference at Kirkcaldy on September 4, 1915, again with Jack Elliott in the chair, they decided to raise contributions to 9d per week; they doubled the period of sick benefit and decided upon a campaign for a 56-hour week. Jack Elliott gave a warning that 'the present boom in trade and inflating wages is only temporary and not caused by any briskness in trade, but by a scarcity of labour'. But his warning seems to have gone largely unheeded with agreement after agreement—over sixty are listed—in effect raising the war bonus universally by 5s. Even some of the most diehard employers were obliged to recognize the Association fully. A wage agreement taking effect in May 1915, signed by D. Y. Abbey for the Edinburgh & District Horse Owners' Association, contained the proviso

'That every facility shall be given to the representatives of the Scottish Horse & Motormen's Association to have access to the stables of employers for the purpose of securing by moral persuasion employees, non-members of said Association, as members thereof.'

Members began to feel that they would not always be the underdogs. A ballad was popular amongst them in Edinburgh that year:

'Maybe in some future date, no very far tae seek,
We'll a' be jolly cairters earnin' five-and-thirty bob a week.
Sae good luck to the cairter, he's a hard workin' chiel,
Frae early morn till late at nicht he works wi' richt guidwill,
An' should ye meet him on yer travels, he aye looks bricht an' gay,
Since he's become a member o' the S.C.A.'

Seven years after the official change of name, the 'old 'uns' still called themselves members of 'the Carters'. Within eighteen months, their wages had risen far beyond 'five and thirty bob a week'. Prices had shot up too, but the carter was still winning by a head.

In the next war year, 1916, there were contrasting views, but the predominant note is the undercurrent of war-weariness and gloom. In his report Lyon remarks that

'the country today has reached the most critical stage in its history, and whatever the rights and wrongs of the war may be it is the duty of every man and woman to do all that he and she possibly can, by giving of his or her best to bring this war to an honourable end.'

From Edinburgh and Leith a somewhat complacent note was struck, however. Their three organizers, A. Mark, John Williamson, and D. Stewart, had

'. . . not much to report this year owing to everything going so smoothly, and also to the fact that everybody seems to be patriotic just now and want to have as little trouble at home as possible.

'We think it is very gratifying when our country is in such a state that they are willing to bear the heavy burdens and sacrifices being placed upon them through the enormous increased cost of living—the necessaries of life having gone up enormously.'

They went so far as to say that they believed disputes were 'now a thing of the past'. They were wrong, even at that stage.

Strikes took place, especially in the earlier war years. The Paisley cabmen struck in May 1915 for some weeks; it was a bitter struggle, during which pickets incurred severe fines. In Edinburgh that year there was a short strike of Corporation employees and a sharp set-to with St Cuthbert's Co-operative Society. Wage negotiations had been in hand, and the society asked for time for further consideration; but, during the respite, the society advertised for vanmen, an action which provoked a lightning strike that week-end, just as deliveries were due to be made. With the help of John Williamson, who was an organizer of the Association as well as a director of the society, a speedy settlement took place. The men got their advance, and the society agreed in future to employ only Association members.

In Leith, men working for the Corporation won their demands after a three-day strike; some 160 of Wordie's railway contractors' men struck against the employment of non-unionists, and gained the day. The Munitions Acts of 1915 and 1916, which restricted the right to strike of those engaged in munitions work, did not stop strikes taking place. In Aberdeen, taxi-drivers came out. They had been working up to ninety-eight hours a week; and, by 1917, their wages at 25s were only 2s 6d above pre-war rates. When the town council agreed to a fifty per cent increase in taxi fares, it was the last straw. The men demanded a 10s increase from the cab proprietors and claimed extra payment for Sunday work; they were finally successful. The Edinburgh cabmen struck for nine days in May 1916, before they could force the employers to arbitration, where they gained an increase in war bonus. Eighteen months later they had to strike again when the employers refused to accept arbitration by Sir George Askwith, Chief Industrial Commissioner.

The Edinburgh contractors were frequently in conflict with the Association; but, after a week's strike, they went to arbitration, where the men's claim was won. The Perth Co-operative men, after a week's strike in May 1918, also got 13s after arbitration. Lyon recalled that there was 'scarcely a week' throughout the war without a case going to arbitration or being brought before the wartime Committee on Production, mostly to win or enforce agreements for war bonus additions.

But the most memorable occasion during the war was in 1916, when a strike at Rutherglen led to legal action being taken against six members, a test case in which Lyon himself became involved.

2. THE CASE OF THE ILLEGAL STRIKE

Six carters at Rutherglen were employed by a contractor to cart coal to 'a controlled establishment for the manufacture of munitions'. The employer had been paying 2s above the rate; at that time there was a shortage of carters, which in an emergency could put a small contractor out of business altogether. On September 28, 1916, a joint conference of the Association with the Glasgow Carting Contractors' & Horse-owners' Association had met under the chairmanship of Sir George Askwith, the Chief Industrial Commissioner, to discuss modifications to their existing agreements. The Askwith award was that, in addition to setting up a Joint Committee to discuss 'irregular time-keeping' as a matter of 'the utmost national importance', men's wages were to be increased by 4s a week and boys wages by 2s on pre-war, the first payment to be made on October 7, 1916. The Rutherglen employer immediately withdrew the 2s which had formerly been paid above the rate, claiming that it had only been a gratuity. This the men denied, and after consulting with their local official, Harry Erskine, and with Hugh Lyon, they ceased work on October 16, 1916, being guided entirely by Lyon's advice to strike until the 2s was paid. The six men were therefore called before the Sheriff and his assessors at the Glasgow Munitions Tribunal and fined £1 each.[1]

Lyon did not believe the Acts applied in such circumstances and took it to appeal as a test case. Under the Acts, before a worker engaged in connection with munitions work could legally engage in a strike, the dispute had to be reported to the Board of Trade. If it was not referred by them,

[1] For contravening Sections 2 and 3 of the Munitions Act, 1915, as amended by Section 9 of the 1916 Act.

within twenty-one days, to an arbitrator, only then would a strike be legal. As every dispute was in fact so referred to arbitration, in practice no wartime strike ever could be legal if the men engaged on it were employed on munitions work. If a worker left such work, no other employer could take him on without the production of a leaving certificate, authorizing the worker to leave his previous employment. Similar restrictions, but with considerable safeguards for the workers, were operative during the 1939–45 war. The argument in defence of the Rutherglen carters was on two grounds: firstly, that they were not employed in a munitions establishment; secondly, that, as the employer claimed the right to dismiss them, they were entitled to go, and without leaving certificates. Lord Dewar found against them. His argument was that what counted was not who paid their wages, in this case a sub-contractor, but what the nature of their employment was; that carting coal to the factory was so directly connected with munitions work that their action

'. . . might have stopped the output altogether, and when they reflect upon that, what it might mean to the nation if any considerable body of workmen were to adopt a similar course, I am sure they will see the impropriety of the course they took.'[1]

Then he drew a distinction between a strike and leaving without a certificate under the Acts.

'Workmen take part in a strike when they arrange among themselves to stop work in a body to force terms upon their employer. It is a combined action which constitutes the offence.'[2]

He took the opportunity afforded by this small case to utter some remarks which were meant to be heard by the shop stewards at that time above the clanging hammers of the shipyards of the Red Clyde, and by the Glasgow housewives and tenants' leaders who had declared a rent strike:

'All strikes at the present time are unseemly, and a strike amongst those who are engaged on or in connection with munitions work is a very grave offence for which there is no excuse, because other means have been created for settling all disputes between workmen and their employers.'[3]

About the action of the Rutherglen employer he said, of course, nothing for publication; it was outside his terms of reference.

That was not quite all: Lord Dewar remarked, in giving judgment, that he trusted 'the authorities may see their way not to proceed with the prosecution which Mr Lyon informed me it was proposed to bring against him'. The local Press were quick to seize upon the significance of this; it

[1] *Glasgow Herald*, November 16, 1916.
[2] *Glasgow Herald*, November 16, 1916.
[3] *Glasgow Herald*, November 16, 1916.

was a threat of action under Article 42 of the Defence of the Realm Act—the notorious DORA—against any person who attempted to impede production or transport of war material. An editorial in the *Glasgow Herald* remarked:

'The importance of Lord Dewar's judgment, indeed, is that he lays stress upon the fact, which is too readily forgotten, that the long arm of the law may reach the instigator of a strike as well as the striker himself . . . there are other means of reaching those who commit what Lord Dewar charitably in the carters' case calls 'a very serious error of judgment', but for which the Defence of the Realm Act has a different name.

'If not in Mr Lyon's case, then in some other case of the sort, we hope the authorities may take such proceedings as will bring home to all who influence opinion amongst working men, by speech or writing, that the law can reach the man who advises coming out on strike, as well as the man who comes out.'

This may have or may not have led to cold feet amongst Scottish trade union officials; but at the Scottish Trades Union Congress in April 1916, meeting on Glasgow South Side, at which the Association had been represented by Hugh Lyon, Walter Lumsden, and Robert Carson, there were two relevant resolutions, both passed unanimously. The first, moved by William Shaw of the Glasgow Trades Council and seconded by Robert Smith, of the Ayrshire Miners' Union, called for 'the immediate repeal of the Munitions Act, as being a gross interference with the rights of the workers' and strongly condemned 'the action of the Labour Party in giving practically unqualified support to the Munitions Act, thereby imperilling the hard-won rights and liberties of the workers, without securing an equivalent sacrifice from the employers of this country'. The second resolution was moved by Tom Mann, up from Poplar for the National Sailors' and Firemen's Union, and seconded by Councillor George Kerr, Workers' Union, which protested against

'. . . deporting trade unionists and munitions workers from Glasgow without trial on any specific charge, and call for their immediate return. Further, that we protest against the vindictive sentence passed on Mr John Maclean, MA, and urge that he be treated as a political prisoner until he is released.'

The famous John MacLean, teacher and educator of Socialist principles to thousands of Clydeside workers, was later to become the first consul in Britain of the first Workers' Socialist Republic in the world, after the October Revolution in Russia, in November 1917, just a year after Lord Dewar's judgment.

In the same month of November 1917, the Association was successful in a case before the Edinburgh and District Munitions Tribunal which arose out of contractors refusing to comply with an arbitration award conceding a war bonus addition. Three men carting rubbish from a controlled establishment went on strike and so were brought before the Tribunal. Hugh Lyon claimed that the strike was legal, and while he was arguing it, the employers accepted arbitration, and the case was dismissed. A week later the remaining Edinburgh employers came into line. Lyon spent most of the war in activities of this kind.

3. FEDERATION AND NATIONAL WAGES APPLICATION

When 1917 opened, forty per cent of the membership had enlisted: before the year ended, another 1,000 members were to be in uniform. The Association was already thinking about the problems of demobilization. The Annual Conference, held on September 2, 1916, had instructed the Executive to 'formulate a plan to meet the difficulty attendant on demobilization of the Army', with special reference to 'limiting working hours per day, cancelling overtime and so on during the period of adjustment'. They were fully aware that the Association needed strengthening. Financially they were in a good position, with their balance of £21,618 increased by the end of 1917 to £27,833. But the membership, with 7,000 in the forces by the end of 1917, had actually decreased, from 8,781 at the end of 1916 to 8,045 in 1917. This trend may have been one factor in leading the Annual Conference of 1916 to 'recommend that the EC take immediate steps to affiliate with the National Transport Workers' Federation'. Lyon wrote in the Annual Report: 'This combination, if properly guided, should be of immense value and importance to the workers' future progress.'

A few months earlier, representatives of the Association and Gillespie's Northern Horse & Motormen's Association had met in Dundee, brought together by the Parliamentary Committee of the Scottish Trades Union Congress, which, as their report for 1916 states, had put forward certain proposals 'for the purpose of getting the two unions joined together'. Their proposals were rejected by both. After that, Robert Williams asked the Scottish TUC to allow his organization, the National Transport Workers' Federation, to 'endeavour to try and arrange matters as between the two Associations'. The proposal was in line with the aims of the Parliamentary Scottish Trades Union Congress, which had appointed a special committee at the end of 1916 to consider an appeal for an effort to increase amalgamation. The committee discussed the question of federating by industrial groups, such as the National Transport Workers' Federation; and all trade unions affiliated to the Scottish Trades Union Congress were asked to consider a special conference on the subject to be held early in 1917.

There was deep concern throughout the movement about the wartime restrictions which were making themselves increasingly felt with each month that passed. The Parliamentary Committee accordingly recommended Congress to authorize Williams's attempts to bring about amalgamation of the two, but with the proviso that there should be 'sufficient power to enforce their proposals should these not be accepted by either one or all of the unions involved'. The Parliamentary Committee complained that they had:

'. . . wasted a great deal of time and spent a large sum of your money in most of these cases without the slightest result. In view of this the power suggested should be given, so that the trade union movement be further consolidated and co-ordinated in the interests of the members of the trade unions.'

But although Robert Williams did not succeed in drawing them both into federating with his organization as a first step, Lyon saw that there could be advantages in doing so. Joining the Federation could be an inducement to persuade the two smaller Scottish unions to amalgamate with the Association, and form a single commercial road transport workers' union in Scotland. This explains the decision for the Association to affiliate to the Federation, in time to take part in a number of important activities in which the Federation was engaging in 1917. The first of these was the adoption by the Federated societies throughout Britain of a National Programme[1] in June 1917.

Throughout the summer, the Federation was holding meetings in seven areas in Britain to popularize the programme, which was in full accord with Association policy. The climax in this campaign came on August 23, 1917, when the Federation held a conference of carters' and motormen's organizations in Salford, attended by seventeen of such societies, which declared for a 20s increase on pre-war rates, with each society agreeing to submit identical demands; and set up a sub-committee to prepare for establishing minimum rates and maximum hours for the whole of Britain.

By the end of the year the Federation consisted of thirty societies covering some 230,000 members.[2] At the same time more and more amalgamations were taking place amongst different sections of transport

[1] Its six points were:
  i. Conversion of war bonus into wages
  ii. Abolition of systematic overtime
  iii. Systematic reduction of hours
  iv. Week-end rest
  v. Payment of travelling expenses
  vi. Abolition of underpaid Asiatic labour.

[2] Besides the groups of seamen's and waterside workers' unions, there were the road vehicle workers. These included the Amalgamated Association of Tramway and Vehicle Workers (30,000) and the London and Provincial Union of Licensed Vehicles (25,000) which were larger than the Association. Those which were smaller included the Mersey Quay and Railway Carters' Union, the National Union of Vehicle Workers, the United Carters' and Motormen's Association, and the Amalgamated Carters', Lorrymen's and Motormen's Association.

workers; by the spring, employers' organizations in some sections of transport had agreed to meet the Federation for negotiation instead of the constituent unions, where this was desired. Above all, the war-time Committee on Production, which the Government had established early in 1915, had issued an award of the 20s. By the time the Federation met for the Annual General Council Meeting in Newcastle on June 6, 1918, they were ready to take the principle of national wages application further and negotiate a big new increase for all transport workers.

On the face of it, there was nothing but good value for money to be gained for the Association in belonging to the Federation. Yet Lyon had suddenly decided to withdraw from the proposal. It is worth noting that for some time the Parliamentary Committee of the Scottish Trades Union Congress, of which Lyon was a member, had been concerned to persuade all unions based in England to affiliate to the STUC in respect of their Scottish members. Hugh Lyon was Chairman of Congress in 1918. The following year the British TUC was due to meet in Glasgow, for the first time since 1892; negotiations took place between Glasgow and London, many months before, urging that Scottish District Councils of English unions should affiliate. Some saw this as an encouragement to strengthening trade union organization in Scotland; others may have had misgivings that it might lead to 'poaching', especially in industries where trade unions were rapidly expanding. Whatever may have been Lyon's anxieties in this respect, the annual conference of the Association meeting on May 18, 1918, supported his withdrawal from the Federation by nineteen votes to four; and at the same time it was unanimously agreed to promote a meeting between the Executives of the Association and of the Greenock Horsemen's Union 'to consider the question of amalgamation'.

Were the events connected? What was the reason for the withdrawal? The official records of the time are by no means explicit; Lyon's announcement is of the briefest: 'We have withdrawn from the Transport Federation for various reasons. They issued a circular condemning us for doing so.' He appended the Association's reply,[1] but not the circular.

Williams had written to Lyon in conciliatory fashion on September 11, 1918:

'Personally, it is extremely regrettable that there should be any difference between your union and the Transport Workers' Federation. I am pro-

---

[1] 'We wish to state that it [the Federation's circular] seems to have been issued with one purpose in view, viz., a deliberate attempt to undermine the influence of our General Secretary and to cause dissension in our ranks. If this is the method or function of the National Transport Federation, the quicker it is disbanded the better for trade unionism. We have no wish to quarrel with anybody, all we ask is to look after our own affairs, as we have so successfully done for the past 20 years.'

After an attack on Williams for being 'a Conscientious Objector,' the statement continues: 'It will be noted we have made no attempt to discuss the statement made by the Federation or why we withdraw our affiliation. Our business is with our members.'

foundly convinced in my own mind, and I am confident that my EC will bear me out, that there is no place or need for dissension between us on the points discussed and considered from time to time.'

He suggested that small deputations of the two executives should meet for 'a frank and free interchange of opinion'; and he hoped that the Association's Executive 'will realize—as I am certain you do yourself—the folly, and, in fact, the iniquity of ill-will and recrimination'. Meanwhile he asked them at least to be present at a hearing before the Committee on Production on September 17, 1918, when an application for 30s on the pre-war wages would be heard. Adroitly he reminded them that they would not be alone amongst Sassenachs:

'The Glasgow Employers' Association is part of the National Employers' Association and it will be clear to you that it is to your, as well as the general, advantage of carters and motormen that your union should be present at the hearing.'

The Association held a Special Executive Council meeting and finally decided to send a deputation to London to the Committee on Production, where the application was successful. It was however, 'much against our will, as we feel we have no right to spend money and time on questions that can be quite easily settled in Glasgow'.

4. ATTEMPTS AT AMALGAMATION IN SCOTLAND

During the next two years, the Association pursued amalgamations in Scotland. Their attempts in 1917 to persuade the Greenock Horsemen to amalgamate with them had failed. At the end of 1919, the Scottish TUC again took a hand, following a resolution passed by Congress in favour of amalgamations. They issued invitations to the Greenock Horsemen to discuss amalgamation with the Association, and once more to Gillespie's North of Scotland Horse & Motormen. The veteran Bailie Robert Lemmon, of the Greenock Horsemen's Union, declined the invitation outright; the Association, of course, accepted. Robert Williams, who was to assist, wrote that if either Lemmon's Union or Gillespie's Association

'. . . should amalgamate with the Scottish Union, the best test of the belief of that organization in the principles of solidarity would be their willingness to affiliate with the above Federation, which is an organization which not only claims, but has achieved, a measure of solidarity for transport workers of all grades.'

He did not think the 'amalgamation movement would have any success or produce any tangible results whilst the policy of the Scottish Union remains as it has been during the past few years'. Gillespie wrote to the Scottish TUC that his Executive endorsed the 'sentiments contained in Mr Williams's letter'; and that they could not 'consider any form of amalgamation with the Scottish Horse & Motormen's Association until such time as that Society rejoins' the Federation. There the matter rested yet once more.

But a year later, the situation became clear-cut during another discussion, once more under the auspices of the Scottish TUC, when the Association met Ben Smith's United Vehicle Workers on September 28, 1920 to consider amalgamation. Peter Webster was the Association's spokesman on this occasion; and he made it clear that their policy all along had been to use the good offices of the Federation to get the still independent Scottish carters' organizations to amalgamate with the Association; beyond that they would not go. He told Ben Smith that:

'An effort was on foot to secure the amalgamation of all transport workers in Scotland, and he suggested that if one union could be achieved for Scotland and one for England, that would, in the first place simplify the problem and lead to the possible amalgamation of all into one, though it would have to be recognized that a strong national feeling existed in Scotland.'[1]

Ben Smith, speaking for 44,000 road transport workers in England, said that progress had been made towards amalgamation of unions there,[2] the 'United Vehicle Workers being now much the predominant factor in the road transport industry'.

'He dealt with the scheme propounded for the formation of one union for all transport workers and explained its scope. He strongly urged, however, that they should go on with the consideration of the organization of all road transport workers into one union, as even though the larger union suggested was accomplished, they would speak with more authority in that body if they spoke as a united body of road transport workers.'

But when Ben Smith went on to say that the National Transport Workers' Federation were fully aware that he and Webster were meeting, Webster drew back in anger:

'Mr Webster expressed his surprise, as he said the Transport Federation had intervened when the Parliamentary Committee of the Scottish Trades Union Congress had last year endeavoured to secure the amalgamation of

---

[1] Scottish Trades Union Congress, 24th Annual Report, 1921.

[2] Just over half a year later, Ben Smith's union was to be one of the eleven unions which first came together to form the Transport & General Workers' Union, dominated largely at first by the dockers' groups, with Ernest Bevin as Secretary; it was finally to take over the remnant of the once powerful Federation.

the Scottish unions of the horse and motormen, and had sought to coerce his society into the Federation.

'Mr Smith repudiated any such notion and hoped the proceedings begun that day could be continued with perfect freedom.'

Discussions then broke down and, despite the efforts of James Walker, the Chairman of the Parliamentary Committee of the STUC, they were never resumed. Instead, the Association sent a resolution to the STUC that they would

'. . . take no part in any scheme of amalgamation or fusion which involves the handing over of their funds and the relinquishing of their independence and individuality as a Scottish Union to any Executive with headquarters in London or in any part of England.'

If the Association's attitude was one of 'ca'canny' at the time, it should be remembered that these were the days when the great vision of solidarity of rails, docks and road transport workers with miners was breaking up. For the Triple Alliance's actions had driven back to work the miners who had yielded up their autonomy in exchange for promise of support in the great strike of mineworkers in the autumn of 1920 and the lock-out in the spring of 1921.

Ironically, it was Robert Williams and his Federation who followed the lead of J. H. Thomas, of the National Union of Railwaymen, in destroying the Triple Alliance. The Federation was to save its members' funds and lose its soul, and soon its existence; the funds of the Scottish Horse & Motormen's Association were never endangered. Lyon did not recall this curious interview between Webster and Ben Smith in his Annual Report. Instead he wrote, in his bitterest style:

'Two years ago, the Transport Federation sent a Mr Robert Williams, from London, up to Scotland to teach us what trade unionism meant, with the threat that unless we joined the Federation we would be extinguished. Now it seems that both the Federation and Mr Williams have been extinguished, as a Mr Ernest Bevin has been sent to tell us that what they want is an amalgamation of dockers, tramwaymen, carters and labourers, and that we hand over all our funds and independence to England, and they will tell us how to run our business. Puir auld Scotland! In the last 21 years our members have looked after their own business fairly well, and have decided to continue to do so.'[1]

Gillespie's society went with Ben Smith's union direct from Williams's Federation into Bevin's general union, and never joined the all-Scottish amalgamation for which Lyon was working. This was the first of many occasions when the question of amalgamation with what was later to

---

[1] Annual Report for 1920.

become the gigantic Transport and General Workers' Union came up. The attitude of the leadership of the Association varied from time to time according to circumstances.

5. THE ASSOCIATION'S SECOND DECADE CLOSES

The First World War was transforming everything, not least the old carting industry, based on local needs and local outlooks; it became increasingly clear to the members that the Association must pay attention to politics, and strengthen its ties with the labour and trade union movement as a whole. The question of affiliation to the Labour Party had been raised in 1914, after the Association had had two years' experience of grappling with the problems and opportunities of national insurance. Present at the Annual Conference in Hamilton in September 1914 was Mr Ben Shaw, then Scottish organizer of the Labour Party, who, six months before, had been insurance clerk in the Association. Although the Annual Conference decided 'that the Executive take a ballot of the members at an early date', this was not followed up. At the Annual Conference at Kirkcaldy in 1915, Jock Urquhart of Glasgow, with the Edinburgh delegate seconding, moved that the Association should become 'affiliated to the National Labour Party'. Next year at Falkirk, on the 'motion of George Irvine of Glasgow and Heiner of Dunfermline, it was agreed 'that immediately the war is ended, a ballot be taken on the question of becoming affiliated to the Labour Party'. This was repeated at the 1917 Annual Conference, where it was decided not to delay the decision until after demobilization, which some thought would be more proper. Rules for taking ballots were registered on December 3, 1917. A ballot was taken for adopting political action as an object of the Association.

Those voting in favour:	1,805
Those voting against:	605
	2,410

The majority in favour was 1,200. Rules providing for a political fund were accordingly registered on April 6, 1918, and the Association affiliated with payment of a £50 fee.

The close of the Association's second decade was approaching. In October 1918, a couple of weeks before the end of the First World War, they were celebrating their twenty-first anniversary. In May of that year, Lyon had asked the Government to set up an Industrial Council for the carting industry. A meeting of the employers and the Association was called, at which the Minister of Labour proposed a Council which should cover the industry both in England and Scotland. This proposal the Association refused to entertain. Lyon said in his memoirs that the Association believed 'the habits and conditions of the carter in Scotland differ materially from those in England'. Nevertheless, marked gains had been made. The Association was recognized by all Scottish corporations and co-operative societies, by the contractors' Associations which were then coming together into a Scottish Federation, and by the Railway Cartage Conference. Weekly wages, with successive war bonuses, had risen by 30s, being about twice what they had been in pre-war days; despite the rise in prices, it was nevertheless a notable advance. Their numbers were 9,334, not counting over 5,000 in the armed forces whose pence cards were being kept clear; nearly 250 members had died on active service. Their assets totalled just over £34,200 or £2 6s 0d per head.

Hugh Lyon presided over the twenty-first meeting of the Scottish Trades Union Congress at Ayr in April 1918. A month later, at Alloa, the Association's Annual Conference passed a resolution about hours:

'Mr Watson moved that it be an instruction to the EC to use every means possible to bring about an 8 hours' working day, with only 5 working days per week, for our members. This was seconded by Mr Alston and agreed to.'[1]

But it was not until six months later, late in November, when the war had ended, that Lyon took any action to approach the employers. What was the reason for this hesitancy? For that it is necessary to look beyond the domestic affairs of the Association and its members' anxiety about post-war conditions.

For the carters with their problems and preoccupations were at the same time to a large extent part of the Clydeside, where the war had brought profound changes in outlook, especially amongst the engineering and shipbuilding workers. Before the war the concern of their shop stewards had been for the most part to check cards and collect dues merely; now they had taken on a new role. Becoming negotiators in their shops over the thousand and one problems which war conditions had brought about for daily decision, they developed into the real and effective leadership. The factories and shipyards had thrown up from their own ranks a new leadership responsive to the man at the bench from whom the old national and district paid officials were becoming more remote. Whilst the carter was not himself part of the shop stewards movement, he was daily in contact with the mood and ideas of the rank and file who had produced the new unpaid, unofficial, although duly recognized, leaders of the Red Clyde.

---

[1] Annual Conference Report, May 18, 1918.

CHAPTER NINE

THE CARTERS AND
THE CLYDESIDE REVOLT

1. THIRTY HOURS, OR FORTY?

EVEN in the spring of 1917 the carters were already anxious about post-war problems; by the spring of 1918 the industrial workers of Scotland, especially those who had earned themselves the title of 'The Red Clyde', were indeed looking ahead. In factories and shipyards there was a powerful movement for a drastic shortening of hours without loss of pay, in order to keep wartime gains, prevent post-war unemployment, and 'never go back to all that'. Under this pressure, the Parliamentary Committee of the Scottish Trades Union Congress called a meeting of trade union officials on March 14, 1918, with Lyon as their main spokesman, which declared for a forty-hour week. But a month later the Scottish Trades Union Congress held their annual meeting, over which Lyon presided, at which an amendment was carried for thirty hours, which was the policy of the powerful Clyde Workers' Committee, made up of shop stewards in the shipbuilding and engineering factories: 'That this Congress declares that the first act of reconstruction after the war should be a reduction of the hours of labour to six hours a day.'[1]

This met with resistance from some of the upper level of trade union officials, many closely involved with employers and government departments on wartime joint committees, who were anxious to revert to the first proposal of forty hours. There was, however, general agreement that a shorter working-week must be won immediately the war ended. The joint Executives of the Scottish Trades Union Congress and the Scottish Labour Party therefore sent a memorandum to the Government in August 1918, and interviewed the Right Hon. G. H. Roberts, MP, then the Minister of Labour, when he was in Scotland on October 24, 1918, putting to him the case for legislative enactment of a shorter working-week as soon as the war should end.

Within less than three weeks the Armistice had been signed. A Conference on Demobilization Problems was called for December 27–28, 1918. It was indeed timely; each day thousands of servicemen were returning to civilian life; war work was brought to a sudden stop; widespread un-

[1] 22nd Annual Report to the Scottish Trades Union Congress, 1918–19.

employment was imminent. But in the seven weeks which passed between Armistice Day and the Conference on Demobilization, new factors kept appearing. There was the disillusionment caused by the snap 'Coupon Election', the results of which were declared while the Demobilization Conference was meeting.

The leaders of the engineering and shipbuilding unions took a controversial step; they made an agreement with the employers to start a forty-seven-hour week on January 1, 1919, and pressed this to a ballot. The men at the bench were angered; there was what the Annual Report to the next STUC describes as 'rampant dissatisfaction'. At the end of the two-day Conference on Demobilization, a resolution was passed, which the Annual Report called 'an unmistakeable mandate to the Parliamentary Committee to take immediate action'. It declared on Saturday, December 28, 1918:

'That this Conference, for the purpose of reabsorbing the sailors and soldiers into civil life, and giving greater leisure to the working classes, demands the reduction of hours by legislative enactment to a maximum of 40 hours per week, preferably five days of eight hours each.'

Having decided on a direct demand upon the Government, the Conference went on to the alternative:

'Failing Government action in this direction, that the Parliamentary Committee be empowered to devise such methods of industrial action as will enforce this demand. Conference demands the right to work or maintenance for all workers.'

Clydeside was in no mood for further delay; the question was, when would a date be fixed for action, since the Government showed no willingness to introduce legislation? The Parliamentary Committee of the STUC continued in what looked like a leisurely fashion, falling far short of the needs of the day.

The truth is that they were in difficulties. On the one hand they were conscious of great pressure from the factories and shipyards led by the shop stewards' movement for immediate action for a thirty-hour week. On the other hand, they were under sharp criticism from some trade union officials, whose attempts to restrain the ever-increasing mass movement led by the shop stewards were having the reverse effect; whenever they reached for the brake, the movement accelerated. Finally, there were ill-paid and more weakly organized sections of workers to whom the reduction of the working week even to forty hours would seem far beyond their wildest hopes of what they could win unaided from their employers. To overcome these obstacles to unity demanded a spirited and determined campaign. The Parliamentary Committee continued to deliberate, whilst the impatience of the shop stewards increased hourly. When the Clyde

District Committee of the Engineering and Shipbuilding Trades, the Glasgow Trades and Labour Council, and the Clyde Workers' Committee invited the STUC to be represented at a conference to organize an early strike for thirty hours, the Parliamentary Committee, 'considering that such a course would be disastrous', sent representatives, led by Lyon, to argue against it. Speaking afterwards in defence of their decision, Bailie Robert Climie, of Ayrshire Trades Council, said: 'They considered it their duty to try to divert that agitation into a general Scottish movement for a forty-hour week.'

At a meeting which followed of shop stewards from all over Scotland on January 18, 1919, to which Lyon was sent to argue the case for confining the demand to forty hours and for calling off an immediate strike, the decision went against them. The conference put Lyon himself on a sub-committee to draw up a strike manifesto and appointed a Joint Strike Committee[1] under the chairmanship of Emanuel Shinwell, then councillor and chairman of the Glasgow Trades and Labour Council. They issued a statement to the Press:

'After careful consideration it was decided to issue a Manifesto of the workers throughout the country calling on them to declare a general strike on Monday, January 27th, for a 40 hours' working week with no corresponding reduction in wages.

'The 40 hours' working week is to be tried as an experiment with a view to absorbing those unemployed consequent on demobilization, and further action is contemplated in the event of the reduction of hours being insufficient for this purpose.

'There was very strong feeling expressed in favour of taking action for a 30 hours' week, and it was only by a small majority that the representatives agreed on a 40 hours' week.'[2]

Finally, after further hesitation although it had gained its point in reducing the demand to forty hours, the Parliamentary Committee called a meeting of trade union officials which decided that the STUC should recommend 'affiliated bodies to do whatever is possible to make the movement a complete success'.

2. 'A CALL TO ARMS'

The irresistible wave swept on. On the afternoon of Sunday, January 19, 1919, mass meetings were held at Govan, Shettleston, Springburn, and

[1] The Joint Committee was described as 'consisting of representatives of the Scottish Trades Union Congress Parliamentary Committee, the Glasgow Trades and Labour Council, the District Committees of the Engineering, Shipbuilding and allied trade unions, the Clyde District Shop Stewards' Committee, the Scottish Union of Dock Labourers, the Scottish Horse and Motormen's Union, Railwaymen, the Municipal Employees' Association, and the Building Trades and Electricians'. (Joint Strike Committee Statement)

[2] *Glasgow Herald*, January 20, 1919.

St Andrew's Hall, Glasgow, to hear and endorse the Joint Strike Committee's *Call to Arms of the Workers*, the manifesto which their sub-committee had drawn up. In Glasgow, Hugh Lyon himself read it to the enthusiastic audience in St Andrew's Hall, where it was unanimously endorsed. A further statement in support declared:

'Thousands of men are being demobilized from the Army and Navy every day. Over a hundred thousand workers in Scotland have been dismissed from civil employment. They are now looking for jobs. There are no jobs for them.

'There is only one remedy. Reduce the number of hours. The time for action is now. Delay means failure. No more than 40 hours per week to be worked. No reduction in wages. No overtime to be worked. No work on Monday, January 27th. No resumption of work until demands have been conceded.'

There were to be no negotiations with employers, as one of the main objects was to press the Government to speed up demobilization. Speaking in support of the manifesto at St Andrew's, on Sunday, January 19th, Hugh Lyon said that:

'. . . the committee were asking all workers, including the police, to come on strike. They were sending telegrams all over the country asking the workers to join up, and they expected Belfast would fall into line with Scotland on the 40 hours' week. Bakers would be allowed to remain at work if they cared to ensure a supply of bread for the women and children.'[1]

The story of the strike; the attack on the Committee and the police charge on 'Bloody Friday', January 31, 1919, in the Battle of St George's Square, whilst they were waiting for their deputation to return from an invited visit to the Lord Provost; the arrest and gaoling of the Strike Chairman, Emanuel Shinwell, the organizer, William Gallacher, David Kirkwood and three others—all this has been told elsewhere, notably in the memoirs of William Gallacher and Emanuel Shinwell. What concerns us at this point is the position of the Scottish Horse & Motormen's Association. The basic facts are that on January 27th the strike began; there was a complete stoppage. On Thursday, January 30th, the railway carters and the co-operative carters returned to work, followed before the end of the week by all the Association's members. Hugh Lyon, who was still on the Joint Strike Committee, had negotiated a forty-eight-hour week on their behalf.

3. THE CARTERS RETURN TO WORK

How did it come about that Lyon had led the carters back to work on a forty-eight hours' agreement at the height of the strike, whilst he himself

[1] *Glasgow Herald*, January 20, 1919.

was responsible for *A Call to Arms* which demanded nothing short of forty hours ? To understand the position, we have to examine the Association's policy on hours. As long ago as the Annual Conference of September 1, 1917, the Association had gone on record 'that the EC take such steps as are necessary . . . to reduce the hours to fifty-six per week'. In his Presidential Address at the 21st Scottish Trades Union Congress at Ayr in April 1918, to which we have already referred, Hugh Lyon said:

'If, with a so-called organized effort at production, we have increased the output to such an extent (even with a shortage of labour) that every thoughtful man and woman recognizes it—then the hours of labour should be greatly reduced. As trade unionists we have a right to demand that no man or woman should be allowed to work more than 8 hours per day and 5 days per week. Man should not live to work, but work to live! This should be the first plank of reconstruction for every trade unionist.'

At the Association's annual conference, a month later, at Alloa, on May 18, 1918, as we have seen, a resolution was carried that 'it be an instruction to the EC to use every means possible to bring about an 8 hours' working day, with only 5 working days per week.'[1]

This resolution for the forty-hour week, a long stride forward from the previous year's demand for fifty-six hours, was naturally a great deal influenced by the Clyde shorter hours' movement. The Executive, however, did not make any move until the war ended. But, in November 1918, Lyon approached all four groups of employers for a reduction in hours, the railway companies, the co-operative societies, the contractors' association, and the Corporation of Glasgow. The demand put forward was not for forty hours, but for forty-eight.

Lyon next notified Sir George Askwith, the Chief Industrial Commissioner, that he would submit the question of hours to the Committee on Production. On Saturday afternoon, November 30, 1918, a conference of delegates from all the stables in Glasgow was held; they resolved unanimously to strike on December 23rd to enforce a reduction of hours to forty-eight. An Executive meeting followed that night of which a report appeared in the Glasgow Press:

'It was stated at the meeting of the men's executive that the union officials had done all in their power to restrain the members from taking advantage of the shortage of labour during the war. Now, however, it was deemed necessary to adopt this course in order to absorb the sixty-five per cent of service members who would be demobilized shortly.'[2]

Here is a pattern of Lyon's tactics with which we have grown familiar; we look for and duly find reaction from the employers to the Press report

---

[1] Report of Annual Conference, 1918.
[2] *The Post*, November 30, 1918.

of a strike threat. On December 21, 1918, the Saturday night before the carters were to go on strike, Lyon reported to the Executive that the West of Scotland Co-operative Wages Board, representing thirty societies, had agreed to grant forty-eight hours from February 3, 1919. This the Executive regarded as sufficient grounds for recommending to the mass meeting of members the next day that there should be no strike, 'owing to the change brought about by the principle of 48 hours now being established for carters. In face of this there would be no need to go before the Committee on Production, and it was agreed that other employers be asked to fall into line.'[1]

The Association had one set of employers lined up for a forty-eight-hour week; there was no knowing what might be the reaction of the other carting employers when they were submerged by the tidal wave from the Clyde engineering factories. But, although Hugh Lyon represented the STUC on the Joint Strike Committee, and, although his Association took part in the conferences held to organize the forty hour strike, it appeared that there was doubt about what Association members would do. Would the carters come out with the rest on January 27th, or would they pursue a separate policy? They had refused to go to arbitration on their own claim for a forty-eight-hour week, which had been granted only by the Co-operative Wages Board to come into effect on February 3rd. Now at the eleventh hour, Lyon was about to recommend his members to remain at work and to come out on strike a week later only if the remaining carting employers failed to concede their forty-eight hour claim by February 3rd.

But zero hour was striking and, as he put it, 'the heather was on fire'. He called a carters' meeting in the St Mungo Halls for Sunday, January 26th, the eve of the great strike. At the last moment, the Town Clerk refused the use of the halls. 'Unknowingly he played into Lyon's hands,' wrote the Association's General Secretary in his memoirs:

'Our men could be advised to take a holiday on the 27th as a protest against the action of the Town Clerk, and also to meet to discuss their business. On Sunday we met at the hall as advertised. Policemen were there to prevent us from holding a meeting. We therefore adjourned to Nelson's Monument in Glasgow Green, where the men unanimously decided to take the following day as a holiday.'

The refusal of the halls had given a pretext for the way out of Lyon's dilemma: the carters could stop work next day with the rest. They rode in on the crest of the tidal wave of the great strike, while the door was left ajar for the carting employers to make a move to detach them from the main body of strikers.

On Monday, January 27th, with the general strike solid, the carters met in St Mungo's Halls and agreed to continue their 'holiday', and ballot

[1] Executive *Minutes*, December 21, 1918.

on Tuesday for or against joining in the general strike. The ballot was taken throughout the day. While a meeting was taking place that night to discuss its result, the carting employers made their move. A letter was delivered by special messenger from the chairman of the Railway Cartage Conference inviting Lyon to meet them. The carters continued their 'holiday' on Wednesday, pending the discussions. The railway employers agreed to grant the forty-eight-hour week, including stable work, to come into force on February 3rd, provided the carters returned to work at once. On Wednesday night, mass meetings of the carters decided that the railway carters should return to work, and that the general contractors' and the Corporation men should remain on strike until their employers also conceded the forty-eight hours. This they did on Thursday, and all the carters returned to work on Friday, January 31st. This was 'Bloody Friday', the day of the Battle of George Square, when the police charged the strikers and arrested the leaders of the General Strike. The carters took no further part in it. But their General Secretary did: he remained on the Joint Strike Committee and was prominent in subsequent events.

The Association was not the only organization represented upon the Joint Strike Committee which did not join the strike. The Municipal Employees' Association also did not answer the 'Call to Arms', having negotiatied a forty-seven-hour week with their employers.

4. THE DEPUTATION TO LONDON

Hugh Lyon attended the Conference next day, Saturday, February 1, 1919, to which all trade unions, whether affiliated or not, had been summoned by the Parliamentary Committee of the STUC. It met under the shock and shadow of 'Bloody Friday', and the arrest of the strike leaders, including the chairman of the Glasgow Trades and Labour Council and of the Joint Strike Committee, Emanuel Shinwell. There was dissension, for the division amongst the trade union leadership was unabated. After an embittered discussion, the conference decided by seventy-eight to sixty-one votes to exclude the Press. Then a resolution was moved:

'That this Congress in its strongest language protest against the authorities and police in their brutal attack upon the strikers, and declare the Lord Provost and the authorities are criminally responsible for that attack upon the defenceless citizens of Glasgow and that the Conference demand the release of Messrs Shinwell, Kirkwood, Gallacher, and others.'[1]

It was carried by a large majority after an amendment had been put that no action be taken. The main opposition came first in an amendment flatly condemning the Parliamentary Committee for 'recognizing and supporting an unofficial strike' and demanding the recall of representatives

[1] 22nd Annual Report to the STUC, 1918–19.

from the Joint Strike Committee. A second line of attack was expressed in an addendum which said that 'the workers have sufficiently demonstrated to their Executive, their employers and the Government their keen determination to secure a forty-hours' week', and that the strike now should be called off. This was defeated by seventy-seven votes to twenty-four. The key resolution, however, which was carried by ninety-two to twenty-two votes, endorsed the Parliamentary Committee's action:

'. . . and recognizing the great volume of opinion in favour of a 40 hours' week urges all Executive Committees to take such steps as will support the present strike and calls upon the Government to take such measures as are necessary to have a 40 hours' week established by legislative enactment.'[1]

That evening the Executive Council of the Scottish Horse & Motormen's Association met to consider the STUC's recommendation; they decided unanimously, however, that their members should remain at work, and decided also to pay strike aliment for the four days they had been 'on holiday'. Lyon reported this to the Parliamentary Committee and asked to be allowed to resign both from that body and from the Joint Strike Committee. This the Parliamentary Committee opposed, on the ground that his resignation might injure the strike. He attended no further meetings of the Joint Strike Committee; but he played a full part in the subsequent meetings of the STUC.

The Parliamentary Committee in its report to the next Congress described the policy it adopted after the February 1st conference: 'While we adhered to the Joint Strike Committee, we maintained an independent line of action of our own.' They pressed the Ministry of Labour to intervene, but at first the Government declined to do so, 'sheltering themselves behind the plea that the strike was unofficial, and that to intervene would be to subvert the authority of the regularly constituted trade unions.'[2]

The National executives of the engineering and shipbuilding trade unions refused to pay strike benefit. Nevertheless, the strike continued for a further week; and finally the Government did intervene, calling an Industrial Conference to 'consider the prevailing unrest', which produced a proposal for a forty-eight-hour week for all workers by legislative enactment.

While the Industrial Conference was in progress, the Parliamentary Committee sent a deputation to London on February 24, 1919 to 'lay Congress resolutions before Ministers and Heads of Departments'.[3] Hugh Lyon was their spokesman at the Ministry of Labour in submitting

[1] 22nd Annual Report to the STUC, 1918–19.
[2] 22nd Annual Report to the STUC, 1918–19.
[3] The interviews were fully reported to the STUC annual meeting in April 1919, and appear in the Report for that year.

the STUC resolution on the forty-hour week. He said that at the many conferences of trade union officials in Scotland, 'practically unanimous opinion had been reached on this question'. Lyon continued:

'The people were not divided on the forty-hour question; they were merely divided on the action being taken.

'There were many cases of unrest, and if the war had not taken place there would have been unrest, and the unrest was caused as the result of the better education of the new generation which was now reaching manhood. The workers realized that the old systems must be changed.'

He went on to put forward arguments for the reduction of hours in terms which every carter would endorse:

'They were demanding not merely a reduction of hours to prevent unemployment; they were demanding not merely a recompense for their sacrifices during the war; they were demanding, apart from all this, better conditions of life generally.

'They felt that this was a great opportunity for the workers. They felt that they should have more time and leisure. They felt that by bringing about the conditions they proposed, they would be able to have a fairer measure of life.'

The Ministry spokesman, Sir David Shackleton, showed a keen awareness of the divisions which had been expressed and there were some characteristic exchanges. It was impossible to have a uniform system of hours; some wanted a six-hour day, others an eight-hour day. Foreign competition had to be taken into account. The railways and the mines were exceptions; there the Government was in control 'as the custodian of the whole country'. What had to be decided was whether one trade would stand the hours which another proposed?

This was coming near to the bone for Lyon's carters. Sir David then asked Lyon:

'You say 40 hours should be the maximum. If the trade representatives on both sides came to the conclusion that the trade could not exist on these hours, what would you do?'

Lyon replied that there was no reason why a trade in which the conditions were exceptional should not have a special scale of hours. He retorted that

'the Government were dealing with the miners and railwaymen, not because the Government happened to be the employers, but because the men had forced them into the position of having to.'

Sir David: 'I think experience will show that those in the industries concerned can best decide what hours and conditions they can afford.'

When the Scottish Trades Union Congress met two months later at

Perth there were still divisions upon which opponents of the trade union movement could play. Some criticized the Parliamentary Committee for having supported strike action at all. Hugh Lyon intervened against those critics:

'They could say whatever they liked, but the fact remained that the strikes in Glasgow and Belfast were a success. There would have been no Industrial Conference or other reforms granted if it had not been for the strikers. All through their history it was the same; whatever they had won had followed in the wake of strikes or threats of strikes.'[1]

In his Annual Report to the Association, Lyon wrote:

'The education gained from the war has opened the eyes of the people. They have learned more in the last four and a half years than their fore-fathers learned in fifty years. A new world must arise from the old. The Government, the guardian of the nation in war, controlled production and consumption in the interests of the people. They must do the same in peace.'[2]

Referring to 'the present discontent', he added:

'If the Government wish to prevent strife, then they should make an announcement guaranteeing that as early as possible they will pass legislative measures making compulsory a maximum working week and a minimum wage, and this will, to some extent, take away the great fear of unemployment.

'Those who today condemn the present strikes and demonstrations should read up history, and they will find that the progress of the world had been made from such.'[3]

The Scottish carters had come a long way since their pre-war degraded levels. Now that the forty-eight hours had been conceded, the carter had got fourteen and a half hours knocked off his week's work. His wage had been exactly doubled in money values since the war began. All town councils, co-operative societies, the contractors' organization, and the Railway Cartage Conference recognized the union.

But there was no clear road ahead for the carters. In the exceptionally favourable circumstances of the war, the employers had been forced to concede some gains to the carters. This was Lyon's advice to them for the first year of peace:

'The Carters must now concentrate their efforts on keeping what they have got. Delegates should be appointed in every stable—men who can be

[1] Debate at 22nd Annual STUC, April 23, 1919.
[2] Financial Report, 1918.
[3] op. cit.

trusted to see that no man is allowed to work unless he is a member. To see that all overtime is stopped, unless where absolutely necessary.

'Any man known to waste his time for the purpose of endeavouring to make overtime is a danger to the whole carting industry, and should at once be reported to the Head Office. We do not want overtime. We want more leisure and time to devote to other interests in life. No man should work overtime while another is going idle.'[1]

They faced an uncertain future, after the Association's first twenty-one years.

---

[1] Financial Report, 1918.

CHAPTER TEN

UNEMPLOYMENT AND THE
AFTERMATH OF WAR

1. 'NEVER AGAIN!'

A PHRASE on many lips in the early post-war years was 'Never Again!'
It had a different emphasis and meaning according to speaker and place,
whether an ex-serviceman returning from the blood and mud of Flanders
to the mines and transport industries, both still under public control;
or those who had sweated and toiled in Britain, and had no intention of
going 'back to all that'. For many employers it meant 'Back to Business
as usual'. For some workers it meant 'peace at any price', and a finish
with strife of any kind. For others it meant looking back on what seemed
a steady climb out of an abyss of pre-war misery, back into which they
feared that employers would be eager to thrust them, once they were rid
of wartime public controls. For some it meant carrying forward these
controls. For some it meant carrying forward their war aims at home,
with no goal too high; and, indeed, believing that nothing short of social
and political revolution would be capable of consolidating the small but
bitterly hard-won gains.

But for the leaders of the Association, the forty-eight-hour-week,
snatched from employers under pressure of what looked like a high and
rising tide of revolutionary strikes, seemed the limit of the possible, and
a good basis for holding fast. Never again would they let themselves and
the thousands of members returning to civilian life 'live and work with the
miserable wages and conditions of labour that existed previous to the
war'. As for the war years, Lyon said in the 1918 *Financial Report*: 'At
long last the horrible nightmare is past,' adding: 'So much has been said
and suffered during the last four years and a half, that everyone feels as if
they wanted to forget it all'.

During 1919 things seemed to be going well for the Association, their
funds and their numbers increasing as the ex-servicemen returned. That
autumn it was decided to celebrate the twenty-first birthday of the Association. At the Annual Conference, held on June 7, 1919, in the Central
Halls, Glasgow, the following decision was taken:

'The question of the celebration of the Society's Coming-of-Age in
October 1919, was considered, and it was agreed to recommend to the

EC that we publish and issue to every member of the Society a copy of the history as compiled by the General Secretary, and also that they should celebrate the occasion in other ways as they think fit.'[1]

In due course the history was distributed, and all branches sent delegates to a celebration dinner in Glasgow, held on November 7, 1919. Mr Ben Shaw, for the Labour Party, proposed the toast of the Association, to which Councillor Jack Elliott of Paisley replied. The Association's chairman, Walter Lumsden made presentations to Hugh Lyon and Mrs Lyon.

But, for Lyon, the great event of 1919 was the setting up on October 13th of an Industrial Council for Road Transport in Scotland, with the contracting employers, the Association being sole representative of the workmen's side. It was one of the joint industrial committees established following the recommendations of the Whitley Committee of 1916, many of which were short-lived. This was separate from any other such council in transport, being exclusive to Scotland and the Association. The chairman of the Scottish Joint Industrial Council for Road Transport was Mr D. Y. Abbey of Edinburgh, President of the Scottish Carting Contractors' and Horse Owners' Federation, a formidable old antagonist. He was a man of the past, one who was said to hate the very sight of motor-cars.

Even in the mid-twenties, Lyon, too, was not convinced that the motor vehicle would dominate the future. There were still well over 10,000 carters in Glasgow alone, and the Association's membership in 1919 was overwhelmingly amongst the horsemen, not the young motormen. This connection was the first step in a chain of events culminating in the establishment of a Sliding Scale Agreement which determined the course of action of the Association for many years, for good or ill. A first result of taking part in the Industrial Council was that it stiffened Lyon's attitude against closer working or amalgamation with other transport bodies. To him the immediate merits were: first, sole recognition, and a further step toward collective bargaining with all that could involve; second, that he could abandon his old weapon of threatening employers with strike action, with its double-edged consequences; third, it could be a means of building up the financial strength of the Association, the funds of which had already reached £42,747. This, with a membership of 14,767 (although Lyon claimed 16,000), meant over £2 17s per head, and, in the 1919 Financial Report, he wrote that the 'financial position is such as has never been before in the history of the carters'. In fact, it was to rise far higher, by accumulation of untouched funds at the same time as its numbers fell catastrophically.[2]

This trend began with the acceptance through the Industrial Council

---

[1] Report of Annual Conference, 1919.

[2] In 1932 membership had dropped by almost half to 7,596, whilst the funds were more than three times as great, at £131,295.

of a sliding scale which was introduced two years later, in 1921. At the early stage, however, favourable agreements were reached, such as those fixing overtime rates and minimum wages for drivers of steam wagons (£4 5s and the second man £4), and 'for drivers of petrol motors' (£3 10s). At the same time the Association was meeting the co-operative societies on the Scottish Co-operative Wages Board. Attempts to reach similar arrangements for the railway carters, however, were met by the argument that there was no power to act, because the railways were still controlled by the Government. Another by-product of the Industrial Council was the stimulus it gave to the formation of branches of the Association far and wide—seventeen were formed during 1919 and 1920, only four of which failed to establish themselves. By the end of 1920 there were in all forty-four branches. But there was much ground to be covered if there were to be any approach to a normal wage standard. Wages varied greatly from one town to another and between the four main types of carting. Wages were still rising up to the end of 1920, but they were uneven; the following table illustrates the absence of a common standard at the end of that year, as quoted in the Association's Financial Report, 1920:

Railway carting	1920		
Cowdenbeath	£3	5s	–
Alloa	3	16s	–
Co-operative Societies			
Rothesay	3	–	–
Kilbirnie	4	15s	–
Corporation			
Stranraer	2	–	–
Kilbirnie	4	2s	–
Contractors			
Maybole	2	18s	–
Motherwell	3	16s	6d

After 1920 wages fell steeply; but in 1919 there was still a strong upward trend and the hours worked were influenced by the forty-eight hours' agreement, even though it was not everywhere observed. The members, whose cards had been kept clear whilst they were in the forces, were coming back to considerable gains. Bob Scott wrote in his report for 1919, from the Anderston and Maryhill District: 'It is gratifying to hear the men who have come home from the war speak so highly of the great changes in the working conditions of the lot of the carter, and they are a great help in convincing young lads to become members of the Association.'

One of the ex-servicemen was John Brannigan, who became the General Secretary twenty-four years later. Coming from a mining family, as a vanman in the Newmains and Cambusnethan Co-operative Society he had joined the Association in 1917 at the age of seventeen, and had sought the help of the Lanarkshire district official, Jimmy Jackson, to organize the stables there. He came back to the same job in 1919 after serving in the Royal Air Force, and strove to get the forty-eight hours' agreement put into practice by his co-operative society. In the course of this he lost his job and applied for a vacancy as full-time official for the Association in Lanarkshire, to which he was appointed in 1920. The district stretched from Harthill to Blantyre, the great majority of the members being horse-men employed by co-operative societies or by local authorities. Yet a transformation of the industry was beginning, with small operators buying up secondhand motor vehicles which were sold off by the government, and road haulage and road passenger transport developing fast. Brannigan was keen to organize the motormen. Years later he wrote:

'I consulted the General Secretary, Mr Lyon, and pointed out the possi-bilities I envisaged in this field. To my dismay he told me to leave them alone, I would only be organizing trouble. . . .

'The great Transport & General Workers' Union who to-day control the whole of the passenger services in Scotland were not at that time in being. It was some two years later they were formed as a result of an amalgamation. Lyon stayed outside the amalgamation and fought the principle bitterly, but in his advice to me he had already conceded the field of activity.'[1]

In the all-too-short post-war period when Lyon was meeting with little resistance from the employers to wage increases, there were some other innovations with which he was preoccupied. The Unemployment Insurance Act of 1920 brought new groups of workers, including carters, into the compulsory contribution scheme, with a provision to enable a union to administer the scheme themselves. The union paid out its own aliment together with the statutory benefit, which was later recoverable from the Ministry of Labour. This scheme, with its specious superficial attractions, was taken up enthusiastically by Hugh Lyon, Peter Webster, and the Association's Executive. However, it was not long before they discovered some of the disadvantages of a scheme, which the Government got administered so economically and which provided a social insurance in more than one sense. At first, the chief criticism by the labour movement was that the trade unions did not have exclusive control, since insurance companies and friendly societies also had a share in administering the scheme. Hugh Lyon was spokesman on this for the Parliamentary Com-mittee of the Scottish Trades Union Congress when Sir Robert Horne, then Minister of Labour, received the deputation in February 1919; and Peter Webster seconded a resolution in a similar sense at the 1919 Scottish TUC. In 1920 the Association's Annual Conference decided by fifteen votes to ten to cease to administer the Act. Lyon gave as the reason

[1] *The Highway*, February, 1955.

5. Horse lorries on the tram lines before the First World War. Dundee.

6. An entry, 'Big Johnny', from the Edinburgh firm of Bruce Lindsay. First Edinburgh Infirmary Charities Pageant, May 22, 1920. The men holding the laed ropes are P. Lamond and R. Aitchison.

[photo: Scottish Studios Ltd.

'Nancy' taken June 27, 1949, for the Fleischmann Distilling Corporation.

'continual alterations and obstacles'. The Association pulled out just in time; with mass unemployment increasing, some unions, which continued to administer it, found themselves owed scores of thousands of pounds by the Government and their coffers empty.

By the end of 1919, the Association was paying £89 a year in affiliation fees to the Labour Party and a number of trades councils; at their conference they were demanding a state medical service, with adequate maintenance allowance for the sick and their dependants, as well as nationalization of all hospitals and infirmaries. This was moved by Peter Webster, who, as the expert on the subject, also sponsored a resolution to that effect carried at the next Scottish TUC. But, as the next year came to a close, it was the end of the short post-war 'paradise'. By the end of 1920, there were already the signs of the scourge of mass unemployment which was to grip Britain and last year after year. To this the transport industry was particularly sensitive; the employers began to attack. Lyon wrote: 'The Carters must now concentrate their efforts in keeping what they have got.' He added:

'Unemployment is rampant in the country today and no man should work overtime while another man is going idle. The incoming year is likely to be a trying one for the workers. Already attempts are being made to reduce wages, while the employers continually urge that the only cure for high prices is to reduce wages. If reduced prices is an argument for reducing wages, how much more so the need to reduce interest, profiteering and other burdens pressed on the workers by the over-wealthy living luxurious lives.'[1]

2. THE SLIDING SCALE AGREEMENT

The employers' offensive, coinciding with mounting unemployment, opened in February 1921, when the Scottish Carting Contractors' and Horse Owners' Federation demanded an increase of hours from forty-eight to fifty-four. They also demanded a wage reduction of no less than 9s a week. After prolonged conferences with their old antagonists, Mr David Murray and Mr Donald Mackay, the Association's leaders came to the sliding scale Agreement, on April 6, 1921, at the Joint Industrial Council, over which Mr D. Y. Abbey continued to preside. The terms included:

1. That the working-week should 'remain as at present'.

2. Wages to be reduced 3s a week immediately and a further 2s when the cost of living should fall to 130 points above pre-war; and that thereafter there should be a 1s increase or reduction for every 5 points variation.

3. There should be a three-monthly revision of wages in accordance with the Board of Trade figures.

[1] Financial Report, 1920.

4. That the Agreement should last a year and after that might be ended by one month's notice.

The Scottish Co-operative Wages Board made a similar agreement. For the next four years, the story is the same melancholy one of continued unemployment and the members clinging to the sliding scale, on the grounds that without it worse would befall them.

When the employers put in for an increase of the hours of labour beyond the treasured forty-eight-hour week which stood for a symbol of a higher life to the downtrodden carter, Lyon considered that they believed 'an opportunity has arisen in which they hope to use the unemployed to defeat the employed'. The road transport workers were by no means the first nor the only workers to suffer the attack. The brunt fell upon the miners. After a long struggle throughout the latter part of 1920 they found themselves faced with a declaration by the Government that it would no longer guarantee the coal-owners' prices, which it had been doing under war-time powers. The miners were therefore met by what amounted to a demand from the coalowners for wholesale reductions. The Miners' Federation of Great Britain had appealed for support to the other two partners in the Triple Alliance, the railwaymen and the transport workers. The Executive of the National Union of Railwaymen declared the attack on the miners was 'the prelude to a general attempt to destroy national negotiations and reduce wages'. The Transport Workers' Federation, from which Hugh Lyon had held aloof, described the situation as 'an attempt to get back to the old days of district negotiations rather than national negotiations, which would affect us in the same way as the miners'.

After each had held special delegate meetings on April 8, 1921, the full conference of the Triple Alliance decided to take strike action in support of the miners. But on the eve of April 15, 1921, when all were to stop, after much behind-the-scenes manoeuvring, the leaders of the Triple Alliance called off the strike and left the miners to fight alone. This 'Black Friday' was long remembered throughout the whole movement, not least in Scotland. Eight days earlier, Hugh Lyon and Peter Webster had accepted reductions under the Sliding Scale Agreement on the Scottish Joint Industrial Council, but had successfully resisted an eight-hour increase in the normal week.

Immediately after 'Black Friday', there began throughout Britain an avalanche of reductions—in building, textiles, agriculture, shipyards, engineering, and amongst seamen and dockers. The miners endured a three-month lockout; transport workers could not ignore this, even though the Triple Alliance had collapsed. Hugh Lyon reacted very sharply to these events. In retrospect that year, he wrote:

'Many strikes took place throughout the country—the most notable being the miners. Many efforts were made to bring our members out in sympathy, but failed, and today this has proved to have been the wisest course to pursue. On the approach of the Lanarkshire miners' officials, we gave them the loan of £11,000 which was more appreciated than bringing our members out on strike.'[1]

Then he let fly once more at Robert Williams's Transport Workers' Federation, soon to become the nucleus, with Ernest Bevin's dockers' union of the Transport & General Workers' Union:

'Throughout the war, we heard a great deal of the power of the Transport Federation and the Triple Alliance, but when the critical moment arrived for the proof of their strength, they absolutely failed to either support the miners or even the Glasgow dockers, who had struck work in sympathy with the miners. I am pleased to say that our members passed through 1921 without any strikes.'[2]

But, to be in a position to criticize the National Transport Workers' Federation for not standing by the miners, it would be necessary for the Association to be able to enter the controversy with clean hands. Unfortunately the Association was under heavy fire, and had to defend itself from a serious complaint by those same Glasgow dockers to the Scottish Trades Union Congress. When that body met at Edinburgh in April 1922, it had before it a report by the Parliamentary Committee, on which the Association was not represented that year, which gives the circumstances; the Association's record is silent on the entire incident. Scottish dockers, acting on the original decision of the Triple Alliance, in May 1921, refused to handle coal brought into the Glasgow docks which had been produced by 'blackleg' labour during the three-month miners' lock-out in 1921. They therefore found themselves in serious dispute with their employers. The Parliamentary Committee reported: 'Blackleg labour was organized by the employing class, and the Parliamentary Committee, at the request of the dockers, sent a deputation to meet their Executive to see what assistance could be rendered.' The STUC report continues: 'It was found that the matter was further complicated by the fact that the Scottish Horse & Motormen's Union were handling merchandise which was being loaded by blackleg labour.' The Parliamentary Committee decided to send a deputation to the Association:

'The sub-committee met Mr Lyon along with a colleague of the union, when the whole position was discussed without, however, any definite progress being made. The position of the Horse & Motormen's Union being that they had instructed their members to continue doing their own work and refuse to touch any work belonging to any other class of worker.

[1] Financial Report, 1921.
[2] Financial Report, 1921.

As is well known, the dockers put up a gallant fight for a good many weeks but ultimately had to accept the position and return to work.'[1]

Shortly after this distressing incident, Lyon, in June 1921, complained to the STUC that the Shop Assistants' Union had been recruiting past members of the Association. In rebutting the charge, the Shop Assistants' Scottish Organizer, William Fraser, described how he had pointed out to Lyon:

'. . . that after the last tramway strike at Edinburgh, the Horse & Motor-men's Union had transferred members from the United Vehicle Workers' Union. In his subsequent letter to me Mr Lyon made no reference to this point, thus leading me to assume that he is willing to indulge in stone-throwing while living in a glass house.'[2]

Fraser knew well that the incident complained of by the Glasgow dockers was still much in the mind of Scottish trade unionists as a whole. Unfortunately this was not the last time that the Association was to come under fire from brother unions, the most notable occasion of which we must refer to in some detail in the next chapter, which deals with the General Strike.

3. THE SCOURGE OF MASS UNEMPLOYMENT

Between April 1921 and August 1923, the Association's members suffered nine reductions amounting in all to £1 0s 6d.[3] Their post-war gains were wiped out. But worse was yet to come upon them. Mass unemployment and short-term working existed side by side, and failure to observe the forty-eight-hour week was by no means uncommon. The news from the district officials in the *Financial Report* year after year gives a dark picture. In 1921, from Tradeston and Pollokshaws, Duncan McGregor writes in sympathy for the 'suffering through unemployment for the last eighteen months, more especially the womenfolk'. Aberdeen had 'more than our

[1] 25th Annual Report of the Scottish Trades Union Congress, 1922.
[2] 25th Annual Report of the STUC, 1922.

		£	s	d
[3] April 11,	1921		3	0
June 11,	1921		2	0
August 6,	1921		2	0
November 5,	1921		2	0
February 4,	1922		3	0
May 6,	1922		2	0
November 4,	1922		2	0
December 2,	1922		2	6
August 4,	1923		2	0
		£1	0s	6d

After ten years of the sliding scale the carter's wage was forced down to £2 10s 0d, the motorman's to £2 19s 0d and the steam wagon driver's to £3 9s 0d.

full share of trade depression in the North'; J. M. Fraser wrote of the Sliding Scale Agreement: 'Whatever may be said against it, a series of strikes has been obviated, which would have been of no advantage to our members.'

From Edinburgh and East of Scotland, Walter Lumsden noted:

'There never was a time more essential than now that we keep together, because the employers of your districts are determined to try and get you back either to the 54 or the 60 hours per week.

'Today, men, in the face of all the sweet and lip promises that were made during the period of the five years' bloody war, we have still that cold, ruthless commercialism which was carried on previous to 1914, and I trust that each and every member in these districts have made up their minds to stand side by side, just the same as they did in the Great War.'

From Lanarkshire District, John Brannigan speaks of 'the great unprecedented spate of unemployment':

'A great number of our members in this district have been without work for considerable periods. Quite a lot of our members are still suffering from periodical suspension, and though not quite so bad as permanent unemployment, it tends to affect the financial position of such members. . . .

'While other workers are compelled to submit to reduced wages at the behest of their employers, it is pleasing to know that the Agreement entered into by our Association with the employers only permits of wages being reduced according to the fall in the cost of living.'

In 1922, the General Secretary recorded 'a successful year', over £8,000 having been added to the funds, 'making a grand total of £74,403 1s 0d'; but continued:

'Unemployment has again played sad havoc. The Industrial Council Agreement with a few exceptions has been loyally carried out by both parties. We have had no strikes worth mentioning and trust there will be no cause for such. There seems to be a genuine feeling at the meetings of Industrial Council to avoid trouble.'[1]

In 1922, the Sliding Scale Agreement had been renewed another year, imposing a further cut of 9s 6d in instalments, but with the forty-eight-hour week nominally unchanged. Most officials in their district reports gave the opinion that, without the Agreement, the state of affairs would have been worse; several complained bitterly of attempts to poach members of 'nondescripts that are masquerading under the title of trade unions' (Jack Elliott, Paisley). John Brannigan wrote from Lanarkshire that 'no great industrial improvement obtained through the year':

[1] General Secretary, *Financial Report*, 1922.

'In common with other districts, our members were obliged to submit to reductions in wages, and no doubt, but for the careful handling of the negotiations by our officials these reductions would have been more substantial.'

From Tradeston and Pollokshaws, Duncan McGregor wrote:

'A great number of our members are yet idle, and from that cause have been forced to sever their connection with the Association meantime, and quite as many, I believe, are yet suffering from periodical suspension.

'And because of those conditions many men find it difficult to act up to the Agreement entered into between our Association and the employers as regards hours and wages, and the employers are not slow to take advantage.

'If we are determined to maintain the 48 hours' week and a living wage, it can only be done by unity and organization, for the employers are as determined to try and get you back to pre-war conditions.'

From Kirkcaldy, W. Taylor reported:

'Taking advantage of the acute depression in trade, and the fact that other unions had submitted to big cuts in the wages, the employers made an attack on us, and after a fight lasting many weeks, we accepted a cut much below that which they suggested.'

In Leith, D. A. Mark and William Brodie noted:

'The year that has just gone started with us very black owing to so much sickness and unemployment. The scenes were terrible. . . . Although unemployment is still rampant in our midst our members have been staunch and loyal and kept their books remarkably well. All credit to them.'

The following year, 1923, Lyon again recorded a large addition to the funds of nearly £7,750, raising the total to £82,153 0s 10d, before he went on to say that 'unemployment still hangs over us like nightmare'.

The advent of the first Labour Government was not received with much cheer by the leadership of the Association:

'We have now for the first time in the history of this country a Labour Government taking over the reins of power. Well, whatever success attends their efforts they cannot be worse than their predecessors.'[1]

In 1923 an agreement was once more signed under the Sliding Scale Agreement. Peter Webster, the Assistant General Secretary, wrote in defence of it that in every industry where agreements had expired or had not been on a cost-of-living basis the employers had made a drive to break

[1] General Secretary, *Financial Report*, 1923.

or end them. The Association had been 'able to keep our Agreement intact, and the whole of our negotiating machinery in operation'. It was, he wrote, the only industrial council which still operated in that industry; elsewhere the employers had 'refused to be bound by any such constitution'. Peter Webster said this was a credit 'to Mr Lyon who laid the foundation, and to the Executive Council and Industrial Council Representatives and above all to the members, whose loyalty is our biggest asset'. He continued:

'When we contrast this with the position of those engaged in the same industry over the Border, and remember that they endeavoured to prevent us from having the right to establish an Industrial Council for Scotland, we have good reason to be satisfied with our ability to look after ourselves in Scotland.'[1]

Relations with the Transport & General Workers' Union were thus already settling into a clear-cut mould; but the Working Agreement on demarcation lines was still four years away, and much was to happen before it was reached. Duncan McGregor writing from Tradeston and Pollokshaws, noted 'a want of unity' amongst the men, and continued:

'The Agreement entered into with the Contractors' Association as regards hours is not being observed in practice by either master or men. Unemployment is very much to blame for this state of affairs. The vexed question of overtime is still with us.'

David Templeton of the Townhead District, bore this out, noting: 'With better trade and less unemployment it would be much easier to ensure that Agreements are faithfully kept.' From Paisley, John Elliott reported:

'Nearly all our members idle in this district. Those who were not wholly idle were only working two days per week, and some fortunate ones three days. Yet all our members stood fast by the union although rival unions were pressing them to come over to their unions, such as the National Union of Railwaymen, who miss no opportunity of making the most of propaganda amongst the railway carters.'

Both Leith and Edinburgh remarked on sickness, 'for which we blame so much unemployment, incomes being quite unfit to reach the necessaries of life'.

By the year 1924, membership had fallen by 3,500 from the 1921 figure to 10,573; but over £7,550 had been added to the funds, which had risen by 35 per cent to £90,416 13s 4½d. There had been no strikes, wrote Lyon 'which is a proof of the harmony that exists between the employers

_____
[1] *Financial Report*, 1923.

and the Association'. But Webster stressed the danger of the non-unionist, and declared that 1924 'was not a good year for trade unionism':

'With a Labour Government great expectations were raised. Very few of our hopes were realized and as a result, there has been to some extent an appearance of a loss of hope in the trade union movement.'[1]

In Paisley the year 1924 was 'the worst amongst the many bad ones since the termination of the Great War . . . very few of our members being employed for a full week at a time'. In Aberdeen they wondered 'when, if ever we are to see an improvement'. In Lanarkshire it had taken a strike to enforce the principle of the forty-eight-hour week. Minimum wages were down to 53s.

At the end of 1925 Lyon wrote that 'the wheels of our Association have gone so smoothly in the past year that there is little to report unless financial figures, which are still mounting up to your credit'. Their total was now £96,590 8s 4d; a Convalescent Home had been set up in Cardross Park, a mansion build by a steamship owner and bought by the Association for £4,000. But reports from the Districts for the most part showed 'no improvement' and much short-time working.

A young official, making his first report, wrote of 'the unprecedented epidemic of unemployment'. This was Robert Taylor, who in May 1925 had taken the place of old John Hair, office clerk, who had first belonged to the old Plantation Branch over twenty-five years before and retired early in 1925. Eleven years later he became General Secretary. Robert Taylor came from Bathgate in West Lothian, an area which produced at that time a number of men who later played an important part in the movement and in the Association itself. One of these, from neighbouring West Calder, was John Murphy, who was part-time collector there for forty-two years; when he retired at the end of 1964 he had served on the Executive Council for twenty-two years continuously, a record only once equalled—by William McKenzie of Leith (1914–36). Another Bathgate man was Peter Hamilton, who served as Edinburgh District Secretary from 1942 to 1962. He played a leading part in forming the branch in Bathgate. An account of what lay members, stable delegates, and branch officials were doing in this area may serve to round off the picture of the Association's activities in these early post-war years.

Hamilton had started life as a moulder and worked throughout the 1914–18 war and the post-war period in the foundries of the Lothians and Lanarkshire. He was active in the affairs of the union and of the Independent Labour Party; he was often victimized and was finally forced out of the industry. Working round the farms during spells of unemployment, he came to drive a horse and got a job driving a bread-van for the Bathgate Co-operative Society. Speaking of the conditions then he said:

[1] Peter Webster, Assistant General Secretary, *Financial Report*, 1924.

'They were very bad at that time. The hours were so long—twelve hours and more, and late on Fridays and Saturdays. Wages were £2 5s. Yet on a horse bread-van the carter might be taking £80 to £100 a week, when it was 6d for two half-loaves. These were the days of unemployment and we sold much bread around the mining villages. The saddest sight of my life was to see an eviction of a miner's family from a company house in Easton Houses, the furniture piled outside, the children crying, and absolutely nowhere for them to go.'

Coming, as he did, from the well-organized foundries, he found the carters very different:

'Out all day on their own they did not meet at work and so they were not quick to stand together like the foundrymen. Then, the commission on bread sales kept the men quiet. They did not get great wages in the Co-op, but they had the security and there was so much unemployment around.'

He noticed also the difference between horsemen and motormen.

'The motormen were younger fellows, many ex-servicemen who had been about a bit. The horsemen were mostly off the farms and were not at all well educated. Customers sometimes took advantage of the ignorance of the old carters; one old roundsman ended up with customers owing £50 and he was made to pay it up himself.'

In 1920 he and some other vanmen decided to form a branch of the Association.

'John Brannigan who had become district official for Lanarkshire that May, cycled over from Newmains to help us set up the branch. Men joined to get shorter hours. Danny Banks became our first secretary. There were around 20 or 30 members. But for years the Bathgate branch really only consisted of the co-op men; the railway carters were in the National Union of Railwaymen and the corporation men were in the Municipal and General. There was only one contractor in Bathgate at that time.'

Robert Taylor joined the Bathgate branch a couple of years later. He was one of a family of twenty-two children and had started life in mining. But, when he was about to take his second certificate as a mine manager in the latter part of 1921, the wage cuts came into force. He left mining, trained for six months as a driver, and found himself working as a co-operative vanman alongside Peter Hamilton and the other founders of the branch. He too had been active in the Independent Labour Party in Bathgate; he stood as a candidate for the town council in 1923.

At the same time, five miles away, John Murphy was active in the West Calder Branch, of which he became secretary in 1923. He too was working as a Co-op vanman around the mining villages, and he found the same conditions in the industry as Peter Hamilton, with whom he shared a deep

F*

regard for the mining community. Looking back when he was retiring after a lifetime of modest service in the trade union movement in West Lothian, he said: 'There are no finer people than the miners; they would never willingly let a neighbour want.'

These two branches had much in common; in both, the majority were co-operative men. Negotiations were with the Co-operative District Wages Board, which included the Bathgate and West Calder Co-operative Societies and five others. Throughout 1924, the branches were frequently corresponding with the Association's chief officers on wages and hours; constant vigilance was needed to ensure that the agreements reached by the Wages Board were honoured. Most of the correspondence was handled at head office by Peter Webster, and it was he who usually conducted the negotiations and visited the branches. There was protracted correspondence in 1924 and again in 1925 with the Bathgate employers, at a time when Robert Taylor was president of the branch. Meeting him in Glasgow, Hugh Lyon suggested that he should apply for the vacant position of office clerk, and Taylor began the job in May 1925. From then on, he spent forenoons in the head office, becoming thoroughly familiar with the administration—or lack of it! and in the afternoons and evenings went out organizing without being confined to any one district. In after years he recalled: 'It gave me exceptionally useful experience; at the time it was a field which no one was handling on an all-Scotland basis. Lyon did not like to go out organizing. I got to know the members all over the country; it was invaluable experience.' He became delegate to the Glasgow Trades Council; and he also acted as secretary to the quarterly meetings of the combined Glasgow branches, a very important section of the membership of the Association, right up to the time in 1936 when Lyon was dismissed from office and Taylor was elected in his place.

But that was a troubled decade later; when Taylor started working at head office in 1925 he was the only man there without memories of the days when the old carter was slowly fighting his way out of degradation and towards recognition. Taylor was of the post-war generation, confronting the new problems: they were considerable. Although the bank balance was rising, numbers were falling seriously.

Year	Bank Balance	Membership
1918	£34,066	9,334
1919	£42,747	16,000
1920	£55,738	14,980
1921	£66,384	13,342
1922	£74,403	11,031
1923	£82,153	10,573
1924	£89,711	10,000
1925	£96,590	9,972

The funds had risen to no less than £9 13s 8d per head; but all the post-war gains in membership had been wiped out. In Oliver Goldsmith's words:

'Ill fares the land, to hastening ills a prey,
Where wealth accumulates, and men decay.'

The Association's affairs had already started on the decline as they entered the fateful year of 1926. The aftermath found them on strained terms with other unions, with their numbers dropping steeply, in no strong position to stand up to the depths of the economic depression, nor to meet the new conditions which were developing in the industry. This decline has to be seen against a background of events in Scotland during and after the General Strike, and the part played in them by the Association's leaders, Hugh Lyon and Peter Webster.

CHAPTER ELEVEN

THE GENERAL STRIKE
IN SCOTLAND AND AFTER

I. THE PREPARATIONS

THE coal-owners in Britain had posted notices declaring that they were locking-out the miners just a week before the twenty-ninth Annual Meeting of the Scottish Trades Union Congress opened at Inverness on April 21, 1926. That meeting passed two motions which determined the policy of the trade union movement in Scotland to the great events, expressing the warmth of feeling for the miners and, at the same time, giving a hint of what differences might later emerge. The first was an emergency motion moved on April 22, 1926 for the National Union of Scottish Miners by Provost Doonan:

'That this Congress of Scottish trade unionists heartily endorses the fight the British Miners are putting up to maintain their present conditions, and calls upon the General Councils of the Trades Union Congresses to continue their co-operation with the Miners' Federation, and as a result secure such terms as will result in no lowering of the living conditions of the working class of this country.'[1]

The mover explained that the miners were fighting a defensive battle for a national agreement, a national minimum with no district settlement and no extension of hours. 'If the miners by any mischance were to go down in this struggle,' he said, 'it was certain that it would affect every industry and trade in the country.' The seconder, James Kiddie, of the National Union of Railwaymen said that 'as one of the rank and file, he hoped workers would profit by the mistakes of the past, and when the struggle was over there would be no more "Black Fridays" behind them'.

Two days later, on the last day of Congress, Peter Kerrigan, on behalf of Glasgow Trades and Labour Council, moved:

'This Congress viewing the steady breakdown of British Capitalism and the expressed intention of the capitalists to stabilize their system at the cost of inroads into the standards of life of the workers, states that effective preparations must be made by the working class. To this end the Congress supports the Workers' Industrial Alliance and instructs its General

[1] 29th Annual Report of the STUC, 1926.

172

Council to lend all possible support to this organization and its development.'[1]

This paragraph of the resolution was accepted by the General Council; but they objected to the next paragraph, which instructed the General Council

'to enter into definite negotiations with the Scottish Co-operative Wholesale Society with a view to drawing the co-operative and trade union movements more firmly together, and to obtain united concerted action from these two workers' organizations in resisting the capitalist attack.'[2]

An amendment to the second paragraph urged that the General Council should 'keep in touch with the British Trades Union Congress General Council in any effort to resist the capitalist attack'. In spite of the mover asserting that the General Council were 'endeavouring to cloud the issue by suggesting that the movers of the motion were going too fast', the motion was so amended and carried.

This difference between the attitude of the platform and what was a typical expression of the policy of the left-wing Minority Movement[3] at that time was in fact to prove significant. On the one hand there were those who were hoping up to the last that J. H. Thomas and others in the British TUC General Council would succeed in getting Government and coal-owners to relent and avoid a showdown; on the other, those who had been campaigning for months for the trade union side to make as detailed preparations for defence as Mr Stanley Baldwin's Government was making for attack.

After it was all over, Ernest Bevin made it clear beyond all doubt that such plans as were made were quite inadequate. On the all-important question of the control of foodstuffs—whether they should be distributed and under what conditions—he stated:

[1] STUC Annual Report, 1926.
[2] STUC Annual Report, 1926.
[3] In August 1924 a conference was held of some 270 delegates from a number of trade union organizations which included vigilance committees, reform committees, and shop stewards' committees still in existence after the engineers' lock-out of 1922, together with miners' minority groups. They set up the National Minority Movement. Its objects were: to unite the workers in the factories by the formation of factory committees; to work for the formation of one union in each industry; to strengthen the local trades councils and the Trades Union Congress, with the ultimate aim of winning 'complete workers' control of industry.' They elected as President Tom Mann, the veteran engineers' leader; and, as secretary, a leading boilermaker, Harry Pollitt. In 1929 he resigned on being elected General Secretary of the Communist Party. His successor was Arthur Horner, later the General Secretary of the National Union of Mineworkers.

Both the National Minority Movement and the Communist Party had been prominent in urging throughout the latter half of 1925 and during 1926 that the British Trades Union Congress should make ready a plan of action to match the Government's preparations. The National Minority Movement held a Conference of Action on March 20, 1926, calling on the General Council to publish a plan of campaign, and putting forward detailed proposals.

'With regard to the preparations for the strike, there were no preparations until April 27th . . . In fact, the Strike Committee did not sit down to draft the plans until they were called together on April 27th.'[1]

It was the lack of a clear-cut policy on the control of food and necessities, together with Hugh Lyon's unauthorized action in this connection, which brought upon the members of the Association the charge of 'blacklegging', which had far-reaching and long-lasting effects on their good name. It becomes essential, therefore, to touch upon aspects of the events in Scotland in some detail.

Immediately after the Scottish Trades Union Congress had risen, William Elger, JP, the secretary, was sent to London. With him was the new President, just entering upon his year of office. This was Peter Webster, assistant general secretary of the Scottish Horse & Motormen's Association. They took part in the historic conference of Trade Union Executives in London on Thursday, April 29th. Thus it happened that, through the critical hours leading up to the declaration of the General Strike, a leading member of the Association was in the closest touch with events. As Peter Webster explained in his Presidential Address to the next annual meeting of the Scottish TUC in April 1927:

'Representatives of the General Council were present at the meeting of members of Executives which authorized the General Strike. At these Conferences it was decided that the organization of and the method of conducting the strike should be controlled by the General Council of the British Trades Union Congress. While the Scottish TUC General Council were not actually for decisive purposes part of the Conference, your representatives were asked to take over the duty of acting as Headquarters in Scotland.'[2]

Peter Webster brought back with him to Scotland the printed memorandum giving the broad lines on which the British TUC General Council recommended the strike should be run. The most important part of all would have to be played by the transport workers—road, rail, and docks. Each trades council established a local strike committee. On Clydeside this was the Glasgow Central Strike Committee, set up by the powerful Glasgow Trades and Labour Council. The chairman first appointed was John McBain of the foundryworkers; but before the first week was out, union business obliged him to withdraw, and the position was taken over by the vice-president, Peter Kerrigan, of the engineers. The secretary was Councillor William Shaw, JP. As with central strike committees in other Scottish cities, Glasgow was under the general guidance of the STUC. Some, however, proved more autonomous than others; distance

---

[1] Report of the Special Trades Union Congress, 1926, Margate.
[2] 30th Annual Report of the Scottish TUC, 1927.

and difficulty in communication made this inevitable. But a special difficulty had to be faced by the Scottish officials of unions whose head-quarters were in London. To whom were they responsible: to the head office of their union in London or to the local strike committee, under the general direction of the Scottish Trades Union Congress? This was of great practical importance, particularly for the three railway unions and the Transport & General Workers' Union, which organized most of the dockers and busmen, when it came to what policy should be adopted towards transporting food, coal, and other essential supplies.

2. THE EVENTS

It is not the purpose of this chapter to describe the remarkable support from trade unionists everywhere, or the general events of the strike in Scotland. It is enough to say that it was an overwhelming success, gaining in power daily, until the General Council of the British TUC in London suddenly called it off on its ninth day, Wednesday, May 12th. It is, however, necessary to dwell upon some of the events if we are to understand the situation in Scotland, where the heroism and initiative of the families of the ordinary miner, railwayman, transport worker, engineer, and shipwright was at least equal to those of his or her brother and sister elsewhere in Britain. In the words of the Executive's report to the 1927 Scottish TUC: 'The response of the workers, organized and unorganized, was beyond all expectation, and when the strike was called off on May 12th, uncertainty and bewilderment were in evidence for the first time.'

On Saturday, May 1, 1926, the lock-out of the miners began; the same day the Conference of Executives of affiliated unions met once more in the Memorial Hall in London. They had before them a memorandum signed by Arthur Pugh and Walter Citrine, Chairman and Acting Secretary of the British TUC, which was the General Strike Order. This they approved by 3,653,529 votes to 49,911, the dissentients being the National Union of Seamen, who a year later were charged with organizing breakaway 'non-political' unions and expelled from Congress. The strike was to begin at midnight on May 3rd, but not all workers were to be called out at once. This was to proceed in two phases. The first phase was to include these industries: all transport; printing and the Press; iron and steel, most engineering industries and heavy chemicals; building, except housing and hospitals; electricity and gas. The respective unions themselves were each to call out their own members, apart from which they agreed to put themselves in the hands of the General Council of the British TUC in the conduct of the dispute. There was a specific guarantee about the conditions under which work might be resumed; the executives of the unions were required by the General Council to declare that in the event of 'trade union agreements being placed in jeopardy, it be definitely agreed that there will be no general resumption of work until those agreements are fully recognized'.

Not only the miners but some of the transport workers, particularly railwaymen and dockers, had bitter cause to remember that guarantee on which the General Council of the British TUC had insisted, and which had been so firmly given by the members. There were also later bitter complaints that the memorandum was insufficiently explicit, and different unions, and even different areas of a union, had different interpretations. The General Strike Order put transport amongst the trades and organizations to cease work:

'Transport, including all affiliated unions connected with transport, i.e. railways, sea transport, docks, wharves, harbours, canals, road transport, railway repair shops; and contractors for railways and all unions connected with the maintenance of or equipment, manufacturing, repairs, and groundsmen employed in connection with air transport. . . .'

'Health and Food Services—The General Council recommend that there should be no interference in regard to these, and that the trade unions concerned should do everything in their power to organize the distribution of milk and food to the whole of the population.'

The vital point was that the distribution of food was to be organized, where possible, by the central strike body in the main regions, and under its authority. All the unions affected by the first mobilization began issuing strike orders. How unprepared the 'general staff' of the unions were, all over Britain, became all too clear. It was not until the third day of the strike, Thursday, May 6th, that the General Council in London established five sub-committees for guidance, including the all-important Transport and Communications and Food Supply Sub-committees. It was not even until the second day, Wednesday, May 5th, that the British TUC published a newspaper, the *British Worker*, using the *Daily Herald* equipment; and then only in response to the Government's publication of the official *British Gazette* on the *Morning Post*'s presses, under the control of Winston Churchill, then Chancellor of the Exchequer. Again, although a system of permits was set up, to authorize pickets to allow the passage of certain goods on the authority of the strike body, there was controversy about what should be permitted. Whilst this was in dispute, regional authorities were advised to use their discretion (May 5th). In London, agreement was reached (May 6th) and reversed (May 10th). In Scotland also there was division in the local Transport Committee. The final decision was not published in the *Scottish Worker* until May 12th, the day the strike was called off.

Scottish trade unionists were certainly not immune to the consequences of confusion and lack of preparedness; but members of the Association suffered even more than others. The General Strike Order charged the trades councils with the responsibility, 'in conjunction with the local officers of the trade unions actually participating in the dispute to assist in carrying out the foregoing provisions and of organizing the trade unionists in dispute in the most effective manner for the preservation of peace and order'. Much was necessarily left to local initiative and there were remarkable examples of brilliant improvisation and organizing ability. But there were also cases in which local trade union officials were torn between different policies; instructions from their head offices, whether in London or Glasgow, being in conflict with what was seen to be necessary by local strike committees. One case in point was in the National Union of Railwaymen, whose general secretary, J. H. Thomas, was one of the leading members of the General Strike Committee in London. In Scotland, leading members of the NUR, such as J. B. Figgins, held views markedly different from those of another official, James Campbell.[1] Again, the Glasgow Central Strike Committee was often at loggerheads with the local full-time trade union officials; and it constantly appealed, though usually without success, to the General Council of the STUC.

This body remained in permanent session from May 3rd to May 15th, with overriding authority from the British TUC, to see that general strike policy was operated in Scotland. One of the first steps which the STUC General Council took was to establish road communications from Carlisle to Congress office in Glasgow and thence to Aberdeen. Relay stations on this chain of communications were meant to be distributing and collecting centres for those Strike Committees which could reach them. The chain of stations was open soon after the strike began and remained so during the dispute. Through it the official bulletins issued on May 5th–8th were delivered with relatively short delay, thanks to the devotion and energy of those who were active with the strike committees and trade councils in each locality.[2]

In Scotland the strikers were probably less well informed and less well equipped to counter the continuous Government propaganda on the radio than in any part of Britain. For although on the one hand the Government's propaganda sheet, the *British Gazette*, never circulated in Scotland,[3] neither did the *British Worker*, the first copy of which did not even

---

[1] Each served as general secretary of the union in later years.

[2] The Report to the 1927 Congress made acknowledgement of this: 'We are bound to place on record the efficient manner in which hastily improvised organization was maintained. The initiative and efficiency displayed by those responsible for local organization was one of the most outstanding features—if not *the* most outstanding—of the strike. It demonstrated clearly the capacity latent in the movement to deal effectively with the problems of the organization with which the trade unions are still faced.' (STUC 30th Annual Report, 1927)

[3] Instead there was produced on the *Glasgow Herald*'s presses from May 5th–13th a journal entitled *Emergency Press*, 'combining the issues of the *Glasgow Herald*, the *Daily Record*, the *Bulletin*, the *Glasgow Evening News*, the *Evening Times* and *The Citizen*'.

reach Congress office until Friday, May 7th, half-way through the dispute. Thus the Government-controlled radio would have had it entirely its own way from the vital first day if it had not been for a number of cyclostyled sheets produced, with only one exception, on a local basis and with a local circulation, usually by strike committee and sponsored by the trades council. It might have been thought that amongst the first self-evident duties of the STUC would have been to publish a Scottish paper in Glasgow, Aberdeen and Edinburgh at least; there were facilities and journalists and print workers eager and willing to do so. Indeed, there were immediately demands for it, especially on Clydeside, and the Glasgow Central Strike Committee kept pressing the General Council to publish or to permit one to be published. This they refused to do—and later came under sharp criticism for it—on the ground that it would 'conflict with strike discipline', until the British TUC itself at length pressed them to print an edition of the *British Worker*. This finally decided the STUC Emergency Committee to produce the *Scottish Worker*. But the first copy was not published until a week after the strike had begun, on May 10th—two days before the strike was called off in London. The paper appeared for six days, starting with a mere 25,000 copies and reaching 70,000.

During that first vital week when there was no official newspaper speaking for the trade union movement circulating in Scotland, members of the Communist Party and the Minority Movement produced and distributed a cyclostyled paper *Worker Press*, which incorporated both the *Worker* and the *Workers Weekly*. When the General Council's Annual Report to the next STUC referred to this as 'the sole exception' to the maintenance of discipline during the strike, there were some exchanges, perhaps the sharpest reproof to the STUC General Council coming from Jim Figgins of the NUR. He said he 'thought the cyclostyled *Worker Press* referred to was necessary, because of the inactivity of the General Council itself, and its refusal to issue any publication until forced to do so'.

Figgins indicated what a need there had been for information and a lead:

'The NUR District Council issued a duplicated paper putting out all the strike news, without which their members would never have had any report. This was not a condemnation of the people who sent out the Paper, but a condemnation of the General Council.'[1]

Then he criticized the General Council for describing the publication of the cyclostyled *Worker Press* as the sole breach of discipline:

'The General Council was talking about discipline, yet they had an affiliated union to this Congress which had not instructed its members and they knew that that organization had issued permits in a reckless

[1] 30th Annual Report of the STUC, 1927.

178

manner and they knew that these permits had been grossly abused. Under these circumstances, he said, the General Council failed in that they did not bring this organization to book.'

The union which Figgins was accusing was the Scottish Horse and Motormen's Association. The Assistant General Secretary, Peter Webster, was Congress Chairman: neither he nor Hugh Lyon rose in conference to answer the charge.

What had happened to lay the Association open to such a charge, and bring them under such grave suspicion amongst their fellow trade unionists?

3. DID THE ASSOCIATION 'BLACKLEG'?

It should first be noted that the published records of the Association are entirely silent on this subject. There is no word, either in explanation, defence or denial. In his general remarks for the year ending 1926, Hugh Lyon has very little indeed to say about the General Strike, nor are the District Reports much more informative. Yet the STUC reports disclose that there were repercussions over the next two years which establish that the belief in the Association's guilt was held amongst members of the Association itself. Certainly there were enough references by other delegates at the 1927 STUC conference to show that there was a case to answer. Why was that answer never given? Officials acting in good faith should have had little difficulty in putting forward a defence, in the light of all the confusion that lack of preparedness, divided counsels—and, indeed, divided purpose—at top levels had caused. But Hugh Lyon did not attempt a defence; he was silent about a charge which was levelled at him for the third time in seven years.

What are the ascertainable facts?

The General Secretary of the Scottish Horse and Motormen's Association did not go so far as Havelock Wilson of the National Union of Seamen, who instructed all his members to continue working. What he did do, on May 3rd, was to send the following letter to all forty-seven Collectors of the Association:

'Dear Sir,

'If a General Strike takes place tonight, our members who are employed driving, either by horse or motor, any kind of foodstuffs or other essentials of life and those driving coal, food or such like to all public institutions and those in the Cleansing Department, are to be given permission to work, as well as those employed on all Housing Schemes.

'Members are also permitted to attend to their horses.

'Yours truly

'HUGH LYON'

179

Here was no call to strike nor explanation of the issues. He had concentrated upon giving instructions to continue working to those of his members who could be brought within the terms of the British TUC's memorandum of those excepted.[1] But there was neither instruction nor advice to any other, or to any in doubt. What, for example, were those employed by the railway contractors or the general contractors, who might well not know what load they were booked for, to do?

The admittedly difficult conditions which must have confronted all transport workers were made none the easier by lack of instructions and aid from their officials. The road transport men were in special difficulties. If they had to fetch their loads from the railway stations, for example, they were dependent upon the attitude of the National Union of Railwaymen, which held the view that it was their province and that nothing at all ought to be transported. With the tremendous response of all workers to the strike call, a transport worker without instructions was in an impossible position. It became obvious at the earliest stage that there must be a system of permits. There were differences of opinion on the course to be followed between the NUR, the Associated Society of Locomotive Engineers and Firemen, the Railway Clerks' Association, the Transport & General Workers' Union, the General and Municipal Employees Society, and the Scottish Horse & Motormen's Association. The Association was not represented upon the Joint Transport Committee with the others. Hugh Lyon, on his own authority, began at once, from the Association's office, to issue permits to employers. A Press report appeared:

'It is learned in connection with the trade unions' organization for food supplies, as distinct from the OMS[2] that Mr Hugh Lyon, general secretary of the Scottish Horse and Motormen's Union, 108 West Regent Street, Glasgow, has been appointed food transport officer for Scotland by the Scottish Trades Union Congress. Permits to employers will be issued by him from the above-mentioned office.'[3]

That morning it was taken up as the first item on the agenda of the STUC Emergency Committee: 'The Secretary reported that a report in the Press of the appointment of Mr Hugh Lyon as permit officer for Scotland was made without authority. Noted.'[4]

By telephone from London, the Scots learnt that 'staple foods were to be released from store for retailers and carted from retailers to customers'. (Item 32.) But did 'store' include railway or depot? On this the National

---

[1] The *Glasgow Herald*, which published on May 4th an item giving the gist of the letter, commented: 'This is tantamount to allowing employees of the Corporation and co-operative society to continue at work.'

[2] The Organization for the Maintenance of Supplies was the body set up by the Government in September 1925, in readiness for the General Strike, for strike-breaking.

[3] *Bulletin*, May 4, 1926.

[4] STUC Minutes, Morning Session, Tuesday, May 4, 1926. Item 29.

Union of Railwaymen insisted that nothing should be moved from the railheads.

At the afternoon session on Tuesday, May 4th, Peter Webster informed the other members of the Emergency Committee that his union 'was carrying out instructions in accordance with the General Strike Plan'. The Joint Transport Committee comprising the other transport unions was received by the STUC:

'The Committee reported inability to reach agreement on transport of food supplies. The National Union of Railwaymen had received instructions to stop all goods: the Transport & General Workers' Union had received instructions to transport only milk and bread; the Railway Clerks' Association and the Locomotive Engineers and Firemen were ready to agree to any decision reached by the Joint Committee.'[1]

The same day, James Campbell, on behalf of the National Union of Railwaymen, Glasgow and West of Scotland District Committee, wrote to William Shaw, secretary of the Glasgow Central Strike Committee:

'We have to direct your attention to the fact that we have been informed by telephone this afternoon from Unity House that Mr Hugh Lyon is usurping authority in issuing permits and has no power to issue permits for the removal of food.'

Hugh Lyon continued to issue permits. Miss Katherine Brown, at that time a young clerk in the office, relates: 'He was in his element. There was a stream of employers, sometimes a queue waiting. Hughie sat there smoking a cigar; sometimes he would not give a permit. It depended upon whether he thought the employer would be co-operative in future'. He was said to hold a generous view of what were 'staple foodstuffs', in which he included whisky. Whilst Hugh Lyon distributed, or withheld permits, his members acted upon them, which brought them into conflict with pickets. Their vehicles were overturned; the drivers were sometimes roughly handled. The *Emergency Press* described many incidents: a food lorry 'mobbed' in John Street, Glasgow, while in Dundee 'the only way of getting food about was by police convoy' (May 6th). In the East of Glasgow, 'since the early hours of Thursday morning' there had been riotous scenes, wrote the journal on Saturday, May 8th, when 'bread vans and food lorries seemed to be specially singled out for attack and many of these were stopped'. There were similar incidents reported from Bonnybrigg, Stirling, and Linlithgow.

Jack Steedman, later an official of the Association, described to the author an incident at Bathgate. As a member of the Edinburgh Central Strike Committee, he was invited to address a mass open-air meeting,

[1] STUC Minutes, Afternoon Session, May 4, 1926. Item 36.

mostly of miners and railwaymen. As he was speaking there was the sound of a lorry approaching; his audience broke up; and, to shouts of 'It's one of Lyon's men!', the lorry loaded with flour was overturned in a field. 'It was not the only wreck there, either,' commented Steedman. 'In Edinburgh we had a better grip of things, but the transport drivers did not know from one day to the next what to do.'

The STUC put out a circular, dated Wednesday, May 5th, that 'no individual union is to be responsible for the issuing of permits'. On that morning, the third day of the strike, the Emergency Committee received a telegram from London: 'General Council have fully discussed difficulties but local Committee must exercise own discretion within terms of printed memo.'[1]

But the local railwaymen for the most part felt themselves bound by their union's instructions from London that nothing should be moved. Although there was still deadlock on what might be moved and in what circumstances, the STUC Emergency Committee could no longer delay taking action against Lyon's independent system of permits, which employers were said to be abusing. The Joint Transport Committee were fully agreed on the need for that:

'Reference was made by the Committee to the position of the Scottish Horse & Motormen who had not been represented on the Committee and whose permit system was not regarded as satisfactory by the Joint Committee.

'The General Council instructed the Secretary to advise Mr Hugh Lyon to issue notices for the withdrawal of all permits and that in future permits were to be issued only on the authority of the Joint Transport Committee. Mr Lyon was to be further advised to be represented on the Committee.'

They agreed to issue a statement about the Joint Committee which would 'be solely responsible for the issuing of permits to transport staple food-stuffs in the Glasgow Area. Permits will be issued only on the authority of the Joint Committee', and that arrangements were being made to set up similar committees all over Scotland. Late that night and much of the next day the struggle went on; only if agreement could be reached with the NUR District Committee could a permit be issued. Finally, on Thursday afternoon, May 6th, it was reported that all transport unions were at last represented on the committee, which had agreed to grant permits for the transport of all staple foods from warehouses to retailers and thence to their customers, on the understanding that 'warehouses' did not include either railway depots or docks. It was left to trade unions to inform their branches.

[1] STUC Minutes, Morning Session, May 5, 1926, Item 40.

The STUC General Strike Bulletin No. 2, dated Thursday, May 6th gave specimen copies of permits.[1]

From Edinburgh it was reported that the new permit system was 'working admirably', with 'a constant stream of applicants in the office and many business firms on the doorstep'.[2] The system current on the east coast and in the Lothians was linked with that of the west coast. But on Monday, May 10th, there was a new crisis; in London the decisions were reversed. It was decided to stop the transport of all goods and call out all transport workers, with the exception of men employed by co-operative societies 'solely for the purpose of delivering bread and milk direct to their members'. In Scotland, the Joint Transport Committee decided to give their members instructions accordingly on Tuesday, May 11th. That same morning the secretary of the STUC agreed, at the request of the NUR, to ask Hugh Lyon to withdraw 'all stablemen employed when scab labour was being employed'.[3]

The next day the General Strike was called off by the General Council of the British Trades Union Congress. Everywhere the workers were shocked and bewildered. The miners were deserted and left to fight on alone. There was victimization, particularly amongst the transport workers, above all the railwaymen, whose leaders, J. H. Thomas, C. T. Cramp (NUR), J. Bromley (ASLEF), and A. G. Walkden (RCA) signed a most humiliating agreement with the railway companies on May 14th, which allowed their members to be reinstated one by one, at the employers' will. Many were months 'on the stones'.

The trade union movement as a whole began to try and learn the lessons. There was a long and confused aftermath. Hugh Lyon's comment was brief:

[1] Central Transport Strike Committee,

Address ....
Date.............

The Bearer .... employed by .... is hereby authorized to handle the following material .... for the period from .... to .... inclusive, from .... to .... This permit does not allow goods to be lifted from docks or railway premises. Bearer MUST produce permit and pence card to picket when requested. On behalf of the Central Joint Committee.

Chairman ....
Secretary....................
Central Transport Strike Committee

Address ....
Date.............

Messrs .... have been issued .... Permits for conveyance of the articles named on permit subject to employment of trade union labour only, and on the distinct understanding that permits will not be used in the uplifting of goods from docks or railway premises. Permits will be withdrawn if the specific permission is abused.

Chairman ....
Secretary....................

[2] Edinburgh Strike Committee Bulletin No. 5, Saturday May 8th.
[3] Afternoon Session, Tuesday May 11th, Item 107.

'In submitting my report for 1926 I have again to record a successful year, less the tragedy that took place in the month of May (the General Strike) over which we had no control and about which the less said the better. . . . No more telegrams from London telling us when to stop and start work.'[1]

Remarking that over £1,200 had been added to the funds during the year, he said: 'The General Strike cost us £4,996 11s 10d.' He explained that the Executive had adopted a resolution, confirmed by the branches and passed by the Annual Conference on September 4, 1926, adding a new rule to the constitution:

'Before a strike can be called which involves a breach of any Agreements between employers and the Association a ballot vote of the members covered by such agreements must be taken and no strike be called unless a decision to strike is carried by a majority of two-thirds of members voting.'

He remarked: 'No more telegrams from London telling us when to stop and start work. Throughout and since the strike no body of members could have been more loyal to their union.' He said no word about the members of the Association who had left it in protest. They were not present nor represented at the Association's Annual Conference, the proceedings of which are, of course, still recorded, in extremely brief style, by Hugh Lyon himself. In turning to the aftermath of the General Strike we must first look at this reaction of members.

4. THE AFTERMATH

The Edinburgh Trades Council issued to delegates a report on the General Strike.[2] It declared: 'The local unions concerned, with one exception, gave a demonstration of solidarity unequalled in the history of the local working-class movement. The exception mentioned concerned commercial road transport.'

The *Labour Standard*, a local weekly newspaper circulating in Edinburgh and the Lothians, made a more detailed criticism. The journal was the organ of the Independent Labour Party, of which Hugh Lyon, John Brannigan, and Robert Taylor had all been members; indeed, Robert Taylor had been an officer of the ILP in Bathgate only a year before:

'The organization of Horse & Motormen, as devised by the Glasgow Headquarters of that organization, was absolutely inadequate to meet the situation here in Edinburgh.

[1] Financial Report, 1926.
[2] 59th Annual Report of Edinburgh Trades Council, Supplementary Report.

'There was no local committee, no local authority, and consequently no local initiative; and the position was further complicated by an almost total absence of instructions from Headquarters.

'The present position is a positive menace to the movement.'[1]

This failure by Lyon to issue instructions to his members was one of the main points of criticism of the Association made later by the General Council of the Scottish Trades Union Congress, when noting complaints brought before it. There were not a few. At their first Executive meeting after the end of the General Strike, the General Council considered a letter from the North-Eastern District Co-operative Conference Association in Aberdeen 'expressing dissatisfaction with the action of pickets during the General Strike'. It appeared that the Association's pickets had advised co-operative society employees to go out with the lorries, whilst the pickets of the North of Scotland Horse & Motormen's Union prevented them: 'For three days the Society was unable to supply its people, while the pickets paid no attention to the private dealers.'[2] The complaint was not, the letter continued, made 'in any carping spirit, but merely to guard against anything similar happening again'. The STUC replied, regretting dislocation caused by 'misunderstanding or conflicting instructions given to pickets by the trade unions'. But at the same meeting of the General Council a much more serious and far-reaching question was raised.

During the next three years the Association lost over seventeen per cent of its members, being reduced in 1929 to 8,720, less than three-quarters of the pre-war figure. The Association was involved in severe jurisdictional disputes, first with the Transport & General Workers' Union and the National Union of Distributive and Allied Workers, and finally in a protracted struggle with the National Union of Railwaymen over the right to organize carters employed by the railway contractors. Each of these disputes took up much time in the Scottish Trades Union Congress. Indeed, the STUC General Council was more often in consultation with the Association over inter-union disputes than with any other organization at this time. All this was part of the aftermath of the General Strike. It had ended with transport workers in a number of cities, including Glasgow, Edinburgh, Leith, and Dundee, leaving the Association because of the situation which has been recounted and which had not increased the standing of the Association in the eyes of their fellow trade unionists.

The Scottish TUC received from Hugh Lyon on May 24, 1926 a complaint against the Transport and General Workers' Union that they had poached Association members. Immediately after the General Strike, men employed by the United Co-operative Baking Society Limited and

[1] The *Labour Standard*, May 22, 1926.
[2] STUC General Council Minutes, June 14, 1926, Item 23.

also some employees of the Scottish Co-operative Wholesale Society in Glasgow left the Association and approached the Transport & General Workers' Union. They asked its officers to hold meetings with a view to organizing them in that union. The Scottish TUC General Council called representatives of both unions together on June 30, 1926. The T & GWU stated that the men had insisted 'that the attitude of the officials and members of the Scottish Horse & Motormen's Association during the General Strike period had led up to the action taken by them'. A statement of 'complaints received from localities of the attitude of the Scottish Horse & Motormen's Association officials and members during the General Strike' was then handed in to the STUC.

After hearing both sides, on July 5, 1927, the General Council made four recommendations. Firstly, they decided that the T & GWU 'should cease accepting contributions from the men concerned', on the ground that to justify their action 'would tend to increase disagreements within the trade union movement generally'. Secondly, the STUC referred in diplomatic terms to the complaints against 'the conduct of the Scottish Horse & Motormen's Association during the General Strike', first stressing that it could have no bearing on the decision: 'Whether or not these complaints can be substantiated cannot bear upon the decision that it is contrary to trade union discipline to organize known members of other unions.' But, the STUC findings continued:

'
At the same time, we feel that the instructions issued during the General Strike by the Scottish Horse & Motormen's Association were not sufficiently explicit, in that no definite instructions to stop work were issued; and, in the matter of permits for the transport of permitted goods, instructions to withdraw permits sent out by this union were not issued to their officials.

'Such lack of definite instructions undoubtedly resulted in confusion in the localities.'[1]

The third recommendation, 'to obviate the possibility of continued friction between the two unions', was that 'a joint working arrangement should be immediately set up'. The fourth recommendation, aimed at placating the Transport & General Workers' Union, introduced the significant word amalgamation: 'Finally, we trust that negotiations with the object of ultimate amalgamation will be opened up between the unions.'[2] There then began a series of manoeuvres between the two unions, with the STUC General Council as go-between, which were not resolved for eleven months.

When, a year later, the General Council presented its Report to the 1927 meeting of the Congress, the terms of this mild rebuke did not go

[1] Scottish TUC General Council Minutes, July 5, 1926, Item 179.
[2] Scottish TUC General Council Minutes, July 5, 1926, Item 179.

nearly far enough to satisfy some of the delegates. For example, J. B. Figgins of the National Union of Railwaymen commented: 'There was no excuse for the General Council allowing one organization to utilize permits for the transport of food and he thought that in part of the report there should have been strong condemnation of that union.'[1] Hugh Lyon and Peter Webster said nothing, as we have seen.

When the General Council made its four recommendations on the jurisdictional dispute, the T & GWU accepted, but later reported to the General Council 'that difficulty was being experienced in getting the position accepted by the men concerned, who refused to rejoin the SH & MA'. Hugh Lyon wrote that he would not discuss the recommendations with the Transport & General until the members had been returned to the Association. Many weeks passed; the men persisted in their refusal, whilst the Transport & General pointed out that their rules prevented them from expelling them. Lyon then approached the employers and informed them of the terms of the first recommendation of the STUC, which had not yet been released since the dispute was still in progress. The United Co-operative Baking Society thereupon wrote to the STUC asking for guidance 'as we understand from Mr Lyon that a few of our motormen declined to rejoin the union and are therefore classified as non-unionists'. The STUC reassured the employers and urged John Veitch of the Transport & General to approach each man individually, explaining that contributions had been accepted in error. The men refused to give way and John Veitch reported that his union's solicitors had advised him that their rules would not permit expulsion. Lyon pressed for a public statement, but the STUC decided to wait. They took the question up with Ernest Bevin, the union's General Secretary in London, after which John Veitch wrote to the STUC:

'While not raising the question of amalgamation to evade the question arising from the General Council's decision, it appears to me that the only way out of the difficulty is for the two unions to discuss the question of amalgamation under the auspices of the General Council.'[2]

Hugh Lyon wrote a characteristic letter to the General Council:

'As the trade union has not put into operation your decision and as your Council has not up to the present taken steps to compel such, I am forced to advise you that tramwaymen, busmen, dockers and 500 men employed in the Clyde Trust have approached us through deputation and otherwise to become members of our Association.

'For 25 years I have abstained from interfering with any class of labour outside of the carting industry, but owing to the attitude adopted by the

---

[1] 30th Annual Report of the STUC, 1927.
[2] STUC General Council Minutes, December 13, 1926, Item 18.

trade union am now being forced through circumstances to inform you that unless we have a definite decision from your Council within seven days whether you intend to force the trade union to accept your decision, or failing such, to recommend their expulsion from the Congress, we shall have no other option but accept all classes connected with transport into our Association.'[1]

Lyon asserted that the Association would be ready for discussions on amalgamation 'when the T & GWU refuse absolutely to accept any contributions from our past members in the United Co-operative Baking Society'.

The STUC appointed representatives to meet the men together with John Veitch to persuade them to change their minds. There were thirty present when the meeting took place on December 27, 1926: 'There was considerable hostility to rejoining the Scottish Horse & Motormen's Association and the meeting terminated by the men deciding to hold a meeting to review the situation.'[2] When the men still maintained their standpoint, John Veitch then announced that he would no longer accept contributions. But the Association did not reply to suggestions that talks on amalgamation should proceed; the men did not rejoin; the deadlock continued.

In the Association's Financial Report for that year, Hugh Lyon wrote briefly about the dispute. He made no reference to the STUC's recommendations about reaching a joint working agreement, nor amalgamation, nor the Association's conduct during the General Strike.[3] But the matter was not at an end for the men who had left the Association. So far from them being 'anxious to be non-unionists', they sought yet another alternative.

In April 1927, ten days before the annual meeting at which Peter Webster would end his year of office as President of Congress, there was a sharp turn. Hugh Lyon agreed at last to meet his opponents to discuss the recommendations on joint working and amalgamation. They met on April 6, 1927; and on April 9th Lyon lodged a new complaint with the STUC. This was against a third union, the National Union of Distributive and Allied Workers, when the Association's former members in the United Co-operative Baking Society had applied to join this union, which admitted them. Together with some four-score former Association mem-

---

[1] STUC General Council Minutes, December 13, 1926, Item 18.

[2] STUC General Council Minutes, January 10, 1927, Item 9.

[3] 'A section of our members employed by the United Co-operative Baking Society decided to join the Transport & General Workers' Union.

'The Council of the Scottish TUC has again decided that all horse and motormen should be members of our Association, with the result that the Transport & General Workers' Union had to expel these men, and the directors of the United Co-operative Baking Society decided that they must either join the Scottish Horse & Motormen's Association or leave their employment.

'This should be a lesson to others who are anxious to be non-unionists.'

(Financial Report, 1926)

bers in St Cuthbert's Co-operative Society, Edinburgh, and a number at the Scottish Co-operative Wholesale Society in Leith who did the same, they became the cause of a long and protracted triangular dispute, which led to a court case and dragged on for over two and a half years.

In this dispute, Hugh Lyon enjoyed the support of his former antagonists who had been forced to disenrol the men. The Transport & General Workers' Union also lodged a complaint stating that they had 'strong objection to tolerating a third union in Scotland catering for transport workers'. Lyon demanded the expulsion of NUDAW; the T & GWU threatened to withdraw from the STUC and 'go out for an intensive campaign among all transport workers in Scotland'.[1] This led to a meeting of the three unions with the General Council on June 10, 1927. The NUDAW representatives denied that they had sought any of these members:

'85 employees at the United Co-operative Baking Society had requested membership forms which had been supplied in accordance with the rules of their union. A clear card of the Scottish Horse & Motormen's Association had been insisted upon and the workers had been enrolled as new members.'

Of the employees in Edinburgh and Leith they said:

'Dissatisfied members of the Scottish Horse & Motormen's Association had held meetings in Edinburgh, but the National Union of Distributive and Allied Workers were in no way responsible for these meetings.'

The General Council gave their decision against NUDAW, but, as the men themselves still refused to budge, this was no solution. That summer of 1927, the Association and the Transport & General Workers' Union, at last, after nearly a year of wrangling, reached agreement on joint working, although not on amalgamation.

These were the circumstances in which the Working Agreement which governed relations between the two unions for fourteen years, was arrived at. It was negotiated between Peter Webster, Robert Taylor, and Jack Elliott for the Association, and John Veitch, Peter Gillespie, and W. Roger for the Transport & General Workers' Union. Lyon published the Minutes[2] of the meeting which completed the agreement in the Financial Report for 1927. Its main provisions were that future organization of commercial grades in towns where either organization held control (and these were listed) was to be left to that organization; that in towns where each had many members there should be a joint organizing effort and members should be advised to join one union. Still the men who refused to rejoin the Association would not shift. When NUDAW, under pressure from the

[1] SHMA Minutes, June 13, 1927.
[2] See Appendix.

STUC, refused to accept further contributions from them after August 13, 1927, three brought a test case. Thomas Connell, David Faulds, and James Dunn asked the Court of Session to declare that they were members of the National Union of Distributive & Allied Workers and that it must accept their contributions. The case was heard on February 3, 1928, before Lord Moncrief, who decided in the men's favour. NUDAW's unsuccessful appeal was dismissed some months later. The matter came constantly before the General Council and successive conferences of the Scottish TUC; and it was not until November 1928, after many meetings between the three unions, that agreement was reached. By this NUDAW agreed not to organize the transport department of the UCBS in future; the transferrees into that department should be allowed dual membership; that the transport workers then there 'should be struck off the books of that union whenever they fall out of compliance with its rules'; and the Association should be informed. In return, a further agreement arranged for extensive joint working between all three unions and allowed NUDAW representation on the joint Trade Union Committee for Road Transport in Scotland.

Nor were these the only post-General Strike jurisdictional disputes to which the Association was a party. During 1929 and well into 1930, there was a long-drawn-out dispute against the National Union of Railwaymen for organizing employees of the railway contractors. The core of the dispute was that the NUR's claim to organize all employed 'in or about the railways' would not be pressed only if men were members in good standing of another union. But the STUC's investigation of the facts made it clear that many who were claimed as members of the Association were long past the thirteen weeks which rendered them ineligible for membership, according to the Association's rules. Yet they had not been lapsed: and the STUC noted that the Association's Executive 'had given general powers to Collectors to excuse arrears'. James Walker, defending the General Council's failure to act against the NUR, disclosed an astonishing state of affairs, which was not denied by the Association's delegates:

'Mr Webster had told them that his organization could keep a man in the union practically for two or three years although he was not paying contributions. That was the General Council's difficulty, because they could not find in the movement any parallel to that.'[1]

All these events were further indication that the Association's affairs were not in a happy condition.

At Quarterly Meetings questions were frequently asked. It is clear that much anxiety was felt, however little was recorded in the Association's annual reports. Anger of members at the attitude taken by the Association's officials had ended in jurisdictional disputes, and the strange position of the Association and the T & GWU being ranged in alliance. That was

[1] 33rd Annual Report of the STUC, 1930.

typical of the aftermath of the General Strike. It was a period when a great controversy was raging in the whole trade union movement.

At first there was a struggle between three points of view. There were those who regarded the General Strike as a great mistake, defended J. H. Thomas and those who had brought it to an end, and whose watchword was: Never again! No more class war! The second point of view was that the collapse of the General Strike was not 'a great mistake', but a great betrayal by men who pursued a policy of accommodation, or 'class collaboration', with the employing class: that conflict between the employing class and the working class was basic to their relationship; and that any progress in the trade union and labour movement would depend upon these men and their policy being defeated and rejected by the membership. The view of the third group, to which Hugh Lyon and Peter Webster adhered, was 'least said, soonest mended', 'no recrimination', and that the priority should be given to restoring formal unity without discussion on policy.

By 1928 the clash of opinion centred round a further development of these lines of argument. This was the policy known as 'Industrial Peace', put forward as a result of the joint talks between Sir Alfred Mond, Chairman of Imperial Chemicals Ltd., on behalf of leading industrialists, and Mr Ben Turner, then Chairman of the British Trades Union Congress. The Mond-Turner talks and the subsequent policy issue took place against a background of increasing mass unemployment, disunity in the trade union movement, and the introduction by the Government of punitive anti-union legislation which followed the General Strike. To the fore in opposing the policy of Mondism was the Minority Movement, in which miners had become especially prominent, and the Communist Party. With the acceptance of the policy of Mondism, the General Council of the Trades Union Congress ruled that no person associated with the Minority Movement should, as from 1928, be eligible to attend the annual conference of trades councils. This was the signal for a number of unions to ban their own members, who supported the Minority Movement, from holding office. The Association immediately followed suit, and a resolution was carried at the annual conference in September 1928.

'That this Annual Conference decides that no Communist or members of the Minority Movement can be eligible to hold any official position in, or be part of any delegation acting for the Scottish Horse & Motormen's Association.'[1]

Opposition was expressed at a number of branches, notably Glasgow; but the rule was adopted. It was later dropped without debate. At the same conference an attempt was made to reduce the contribution which had recently been raised to 10d. The initiative came from the Glasgow branches,

[1] Report of the Annual Conference, 1928.

where it had been argued that 'half of the transport workers of Glasgow were not members of any trade union', and that the Association was becoming 'more of a Friendly Society than a trade union'. The resolution was unsuccessful.

These were unhappy times of dissension, ever-increasing mass unemployment and falling membership. By 1931 the Sliding Scale Agreement was still in operation, and Glasgow wages had fallen to £2 10s. The railway carters were cut still further. The bottom was touched in 1932 when the membership stood at only 7,596, although the funds had risen to £131,295. At the same time conditions in road transport were changing at remarkable speed. The first of the Road Traffic Acts, which were to make a great difference in conditions, was shortly to be in operation. The Association had been deeply concerned with this question over a long period. Association members had played an important part in Scotland in efforts leading up to the Road Traffic Acts. That legislation in its turn was to lay the basis for the gradual transformation of the Association itself. It called for different capacities in the Association's leaders, for men able to exploit new possibilities and meet new problems. The new men began to come forward, first Peter Webster and later Robert Taylor. A third man, by no means lacking in ability, was not then available. This was the organizer, John Brannigan, who left the Association's employ at short notice in 1927 and went to the United States, returning in the early thirties to Scotland but not to the industry. Eight years later he returned as Assistant Secretary to Robert Taylor, who replaced Hugh Lyon in 1936: and in fourteen years he himself became General Secretary.

But the man who was most prominent at this time was Peter Webster. For years he had taken more and more of the work upon his shoulders. It was rare indeed for Lyon to attend the quarterly meetings to introduce the Executive Minutes: Webster almost always went to those in Aberdeen, Edinburgh, and Glasgow. When it came to the new legislation, it was he who mastered it and explained its complexities to the members. When the Scottish TUC sent a deputation to the Minister of Transport to discuss a proposed Road Traffic Bill, Webster made the case. Unlike Lyon, he was aware of the growing importance of the motorman in the fast-changing condition of the industry.

[photo: Robert L. Nicholson]

7. Hugh Lyon (Second General Secretary) when Chairman of the Scottish TUC Parliamentary Committee, 1918. Centre seated. Back Row (*left to right*) W. G. Hunter, Vice-chairman (Operative Bakers' National Federal Union), William Shaw (Glasgow Trades Council), J. O'Hagan (Amalgamated Steel and Ironworkers), N. S. Beaton, Treasurer (National Amalgamated Union of Shop Assistants), R. Climie (Ayrshire Trades Council). Sitting (*left to right*)—J. C. Hendry (Brechin Mill and Factory Workers), R. Allan (Edinburgh Trades Council), H. Lyon, Chairman (Scottish Horse and Motormen's Association), George Carson, Secretary and J. Houghton (Scottish Union of Dock Labourers).

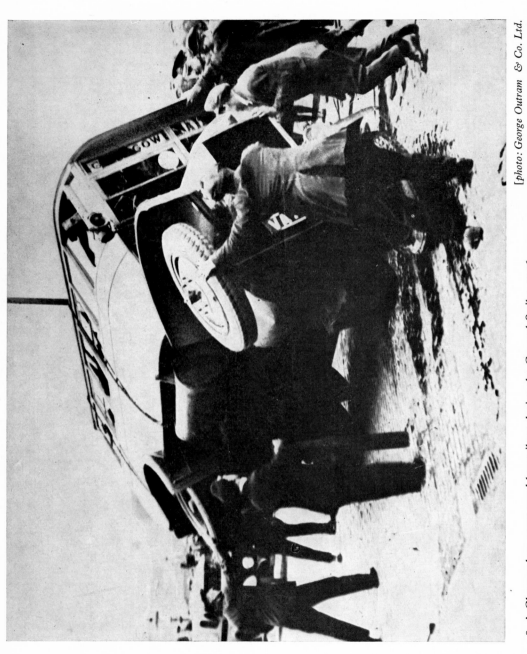

8. A Glasgow bus overturned by strikers during the General Strike, 1926.

APPENDIX

Working Agreement with the Transport & General Workers' Union

MINUTES OF MEETING

of the Joint Committee representative of the
Scottish Horse & Motormen's Association and
the Transport & General Workers' Union, held
in the Area Office of the latter union, 11 Bridge
Street, Glasgow, on Monday, August 15, 1927,
at 5.30 p.m.

CHAIRMAN: Bro. J. Veitch.

PRESENT: Representing Transport and General Workers' Union, Bros.
J. Veitch, P. Gillespie, and W. Roger. Representing Scottish
Horse and Motormen's Association, Bros. P. Webster,
R. Taylor, and J. Elliott.

Bro. P. Webster, on behalf of the Scottish Horse and Motormen's
Association, stated that his Executive Council had accepted and endorsed
the Minutes of the previous meeting.

Bro. J. Veitch, on behalf of the Transport and General Workers'
Union, stated that he had submitted the Minutes to his headquarters, but
their Executive had not yet met, but were doing so at an early date. (The
Minutes have since received the approval and endorsement of their
Executive Council.)

The Committee then went on to discuss the best methods of co-
ordinating organizing work, and the prevention of overlapping, and the
allocation of this work by towns and districts.

In regard to this matter, Bro. Webster submitted certain suggestions,
as follows:

1. All further organization of Commercial Grades in towns where Scottish
Horse and Motormen's Association hold control to be the work of, and
left entirely to, Scottish Horse and Motormen's Association;

2. All further organization of Commercial Grades in towns where Transport and General Workers' Union had control to be left entirely to
Transport and General Workers' Union;

3. In towns where both Unions have a considerable membership, joint
organizing work to be undertaken jointly, and men to be advised to
decide that all men in such to be members of one organization;

4. For the purpose of consolidating organization in the Road Transport
Industry (Commercial and Passenger) joint Committees of both
organizations to be established in all districts to carry on joint propaganda
efforts;

G

5. That a small Committee be appointed nationally whose work shall be to deal with questions of organization referred to them by districts, and to consult and advise on the general position in the industry;

6. That the Scottish Horse and Motormen's Association act along with the Transport and General Workers' Union when the question of legislative and Parliamentary action is being considered. Each party to bear proportion of general expenses on the basis of membership in the Road Transport Sections of the Transport and General Workers' Union, and the membership of the Scottish Horse and Motormen's Association. Each party to pay expenses of their own representatives on delegation;

7. That in cases of dispute by any action of either of the organizations the local or national Sub-Committees meet to decide on what joint action is considered necessary;

8. That both parties agree to co-operate towards better organization, and where and when considered advisable tests to be made of membership such as by a show of pence cards or other methods where such is considered advisable;

9. That both parties shall constantly work towards creating a better understanding, and a closer unity among the workers engaged in the Road Transport Industry in Scotland.

With reference to points 1 and 2 the allocation is as follows:

Scottish Horse and Motormen's Association:

Aberdeen	Dundee	Kirkcaldy	Perth
Airdrie	Dalkeith	Lanark	Pitlochry
Ayr	Edinburgh	Leith	Rothesay
Alexandria	Falkirk	Largs	Stirling
Alloa	Fauldhouse	Motherwell	Stranraer
Bathgate	Glasgow	Old Cumnock	Tranent
Cowdenbeath	Kilmarnock	Musselburgh	Uddingston
Dumbarton	Kilbirnie	Paisley	West Calder
Dunfermline	Kirkintilloch	Penicuik	Wigtown

Transport and General Workers' Union:

Alyth	Cupar-Angus	Greenock	Newport
Arbroath	Dundee	Hawick	North Berwick
Berwick-on-Tweed	Glasgow (News-	Kilmarnock	Peterhead
Blairgowrie	paper section)	Kirkcaldy	Port-Glasgow
Brechin	Dumfries	Kirriemuir	St Andrews
Campbeltown	Forfar	Lerwick	Stornoway
Carnoustie	Galashiels	Melrose	Tayport
Cupar-Fife	Gourock	Montrose	

No. 3. With reference to point 3, this takes into consideration towns such as Dundee, the intention being to have local meetings. Arrangements were made by Bro. Webster and Bro. Gillespie to hold a meeting in Dundee on August 24th for the purpose of explaining the position to the members with a view to getting agreement with them to the effect that the Scottish Horse and Motormen's Association cease organizing in this locality.

No. 5. This point is already in operation.

No. 6. The subject of representation and expenses has already been agreed by both Executives.

Nos. 8 and 9. These are self-explanatory.

It was further agreed that the Minutes of all local Joint Committees be submitted to the National Joint Committee for approval.

Signed as a correct Minute:

(sgd) PETER WEBSTER
Scottish Horse and Motormen's Association
(sgd) JOHN VEITCH
Transport and General Workers' Union.

CHAPTER TWELVE

ATTEMPTS TO CONTROL ROAD CHAOS

I. FROM HORSE TO HORSE-POWER

ONE factor distinguishing the years after the First World War from those that preceded it was the great impetus to technological change that set in. To maintain the millions of men who were bogged down in trench warfare for over four years immense quantities of heavy munitions of war had to be made and hauled great distances, as quickly as possible. For warfare on this hitherto unimagined scale, the internal combustion engine had to be developed on land and sea and in the air to an unprecedented degree. Every form of transport was in huge demand; in particular, motor transport expanded vastly. When the war was over, with much of Europe devastated and industry in the other half geared to war production, which came to a sudden stop, what would happen in road transport? New industries came into being. Dominating all were the oil trusts, controlling the supply of a fuel which was to expand in importance to levels undreamed of. But what of the other new industries?

Firstly, there were the engineering firms which had sprung up in the war, now anxious to turn from producing war transport vehicles, to capture a new civilian market, and to create a new industry, the motor industry.

Secondly, hundreds of thousands of men trained as motor drivers and motor mechanics during the war came pouring out of the forces, seeking a a living in 'Civvy Street', with a new skill but no capital to exploit it for their own benefit. Haulage contractors had learned that not only could a motor-lorry carry more than a cart could in a single journey, but, being so much quicker, could make many more journeys in the same time, and much longer hauls. This had a number of important effects. One was that the haulage contractor could get more business and operate further afield. But to realize the big profits that were there to be made, he had to command more capital; if he had that, all he needed was the motor and the man to drive it, and both were in the market.

The scene was set for a big expansion in motor vehicular traffic, and that was the picture in the first post-war decade, whether in boom or slump. The total number of motor licences rose from 952,474 in 1922 to 2,217,609 in 1930. For the same years, those for goods vehicles rose from

150,995 to 334,237. In decisive sections of road transport, the motor was taking over from the horse-drawn vehicle, above all with the beginning of long hauls by road. Of course, this did not happen all at once, nor did it begin only after the First World War; in the first years of the century, the electric tramway and the motor vehicle were already in use, especially in public passenger service. The horse and cart or dray remained for many years, even into the second half of the century; but the horse could not be worked twenty-four hours a day and had to be cared for when it was not in use. It was doomed to disappear altogether from the roads; and, slowly, with his horse, the old carter, too, was to disappear from the scene. In the words of the folk song:

> When I was young and in my prime
>   And in my stable lay
> They gave to me the very best corn
>   And eke the choicest hay,
>   Poor old horse, poor old mare!

> Now I am old and past my prime
>   And good for nothing more
> I am not worth a peck of corn
>   Nor scarce a wisp of straw,
>   Poor old horse, poor old mare!

The carter sang the song about his horse, but he thought of his own life as he sang.

The foundations of big fortunes and very large concerns in the road haulage industry were thus laid, giants which in Scotland today can be counted on one hand. But technological advance and the march of progress brought no automatic solution to the problems of the road transport workers, whether horsemen or motormen. On the contrary, they were confronted with unemployment on the one hand and over-work on the other, to be found—as always—side by side where the motive is private profit. When in work the motormen endured almost incredibly long hours; the chaotic uncontrolled development and the unbridled competition of free enterprise made this inevitable in the economics of the new conditions in road haulage.

Throughout the twenties there were examples of men working desperately long hours, killing to themselves and also a cause of accident and public danger. Ten or twelve hours continuous driving of heavy passenger or goods vehicles without a break were usual; it was not uncommon for motormen to be continuously at work for nineteen or twenty hours. On the profitable runs—particularly in Scotland—the competition was so keen that drivers were obliged to race each other; especially was this the case with passenger vehicles, where companies' time-tables were scheduled so as to capture each others' passengers in circumstances which forced excessive speed on the drivers. It was the men alone who suffered the legal consequences. Not only was there no rest for the drivers; there was often virtually no maintenance of the vehicles, until they fell to pieces. The conditions were reminiscent of the railways some generations earlier, when they were developing at fast speed, and the rival companies raced between London and Scotland, until they were warned by a Home Secretary that if an accident occurred, the directors of the competing companies would be prosecuted. Railway racing ceased abruptly.

Early in the twenties, the state of road transport became so chaotic that it began to be plain to those who sought their living or their profit on the road, to those who needed to travel on it or to have their goods transported quickly and efficiently, as well as to those who merely wanted to cross the road without being killed or maimed, that something would have to be done to regulate it. Road transport organizations were not strong enough to impose a change, nor were the employers who, indeed, by no means universally favoured organization in their own ranks, where there was ineradicable conflict of interests. A feature of the fast expansion of road transport was that very large numbers of very small employers started up with the minimum of capital, ready, as long as they were solvent, to undercut tonnage rates and to work the drivers for the longest possible hours. Unbridled competition and undercutting began to convince a section of the larger employers that regulation might be to their economic advantage.

Within the scope of a history of a single union, it is possible to give only the briefest sketch of some of the events which led at last, after two Conservative and two Labour administrations had had the problem increasingly forced upon their attention, to the appointment of a Royal Commission[1] (which is the subject of later sections) and to the appearance on the Statute Book as late as 1930 of the first of a series of Acts regulating road traffic. In time, this not only led to very big changes in the conditions and status of road transport workers, but also transformed their unions, not least the Scottish Horse & Motormen's Association. Having regard to the haphazard development of road transport against a background of cut-throat competition, of private monopolies opposing municipal undertakings, of the position of the railways and air transport both under private ownership and when nationalized, of the unplanned development of civil engineering and the motor industry and, above all, of the politics of oil, a rational transport system could scarcely result. But its history, with all the mistakes and setbacks, makes it very clear why today, when the problems left unsolved have led to infinitely more complicated conditions, the transport trade unions have come to support an integrated transport

---

[1] Royal Commission on Transport, 1930. (Final Report: *The Co-ordination and Development of Transport*. 1931. Cmd. 3751.)

system as a public service. The first, primitive attempt in the twenties to get the rudiments of traffic regulation to replace the law of the jungle casts light enough on the problem and its solution.

Basically the economics of transport depend upon how to meet the problem of 'empty running', whether of wagons and coaches in railway marshalling-yards, peak-hour running in rail and road passenger services of densely populated areas, or the search for 'return loads' in road transport. Although there were no statistics, there was much evidence on this before the Royal Commission on Transport of 1930.[1]

'I should estimate that between 30% and 50% of the total mileage run by goods vehicles in this country are run empty; and that quite a considerable portion of the mileage, possibly anything between 10% and 15% could be added for vehicles being run not fully loaded. You will frequently get the position of 2 or 3 drivers, each knowing the other is to make a similar journey, arranging to do the journey together for companionship. Probably not one of them has got a full load; they are traversing anything from 5 to 100 miles together, and each is doing that journey, whereas, possibly one vehicle could have carried all the goods.'[2]

A feature of the rapid post-war growth of the motor industry was that vans, lorries and small coaches could be bought on hire-purchase terms. In addition, masses of army transport vehicles were sold off cheaply by the Government Disposals Board. Many ex-servicemen invested their gratuities in these, sometimes running them as goods vehicles during the week and converting them with seats for passengers for week-end hire. Owner-drivers of these surplus vehicles and of the new ones on hire-purchase worked themselves and their vehicles into the ground. There were no regulations and nothing to prevent anyone from buying, hiring,

---

[1] 'It can be accepted that between one-third and one-half of the miles operated are run empty. This is a loss that is met by one or both of the following expedients: (i) by passing the cost on to the trader; (ii) by operating with cheap and hence dangerous equipment and/or cheap and consequently dangerous labour.'
(John Cliff, Assistant General Secretary of the Transport & General Workers Union. March 20, 1929. 20th Day. Para 33.)

[2] Archie Henderson, National Secretary, Commercial Services Group, May 15, 1930. 43rd Day, Q.14638.)

The same witness was speaking of London up-town wharves; it could be dockland anywhere in Scotland:

'The approaches to the wharves are unsuitable for modern traffic and they are rendered more congested than necessary by the fact that there are possibly three times as many vehicles calling there for goods than there need be. A small carrier, say, gets an order to pick up a chest of tea at one place and a case of oranges at another wharf. To make up a load he visits half a dozen different wharves, whereas instead of half a dozen different vans doing this in half a dozen different places, we suggest that with proper co-ordination the thing could be done on a more systematic basis and you would find that all this heavy congestion which takes place at the docks and wharves and the approaches to them could be avoided.'

(Q.14639.)

or borrowing a vehicle and offering himself for hire as a carrier. There was no age limit and no physical or other test on drivers; nor was there any test for the vehicles. A small number of owner-drivers succeeded in building up small businesses in the new road transport industry, but the vast majority failed, through lack of capital, fierce competition, and inexperience. Before they were driven out, they had played their part in intensifying the chaos in the industry. The Report of the Royal Commission relates that witnesses from amongst the road hauliers gave evidence of conditions which were caused, in their view, by ex-servicemen setting up as carriers.[1]

Some struggled on by undercutting prices and overloading unfit vehicles. Of the small owner-drivers who were squeezed out by stronger rivals, some went to other industries; many joined the hundreds of thousands of unemployed in the dole queues; and others went to work for the ever-growing more powerful haulage contractors, or for the clearing-houses, which sprang up from the need of hauliers to reduce the losses from empty running by ensuring return loads. They owned no vehicles and needed no capital. They touted for hauls from traders and then gave the work to a haulier who was often willing enough to take it at an uneconomic rate to ensure a return load instead of an empty truck. Some firms imposed the job of canvassing for return loads on their drivers. The clearing-house meant an opening for those who could set up to make a quick profit 'by underquoting the organized hauliers and railways and then beating down the owner-driver to the cut rate less the clearing-house commission', to quote Sir Maxwell Hicks, the representative of road hauliers:

'The haulier has no option but to accept these terms, return empty or waste some days in idleness until finally he consents to the dictation of the clearing-house. One result of this system is that the cut rate obtained by say, a Manchester haulier for a return load from, say, Hull to Manchester, becomes a standard outward rate obtained by a Hull haulier proceeding to Manchester.'[2]

There were other profitable deals in which the clearing-house could indulge before monopoly became so far advanced in the industry that its

[1] 'The ease with which second-hand vehicles could be acquired from the Disposals Board, together with the fact that railway rates had materially advanced, brought about transient and fictitious conditions which encouraged many who were without either the necessary resources or training to embark in the business of road transport. The large number of new-comers created a condition which amounted almost to complete chaos and it was not until comparatively recently that the business of road transport settled down into a condition of relative stability in comparison with that which previously existed; but the process was painful and, although some survived, a great number of the small operators were submerged.'
(Royal Commission, 3rd Report, Chapter IV, Para. 300.)
[2] Royal Commission, M.58.14.

work could be conveniently and profitably taken over by the hauliers themselves. But they had a long innings in which their activities played a key part in forcing the owner-driver and the small firm out of business.

As well as duplicated services, price-cutting and the speeding and overloading of unfit vehicles, Scotland suffered from other excesses of a special kind. The poor development of her roads and bridges was always notorious[1] and remains so today. They were less equipped even than roads elsewhere to take the vastly increased size and weight of motor vehicles and their loads. During the war much damage had been done to road surfaces by the heavy war transport, and in peacetime the vast articulated vehicles and 'tenders' began to make their appearance, sometimes with several trailers, on roads which were narrow even for wagons. Still less were the roads in Scotland equipped to take traffic at the high speeds which intense competition promoted. Scottish transport workers were troubled not only by the racing and high speeds they were obliged to maintain to keep to the schedules imposed by the employers, but also by onerous local by-laws and customs and the draconian administration of justice and by police action. Examples were by-laws affecting slow-moving traffic in the cities; the practice of one carter being forced to drive two vehicles simultaneously, about which the Association had been complaining bitterly since 1898, and which in modern road conditions had become a serious danger.[2]

Another point which especially troubled the Scottish transport workers was the frequency with which the police chose to arrest drivers for trivial offences under the Motor Car Act, 1903, under which a magistrate was unable to grant bail. Finally, from the early twenties, horsemen and motormen alike lived in fear of the double effect of unemployment. Poor trade and slump conditions threatened their jobs directly, whilst the existence of mass unemployment and short-time in mining, textiles, and engineering meant that many men were seeking jobs where they would not be handicapped by lack of specialized skills. Anyone could drive a horse;

[1] Some light is thrown by travellers' tales, such as their books describing their visit to Scotland in 1773 of the Englishman, Dr Samuel Johnson in *Journey to the Western Isles* and his Scottish companion James Boswell in *Journal of a Tour to the Hebrides*. More authoritative is the *Journal of a Tour in Scotland* which the English poet Robert Southey made in company with the great Scottish civil engineer, canal, bridge, road and railway builder, Thomas Telford, in 1819, the year of Peterloo.

[2] When the Scottish Trades Union Congress sent a deputation to Parliament on February 24, 1919, on a number of matters, Hugh Lyon put the question to the Home Secretary, Mr Edward Shortt. After dealing first with the cruelty to the horse of such a system, he referred next to 'the introduction of motor traction, which had made it dangerous not only for the driver but also to the public, especially in large industrial cities'.

The account in the 1918–19 STUC Report of the interview notes that the Home Secretary 'was surprised to learn that such a system still existed in Scotland, as it had practically become extinct in England through legislation. He expressed the opinion and promised that at the first opportunity legislation should be introduced to prevent such a system, especially in large industrial centres.' Eleven years later the Association was still patiently pressing for it to be made illegal.

many could drive a lorry, or at least thought they could. This was the background to the reaction to the new conditions in road transport, to which Scottish trade unionists responded earlier than in most parts of Britain.

2. THE ASSOCIATION TAKES THE LEAD

At the Association's first post-war Conference, held on June 7, 1919, resolutions were passed condemning the overloading which had become common practice, demanding that all drivers, whether horsemen or motor-men, should be licensed, and demanding the prohibition of the system of one man being obliged to drive two carts simultaneously. The following year's conference demanded legislation 'to establish a legal maximum working-week of no more than forty-four hours', and the Association continued to support demands to establish a maximum working-week by law, when the movement had failed to achieve it by other means. In 1921, the Association formulated three demands which were to be re-peated practically every year until legislation was achieved. These were:

(1) licensing all drivers;
(2) prohibiting one man driving two carts; and
(3) the outlawing of all trailers on Scottish roads.

In January 1924 the first but short-lived Labour Government took office, which aroused hopes that a sympathetic hearing, if not legislation, could be obtained at last from Westminster. There was consultation with other transport unions immediately; and at the Conference of the Scottish TUC in April 1924, a joint demand was put forward for a consolidating Act governing transport services, listing the most urgent changes, and demand-ing that the Motor Car Act be amended to allow bail to be granted. The resolution, moved by Peter Webster, ran as follows:

'That this Congress calls for the amendment of the Motor Car Act 1903, so that power be given to a Police Magistrate or even a Police Officer to grant bail in the event of a motor driver being apprehended for a trivial breach of the Act, or where there is no fear of the accused party de-camping.'

He said it was a serious matter for his members:

'Any man could be arrested and lodged in cells. They had three cases, men of high moral character, who were lodged in cells and afterwards dismissed. The Chief Constable had been interviewed and he had frankly admitted he had no powers to grant bail.'

But although there was a Labour Secretary of State for Scotland at the time, Mr William Adamson, the reply was of little comfort. It asserted that:

'It is not the practice to arrest in a case where the breach is trivial and where there is no risk of the accused absconding. Accordingly there appears to the Secretary of State for Scotland to be no occasion for the proposed amendment of the law.'

When, at his request, particulars of cases were forwarded, they reached the hands of his Conservative successor, and the reply was in almost identical words. The new Secretary of State for Scotland was of the opinion 'that there is no occasion for altering the law either as to the court having jurisdiction in such cases or in the direction of empowering the police to grant bail'. The Scottish TUC gave up, but the Association continued to press the point as late as 1929.

Then a multiple resolution, which became the basis of the policy of the Scottish trade union movement for the next years, called for a consolidating Act to regulate the conditions under which driving licences should be granted and the number of people to be employed on heavy lorries and trailers; to make employers legally liable when time-schedules caused excessive speed; to impose a limitation on excessive hours and to make adequate provision for rest and 'that an Advisory Committee to the Ministry of Transport be established, with representatives of organized workers as members'. In this last proposal we may see the hand of Ernest Bevin, then busy amalgamating all smaller transport groupings into one big authoritative union. Although Hugh Lyon was not willing for transport unions in Scotland to be brought together into any organization but his own, he was nevertheless prepared to co-operate with Bevin's union on this occasion; and, at the Scottish Trades Union Congress in April 1924, this multiple resolution was moved by the Transport & General Workers' Union and seconded by an Association delegate. This was all the more remarkable since the Transport & General Workers' Union representative was none other than Bailie Peter Gillespie, the former Association member who had engineered a breakaway from the Association in Dundee before the war, and against whom the bitterest animosity continued to be expressed. Later, Gillespie's breakaway union had joined up with the 'big union', and it was not long before Gillespie was a leading lieutenant of Ernest Bevin.[1]

---

[1] Only six months before this debate, Bevin had written to Gillespie as follows:

Transport & General Workers' Union,
3 Central Buildings, Westminster,
London S.W.1

Private & Personal   EB/MF
Dear Peter,
   For your private information I give you herewith copy of letter I have received from the Minister of Labour (Belfast).

Kindest regards,
Yours sincerely,
ERNEST BEVIN

Copy   Belfast, September 14th.
Dear Mr. Bevin,
   I want to thank you very sincerely for sending over Mr. Gillespie to help us out of an

The day before moving the multiple resolution on road transport at the 1924 Scottish Trades Union Congress, Peter Gillespie had spoken in the debate on 'The Functions of Congress' on the virtues of the 'One Big Union for the transport industry of Great Britain'. 'That,' he said, 'has almost been accomplished.' There were one or two delinquents which he hoped in the very near future would see the error of their way and come into the fold. He argued Bevin's case for 'one large union, sectionalized and departmentalized, catering for all sections'. Peter Webster and the rest of the delegation of the Scottish Horse & Motormen's Association sat silent throughout that debate. But the high hopes of those who aimed to establish trade unions as a single monolithic power, capable of talking with authority to the government of the day and achieving any legislation it thought necessary, were to suffer a setback. By October 1924 the first Labour Government had fallen, after only a few months in office, before the Association's executive could carry out an instruction to seek an interview with the Home Secretary for legislation on special topics. The days were past when government departments, and even the Prime Minister, were eager to receive deputations from the Scottish trade unions, as they had been during the aftermath of the great mass movements on the Clyde of the 1914–18 war.

3. INTERMINABLE DELAY

But although the Labour Government was out, the pressure was maintained. Thus, in April 1925, the Scottish TUC had before it once again the points passed earlier, but with modifications; and in some cases there was opposition. Thus, when Webster moved that the use of trailers on Scottish roads should be made illegal, Gillespie opposed it, on the ground that it was not practicable. 'Trailers had been on the roads since he could remember, and the suggestion of the resolution was trying to put back the hands of the clock.'[1] The votes were equal, and as the Chairman gave his casting vote against the motion, it was lost.

There was a similar clash when Gillespie moved that three tons should be the weight over which it should be obligatory to employ a second man, on the ground that to make the limit two tons, as the Association always

---

embarrassing tangle. In fact, what was needed was someone with sufficient power and personality to reinforce with strength the men's leaders here, as the rank and file had got so out of hand that the local officials were in a very difficult position. Mr. Gillespie created a most favourable impression with both the men and the employers, with the result that a stoppage of work, which, I believe, under existing conditions, would have developed into a serious struggle, has been prevented.

Yours sincerely,
JOHN M. ANDREWS.

[1] 28th Annual Report to the STUC, 1925.

insisted, 'was to ask for more than had been in practice for half a century'. Here again the Association's view was defeated by a narrow margin. Another resolution was moved by Gillespie and seconded by Willie Hunter of the Association, that:

'. . . the employer should be held liable in law, instead of the drivers, as at present, in all cases where a driver driving to time schedules or under issued instructions, is required to exceed the stated speed limit, thereby causing him to drive to the danger of the public.'

There was some opposition to this, some delegates arguing that if drivers were relieved of responsibility by throwing blame on to their employers it would endanger public safety. The resolution was carried; but at later conferences the terms were modified, seeking to make the employer liable as well as the driver.

The Scottish TUC sought an interview with the Conservative Minister of Transport, but meanwhile the General Council of the British Trades Union Congress had already been received by the Minister on May 13, 1925 'for the purpose of discussing proposals identical in character with those which form the subject of the resolutions forwarded by you'. The Scottish TUC was informed that the Government's intention was to introduce a Bill but not in the current session, and that the General Council of the Scottish TUC would be given an opportunity of expressing its views. The whole question was discussed by the BTUC in 1925, to which the T & GWU had submitted a 'Transport Programme', and also at the Labour Party Conference, where some of the points which they had been pressing in Scotland were put forward. When the delegates met at the Association's Rothesay conference on September 5, 1925, it was learned that the Government had agreed to receive a deputation from the union on the proposed legislation. The delegates decided that the points to be put forward should include those on which they had not yet won the Scottish TUC's support: the total banning of trailers on Scottish roads; that there should be two men on vehicles of over two tons; that all drivers of horse and motor vehicles be licensed. To these they also added two new points: compulsory insurance of not less than £3,000 to cover all risks; and that no driver should be allowed to work more than nine hours at a stretch without an adequate rest period. This last the Association fought for stubbornly, long after Section 19 of the Road Traffic Act 1930 limiting hours to eleven, had appeared and was found to be unsatisfactory and unenforceable. Year after year proposals were considered, modified and brought forward again and again; all the Association's points, except that for the abolition of trailers, finally gained support in the Scottish TUC.

It soon became clear that there would need to be considerable increase in pressure if the Bill was ever to see the light of day. Early in 1927 an advisory committee of transport unions was set up in London. By March

1927 the Conservative Government at last produced its promised draft Bill, on which the British TUC and the Scottish TUC were invited to comment. On November 3, 1927, a delegation from the Scottish TUC, which included Peter Webster, met the Minister of Transport for detailed arguments on the draft Bill. They objected both to what the Bill contained and to what it omitted. It contained clauses dealing with 'dangerous driving' and with 'careless driving', which last the Scots wanted deleted, believing that it would lead to trivial charges being made against drivers. The Bill did not provide for a trailerman to be employed on the first trailer, for provisional licences, driving tests, and physical fitness, nor for limitation on hours and the provision of rest periods. Furthermore, the lower age limit for a person to drive a commercial motor vehicle was only seventeen. But the bill did at least insist upon compulsory insurance.

The Minister claimed that it was unnecessary to insert a clause making an employer liable when instructions were given which resulted in breaking the law; but the delegation pointed out that not only were bus proprietors forcing their drivers to use excessive speed if they were to keep up to advertised time-tables, but also that they were paying commission to drivers and conductors upon takings, which was a direct inducement to speeding and overcrowding. The deputation quoted cases in Scotland where drivers had produced in court schedules to prove their case and where no proceedings had been instituted against the employers. They complained of considerable variations among Scottish burghs in the administration of the law; and that in some the police took action for very trivial offences. This led the Secretary of State for Scotland to write, on December 3, 1927, asking for particulars of the cases, which were duly sent to him.

There was still no Act. Instead, on February 20, 1928, Prime Minister Baldwin announced that it was proposed 'to institute an investigation into the need for the better regulation of road traffic and the possibility of greater co-ordination of means of internal transport', though he did not go so far then as to admit that the Transport Bill was, after all, being dropped. Pressure began to mount throughout Britain. That year there was a steep increase in road casualties; the figure rose by 22,000 to 156,000, with 5,489 fatalities. On August 4, 1928, the Government appointed a Royal Commission on Transport, which made its Final Report in December 1930.

4. THE ROYAL COMMISSION ON TRANSPORT

Beginning on November 14, 1928, the twelve-man[1] Royal Commission took written and oral evidence which occupied three large volumes. They

---

[1] Sir Arthur Griffith Boscawen; The Marquess of Northampton; The Earl of Clarendon; Major J. J. Astor (later replaced by Sir Robert Donald); Sir Matthew Wallace, Bart; Sir Ernest Hiley; Sir William Lobjoit; Mr. Isidore Salmon; Major Horace Crawfurd; Mr James Learmonth; Mr Frederick Montague and Mr Walter Smith, who were replaced later by Mr William Leach and Mr Frank Galton.

issued three reports, the last in December 1930; it was this which contained special recommendations about road haulage vehicles.

The Commissioners' terms of reference were wide:

'to take into consideration the problems arising out of the growth of road traffic; and, with a view to securing the employment of the available means of transport in Great Britain (including transport by sea coastwise and by ferries) to the greatest public advantage, to consider and report what measures, if any, should be adopted for their better regulation and control; and, so far as is desirable in the public interest, to promote their co-ordinated working and development.'

They dealt with railways, tramways, canals and inland waterways, docks and harbours, highways, and the co-ordination of transport, as well as with road transport. This last they divided into three categories; the private vehicle, which was the subject of their First Report, dated July 19, 1929; the public service 'which carries passengers for hire or reward', covered by their second report, dated October 18, 1929, the main conclusions of which were incorporated in the Road Traffic Act, 1930; and commercial vehicles for the transport of goods by road, which were dealt with by their third report. 'The primary reason for our appointment', they explained, was the growth of road traffic resulting from 'the remarkable development of the internal combustion engine which, during the present century, has not only revolutionized road transport, but has completely altered the whole economic situation'.[1] Amongst the statistics quoted by the Commission's third report to illustrate the immensely rapid development of road transport, perhaps the most striking is one which brings home particularly the increase in weight of traffic on Scottish routes. A table[2] compared the increase in road traffic from records showing pre-war and post-war traffic censuses. Here are five typical instances showing the weight of traffic passing certain census points:

Class I Roads	Census Points	Tons Per Day			
		1911–12	1922	1925	1928
A.57 (Liverpool–Manchester–Lincoln)	Sankey Bridges (Lancs)	1,150	8,250	11,610	15,800
A.24 (London–Worthing)	near Findon (Sussex)	700	1,920	3,600	5,040
A.1 (London–Edinburgh)	Framwellgate Moor (Durham)	650	3,350	5,350	8,540
A.7 (Edinburgh–Carlisle)	near Moorville (Cumberland)	650	1,920	4,330	5,740
A.944 (Moffat–Aberdeen)	Lock of Skene (Aberdeen)	297	473	717	985

On the Edinburgh–Carlisle road traffic had nearly trebled in the six years 1922–8; and it had more than doubled on the Edinburgh–London

[1] Para. 285.
[2] Para. 291.

road and between Aberdeen and Moffat. It was more than evident that some form of regulation was needed.

The second Labour Government took up points from the Royal Commission's earlier reports to legislate about the sector on which the general public might be expected to feel most strongly: the public service vehicles. Some of the provisions also applied to motor vehicles generally. The Act set up machinery and established principles which could later be applied to other types of vehicles. There were four main types of provision in the Act, which received the Royal Assent on August 1, 1930.

1. A system for the regulation of traffic on the roads, with particular reference to public service vehicles.
2. Compulsory insurance 'for the protection of third parties against risks arising out of the use of motor vehicles'.
3. Far-reaching provisions limiting hours and regulating the wages and conditions of the drivers of public service vehicles.
4. Powers of local authorities were extended to enable them to provide public service vehicles.

This last—'municipal socialism', as it was sometimes optimistically described—was a favourite scheme of Herbert Morrison (later Lord Morrison of Lambeth), the then Minister of Transport. His theory at the time was that municipal ownership would provide 'socialism by instalments'; municipally-owned buses were to be a first instalment. The Act contained provisions about licences for drivers, fixed a minimum age and required a declaration, but not a certificate, of physical fitness; imposed speed limits; gave power to endorse licences and to disqualify for certain offences; and made employers liable where employees, in complying with their orders, were obliged to commit offences. There was, for example, the famous provision, section 10 (b), that if an employer published a timetable under which a journey could not be completed 'without an infringement', it could be used against the employer as evidence of an offence. Other offences included: 'dangerous' driving; 'driving without due care and attention'; driving 'under the influence of drink or drugs'.

One of the most important sections was Section 19, which sought to limit the hours during which drivers might remain continuously on duty. This was for the purpose of 'protecting the public against risks . . . where the drivers . . . are suffering from excessive fatigue'. It was declared an offence to employ drivers for more than eleven hours out of twenty-four, or without a break for rest and refreshment after $5\frac{1}{2}$ hours continuous driving. The enforcement of this section was to prove notoriously unsuccessful, particularly for road transport men.

The machinery which the Act set up divided the country into Traffic Areas, with Traffic Commissioners charged with responsibility for licensing, controlling, and examining public service vehicles, and with the control of routes, competition, fares, etc. Finally, Section 93 laid down that there should be minimum wages and conditions of service for those employed on public service vehicles; with the right of their organizations to make representations to the Commissioners, and for disputes to be referred by the Minister of Labour to the industrial court. An employer in breach could be treated as having failed to comply with the conditions of his road service licence.

These, briefly, were the main provisions of the Act, which did not provide for any system of licensing haulage vehicles, nor with wages and conditions of service for those operating them. As far as it went, however, the Act was of considerable importance; it did move towards the beginning of a nationally co-ordinated transport policy, and resulted in the establishment of municipally-owned bus services in most of the larger towns. But, with the railway companies as well as the long distance motor-coaches still in private hands, this was not a decisive factor even in passenger traffic; it was still a far cry to a nationally-owned system on socialist lines. Whilst the minimum age at which a driver's licence could be held was as low as seventeen on some vehicles, there were still no provisional licences, nor tests of physical fitness or ability to drive. Yet there was some control of employers' practices and on the fitness of their vehicles; the employment of mates and trailermen was made compulsory; and at least a start was made in the battle for limiting hours of continuous driving, even though the ten hours with a rest break after each five in the original Bill was increased to eleven and $5\frac{1}{2}$ by the House of Lords.[1] How to enforce the limitation of hours in practice was an issue to be bitterly fought for years to come.

At least the 1930 Act was the thin end of the wedge towards some degree of control of the chaos and danger of the roads. It certainly did some jobs with maximum efficiency: it stopped undercutting and competition and regulated fares in sectors of passenger traffic; and it provided that, by compulsory insurance for third party risks, compensation for damage to property and for injury to innocent parties in accidents should not be evaded because the owner of the offending vehicle was a man of straw. From an economic point of view, it accelerated the trend towards monopoly in the industry and strengthened it in the battle for traffic against the private railway companies. It gave much greater importance to the biggest concentration of trade unionists and, therefore, favoured the big general union which Ernest Bevin was building. The bigger the union the more thorough was its recognition by the Traffic Commissioners, which in itself was a powerful lever for forcing recognition upon employers who

---

[1] It may be noted that the other section against which that Chamber put up a major obstruction was Section 101, extending the powers of local authorities to run their own buses. When the bill came back to the Commons, Herbert Morrison did not yield on that point.

still refused it. Most of these trends, of course, had already been evident; the series of Acts, of which the Road Traffic Act 1930 was the first, were to give immense impetus to them.

When it came to the third report and the transport of goods by road, the standpoint of the unions about the Road Traffic Act 1930 was expressed mainly by Archie Henderson, then National Secretary of the Commercial Services Group of the Transport & General Workers' Union. He said in evidence on May 15, 1930 that 'the scheme for licensing the Road Transport Goods Services could now much more easily be operated and could be accomplished by an extension of the powers of these new licensing regional authorities'. That, broadly speaking, with some omissions and modifications, was what took place.

Before considering the major criticisms, about which the Association was in general agreement with the spokesmen for the Transport & General Workers' Union, whilst reserving its own position on a number of points, it is necessary to see what was the approach of the Royal Commission and the varying standpoints of the interests which gave evidence before it. The Royal Commission considered that problems involved in the transport of goods 'undoubtedly present much greater difficulties'. There were two serious flaws. The first was that the case for public ownership was not seriously argued. Whilst, in the original memorandum, the Transport & General Workers' Union had stated that it was 'the considered opinion of the union that the essential transport services of the country should as public services be operated under public ownership', they did not put forward any proposals for this. When questioned on the point, John Cliff, the Assistant General Secretary, said in general terms that public ownership might be national or municipal, but in his opinion 'a municipality is rather too limited a boundary'.[1] He was in favour of public ownership of goods vehicles 'in principle'; but continued: 'We agree that the public ownership of freight goods presents much greater difficulties than that of road passenger services.'[2] He was ready to accept the idea 'of what is called a controlled monopoly'. This was also accepted by the organizations of the big haulage firms, but not by the smaller employers.

The conclusion of the Royal Commission on this first and basic point should be noted. Railways, inland waterways, and shipping are all organized agencies of transport, each claiming to suffer from the 'unfair competition' of road transport, being bound by 'statutes, agreements, rules, practices and all other adjuncts which are associated with a highly organized business'. On the other hand, the Commissioners remarked, goods transport was 'in a condition which lacks all unity and is operated by a number of independent firms and individuals who, while endeavouring to compete with other forms of transport, are at the same time engaged in

[1] Q.7089.
[2] 7091.

bitter and uneconomic strife with each other in their own particular branch'.[1] The Commission's conclusion was that it would not only be greatly to the advantage of the road haulage industry to be put on an organized basis, but that it was 'an essential precedent to any attempt at general co-ordination with other forms of transport'. Such organization, in their opinion, could be brought about only by a system of licensing under the Area Traffic Commissioners. They recommended that it should be applied to every road haulier, defined as 'any person, firm or company who holds himself out as willing to carry the goods of others for hire or reward'. They excepted firms on contract for one employer only. This definition deliberately excluded those who were later to become known as 'C-licence-holders'. The Report pointed out that, although road transport vehicles had increased from 150,995 in 1922 to 334,237 in 1930, they regarded the greatest increase as being in those 'owned and operated by manufacturers and traders for the conveyance of their own products, and in the number owned by contractors working exclusively for particular traders'. Whilst admitting that statistics were not available, they accepted the evidence of one of the employers' organizations that eighty per cent of road-borne goods were carried in such vehicles, and only twenty per cent in road hauliers' vehicles.[2] The Commissioners thought that 'in all probability the bulk of it is for local delivery', which they considered 'unsuitable for any other mode of conveyance'. They therefore concluded that they would not 'make any recommendations regarding the control or regulation of this particular type of transport which would interfere with its natural development, since we believe that its future depends solely on its economic value to traders'.

In their written memorandum the Transport & General Workers' Union had already made it clear that they would not even put forward an argument for it: 'We do not propose that registration should be imposed upon traders using their own vehicles for transporting their own merchandise.' Asked whether bigger firms would not be encouraged to use their own private vehicles, Archie Henderson agreed that it might do, but continued: 'There are a very large number of businesses which could never properly employ their own transport; the nature of the business is such that it would not pay them.'[3] Here was a second fatal flaw. What was to prove the main obstacle not only to effective control but later to public ownership—the C-licence vehicles—was from the start to be excluded from control, with the full acquiescence of the workers' representatives. They were to pay dearly for this.

[1] Para. 331.
[2] Para. 296.
[3] 14681.

5. DIVERSE INTERESTS AND THEIR ORGANIZATIONS

It would now be timely to glance at the categories of interested parties who gave evidence before the Royal Commission, noting their standpoints and where there was community or clash of opinion. On the workers' side, the Royal Commission accepted the Transport & General Workers' Union as representing 'the majority of the organized transport workers employed in the conveyance of goods by road'. Their main spokesman on this section, as we have seen, were John Cliff and Archie Henderson; whilst Ernest Bevin also gave evidence, he spoke only about the docks. The small employers were represented by the Commercial Motor Users' Association, with a membership of 5,000 to 6,000, owning only 100,000 road vehicles between them. Of these, only fifteen per cent were haulage contractors; sixty-five per cent were traders with their own motor transport and ten per cent were bus and coach proprietors. On the average, each owned between seventeen and twenty vehicles. The National Road Transport Employers' Federation represented haulage contractors in England and Wales, with 3,000 members employing 'at least 150,000 people' and owning 80,000 horse-drawn vehicles and 50,000 lorries. These were the bigger hauliers, with much short-haul business, each employing fifty people on the average. Finally there were the really big men, the long-distance hauliers; they were represented by a special *ad hoc* six-man committee which came into existence at a conference held on April 29, 1930 consisting of 'influential members of the transport industry who were engaged in long-distance road haulage work', for the purpose of examining their own position and agreeing upon proposals to put before the Commission. They were described as having a full knowledge of long distance work all over Great Britain, 'and definitely representing the majority of the principal firms engaged in the business and supported generally by many others'. Their title was The Long-Distance Road Haulage Committee of Inquiry, and their spokesman was Sir Maxwell Hicks. These two organizations of the big employers concentrated their criticism upon the small hauliers.

Sir Maxwell Hicks claimed that the organized companies had built up their business by 'securing a regular flow of traffic operated by efficient vehicles at economic rates'. He claimed for them 'a proper sense of their responsibilities both towards their employees, their clients and road users generally'. He said that the owner-driver was usually a newcomer to the trade, with little business experience or knowledge of costs. As to return loads, said Sir Maxwell, the owner-driver

'is almost forced to accept any rate that may be offered and is certainly tempted to canvass for traffic at a rate which will obtain the traffic irrespective of whether the transaction is a paying proposition in the long run for himself'.

This especially applied to those buying their vehicles on hire-purchase. 'The only way in which the small man in this position can keep going is to increase his hours of labour and try and make man and machine do an abnormal amount of work.'

His view was supported by the National Road Transport Employers' Federation, which complained of great disparity in wages throughout the country and 'grossly unfair competition' in large centres from owners who undercut because 'they do not pay anything like the same rate of wages and recognize no restrictions as to working hours'.

It was possible for a large measure of agreement to be reached, if from differing viewpoints, between the large and middle-sized employers and the Transport & General Workers' Union. Determined opposition came from the small employers represented in the Commercial Motor Users' Association. At the heart of the whole question was the scheme of registration of road haulage operators put forward by the Transport & General Workers' Union, which had been approved by the National Joint Road Transport Council which represented employers as well. If Area Traffic Commissioners were to establish a register of licensed operators, with power to refuse a licence where they were not satisfied that the needs of the area demanded additional facilities, this meant that entry to the industry was restricted. It meant a long step towards reducing competition. The union put it forward; the larger employers accepted it. The medium-sized employers of the National Road Transport Employers' Federation, it is true, viewed it with some caution. They stated that they would strongly approve efforts in the direction of regulation of the industry provided it 'would not force rates up to an uneconomic level'. Their suggestion was that 'consideration should first be given to the unification of wages and working conditions so that these should be standardized throughout the country'. They criticized sharply those vehicle owners who 'engage intermittently in the industry without regard to economic cost, a practice that is most mischievous in any trade and enormously increases the difficulties of responsible transport interests, and in the opinion of this Federation the industry cannot be properly regulated whilst this element exists'. They therefore accepted licensing, but urged that 'licences should be issued only to bona fide contractors'.[1] They were emphatic that 'unrestricted competition of the present day is conducive to waste and cannot be said to be in the public interest'. The biggest employers, the Long-Distance Road Haulage Committee of Inquiry, for whom Sir Maxwell Hicks spoke, had no reservations against the licensing system. Indeed, they wanted it also applied to the clearing-houses, so that licences should be granted only to those whose record, capital, and knowledge of the industry were 'satisfactory', and having regard to competition with other clearing-houses in the area.

[1] Para. 324.

But the small employers of the Commercial Motor Users' Association were as bitterly opposed to any form of regulation as the Road Haulage Association was to be to nationalization seventeen years later. Many of their arguments, for that matter, were identical; these they put forward in a lengthy memorandum[1] submitted in September 1930, after the Long-Distance Road Haulage Committee of Inquiry had given evidence before the Commission and had opted for registration without reserve. The memorandum argued that the industry was young and growing and 'should be left free and untrammelled'. The convenience and demands of the general public could not be met unless freedom of development and expansion were allowed to road transport:

'Cheap road transport is essential to the nation and is only possible by the full development of motor traction. It affects costs through innumerable phases of industry as well as throughout the whole process of distribution of foodstuffs and materials.'

They argued that regulation of the carriage of goods was 'impracticable'; and that 'the choice in these matters should still rest with and be exercised by the producing and trading communities'. Any further regulation would act as 'a restriction of trade and an added cost to the commercial activities of the community'. Feeling the need to defend the fact that many vehicles at that time were idle, they explained that that was 'common to commerce generally, owing to the prolonged depression in trade throughout the world', but that it was no time for imposing regulations which would limit the industry's competitive powers. They favoured no system of licensing haulage contractors of any kind, and thought the industry should be left to competition, where 'the one who gives the best service at the cheapest price obtains the business'. Referring to evidence which had been given that, in the United States, a similar system of control had broken down, largely because the manufacturer or trader at once provided himself with his own transport, they predicted a similar outcome here. There was no need for inspection and supervision of goods vehicles; here again this would be taken care of automatically by 'keen competition between individual operators and with alternative forms of transportation', which would demand a high standard of efficiency. With a final flourish, the small road users concluded: 'It is submitted that the operation of economic laws can be relied upon to prevent redundancy of transport far more efficiently than any regulative action of officials.' Unfortunately, war to the death, according to the law of the jungle, was taking place on the public roads, where the innocent bystander was losing life and limb.

The Commission proceeded to recommend a system for licensing road haulage operators, with especial reference to provisions for securing the fitness of the vehicle and that the wages and conditions of service of the

[1] M.62.

men who worked with them should at least reach minimum and standardized levels. On this the Commissioners had some special points to under-
line. They did not disregard the plain fact that 'wages and general conditions
of service in the industry leave much to be desired'; with a graceful nod in
the direction of the firms to whom such criticism would not apply, the
Commissioners continued:

'We cannot but feel that there are others whose profits, if there be any,
represent to a considerable extent the difference, expressed in terms of
money, between the wages paid and the conditions obtaining, and the
wages which should be paid and the conditions which should obtain, if
proper standards were maintained.'

The Commissioners therefore agreed with the union and the larger
employers that improvements here 'will go far to weed out the less desirable
operators and to place the industry on a sounder basis by removing the
element of uneconomic operation which undoubtedly exists'. This was
why they recommended that Section 93 of the Road Traffic Act 1930,
applying the 'Fair Wage Clause', should be extended to employees of
road haulage contractors.

As to the clearing-houses, the Commission would not make recommendations. It did not question the opinion of the Long-Distance Road
Haulage Committee of Inquiry that 'the ideal clearing-house would be an
organization controlled by hauliers and traders, limited as to profits and
debarred from selling lorries on the hire-purchase system'. But they
thought that once the industry was on 'a more stable footing, it should
itself organize its own clearing-houses and not, as at present, leave this
part of its business to the activities of others, some of whom, we have been
informed, are not always particularly scrupulous'. The industry took the
tip. With the accelerated growth of monopoly it was not long before the
biggest firms had squeezed out or bought out the clearing-houses and
converted them into part of their private network for getting traffic.

6. HOW TO CO-ORDINATE TRANSPORT

Before leaving the Royal Commission, however, it would prove instructive,
if tragic, to look back from the sixties to see what were the conclusions of
the Commissioners on their final task: to decide what steps should be
adopted to promote in the public interest 'the co-ordinated working and
development' of the available means of transport. They said frankly that
they were confronted 'with very great difficulties'; but with the question
of goods traffic, they said, 'the difficulty of co-ordination is infinitely
greater'. Many problems would disappear if every passenger travelled,
and all goods were carried, by the most economical route and form of
transport:

'But, as things are today, is such a state of affairs or even any approach to it practicable? Who is to decide, for example, what rail services are desirable in the public interest and what amount of coastwise shipping? Or what goods should in the national interest be sent by rail, road, canal, or ship?'[1]

They discussed four methods to secure what today would be called 'integration', which they described as 'unification', without which 'no attempt to bring about complete co-ordination would be successful. One method was nationalization, which would mean merging all existing transport into one huge combine 'for the purpose of spreading overhead charges over the whole field of transport and eliminating unnecessary competition'. This, they found, would involve much governmental control, 'since otherwise the whole of the essential services of transport would be in the hands of a huge uncontrolled monopoly'. Another scheme would be a combination of nationalization and rationalization, and would mean 'national ownership with private operation'; railways and road vehicles would be bought by the State, vested in a government department or public trust, and operated under licence by private companies. Another method would be a Public Transport Trust, which would not work for profit, but would pay a fixed rate of interest on the capital with surplus funds 'devoted to the improvement of facilities. It would be entirely divorced from political action'. Those who supported that method

'feel that transport should be carried on not for profit in the ordinary sense but as a great national service—a policy which was deliberately adopted by the German Empire and some other countries before the war.'

Of nationalization: the Commissioners had this to say: 'Unfortunately, it is impossible for us to discuss nationalization . . . without raising political differences of a party character upon which agreement would be impossible.'

Agreement was equally impossible on any other alternative, for some members were extreme exponents of *laissez-faire*, as this paragraph discloses:

'Other members of the Commission . . . are frankly opposed to direct government action, either through nationalization or the formation of a National Trust, believing that industry and the public in general would be less well served under such a system than they are today; that such further co-ordination of the various forms of transport as may be advantageous will come about naturally through the play of economic forces; and that co-ordination so reached will be a better solution than co-ordination enforced by the creation of a huge monopoly even though it be subject to governmental control.'[2]

[1] 500.
[2] 534.

They therefore found it impossible to make any recommendation at all.

One warning the work of this Royal Commission gave was that the problem was not capable of being tackled piecemeal. As they remarked about proposals for nationalizing the railways: 'The nationalization of the railways alone—leaving other forms of transport in other hands—would certainly not produce any real co-ordination of transport.' Thirty-five years later that lesson had still to be learned. But road transport workers at the beginning of 1931 were occupied in watching the first months of operation of the Road Traffic Act 1930 and in formulating their demands following the publication of the Royal Commission's third report about improving its provisions and extending them to road haulage. Yet before this could come fully under way, the second Labour Government had fallen, and fifteen years were to pass before another Labour Government was in power. In the confusion caused in 1931 by the Labour Premier, Ramsay MacDonald, and his associates dismissing the Labour Government, and leading in a 'coalition' adminstration which was essentially Conservative, the situation was changed; from then onward every improvement had to be hard won. Some were slow to realize this hard necessity.

CHAPTER THIRTEEN

PRIVATE RAILWAYS VERSUS
PRIVATE ROAD HAULAGE

I. THE SALTER CONFERENCE

THE standpoint of the Association to the Royal Commission, to the legislation dealing with road traffic, to the question of national negotiation and status as well as relations between unions, is discussed fully in later sections. It is necessary here first to give the briefest summary of the forces brought into play and a sketch of the general sequence of events. The abortive Conservative Transport Bill was issued in March 1927; the Road Haulage Wages Act came into force in July 1938, a decade later, whilst the first product of the whole complex machinery did not appear until January 1940. Yet that dozen years saw the recognition that a new industry had come into being.

The Royal Commission had produced half a loaf, with some control achieved over the owners of road vehicles carrying passenger traffic. More years passed before further crumbs were available in partial, but largely unsuccessful, attempts to introduce firm control over road haulage operators, even though the largest amongst the employers had indicated willingness to accept a licensing system which would tend to hinder the entry of small men into the industry.

But the pressure of forces continued. On the one hand, the road haulage transport 'explosion' did not let up; there was even more undercutting of rates. Road transport was 'stealing' traffic from the railways, which mounted a major counter-offensive, with the private railway companies and their newly imported business efficiency experts going further into road transport themselves, as a method of diverting traffic back on to the railways, and checking the tearaway development of road transport. If ever there was a case for nationalizing both forms of transport, here it was: on the one hand, the old railways, long since in decline and neglected under the private monopoly ownership of the big four and, on the other, the chaotically expanding new industry, where vast private fortunes were being made. The national interest required that all transport should be immediately and fully integrated into a well-run and efficient public service, capable of moving people and goods safely and quickly to every part of this small but densely populated island; that it should allow for the development of new methods, from air to monorail; and that it should be capable of keeping pace and expanding with the immensely increased production potential which science had already made technically possible. Against this were the vested interests on both sides; and it must be remembered that behind both protagonists was the shadow of the vested interest of oil, which at this stage heavily favoured road transport for quick returns, and had not yet succeeded in impeding electrification of the railways by developing the diesel engine.

In these circumstances, who was to do battle for the interests of the nation? Certainly not the government of the day, which could be expected only to react in support of whichever should finally prove the stronger vested interest. Here was indeed an opportunity for the Labour movement to conduct a massive national campaign. What a chance, indeed, for the unions of the railway workers and road transport workers to take the initiative, and so defend simultaneously their short-term and long-term interests, whilst making the general public fully aware of their community of interests. But the opportunity was not taken by a Labour Party Parliamentary Opposition, bewildered by the consequences of the policies, or lack of them, which had brought about the downfall of the second Labour Government. There was some tendency for unions to concentrate upon minimum standards of wages and hours and for national recognition each within their 'own' industry. However, the National Union of Railwaymen and the Transport & General Workers' Union reached agreement not to poach members when railway companies put vehicles on the road. There were many arguments put forward asserting that this was the day of the big battalions and that while the biggest unions would reap big advantages, the smaller unions would be squeezed out. The officers of the Association finally agreed, with some reluctance, to a greater measure of joint working with the Transport & General Workers' Union.

The railway companies had already been feeling the draught with some loss of passenger traffic; but the loss of freight could be decisive. When freight, already hit by the world economic crisis, was fluctuating in the early thirties, and manufacturers sought the cheapest possible transport, the most prominent question was who should pay for the big increase in the cost of maintaining and building highways used by motor traffic? The pressure from the old vested interests in the railway companies for large contributions from the big road haulage operators to this cost made the hauliers anxious to raise freight rates, kept down by competition of the small men. As we have seen, a big factor in the cut rates was the lack of regulation of wages and hours; once these could be controlled and standardized, the smaller men could be eliminated and the rates raised, to offset the increased share of paying for the roads, if the railway companies had their way. The control of wages and hours, therefore, had now become a not unimportant factor in the struggle between the big road and rail interests, and the Royal Commission's recommendations for licensing and regulating wages and hours came back into the picture. It had taken over two years since their third report.

On March 8, 1932, the railway companies delivered a powerful broadside by publishing a booklet demanding legislation to give them a 'Square Deal' to meet road competition.[1] The Minister of Transport met representatives of both sides and decided to convene a Conference on March 22, 1932, of four representatives of each side, with joint secretaries, under the chairmanship of Sir Arthur Salter, later Lord Salter.[2] The terms of reference of the Conference were to seek to establish a fair basis of competition and division of function between rail and road transport of goods, and also to assess an equitable allocation of the cost of maintaining highways. When the Salter 'Report of the Conference on Rail and Road Transport'[3] was issued in the middle of August 1932, it came under fire from the smaller road haulage men and others. The Salter recom-

---

[1] They recalled that the Royal Commission had expressed the opinion that in the year 1930, as compared with 1924 the railways had lost £16,000,000 of goods traffic to the roads; they had had to put their freight rates up by 7% in 1927. This would have been 'unnecessary except for road competition'. They pointed out that the permanent way had cost the railways £800,000,000, whilst road users had been presented with £490,000,000 spent on the roads in the nine years up to 1929 which they were using as their 'permanent way', although their taxation contribution to it had been only a quarter of the sum. The railway companies demanded legislation which would ease their statutory obligation to carry whatever traffic offered and would enable them to fix agreed prices with traders. They also demanded that road users should pay the total cost of construction and maintenance of highways, divided amongst them according to user.

[2] The members of the Salter Conference were all men of outstanding influence in their organizations.

The joint secretaries were well matched: Mr Gerald Cole-Deacon formerly on the legal staff of the London Midland & Scottish Railway, and at that time the Secretary of the Railway Companies Association. His opposite number was Mr Frederick G. Bristow, who had been chief executive officer of the Commercial Motor Users' Association since 1906, secretary of the Standing Joint Committee of Mechanical Road Transport Associations since 1912, secretary of the Motor Transport Employers' Federation since 1918, and secretary of the Empire Motor Fuels Committee of the Imperial Motor Transport Council from 1920 to 1930. Mr Bristow had also been secretary of the Joint Industrial Council for the Road Transport Industry between 1912 and 1920; an old campaigner.

The official representatives of *the railway companies* were: Sir Herbert Walker, Chief General Manager of the Southern Railway; Sir James Milne, General Manager of the Great Western Railway; Sir Ralph Wedgwood, General Manager of the London & North-Eastern Railway; and leading them, Sir Josiah Stamp, later Lord Stamp, President of the London Midland and Scottish Railway. He was a formidable figure; formerly a civil servant in the Inland Revenue, he had left government service to become director of Nobel Industries in 1919 and of Imperial Chemicals in 1927; he had become Director of the Bank of England and President of one of the largest building societies.

The four representatives of *road transport* were: Mr W. H. Gaunt, distributive manager of J. Lyons Ltd; C. le M. Gosselin, a past president of the Commercial Motor Users' Association; P. R. Turner, President of the London Haulage Contractors' Association; and, finally, Mr E. Graham Guest, President of the Scottish Commercial Motor Users' Association.

[3] Dated July 29, 1932. Ministry of Transport, 1932.

mendations were that road-users should bear £60,000,000 of what was needed for maintaining highways, divided as to £23,500,000 to be borne by commercial goods haulage and as to £36,000,000 by all other road vehicles. That was £2,500,000 more than the current yield of motor and petrol taxation; it meant that the heavier vehicle would be taxed at a considerably higher rate than it had been. Some critics accused the Salter Conference of having remained silent on the question of setting a fair basis of competition between rail and road traffic, which was, of course, the key problem, but one which was wholly insoluble by competing interests. The Salter Report proposed relaxing restrictions on the freedom of railway companies to select freight and negotiate with traders on rates. But they also indirectly touched on the question by supporting the Royal Commission's recommendation for a system of licensing to be introduced which would be conditional upon the payment of reasonable wages, the observance of proper conditions of service, and the maintenance of vehicles in a proper state of fitness.

A week later, on August 22, 1932, the Commercial Motor Users' Association called its National Council together and passed resolutions rejecting the Salter recommendations. They regarded the proposals on highway costs as 'not equitable'; and, as to regulating the industry, they declared that

'. . . while supporting the principle that commercial motor vehicles should be maintained in a satisfactory state of mechanical fitness and that drivers should be in receipt of adequate wages and work under proper conditions of service, [we] do not support the special system of licensing and control recommended in Part III.'

Five weeks later still, whilst some sections were still campaigning vociferously, all the road transport interests came together to regroup and plan the next stage of the battle. On September 29, 1932, over 150 representatives of seventy organizations concerned in passenger and goods transport came to a conference in London called by the Commercial Motor Users' Association, and decided to put out a considered report based on the views of a whole number of interests, including agriculture, the motor manufacturers and road constructors. On the same day, the British Road Federation was formed, to unify commercial interests concerned with road traffic and construction. Its main aim was

'to create a common liaison between interests concerned in transport operation and road traffic and in the improvement and maintenance of roads, with a view to presenting a united front upon present and future basic problems affecting transport in the interests of the public and of the trade and industry of this country.'

F. G. Bristow became secretary, with a wide range of interests represented on the provisional committee.[1]

A month later, on October 27, 1932, the Conference of National Organizations of Trade and Industry denounced the Salter recommendations, saying that the only reference to the railways was the proposal to relieve them of certain obligations; and that the result of the proposals would 'eventually deprive trade and industry of any effective alternative means of transport, destroying the same and the reasonable competition which is their safeguard.'

Whilst the Salter report was criticized both for what was done and for what was left undone, the main public battle continued to rage round the recommendation that road-users should bear a greater share of the road costs. It was eight months before the Government announced in April 1932 that it was adopting the Salter Conference recommendations; that taxation on motor vehicles of over five tons would be increased, and that a Road and Rail Traffic Bill would be introduced. This was to lay the basis —a shaky one as it proved—for control of goods transport by road; but it did not come into operation until many months later still.

2. THE ROAD AND RAIL TRAFFIC ACT, 1933, AND AFTER

In setting up a licensing system for goods haulage operators, the Act divided them into three categories. A public carrier's A-licence entitled the holder to use the vehicle to carry goods for hire or reward. A limited carrier's licence, the B-licence, entitled the holder to carry goods either in connection with his own business or for hire or reward. Thirdly, the C-licence, or private carrier's licence, entitled the holder to use the vehicle for the carriage of goods in connection with his own business only. The granting of all three licences was conditional upon the vehicles being

[1] National Petrol Distributing Companies: George N. Wilson
Cement Makers' Federation: Brig. Gen. A. C. Critchley
Asphalt Roads Association: F. M. Bond and J. S. Killick
British Road Tar Association: R. G. Clarry, MP
Road Machinery Manufacturers: J. M. Johnston
Road Improvement Associations: W. R. Jeffreys
Society of Motor Manufacturers and Traders: Norman A. Hardie (Vice-President), Colonel A. Hacking, and Colonel D. C. McLagan
Whittington Trust: J. D. Marks
McNamara & Co: Sir Maxwell Hicks
National Road Transport Employers' Federation: W. H. Hixson
Road Haulage Association: J. S. Nicholl and R. W. Sewell
Commercial Motor Users' Association: F. G. Bristow, E. W. Rudd, and G. Shave
Motor Hirers' & Coach Services Association: William Birch and Major J. B. Elliot, and Furniture Warehousemen's and Removers' Association: F. C. Skinner.

Amongst these, not the least important was Major Elliot (later Sir John Elliot) of the London Transport Executive, Thos. Cook & Sons Ltd., Pullman Car Ltd., Thomas Tilling Ltd., and the Southern Railway. From early days he had been a skilled publicity and advertising expert.

maintained in fit condition and upon driving hours being limited. Section 31 sought to amend the hours that might be worked and the obligatory rest periods, theoretically brought into operation by Section 19 of the Road Traffic Act, 1930. The Act insisted that log-books should be kept (Section 16) with full details of the journey and load, which had to be available for inspection on demand (Section 18). Efforts were made to stop up the holes in the first Act when it came to apply it to road haulage vehicles. The payment of fair wages, however, was made a condition only of A- and B-licences; C-licences were excluded from these provisions. In theory any employee of an A- or B-licence-holder could complain to the Area Traffic Commissioners that his wages were unfair. If the complaint were not satisfactorily disposed of, it was to be referred by the Minister of Labour to the Industrial Court for settlement. Part II of the Act permitted the railways to negotiate agreed charges with customers. Part III provided that a Transport Advisory Council should be set up with members appointed by the Minister. The Minister finally made an order bringing the licensing machinery into effect on January 1, 1934.

But what was to be the standard of fair wages? What protection would be afforded to men making complaints, individually or through a trade union recognized for the purpose? What about the wages of the workers of C-licence-holders? And how, in any case, was it all to be enforced? Ernest Bevin had tried unsuccessfully to get a national wages board incorporated into the Act, instead of the 'Fair Wages' clause. The nearest approach to this was that Section 32 required the Industrial Court when dealing with a case referred to it to

'have regard to any determination brought to its notice as to rates of wages and conditions by a Joint Industrial Council, Conciliation Board or to an agreement between organizations representative of employers and work-people.'

With some difficulty, voluntary collective bargaining of this sort was brought into being. A National Joint Conciliation Board was set up with Sir Richard Redmayne, former Chief Inspector of Mines, as its independent chairman; and, as we shall see, after great anxiety on the part of the Association, the Minister of Labour called together a separate Industrial Council for Scotland, with eight Association members amongst the twelve members of the workers' side, which met in August 1934. After prolonged negotiations, which in Scotland were held up by differences between the employers themselves, the first national agreement on scales and conditions was reached on February 25, 1935. Similar agreements were being negotiated all over the United Kingdom in Area joint conciliation boards. But only a quarter of the A- and B-licence-holders were members of employers' associations. No method of forcing them to comply had been provided for. In practice, therefore, these agreements proved ineffective; their provisions were widely disregarded, and the victimization of employees who lodged complaints was all too easy. Hours of work were grossly exceeded, sometimes through the bribe of overtime pay to supplement miserably low wages. Until they could be fully organized, some men could not readily see an alternative; log-books were falsified to a very considerable degree. The chaos was rendered worse by the practice, particularly prevalent in Scotland, of employing casual labour in the industry, and of course by the fact that employees of the C-licence-holder got little help in trying to eliminate unfair wages. The effect of the exclusion of C-licence-holders thus began to be felt early in the thirties, long before their number had increased as startingly as it did at the time of nationalization and after.[1] Instead of the wages of these men being raised, they pulled down the level of the A- and B-licence men.

Why had the C-licence-holders been excluded? Firstly, since they carried only their own goods and largely in these early years were concerned with local deliveries, they offered no competitive threat to railways nor to big haulage operators, neither of which were likely to get their traffic nor would find it profitable enough to fight over; at the time, therefore, there was no pressure for their regulation from those influential quarters. On the other hand, the transport unions were not concerned with them to any considerable degree; indeed, as we have seen, the spokesman for the Transport & General Workers' Union before the Royal Commission had specifically excluded them? Why? The view has been expressed, and denied, that one reason was that one of the largest single group of C-licence-holders were the co-operative societies, with their delivery vans and vehicles. There was said to be reluctance by the leaders of the Labour Party, by then on the Opposition Front Bench, to embark upon the political hazards of interfering with the co-operative societies. Again, in some cases relatively satisfactory agreements existed with representation on wages boards between most of the co-operative societies and the transport unions, which did not see that any initiative which might upset relations was called for from them. In the early stages the proportion of co-operative society vehicles amongst the total C-licences was higher than it became later. When it came to 1960, for example, there were 1,400,000 C-licences but only 60,000 co-operative vehicles, or some 4·3 per cent. Mr Robert Taylor, one time secretary of the Association, and later president of the Scottish Co-operative Wholesale Society, pointed out that in 1960 there were only 4,000 vehicles on C-licence owned by the Scottish co-operative societies. In Scotland the co-operatives were perhaps slower in changing over to motor delivery;

[1]

Year	Goods Vehicles Licensed	C-licences	Percentage
1938	513,000	365,000	71·1
1948	757,200	591,400	78·1
1958	1,222,700	1,049,100	85·8

in 1925 there were still 9,000 to 10,000 horse-drawn vehicles in Glasgow. In any event, it was the London-based leaders of the Transport & General Workers' Union who had the decisive voice at the time.

So unsatisfactory were the results of voluntary collective bargaining, following the Road and Rail Traffic Act, that the National Joint Conciliation Board asked for legislation to give effect to their decisions and agreements in future; and also to bring the C-licence-holders into the picture. This led finally to the Ministries of Labour and Transport jointly setting up a 'Committee on the Regulation of Wages and Conditions of Service in the Road Motor Transport Industry (Goods) 1936', under the chairmanship of Sir James Baillie. The Baillie Committee reported on April 24, 1937, and most of their recommendations were incorporated into the Road Haulage Wages Act, 1938. This established government supervision for wage negotiations; it was a major change. The Association had to face quite new opportunities, and new problems as well as many of the old problems. What were the obstacles in the way of the old leadership facing up to this challenge?

The dozen years which passed between the appointment of the Royal Commission on Transport late in 1928 and the first Road Haulage Wages Order in January 1940 began with the Association at low ebb, with power still largely centralized in the hands of a General Secretary whose ideas, policies, and practice had been unchallenged for twenty-five years. In his earlier years he had earned the confidence of the downtrodden, often ill-educated carters, some of whom were slow to learn that tips, thieving, and a rough understanding about the number of breakages on the loads were no substitute for a strong organization and negotiated living wage.[1]

Hugh Lyon found it hard to recognize that the old days were passing and that his ideas and methods were typical of the era before 1914. His health was beginning to fail; he relied increasingly upon Peter Webster, the Assistant General Secretary whom he had trained up for over fifteen years as the 'crown prince' of what appeared to be yet another disappearing empire.

In the late twenties and early thirties the membership was at a very low ebb. Unemployment and short-time working were rife in every district of Scotland. Membership figures fell; branches closed down. The membership tended to remain strongest amongst the carters, and in the stables traditionally organized by the Association: the railway contractors; the co-operative society stables, much of it local delivery; the local authorities. The basic organizing work amongst the new type of transport worker was

---

[1] A collector of the early days tells of an old carter, Tom M——, 'He had a good reputation; yet he handled a large number of stolen cheeses and had never been caught. His card was always paid up on the nail. He was respected and self-respecting. He knew he was being robbed; it took a long time for him to learn that to be a Rob Roy was not the answer.'

not being done by the Association. In 1929, of every 10d contributed 6·5d went on sickness and funeral benefit and the convalescent home; salaries and commission accounted for another 2·8d. Organizing expenses were conspicuously absent; organizing work costs money. As he grew older, Hugh Lyon came more and more to dread parting with money, especially on organizing. Whilst the membership dwindled, the funds piled up. In 1932 the membership had dwindled to 7,596, below the 1912 mark; with assets totalling £131,295 there was over £17 per member; the Association was described as 'the richest trade union in Britain'.[1] From the Glasgow branches came the gibe that the Association had become the money-lender to the Scottish movement, and that it had deteriorated into a mere friendly society.

With much unemployment and the majority of Glasgow transport workers unorganized, why did the officials not launch out on an organizing campaign, instead of increasing the amount of the dues and piling up large resources? Such suggestions caused intense resentment in Hugh Lyon, who was able to do less and less through failing health. He had for many years relied upon the old Joint Industrial Council, where the Sliding Scale was sliding downwards at the close of the twenties, as employers again began calling for wage decreases. Whilst some members took occasion to demand that the Association should withdraw from it and negotiate for wage stabilization, others clung to it as to a raft in stormy seas. Lyon's view was that the moment was inopportune to seek stabilization of wages.

Then came the economic and politic crisis of 1931, which saw the proposed introduction by the Labour Government of economy cuts, the demand by the bankers for economy measures which would go beyond those the Labour Government had agreed to, Ramsay MacDonald's agreement to call in the Conservatives and to operate the cuts, and the fall of the Labour Government. The records are altogether silent on those events; but six months before, in the spring of 1931, the Association's delegates to the STUC had expressed sharp criticism of the Labour Government. It was on a favourite theme of Lyon's; that the way to deal with unemployment was to limit the hours of labour by legislation. Twelve years after the great post-war 'hours strike', he was pressing for a forty-hour week by Act of Parliament. The Association had put down a resolution at the STUC at Elgin in April 1931, pressing the Labour Government

---

[1] A columnist described how Lyon was 'not now much in the public eye', and wrote: 'An examination of the accounts reveals that the union is conducted without expense to the members. The balance sheet shows an expenditure of £4,425 for wages, salaries and commissions to officials, organizers and clerks.

The interest from investments was £4,325, so that the union pays expenses of management from the profit on investments.

It is probably the only trade union which succeeds in making investments pay for the costs of administration.

(*Glasgow Herald*, September 2, 1933)

to proceed immediately with the Hours of Industrial Employment Bill, which had been introduced but held up. Lyon suddenly intervened in the debate to make a scathing attack on the Government:

'They had been filled up with excuses about the Government being in the minority. Were they content to go on taking that as an excuse for doing nothing? What would they have said to a Conservative Government, had it evaded its responsibilities in this matter?

'In the Corporation of Glasgow, with 40 representatives, they had men working 20 to 40 hours a week overtime while thousands of people walked the streets unemployed.'[1]

He called for a deputation to interview the Premier, Ramsay MacDonald, and 'to suggest to him that it would be far better for the Labour Government to be defeated on a question which affected the working class directly instead of going on doing nothing, as was the position at present'. Earlier that week Lyon had engendered heat in Congress by accusing the National Union of Railwaymen of poaching members. Now he came out with what lay behind that: 'For over thirty years they had been asking for the nationalization of the railways, and today they found a Labour Government giving powers to those same railway owners to go on the roads.' Then the former Independent Labour Party supporter burst out against the Premier. 'Twenty years ago,' he exclaimed 'Ramsay MacDonald was suspect of being a Liberal, and he is very near it now.' Within six months the Premier had dismissed his Labour colleagues; and with a handful who clung to office with him, invited the Conservatives and Liberals to help him form a new government.

The records of the Association are full of the grave consequences throughout 1932 of local authorities operating economy cuts in the wages of their employees. The Industrial Council demanded cuts, and many co-operative societies were unable to maintain wages. That year things were indeed at a low ebb.

Lyon did not take the lead after his sensational speech at the STUC in 1931; the day-to-day work fell largely on Peter Webster. But whilst fighting the rearguard action to resist decreases in wages as far as possible, Webster was also busy attempting to come to grips with the new legislation. It was he who went from branch to branch explaining the terms of the Road Traffic Act, 1930, taking up the points under Section 19. It was Webster whom the Executive sent to represent them in London at two conferences in January 1931, at which the employers were aiming to undermine the conditions limiting hours under Section 19 of the Road Traffic Act, 1930. The employers had suggested varying the terms to enable a longer day to be worked. After hearing Webster's report, the Executive, on February 7, 1931, 'decided to stand by the Act, and further,

[1] 34th Annual Report of the STUC, 1931.

'that we take no part in any negotiations to amend the Act'. Webster made himself the Association's authority on the struggle with the railways which led up to the Salter Report and finally to the Road and Rail Traffic Act, 1933, which he mastered.

That year's annual conference at Kirkcaldy, in September 1933, demanded that the Rail and Road Traffic Act, 1933 should be extended to C-licences. Once again Hugh Lyon returned to his favourite question of the limitation of hours, but he did not raise it in the context which was of urgent concern to the motorman under the Road Acts. Lyon put forward a resolution that 'in view of the advance of science and the development of machinery with a consequent displacement of labour, this conference presses for the establishment of the 40-hour working week'.[1] It was Webster who explained all the new legislation in a comprehensive speech, which resulted in conference objecting

'to the appointment of representative members of the Transport Advisory Council, and demands an increase in the number of representatives of Labour, and further, that at least one such representative should be appointed for Scotland.'

They could congratulate themselves on the fact that the Salter Report had recommended a number of proposals on registration and conditions of service for which the Association had been pressing years before.

Webster attended both the branch quarterly meetings and also some special mass members' meetings to explain legislation. Typical of these was one held on May 13, 1934, at the Free Gardeners' Hall, Edinburgh, which was 'a Mass Meeting of motor drivers and assistants employed in the commercial or goods road transport service'. The chairman was Councillor Cathcart, later Bailie Cathcart, then District Organizer, who introduced Peter Webster as having 'made a special study of the question' of the Road and Rail Traffic Act. After going through the Act in detail, Webster went on to deal with the Conciliation Board, and pointed out that the Association:

'would have the majority of the representation on the employees' side. Individuals would have no standing in these matters except as members of their appropriate organizations.

'He made a strong appeal to all present to strengthen the position of the organization in the matter by becoming members or inducing others to do so.'

But what was needed was that time and money should be spent on rapidly organizing the thousands of unorganized motormen.

[1] Annual Report of Conference, 1933.

3. RELATIONS WITH OTHER UNIONS

While the Royal Commission was at work during the years 1928 to 1930, as we have seen, a large proportion of the Association's members were still carters. When the railway companies in search of traffic had gone on to the roads, and were engaging in traffic, it affected Association road members directly, because of their agreements with the companies and the railway contractors in Scotland. If the railway companies were running their own transport vehicles, it was not surprising that the industrial union, the National Union of Railwaymen, had views as to which organization was appropriate for them. This brought the National Union of Railwaymen into direct conflict with the Association; and also into conflict with the Transport & General Workers' Union. Whilst Lyon usually favoured industrial unionism as against both craft and multiple unions, he regarded the National Union of Railwaymen as a greater menace at the moment than the multiple Transport & General Workers' Union with a strongly established road transport section. At this moment, from his point of view, the railways were a separate and competing industry, as he clearly expressed when he addressed the Annual Conference in September 1929 on the subject, referring to 'the present action of the National Union of Railwaymen in relation to workers other than purely railway employees'. He argued that 'this was a common danger to all those employed in the industry' and 'it was necessary to meet the trouble by a united front among other unions catering for transport workers.'[1]

Thereupon a resolution was moved by J. M. Fraser of Aberdeen, where the bulk of the membership were carters employed by the railway contractors and seconded from Glasgow, recognizing

'the need to co-ordinate and equalize wages and conditions in all sections of the industry: and for this purpose to give power to Executive to co-operate, and if necessary to initiate, proposals for joint consultation and joint action with other unions catering for road transport workers.'[2]

The Association's attitude to co-operation with other unions fluctuated with changing pressures. When the Royal Commission (1928–30) took evidence from the workers' side, there was some heart-burning at the degree to which the Transport & General Workers' Union—by far the biggest organization, with over 300,000 members—held the limelight. It rankled, and was remembered for some time against Ernest Bevin's organization. At the 1931 British Trades Union Congress, when the Liverpool & District Carters' & Motormen's Union moved a resolution

---

[1] Annual Report of Conference, 1929.
[2] Report of Annual Conference, 1929.

that the Road Traffic Act, 1930 should be extended to the commercial section, their spokesman took the opportunity to make a sharp complaint that the Royal Commission had said that their union's evidence should merely be submitted in writing, instead of being led before the Commissioners, as that of the Transport & General Workers' Union had been. He said:

'It seems to me that because we are a small union 7,000 strong, we were left out in the cold, while the organization that is 300,000 strong had a representative there. Mr Bevin printed a handy little book for the members of his organization, which is very useful, and in this book it states that this was the only union which gave detailed and unremitting attention to the problems of road transport and the welfare of the men employed on the road.'[1]

That handbook, although no doubt informative and stimulating to Mr Bevin's road transport members, was scarcely tactful; it was likely to irritate the Liverpool Carters, the Manchester-based United Road Transport Workers' Association of 10,000 members, and the Scottish Horse & Motormen's Association's 7,000 or 8,000 farther north again, where wages and conditions were even worse than those which the delegate went on to describe:

'The wages paid to these men are disgraceful. Mr Bevin knows, as we all know, that the competition between road transport workers is horrible. I have been a worker in my union for the past 20 years and our wages are £3 10s a week for driving; but there are men driving today at from 35s to 50s a week.

'I think if we could get support by setting up a National Board to discuss this problem we might do something. As isolated unions we can do nothing, and the quicker we realize that fact the better.'[2]

The Association officials did realize that all too well; but at the same time they were equally conscious that all this implied centralization, and that negotiations for ever centralized in London could mean the end of the Liverpool, Manchester and Scottish organizations. Also there was solid ground at the time for noting the differences area by area; employers' organizations then were also tending to resist anything but area grouping. Any scheme which took into account area organization as well as central negotiations, and found a formula for putting them on a parallel footing, would prove of keen interest. At the same time, as we have seen, the National Union of Railwaymen had its own interests, just as the railway employers and road haulage employers were in conflict.

This is the background to the zigzag moves in the Association's relations

[1] British Trades Union Congress Annual Report, 1931.
[2] British Trades Union Congress Annual Report, 1931.

with other trade unions during the thirties, a decade of such importance to road transport.

Already, in early 1929, the Executive of the Association had decided to call a special conference of the Executive Council and officials 'to consider the position of trade unionism in regard to the present developments in the transport industry'.[1] By summer a Glasgow member was threatened with expulsion for acting as Chairman of a meeting called by the National Union of Railwaymen for railway contractors' men. The Glasgow Trades Council had passed and circulated throughout the Scottish trade union movement a resolution which declared that 'an agreement between all the unions catering for railways and transport workers is absolutely essential if effective organization is to be attained'. Meanwhile there was strong pressure by railway companies and by railway contractors for a decrease in wages; something had to be done. On November 30, 1929, there was a Special Conference of the Executive and officials to discuss 'whether we should consider having closer agreement with the Transport & General Workers' Union, an agreement with the National Union of Railwaymen, or whether we remain as we are'. But the decision was once again to delay, for it was 'agreed to submit a resolution to the Annual General Meeting' ten months ahead, when a resolution sponsored by the Executive was moved to 'have a closer agreement with the Transport & General Workers' Union and that the Executive be empowered to negotiate conditions'. It was carried only by seventeen votes to seven.

By March 1931 the employers were pressing the Industrial Council to cut Glasgow wages by 1s, leaving them below £2 10s, which from October 1, 1931 was to be the minimum wage for carters throughout Scotland. In April 1931, railway companies reduced wages by 1s 6d and the cut was accepted by the railway contractors' men. The Transport & General Workers' Union wrote to the Association regarding the 'proposed alteration in the present working agreement'. But it took until the autumn of 1931, after the fall of the Labour Government, for a measure of agreement to be reached between the Transport & General Workers' Union, the National Union of Distributive and Allied Workers, and the Association, following correspondence and joint meetings about what they should do on the Co-operative Wages Board; they finally agreed to make joint representations. The amicable arrangement did not last long under the pressure of the economic crisis, when 'economy cuts' had been introduced in all Government services, and many other employers seized the opportunity to reduce wages. There were many piecemeal reductions in wages. Even when the crisis receded, the reductions remained for a long time; indeed, it was late in 1934 before the Edinburgh Corporation would agree to 'restore' even half the cuts they had imposed at this stage.

[1] Executive *Minutes*, February 2, 1929.

By March 1932, despite the agreement on joint negotiation on the Co-operative Society Wages Board, the Transport & General Workers' Union and the National Union of Distributive and Allied Workers had nevertheless made separate agreements, pending the completion of negotiations. The joint negotiations were therefore cancelled. It was a sharp set-back and, when the Executive considered in January 1933 an invitation from the Co-operative Wages Board to discuss a new agreement, it was decided to notify the other two unions that on this occasion they would have 'to adhere strictly to any agreement arrived at covering joint action'.

With the attack on wages at this time coming from all sides, the National Union of Railwaymen wrote, on July 19, 1932, to suggest a joint conference to deal with grievances amongst the railway contractors' men, but the Association refused to have anything to do with them. The next month Liverpool & District Carters wrote saying that their employers were trying to get reductions and asking how things were in Scotland. In September 1932 when the Glasgow Corporation decided to cut wages, the Glasgow Trades Council convened a conference of all the trade unions involved. Yet when, in January 1933, the Transport & General Workers' Union proposed a joint meeting to discuss the position of the railway contractors' men, the Executive again refused.

Meanwhile the struggle was continuing between railway and road transport employers, before, during, and after the Salter Report and the Rail and Road Traffic Act, 1933, which followed from it. An important question for the Association was what unions would be represented on the Conciliation Board for Scotland under Section 32 of that Act. During the passage of the Road & Rail Traffic Act, 1933, the Government had promised in the House of Lords that there should be 'a joint voluntary body or bodies' and four 'experts' were named to advise the Minister of Labour about setting up the voluntary machinery. They included Ernest Bevin, General Secretary of the Transport & General Workers' Union, and Albert Denaro of the Liverpool Carters. The National Joint Conciliation Board was inaugurated in London on March 16, 1934, but still no news reached the Association. Would there be a separate Scottish Board, or merely local Boards for the two Traffic Areas in Scotland? Then came the beginning of the breakthrough. On April 7, 1934, the Executive Minutes record that

'It was reported that a committee was to be established for Scotland to deal with questions arising out of the Act. The first thing to be done was to deal with the question of what standard would be adopted to meet the requirements of Section 92, which deals with the Fair Wage clause as defined in Section 93 of the 1930 Act.

'Thereafter the Committee would consider any other questions raised under the Act for the regulation of road transport in Scotland. The Association will be represented on the Committee.'[1]

But the question remained: what would be the strength of the Association's representation? By July 1934 the worst doubts were over: they had received an invitation to the preliminary meetings: 'It was decided that Messrs Webster & Lyon attend meetings to deal with the establishment of the Conciliation Board under Section 32 of the Rail and Road Traffic Act, 1933.'[2]

It seemed that the Association was surviving and successfully staking a claim for recognition in this new world. They felt their strength. A month later, the National Union of Railwaymen wrote suggesting 'the formation of one union for all transport workers'. Two Executive members moved that 'the letter be allowed to lie on the table', but the majority decided, by ten votes to two to remit it 'to the officials for inquiry'. The Scottish Conciliation Board continued to meet at the Central Halls, Glasgow, during the early months of 1935 to fix immediately temporary rates, pending the setting up of permanent rates. This confrontation with the main Scottish employers, or, rather, with those of them who were organized, had begun a long drawn-out struggle.

Into the trials and tribulations and difficulties of the voluntary Conciliation Boards we cannot, at this stage, go in detail. It is enough to say that the difficulties were not less in Scotland, where wages and the level of organization both of workers and employers were lower than in England and Wales. The measure of failure of the voluntary principle was the need to set up the Baillie Committee, whose main provisions were finally incorporated into the Road Haulage Wages Act, 1938. Four years passed in struggle, frustration, diehard obstruction from certain employers, and continued low wages for the transport men. But at this stage we must concentrate on the relations with other unions, which took their zigzag course during this prolonged struggle.

4. BEVIN COMES TO GLASGOW

In the Annual Report of 1934, written in the early months of 1935 in the first exhilaration of joint negotiations, Peter Webster indicated the policy of the Association[3] and weighed up the advantages and weaknesses of the legislation. He stressed that the industry's problems were not yet solved, saying:

[1] Executive *Minutes*, April 7, 1934.
[2] Executive *Minutes*, July 7, 1934.
[3] He was the admitted master; for, as Hugh Lyon wrote in the same report: 'In the past year I have really only played the part of stage manager. . . . He has done all the negotiating on behalf of the motormen in Scotland, dealing with one of the most complicated Acts of Parliament. He has not only mastered the contents, but he has all the details at his finger ends.'

(Annual Report, 1934)

H*

233

'Competition between road and rail will in all probability become more intense. In spite of all this I am convinced that we will steadily get nearer the point of having transport organized as a national service.

'This will call for a new outlook on the part of employers and men engaged in the industry and may call for the consideration of new methods of organization.'

The Transport & General Workers' Union made approaches.[1] On February 2, 1935, the Executive Council received a deputation headed by Ernest Bevin, with Stanley Hirst, Financial Secretary, and J. Edwards, Chairman, together with John Veitch and two others from the Scottish Area of the Transport & General Workers' Union. Mahomet had come to the mountain in West Regent Street, Glasgow.

'Mr Bevin addressed the meeting, dealing with the problems confronting the road transport industry at the moment and the probable trend and result of legislation, and suggesting the need for closer unity among the organizations representing the workers. He instanced several methods by which this object would be achieved.

'After a full discussion and questions the deputation were thanked for their attendance and withdrew.'[2]

The Association remained wary. Two months after the deputation the subject 'was remitted to the Rules Committee for inquiry and report' (Executive Minutes, April 6, 1935); and it was decided to put a proposed alteration to rule[3] to deal with 'amalgamation or working agreements'.

When it came to the Annual Conference on September 7, 1935, Peter Webster once more was the spokesman on this delicate subject; and 'after a full discussion', the following resolution was unanimously adopted:

'1. That the Executive Council be empowered to discuss proposals for amalgamation with any other unions or group of unions with a view to amalgamation.

'2. Establishing of closer relationship with other unions on the basis of any

---

[1] 'A letter was read from the Transport & General Workers' Union suggesting that in consequence of the position created by dealing with motor and general Transport Acts it was desirable that a closer unity be effected between the two unions and offering to appoint a sub-committee of their executive to meet our Executive Council to discuss this. Mr Muir moved and Mr Bishop seconded that we agree to this request. Messrs Heslin and Hammett moved that the matter be left on the table and that no action be taken. The motion was carried by 11 votes to 2.

(Executive *Minutes*, January 5, 1935)

[2] Executive *Minutes*, February 2, 1935.

[3] 'Rule 19a. Add new clause 3. An Annual or Special Delegate Meeting shall on behalf of the Association have power to proceed to amalgamate the Association with any other trade union or group of trade unions, provided that this power can only become operative after a ballot of the members has been taken and the results of the ballot shows that a majority of two-thirds of the members voting are in favour of the proposed amalgamation.'

(Executive *Minutes*, June 8, 1935.)

such proposals being submitted to the members for their approval or otherwise.'[1]

Lyon was absent ill, and young Robert Taylor appeared for the first time. It was Webster's twenty-first year of service, and the Conference recommended that the Executive make him a suitable testimonial, after hearing his speech.

Many months passed with the door to 'closer relationships' left ajar, until it was slammed shut by the attitude which Ernest Bevin took about separate Scottish representation during the deliberations of the Baillie Committee.

5. THE BAILLIE COMMITTEE

The Baillie Committee whose recommendations were the basis of the Road Haulage Wages Act, 1938, had to be set up by the Government when it became clear that the decisions of the 'Salter' National Joint Conciliation Board and the Area Boards were being ignored. It was a small committee, but extremely important, because it not only expressed the lines of development on all sides but partly, perhaps, by the very act of expressing them, it also moulded them. The leading employers and trade unionists were obliged to sit cheek by jowl, as well as face to face across the table. Perhaps it provided some employers with insight into the mind of trade union leaders which they put to use in their campaign, first to oppose, secondly to reverse, the nationalization of road haulage. A remarkable feature of the Baillie Committee was the significant passages affecting Scotland and we must give a brief indication of the character of some of the evidence set before it.

A joint committee was set up by Mr Ernest Brown, Minister of Labour, and Mr L. Hore-Belisha, Minister of Transport, on July 21, 1936; its terms of reference were

'to examine the present position in regard to regulation of wages and conditions of service of persons employed in connection with the carriage of goods by road (whether in vehicles authorized under A, B or C licences) and to make recommendations as to the action which it is desirable to take.'

It was under the chairmanship of Sir James B. Baillie, a philosopher and vice-chancellor of Leeds University, with long experience of conciliation, arbitration courts, and Trade Boards. The other members were Sir Gerald Bellhouse, CBE, and Mr John Forster (later Lord Forster).

They had before them written memoranda from a very wide range of interests, as well as from the National Joint Conciliation Board, the Scottish Conciliation Board, and others. Seventeen days were taken up with oral evidence from representatives of the organizations submitting

[1] Report of Annual Conference, 1935.

memoranda, and it lasted for ten months. The railway companies and the National Union of Railwaymen submitted evidence, as did the employers and unions in the steel trades and shipbuilding and engineering unions, as well as a number of other trade unions, such as the Amalgamated Engineering Union, the General & Municipal Workers, and the Distributive and Allied Workers. The industrial interests included the Mining Association, the Cement-Makers' Association, a large number of such bodies as Chambers of Commerce and employers' federations, which included the Scottish Federation of Aerated Water Manufacturers and the Bottlers Association; the Scottish Association of Master Bakers; and the Scottish Federation of Grocers and Provision Merchants' Associations. In the C-licence section there was extremely important evidence from two contrasting organizations: the Joint Parliamentary Committee of the Co-operative Congress, whose 9,000 mechanically or electrically propelled vehicles belonging only to retail societies accounted for three per cent of all C-licences at the time, and were expected to double in the next five years, and Unilever, with a special carrying company and over 1,100 vehicles. On the state of the low level of organization, the Baillie Report remarked:

'The state of the organization of the industry at the time of the institution of the Board was such that it could not claim to represent the majority of the employers. . . . Being a highly competitive industry the attempt on the part of the Board to lay down a scale of wages met with hostility in many localities and led to local attempts to defeat the purposes of the Board. . . .

'The trade unions represented on the National Board could not claim to have in membership a majority of the workers concerned in the industry . . . (but) until the scheme of wages and conditions was published by the Board, no suggestion was made that it was not fairly representative of the industry.'[1]

The National Board had set up three grades of wages, ranging from those to be applicable to chief ports and industrial centres (Grade 1); other industrial centres (Grade 2); and rural areas (Grade 3). An interim value for these Grades was fixed and the Area Boards left to fit their towns into the grades, but not to vary them. There was much local opposition to this 'hasty procedure', which created 'discord from the first', resulting in long delay, of which the employers took full advantage. The Baillie Report commented

'It was possible for employers, soon after the Board was established, to set up an entirely different district rate of wages from that laid down by the Board for the purpose of circumventing its decisions.'[2]

[1] *Report of the Committee on The Regulation of Wages and Conditions of Service in the Road Motor Transport Industry (Goods).* May, 1937. Cmd. 5440. Para. 25.
[2] op. cit., para. 24.

A classic example was known as 'the Oxford Case', in which an Industrial Court held that it was obliged to 'have regard to any existing district rate', so that when the Board referred to it a complaint of unfair wages, it decided that the rate of wages in the area had already been determined. (22 September 1936. H. Tuckwell & Sons Ltd., Oxford 1659)

'The unreality of the present statutory backing offered to the decisions of the Board was fully exposed by the decision of the Industrial Court in the Oxford case, two years after opposition to the Board's decisions had appeared.'[1]

But what was much more widespread was that the decisions of the Board were simply ignored. The enforcement machinery was 'cumbersome;' only two cases had been before a court and there was no case at all of a licence having been withdrawn or suspended.

The Baillie Committee 'heard many allegations of neglect to keep in proper form the records of journeys' which, it was 'repeatedly stated', were being 'frequently falsified'.[2] Similarly the statutory limitations of hours 'are often not being observed'; whilst the Committee considered that in any event the hours laid down in Section 19 of the Road Traffic Act 'cannot be regarded as prescribing a suitable standard of normal working hours', and recommended that 'steps should be taken, either by amendment of the Act or otherwise, to secure a greater measure of effective control of driving hours.'[3] One of the most brazen and ingenious methods of evasion was given in Appendix G of the main Report; it quoted a contract of employment introduced by an employer, stating that 'as from 14 August 1936 . . . all drivers will be employed as daily servants'. That was defined as meaning the hours permitted under the Road Traffic Act, 1930; and therefore there would be no overtime, and the worker would be subject to one day's notice.

Recommendations, however important, by committees sitting round Ministry tables in Whitehall are one thing; the difficulties in garage and stable, on the job, are another. The problem and what it meant came to life in a list of cases in Scotland included in the memorandum of the Scottish Conciliation Board, gathered by the workers' side. We quote only four, terse and tough, from Appendix J:

'*Case 6*. Two-ton lorries. 45s per week. Firm doing public contract work.'

These are not merely cases of struggling firms, with perhaps an owner-driver and only a couple of vehicles:

---

[1] op. cit., para. 30.

[2] In 1933 a lorry driver was killed in an accident after being at work for 54 hours out of a period of 98 hours. In 1935 a Traffic Commissioner pointed out that a haulier, who had been censured by a court when one of his drivers had died after 24 hours at the wheel with less than an hour's break, was caught breaking the law again within a few months.

[3] op. cit., para. 130.

'*Case 10*. Eight drivers on long-distance work. Minimum wages 30s. Maximum 60s per week. No overtime. Threatened with dismissal if they negotiated with the union.'

Behind that case history, there is the memory of years of appalling unemployment and short-time working. The short wage packet is matched by the long hours:

'*Case 11*. Three drivers worked 90 hours per week. Two youths at 30s. One driver at 60s. On one occasion the week's work consisted of 90 hours. Only 5s allowed for 30 hours booked off. No extra Sunday rate. Run booked so that the speed limit must be exceeded.

'*Case 12*. Three drivers: maximum 50s per week. Average hours 80. No extra payment for Sunday or overtime.'

Ernest Bevin, General Secretary of the Transport & General Workers' Union, who had just become chairman of the British Trades Union Congress, and William Edwards, President of the National Road Transport Employers' Federation, a shrewd employer from north-west England, gave evidence as spokesmen for the National Joint Conciliation Board. They were examined on the National Board's memorandum, one of the recommendations being that the statutory machinery, which they were asking should replace the voluntary Conciliation Board, should not continue separate machinery for Scotland. The spokesmen for workers and employers in England and Wales were both strongly in favour of cutting out the Scottish Conciliation Board, and of having the two traffic areas in Scotland merely send representatives to the National Board like all other traffic areas. The Scottish employers and workers were equally emphatic that Scotland should have a separate Board.

The Scottish Board which had only been set up after strong representations by the Association, had negotiated an interim agreement, only to have the National Board come out with the grade system. Scotland had then adopted Grade 2, which they made applicable throughout Scotland, leaving any employer who thought it too high to make the case for it to be varied in respect of his particular town or district. When questioned on the first day of evidence, September 29, 1936, Ernest Bevin said:

'It has been rather difficult to get a uniform approach to the problem, as between Scotland and England. . . . We have made a report which was not applied in Scotland. Now transport is a very mobile thing. The traffic cannot be divided by a border.'[1]

He said that there was unrest and competition between the English areas and the Scottish areas; decisions of the Board should be equally applicable all through:

[1] *Minutes of Evidence*, Q. 21.

'You get vehicles running from Newcastle, Hull, London and everywhere else to Glasgow and to the North, and equally their vehicles running down. It becomes a tremendous competitive factor unless the Board's decisions apply to both.'

He was doubtful if 'closer co-operation on an agreed basis' would meet the case; loads had to be split up in Glasgow. The Railway companies had never been able to do it and had applied their grades to Scottish towns 'in proportion to their importance, exactly as they did in England; and on the passenger side of our industry we have had to do precisely the same thing'.[1] If there were two Boards, one would have to give its decision first

'England and Wales being the largest area, the National Board would have to give its decision and Scotland would have to co-operate; and Scotland would say: 'We were not in at the making' and there would be the opportunity for a sheer nationalist attitude to some extent, if I may say so, that would block the co-operation. Whereas if the Scottish representatives have proper representation on the Board and are in on the making they would give effect to it exactly the same way as the other areas in England.'[2]

One of the leading English employers, Roger W. Sewell, giving evidence on October 12, 1936, objected strongly to Scotland's having a separate Board. He said bluntly: 'At the present time the Border raids are being repeated, that is to say, Scotsmen come over the Border and raid Newcastle and other Border towns.'[3] The basis for this was that the Scottish transport worker was more severely exploited even than those in England and Wales. The Scottish employer could therefore compete to advantage against the English employers, even if some of the latter were more highly capitalized. But, if the wage-grading were fixed in London? As it stood, all Scotland, including Glasgow and Edinburgh, were Grade 2 only: Newcastle, Liverpool, and Manchester were Grade 1. Here was the basis for the display of the 'nationalist attitude' on either side of the Border.

6. WEBSTER'S EVIDENCE

The Scots gave evidence on October 19, 1936. Mr T. Worsley, who led for the employers, having said that the Scottish Conciliation Board might represent sixty per cent of the total licence-holders, was asked whether the Scottish employers wanted a separate Board. He replied: 'The opinion is practically unanimous in the trade that Scotland ought to have its own Board.'[4] There were, he said, 'separate characteristics' and different legal procedure. Peter Webster was closely questioned as to how they had

---

[1] op. cit., Q.23.
[2] op. cit., Q.24.
[3] op. cit., Q.459.
[4] op. cit., Q.986.

arrived at the interim agreement and finally reached the Grade 2 figure. He explained that earlier they had established a minimum for drivers of two tons and upwards of £2 19s, and had built up scales for lighter and heavier vehicles round it, and it had been agreed with the Scottish Horse & Motor Contractors' Federation. That was their starting-point on the Scottish Conciliation Board.

CHAIRMAN: 'And you were satisfied that that was a fair standard of wages to start with?'
WEBSTER: 'We were satisfied that it was the best wage we could obtain at that particular time.'[1]

They had finally reached the figure by taking this and wages in the South, and by concessions between the parties. Even so, the Dumfries employers had thought it so much too high that they had withdrawn from the Conciliation Board. When Webster was asked whether the wages being paid were 'much below your standard', he replied that in the industrial centres the standard wage was being paid by seventy per cent of the employers, but there were 'continuous evasions' in the rural areas. But, where the wages were paid, what of the hours? Webster described conditions in the West Lothian district, instancing an employer who was paying wages 'not for 40 hours, but for round about 65–70 hours; but I could not take him to the industrial Court, because he is simply paying what every other body is paying and that is why we want the Fair Wages Clause amended.'[2]

He said that the Association represented 10,000, and John Veitch some 4,000 in the Transport & General Workers' Union in Scotland: 'Generally speaking we are not so badly off in Scotland about the wages, but on the question of overtime and the other conditions of the agreement observance is practically 20 per cent.' It was not, he said, 'a blank refusal to pay overtime; but it is just that the employers, generally speaking, give a man so much as he has earned, so much for a day's work, but they do not get the number of hours that the log sheet shows'. He insisted:

'I am not worrying so much about wages. It is our particular work to fix the wages, and I am not asking the Government to fix wages. I certainly agree there should be a minimum under which no man should be paid, and I am prepared to take the responsibility of fixing the wages. But I do want some method that, the wages having been fixed, they should become compulsory on the industry and forced to be applied in a manner we cannot have at this time.'[3]

When asked why he objected to the proposal that it should be a condition of the licence that an employer should join an organization, he replied:

[1] op. cit., Q.996.
[2] op. cit., Q.1053.
[3] op. cit., Q.1051.

'Because we fear that it would lead ultimately to compulsory arbitration.'[1]

Now that we can see what was the background of the 'separate characteristics' of the industry in Scotland, it is of interest to compare what the Scottish employers' and workers' representatives had to say as to whether there should be a separate Board for Scotland. Worsley replied:

'While we have no disrespect for the South we feel it is a rather cumbersome matter that our local negotiations should be conducted so far away as London. We find in Edinburgh or Glasgow we can get a better expression of local opinion and there would be no objection at all after the whole matter has been thrashed out to adjust our proposal with those in the South.

'We quite appreciate that the Board has a desire of uniformity, but we do not think it would be helped by a system that would largely savour of a dictatorship; because after all, the tail cannot wag the dog and there are many more interests in the South, and we feel we might be swept into the welter.'[2]

Webster said that he noted all the Areas were cleaning up their own difficulties:

'We in Scotland think we can clean up ours, and we should always be ready to collaborate, and if possible in a saner method than has been adopted. Today we might very favourably consider further linking up. But we were told quite definitely that England and Wales were to have a Board and that we in Scotland may not get one.'

Sir Gerald Bellhouse asked him whether he did not think there was real dissatisfaction, and whether they would be prepared to 'receive orders from the Board as to what you are to do in Scotland?' Webster replied: 'The real reason behind our opposition is this: that we feel that it is a big enough job for Scotsmen to clean up the present chaotic conditions in Scotland before we hand over our troubles to someone else and take over other people's burdens.'[3] When the Baillie Committee came to report, they considered that virtually all the problems applied equally to Scotland, and one of the factors they took carefully into account, when considering whether independent machinery should continue to operate in Scotland, was the question of unfair competition. Their conclusion was as follows: 'It has been reported to us by employers in England and particularly in the Northern Traffic Area that they are at present subjected to unfair competition by reason of the fact that Scottish employers whose vehicles run into England pay lower wages, and we are satisfied that the fact of competition is established. We do not consider

[1] op. cit., Q.1128.
[2] op. cit., Q.1029.
[3] op. cit., Q.1032.

that competition in itself is undesirable and it is perhaps inevitable. We do however consider that steps should be taken to ensure that it occurs on a common basis of fair wages.'[1]

They recommended that Scotland should not have a separate Board.

That spring, the Transport and General Workers' Union had submitted to the Association a provisional scheme for amalgamation; now it was unanimously agreed by the Executive 'to have nothing whatever to do with the scheme'.[2] After considering the Report of the Baillie Committee, which had adopted Bevin's standpoint, the Executive decided to put all possible pressure to persuade the Government to accept the policy of separate machinery for Scotland, for which Peter Webster had argued so forcefully, though unsuccessfully.

But there had been some notable changes at the Association's head office. Hugh Lyon had been dismissed after thirty-four years in office; Robert Taylor had defeated Peter Webster in the election for a new General Secretary; Peter Webster himself had been demoted from the position of Assistant General Secretary, which he had held for sixteen years, and put in charge of the Insurance Department. It was, therefore, Robert Taylor, the new General Secretary, who took over negotiations with the Ministries.

At that year's Annual Conference, Taylor spoke on the 'suggestion that the sole right of initiating proposals should rest with a central authority in London, and asked conference to register its emphatic protest against such a principle'. It did so, affirming

'its belief in the right of men in Scotland to be responsible for the initiation of and negotiating for wages and conditions affecting themselves without reference to a body in London. This conference further declares that nothing short of the establishment of a rate-fixing tribunal for the industry in Scotland will eliminate the unfair competition which is being experienced by decent employers by the worst type of employer in the country.'[3]

Pressure was kept up; when the Road Haulage Wages Act 1938 was finally passed in July, Scotland had its Wages Board as well as representation on the Central Wages Board, even if it did not have the right to initiate claims.

7. THE ROAD HAULAGE WAGES ACT

The Road Haulage Wages Act which was to bring with it national status for the road transport unions, came into force on July 13, 1938, and set up machinery through a system of national and area wages boards on which both sides were represented, their decisions having the force of law. With relatively minor changes, its machinery was still in force twenty-five years later. As well as ensuring minimum wages and conditions for

[1] Baillie Report, para. 63.
[2] Executive *Minutes*, April 4, 1937.
[3] Report of Annual Conference, 1937.

those employed by A- and B-licence-holders, it made parallel provision for protection of those employed by C-licence-holders. The Minister of Transport was empowered to set up a Road Haulage Central Wages Board, a Scottish Road Haulage Area Wages Board, and boards for other areas. The Central Board was to have the power to submit to the Minister proposals for fixing wages and holiday pay for workers employed by A- and B-licence-holders, after first sending a draft to every area affected. The Board was to have power to specify the time to be worked 'in any day or in any week respectively in order to render payable any daily or weekly rate proposed by the Board; to specify the number of hours of employment by his employer after which any overtime payment proposed is to be payable, and generally to make such provision as may be necessary for specifying the work in respect of which any remuneration proposed is to be payable and for enabling the remuneration payable to any worker to be ascertained.' This was a most important clause; for, in the event, the road haulage employers proved to be far keener to resist limitation of hours than increase of wages. Other powers of the Central Board included making recommendations about safety on the roads, 'the health and comfort of workers', and any other matter 'affecting the efficiency of and conditions of work in connection with the transport of goods'. As soon as the Minister should make 'a road haulage wages order', its terms and the sum mentioned in it should come into force as 'statutory remuneration'. Employers were then bound to observe it.

If a worker employed by a C-licence-holder considered his remuneration unfair, he or his trade union, 'or a trade union which in the opinion of the Minister represents a substantial number of workers employed in road haulage work', could apply to the Minister for him to refer the dispute to the Industrial Court[1] for settlement.

[1] The Industrial Court is not a court of law, neither are its decisions legally enforceable; it has, however, been held that, where a decision had been accepted or acted upon, it forms a term or condition of the contract of employment. Its history arises from events which took place in Scotland. It was an indirect outcome of the power of the Shop Stewards' Movement on Clydeside during the First World War. In October 1916, the government set up 'the Whitley Committee', under the chairmanship of Mr J. H. Whitley, MP, the Speaker of the House of Commons, to make recommendations 'for securing a permanent improvement in the relations between employers and workmen.' One of its recommendations was that there should be set up a standing Arbitration Council to which 'differences of general principles' could be referred where the parties had failed to agree 'through their ordinary procedure and wish to refer the differences to arbitration'.

Accordingly, immediately after the war, following the great Clydeside campaign on hours, briefly described in Chapter Nine, the Industrial Court was established under the Industrial Courts Act, 1919. The President is appointed by the Minister of Labour and the two full-time members from panels of employers and workers. Where the Court's members cannot agree, the President has the powers of Umpire. The Court may also be asked to advise the Minister on any question, usually about a trade dispute, which he may refer to it.

Industrial agreements often provide for reference of outstanding disputes to the Court, both parties agreeing to abide by the decision. Increasing use has been made of it in Acts of Parliament, notably the Road Traffic Acts.

The standard of fairness by which the Industrial Court should be guided was whether the wage was equivalent to what would be payable under a road haulage wages order; or in accordance with any agreement in force between employers and trade unions in the same trade; or equivalent to similar work of other employers where a wages agreement was in force in the district; or following a decision of a joint industrial council or the like, or a decision of an Industrial Court.

The Act put transport unions into a wholly new position. To begin with, it forced recognition upon employers; it obliged them to accept collective bargaining and agreements; it gave wage awards statutory enforcement; and, whether they liked it or not, in the last resort employers had to go to arbitration. It was bound to give a considerable impetus to recruitment to a union amongst the very large number of motormen who were not organized. A union which was already strong enough to rank, in the Minister's opinion, as representing a substantial number of employees, was well in; any other was—out. On the one hand, there was national recognition by Government and employers alike; on the other, total eclipse. Wages Board negotiations thenceforth would occupy a very important place in the activities of any road transport union. Decisions there would influence negotiations with all other types of employer and other transport workers. Eighteen months of hard negotiation still had to be gone through before the Act yielded its first-fruits in the shape of the first Road Haulage Statutory Order, which did not take effect until the fifth month of the war, on January 29, 1940. To some it seemed at that stage of more absorbing importance than the Second World War. Years of hard and intensive bargaining had been necessary before the machinery was complete and in action.

CHAPTER FOURTEEN

THE OLD LEADERS GO

I. LYON IS CALLED UPON TO RETIRE

After the Baillie Committee had reported in May 1937, there were more battles before the Act was passed fourteen months later, and Scotland was assured the separate machinery for which the Socttish employers and the Association continued to fight, the Transport & General Workers' Union being amongst their antagonists. Many more months were still to pass before the first statutory wages order had been forced through the new machinery. By that time the expected war had already begun, if taking an unexpected course, and the new problems of wartime were troubling transport workers. But the earlier leaders were not there to meet these problems; both Hugh Lyon and Peter Webster had been ousted from the leadership within months of each other. Hugh Lyon, it is true, had been in failing health and occasionally threatening to resign for seven years or more, and as he himself said back in 1934, he had left all the disputes and the negotiations to Webster. It was obvious enough that Lyon was not capable of dealing with the new types of problems and opportunities facing transport workers. But Peter Webster was a different matter. He was younger; he had had over twenty-one years of experience as an official of the Association, in which he served as Assistant General Secretary for sixteen years. He was well known throughout the Scottish labour movement, having served for six years as a General Council member of the STUC, as well as being a past President. He was a director of the Cowlairs Co-operative Society for ten years, and was a director and chairman of the Civic Press. For half a dozen years he had carried virtually all the executive work on his shoulders, at a time when the ageing Lyon had shown himself almost pathologically opposed to spending any sum at all from the hoarded funds of the Association.[1] Yet the busy Peter

[1] The following table shows the net membership, the general fund (only), and the funds per head for the years 1930 to 1936.

Year	Membership	General Fund	Per Head
1930	8,261	£118,686	£14·3
1931	8,079	£124,345	£15·3
1932	7,596	£131,295	£17·4
1933	8,549	£136,691	£15·9
1934	8,824	£143,193	£16·2
1935	9,042	£145,776	£16·1
1936	8,857	£149,174	£16·9

Webster, the obvious successor, who had led the Association members through the complexities of this decade of legislation and struggle for national recognition, was not at the wheel when the way ahead reached open country at last.

The main drive to shift the two leaders came from the West Coast branches, such as Glasgow and Paisley; the strong support for Lyon was in Edinburgh, Aberdeen and Kirkcaldy. These were the five biggest branches. Edinburgh was two-fifths the size of Glasgow, but had double Aberdeen's membership. But Glasgow had more members than all other branches put together. Robert Taylor had been their Minute Secretary since before 1927; in the thirties he had been their delegate to the Glasgow Trades Council. Dissatisfaction with Lyon's leadership or lack of leadership, was expressed in a number of ways. Glasgow had pressed unsuccessfully since the early thirties for a Rules Revision Committee; they objected to officials being eligible to be appointed chairman of annual conference, and to conference delegates being prohibited from becoming candidates for the Executive; and they took the strongest exception to a favourite plan of Lyon's, to sell part of the ground of the Convalescent Home at Cardross to the Dumbarton County Council. Above all, they wanted a vigorous campaigning trade union, which would give a militant organizing drive priority over friendly society benefits. Older members of the Association described Lyon's reaction: 'To Lyon this seemed the Communist bogy, which made him see red, and reduced him sometimes to incoherent rage.' Signs of friction mounted through the early thirties, but they should be seen not only against the background of years of unemployment, short-time working, and wage cuts: the composition of the membership, a large proportion of whom were still horsemen, was also important. Lyon was inactive; Webster's main concern could be represented as being overmuch for the motormen, since, as we have seen, the well-publicized struggle with the road transport legislation was in progress all this time. It was perhaps significant that we find, in Robert Taylor's neat handwriting, this minute of the Glasgow quarterly meeting at the Central Halls, just after Webster had triumphantly forced an agreement through the Conciliation Board: 'Mr Webster gave a lengthy report of the wages negotiations with the Conciliation Board and explained the interim agreement which had been arrived at. . . . Many questions were asked and answered and there was a general expression of opinion that the next move should be to do something for the carters.'[1] This emphasis was repeated more than once, and not only in Glasgow.

But from 1935, a new factor arose in that a number of permanent collectors defaulted in several of the big centres, including Glasgow, Paisley, and Kirkcaldy. The south-east was particularly unfortunate, both

[1] Glasgow Minute Book, March 10, 1935.

Leith and Edinburgh suffering severe losses. Whilst methods of meeting the situation gave rise to differences of opinion, these events became the occasion for bringing up an old grievance: the lack of resources devoted to organizing work. There was strong pressure for the appointment of organizers, especially from the East of Scotland. It was hoped that a new organizer would be appointed in Edinburgh, but, in November 1934, Lyon appointed Councillor Alexander Cathcart, who was an extremely busy man on the Edinburgh Town Council, not as an organizer but as collector only. A newcomer to the Executive from Edinburgh, Alex Bishop, unsuccessfully objected to Cathcart's appointment as collector, and a major storm blew up on the Executive, which lasted almost without pause from January 1935 until Lyon's suspension in August 1936. Supported by some of the Glasgow Executive members, Bishop urged that Cathcart should be called upon to resign, on the ground that, with his town council work, he could not devote all his energies to the Association, and the Executive agreed upon this by six votes to five. The decision was opposed in Edinburgh when Webster went to the next quarterly meeting there, but he failed to convince them. It had to be recorded that 'one of our officials has definitely decided not to act in accordance with decisions of the Executive Committee and officials at Head Office were instructed to take all necessary steps to deal with the position in Edinburgh'.[1] Webster had to deal with this, because Lyon at that August meeting had been granted 'leave of absence for three months, or such longer time as may be required to restore his health', and Webster was unanimously 'appointed Interim Secretary during the period Mr Lyon is off'. At the next Executive, a Trade Committee reported 'that Mr Cathcart has refused to resign and the committee recommend his dismissal; that as the applications had not thrown up any outstanding applicants . . . no organizer be appointed in Edinburgh meantime; that a new Collector be appointed for Edinburgh; and that the whole position in Edinburgh and the East of Scotland be reviewed at the beginning of next year.'[2]

This was calculated to cause some comment on the eve of Annual Conference, to which Cathcart was a delegate and which Robert Taylor attended for the first time, Webster acting as General Secretary in Lyon's absence. With Lyon out of action on indefinite sick leave, pressure against him eased during that autumn, and the rebels concentrated their fire on the Interim General Secretary, Peter Webster. One of the recommendations from the 1935 Conference had been that the incoming Executive should 'suitably recognize' the completion of Webster's twenty-one years as an official. This led to a discussion at the next Executive which should have served as a warning signal. The chairman, R. S.

[1] Executive *Minutes*, August 3, 1935.
[2] Executive *Minutes*, September 7, 1935.

Anderson, from Hamilton, raised the question, remitted from the Annual Conference, of the testimonial. There was opposition from the Glasgow delegates.[1]

Then the whole weight of the attack swung back against Hugh Lyon. At the Glasgow Quarterly meeting in November 1935, where 'there was an exceptionally large attendance', Taylor was absent and Webster presented the Executive minutes, reported on the Annual Conference, and himself took the minutes of the meeting. These were later challenged in that he had failed to record a resolution 'to the effect that Mr Lyon had to attend the next meeting of this branch'. When Lyon did not attend the next meeting, at which Taylor, in Webster's absence, presented the Executive minutes, the storm broke: 'The question of the work done by officials of the Association was then raised and Mr D. Connell moved: "That we call upon Mr Lyon, General Secretary, to retire and make him an honorary President of the Association." Mr McKenna seconded and after some discussion the motion was carried unanimously.'[2]

A fortnight later, with Lyon back from sick leave, the next stage of the battle was fought out in the Executive. Hammett and Hyland moved 'that Mr Lyon be asked to resign and make him an honorary President of the Association'. Bulloch (Ayr) and McKenzie (Leith) led the opposition, but the motion was carried by five to four, with some six abstentions. The decision was, however, modified, on the motion of Hamilton and Kirkcaldy members: 'A further amendment was moved by Messrs Irvine and Connolly that no action be taken till this matter has been submitted to all the branches.'[3] This was agreed by eight to six. The rebels followed this up by an attack on Webster's testimonial: 'Mr Webster was asked to retire as it was proposed to give further consideration to the question of the testimonial. Mr Webster intimated to the EC that he did not desire this matter to be raised again.' But the Lanark protest ended in the doubling of the grant.

Now the dog-fight switched to the branches. Lyon began to see danger ahead and felt the need to rally his supporters outside Glasgow. He wrote to J. M. Fraser, secretary of Aberdeen branch:

[1] Messrs Hyland and Hammett moved that no action be taken; Messrs Heslin and Bannatyne moved that a grant be made. Four members voted for each proposal and the Chairman gave his casting vote in favour of making a grant.'
(Executive Minutes, October 5, 1935)
Support for Webster came at this stage from Hamilton and the old Paisley member, H. Heslin, who then moved, seconded by W. McKenzie (Leith), that a grant of £25 should be made, which was agreed. When this minute went for approval to the quarterly meetings, Lanark took objection 'to the meagre grant given to Mr Webster's testimonial', and the Hamilton delegates on the Executive narrowly succeeded in forcing it to be rescinded and the sum raised to £50.
[2] Glasgow Branch *Minutes*, February 23, 1936.
[3] Executive *Minutes*, March 7, 1936.

March 10, 1936

'PRIVATE

Mr J. Fraser,

Aberdeen

'Dear Fraser,

'We are having some trouble here with some of the Executive, especially four or five of them who have stood for jobs and didn't get them. Webster will give you full details, but meantime you might try and get the best of your members to turn out to the meeting. I would have come up to this meeting, but don't think it wise, but hope to be at your next one. I would like also to see you appointed to the Annual Conference which is to be in Aberdeen this year, as some very important questions are likely to come up.

'Yours truly,

H. LYON'

There was a full meeting at Aberdeen when Webster went to put the Executive's resolution to the third largest branch: 'Mr George Paterson moved that this meeting of Aberdeen members having learned from the minutes of the EC of a proposal that Mr Lyon be asked to resign the post of General Secretary as such, and regrets that such proposal had been made and instructs Mr Fraser, local secretary, to inform the EC that in the meeting's opinion Mr Lyon should not be asked to resign the General Secretaryship; and places on record their appreciation of his long and valued service to the Association.'[1]

This was seconded by William Middleton, while Robert McIntyre moved no action; but the protest in favour of Lyon was carried by thirty-one votes to five. Lyon's opponents were even less successful at the quarterly meeting at Edinburgh and Leith, the second largest branch. Unlike Glasgow, which was overwhelmingly against Lyon and also, as it proved, against Webster, Edinburgh was divided. At the Free Gardeners' Hall, after Webster had read the Executive Minutes, there was a sequel: 'Mr Annal moved that the meeting express its complete confidence in Mr Lyon as General Secretary. Mr Mitchell seconded. Mr Cathcart moved as an amendment that EC members be instructed to support the demand for the resignation of the General Secretary. Mr W. Bryden, jun, seconded.'[2] But only Bishop voted with the opponents and the vote of confidence in Lyon was carried by forty-four votes to three. Of the Edinburgh District representatives on the Executive, William McKenzie of Leith voted consistently with 'the Lyonites', and Bishop as firmly with his opponents. Now the counter-attack was taken further: 'Mr Annal raised the question of Mr Bishop's conduct as an EC member in supporting

[1] Aberdeen Branch Quarterly Meeting Minutes, March 15, 1936.
[2] Edinburgh & Leith District Quarterly Meeting Minutes, April 4, 1936.

the motion calling for the resignation of the General Secretary and moved that he be no longer regarded as representing the District on that body. Mr Henderson seconded and on a show of hands 19 voted for the motion and 13 against.'[1]

Bishop's term of office did not expire until the end of the year, and any new nomination would have to go before the Annual Conference in September. Lyon, however, thought he could seize the opportunity to reduce the number of his opponents on the Executive, by treating Bishop as no longer a member and ceasing to call him to their meetings. This side issue was to cause the final rift, and to range the majority of the Executive against Lyon. At the July Executive 'the question was raised why Mr Bishop, Edinburgh, had not been notified to attend meeting'. Lyon quoted the Edinburgh decision 'that he was not to remain on the EC as their nominee'. The leading Glaswegians, Hammett and Hyland, moved that, notwithstanding, Bishop 'be notified to attend the next meeting, and this was agreed to'. When Muir (Glasgow) and Connolly (Kirkcaldy) moved that the meeting adjourn until Bishop had been notified to attend, the motion was lost only by a margin of four votes to five. Main (Glasgow) and Irvine (Hamilton) went on to move 'that Mr Lyon, General Secretary be censured for acting on the instructions of the Edinburgh meeting, as such in their opinion was contrary to rule'.[2]

2. LYON IS DISMISSED

But Lyon dug his heels in; he did not summon Bishop to the next month's Executive, nor did he attend himself. Thereupon, Hyland and Hammett moved that they adjourn at once 'and that the General Secretary notify Mr Bishop to attend'; in addition Lyon himself was also 'instructed to attend'. The motion was carried by seven to four, and the meeting closed. When the Executive next met, it was the final breach. Hammett and Hyland immediately moved 'that Mr Lyon, General Secretary, be suspended. As an amendment Messrs McKenzie and Bulloch moved that this matter be delayed until next EC meeting. The motion was carried by 9 votes to 3'.[3] The same members then moved 'that Mr Webster be appointed Interim General Secretary, and this was unanimously agreed to, and further that Mr Taylor be Assistant Secretary'. The next day was the Glasgow quarterly meeting, with Hyland presiding and Webster speaking to the Executive Members. Over 200 were present. In discussing the Annual Conference, two weeks ahead, they decided: 'On the motion of Messrs Wilkie and Jardine it was unanimously agreed that the delegates be mandated to vote for the resignation of the General Secretary.'[4]

[1] Edinburgh and Leith District Quarterly Meeting Minutes, April 4, 1936.
[2] Glasgow Branch *Minutes*, August 23, 1936.
[3] Executive Minutes, July 4, 1936.
[4] Executive *Minutes*, August 22, 1936.

On Monday, August 24, 1936, after this momentous week-end a letter was written to Hugh Lyon telling him that he had been suspended. Lyon then began a campaign both public and private. He called in aid the secretary of the Glasgow Trades Council, Ben Shaw, the Secretary of the Scottish TUC, William Elger, and the Lord Provost, Patrick J. Dollan. There were private conferences and counter-conferences, and much correspondence. Lyon kept in close touch with his key supporters, such as Fraser.[1]

He went to see Dugald Connell who had moved the resolution against him in Glasgow, and produced a letter of withdrawal for Connell to sign. Connell refused to withdraw, and there were vehement exchanges. When he found the tide running against him, Lyon sent a circular letter to every delegate attending the Annual Conference at Aberdeen on September 5th. It was a belated appeal to the members, from whom he had been so long remote.

This intemperately-worded letter was too much. At the eve-of-conference Executive meeting, even his most ardent supporters, Bulloch (Ayr) and McKenzie (Edinburgh), had to confine their efforts to winning for him the right to resign. They pleaded for a committee 'to consult with Mr Lyon on the basis of his resignation'. But the motion carried, by eight votes to three, was 'that Mr Lyon be dismissed and hand over all keys'.[2] At the Annual Conference later in the day, at which Hammett of Glasgow was elected Chairman, there were thirty-six delegates; sixteen were officials, four being full-time. One of these, the old Lyonite, J. M. Fraser of Aberdeen, tried to move in his defence, but he was ruled out of order, whilst the Paisley delegate, Tom Berrey,[3] 'congratulated the EC on the manner in which they had tackled this question and submitted that as a result of the decision of the Executive the matter was one which the Conference should not discuss.'[4] Supported by Willie Hunter of Glasgow, he then moved the next business, which Conference supported. At the close of the meeting, Fraser asked that 'the Executive should consider sympathetically the suitable recognition of the long service of Mr Lyon with a view to providing a retiring allowance'. The last word was with Tom Berrey. Supported again by Hunter, he moved that 'the time was now opportune for a revision of the rules of the organization', and that 'an opportunity be given the branches for sending in amendments'. This

---

[1] He wrote to him on August 26, 1936:
'I think your letter has summed up the position very well, and I will have a talk with you before the Conference.

'You will have learned of the difficulties we are having down here, but I think everything will come all right.

'However, I can tell you in confidence that this matter was not discussed at any meeting of the EC and must have been a private meeting, not under the auspices of the Society.'

[2] Executive *Minutes*, September 5, 1936.

[3] Fourteen years later, Tom Berrey was himself to preside over an annual conference when there was bitter dissension in the Association, and the assistant to the fourth General Secretary had been dismissed.

[4] Annual Conference, September 5, 1936.

attitude was typical, especially on the West Coast, amongst the active members. The basic reason why Lyon's dismissal was accepted by the membership without protest lay in the general feeling that a complete overhaul was needed of everything savouring of the old Carters' Association, and that Lyon's continued existence as chief official blocked progress. Where there was uneasiness and misgiving about the methods used, they were quickly overshadowed by the lengths to which Lyon himself went in his rough fight back. At an early stage he wrote to say that he proposed, later, to resign, and the Edinburgh quarterly meeting gave him some support by a vote of forty-seven to thirty-five. But he followed this by a Press announcement on Sunday, October 25, 1936, in which he insisted that he was still General Secretary; at this the Executive had to call a special meeting, and send a letter drafted by their legal adviser, Mr Peter Doig.

Lyon's campaign was at its height during October 1936, when the branches were holding special meetings, each with an EC member present, to decide on nominations for the new General Secretary. There are no records of the largest at Glasgow; but their branch nomination went to Robert Taylor, their own minutes' secretary. At the second largest, Edinburgh and Leith, Webster received the nomination by eighty-four votes to Taylor's thirty-six. But at Lyon's stronghold in Aberdeen, there was a different opinion. Mr William Grant 'intimated that as chairman he felt that the minutes of the EC containing a decision on their part to dismiss Mr Lyon ought to have come before a meeting for full discussion before nominations for a successor were in order; and in addition that it was his opinion that it was the members who must have the right of dismissal'. There was considerable discussion; and finally a resolution was carried, with only one vote against,

'that no nomination be made until a meeting was held giving full explanations as to Mr Lyon's dismissal'.[1]

3. THE LAST OF PETER WEBSTER

During this period, Peter Webster had been preparing the case to be submitted to the Baillie Committee, before which he gave evidence on October 19, 1936. A fortnight later the nominations were considered at a special meeting of the Execution Council on October 31, 1936, the minutes of which were taken by the Association's legal adviser Peter Doig. It was found that nine branches had nominated Webster and thirteen Taylor, whilst Aberdeen with two others had made no nomination.[2] With the

[1] Aberdeen Branch *Minutes*, October 18, 1936.

[2] For Webster: Edinburgh, Kirkcaldy, Falkirk, Kilmarnock, Inverness, Alexandria, Motherwell, Lanark, and Musselburgh.

For Taylor: Glasgow, Paisley, Perth, Dunfermline, Ayr, Bathgate, West Calder, Stirling, Dundee, Airdrie, Dumbarton, Wigtown, and Cowdenbeath.

No nomination: Aberdeen, Alloa, and Rothesay.

exception of Dundee and Bathgate, which was his home town, Taylor's support was overwhelmingly from the West Coast.

The election was carried through with every precaution to avoid occasion for criticism, Peter Doig being Returning Officer; the votes were counted and the results declared at a special meeting of the Executive Council on November 29, 1936. It was the first entry in the EC Minute Book in Taylor's hand. Doig reported that of the 7,760 ballot papers duly distributed, 6,109 were returned, of which 208 were spoiled. There remained 5,901 valid votes. The result was

Robert Taylor	3,645
Peter Webster	2,256
Majority	1,389

In an extraordinarily high poll for a trade union election of seventy-eight per cent, Taylor had received sixty-one per cent of the valid votes cast. 'It was thereafter agreed that the General Secretary be instructed to call in an independent auditor for the purpose of examining the Association's books and submitting a report thereon, if possible, by Saturday, December 5th,'[1]

The Association had now got its third General Secretary. The first General Secretary, John Sampson, might well have reflected that Lyon had been treated with infinitely greater forbearance than he had used towards his predecessor: there had been no question of the membership being consulted when Lyon had ousted Sampson. But the spectacle of an important trade union having a public brawl with a man who had been its General Secretary for thirty-four years was not at all edifying for the Scottish labour movement. It was bad enough to have to resort to lawyer's letters and to take legal advice on possible actions for slander and libel; now there had been the election conducted by lawyers, at a cost of £128 5s 0d. In the short term, this upheaval was doing the Association's name no good. At the first meeting under the new régime, the Executive Council took energetic action. First, steps were taken to put the banking arrangements in order; Lyon had kept no current account, moneys being put in from time to time on a deposit receipt in his name. However, it had been reported 'that everything was in order although the auditor would submit a report recommending certain changes in the system'.[2] Legal advice was centralized in Mr Peter Doig's firm. A committee of five was appointed 'to consult with the General Secretary upon the question of staffing the Association'. Finally, 'It was agreed to place on record the appreciation of the Executive Council and members of the work which

[1] Executive *Minutes*, November 29, 1936.
[2] Executive *Minutes*, December 5, 1936.

Mr Lyon did in the early days of the Association and the success which had attended the organization under his guidance.'[1]

When it came to expressing it in money, a decision to make a pension of half-salary (£5 a week), and to review it at the end of the year, was carried by eight to five, against a proposal to make a £250 grant. This might have been thought likely to have a soothing effect on the membership, but the proposal did not have a wholly easy passage. In Glasgow there was strong objection to the payment and approval of the minute as presented by Taylor was carried by 157 to 52 only 'after a long discussion'.[2] In Aberdeen, Taylor met resistance from the opposite point of view. At their December quarterly meeting, Taylor had to explain 'in detail generally the reasons leading to the decisions of the EC both as to the suspension of Mr Lyon and ultimately his dismissal. Numerous questions were put by the chairman and others regarding Mr Lyon's position and these were answered by Mr Taylor and Mr Hammett. There being a difference of opinion regarding the EC's powers to dismiss the General Secretary Mr Taylor intimated that the EC had obtained opinion of counsel and had been advised that they had such powers.'[3] After members had had pointed out to them that the Executive proposed the pension, they agreed to adopt the minute. Taylor also attended Edinburgh's meeting: it may be noted that Peter Webster was never again sent to address a branch meeting, although he had almost always taken the quarterly meetings in the four main cities for the past dozen years. At Edinburgh no objection was raised to the Executive Minute which covered Lyon's pension; but Taylor was pressed with questions about the need for an organizer for the East of Scotland, and also about the small representation of the East Coast on the new Executive Council, where there were only two members, Cathcart of Edinburgh and Fraser of Perth. Out of fourteen members, no less than eight were from Glasgow, Hamilton, and Paisley.

At their first meeting on January 9, 1937, the Executive appointed the long awaited Rules Revision Committee, and asked branches for amendments. Hammett and Hyland were elected chairman and vice-chairman. But most important was the recommendation of the Special Committee on Staff, which had agreed 'to advertise for two Organizers who would be under the immediate control of Head Office, and a man for the office to look after the register of members, contributions and claims'. Before the end of the month the three appointments had been made. Two were Glasgow men: Willie Hunter, Taylor's former fellow delegate to the Glasgow Trades Council, and W. Fulton, who had succeeded Taylor as Glasgow minutes secretary. The third, now appointed organizer, was John Brannigan, who, ten years before, had been collector at Motherwell;

[1] Executive *Minutes*, December 5, 1936.
[2] Glasgow *Minutes*, December 13, 1936.
[3] Aberdeen *Minutes*, December 20, 1936.

in seven years' time he was to succeed Robert Taylor as General Secretary. His appointment did not go unchallenged; at the next Executive, Mr R. S. Anderson (Hamilton), who had not been present when the organizers had been selected, 'raised the question of Mr Brannigan's appointment and asked several questions which were answered by the General Secretary'. In the Glasgow branch his appointment as organizer was also challenged: 'questions were asked . . . as to when he joined the Association and the reason why he left to go to America'.[1]

John Brannigan addressed the meeting and won a unanimous vote of confidence. The background to this uneasiness was the story, widely believed amongst the older members, that, owing to the alertness of the young Robert Taylor when a clerk at Head Office, Lyon had been made aware of irregularities in the accounts for which Brannigan was responsible as collector, and had given him the choice of resignation or dismissal. Brannigan insisted that he had gone abroad for personal reasons, being unable to tolerate Lyon's dictatorial distrust and hostility.[2] But the fact remained that, at the time he was appointed organizer, he had not been a member, nor active in the union, for a decade. Nevertheless, he was an energetic and capable organizer and speaker, and unlike a number of the staff, he had no loyalties to either Lyon or Webster. The first meeting he attended as organizer was the Executive of February 7, 1937, where Webster's position was the central theme. Taylor submitted a medical certificate and two letters 'in which Mr Webster intimated he was going away for two or three weeks for a change of air. He further reported interviews he had had with the Government auditors on the state of affairs in the health insurance department and on the position of the work at head office.' There was 'a long and protracted discussion', after which Messrs Hyland and D. Connell (Glasgow) moved Webster's suspension which was carried by nine votes to five. However, this clearly was felt to go too far; because after correspondence between Webster, the Treasury Auditor, and the General Secretary, a special Executive decided upon reorganization of the Health Insurance Department 'with a view to having

---

[1] Glasgow *Minutes*, March 21, 1937.
[2] He published his own account many years later in *The Highway*:

'I tendered my resignation at the beginning of October that year, sold off my comfortable little home in Newmains, and on Hallowe'en night, with my wife, left for the USA and pastures new. You may ask why! The position was that life under the General Secretary, Mr Lyon, was becoming intolerable.

'He had not only ceased to co-operate with me, but at a special meeting he actually asked the Lanarkshire branch to recommend my dismissal, which recommendation a largely attended meeting in the Masonic Hall in Motherwell refused to act on.

'There were over 200 members at the meeting, and Lyon, who in those days was a virtual dictator and almost dismissed or appointed at will, walked off the platform while I was speaking.

'I had been on good terms with Lyon for many years, and why he took up this attitude to me remains unknown.'

(*The Highway*, November, 1955)

the work done in a more systematic fashion', and that Peter Webster should be reinstated and, surprisingly enough, 'put in charge of the Insurance Department only', the very work which he had been charged with neglecting. The main consequence was that Peter Webster was no longer Assistant General Secretary. It was not Webster, therefore, but John Brannigan who was appointed to the Road Haulage Wages Board when it was first set up. By October 1938, John Brannigan had been appointed Assistant General Secretary and Peter Webster was no longer in the employ of the Association. Less than six months later, on February 7, 1939, Peter Webster was dead. There was no reference to him in the General Secretary's Annual Report nor at the Annual Conference. As a past President he figured in the obituaries at the Scottish Trades Union Congress, of which Robert Taylor was President that same year; but only two references to his death appeared in the records of the Association in which he had served for twenty-five years.[1] That was the last of Peter Webster: Hugh Lyon survived him by eleven months.

4. ROBERT TAYLOR'S AIMS

There had been serious dangers to the Association while Lyon and Webster were being dislodged, as Robert Taylor frankly admitted six years later, when there was another struggle amongst the leadership on the next change of general secretary. In his valedictory article, on leaving to become a director of the Scottish Co-operative Wholesale Society, he wrote:

'There is no doubt . . . that the shock which the Association suffered at the time of the change threatened to divide the membership into two parts. Fortunately, however, we weathered the storm and proceeded to build upon the very solid foundation which had been created for us.'[2]

When asked his opinion of Lyon many years later, Robert Taylor said that his great weakness was that he did not see a changing situation. 'For a long time he resisted the new Joint Industrial Council, being satisfied with the old sliding scale agreement. He was bitterly against amalgamation; he would not hear of it, whatever the advantages. He objected less to a working arrangement or even a loose federation. It was long before he

---

[1] The Aberdeen Branch expressed their appreciation:
'The Chairman referred to the death of the late Mr Peter Webster, late Insurance Secretary, and Mr Fraser was instructed to send to his son, Mr Peter Webster, a message of sympathy in the loss that the family had sustained and our appreciation of services while an official of this Association.' (Aberdeen *Minutes*, March 12, 1939)
The Executive Council also noted the occasion:
'Before the commencement of the meeting, Mr Taylor made reference to the death of our late Insurance Secretary, who had passed away that week (Mr Webster), and it was decided to record our sympathy in the minutes.' (Executive *Minutes*, March 1, 1939)
[2] *The Highway*, November 1943.

9. A line-up of working horses belonging to McEwans, the Brewers at Fountainbridge, Edinburgh, 1936.
From left to right: W. Fairgrieve; W. Hood, Foreman; 'Welshie' led by W. Newberry; 'Tommy' led by J. Hay; 'Snozzle' led by A. Hardie; 'Charlie' led by G. Bell; 'Darkie' led by N. McCormack; 'Donald' led by T. Watson; 'Massie' led by E. Fairgrieve; 'Hector' led by J. Brown; 'Davie' led by J. Lardles; 'Dobbin' led by J. Whigham; 'Sonny' led by W. Pinkerton; J. Thomson, Stableman.

[*photo: The Scottish Farmer*

Horse-drawn vehicles belonging to James Buchanan & Co. Ltd., Glasgow, giving a display at Falkirk Ice Rink in 1958.

[*photo: Robert L. Nicholson*

10. Portrait of Robert Taylor, the Third General Secretary, reproduced in *The Highway*, February 1943.

could be brought to believe that the motor vehicle had come to stay and would oust the horse and cart. In this he had something in common with D. Y. Abbey, President of the Edinburgh contractors, who hated the very sight of motor-cars.' Of the struggle to get the change in leadership, Taylor recalled: 'It was a major operation getting rid of Lyon. He was doing nothing; the union was just falling to pieces. I had a lot of help from people who finally got on to the Executive, because that was where the change had to come. Amongst those who were very helpful were Hamilton of Ayr, Bishop, Hastie, Rutherford, and Willie Watson of Edinburgh, all the members from Glasgow, and also Bob Anderson from Hamilton. The branches soon accepted it when they realized that the new General Secretary took a reasonable view. Besides, they quickly got the benefit of the improved administration. I saw the necessity of first getting the administration working normally and in an efficient and business-like way; I had been in the office closely studying it for some time.' Above all, Robert Taylor saw the need to pay out money to send out organizers. Soon they had five organizers at work, and the effect of this basic work was soon apparent; Brannigan was put in charge of all organizing work.

Robert Taylor, who was born on October 30, 1900, at Bathgate, came of a family of twenty-two; his father had four children by his first wife and eighteen by Robert's mother. He went into mining and was about to take his second certificate as oil and shale mine manager when, in July 1921, on coming back from his honeymoon, he was informed that his wages had been cut by half. He, therefore, trained for six months as a driver and went into the motor industry as a van driver with the Bathgate Co-operative Society. He had joined the Independent Labour Party in Bathgate on his seventeenth birthday, and had been chairman there at twenty; he remembered chairing a steelyard meeting for MacDonald and Snowden. He stood for the Bathgate Council in 1923. In March 1925, he visited Glasgow to see old Ben Shaw of the Labour Party, which occupied offices in the same building as the Association. When he had finished his business, Shaw asked him whether he was 'going into the neighbouring office to see your Union secretary, Hugh Lyon', and pressed him to pay a courtesy call. Lyon and Webster were there. Lyon said: 'We are looking for a man like you to do an organizer's job. Why don't you apply?' He got the job and started on May 25, 1925. 'At first I would spend the forenoon in the office doing the work of John Hair, the Chief Clerk, who was past it. In the afternoon and evening I went out organizing, which gave me exceptionally useful experience; at the time it was a field which no one was handling on an all-Scottish basis. Webster specialized on the new insurance work; Lyon did not like to go out organizing. I was the Glasgow branch minutes secretary until my election as General Secretary. At that time there were still 10,000 carters in Glasgow, where the Association had been early stamped by close connection with dock work. It was nothing unusual in Glasgow to have members' meetings of 150 to 200; and when it was an occasion for explaining an agreement, the meeting would be packed out. You got to know many members at quarterly meetings.' Soon he was on the Glasgow Trades Council with Willie Hunter, Louie Finnie, and others. He served on its executive, and got valuable experience when he was vice-president to Tom Scollan, who rarely attended.

What were Robert Taylor's main objectives when he became General Secretary? 'In the union, when I took over, we were gearing ourselves to a new type of activity, to negotiating machinery. Lyon could not possibly have done it. My biggest struggle was to break down the prejudice, because we had come to be regarded as a mere friendly society. I had to try and make them understand that only by appearing before the workers as a militant body could we get anywhere and break down the bad reputation and go forward. At the Annual Conference in 1938—my second as General Secretary—it was decided to accept an invitation from the Soviet trade unions to attend the twenty-first celebration of the October Revolution. I went representing the Association, together with Alexander Smith of Paisley, who was President that year.'

In the first months of the war, Taylor was a great deal in London, called in for consultation with ministries, especially the Ministry of Transport. There was every kind of organizational problem affecting transport workers: the 'black-out', the call-up, deferments, and regulations affecting motor vehicles in wartime. The basis for their smooth passage, with the Association's views given due weight, was laid during the struggle to establish the statutory machinery for the road haulage men, which claimed Taylor's attention continuously from the time he became General Secretary, as it, before him, had claimed Webster's.

5. BUILDING UP THE WAGES BOARDS

Now that the active membership no longer needed to be preoccupied with the struggle amongst the leaders, and Executive Council meetings were no longer a continuous battlefield, it was possible to get down to the very urgent needs of the Association. In the past decade, the Association had not stood still; it had declined, as can be seen from this comparison between the state of affairs at the end of 1926, when membership was on the point of a further sharp decline, and 1936.

MEMBERSHIP			STAFF		
			Permanent	Part-time	
		Organizers	Collectors	Collectors	Assets
1926	10,561	1	16	31	£97,804 12s 11d
1936	8,857	1	14	31	£149,174 17s 4d

Of the 1926 permanent collectors, no less than four had been recently dismissed for shortages in their money. John Brannigan, who at his best was a skilful propagandist, with an orator's effective turn of phrase, had last written in the 1926 Financial Report. Now, after eleven years, he wrote in the 1937 Report: 'Unfortunately, within the last decade, numerically we were becoming weaker, and it seemed that ere long there would only be a skeleton of organization for which our huge funds might provide a Golden Casket. But that was not to be our experience. During the year 1936 the canker was discovered and towards the close of the year the members very wisely decreed the policy should be changed, and so we started 1937 with that altered policy manifest in the leadership of the new General Secretary.'[1]

Whilst membership dropped to 83·8 per cent of the 1926 figure, the reserves had risen to 152·5 per cent, with fewer organizing officials. It was more than time some of this accumulated money should be used to build up membership. The recent developments, particularly in road motor haulage under the new Act, made it essential to recruit. During 1937 no less than 2,753 new members joined; and although the net increase was only 1,347, the membership rising to 9,954, it was significant, because the increase was largely amongst the motormen, whose total numbers were increasing, rather than amongst the carters. A 'Carters' Charter', fixing a minimum wage and providing a week's annual holiday throughout Scotland, had been reached before the change in leadership. Now it began to be realized slowly that the stronger position of the motormen could be used as a lever for improving the conditions of the horsemen, whose numbers, although dwindling, were still considerable. The passing of the Road Haulage Wages Act, 1938, did not solve all the problems; competition continued tense, at the expense of the wages and conditions of the road transport worker. Speeding, the falsification of log-books, and long-running were common. Although by 1938 the armament programme was beginning to have some effect on the economy and therefore on the transport industry, the fear of victimization was strong enough to make men hesitate to complain. The industry had yet to see how the Act would work in practice, and whether employers could evade it. The Scottish Board was established before the Central Board, but it was not in action until 1939. There was hard bargaining to lay down the principles and get the proposals through for the first agreement, Road Haulage Order No. 1. In the first eight months of 1939 Robert Taylor had to attend thirty-seven meetings of the Scottish and Central Wages Boards. Together with all the other negotiating machinery of Wages Boards, Conciliation Boards and Joint Industrial Councils which was springing up in those years, it took up much of the officials' time. John Brannigan, the recently appointed

[1] Financial Report, 1937.

259

Assistant General Secretary, for instance, was responsible also for the Association's organizing work.

Robert Taylor gives an interesting picture of the early days of the Central Wages Board: 'In 1939, under the Road Haulage Act, I was down in London every week, working on the first agreement very closely with Ernie Bevin. He would meet me often off the train and we would go to Lyon's Corner House. We worked out all sorts of problems. What was the measuring-rod to be—tonnage basis or what? Others on our side were Albert Denaro, of the Liverpool & District Carters, whose members were all passenger men, Jimmy Francis, of the United Road Transport Workers' Association of England, who had members both in passenger and transport, and Jack Corrin, if Bevin were not there.' Amongst those on the employers' side: 'Roger Sewell was prominent, Hanson of Leith and Charlie Holdsworth. But by far the most capable was old Edwards of Liverpool, a very big haulage contractor, small and dapper, always very friendly to Bevin and myself.' The points that Mr Taylor recalled when it came to the bargaining were these: 'It was noticeable that Edwards and Sewell never struck on wages. They were not interested; it was hours and overtime which concerned them. When the long haulages began to increase and there were provisions for a break in the hours, it involved overnight allowances. Bevin used to taunt them: "You value your vehicles and loads and employees so low that you are willing for them to go into common lodging-houses." Bevin would argue: "You're not operating with men in a fixed job, in a fixed building; the whole point of your business is that your men are mobile." The employers were making vast profits at that time. I never once heard them put up a case that they could not afford to pay; old Edwards never put that one up. They could steal the railway traffic.'

It took eighteen months' hard negotiations before the first Road Haulage Order was issued on January 29, 1940. During that time, whatever may have been the personal relations between Ernest Bevin and Robert Taylor during negotiations on the Board, friction between the organizations was never far from breaking through the surface, and did, in fact, break through later with grave consequences.

Close working together on the national machinery and in areas made clear the need for unity of purpose and the disastrous consequences of division; but at the same time it sharply focused differences in policy and tactics. It may be that it overstressed them. There were several factors. The first was that in general the standard of wages and conditions had been lower in Scotland than in the other main industrial areas in Britain. At an early stage in negotiations for the national machinery there was certainly an anxiety felt in Scotland lest high grading and consequent steep rise in wage rates might grade transport workers out of a job and send bigger employers over the Border. Hence the Association moved quickly to get a low but uniform grading for all Scotland. This by no means chimed with the strategy and tactics of the London Headquarters of the Transport & General Workers' Union. The level of grading was therefore a bone of contention. A second factor was that the Association most certainly regarded itself, and rightly, as a specialist in organizing road transport workers, which it considered to be a self-contained industry. There was a strong feeling that a general union would not and could not give any particular section the same attention. At the back of some minds was a fear that road transport workers would be drawn into action in connection with disputes in other industries, in the conduct of which it would have no say. The past record of the Association made it particularly sensitive on this point. Whilst such trends were, of course, far from un-common in other unions, what was usually a powerful counter-argument did not come into play with the Association. Most smaller unions are beset with financial weakness which makes amalgamation with a larger unit appear as a rescue operation. This was not true of the Association, which for years had boasted that their assets per head were higher than in any other trade union in the country. A further factor was that there had been a long history of special Scottish conditions in transport which called for local knowledge and local tactics, and the ability to decide problems upon the spot. It was frequently claimed that officials of the Transport & General Workers' Union in Scotland were obliged constantly to refer to their London headquarters where the problems would not be under-stood, and delay and confusion resulted. As the industry developed, and long distance haulage increasingly dominated it, local differences tended to be reduced if not eliminated; but this trend was slowed up by the con-ditions of wartime. The differences were rarely fought out on the real main factors, such as have been indicated, but often on the ground of Scottish nationalist feelings. This confused the issues instead of clarifying them. There were some typical and sometimes unfortunate wartime examples. Whether the differences were over major points of principle and policy or minor issues of fleeting importance, they did not usually reach the public light of day until matters had reached charges of poaching or demands to denounce the Working Agreement.

In September 1938, it was reported to the Executive that there had been meetings between the two unions on organizing activities. But when next month new agreements were put forward 'it was agreed that this be discussed after further information had been obtained, at a future date'. Nothing came of it; and when, two months later, the Association's chair-man, James McMillan, gave his end-of-year report for 1938 to the Execu-tive, he made some outspoken remarks: 'We do not require to seek guid-ance or advice from anyone over the Border: we believe that Scottish people are perfectly able to conduct their business efficiently and well without dictation from England. I say this not in any spirit of narrow economic nationalism, but with a full understanding of how some national organizations operate.'[1] He recommended members to strengthen 'an organization with its headquarters in Glasgow, where decisions are arrived at and put into operation without the need of consultation elsewhere'. The following spring members were complaining in Glasgow of 'the tide of poaching which is militating against the best interests of workers employed in the industry'.[2] That month Robert Taylor approached the Scottish Transport and Allied Trades Association, a breakaway from the Transport & General Workers' Union led by Norman MacPherson, a man of spirit and force. For three years past there had been restiveness in the passenger section in Scotland, which was the sphere of the Transport & General Workers' Union. A strike of bus workers over split duties in 1937 had not received the support from London which they had expected; those who did not join a breakaway on the East Coast nevertheless remained deeply critical of the English union. In the Glasgow passenger field the energetic and rebellious MacPherson had formed the Scottish Transport and Allied Trades Association; into it he recruited the men who worked on runabout trucks at the Empire Exhibition of 1938-9, the 'Liston drivers'. By the spring of 1939 his organization was financially in low water and membership was sinking. They were ready to accept overtures from Robert Taylor with the aim of sinking their identity and joining the Association. It might be thought a marginal case of how 'the Liston drivers' fitted into the Working Agreement. Whilst preliminary discussions were going on, the Executive Council *Minutes* related that the General Secretary was 'instructed to intimate to the Transport and General Workers' Union that in view of their actions in several districts during the past few months, we should terminate the Joint Working Agreement'.[3] The following month the Executive received a deputation from the Scottish Transport and Allied Trades Association; when negotiations were complete MacPherson's union dissolved itself and some 150 men, who would or could not return to the Transport and General Workers' Union, were accepted into membership of the Association, for which their leader became an organizer and expert on legal affairs.

At the same Executive meeting of July 5, 1939 when Robert Taylor reported about a meeting of the Scottish Road Haulage Wages Board, 'it was agreed that our representatives be instructed to support a policy of securing a decision on grading within the Scottish Board'. John Veitch, of the Transport and General Workers' Union, wrote an article in the *Daily Herald* on July 19, 1939 sharply criticizing the Association's attitude on the Wages Board about grading in Scotland, to which the Association as fiercely replied, the chairman James McMillan once again hitting out

[1] Chairman's Report, 1938.
[2] *The Highway*, May 1939.
[3] Executive *Minutes*, June 7, 1939.

in *The Highway*, the Association's new journal.[1] The Executive appointed a deputation to meet the other union; it was delayed by the outbreak of war in September, and in the meantime there had been correspondence from Dundee asserting that a strike there had been broken by their opponents. Discussions continued until the end of the year. Bevin wrote suggesting amalgamation. A special Executive meeting was called on December 23, 1939 to discuss his letter and a proposed working agreement. They decided to write outlining the basic principles upon which the Executive Council were prepared to effect a working agreement. As for the proposed amalgamation they asked 'Mr Bevin to submit details of the scheme he had in mind'. There the matter rested, leaving ill-feeling smouldering beneath the surface.

The Executive did not record any further discussion, and it was left to go to the Annual Conference. But before the proposal reached the Annual Conference, an article appeared in *The Highway* by John Brannigan, discussing an issue of sharply divergent policy. He was writing about the history of negotiations since the Joint Industrial Council for Local Authority Services had come into operation in Scotland in 1937. In addition to the Association and the Transport & General Workers' Union, the National Union of Municipal & General Workers, and the National Union of Public Employees were represented on it. For two years there had been a struggle to win a standardized scheme on basic rates. A com-

[1] 'First of all, let every Scottish road transport worker remember that the powers of the present Scottish Board were granted under the Road Haulage Wages Act, 1938, against the wishes and, indeed, the representations of the Transport & General Workers Union.

'Their attitude all along has been that the Scottish Board should do nothing and that everything should be left to the Central Wages Board which sits in London and where Mr Bevin can control the whole thing.

'This was their attitude before the Scottish Board was actually established, and many of our members will remember that when our General Secretary was making representations to the Ministry of Labour for certain powers of initiation being given the Scottish Board, an official of the Transport & General Workers Union from Scotland actually told the Ministry that his organization did not agree with the representations and preferred that such powers as we were seeking should only be vested in the Central Board located in London.'

Then he turned to the wages question and grading.

'When the Boards were established and came to discuss wages, their position was exactly similar, leave it all to London, but the cause of the present controversy surely created the most absurd situation of all.

'The Central Board *asked* the Scottish Board to grade Scotland in order to give effect to their draft proposals, and the Transport & General Workers Union was actually anxious to prevent the Scottish Board doing this job, and referring the whole matter to London.'

The President concluded his fiery article with this paragraph:

'My advice to road transport workers in Scotland is to look after your own affairs and let it be known throughout the country that the Scottish Horse & Motormen's Association does not require to write to London to secure permission to do this or that. It has its headquarters in Glasgow. It is run by Scottish people. Its Executive Council is composed of men working in the industry. It does not seek to be a jack-of-all-trades. In short, it specializes in transport and consequently is familiar with all the problems in the transport industry.'

(*The Highway*, August 1939)

promise scheme was finally reached and was to come into effect on January 1, 1940. When the war began claims were immediately put in for wage increases, and finally the employers agreed to a war bonus on a flat basis, but only provided that the scheme for standardizing basic rates should be 'temporarily abandoned'. The Association's representatives opposed acceptance, but it was carried by a majority on the trade union side:

'And so two years' hard work in striving to secure what in essence is fundamental principles in trade unionism went "Down the stank" in favour of acceptance of a miserable measure of what may amount to transient amelioration. I regret to say that some trade unions did not cover themselves with glory there.'[1]

Two months later at the Annual Conference on April 6, 1940, after Robert Taylor had reported on the scheme submitted for amalgamation, 'it having been advocated that amalgamation would assist in bringing greater pressure to bear on the employers in the industry', it was debated on the understanding that it would have to go before the branches, be returned to the next Conference, and be subject to a ballot vote:

'Many delegates then expressed their views on the matters raised by Mr Taylor who replied to numerous queries, after which it was agreed that we reject the offer to amalgamate.'[2]

The outstanding achievement of the decade, however, was that the new machinery did, finally, work; and while the first agreement was passing from Boards to Ministry, Robert Taylor wrote:

'When this procedure has been followed, we will enter a new era in the transport industry.'[3]

It had been a long struggle; looking back, as he was ceasing to be the Association's General Secretary, Robert Taylor wrote:

'The growth of statutory machinery, and particularly the Road Haulage Wages Board, has created a mild revolution in road transport in this country. There is no doubt that, but for the war, we would have perfected a much more complete organization throughout the whole country.'[4]

He had seen this machinery as a method of recruiting to the Association the many non-unionists among the motormen; so had other unions.

At the close of the fourth decade there was a very different picture from ten years before: the General Secretary and Assistent General Secretary

[1] *The Highway*, February 1940.
[2] *The Highway*, May 1940.
[3] *The Highway*, November 1939.
[4] *The Highway*, November 1943.

had gone; all the Executive Council members were different; all the senior head office staff had gone, including Miss E. Munro, who had been treasurer for over twenty-one years. Of the permanent collectors seven out of sixteen, and of the part-time eleven out of twenty-four were all who had survived the years. Membership, which had been 9,621 in 1928, rose to 10,804 in 1939; the general fund had moved from £107,543 to £161,355. Negotiations at this stage were much further developed than in 1928 and 1929. The wages and conditions of transport workers in retail co-operative societies were governed by the Scottish National Co-operative Wages Board in general, with some eleven area boards dealing with detail; it was war conditions which finally led to a National Wages Council for co-operative workers. The National Joint Industrial Council for Local Authority Services (manual workers, non-trading) was set up in 1937, the Association being one of the four unions represented on it, but it was still working out the machinery, like the Road Haulage Board. Its first agreement came into force on January 1, 1940. Most of the other agreements were still with individual employers; but there had been some important successes. The railway contractors' carters had achieved what would have seemed unbelievable to their fathers, when John Sampson and Hugh Lyon had patiently tackled the stables, thirty-five years before: a week's holiday with pay was theirs at last. A year later, in 1939, the same was agreed for motormen employed by general contractors and for carters employed by members of the Scottish Carting and Horse Owners' Association; it was the last summer of peace.

CHAPTER FIFTEEN

TRANSPORT IN SIX YEARS OF WAR

I. UNEMPLOYMENT IN WAR-TIME

MEMBERS of the Association had seen the war coming, as who had not? During 1938, district officials' reports generally observed a rise in employment; and William Purcell of Lanarkshire notes wage advances 'consequent on the stimulus in trade created by the Government's armaments programme'. But the sense of crisis and anxiety mounted also. When on April 26, 1939, Robert Taylor stood up at the Pavilion, Rothesay, to give his Presidential Address to the Scottish Trades Union Congress, he was aware that every delegate's mind was on the announcement that morning that the Government proposed to introduce peacetime conscription. It overshadowed the conference and led to a fierce debate and a declaration of protest. In his Address Taylor noted improved employment was 'largely because of the artificial stimulus to trade due to the rush of armaments manufacture'. He added: 'It is a sad commentary on the life of any nation when it records progress only under such circumstances.' He described the efforts 'being made to attract new industries to Scotland':

'But so long as the chief object of industry is to be remunerative to capital, instead of meeting the needs of the community, I am afraid we are only tampering and tinkering with the problem. The whole capitalist system must be cited as the major cause of industrial confusion. . . . It is worthy of note that capitalism can, and will, attempt to bring some order and thought into the industrial life of the community in a time of war, and will attempt to convey the impression that while doing so they are anxious for peace.'[1]

The contrast with the first Socialist country which he had just visited as delegate from the Association, was in his mind when he said that every worker should be afforded 'the right to live':

'Any policy which prevents that elementary right must be destroyed and replaced by a saner and more equitable one. We must secure a shortening of the working day, and in this connection we can learn something from our Russian friends who, after 21 years of working-class government,

[1] Presidential Address, Scottish Trades Union Congress, 42nd Annual Report, 1939.

266

have established a seven-hour working day for day workers and six-hour day for night and under-ground workers, and above all, have abolished unemployment in a country with a population of 180 millions.'

His speech was characteristic of the attitude of the majority of the members of the Association at the time. The Prime Minister, Neville Chamberlain, announced that Britain had declared war three days before the Annual Conference met at Cardross, where all resolutions were abandoned. Although the annual conference curtailed its business, it took two steps which indirectly had a bearing on their determination that this time, at least, trade unionists should be consulted, and for that purpose the Association ought to see that it was not isolated. They agreed to apply for affiliation to the British Trades Union Congress and therefore to alter the time of the annual conference from September to April in future, so as not to clash with Congress. Secondly, in pursuance of the ballot they had been conducting as to whether to renew their affiliation to the Labour Party once more, which they had dropped after the General Strike, they agreed that the proposed new Constitution for the Association should be submitted to the branches throughout the year. Two statements were made on the war at this conference; Richard King, the Vice-President, in his address

'briefly referred to the war, pointing out that the trade union movement in no country can benefit from armed conflict. Mr King concluded by appealing to the delegates to render their assistance in the establishment of a great free trade union movement throughout the world.'[1]

Robert Taylor also spoke briefly:

'Referring to the war, Mr Taylor said that the common people of all countries should clearly understand that, so long as the capitalist system exists, wars will be inevitable. . . . It was dangerous for the whole civilized world to continue to allow themselves to be dominated by international capitalism. It is the desire of all common people, he concluded, to live in peace and harmony, one with the other.'

Some weeks later, in his editorial review in the same issue, Robert Taylor elaborated on this theme.[2]

As months passed in passivity, an increasing measure of doubt and deep-rooted suspicion of the Government's good faith can be observed in the resolutions, reported speeches, and articles of the members; it took

[1] Report of Annual Conference, 1939.

[2] 'This war, we are told, is to preserve democracy and smash Hitlerism, but as I write our Government is proposing to take unto itself powers which will out-Hitler the Fascist régime in Germany. I cannot escape the conviction that the present legislators in this country are not so anxious as they would have us believe to establish throughout the world machinery which would prevent war at all costs.'

(*The Highway*, November 1939)

particularly the form of a demand for the definition of war aims. The shock of the overrunning of the Low Countries and Scandinavia and of the fall of France seemed merely to accentuate this viewpoint. Even when on May 10, 1940, Winston Churchill became Premier and the Labour Party assisted him to form an administration, the membership seemed slow to show consciousness of any marked change. With the appointment of the General Secretary of the Transport & General Workers' Union as Minister of Labour & National Service, however, a new factor had emerged which affected their interests directly. Ernest Bevin brought into full use the National Arbitration Tribunal, and produced powerful weapons which could be used by the workers to induce reasonableness amongst employers in certain kinds of industry. This was particularly true of the road haulage employers. As Robert Taylor remarked: 'It provided the most valuable opportunity for reference; whether the employers liked it or not, they had to lump it.' With a trade union leader at the Ministry of Labour and National Service, joint negotiations in the industry began to go more smoothly. If the employers were not broken in, at least the bridle was on.

The outbreak of the war meant considerable dislocation in trade and therefore in transport. For some months there was a marked increase in unemployment and upheaval in many directions. Early there was the first evacuation of the children from vulnerable areas to what were, at the time, regarded as areas unlikely to be within range of attack. Then there was the first evacuation of firms, and the decentralization of certain Government Departments and their staff. There was, of course, the movement of troops and equipment, the biggest single operation being that which transported 158,000 men and their equipment to France in the five weeks between September 3rd and October 11th; in 1914 it had taken a week longer to transport 10,000 fewer. Month after month passed; it was nine months before the troops had their first engagement; and that was the retreat and re-embarkation from the Dunkirk beaches of those not taken prisoner of war. It was exactly a year before there were massive air attacks on cities, although airfields and selected war factories had been raided by day. During the period of the 'phoney war', there was a large drift back from evacuation, only for the movement to be reversed on a big scale in September 1940, when the bombs rained down. Already, by November 1939, unemployment was 1,400,000, being 100,000 higher than before the declaration of war. The cost of living rose by ten per cent in a matter of weeks. Those with low incomes were in a serious condition: the then Prime Minister, Neville Chamberlain, told the House of Commons that the country could not afford any increase to the old age pensioners. The wages of the transport workers lagged far behind the rising prices. The road transport men were in a special position, since their first agreement was being negotiated under the Wages Board. It may be, however, that, if it had not been for the unanswerable argument of rising costs in wartime, there would have been an even stiffer resistance put up by the employers. As it was, when the first agreement was announced on January 29, 1940, it was already more than time to put in for a war bonus.[1] For the next six years this became necessary every few months throughout the collective machinery of all kinds, which covered different classes of road transport workers and their employers.

Whilst wage rates on the average rose fairly substantially during the war, the question was: what would be the position of those admittedly starting as the lowest paid? Transport workers were certainly amongst these. Nor should it be supposed that the existence of the statutory machinery meant that transport workers automatically got all to which they were entitled. The Association was forced to take action against three Aberdeen firms who paid below the rates set up by the first Road Haulage Order, and several hundred pounds were recovered. Up to December 31, 1943, some twenty per cent of the workers in road transport establishments which were visited were found to be underpaid:

Number of workers whose wages were examined	Number underpaid	Amount of arrears recovered for workers through the Department
52,600	10,900	£82,300[2]

Yet, during the four years from 1940 to 1943, only ten employers were convicted in the courts for infringement of the Act. There was no sign of any road hauliers undergoing a Pauline conversion in a blaze of light on the road to Damascus at any of the war's many stages.

The first anxiety, however, was the dislocation of employment and the very difficult driving under war conditions in the black-out, long before bombing brought additional hazards. The Government requisitioned vehicles to transport troops and materials, which led to drivers being dismissed. John Brannigan wrote that 'Many contractors are reaping a rich harvest these days'.[3]

---

[1] In 1941: 'wage rates were 21 to 22% above the level of September 1939. In 1943 the increase had reached 35% to 36% on the average of the year.' (Sir John Anderson, House of Commons, April 25, 1944.)

By spring 1944, wage rates were up 40%, with actual earnings of course being much higher. But the cost of living had risen much faster than wages. In July 1941, wage rates were 6% less than the rise in the cost of living. By the fifth year of the war, however, wage rates had risen 11% more than the cost of living and the Government was attempting to keep the cost of living index down to not more than 30% to 35% over pre-war.

[2] *Industrial Relations Handbook*, 1944, p. 156.

[3] 'If we exclude the requisitioning of vehicles it might be truthfully said that contractors are receiving a greater share from the industry today than has been their experience since the lean years of 1930–1.

'Many are finding work of a more lucrative character from the War Department, or the Civil Defence Services; indeed, this "plum" seemed so ripe that Motor Trade journals have been consulted by the hauliers to see how far they might be permitted to charge the Government before it was likely to squeal, and it is interesting to note that the advice

The Association at once put in for increases generally. Robert Taylor noted one of the special problems:

'This war has brought peculiar problems for our industry—the lighting restrictions imposed on our members who are doing night driving is a very heavy strain. In this connection we have been attempting to secure a substantial reduction in the amount of transport by night, and the employers have co-operated with us on the question. It has been found impossible to completely eliminate night driving, but during the month of October it was very much diminished.'[1]

By the time of the Annual Conference on April 6, 1940, there were 3,000 members in the forces. That spring the officials were 'busily engaged meeting the employers in the various sections of the industry for increased wages to maintain the standard of living enjoyed by our members prior to the war. At the outset we resolved not to hitch our wages to the cost-of-living figures.' The policy of fighting for flat increases instead was to bring them once more into sharp conflict with the Transport & General Workers' Union.

2. THE 'WAR' BETWEEN THE UNIONS

The decision to reject amalgamation taken by the 1940 Conference, as Robert Taylor wrote later, 'appeared to cause the Scottish officials of the Transport & General Workers' Union some concern'. Relations became unpleasant; poaching and counter-poaching which had been going on below the surface came into the open. On January 13, 1941, the Association complained to the Scottish Trades Union Congress that twenty-three members were poached from the Cleansing Department of the Glasgow Corporation, which had been the Association's territory for many years. The Transport & General Workers' Union retorted that, on their application forms, the men had stated that they were not members of any other union. Just before the STUC Annual Conference, the Executive of the Association decided: 'that we should advise the STUC, that they should not proceed further on this reference'.[2] At the STUC Annual Conference, John Veitch of the T & GWU complained bitterly at the reference having been withdrawn without apology, which he said 'was not playing the game'; and he pressed for a decision. Within the next few days, it was clear that the Association had decided to fight the problem out in a different way.

---

tendered would not only permit of a very substantial profit, but in many instances would enable them to write off the entire cost of the vehicle itself in a year's time; at the same time the Government are asked to pay the driver's wages and meet the cost of fueling and maintenance.

'It is obvious from this that some employers have only one interest in the war and that is profit for themselves. The promised vigilance of the Government against profiteering seems to hold no terror for those profit-mongers.' (*The Highway*, November 1939)

[1] *The Highway*, November 1939.
[2] Executive *Minutes*, April 5, 1941.

They decided to go all out in organizing passenger workers, the bulk of whom were within the orbit of the rival union, according to the 1927 Working Agreement.

'We have now decided to extend our field of activity to embrace all forms of transport. We regard the action of the Transport & General Workers' Union as being a challenge, firstly, to the right of our delegates to the Annual Conference to reach a decision which they regard as being in the best interests of the Association; and secondly to the future welfare of the Association itself.'[1]

Many busmen were still smarting under memories of the 1937 strike, when leading officials of their union had come from London to order them back to work. Now John Brannigan went first to Airdrie, where he and the local leader, Gordon Forsyth, organized the busmen; then to Edinburgh where ninety-five per cent of the busmen in the Scottish Motor Traction Company's depot joined the Association; from thence to Falkirk, Bathgate, and Broxburn. Whilst William Elger, the General Secretary of the STUC was calling both sides together in Glasgow and getting agreement to suspend hostilities until discussions on the basis of the 1927 Agreement could be opened, the situation again deteriorated. The Scottish Motor Traction Company had an agreement with the Transport and General Workers' Union, unknown to their employees, only to recognize membership in that union. This led to a strike in Airdrie under Gordon Forsyth's leadership; and when 'black' buses came through Edinburgh, the men there stopped work and the strike spread. The younger strikers were threatened with being called up for the armed forces. 'Robert Taylor came through to Edinburgh with £300 strike pay,' recalled Jackie Steedman, later an Association official and Labour councillor in the George Square and Giles Wards of Edinburgh. 'John Brannigan told us that he intended to extend the strike, but some of us had our doubts as to whether full backing would last.' The truce was over and, by the end of June, John Veitch notified the STUC that 'owing to the difficulties created in the bus industry', he intended to open an organizing campaign to get one hundred per cent membership. The Association retorted that they would 'continue organizing in the passenger transport industry'.[2] They also began to organize commercial transport workers (Dundee, Port Glasgow, Gourock, and Greenock) who came into the rival union's sphere. As the STUC report to the 1942 Annual Conference declared: 'It became evident that the whole question of the relationship of the two unions in their organizing activities in Scotland was involved.'[3] Yet another month had passed before this unhappy state of affairs came to an end. On August 13, 1941, eight months after the outbreak of hostilities in this 'wrong war', a new working agree-

[1] *The Highway*, May 1941.
[2] Executive *Minutes*, July 2, 1941.
[3] 45th Annual Report, STUC, 1942.

ment was negotiated, and was finally signed two months later, on October 10, 1941. This allowed the Transport & General Workers' Union the sole right to organize road passenger transport workers in Scotland, and the commercial transport industry to be organized by the Association, with certain exceptions. It provided that there should be no notice to terminate the agreement before January 1, 1943; it ruled out retaliatory measures if there were any breach, and laid down that there should be arbitration by the STUC.

This union 'war' had had its casualties, which leaders like Gordon Forsyth of Airdrie and Jackie Steedman and 'Sandy' Falconer of Edinburgh did not quickly forget when there were difficulties in the Association ten years later under the fourth General Secretary, John Brannigan. For he had urged the strikers in Edinburgh to return to work in circumstances which did not provide against victimization. The Scottish Motor Traction Company refused to take back the ten members of the strike committee, including Steedman and Falconer, and others. Some men felt that they had been 'let down' for the second time, by a second union. But, for the road transport workers at large, the struggle between the two unions had been 'the wrong war' in which there was no future. A short article by James Revie of Aberdeen appeared in *The Highway* which may have summed up the thoughts of the ordinary member. He wrote that the news of an amicable working agreement had 'sent up a glad song in my heart':

'Why? Because there are members of the rank and file who devote every ounce of energy and spare time they have to the furthering of the trade union movement. They do not tell of its aims and benefits in flowing flowery language, but in their scanty everyday vocabulary; yet it comes from their hearts, and they never sit on the fence, as I have seen suggested some officials do. These members are the very backbone of the movement. When a step towards unity, such as this is, is taken it gives more power (as it were) to their elbow to carry on with their simple but effective propaganda. I would make bold to say, without fear or favour, that if the leading lights of the labour and trade union movement had only been half as enthusiastic as their devout following, there would have been a Workers' Government in power long ere this, and the terrible catastrophe which mankind is now faced with would never have happened.'[1]

This was the spirit which prevented any further serious disturbance, even though everything could not be expected to move smoothly after such bitterness had been generated.

It, however, did not alter the general opinion about amalgamation. When, three years later, a circular was received from the British TUC on 'Trade Union Structure and Closer Unity' and considered at the 1944 Annual Conference, there was an echo of the past in the debate:

[1] *The Highway*, November 1941.

'A great deal of varied discussion ensued, in which Messrs Falconer (Edinburgh), Carson (Glasgow), Brown (Dumbarton), Barbour (Perth), White (Glasgow), Campbell (Edinburgh) and Ferguson (Glasgow) took part. The delegates were of the opinion that there should be no amalgamation between our Association and any other trade union, but while they were of this mind, they were anxious to promote friendly relations and work within the trade union structure with any other union solely interested in transport workers.'[1]

The sting was in the tail; the last five words—'solely interested in transport workers'—showed that they were excluding the Transport & General Workers' Union.

3. A LABOUR MINISTER OF LABOUR

With the fall of France, Chamberlain's resignation and the formation of an administration by Winston Churchill, with Labour Party support, on May 10, 1940, there were new developments. Ernest Bevin became Minister of Labour & National Service. A Joint Consultative Committee was appointed on May 22nd, consisting of seven representatives of the British Employers' Confederation and seven from the Trades Union Congress, to advise and assist him.[2] After consulting this body, Ernest Bevin made the famous anti-strike 'Order No. 1305', under the Defence Regulations authorized by the Emergency Powers (Defence) Acts, 1939–40[2] entitled Conditions of Employment and National Arbitration Order, 1940 (SR & O 1940, No. 1305). At that time, few would have believed that it would continue into the 1950s and be invoked in peace-time. Its main purpose was to prevent work from being interrupted during the war by strikes (or lock-outs), and it also provided that existing joint negotiating machinery should continue to operate in regard to wages and conditions. The Essential Work (General Provisions) Order followed some ten months later, the main purpose of which was to prevent anyone employed on what might be declared essential work from leaving or being dismissed. It was a long time before it was applied to war transport. But, at a much earlier stage in the war, the Regional Transport Commissioner had powers to relax the restriction on continuous working under Section 19 of the Road Traffic Act, 1930. It was necessary for the Association to be vigilant about abuses of any relaxation agreement. The difference, however, was that, with the new administration, transport problems were now being submitted to the appropriate trade unions for consideration. Taylor was invited to serve on the Road Haulage Consultative Committee,[3] and, as

[1] Report of Annual Conference, 1944.
[2] How these worked in practice is briefly described in *Civil Liberty and the Industrial Worker*, by Angela Tuckett. National Council for Civil Liberties. 1942.
[3] Executive *Minutes*, December 4, 1940.

Minister of Labour & National Service, Bevin was holding a number of conferences of officials and executive members, some of whom came from the Association.

The effects of the war were now being directly felt. There were two bombing raids on the Clyde in March 1941, and evacuees were taken in at the Association's Convalescent Home, which on May 5, 1941 was itself damaged by bombs. Fire-watching and fire-watching orders were universally causing trouble. It took some persuasion to make men who had done a long day's work feel that it was more important to care for the employer's premises than to defend their own home. Slowly the position of transport, which had also been dislocated to some degree by the bombing, began to be a serious matter. In April 1941, a War Transport Council was set up by the then Minister of Transport, Lt-Col J. T. C. Moore-Brabazon.[1]

A month later the Ministry, which had become the Ministry of War Transport, was under Lord Leathers. Need for a change was felt widely. Taylor wrote on Leathers' appointment:

'Competition in transport must come to an end. The whole of its resources must be mobilized effectively and efficiently. If the appointment of Lord Leathers to be Minister of War Transport envisages this then we welcome the move. If it does not, we will continue to press for the complete nationalization of transport as we have done for many years. . . .

We have freely given up certain rights to achieve victory and it cannot be made too clear that, having done so, we will not approve methods which hinder and hamper that victory.'[2]

That summer it was announced that the railways would be finally taken under complete government control, and all transport services reorganized to eliminate waste. It was high time; two years of war had passed. Now at last a large number of transport undertakings were scheduled under the Essential Work Order, which brought upon the head of the transport driver yet another set of regulations. No less than 840 cases, mostly offences under the Road Acts, were dealt with in one year by the Association's legal representatives for members in all parts of Britain.

But the increased output of regulations and orders did not necessarily achieve the full development of the war effort. As late as August 1942—the

---

[1] It consisted of the Chairman, Sir Arthur Griffith Boscawen; Lord Stamp of the London Midland and Scottish Railway; John F. Heaton, the managing director of Thos. Tilling Ltd; Lt-Col Sir Maxwell Hicks, the chartered accountant who gave evidence before the Royal Commission, later chairman of McNamara & Company and of Allied Transports Ltd; Sir William Prescott, chairman of the Lea Conservancy Board; J. D. Ritchie, general manager of the Port of London Authority; W. P. Allen, general secreatry of the Associated Society of Locomotive Engineers and Firemen; and Fred Montague, the Labour MP who became the Parliamentary Secretary to the Ministry of Transport. There were also two other 'men from the Ministry', Sir Leonard Browett and R. H. Hill.

[2] *The Highway*, May 1941.

third year of the war—a strange state of affairs existed in the road transport industry in Scotland. Taylor wrote in *The Highway*, in August 1942:

'For the past three months many employers in the industry in the West of Scotland have found great difficulty in finding employment for the men on their books.'

At the same time, there were heavy delays in deliveries of essential war material. Where was that essential, drastic reorganization of transport services under public ownership and control? Taylor commented:

'How much longer are we to permit vested interests to prevent the fullest possible use being made of the men and material in the best interests of the community?'

One of the provisions of the Essential Work Order prevented the worker from changing jobs without permission, but also protected him from dismissal except on grounds of 'serious misconduct'. Yet, Alexander Irvine, one of the Association's organizers, described what happened when firms scheduled under the Essential Work Order had redundant staff:

'The worker is subject to pin-pricking complaints, which can truly be described as trivial, and dismissed on the slightest pretext. . . . We have been consulted frequently by members recently dismissed under these conditions.'[1]

The Association conducted appeals and sometimes had long-drawn out struggles to force the employer to reinstate the men. In Kirkcaldy, carters employed by railway cartage contractors, scheduled under the Essential Work Order, were dismissed for refusing to go to work for general contractors. There were wide fluctuations in conditions and in administration. As late as May of 1943, John Brannigan described a serious situation in long distance haulage:

'A considerable number of men who were formerly employed as long as 66 or 77 hours per week, now find themselves confined to one or two trips or none at all. . . . All this has resulted from the control of traffic beyond 60 miles by the Government under the Ministry of War Transport's new Road Haulage Organization.'[2]

Its purpose was to concentrate vehicles and centre them on firms within twelve areas, to put as many vehicles off the road as possible. Special safeguards were negotiated by the unions to safeguard the men rendered redundant. But the road transport workers were watchful: 'lest our wartime rationalization should be perverted into a profit-making source for the combines and cartels after this war.'

[1] *The Highway*, August 1942.
[2] *The Highway*, May 1943.

The war emergency had led to an immense increase in collective agreements for Association members. Trade boards, joint industrial councils, voluntary wages boards covered almost everyone, in addition to those coming under the Road Haulage Wages Board, the Joint Industrial Council for Local Authorities or the National Co-operative Wages Council. Everything seemed to be centralized and negotiated at national level.

An important lesson for the membership to learn throughout the whole course of the war was that national machinery, although capable of providing a great access of strength, could not be relied upon as a substitute for a vigorous rank and file and strong organization at stable and garage. Under the overriding pressure of the need for efficient and vastly expanded transport, if the war was to be successfully prosecuted, the trade union side at national level found themselves in the novel position of receiving frequent support from Government Departments. Agreements could be reached and orders issued centrally and in the areas; but the degree to which they were operated depended upon the vigilance of the men on the job and the efficiency of local officials, not all of whom found it easy to adapt themselves to the new conditions. Some were replaced, and others were superannuated. This did not always commend itself to the members; their opposition was expressed on the Executive Council, notably by James White, Jnr, of the Glasgow Scottish Co-operative Wholesale Society section. Charges of 'dictatorial methods' were levelled by him against the leading officers. Similar charges, with some justification, had been brought against Hugh Lyon at some stages of his career. It would be easy to lay too much stress on such charges; but it may, perhaps, be safely said that such criticisms, if persistent, usually indicate a gap between members and leaders which is a sign of weakness in leadership and a lack of vigorous democracy and clear understanding of objectives. They should therefore be noted as a symptom of mistaken methods which need early correction.

4. THE FOURTH GENERAL SECRETARY IS ELECTED

An occasion when charges and counter-charges came to the surface was at the end of 1943, when there was another change of General Secretary. At the opening of the war a new constitution was being contemplated; but it was decided to abandon it during the war because of the difficulties of war-time organization. Later the proposal was revived when it was found necessary to alter the rules to make possible a political fund and to enable affiliation to the Labour Party to be carried out, which had already been the subject of one ballot. The occasion was therefore taken also to amend the rules for election of the Executive and the General Secretary. The subject came up at successive conferences, and at last the new constitution was ready. It was registered on August 11, 1943. Then, at the Executive meeting of September 1, Robert Taylor formally 'intimated that he had been elected to the Board of Directors of the Scottish Co-op Wholesale Society Ltd.' He gave three months' notice, which would expire at the end of November 1943, and offered to remain until the end of the year. When John Murphy and Tom Berrey moved that his proposal of four months' notice should be approved, there was disagreement, led by James White, Jnr, of the Glasgow Scottish Co-operative Wholesale Society branch:

'Mr J. White moved an amendment that the Rules in connection with the resignation be strictly adhered to and that the General Secretary be given six weeks' wages in lieu of notice as from 4 September 1943. This was seconded by Mr P. Callaghan. At this point the General Secretary retired from the meeting and on a vote the motion that the period of notice extend to four months was carried by 12 votes to 2.'[1]

It had been known since June that Robert Taylor was standing for election to the Scottish Co-operative Wholesale Society; and in the Glasgow sections in particular there was a not inconsiderable body of opinion which held the view that he ought not to occupy the two positions simultaneously, even for a short time. Some believed that he intended to hold down both jobs permanently. Before the minutes declaring the election and the call for special branches to nominate had reached quarterly meetings, a petition was sent to head office signed by James White, Snr, and seven other members, expressing the opinion that the extension of notice to the General Secretary and rules regarding election had been violated and asking that this be put to arbitration. The Executive considered this request, and rejected it on October 10, 1943. The Glasgow Co-ordinating Committee objected to the Executive Committee's procedure, and agreed that a mass meeting of all Glasgow Sections should be called. At this meeting, a unanimous resolution was passed which was considered by the Executive at its November 1943 meeting; it sharply criticized the Executive and included these expressions:

'That we deplore the irresponsible conduct and general incompetency of the EC and call for their immediate dismissal from office and the election of a new EC.

'That Mr Robert Taylor having accepted an SCWS directorship and being now fully employed in that capacity be requested to forthwith relinquish his position as General Secretary with the Scottish Horse & Motormen's Association.

'That we wholeheartedly endorse the action of the Co-ordinating Committee in convening this gathering and pledge ourselves to assist it in every possible way until the crisis that has developed has been satisfactorily resolved.'[2]

[1] Executive *Minutes*, September 1, 1943.
[2] Executive *Minutes*, November 3, 1943.

By a vote of nine to three the Executive decided not to entertain the Glasgow resolution. The special meetings of branches to receive nominations had been in progress, and the results were received at the same Executive Council meeting. These were:

David Johnstone, who received seventeen nominations, mostly from Fife, Perth, and the North;

John Brannigan, who received fifteen, mostly from Clydeside, Aberdeen and Edinburgh;

Alexander Irvine, with four, whose strength was mainly in the south-west; and

James White, Junior, who was nominated by his own branch, Glasgow SCWS.

During the election and the struggle around it there was only one issue of *The Highway*, that of November 1943. It contained two references to the controversy, one from the retiring General Secretary and Editor, and one from the President, George Little. Robert Taylor wrote:

'May I offer a word of advice about the future. Recently, certain elements within the Association, whose volubility is their only commendation, have been seeking to impose their minority will on the members. I warn you to beware of these people, some of whom had never been in the transport industry in their life.

They are aiming at the destruction of the Association, because it is ever so much easier to criticize destructively than to offer constructive suggestions for the continued building of the Association in the future. I am satisfied that our members, with their usual good sense, will not be taken in by gangster tactics of these people.'

No name was mentioned; but on the facing page George Little was explicit in an article entitled '*A Word of Warning*'. Having referred to a 'torrent of abuse from one of the minority on the Executive', he continued:

'This country, with all its allies, is fighting for democratic rights, and here we have in our midst an Executive member who, because he cannot get his own way, and dictate to everyone else, is indulging in mendacious propaganda against the majority. The position is not improved by the fact that this individual is also a candidate for the office of General Secretary and Treasurer, and I therefore appeal to you very strongly to support the majority of the Executive Council.'

After referring to arrangements to recognize the services of Mr Taylor, who was to be presented with a cheque for £150, he continued:

'This was a unanimous decision of the Executive Council, but apparently Mr White, with his advisers outside the Executive room, feel that we made a mistake here, and we are again told that we are doing wrong.

'Incalculable harm is being done the Association by this individual and the few who associate with him. Be on your guard, fellow-members, and retain above all things, the prestige, dignity and influence of this great union.'

James White replied in the next issue of *The Highway*, in February 1944, but the voting had already taken place. The results, declared on December 28, 1943, were as follows:

John Brannigan	5,157
David Johnstone	1,746
Alexander Irvine	1,176
James White, Junior	912
Spoiled papers	312
	9,303

The total voting papers issued were 12,713. The fourth General Secretary was elected by fifty-seven per cent of the valid votes cast. He had a clear lead; but, in the circumstances, James White's surprisingly high vote of ten per cent was a warning signal of uneasiness amongst the membership, of which a new General Secretary should have taken careful note. In his 'Open Letter to the President of the Association', James White expressed the view that the attack upon him was intended to influence the election, and remarked that

'an unbiased editor, without any axe to grind, and especially one editing a quarterly magazine, would have given the attacked person an opportunity of replying in the issue containing the attack'.[1]

He claimed that there was a 'similarity in technique employed against me with that used against former applicants for a union post'; and that the incident 'disclosed the urgent need for an Editorial Committee to control the policy of the magazine and all subject matter submitted for publication'. Under Taylor's editorship, he insisted, 'it had no real trade union appeal and was practically used as a medium for advertising prominent road haulage contractors'. Under Taylor's régime 'independence and all initiative was suppressed and every particle of democracy assassinated'. White's closing remarks were:

'Unfortunately there are far too many individuals in the working-class movement who prefer the trappings of office and the shoddy of power to a new social order.'

The new Editor and General Secretary, John Brannigan, printed White's Open Letter about his predecessor without comment.

[1] *The Highway*, February 1944.

Robert Taylor had been employed by the Association for eighteen and a half years and for a little over seven years he had been General Secretary. He was of a very different stamp both from his predecessor, Hugh Lyon, and from his successor, John Brannigan. He was not an outstanding mass orator nor a field organizer of long experience who could carry away men at stable or garage. But he had very considerable gifts as an administrator; he could leave the others standing in that sphere; he knew the internal affairs of the Association intimately. Most of the changes in the late thirties which brought the administrative methods of the Association from those of a pre-1914 society to those of a modern trade union were introduced by him. He had been fully aware of the need for gifted field organizers.

John Brannigan had no flair for administration like his predecessor; but he was highly skilful at organizing both the carters and the new motormen, and his intimate knowledge of the membership went back to the early twenties. Fifteen years later he wrote:

'While I knew much about the membership and their requirements when I took office on January 1, 1944, I must confess that my knowledge of the internal administration of the Association was rather scant. . . . At that time I was dependent on a rather small coterie of loyal people, because within the Executive Council, and within the officials, I was in grave doubt as to where some of them stood.'[1]

When the union under Robert Taylor embarked on a new policy of organizing, Brannigan was brought into a sphere of work which suited him. After five years as Assistant General Secretary, he had now achieved the senior post.

There were eighteen more months of war-time; but after that a period was going to open for the Association which was very far from that to which John Brannigan had been accustomed since his early days. In abilities he had much in common with Hugh Lyon; at the age of twenty-five each must have been similar in outlook and ambition. But twenty-five years also separated them in age. The conditions in which a young Hugh Lyon could flourish had gone for ever. When John Brannigan became General Secretary he was already forty-three years of age.

5. LOOKING FORWARD TO PEACE-TIME PROBLEMS

In 1944, the Association had been much preoccupied with the problems of peace for some months. Members were deeply concerned with such questions as defending wages and hours; guarding against the post-war problems that some of them remembered from the first war; pressing for political objects to be added to the aims of the Association; and above all,

[1] *The Highway*, May 1958.

they were considering what measures should be taken towards nationalization and public control of the industry. They were not, however,
regardless of international problems, nor the difficulties of their fellow
trade unionists in post-war Europe.

Just a year before the end of the war, and two months after British
troops had at last invaded Nazi-occupied Europe from the West, the
Executive Council defined the Association's attitude. A resolution moved
by Alex Falconer and seconded by P. Callaghan, expressed the opinion
that 'the Nazi régime is cracking up'. 'We call upon the whole German
people to support those men who have had the courage to fight the Nazis.'[1]
After appealing to them to overthrow the Nazi Government and 'so save
Germany from utter destruction', the resolution took up the position of
the anti-Nazis living in Britain:

'We record our conviction that the anti-Nazi Germans living in this
country can be of tremendous assistance to the cause. We urge the BBC and
the War Office to make more use of these men by allowing them to act
as front-line propagandists to the German Army; to appeal more frequently
to their own people in BBC broadcasts to Germany; also allow them access
to Prisoner of war camps for the purpose of re-educating German prisoners
of war.'[2]

Underlying the resolution, which was carried unanimously, was suspicion
that obstacles were being put in the way of anti-Nazi trade unionists; this
seemed to be well-founded when, after hostilities had ended in Europe,
the British Government prevented their return to Germany for many
months, at a time when the destruction of the Fascist régime and the
reconstruction of the trade unions was essential. It was an indication that
to realize post-war aims abroad, if not at home, might not be all plain
sailing.

During the war the Association had been in close contact with anti-
Fascist refugee trade unionists, some of whom were working in transport
in Scotland and had joined the Association. An example was a member in
the Glasgow Scottish Co-operative Wholesale Society section, Ernst
Langguth, whose home was Berlin. He proved himself to be an active
member of the Association, and was elected as shop steward and also as
delegate to the Glasgow Trades Council. At the Aberdeen Scottish Trades
Union Congress in 1945 he represented the Trade Union Centre of the
German Workers in Britain. As Editor of *The Highway* John Brannigan
asked him to contribute an article in Nobember 1945 on 'Rebuilding
German Trade Unions'. His account affords an interesting parallel to the
preoccupations of the Scottish transport workers. But, in his country, all
trade unions had been destroyed for twelve years, and many of their

[1] Executive *Minutes*, August 2, 1944.
[2] Executive *Minutes*, August 2, 1944.

officials, if they had survived the death camps, were in poor health or in exile. Nevertheless, he wrote, in Germany

'United, free trade unions are already in existence. They have overcome and done away with the old disunity and we hear from Berlin that 17 new trade unions have been founded there. There is, for instance, the union for the traffic industry; this includes, all road, sea and river transport, as well as dockers and commercial workers.'

Then he set out in detail the Four-Point Programme adopted in Berlin, which was very close, in fact, to the post-war aims of the Association's members.[1] He added that almost similar developments were taking place in all four zones of occupation, in Hamburg, Munich, the Ruhr, Frankfurt, and elsewhere, and concluded:

'They need militant democratic trade unions with a leadership able to solve the problems of economy in a regenerated German democracy, where Nazism and militarism will be rooted out for ever.'[2]

Fifteen months after the end of the war in Europe, John Brannigan having made representations on his behalf, Langguth was allowed to return to his own country; and the Executive Council 'unanimously agreed on motion of Messrs G. Little and McDiarmid to grant £10'.[3] In an article entitled 'Farewell Brothers and Comrades', Langguth gave details of some of the Nazis who were at that time still holding official positions in the British Zone, and ended:

'Trade unions must be properly recognized and united over the whole country, working in close collaboration with all genuine anti-Fascist parties. There must be complete unity of all true anti-Fascist forces, just as it says on our Scottish Horse & Motormen's Association badge: "Unity is Strength".

'Let us work together in this spirit, you in Britain we in Germany, and a peaceful, democratic Germany with a strong trade union movement will be on your side for peace, prosperity and Socialism.

[1] 1. To fight against Nazi ideology and the poison of German militarism, and to purge the administration and factories of Fascist elements.
2. To employ all manpower for the welfare of the population and for reconstruction.
3. To organize the protection of labour and employment and the conclusion of wage agreements, to collaborate in the rebuilding of German economy and social insurance, and to safeguard the democratic rights of workers and employees to be consulted on all questions concerning them.
4. To educate the German workers in the spirit of anti-Fascism, democratic progress and acknowledgement of their social position and of their joint interests with the workers of other countries and the consolidation of friendship with other countries.
[2] *The Highway*, November 1945.
[3] Executive *Minutes*, August 7, 1946.

'This shall be my farewell to you, my friends in Scotland, the great country of Robert Burns, Keir Hardie and John Maclean.'[1]

Brannigan's first peace-time editorial, expressed a sense of relief at reaching 'the long sighed for time—peace-time', and the general feeling that there remained stern battles ahead:

'The time has now arrived to start work in implementation of many of the fine promises which have been made for the building of a new world, and if we carry with us the memory of the fear of destruction which clouded our lives during the most difficult years of the war, we will be resolute in our determination that the new world shall be established and that nations are bound together in such a manner that mankind will never again experience the horror of war.'[2]

John Brannigan had written earlier in the war pressing for the Government to state their peace aims. The workers, he declared, had a national plan:

'The plan is the public ownership and control of *all* means of production, to ensure that production would be for use rather than for profit. This would mean the complete reorganization of the economic life of the country. The government should take the financing out of the hands of the usurers. They should take over the land, all forms of transport, coal and power and an equitable and plentiful distribution would follow.'[3]

War-time control of the means of production should be maintained and extended to cover the whole economic life of the country.

By the beginning of 1945, the membership was 14,247, with an additional 4,000 members in the forces. A political ballot had been conducted to decide upon including 'political objects' within the constitution, and the Association had committed itself to post-war political action. One of the biggest political issues of their history was ahead; nationalization of the road haulage industry.

[1] *The Highway*, August 1946.
[2] *The Highway*, May 1945.
[3] *The Highway*, November 1942.

CHAPTER SIXTEEN

TOWARDS NATIONALIZATION

I. THE CAMPAIGN FOR NATIONALIZATION

THE Association had early gone on record as being in favour of bringing transport under national control. During the First World War, members had not been unmindful of the case for nationalizing some institutions and industries which needed to be developed as public services. For many years they had called for nationalizing hospitals and medical services. Observing the effect of government controls in war-time, and taking the lead of the Scottish Trades Union Congress at their 1916 meeting, the Association went on record for the general principle in September 1917, when delegates met at Leith:

'The Conference agreed that the time had now arrived when the State should own and control Land, Mines, Shipping and Railways of this country.'[1]

But road transport industry at that stage, was a different matter. A Glasgow veteran, John Connell, recalled that in 1922 a member suggested at a meeting that the Association should submit a resolution to the Scottish Trades Union Congress which would include road transport amongst other forms which should be nationalized:

'This caused a sensation at the meeting, some of the members telling the mover he was daft, and that it could never come about. The mover of the motion may have been a dreamer, but his dream has come true.'[2]

But within six years the project was no longer sensational; it was beginning to be regarded as essential. A resolution demanding the national co-ordination of the transport services was sponsored by the Association and moved by Peter Webster at the Scottish Trades Union Congress at Perth in April 1928. A similar resolution was moved at the Association's Annual Conference at Cardross on September 1, 1928, by two west-coast members, Louie Finnie of Glasgow and Alex McCallum of Dumbarton:

'That this Conference, being of opinion that the present position of the transport services in the country is unsatisfactory, demands that legislation

[1] Report of Annual Conference, 1917.
[2] *The Highway*, August 1958.

be introduced with a view to co-ordinating all transport services under a central transport authority.'[1]

If the emphasis was rather on technical co-ordination than on public ownership, it should be remembered that, at the time, the appointment of the Royal Commission on Transport was much in their minds. The following year a strong composite resolution was moved at the Scottish Trades Union Congress at Aberdeen in April 1929 by a railway delegate, seconded by the Transport & General Workers' Union, and supported by Peter Webster, speaking for the Association. This showed the influence of the old demand for all-out nationalization of the railways; the demand was now for steps to be

'taken to co-ordinate and organize under public ownership and control all forms of transport, whether by rail, road, water or air'.[2]

In the autumn, at the Association's conference at Dundee, the previous year's resolution was repeated, with minor changes.

After the Royal Commission had reported, but without recommending public ownership, the Scottish TUC came out steadily in favour of 'national transport services', year after year with hardly a break up to 1940. Almost always the resolution was moved by a delegate of the Railway Clerks' Association and seconded by the TGWU or the National Union of Railwaymen. At the 1938 Congress at Girvan, John Brannigan remarked upon the increasing interest in road transport of the railway companies: Wordie & Company 'was now virtually owned by the railway companies', which were 'seeking to control the whole of road transport in Great Britain'. He concluded: 'If we do not get public ownership soon, the railway companies will own the whole business.'[3]

The Association at its own conferences adopted resolutions with unfailing regularity demanding nationalization, usually including the phrase 'co-ordination under public ownership and control of all forms of public transport'. The terms of the resolutions varied with the preoccupations of the time. The Perth Conference of 1942 stressed that 'the recent muddle in transport services' showed that complete co-ordination was 'only possible under a system of public ownership and control'. In 1943, at Edinburgh, conscious of the 'immeasurable part' the aeroplane would play after the war, and 'of the political dangers arising from civil aviation becoming the monopoly of private capitalist interests', Conference brought civil flying into the forefront of their transport resolution. The Aberdeen Conference of 1944 declared that 'the national need during the circumstance of war has amply proven that all forms of transport are

[1] Report of Annual Conference, 1928.
[2] 32nd Annual Report of the Scottish TUC, 1929.
[3] 41st Annual Report of the STUC, 1938.

essential and indispensable', and, fearing that the advantages of scientific improvements 'might be usurped for private profit', sought national control as a step towards 'complete international control'. When the Association met at Millport in April 1945, just before VE-day, they made this more explicit by demanding 'a European Transport Board of Control'.

The Association's attitude, therefore, in twelve years of uneasy peace and six years of war had become clearly defined. In the early days, their approach may have been coloured by regarding public ownership as a method of controlling the road hauliers and reducing the chaos and competition on the roads, or as necessary to resist the railway companies which were themselves seeking road traffic. Experience during the war, first of the lack of integration, then of partial integration, and finally of fairly complete public control, brought a more clear-cut attitude. Towards the end of the war they were concerned with what would happen if the controls were ever taken off. The older men vividly remembered the early twenties, when the railways were handed back to private owners, freed from the government control which had proved necessary during the war, and they were suspicious of any sign that this might happen again. An inevitable effect of centralized national war-time control was that they had to look across the border to see what was afoot in the main centre of political power. This meant inevitably that they were increasingly affected by the climate of opinion in the whole British trade union movement, especially after affiliating to the British Trades Union Congress in 1940.

At an early stage of the war before the Labour Party entered the administration formed by Winston Churchill, there had been an important debate in the House of Commons on war transport. The Labour Opposition were strongly critical of a war-time arrangement financially favourable to the railway companies which had been arrived at by Neville Chamberlain's Government. The Labour Party therefore put down a motion in February 1940, calling for the establishment of a permanent National Transport Authority to own and control all forms of inland and war-time transport.[1] Within three months of the debate came the fall of France, Dunkirk, and the first big air raids.

The intensification and extension of the war brought a new outlook, with much thought and anxiety about war aims and post-war aims. At the 1941 Labour Party Conference, the National Executive gave delegates a pledge to set up a Central Committee on Post-War Reconstruction

---

[1] Mr Herbert Morrison was the main spokesman: 'In our view during war-time the case for the State taking over the effective control of all transport is strengthened. In view of the possibility of air raids it is more than ever important that there should be somebody in authority over every form of transport. There is still friction between competing services and that does not make for effectiveness in the national effort. National ownership and control would get rid of that friction. An important chance has been missed to pool all forms of competing transport on reasonable terms.'

Problems. There was a Transport Sub-Committee of this under the chairmanship of Emanuel Shinwell, MP. Then came a resolution by the Railway Clerks' Association, adopted by the Edinburgh Trades Union Congress in 1941, which, while 'appreciating that the Government have recognized railways as a national necessity by controlling them in war-time', declared that Britain's transport problems could 'be permanently solved only by the co-ordination under public ownership and control' of all forms of transport. It ended with a demand that the General Council insist that 'as a preliminary to a proper nationalized transport service' the railways should 'not again be taken back into private control'. That set the tone for the war years. When on December 4, 1941, the Government announced that nothing would be allowed to hamper the successful prosecution of the war, similar resolutions concerned with post-war reconstruction were adopted in most industries. At the Labour Party Conference at Westminster in May 1942, a TGWU resolution called for co-ordination 'under national ownership with special emphasis on the need to take immediate steps to meet the war-time requirement for an effective transport system'. In moving it, the then General Secretary, Arthur Deakin, said that co-ordination was possible only under national ownership, and remarked: 'As a member of the War Transport Council I have seen from time to time specious arguments put forward designed to protect the long range interests of the present owners.' His seconder, Alfred Balfour, for the National Union of Railwaymen, declared: 'There is a definite intention which has been manifest right from the beginning of the war that the policy of vested interests should be maintained and that we should get no further in the direction of Socialist organization for fear that a position might be brought about at the end of the war that would make it impossible to revert to the old system.'[1] His colleague T. Hollywood, who seconded a resolution on similar lines moved by Harold Clay of the Transport & General Workers' Union, at the Edinburgh Trades Union Congress that year, put it in characteristic terms: 'During the last war statesmen had talked in terms of nationalization until the war finished, and then they substituted for it grouping under private enterprise.'[2]

By the time of the Southport Trades Union Congress in 1943, the mood was seen to be almost universal. Resolutions from a number of unions were 'composited' into a demand that the General Council should bring to the next Congress a comprehensive plan for post-war reconstruction, and recommend 'the degree of national ownership or control to which each industry shall be subject'. In supporting the resolution for the General Council, George Chester, the Chairman of the Economic Sub-committee, said: 'Workers and members of the general community were all anticipating

[1] Report of the 41st Annual Conference of the Labour Party, 1942.
[2] 74th Annual Report of the Trades Union Congress, 1942.

they were not going back to the conditions which prevailed prior to the war.'[1]

The Economic Sub-committee[2] then got down to work. The result was the *Interim Report on Post-war Reconstruction*.[3] Presented to the Blackpool Congress in October 1944, it was based upon a report prepared in the course of an earlier national crisis, adopted by the 1932 Congress.[4] This had been prepared by a committee which had included Ernest Bevin, John Bromley, the Locomotive Engineers' Secretary, C. T. Cramp (Railwaymen), A. G. Walkden (Railway Clerks), Arthur Pugh (Iron & Steel Trades), Ebby Edwards (Miners), George Gibson, and Walter Citrine. They had indicated three categories of industries:

(1) Those immediately ripe for socialization.
(2) Those less important or less unified, but needing some measure of regulation.
(3) Those of minor importance which can for the time be left under completely private enterprise.
(Para 208, Clause 4)

The 1932 Report had decided that the 'criteria of fitness' for socialization or public control would include:

(a) The importance of the industry or service to the life and safety of the community.
(b) The existence of monopoly or unification in an industry or service serving a wide demand.
(c) The importance of the industry or service as a source of demand for new investment.
(Para 208, Clause 6)

Whilst adopting this general approach, the 1944 *Interim Report* went into greater detail. It picked out two groups of industries as coming within the category for immediate public ownership. One of these was 'Transport (including railways, canals, road transport, coastwise shipping and internal airways'. The *Interim Report* was debated by Congress on Thursday, October 19, 1944.

It was the first time that John Brannigan had been a delegate to the

[1] 75th Annual Report of the Trades Union Congress, 1943.
[2] It consisted of J. Brown (Iron & Steel Trades Confederation), G. H. Bagnall (Dyers & Bleachers), H. Bullock (General & Municipal Workers), George Chester (Boot & Shoe), Arthur Deakin (Transport & General Workers), George Gibson (Mental Hospitals and Institutional Workers), George Isaacs, MP (Printers), Sir Walter Citrine, and George Woodcock who acted as its secretary. Professor Harold Laski and Percy Collick (Locomotive Engineers) worked on the committee, too, representing the Labour Party National Executive, which was also busy on a project of the same kind.
[3] Appendix D of the General Council Report to the TUC, 1944.
[4] *The Public Control and Regulation of Industry and Trade*, paras 208–10, General Council Report to the TUC, 1932.

11. The First National Staff Council of the Road Haulage Executive, 1950, which includes (*left to right*)—S. E. Raymond, *sixth standing*. John Brannigan, Fourth General Secretary, *eighth standing*. Harold Clay, *first seated*. A. E. Tiffin, former General Secretary of the TGWU, *third seated*. Major-General G. N. Russell, Chairman, *centre seated*. Arthur Deakin, former General Secretary of the TGWU, *seated left of Chairman*. Frank Cousins, MP, General Secretary of the TGWU, *seated second from right*.

[photo: *Edinburgh Evening News*

12. A. H. Kitson, Fifth General Secretary, appointed as Organizer in 1956. Clock presented by E. Cairns, Chairman of Edinburgh Branches, also shown are Mrs Kitson, J. Carabine and J. Murphy, Executive Council members, William Campbell, Organizer, and William Tollick, P. Hamilton and G. Wilson, District Secretaries.

British Trades Union Congress; and he put the Association's viewpoint during the debate on the resolution welcoming the Interim Report:

'During the last war no one saw the possibilities arising from the development of the internal combustion engine. The inevitability of railway travel seemed generally accepted, and the Railways Act of 1921 was an attempt to bring some administrative order into a badly-managed industry. Only the profit-makers, redundant labour, and distraught wage-earners were alive to the birth of a new industry.

'If ever an industry shrieked for control, that industry was transport. Businesses had grown up on the road in passenger and goods traffic, and throughout this growth there was unleashed on the public the fiercest competition, short of war itself.'

The Association's General Secretary then referred to the road traffic legislation:

'The Government recognized this state of affairs and tried to steady the position by introducing the Road Traffic Act of 1930. Some measure of equanimity was brought about by this control. But creeping up behind all this was the demonstration by road haulage contractors that they could transport anything from a sponge to a steam engine by road. Then came the squealing of the railways for a 'square deal'. So the story went on through the various Acts of 1933, 1934 and 1938 and the multiplicity of regulations designed to protect the workers and the public and to ensure the steady running of the industry.'

Then he dealt with co-ordination and central control: 'With this experience behind them of the vagaries which beset the productions of the modern scientific mind, it was time to tell the Government that all forms of transport should be co-ordinated and controlled under one central authority, namely, the Government itself.' John Brannigan concluded his first speech at the British Trades Union Congress in these words:

'The most important factor in post-war reconstruction would be the control of transport, and therefore they should call upon the Government not only to control its internal transport, but to ensure that no transport left this country without its control.'[1]

Writing later in the Association's journal, Brannigan and Alex Smith, his President and co-delegate, gave impressions of their 'initial experience of representation at the British Trades Union Congress'. Their final conclusion was

'While we are afforded our democratic rights within the Constitution, it would seem, allowing for elections and votes, that the Congress is virtually dominated by the larger organizations.'[2]

[1] 76th Annual Report of the Trades Union Congress, 1944.
[2] *The Highway*, November 1944.

This Congress had also adopted an *Interim Report on Trade Union Structure and Closer Unity*[1] which had been discussed for six months by affiliated bodies and to which the Association had paid a great deal of attention at its Annual Conference that spring:

'The delegates were of the opinion that there should be no amalgamation between our Association and any other trade union, but while they were of this mind, they were anxious to promote friendly relations and work within the trade union structure with any other union solely interested in transport workers.'[2]

Once again they were expressing their doubt of the great general unions with a multiplicity of sections, such as the Transport & General Workers' Union, whilst throwing out a feeler towards those specialist unions which, like the Association itself, were 'solely interested in transport'. It looked as though public ownership would favour the London-based 'larger organizations' amongst trade union bodies, and that it would not do to remain too much aloof from Smith Square and Whitehall. A ballot of the Association was taken with the aim of affiliating once again to the Labour Party, from which the Association had withdrawn after the General Strike. The result of the ballot, which was declared by the Executive on February 7, 1945, favoured political affiliation by a large majority, with only a third of the membership voting.[3,4] But the necessary alteration to rules meant that the Association could not send delegates to the Labour Party Conference until 1947. During November 1944, the General Council of the British Trades Union Congress held formal meetings with the transport unions about the next steps, and John Brannigan must have had ample opportunity for sounding out the other unions catering for road transport workers. Apart from the giant Transport & General Workers' Union, these were the United Road Transport Workers' Association, based on Manchester, whose secretary was J. C. Francis, affiliated on a membership of 9,430, and the Liverpool & District Carters' and Motormen's Union, affiliating at 8,150, whose secretary was Albert Denaro. At this time the finishing touches were being put to the Labour Party's document, *The Post-war Organization of British Transport*, an interim report adopted by the postponed 1944 Conference in the second week of December 1944. This was followed by a memorandum prepared

---

[1] Appendix A of the General Council Report to the TUC, 1944.
[2] Report of the Annual Conference, 1944.
[3]

Ballot for political affiliation	3,846
Against	715
Spoilt Votes	27
	4,588

13,000 ballot papers issued, 8,412 not returned.
[4] Executive *Minutes*, February 7, 1945.

by the TUC's Economic Sub-Committee entitled *Financial Aspects of the Transfer of an Industry from Private to Public Ownership with Particular Reference to Transport*,[1] which was submitted to the Labour Party's sub-committee in March.

All these documents were reflected in the Labour Party's post-war election programme *Let Us Face the Future*, which was adopted at the Blackpool Labour Party Conference on May 24, 1945, and included the public ownership of inland transport:

'Co-ordination of transport services by rail, road, air and canal requires unification. This, without public ownership, means a struggle with sectional interests or the enthronement of a private monopoly which would be a menace to the rest of industry.'[2]

Forty days later, the General Election took place; and two months after Blackpool, Clement Attlee formed the third Labour Government, on July 27, 1945, with 392 Labour seats, and an overwhelming Labour majority. When the Trades Union Congress met at Blackpool in October, George Chester said in moving their final memorandum: 'Those sections of the industry which have been taken over for unified operation during the war should be acquired forthwith and should serve as the nucleus on which a more comprehensive national transport system should be built.'[3] Six weeks later, on November 1, 1945, the new Minister of War Transport, Alfred Barnes, met representatives of the transport unions in London and explained what were the proposals. John Brannigan was present. But when the Lord President of the Council, Herbert Morrison, announced the new Government's programme for reconstructing essential services, it became clear that road transport would not come into the programme for nationalization during the first session. This at least gave more time for the unions to consider practical details. In London a Transport Consultative Committee was set up to advise the Minister 'as to any individual unions which should be brought into the discussion', and to see the Bill through when the time came. But none of the smaller transport unions were represented upon it; it was composed of seven members of the General Council of the British TUC, including representatives of the three railway unions and of the Transport & General Workers' Union. While they were deliberating with the Minister, the Association had taken the initiative in Scotland. The Annual Conference met early in April 1946 in Inverness, when the discussion on nationalization showed that delegates felt that the proposals did not go far enough. At the Scottish TUC at Dunoon later in the month, the Association sponsored an important resolution which noted: 'that these proposals only constitute a limited form of nationalization, and

[1] Paras 297–303, General Council Report to the TUC, 1945.
[2] *Let Us Face the Future*, section IV.
[3] 77th Annual Report of the TUC, 1945.

believing that all transport is purely a public service, recommends the Government to keep in view the ultimate complete nationalization of every form of transport.'[1]

As well as the limited scope of the Bill, which is discussed in section 4 of this chapter, there were other doubts. For the Minister had made a speech in which he had not used the word nationalization, but had said merely that 'legislation would shortly be introduced to co-ordinate all forms of transport'. The employers' organizations had made full play of this: co-ordination without public ownership was their programme. Again, the Association felt uneasiness when it emerged that, as from August 15, 1946, the Minister had decided to end the war-time Road Haulage Organization. The release of the hauliers from control before firm steps had been taken towards nationalization was another shock. The members' feeling was expressed in an article in the journal by Charlie Bruce, who wrote:

'The question has to be asked: Why toss overboard a system of Government control which has advantages, despite limitations, and then give private enterprise the right to run the industry in its own interest, if nationalization has to come anyhow?'

He claimed that this demonstrated a tendency to use 'the best brains of the upper class in preference to workers' control', which would retard nationalization:

'If the government seeks brains to run the industry, I say give me Jimmy White and another ten or twelve comrades from the ranks and we'll run the Scottish road haulage industry efficiently, but in the interests of the people and, incidentally, the interests of the Labour Government.'[2]

Some of these anxieties were allayed when the publication of the text of the Transport Bill on November 28, 1946 put it beyond doubt that nationalization of road transport would be dealt with in the second session of the new Government. But by then the Association had other anxieties, one of which was the old problem of the relations between the unions catering for road transport workers. The 1944 Annual Conference had left the way open to 'promote friendly relations' with other unions, 'solely interested in transport workers', and John Brannigan joined in a number of discussions both in Scotland and in London. In the Summer of 1944, the Executive Council decided to instruct the Association's organizers and collectors that 'the whole of the commercial field of transport in Scotland, within the terms of the Agreements with other unions, was the sphere of activity of this Association, and that they should work towards securing the complete recognition of this union within that sphere'.[3]

[1] 49th Annual Report of the Scottish Trades Union Congress, 1946.
[2] *The Highway*, November 1946.
[3] Executive *Minutes*, July 5, 1944.

At the 1945 Annual Conference, Edinburgh delegates called for immediate talks with the Transport & General Workers' Union for a revision of the working agreement in a resolution moved by Jackie Steedman and J. Carabine of Edinburgh. John Brannigan pressed that it should be remitted. There was difference of opinion on the Executive when they came to discuss it, and it was not until August 1945 that they could agree on the next step:

'It was moved by Messrs Falconer and Wilkie, that the General Secretary open up negotiations to terminate the present Agreement. After a considerable amount of discussion and a statement by the General Secretary, this was agreed.'[1]

On September 7, 1945 John Brannigan and David Johnstone met with A. Paterson and T. B. Meikle of the Transport & General Workers' Union; it was four months before any results came of that, and even those were unsatisfactory. Discussions with these Scottish Area officials had shown that they 'took the view that if the Agreement was altered in any way it should also permit them to organize in spheres of activity which were presently the sole right of the SHMA. After a considerable amount of discussion it was decided on the motion of Messrs Little & Callaghan that the present time was not opportune to proceed with these discussions.'[2]

It would scarcely have escaped John Brannigan's notice that, all through these months, the TGWU over the Border had been in dispute with one of the smaller transport unions, the United Road Transport Workers' Association. It was complained that a number of Yorkshire coal employers' associations had been induced to sign agreements with the small union although it was not the representative organization, and at rates lower than those under the Road Haulage Order. When it was requested that these agreements should be jointly re-negotiated, the reply was that the TGWU should first 'give consideration to and concede the right of the United Road Transport Workers' Association to representation in the various agreements which the Transport & General Workers' Union had negotiated governing transport workers in various sections of industry in which they had considerable membership.'[3] The difference dragged on, and, just before the 1946 TUC, a new development was reported to the Association's Executive Council. The United Road Transport Workers' Association had approached John Brannigan, 'suggesting that that Union and ourselves should consider the advisability of federating, in order that we should press for the whole country a more united front on policy in respect of road transport'.[4] It was decided to hold a special meeting of

[1] Executive *Minutes*, August 1, 1945.
[2] Executive *Minutes*, January 9, 1946.
[3] 77th Annual Report of the TUC, 1945.
[4] Executive *Minutes*, October 2, 1946.

the Executive Council 'to consider the whole matter'. Before they could do so, however, the Brighton TUC had met, at which delegates had debated a controversial subject, on which the General Council had sent round a circular entitled 'The Closed Shop'.[1] It was a subject which some delegates saw as a 'real danger of abusing present power at the expense of the smaller unions associated with this Congress', in the words of Bob Edwards, General Secretary of the Chemical Workers' Union, whose organization was frequently in dispute with the Transport & General Workers' Union.

Correspondence had passed between John Brannigan and J. C. Francis, General Secretary of the United Road Transport Workers' Association, on whether they should make a joint declaration of policy 'in view of the attitude of certain of the bigger organizations on the question of Closed Shop policy'. Now the Association's special Executive meeting 'gave long and serious consideration' to this. They had before them 'a document which showed that this union had actually been considering amalgamation with the Transport & General Workers' Union as far back as 1937'. Finally it was unanimously decided:

'(1) That in view of the declaration of policy by the British TUC General Council on the principle of the Closed Shop, there was nothing to fear in so far as a smaller union was concerned and that it would be injudicious for this union, in these circumstances, to make any public declaration.

'(2) In any event, this Association would be celebrating its Jubilee in the year 1948, and it was generally felt that our independence should be preserved until such celebrations were over.'[2]

There the matter rested; but, at the 1946 Annual Conference of the Association, there was some dissatisfaction at the failure to end the working agreement with the Transport & General Workers' Union. John Brannigan told delegates that, while the Executive were in sympathy with the view of the small trade unions which feared their existence might be endangered by action of the large unions, 'we could not in the meantime agree to any principle which might involve the Association in any conflict with another union'. He said that the existing working agreements with the distributive workers and the TGWU gave 'no immediate cause for concern'. One argument which he used to reassure delegates that there must be co-operation with the other unions, was: 'On the various wage-fixing bodies we meet with these people and if the industry is to be nationalized, then it is obvious there will be a common front required.'[3] Two Glasgow members, Jimmy White, Jnr and Geoffrey Sheridan, pressed for a committee of conference delegates who should be appointed to go into the whole matter with the Executive; but this was finally defeated by fifteen votes to forty-

[1] Appendix A of the General Council Report to the TUC, 1946.
[2] Minutes of special Executive Meeting, November 2, 1946.
[3] Report of Annual Conference, 1947.

three. Before the end of that year, one of the two remaining small transport unions, the Liverpool & District Carters' & Motormen's Union, had been absorbed into the Transport & General Workers' Union.

While the Association had had these doubts and anxieties about the future, they were, nevertheless, fully in favour of nationalization, and their criticisms were directed towards wondering whether the scheme would go far enough. The road haulage employers, however, had been mounting a powerful campaign against it for many months. Theirs was perhaps the most skilful of all the anti-nationalization campaigns which the third Labour Government had to meet.

2. THE CAMPAIGN AGAINST NATIONALIZATION

The hauliers formally opened their anti-nationalization campaign on November 20, 1945, the day after Herbert Morrison had announced that the nationalization of road transport would be included in the new Government's programme. But, in fact, preparations for it had been laid years before. Employers knew as well as the transport workers that war-time needs made measures of centralization and co-ordination inevitable. The questions for them had been: under whose auspices—private mergers or public control? At what price? Could the eggs be unscrambled afterwards? After the railway companies had received favourable treatment for war-time Government contracts, some of the big hauliers known as 'the Waldorf Group', already closely associated with the railway companies, put in a memorandum to the Government offering to run a war-time Road Haulage Organization. They included such firms as McNamara, Bouts-Tillotson, and Pye. On April 5, 1941, the War Transport Council was set up to advise the Minister. It included Sir Maxwell Hicks, chairman of McNamara, who had been spokesman for the big hauliers before the Royal Commission and, with his colleague, J. S. Nicholl, had been prominent in the British Road Federation formed after the Salter Conference of 1933. The smaller firms also banded together for self-protection; and in January 1943 a number of them who were handling traffic co-operatively formed a national association. The same year a pamphlet[1] was published by a number of big independent firms which argued that firms owning fewer than twenty six-tonners should be set a time limit within which they should increase their fleets or join up with bigger firms. Amongst those who signed it were J. S. Nicholl (McNamara), Isaac Barrie (Glasgow Hiring Co.), H. T. Dutfield (H. & G. Dutfield), G. T. M. Fairclough, and J. F. E. Pye.

When the post-war reconstruction reports had been endorsed by the British Trades Union Congress and the Labour Party Conference in October and December 1944, it was a public declaration that there was every

[1] *The Road Carrying Industry and the Future.*

intention to carry war-time co-ordination through into peace-time public ownership. Immediately, in January 1945, the Road Haulage Association was formed, with H. T. Dutfield as chairman; and they set to work extremely vigorously. When nearly twenty-two months later the Transport Bill was published, the Road Haulage Association was able to mount a powerful anti-nationalization campaign which must have cost a very great deal of money, indeed. By May 1945, Lord Leathers, Minister of War Transport in the 'Caretaker' Government, encouraged discussions between representatives of the railway companies and the Road Haulage Association. A considerable measure of agreement was finally reached between them; they worked out a degree of co-ordination which could be represented as an alternative to nationalization and would also eliminate the small competitors.

The first action of the Road Haulage Association after the third Labour Government had announced its intention ultimately to nationalize road haulage was to launch a fighting fund; and to issue warnings against nationalization by Press and circular. They paid the greatest attention to publicity, and appointed sixteen public relations officers to work on the campaign. There were posters on the hoardings everywhere. Free film shows were provided. A feature of the campaign was a nation-wide petition. The Road Haulage Association appealed to the general public, to the small hauliers, and even to the road transport workers.[1] The editorial comment in *The Highway* noted 'with some amusement the belated whine that is being set up'. Of the anti-nationalization campaign just begun, it continued:

'It is too late in the day to argue on the merits or otherwise of the principle of nationalization, as if ever an industry in this country proved by the multiplicity of legislation which had to be introduced since the last war to control the industry that it was heading for nationalization through mismanagement and cut-throat competition, that industry is the road haulage industry.

'We are not concerned nor are to be influenced at this stage with the sentimental whine that it is the small man who is going to suffer (and no one will be robbed in the process of nationalization), because in any great State scheme that is designed for the public good, with the knowledge and approval of the public, while there should be consideration for the *rights* of individuals during any period of transition, the scheme itself must inevitably find its way to the Statue book.'[2]

The employers did not slacken their efforts; the Road Haulage Association produced two documents in 1946. The first, *Road Carriers' Licensing*,

[1] The Association's Journal *The Highway* of February 1946 carried a prominently displayed notice:
DO NOT SIGN THE EMPLOYERS' PETITION AGAINST NATIONALIZATION
[2] *The Highway*, February 1946.

provided for an agreement between the big hauliers and the railway companies not to oppose licences for applicants endorsed by themselves. The second was a major policy document. It was called *Co-ordination of Road and Rail Freight Transport*, published on July 17, 1947, and signed by Sir Charles H. Newton, chairman of the Railways Managers' Conference, and by H. T. Dutfield, chairman of the Road Haulage Association. These echoes of the 'Square Deal' were put forward 'not as an alternative to nationalization, but as a better plan'. The document, it was claimed, proved that road hauliers had accepted the obligations of a public service. To summarize its main points:

1. The road hauliers would accept the same statutory obligations as the railways to carry whatever goods were offered.
2. Haulage should have a national rates structure 'capable of correlation' with railway rates.
3. An area haulage organization should be set up to carry goods which individual hauliers could not conveniently handle.
4. Observance of 'integration' was planned, in these terms:
   'The railways will continue their present policy of concentrating their general merchandise traffic on few railway stations and of establishing railheads throughout the country, these to be served by road for collection and delivery purposes'.
   Express wagons should be put at the disposal of hauliers and consideration would be given to new organizations, owned jointly by the railways and hauliers, to handle railway collection and delivery.

Here was an early statement of the freight 'liner' project put forward by Dr Beeching as part of the policy of the Conservative Government in 1960, after the 1959 General Election. It was not calculated to be to the disadvantage of the road hauliers, even when the railways too were still in private hands. This document made a rallying-point for the anti-nationalization campaign, and was not without its effect.

Within a month of its publication, on August 15, 1946, government control of road haulage ended, which gave rise, as we have seen, to some anxiety in sections of the trade union movement about the Government's intentions. The RHA's joint plan won the approval of the Association of British Chambers of Commerce, the Federation of British Industries, the National Union of Manufacturers, and the British Road Federation. On December 12, 1946, a Liaison Committee of these organizations, the Road Haulage Association, and others was set up to press for an inquiry before the Bill became law; and three days later, on the eve of the Second Reading, the Central Committee of Transport Users, with the Traders' Co-ordinating Committee on Transport, and the Trades' Road Transport Association came out with detailed criticisms of the Bill. Next day H. T. Dutfield announced that the Road Haulage Association's petition had been signed by 600,000 people 'including many lorry drivers'. This was the culmination of Act One of their campaign: the points on which they had campaigned so energetically were to be the Conservative Opposition's brief during the Second Reading, when their main speakers were Sir David Maxwell Fyfe, Sir Cuthbert Headlam, Colonel G. Hutchinson, R. H. Turton, Lady Davidson, W. S. Morrison, R. Assheton, and Anthony Eden. Presenting and supporting the Bill were Alfred Barnes, Minister of Transport and a leading Co-operative Member of Parliament, Hugh Dalton, Herbert Morrison, the Parliamentary Secretary, G. R. Strauss, Ernest Davies, R. J. Mellish, F. McLeavy, and W. A. Wilkins.

As the Christmas recess ended, the Road Haulage Association and the British Road Federation published a manifesto on January 17, 1947, which described the scheme as 'a huge State monopoly', 'red tape and impersonal control', 'an act of political folly'; the authors insisted that no compensaion would be enough for the little man's loss of business 'built up by thought and hard work'; and finally, that the Bill would 'perpetrate a social injustice without parallel in British history'. This did not make much impact upon the road transport worker, because in the meantime something harder than hard words had overtaken him: the intransigence of the employers' side in the Central Road Haulage Wages Board had precipitated a serious strike, and had led the Labour Government to take the decision to use troops to distribute merchandise from the London markets and docks.

3. THE TRANSPORT STRIKE

In May 1946, the unions had put in a claim to the Central Road Haulage Wages Board for a forty-four-hour week, for an increase of annual paid holidays from six to twelve days, and for the modification of the accumulative week. Under this system overtime was paid on a daily basis only after ten hours; on a weekly basis, after forty-eight hours. Employers could make their men work ten hours for four days and then two days for only four hours, and still not have to pay overtime rates. Traffic conditions were already such that to run an hour over the time was very frequently both inevitable and unpredictable. The transport worker's father and grandfather might have been obliged to spend hours over schedule waiting at congested docks and bridges, and to unload without being paid for delays which were not within his control; the driver in 1946 would have none of it. Some might have been tempted to go slow at the end of the day to steal a late hour on overtime rates, but the vast majority was penalized unfairly by the accumulative week system; and employers were not lacking who would so arrange the weekly schedules as to make it impossible ever to get overtime for extra hours worked. The system put a premium upon evasions and friction; it was high time that the unions should call for its revision. The proposal, therefore, was to fix the week as eight hours for five days and four hours for one day, with a guaranteed number of hours to be worked each day.

The haulage employers turned down the application on September 26, 1946; negotiations dragged on through further meetings in October and November, but finally broke down. John Brannigan commented:

'It is perfectly obvious that no improvement will be brought about without a fight. Our members can rest assured, however, that the principles involved in this application are so important to us that the fight for their establishment will be pursued to the bitter end.'[1]

Once again the haulage employers had dug in against any reduction of the working-week or regulation of the working-day. Finally, on December 31, 1946, the Central Road Haulage Wages Board announced Road Haulage Order No. 21, which rejected the shorter week, conceded nine days' holiday and made some minor changes which went nowhere towards meeting the men's main grievance, which was the accumulative working-week for overtime. London transport workers at once decided upon a strike, and it began in the London Area on January 6, 1947.

The actions of the haulage employers had at one and the same time confronted the Labour Government with a powerful Parliamentary struggle against nationalization and a major strike of transport workers, who might well have been expected to be the main basis for support as the struggle for the Transport Bill developed.

The Transport & General Workers' Union appealed to the strikers to return pending an emergency meeting of the Central Wages Board; the men decided to stay out and to call for official recognition of the strike by the union. The strike spread and, by January 8, 1947, there were 13,000 men on strike in London, including the firms of McNamara, H. & G. Dutfield, which belonged to the chairman of the Road Haulage Association, Carter Paterson, and Pickfords. The strike began to spread to Bristol, Ipswich, Oxford, Leeds, Birmingham, Coventry, and the county of Kent. With the docks and markets in London stopped, 400 Smithfield provision drivers came out in sympathy. On January 9th, Minister of Labour, George Isaacs, told the men to go back, since he would refuse to confirm any proposal from the Wages Board while the strike was still on. The Minister of Food, John Strachey, said that food rations could not be honoured and that if the men did not return, troops would be used to distribute the food, on Monday, January 13th. The Smithfield Market porters replied that they too would strike if troops were brought in, and the strike spread to Southampton, Norwich, Liverpool, Cambridge, and Glasgow. The London strikers issued a statement explaining why they were so deeply opposed to the accumulative week system, and declared that they had no confidence in the impartiality of the Central Wages Board. The

[1] *The Highway*, November 1946.

Road Haulage Association, on the other hand, issued a statement saying that the strike was a challenge to constitutional machinery. By now, 1,500 employees of Thomas Tillings had joined the strike, which brought the number out in London to 20,000. In Ayr, on Saturday, January 11th, the Executive Council of the Association held a meeting, at which it was reported that transport workers employed by Garlick, Burrell & Edwards Ltd. in Glasgow had been asked by the London men to strike in sympathy. Several meetings were held with the Glasgow men and finally, 'they had agreed to await the decisions of the central RHWB on 13th inst, and it was unanimously agreed on the motion of Messrs J. McQuade and Wilkie that we demand the implementation of the claims which are presently before the CRHWB in their entirety and that failing the granting of these claims, a special meeting of the Executive Council be held to determine the Association's policy in the light of the decisions of the CRHWB.'[1]

At the week-end, the London men held a delegate meeting, at which, despite the appeal of Arthur Deakin, they voted to continue the strike. Next day, Monday, January 13th, some 3,500 troops were moved into Smithfield Market with 600 lorries and began deliveries; meat porters and provision drivers stopped work there and in Covent Garden and other London markets. The Central Wages Board held its emergency meeting, but the employers would not budge. As the machinery of the Board would not allow a new Award without its going first to the Area Boards, George Isaacs, the Minister of Labour, put to both sides a proposal made by Arthur Deakin that they should agree to a voluntary Joint Industrial Council. This was set up with ten representatives of the Transport & General Workers' Union, the Association, the United Road Transport Workers' Association, and the Liverpool & District Carters' and Motor-men's Union, with H. T. Dutfield appointed chairman and J. E. Corrin, of the Transport & General, as vice-chairman. It was due to meet on January 19, 1947. By Wednesday, January 15th, there were more than 30,000 road transport workers, 11,000 dockers and 2,000 lightermen out in London, and some 23,000 transport workers in provincial towns, either on strike or about to stop. Another delegate meeting was called, which lasted for six hours and ended in a vote against a return, as the men demanded some guarantee that their claims would be met. The delegates finally agreed to return to work on the eve of meeting of the Joint Industrial Council. When this met on January 19th, the employers were still adamant and the JIC reported to the Minister of Labour that they had failed to agree. He appointed a Court of Inquiry,[2] whose findings were reported on January 23rd. They recommended a forty-four-hour week without loss of pay, and a regulated working-week of five or 5½ days, all hours in excess to be paid

[1] Executive *Minutes*, January 11, 1947.
[2] Lord Torrington, Chairman; J. E. Greenwood (director of Boots); James Young (Gen. Sec., Association of Engineering and Shipbuilding Draughtsmen).

as overtime, and approved the employers' offer of nine days' holiday. Next day, a Joint Industrial Council accepted this and so did the Road Haulage Association. It was victory at long last.

In the Association's journal, John Brannigan commented:

'The resentment of some strikers can best be understood by those of us who were engaged in the negotiations and were eternally confronted with the definite attitude of the employers on the question of the regulated week, and although great concern was felt in all quarters for the disaster which faced the country as a result of that strike, it must be conceded that the claim would probably not have been met for many months had it not been for the action of the men.'[1]

He also remarked that the strike 'only stopped short of spreading to Scotland by the careful handling of the situation by the union's leadership'. This statement was not quite accurate: the Executive Minutes for the same month record that 200 men came out in Glasgow.

The effect of the national strike was far from negligible. Its influence could be traced in a number of ways in Scotland, as elsewhere; the determination with which the coalmen pursued their strike in Aberdeen to limit the weight of sacks carried up flights of stairs, and the demand for a speed-up of negotiating machinery in every branch of the trade are examples of the long-term and indirect effect of this defeat of the most powerful group of road transport employers. These events took place in the very severe and prolonged winter when the serious fuel crisis had damaging effects on post-war reconstruction of the economy, and showed how long overdue was the modernization and technical re-equipment of the basic industries. No small responsibility for the coal shortage could be laid on the failure in transport, both by rail and by road. Again, the need to set up voluntary machinery was an important lesson, which was not lost on members of the Association. Some drew from it the conclusion that, in the last resort, they must depend upon their own strength in organization and free negotiation to come to grips with employers, and not upon complicated compulsory machinery. Fifteen years later they were to remember it vividly, and turn to it again.

An immediate and direct effect of the transport strike was upon the drivers employed by C-licence-holders to whom the findings of the court also applied. It was upon their exclusion from the final draft of the Transport Bill that the Association concentrated its sharpest criticism.

4. THE TRANSPORT BILL

The Bill proposed a British Transport Commission having power to acquire a wide range of transport undertakings, with separate Executives

[1] *The Highway*, February 1947.

to run the nationalized railways, road passenger transport, road freight transport, and other undertakings. A Transport Arbitration Tribunal was provided to consider and confirm acquisition notices, as well as Transport Users' Consultative Committees' What the labour and trade union movement had been looking for was a scheme for taking all forms of transport into national ownership, and then co-ordinating them. The text of the Transport Bill, when it was published on November 28, 1946, was eagerly studied; but it was found to fall short of this aim. All the property of the unprofitable railway companies, including their road vehicles and interests, the main canal companies, and the London Passenger Transport Board was to be nationalized by January 1, 1948; but important sections of road and passenger transport were to be exempt or partially excluded. No road transport vehicle ordinarily operating less than twenty-five miles from its base was to be taken over. A- and B-licence vehicles belonging to firms engaged in activities 'to a predominant extent[1] of ordinary long distance carriage for hire or reward' could be brought under the Act. The criterion of 'long distance' stipulated vehicles which operated over twenty-five miles from their home base and that goods should be carried for more than forty miles. Vehicles for specialized traffic were excluded altogether; these were vehicles for bulk liquids, meat and livestock, furniture removal, and 'abnormal indivisible loads'. The Commission was to have power to issue permits allowing firms to continue to license vehicles 'having a single specified operating centre', which would otherwise be acquired, until such permits were revoked. The intention was to space out the acquisition of undertakings; this provided a big loophole, and, in the event, many escaped altogether. Furthermore, C-licence vehicles of traders and manufacturers carrying their own goods were exempted from nationalization; it was proposed in the first draft that at least they should be limited to carrying not more than forty miles from their base without a permit from a licensing authority. When it came to road passenger transport, the Commission was to take over those belonging to the London Passenger Transport Board and those in which the railway companies held a share. There remained all the vehicles owned by the local authorities and the private bus companies. For these, the Commission was only to begin by preparing schemes of co-ordination in consultation with local authorities. These schemes allowed either for public ownership or for co-ordination under private ownership, and provided another sizeable loophole. As the Scottish transport workers were not slow to point out, the Scottish Motor Traction Company and its subsidiaries controlled almost one hundred per cent of the private bus companies in Scotland, including the operation of many municipal services.

[1] A firm was regarded as being so engaged 'to a predominant extent' if either more than half the weight of the total goods it carried was on long distance work, or more than half its takings were derived from such work.

This was far from being comprehensive nationalization of transport as a public service. Its limited scope provided loopholes. The employers saw many opportunities for evasion; but their main line of attack was to widen the gaps provided by the exemptions until a twenty-tonner could be driven through them. On the other hand, the transport workers hastened to put their weight behind reducing the exemptions and closing the gaps. There were, of course, other points of difficulty, ranging from the financial aspects, both of the level of rates and of compensation, to consultative machinery and control: but the first main battleground was the scope of nationalization itself.

The first need, while the Bill was before Parliament, was to counter the propaganda of the Road Haulage Association which had been so quickly and effectively off the mark. The Scottish Horse & Motormen's Association had been one of the first bodies in Scotland to become alive to the need for this, especially after the joint policy document of the Road Haulage Association and the railway companies in July 1946, which had shown that they were capable of getting together to demonstrate that co-ordination of these conflicting interests could be achieved under private ownership. The Glasgow Co-ordinating Committee of the Scottish Horse & Motormen's Association took up the matter and pressed the Glasgow Trades Council to stage a large-scale demonstration. But although discussions went on all through the autumn and early winter, it was not until February 2, 1947 that this demonstration took place in St Andrew's Hall. The main speakers were C. N. Gallie, General Secretary of the Railway Clerks' Association, and Alfred Robens, then Parliamentary Private Secretary to the Minister of Transport. John Brannigan was in the chair. Ten days later, on February 16th there was a conference called by the Labour Party Scottish Council, when Alfred Barnes, the Minister of Transport, spoke on nationalization. The Association appointed half its Executive Council as delegates to this conference; these were Messrs Berrey, Callaghan, Ferguson, Hendry, McQuade, and Wilkie.

The day before, the Minister had met in Edinburgh representatives of the General Council of the Scottish TUC, on to which John Brannigan had been co-opted the same day, to discuss a memorandum on the Transport Bill which they had submitted. Their main points were to press for a Scottish Transport Executive, which was not conceded, and also for a permanent Scottish Transport Users' Consultative Committee, on which the Minister agreed subject to several modifications. But these were points of detail. The sharpest criticism was provoked a month later, on March 13, 1947, when the Bill reached the Committee Stage in the House of Commons. The road haulage employers scored an important victory when Alfred Barnes yielded to Opposition pressure and announced that he was dropping the proposal which would prevent C-licence-holders from carrying beyond forty miles from their base, without approval of the licensing authority. This was the most serious of a number of concessions on the scope of the Bill, and the Association reacted strongly. An emergency resolution was adopted by the Annual Conference on April 6, 1947 and telegraphed to the Ministry of Transport:

'The Annual Conference of the Scottish Horse & Motormen's Association, assembled this week-end at Dumfries, unanimously protest against Government action in granting concessions to C-licensed operators under the Transport Nationalization Bill.'[1]

It was moved by J. White, Snr (Glasgow), and seconded by Charlie Bruce (Glasgow). The General Secretary intervened to say, for the Executive Council, that all transport, being a public service, should be owned by the people who used it. The resolution demonstrated that the Association was not satisfied that the Bill was sufficient. He referred to the widespread belief that, in taking C-licence vehicles out of the scope of the Bill, the Minister had 'succumbed to the Co-operative movement', which at that time was one of the biggest holders of C-licences. He went on: 'The Co-operative movement, so far as this Association is concerned, is an employer the same as any other and must be regarded as such. It is fitting that from this Conference the Ministry of Transport should be advised that we are the practical people; we know what we want, and nothing less than the complete and entire nationalization of all forms of transport in this country will suffice.'

Another resolution, from Glasgow Co-operative Wholesale Society and Retail Branch, welcomed nationalization but added 'that to ensure the success a generous measure of workers' control is essential'. A resolution by the same branch was also moved calling for an amendment to the Bill 'to allow for a shorter working-day', after speakers had remarked that 'working fourteen hours out of twenty-four is not in accordance with present-day principles of the trade union movement'. Yet another resolution, moved by Alex Kitson—it was only his second Conference—and seconded by J. Rowan of Lanarkshire, demanded that representatives on the Central Road Haulage Wages Board press for recognition of Saturday afternoon 'as the weekly half-holiday', and that work after noon should be at double time rates. These and other resolutions showed deep concern with the nationalization of road haulage and the possibilities and problems arising from it.

A fortnight later, at the 1947 Scottish TUC at St Andrews, a comprehensive composite resolution was moved by William Ballantine for the NUR and seconded by David Johnstone, who had become the Association's Assistant General Secretary. Four main points were made in it; that Scotland had special needs; that privately-owned passenger services should be brought 'within the control of the Transport Commission in the same

[1] Report of Annual Conference, 1947.

way as rail transport', with special reference to the Scottish Motor Traction Co.; that road freight exemptions should be cut; and that the Bill was only a first step towards complete nationalization. The wording of these last two points shows the influence of the Association:

'(d) that with regard to road freight services the exemptions contained in the Bill should be cut to the minimum and all road haulage co-ordinated with rail services to achieve the maximum efficiency in the industry;
(e) that this limited form of public ownership and control is only the first step towards the complete nationalization of all transport services.'

David Johnstone spoke especially on the exemptions and the need to co-ordinate road haulage with the rail services:

'He did not desire to see a "black market" established within the nationalized transport industry and condemned the issue of licences for the carriage of goods with certain limits. He concluded by urging the Government to nationalize the entire haulage industry to ensure the greatest good for the community.'[1]

In the Association's journal, Charlie Bruce wrote how 'dismayed' members were 'by the concessions which were being handed out to the employers'. He described how the loopholes were making it possible for employers to work a black market in road haulage:

'As an example, I can give an instance of one Glasgow fishing firm which owned only one vehicle; now it operates eight, all new vehicles, and another four are on the way. Moreover, it is openly claimed that a well-known long distance firm is connected with this enterprise; thus it is easy to understand how the racket is going to work.'

But he insisted that the most significant weakness was 'the absence of a general plan relating to the co-ordination of transport as a whole'. He argued that

'The trade unions operating in the industry should at least be drawn into any discussions on this and that they in turn should seek to find the necessary data to assist the Government from amongst the actual transport workers themselves, for in the final analysis the workers alone know from experience how best the job can be done'.[2]

All through spring and summer there were fierce battles in both Houses of Parliament as the Conservative Opposition put the employers' arguments. There were, for example, no less than forty-seven amendments aimed to exempt various sections of road transport from the Act. When the Government gave way on C-licences and exempted them from the

[1] 50th Annual Report of the Scottish TUC, 1947.
[2] *The Highway*, May 1947.

former mileage limit on free operation, one Labour member tried unsuccessfully to counter it by proposing that C-licence-holders should be required to show need before being exempted. He was Ernest Davies, MP for Enfield. In an important book[1] published at this time, he made two main points on the management of nationalized industries and upon its finances. In his view, the success of a nationalized industry would depend upon local managers, technicians, and workmen, and it was from these that the Boards of nationalized industries should, in the main, be drawn.

'The past mistake has been the belief that the ablest and most efficient industrialists, with a financial stake in private enterprise, are the best men available for the operation of public enterprise. This cannot be assumed and the practice of seeking to buy them at inflated salaries should end. The field is not so limited.'

He prophesied that the danger of approaching nationalized industries on orthodox financial lines would end in 'State capitalism, with many of the faults of private capitalism'. As long as the standard of success was financial solvency, the public corporation would be handicapped:

'Admittedly, nationalization must be efficient and economically run, but the final test of its success is not the annual balancing of its budget, the meeting of interest on its capital or the building up of its reserve funds. In the last resort, the community will judge nationalization by the service it provides.'

His views were close to those of the Association, but they were not accepted by the Government.

When Alfred Barnes had moved the Second Reading of the Bill on December 16, 1946, he had said that £1,065,000,000 would be involved in taking over the railways, the canals, and the London Passenger Transport Board, by 'the largest and most extensive socialization measure ever presented to a free and democratic Parliament. . . . Parliament, in my view, in looking at transport, should look at it as a major overhead cost on the whole of British trade and industry.'[2] The Bill did not finally receive the Royal Assent until August 6, 1947. Two days later, the Minister announced those who were to compose the British Transport Commission. These were: Sir Cyril Hurcomb, Chairman, a civil servant who had been Director-General at the Ministry of War Transport from 1941 to 1946; Lord Ashfield, Chairman of the London Passenger Transport Board, formerly of Imperial Chemical Industries, the Midland Bank, and a number of gas and power undertakings; John Benstead, General Secretary of the National Union of Railwaymen; Lord Rusholme, General Secretary

[1] *National Enterprise: The Development of the Public Corporation.* (Gollancz, 6s.)
[2] *Hansard*, December 16, 1946.

of the Co-operative Union; and Sir William Wood, of the London Midland & Scottish Railway Company.

Some days later, came the announcement of a part-time member, Captain Sir Ian Bolton, OBE, a chartered accountant and a director of the London Midland & Scottish Railway Co., the Coltness Iron Company, the Scottish American Investment Co., and the Scottish Widows' Fund and Life Insurance Society. The members of the Road Transport Executive were also announced. The chairman was a man with experience of army transport, Major-General G. N. Russell. The full-time members were: Claud Barrington, Managing Director of Transport Services Ltd; George Cardwell, of Thos. Tilling Ltd, and other bus and coach interests; Harold Clay, the National Passenger Group officer of the Transport & General Workers' Union; and Archibald Henderson, formerly of the TGWU, but recently chairman of the Traffic Commissioners in Scotland.

The part-time members were headed by Henry Dutfield himself, the chairman of the Road Haulage Association; Percy J. R. Tapp, chairman of the Meat Transport Organization Ltd; and William L. Beckett of Preston. Some of these appointments did not meet with the approval of the Association. A resolution was sent to the Ministry:

'That the appointment of Sir Ian Bolton, Bt. to be Scottish spare-time member of the new National Transport Executive is positively unacceptable to the 22,000 members of the Scottish Horse & Motormen's Association. The Executive Council on their behalf respectfully requests the Minister of Transport to reconsider this unfortunate appointment.'[1]

Although the Act came into formal operation on January 1, 1948, it was very long indeed before the process was completed of taking over such firms as were to be nationalized; it was longer still before the managerial changes and decisive steps towards integration were undertaken. These were not fully under way until the early months of 1951. A few short months passed and, by November 1951, a Conservative Government had been returned to power, pledged to denationalize road transport. Even the limited degree of national ownership had scarcely had any run. Above all, the essential integration of all forms of inland transport had not taken place.

---

[1] Executive *Minutes*, September 19, 1947.

CHAPTER SEVENTEEN

POST-WAR PROBLEMS

I. POLITICS IN THE ASSOCIATION

THE immediate post-war mood of optimism, unity and progress was strongly felt by members of the Association. The journal which went to press just after the end of the war in Europe commented in the Editorial Review:

'The time has now arrived to start work in implementation of many of the fine promises which have been made for the building of a new world, and if we carry with us the memory of the fear of destruction which clouded our lives during the most difficult years of the war, we will be resolute in our determination that the new world shall be established.'[1]

Before the war, the desire had been steadily rising for a new and progressive outlook, which Robert Taylor had encouraged; war-time experiences of transport workers, not least of those who were now coming back from the forces, had greatly increased their determination that their status within the industry should be improved. Many believed that a new social system was within reach and Britain would be transformed by the industrial workers, the transport men taking their place amongst them. It was expected that the new Labour Government, elected with an overwhelming majority, would curb the employers, nationalize all forms of inland transport and integrate it.

But the Scottish transport workers who were organized in the Association had much leeway to make up. Ever since 1926, when Hugh Lyon had broken the ties with the British Trades Union Congress and the Labour Party, following the aftermath of the General Strike, the Association was somewhat out of the main stream. The struggle of the road haulage sections and representation in the new national negotiating machinery brought them over the Border to Whitehall and Westminster, face to face with the biggest employers and alongside the biggest trade unions. Politically they had remained in the wilderness, despite moves under Robert Taylor at the beginning of the war. Changes in policy, in structure and in political education were urgently necessary if they were to grasp

---

[1] *The Highway*, May 1945.

new opportunities. Instead, when it turned out that nationalization was to be only partial and, in effect, to apply only to long distance haulage, no firm lead with a clear prospect of the way forward was given in other sections of transport, although amongst the co-operative men there were some important advances. The impression gained is that there was some tendency to wait upon events, perhaps in the expectation that even partial nationalization in the road haulage section would automatically seep down and gradually produce improvements elsewhere.

But denationalization was imposed before an end could be seen to the problems of transition, and before national ownership could lead to integration which had been for so many years admitted to be the essential need in transport. At the same time, the introduction of the Government policy of wage restraint had coincided with the transitional problems of nationalization. It was imperative that the gap between members and the 'heid yins', which had proved nearly disastrous in Hugh Lyon's later days, should not be allowed to open wider. If confusion and disillusionment amongst members were to be avoided, dynamic leadership was called for which could forge a new relationship with the members, drawing all into active partnership on a progressive policy, in a new and democratic spirit. The situation demanded a new outlook and new thinking, and an alertness to welcome and initiate innovations.

John Brannigan was witty, an engaging speaker, with a quick brain and tongue, and he could be a shrewd negotiator; but he did not show himself an innovator on the scale to match the immense post-war possibilities. His attitude to the post-war co-ordinating committees, set up in the cities where there was more than one branch, ranged from lack of encouragement to positive opposition. Despite difficulties, the Glasgow Co-ordinating Committee, of which the secretary was James White, Snr, played an important part, and could have played a greater one. It discussed questions of general interest and sent them back to the branches; it could have the effect of the lively branches stimulating the more slow-moving. The Executive Council had appointed branch delegates to trades councils; the co-ordinating committees took this over. In some respects they began to develop almost like district committees. It was the Glasgow Co-ordinating Committee which got the Glasgow Trades Council to call an important meeting at which Alfred Robens, later Lord Robens, spoke on nationalization. Certainly the co-ordinating committees expressed the mood for change; however restricted their development, they stimulated action for improvements of structure and administration. Contributions at annual conferences showed that a number felt that the starting-point for progress might be found in giving the structure of the Association a good shake-up. Many were eager for the members to take more interest in political affairs, since events had shown how closely industrial progress was linked with politics. Reaffiliation to the Labour Party, for example, was presented as a measure necessary to prevent the Association from remaining out of things.[1]

A certain pattern is discernible even in the structural and organizational changes. At the 1945 Annual Conference there was pressure for an Assistant General Secretary to be appointed, strongly resisted by John Brannigan, who himself had held that office for six years under Robert Taylor. At the next Executive meeting, on May 2, 1945, the step was taken, but not without conflict of opinion. Alexander Irvine was nominated as Assistant General Secretary by George Little and seconded by Allan Hendry, while Peter Callaghan and John McQuade moved and seconded David Johnstone.

By the narrow margin of six votes to five, Johnstone was chosen. His name first appeared in the records when he was elected to the Executive Council from Perth at the Annual Conference of 1937. In 1942 he was appointed organizer. As soon as he had become the Assistant General Secretary he went into politics and with the Association's backing stood for the Glasgow Town Council as a Labour Party candidate. But, after becoming Assistant General Secretary, Johnstone held office for only a little over four and a half years before he became the focus of an unhappy and profitless struggle within the leadership of the union. The following month the Executive made an appointment which turned out very differently: they approved the decision of the Organization Committee making Alex Kitson a full-time collector in Edinburgh.

There were three other debates at the last war-time Annual Conference, which met four weeks before VE-day. The Edinburgh delegates called for greater decentralization of administration to give area offices autonomy to deal with local problems, anticipating that many 'will require to be faced when demobilization takes place'. John Brannigan spoke against that and it was defeated by thirty-eight votes to nine. Again, objection was raised to officials and members of the Executive Council being allowed to join in the discussions at Conference: the President ruled that only the General Secretary and delegates should be allowed to speak. Finally, a new method of controlling the business of conference was introduced, on the motion of Willie Campbell of Edinburgh and James White, Jnr of Glasgow:

'It was agreed unanimously that a Standing Orders Committee be appointed at this and future conferences. It was thereafter agreed that

---

[1] The President elected in May 1945, Archie McDiarmid, said in his address the following year:
'For some time now it has been obvious to the Executive Council that whether under Conservative or Labour administration, the methods in trade union negotiation and the standing of the trade unions within the State is rapidly changing; and as the Association is becoming so frequently affected by legislation, it is considered advisable that we should at the earliest possible moment have a say in the fixing of legislation.' (Report of Annual Conference, 1946)

Messrs J. Barbour (Perth), J. White, Senior (Glasgow) and W. Campbell (Edinburgh) be appointed to the Standing Orders Committee.'[1]

At the Inverness Annual Conference next year, when he attended as a delegate elected by the Edinburgh Branch, Alex Kitson was chosen to serve on the Standing Orders Committee together with James White, Snr and James Barbour; he continued to be elected to this important post, year after year, from 1946 to 1953, with one break.

How any delegate should be selected to the Labour Party conference led to a long debate. There was a strong body of opinion which held that he should be appointed by conference and not by the Executive, which John Brannigan strongly resisted. In the same mood a motion from Glasgow called for more frequent meetings of the Association, which he also opposed with a sharp glance at the Glasgow Co-ordinating Committe; the Executive, he said,

'had already had experience of the results of meetings held without an officer being in attendance. It is necessary that branches at their meetings should be guided on major policy'.[2]

The motion was defeated by nine votes to forty; but the sentiment for a greater degree of democracy and of participation by the members continued to be expressed more and more vigorously in the next three years and in many different ways.

At the Dumfries Conference in 1947, for example, Andrew Inglis (Kilmarnock) asked that resolutions for Conference should be sent to the quarterly meetings for discussion; proper regard could not be had to them, he argued, if they were merely read out by the official attending the meeting. Glasgow scws and Retail Branch moved through James White, Jnr, that there should be a review of the whole structure of the union to make it 'adequate to grapple with the numerous problems the new legislation will throw up'. At the request of the General Secretary, this was referred to the Executive and little more was heard of it. Next, there was considerable discussion as to how the political fund accounts should be submitted, the aim of the floor being to exercise the maximum degree of branch supervision in this respect and the platform to resist it. The main debate at this Conference, however, arose on an Ayrshire resolution instructing the Executive 'to prepare rules for the administration and operation of the political activity within the Association. The proposed rules to be then submitted to the branches for their endorsement or amendment'.[3] It was moved by Andrew Inglis (Kilmarnock), in view of the Association having become politically affiliated, 'as under the present constitution no provision is made for political activity within the Associa-

[1] Report of Annual Conference, 1945.
[2] Report of Annual Conference, 1946.
[3] Report of Annual Conference, 1947.

tion'. It was seconded by Peter McGarry (Ayr). Amongst those supporting it, James White, Jnr said that 'under the present constitution no avenue is open whereby delegates can be elected to the Conferences of the National and Scottish Labour Parties'. Brannigan asked delegates to reject the resolution, but it was carried by thirty-five votes.

This 1947 Conference, meeting in March, was held in a tense atmosphere: the background to it was a fuel crisis, precipitated by severe weather, delay in re-equipping the mines and inadequate transport; a White Paper on the economic crisis had just been issued; the US President, Harry S. Truman, had, a week before, made his first speech in 'the cold war'. A foreign policy resolution from Glasgow, moved by James White, Snr, and seconded by W. McKay, viewed with alarm 'the constant quarrelling indulged in by the three big Powers' and, 'believing that Russian and American expansionist policy gravely endangers any hope of permanent peace, calls upon the Labour Government to drop its "continuity of foreign policy" and henceforth work for a Socialist Britain as a prelude to a Socialist world—the only possible alternative to another world war'.[1] An Edinburgh amendment moved by Joe Carabine and Jackie Steedman, supported the Government's foreign policy of close association with the United States and declared that the quarrelling was 'only a genuine endeavour to have all international points of difference straightened out before any peace treaties are signed'. There was a long debate in the course of which the General Secretary asked unsuccessfully that it should be referred back, after which J. Rowan (Lanarkshire) said that to celebrate the Association's golden jubilee a delegation should be sent to the USSR during 1948. In the event, the fact that the delegation ultimately went to the United States instead, after two years' delay, did not improve relations between some members and the General Secretary.

A controversial note had begun to creep into the annual conferences. At the end of this 1947 conference, Alex Kitson called for a four-day conference in future. 'Mr Kitson felt that insufficient time was being allowed for discussion on resolutions, and other important business arising from the conference agendas. This suggestion was seconded by Mr G. Sheridan.'[2] The General Secretary did not agree, and the question was left to the Executive to consider.

James White, Snr was elected to the Executive from this conference. At his first Executive meeting, when he was appointed to the Home and Editorial Committees, he took up the question of the Labour Party Conference agenda: had it 'been gone through for the purpose of instructing our delegate on certain items arising therefrom?' When it was moved that this be left to the General Secretary to handle, Tom Berrey and James White moved an amendment that it be dealt with by the Executive,

---

[1] Report of Annual Conference, 1947.
[2] Report of Annual Conference, 1947.

which was lost by three votes to six. James White, Snr had not served on the Executive before; but his son had been on it in 1943, when he had been at loggerheads with Robert Taylor. Both father and son, who were busy members of the Independent Labour Party, tended to make their presence felt.

Although the Organization Committee had had referred to it the resolutions about a changed structure for the union and for regulations to be drawn up for the political section, nothing came of it all throughout 1947. Finally, the next Annual Conference decided that a political Conference should be held to which branches should be asked to send a delegate and from which a political committee would be formed. It was not the only proposal on administration at the 1948 Conference. Alex Kitson moved that there should be a change of rules to enable Annual Conference, rather than the Executive, to elect the President. This was opposed by the General Secretary and lost by twenty-one votes to thirty-four. A motion from Ayr that an official should not be eligible to be appointed delegate to Conference was also defeated, this time by forty-nine votes to two. Both these were repeated, unsuccessfully, the following year. Although these were only straws in the wind, they did show that the membership was ready for changes and sought a greater measure of control for the Annual Conference. But the big domestic development in 1948, which was the golden jubilee year, was the creation of the political conference, despite opposition.

2. THE POLITICAL SECTION IS FORMED

Yet five months passed before the Executive put in hand the preparations for the Political Conference. There was a strong feeling in the Executive, over which Allan Hendry presided that year, that they should take precautions to control any tendency towards autonomy.

The Political Conference took place at the Grand Hotel, Charing Cross, Glasgow, on Sunday, October 17, 1948. The differences of opinion which came into the open centred round the powers of the Political Committee, how the work should be financed, and who would control the finances. Were they to be elected or appointed? And by whom? The Executive was insisting upon appointing a block of executive members. Adam Suttie (Glasgow) was doubtful what authority the Political Committee would have and so argued 'that the formation of same should not be made by conference today, but taken back for further consideration and its relationship with the Executive Committee'.[1] To this Brannigan replied: 'Were the conference today to appoint an *ad hoc* Committee to deal with the political objects within the Association, and any attempt is made to take away authority of the Executive Council, in so far as the management of

[1] Report of Political Conference, 1948.

the affairs of the Association are concerned, the Executive Council would have no alternative but to call a Special Delegate Conference to go into the whole position.' Finally a motion calling for a committee of twelve with five appointed Executive members was carried by twenty-two votes to seven. It was not the last difference of opinion. Some delegates argued that eligibility for membership of the union's Political Committee should be restricted to individual members of the Labour Party; an amendment stressed that 'members so long as they were political contributors to the Association, should be eligible for membership of the Political Committee', After 'considerable discussion' and after the previous question had been moved unsuccessfully, 'the President in view of the wide division of opinion and that the matter was new, ruled same out of order.'

Those elected to the first Political Committee[1] of the Association were: Peter McGarry (Ayr), John Kyle (Dunfermline), Geoffrey Sheridan (Glasgow), B. MacDougall (Lanarkshire), Adam Suttie (Glasgow), Thomas Gowans (Airdrie), and W. Carty (Leven). The still unsettled question of their powers and functions was left for further discussion with the Executive.

The background against which they met was that economic events, the international situation and the gathering clouds of the cold war had brought into the Association's ranks also some unease and anxiety, and not only in strictly domestic matters. Just a month before, in September 1948, sterling had been devalued under pressure from the dollar. In the same month the British TUC had announced that it had withdrawn from the World Federation of Trade Unions. The following day, John Brannigan called a Special Executive to get a decision about sending a delegation to the United States to attend the convention of the American Federation of Labour, which had been in long-drawn-out dispute with the World Federation of Trade Unions and was leading the breakaway from it. He had had correspondence with the International Brotherhood of Teamsters, Chauffeurs, Warehousemen and Helpers of America and the Brotherhood of the Executive Railway and Steamship Clerks, whose representatives he and two members of the Executive had met in Oslo in July at the International Transport Workers' Federation. The visit to the Soviet Union which the 1947 Annual Conference had decided upon had hung fire for eighteen months and that had given rise to criticism. A decision to go to the USA, which had not been discussed at Conference, instead of to the USSR, which had long since been decided upon, was bound to be challenged. Indeed, the Glasgow branches had already recorded a remit of a minute of the Executive where it had been mooted. It was not now a unanimous decision of the Executive:

[1] More than fifteen years later, John Kyle recalled the first meetings of the Political Committee: 'It was like Early Christian conspirators! We had to meet in the attic of Highway House, by candlelight.'

'There followed a very lengthy discussion on this, during which Mr J. White expressed the opinion that the rules did not permit of a delegation being sent to the USA and moved that no action be taken. This failed to find a seconder and Mr White asked that his dissent be recorded in the Minutes.'[1]

On this occasion he was alone in his opinion on the Executive, which was divided only about the number of members who could go, and whether arrangements could be rushed through in time. It was finally agreed that the General Secretary and the President should 'carry on with all arrangements for their journey'. The issue of *The Highway* which carried the report of the Political Conference also contained the full text of the British TUC circular *Trade Unions & Communism*,[2] with special reference to the economic problems.

The political activities of the Association, therefore, were not being started at a happy moment. The organization proceeded only slowly. The Executive's five members were appointed to the Political Committee; these were Tom Berrey, Alex Falconer, George Little, John McQuade, and James White, Snr. When the first meeting was called on January 30, 1949, there was a long discussion before they agreed 'that the principal object of the Committee would be to further the political objects of the Scottish Horse & Motormen's Association within the constitution of the Labour Party'.[3] They left the administration of the finances of the Political Fund to Head Office. The main points on which they agreed were:

(1) To set up local political committees.
(2) To affiliate to and seek representation upon every constituency Labour Party.
(3) To hold meetings for 'political propaganda purposes outwith the ordinary branch meetings'.
(4) To set up a panel of candidates for nomination for parliamentary and local elections, through special meetings of the branches, with the power of the Political Committee to examine them.
(5) That committee members should remain in office for two years and that there should be a biennial conference of representatives of the political section 'to consider policy and to elect the lay representatives to the Political Committee'.

But in fact the Political Committee had remained inactive, as some members had supposed must be so, if there were no Political Secretary to give full-time attention to the organization, and especially to the collection of the political levy. Locally, however, the more active spirits held a number of meetings 'outwith the ordinary branch meetings'. Political

---

[1] Executive *Minutes*, October 28, 1948.
[2] Para 370, General Council Report to the TUC, 1949.
[3] Political Committee *Minutes*, January 30, 1949.

action was certainly very much in the air on many issues; but the subject which was to rouse the most prolonged and far-reaching controversy was the Government's policy of wage restraint.

3. THE FIRST 'WAGE FREEZE'

The effects of the unbalance of Britain's economy, temporarily masked by post-war reconstruction, soon began to weigh heavily upon the trade union movement. It was complicated by the unfavourable terms of the American loan and by the alignment of British policy with that of the United States. This policy comprehended the American Marshall Economic Plan and legislation which impeded trade with the Socialist countries. There was a run on sterling in the late summer of 1947, cuts in capital expenditure, a drive for increased exports and an appeal by the Government for 'incomes restraint'. This was referred to a Special Economic Sub-committee of the British TUC who issued an *Interim Report on the Economic Situation*, circulated at the end of December 1947, to all affiliated unions. When, on February 4, 1948, a new white paper[1] was issued by the Government, the British TUC convened a conference of Trade Union Executives and circulated a report with recommendations to all affiliated unions.

It was decided that the whole Executive Council of the Association should go with John Brannigan to the British TUC Conference. At the Central Hall, Westminster, on March 24, 1948, some 1,550 delegates attended from 155 unions. The white paper had called for acceptance of the general principle that there should be 'a temporary stop' to further increases in personal incomes from whatever source. The General Council of the TUC recommended that this principle should be accepted by affiliated trade unions, subject to five reservations,[2] and this report was approved by 5,421,000 to 2,032,000. It was widely reported that many leaders who cast their union's vote with the majority counted on one or more of these escape clauses to exclude his own union: that, in effect, they were voting in favour of wages restraint for their brother trade unionists but not for

[1] *Statement on Personal Incomes, Costs and Prices*, Cmd 7321.
[2] The Government should:
(a) recognize the necessity of retaining unimpaired the system of collective bargaining and free negotiation;
(b) Admit the justification for claims for increased wages where those claims are based upon the fact of increased output;
(c) admit the necessity of adjusting the wages of workers whose incomes are below a reasonable standard of subsistence;
(d) affirm that it is in the national interest to establish standards of wages and conditions in undermanned essential industries in order to attract sufficient manpower; and
(e) recognize the need to safeguard those wage differentials which are now an essential element in the wage structure of many important industries.

(General Council's Report to the TUC, 1948)

themselves. The Association's Executive Council voted with the majority; and ten days later John Brannigan explained their standpoint to the 1948 Annual Conference at Hawick. After giving the anti-inflationary argument, he said: 'As a union the Scottish Horse & Motormen's Association is not greatly affected at the moment and are protected within the reservations by the British TUC.'[1]

Andrew Inglis (Kilmarnock) argued that the effect of the white paper and the recommendations was that the workers would not get advances except where output was increased or the industry was undermanned:

'When applications were made by the trade unions for increased rates, or when a case was heard before the National Arbitration Tribunal, Mr Inglis was of opinion heed would be paid to the policy of the Government and that trade unions would experience difficulty with their application.'

Some delegates regarded the Executive's action as hasty; others argued that delegates were not mandated, as it had not yet been before the branches, and thought the Executive should have waited until the Annual Conference before casting the Association's vote in favour of the British TUC's proposition. George Little for the Executive intervened to say that, 'in approving the BTUC Report the Executive Council had in no way committed itself or made any final decision on the matter'. John Brannigan declared that they

'had not agreed to any freezing of wages. . . . Every union is left entirely free to use its own judgment in so far as applications for increases in wages are concerned.'

On this assurance, the Executive's action was endorsed by forty-three votes to eleven.

That same month, at the Scottish Trades Union Congress at Perth, John Brannigan moved a resolution on the white paper supporting the Government, and opposed an unsuccessful amendment moved by the miners' delegation, which urged 'the Government not to depend on voluntary appeals' to employers to reduce prices and profits, 'which appeals have proved futile in the past'. It was a subject which figured increasingly in trade union conferences, and not least in Scotland, as prices and profits continued to rise, and misgivings that restraint would prove applicable primarily to wages began to appear justified. Two years later, those opposing wage restraint had become the majority in the BTUC, although it was some time longer before the Association reversed its decision.

Each year, at the Association's annual conference, the vote against wage restraint increased—fourteen votes to thirty-six in 1949, twenty-four to thirty-one in 1950—until 1951, when a Glasgow A, B and C Branch

[1] Report of Annual Conference, 1948.

resolution declared: 'That this Conference urges the Government to implement immediately their policy on prices and profits thus ensuring a reasonable standard of life for the people of this country.'[1] This was carried by fifty-three votes to ten, and reflected a gradual reversal of viewpoint. By the 1952 conference, the first after the return of a new Conservative administration, an Edinburgh resolution moved by Alex Kitson was carried unanimously:

'That this Conference is concerned with the rapid rise in the cost of living and calls on the Government to make more controls on profits and take steps to break down the price rings that are in operation in industry.'[2]

At the same time Conference declared its opposition to 'any form of wage restraint'. Unanimity had been reached in the Association after four years of divided opinion.

4. DISSENSION IN THE ASSOCIATION

But in 1949 there grew up in the Association another rift which led to a period of grievous dissension. The outcome reflected no credit on the union, and the Association's reputation in the Scottish trade union movement was inevitably tarnished. No question of trade policy nor of difference of political opinion was at issue. At the core were individual failings: excessive personal ambition and attempts to advance ambition by less than straightforward means on the one hand, erratic behaviour on the other. Well-intentioned prominent members of the Association, both inside the Executive Council and outside it, failed to resolve a squalid tangle; and in some cases their efforts were unwise, ill-judged, or ill-timed. It would have been preferable to disregard altogether the detail of a series of incidents which included two charges under the Road Traffic Acts against the General Secretary of the leading union of transport drivers in Scotland, the dismissal of the Assistant General Secretary, two long drawn-out legal cases, and the expulsion of several highly respected members, who had given eminent service to the Association. Unfortunately, there were side effects from which it took years for the Association to recover. The great test was whether the Association could face up to the new problems in the industry; unfortunately the effect of these unhappy domestic events was to divert the energies of the members from meeting this test and to delay essential advance for a decade.

The beginning of these years of trouble can be dated, ironically enough, from the golden jubilee year of 1948. At that time, the General Secretary entertained political ambitions. In the summer two by-elections were pending, one in the Gorbals Division of Glasgow, the other in West

[1] Report of Annual Conference, 1951.
[2] Annual Conference Report, 1952.

Stirling. The Glasgow City Labour Party invited the Association to make a nomination for the Gorbals, and John Brannigan called a special meeting of the Executive to discuss it. It was decided to put his name forward for the vacancy, 'provided such nomination was in accordance with the constitution and rules'.[1] As Rule 12, clause 2 required that a general secretary should 'devote the whole of his time to promote the welfare and interests of the Association', it seemed necessary to seek counsel's opinion. A week later came the legal answer:

'Counsel's opinion which had now been received indicated that in the opinion of counsel the General Secretary if he were elected to Parliament would not be complying with the terms of Rule 12, Clause 2. The Executive Council in accepting the opinion of counsel agreed that an alteration of the rules in this connection be recommended to Annual Conference.'[2]

At the following meeting James White, Snr, tried to move that the rule should not be altered, but failed to find a seconder.

Attending each of these Executives, as he did every meeting, was David Johnstone, the Assistant General Secretary, on whom so much more responsibility must necessarily rest, if this should go through. Indeed, it might be that the leading office would shortly be open to him, if anything occurred to incapacitate John Brannigan, whose health at that time was beginning to be impaired. By that time Johnstone was not only a member of the Labour group on the Glasgow Town Council, but he was also becoming known in the broader trade union movement, being frequently spokesman for the Association at the Scottish Trades Union Congress. At the 1949 Annual Conference, an alteration to rule was put forward by the Ayr branch and supported by the Executive which would permit a General Secretary to 'take political or other appointments with the consent of the Executive Council'. Andrew Inglis (Kilmarnock) did not think this could be reconciled with the rule which said he must be elected by a ballot of members. John Brannigan replied: 'The Executive Council felt that something should be done to make the rule more explicit, in allowing him to stand for Parliamentary election if he so desired.'[3] The change was opposed by two Glasgow members, T. Hunter and Geoffrey Sheridan; but only three voted against it. It was put through at once and duly registered and operative on August 25, 1949.

In the summer and autumn of 1949, with instability and unease in the economic and political spheres, there were also changes and unrest in the internal affairs of the Association, some of general application, others local and transitory. The elections to the Executive had given rise to a number of irregularities or breaches of 'gentleman's agreements' in areas sharing

[1] Executive *Minutes*, July 27, 1948.
[2] Executive *Minutes*, August 4, 1948.
[3] Report of Annual Conference, 1949.

Executive members; there was criticism of officials in respect of this for 'interference', which decided the Executive to send out a warning circular.

Glasgow's proposals for reorganizing the structure of the union had received scant attention, some felt. Much against the General Secretary's advice, Geoffrey Sheridan and George Little won the Executive's agreement for certain changes in organization, to make each organizer responsible for a particular area and obliging each to put in regular reports. There were criticisms of the method of allocating the new districts. A full-time collector was dismissed for negligence, and there were complaints about how his successor was chosen. Another was reprimanded and put on probation, to which strong objection was taken by some Executive members.

Such events were indications both that the administrative reins were slack and that members were seeking more control. The Association was, in fact, on the brink of a domestic explosion, in which discreditable allegations, which were quite without foundation, were mingled with others which were patently true. The domestic affairs of the Association were in the public eye from September 1949 until the spring of 1952, but the wounds of the dissension persisted for a long time to come. Here it is necessary to give a brief outline of the facts of a sorry affair.

The prevailing climate became one of mutual distrust of leading officials and some of the leadership at Executive and branch level. The Executive Council itself was not in a strong position either to check on administration or to be quickly responsive to the feeling of the membership; the important factor was that, regardless of the qualities of any individual member, the Executive Council as a whole, in the key year of 1949–50, was, in its composition very far from reflecting the weight of the membership. One Executive member was a retired man; three held managerial posts; and representation of sections was markedly unbalanced, there being only one road haulage motor-man as against seven in co-operative society employment.[1] The trouble flared up in early autumn, when one of the four organizers, Alex Irvine, was appointed Labour Officer under the new Road Haulage Executive; amongst the seven applicants as his successor was James White, Jnr, whose father was carrying the banner for reform on

[1] Name	Place	Section	Job
J. Murphy	West-Calder	Co-operative	Vanman
J. Lumsden	Dunfermline	Co-operative	Vanman
A. Hendry	Lanark	Co-operative	Vanman
G. Sheridan	Glasgow	Co-operative	Vanman
A. Falconer	Edinburgh	Co-operative	Manager
G. Little	Kilmarnock	Co-operative	Catering Manager
A. McDiarmid	Perth	Co-operative	Stableman
T. Berrey	Renfrew	Local Authority	Cleansing (Retired)
W. McKay	Glasgow	Local Authority	Cleansing
P. Callaghan	Glasgow	Railway & General	Foreman stableman
J. McQuade	Glasgow	Glasgow A, B & C	Road haulage driver
J. Young	Aberdeen	Railway & General	Carter

the Association's Executive as well as in the Glasgow Co-ordinating Committee. The result was not a unanimous decision of the Executive, and many in Glasgow certainly drew the conclusion, when John Connell was appointed, that prejudices had been in play to keep Jimmy White from being appointed organizer of the decisive west coat area. On September 8, 1949, nine days later, Jimmy White, Jnr wrote to the Chairman, John Murphy, saying that he had charges of maladministration to level against the senior officials which must be investigated.

The Procurator-fiscal[1] began private inquiries. It was known that he had interviewed James White and John Murphy; but for many weeks it was unknown to John Brannigan or to the Executive that David Johnstone was also interviewed. The Procurator-fiscal advised the Chairman, John Murphy, to give White an interview with the Executive. Brannigan was not the only target for criticism; one of White's fellow full-time collectors in Glasgow, Adam Suttie, who had himself been on the Executive six months before, complained that David Johnstone had threatened to get him ousted from his position. Suttie, too, demanded to attend the interview with the Executive.

Three days before it took place, however, John Brannigan had a serious motor accident. At the police station, where he was charged with driving under the influence of drink or drugs, he collapsed and was taken to hospital, and remained there for four weeks. At the next Executive meeting on October 5, 1949, White refused to make any statement, 'at this stage because of the fact that certain members of the Council were involved'; but he offered to do so to an impartial body, consisting of a member of the Scottish TUC, a lawyer and 'an intelligent member of the rank and file'. The circumstances, he said, had changed since he had written the letter. David Johnstone was by then in control, and the General Secretary had a charge hanging over his head, the consequences of which might be very grave. White, Suttie, and the head office caretaker, together with the cashier, Mrs Joyce Smith, two organizers, William Cockburn and Norman Macpherson, and another Glasgow official, W. Lang, were called again to an all-day Special Executive, after which it was recorded: 'It was felt by all present that as no one could give any evidence of misappropriation, no firm line of action could be taken in the matter.'[2] A Committee of Management, consisting of the chairman, John Murphy, George Little, Geoffrey Sheridan, and Tom Berrey was appointed to go into it all, with full powers. All those who had been interviewed were told that Johnstone was

'to continue in his capacity as Assistant General Secretary and carry on negotiations in the best interests of the Association. Any member con-

---

[1] In Scotland, the equivalent of the English Public Prosecutor.
[2] Executive *Minutes*, October 9, 1949.

nected with anything contrary to the well-being of the Association would be instantly dismissed.'[1]

The Committee of Management then decided themselves to see the Procurator-fiscal. No minutes exist of this special committee reporting to the Executive.

With White unwilling at that stage to disclose the detail of his charges of maladministration, it was long before it became known to the membership at large that much of what he wanted to have investigated rested on material which had been brought to him by the head office caretaker, Alex Lamb. This consisted of what he asserted were torn up audited accounts sheets extracted from the General Secretary's waste-paper basket. These appeared to refer to what White held would be unjustifiable expenses, in which a number of Executive members' names figured. Rumours continued for many weeks, ranging from stories somewhat on these lines to complaints of favouritism and unjustified treatment of staff and threats to dismiss officers and members who were thought to be attempting to get an investigation. Certainly many members in Glasgow regarded James White, Jnr as being the man who would insist upon an investigation.

One of the actions of the Committee of Management was to have a special audit taken; although this was declared finally to be satisfactory, uneasiness amongst the membership was not allayed. On the contrary, rumours increased week by week; it was asserted that they were being fostered deliberately by some well-informed quarter.

Weeks passed without this question being cleared up. John Brannigan returned to work from hospital with proceedings in connection with the drunken driving charge still hanging over his head. The case was heard on December 14, 1949, two months after the incident, when he pleaded guilty and was fined £15 with his licence suspended for a year.[2] At long last a special Executive was called for December 28, 1949 to go into two points; firstly to decide what should be done to meet White's demand for an impartial body to examine the facts, the details of which he still continued to refuse to disclose to the Executive; secondly, to consider Brannigan's position in the light of the Road Traffic Act conviction. This war four months after James White had first written to the Executive.

There were dramatic changes of fortune when the special meeting of December 28, 1949, took place. The Association's solicitor, Harold Dykes, attended and explained all the correspondence he had had with James White's legal representatives. White was demanding arbitration under rule and for this to be begun before he stipulated his charges, whilst Brannigan and Johnstone both refused to accept arbitration until they knew the

[1] Executive *Minutes*, October 9, 1949.
[2] Only a year earlier, on a similar charge he had lost his licence for six months.

complaints 'which at the moment were called maladministration'. Mr Dykes recommended that the Executive should choose between three courses: to call a delegate conference; to enter arbitration with White; or to drop the dispute with him. It was decided unanimously to enter arbitration with White:

'the reason for the decision was to have a record of all facts that might have a bearing on the conduct of officials and so that every step should be taken to safeguard the good reputation of the Association.'[1]

Then they discussed the second item on the agenda, the recent charge under the Road Traffic Act against the General Secretary:

'it was moved by Messrs Falconer and Callaghan that the General Secretary be severely reprimanded. An amendment was moved by Messrs Little and Sheridan that the General Secretary be suspended from December 28th for one month under terms of Rule 15.'

This was carried on a poll vote; Hendry, Young, McDiarmid, Sheridan, Lumsden, Berrey, and Little voted for suspension, and Falconer, Callaghan, McQuade, and McKay for reprimand: Chairman Murphy abstained. Then came another poll vote on who should take charge in his absence. Falconer and Callaghan moved that it should not be Johnstone; Murphy and McKay abstained; but the remaining eight voted that Johnstone should be in charge. Then there was a dramatic intervention:

'At this stage the General Secretary entered the meeting and asked leave to submit a statement contents of which were most urgent. The General Secretary read a photographic copy of a letter written by a member of the Association Mr Barbour of Perth outlining certain allegations which had been made by the Assistant General Secretary.

'Members of the Executive Council expressed the opinion that this letter put a different complexion on matters. After hearing the General Secretary concerning the current work within the Association it was decided on the motion of Messrs Falconer and Callaghan that the date of suspension be postponed for one month.'[2]

The tables were turned; Brannigan's suspension was postponed, and the meeting ended with the Executive deciding to summon both Johnstone and Barbour to appear before them a week later. This letter, Brannigan said, was handed to him by James White, who claimed to have been shown it by the Scottish Industrial Organizer of the Communist Party, to whom it had been written by James Barbour of Perth, a highly respected member of the Association who was also a member of the Communist Party. It was dated November 23, 1949. It dealt with the Road Traffic charge,

[1] Executive *Minutes*, December 28, 1949.
[2] Executive *Minutes*, December 28, 1949.

remarked that 'a drastic clean-up is long overdue', and contained this passage:

'I have been told that the Union car has been used to transport stolen whisky from a bonded warehouse at the docks and the Union offices used to store and get rid of it, and that Brannigan and members of the Executive, names not given, are all in this together; remember this information will have to be very carefully handled. I received it from Johnstone, the Assistant Secretary, and I put it to him that it was his job to place all his knowledge before the Executive Council, but he mistakenly in my opinion feels that it will create the impression that he is anxious to have Brannigan's job.'

To the Executive this letter came as a great shock; they took it as positive proof that the Assistant General Secretary, David Johnstone himself, was the one who from the first had been responsible for disseminating rumours and information against the administrators of the Association in general and the General Secretary in particular. The letter had been in Brannigan's hands for ten days or more; but he did not disclose it until the majority of the Executive Committee had voted his suspension and put Johnstone in charge in his place.

Two years later, in the course of litigation between Johnstone and the Association, both Brannigan and Johnstone were asked by the Judge why they did not earlier bring out into the open all the facts that each knew or alleged. Johnstone said the Executive was trying to get rid of him:

LORD MACKINTOSH: 'Why should they want to get rid of you?'
JOHNSTONE: 'The reason was to hush up allegations against the General Secretary.'[1]

The General Secretary was also examined on the same point:

BRANNIGAN: 'I believed there was a plot outside the Executive to get me suspended. It was to be a steam-roller to have me suspended.'
LORD MACKINTOSH: 'Johnstone thinks there was a plot to get rid of him. So do you now. Were there plots on both sides to have each other suspended?'[2]

Brannigan's dramatic production of this letter at the eleventh hour certainly came as a bombshell. Johnstone and Barbour were both summoned before a special meeting the following week. James Barbour was expelled from the Association and David Johnstone was suspended from office indefinitely. While he persisted in denying that he had passed on to Barbour information 'injurious to the Association and which was unknown to the Executive Committee', Johnstone admitted that 'he had

[1] *Evening Citizen*, October 31, 1951.
[2] *Scottish Daily Express*, October 31, 1951.

been interrogated by the police' about the story of the stolen whisky, but claimed that there was no 'lack of duty in not advising the Executive on this matter'.

After his suspension, Johnstone got affidavits from the caretaker's wife and her sister which purported to give chapter and verse for how stolen whisky had been brought to the premises from a bonded warehouse over a period of two years, directly naming the Executive members Callaghan and Falconer as being involved in it, and alleging that it was within Brannigan's knowledge. During litigation two years later Johnstone asserted that he had been fully expecting that Brannigan, Callaghan, Falconer, and the caretaker, Lamb, would be prosecuted. It was claimed, too, that Johnstone had learnt the story of the whisky from the caretaker's household early the previous September, i.e. in 1949; and, indeed, that he had at that time forced an admission from Callaghan. All these charges and counter-charges were, of course, denied, including the authenticity of the Barbour letter. Two points should be noted: Johnstone took no step towards having these scandalous charges investigated within the Association, as James White had attempted to do over the complaints of mal-administration; and the Procurator-fiscal brought no proceedings.

5. THE GLASGOW MEMBERS TAKE ACTION

During all these painful and damaging months, what had been the attitude of the Association's rank and file members? Rumours of all sorts had been rife; there had been no statements or reassurance from the Executive. The Committee of Management had made no report; indeed, early in December, Falconer had proposed that it should be disbanded:

'As two months had elapsed since the Special Committee had been appointed and further that during that time two Financial Reports had been submitted and approved, the Committee had served its purpose and should now be disbanded, when the Executive Council should take full control of the matter.'[1]

On a poll vote only Callaghan voted with him, and the Committee had remained in being with George Little as convener, although no records of their proceedings can now be traced. Even James White's first initiative had gone no further since his unanswered demand for arbitration. It may be that he was waiting the outcome of the Road Traffic prosecution and any disciplinary action that the Executive might impose on the General Secretary before making his next move. He was still widely regarded as the champion of an orderly investigation within the Association, and no doubt many complaints had been brought to him, as well as Lamb's gleanings from the waste-paper basket and the 'Barbour letter'. He seemed

[1] Executive *Minutes*, December 7, 1949.

to fear that Johnstone might attempt to use him as a cat's-paw. The entire atmosphere was one of mistrust and suspicion; what was clearly the greatest need was that this should be cleared up. After the Executive meeting of December 28, 1949, the Glasgow shop stewards began to hold meetings; one of the points which had most taken them aback was the postponement of Brannigan's suspension. Finally they called a meeting for Sunday, January 15, 1950, at the St Mungo Halls. The notice read as follows:

'Scottish Horse & Motormen's Association

'A MASS MEETING

will be held under the auspices of

The Glasgow Shop Stewards'
DISTRICT COMMITTEE

IN

ST. MUNGO HALLS
MOFFAT STREET, S.S.
Sunday 15th Jan. 1950
at 2.30 p.m.

'A CRISIS Has Arisen In the Conduct of the Affairs of this Association, culminating in the suspension of the Assistant General Secretary, and the expulsion of Bro. J. Barbour.

'The view of the committee on these matters will be placed before the meeting for your consideration.

G. FORSYTH	Chairman
S. BROWN	Secretary

Gordon Forsyth, who had taken an active part during the inter-union 'war' in 1941, had become a well-known shop steward at Taylor's Transport, Sam Brown was at Hays Wharf. They had invited John Murphy, as the Association's Chairman, to preside, but he had declined. Brannigan issued a counter circular under the name of himself and the chairman, which the Executive later endorsed, which described the shop stewards' notice as 'illegally circulated', and appealed to members not to attend.[1]

---

[1]   'Scottish Horse and Motormen's Association
'Our attention has been attracted to a bill which has been illegally circulated under the name of the Scottish Horse and Motormen's Association and the signatures of G. Forsyth and S. Brown, calling a meeting in St Mungo's Halls, Moffat Street, Glasgow.
'The sponsors claim that a crisis has arisen in the conduct of affairs in the Association.
'THERE IS NO CRISIS
'We have just finished the most successful year in the history of our Union. The total funds of the Association now stand at £302,625. After allowing for increased benefits, increased expenditure, many items of which have been more than trebled on the same contribution, there has been added during the life of the present régime almost £80,000.

Brannigan also informed the Press, disassociating the Executive from the shop stewards' meeting; all officials were warned to stay away. The meeting was held, none the less. James Barbour of Perth was introduced and spoke on the need to clear up the scandals; he got an appreciative hearing from the 800 members present. A resolution was moved by James Barrie, shop steward of the Glasgow Hiring Company, a trades council delegate and at that time a member of the Communist Party, who was voted on to the Executive a couple of months later. It read as follows:

'RESOLUTION

'This representative gathering of the SHMA is of the opinion, that due to certain incidents in which the General Secretary has been involved and actions recently taken by the General Secretary and Executive Council affecting the persons of the Assistant General Secretary and a lay member from Perth and the concern of members regarding the unsavoury atmosphere in and around our union over the past period, that to this end a members' committee of inquiry be set up to clarify the situation and bring our organization into relation to other trades unions, without blemish on its officers, executive and membership, and that pending this investigation we ask for the immediate reinstatement of the Assistant General Secretary and the member for Perth.'

The resolution was carried by an overwhelming majority. A working committee was set up which was composed of Sam Brown as secretary, Gordon Forsyth as chairman, James Barrie, Jimmy Cox of Cowans, and Walter Grieve of Holdsworth & Hanson. The startling feature of the meeting, however, was the presence of the Executive member from Kilmarnock, George Little. He was, it must be remembered, the convener of the special Committee of Management; what he had to say was bound to carry a great deal of weight when he told the audience with some emphasis that the 'whole union needed cleaning out from top to bottom'. At this, 'some of the men got carried away', an eyewitness recalled years

---

'We appeal to the members to believe in the wisdom and good managership of the Executive Council, rather than be stampeded by the *unofficial* action of people who are attempting to sow the *seeds of disruption*.

'The matter which has apparently provoked criticism was on two occasions the unanimous decision of the Executive Council when they decided to deal with two members of the Association. When this matter is completed the full facts will be furnished to the whole of the membership.

'A continuance of the confidence and loyalty you have always displayed towards your Union will ensure its permanent success. *Please pay no attention to the calling of meetings unless they are officially called under the Constitution and with the authority of the Executive Council.*

'(Sgd) J. MURPHY, Chairman
'(Sgd) J. BRANNIGAN, General Secretary.'

later. 'Unfortunately Gordon Forsyth let them get out of control. A resolution was put up calling for Brannigan's resignation, which undid all the good work we had done. It was no time to call for resignations and expulsions; on the contrary. What was needed was a proper investigation, as our main resolution demanded.'

Brannigan reacted quickly. He suspended Forsyth and Brown from membership under Rule 15, clause 1, for calling and attending an unconstitutional meeting. He suspended Little from office and from membership for participating in it. At the Glasgow A, B and C branch, James Barrie moved a resolution against the suspension of Forsyth and Brown. He preserved the notes of his speech, in which he said:

'During the last few months there has been considerable unrest amongst the Glasgow membership created by reports of misconduct of union affairs. I doubt if we will ever know who started it all.

'I am positive, however, that it was not the two members who have been expelled from this branch and who are, and should be, our first concern. I am not prepared to accept the suggestion that is implied in discussion that there is a connection between all the expulsions.

'Our two members have committed no great crime, we know that. We can fight for them because we understand the circumstances which overcame them and the sincerity of their intentions which were to assist, not injure the Association. Their weakness, and ours possibly, was the fact that we were not getting the truth from all sources.'

The resolution, which was passed unanimously, declared:

'That this Glasgow A B and C branch rejects the minute affecting the suspension of Brothers Forsyth and Brown and protest at the harshness of the penalty inflicted upon them, as in our opinion the responsibility for the state of affairs which led to their expulsion lies in part with the Executive Committee, which by its lack of finality in its decisions, its shilly-shallying between one officer and another, bewildered and confused the membership of this branch and so exposed to indiscretion two lay members whose enthusiasm was in greater measure than their knowledge of the constitution.'

But when Brannigan reported the suspensions to a specially summoned Executive meeting: 'It was unanimously agreed on the motion of Messrs Callaghan and McQuade that the constitution had been violated and that the action of the General Secretary in suspending Messrs Forsyth, Brown and Little be homologated.'[1] He called the old Glasgow Co-ordinating Committee once more, on February 3, 1950, together with Executive members and the Glasgow collecting staff, which included James White, Jnr and Adam Suttie. They elected James White, Snr as chairman and

[1] Executive *Minutes*, January 22, 1950.

Adam Suttie as secretary. For the next two years the Co-ordinating Committee acted as a sounding board for what was in the minds of the Glasgow members; but its decisions were almost always reversed by the Executive Committee.

Meanwhile Johnstone had been busy with the affidavits he had obtained from the caretaker's wife and her sister. These affidavits, it was alleged: 'he was using among the membership as though this were a proved fact'. In the chairman's view:

'it was his duty to present information of this character to his employers the Executive Council, in order to give them the opportunity of proving or disproving such allegations, instead of using them to the detriment of the Association.'[1]

The Executive decided by seven votes to four to dismiss Johnstone from office; Forsyth, Brown, and Little were all expelled from membership; and they rescinded the proposed postponed suspension of Brannigan. Only Berrey, Murphy, and Sheridan voted for continued suspension.

Brannigan had weathered the storm which had blown up from many directions: six weeks after his conviction and loss of his driver's licence he appeared to be more firmly in the saddle than ever. Tom Berrey was instructed by the Executive to 'hand over to the General Secretary all papers which he had held on behalf of the Committee of Management', which was to cease to function. Brannigan obtained unanimous votes of confidence from the Perth Quarterly Meeting which he had attended in person and from the monthly meeting in Edinburgh, Falconer's branch. George Little asked for arbitration under rule, but was refused it on the ground that 'it was a right afforded only to members of the Association', and that since his expulsion he was not a member and so disentitled to arbitration.[2] Negotiations were proceeding with White's solicitors regarding arbitration, which would preclude public discussion at the Annual Conference which was held at Oban.

There were different standpoints at that unhappy conference. George Little and Gordon Forsyth came seeking to be heard by the delegates, as did David Johnstone. The Executive ruled that none should be heard. George Little wrote a letter making 'a strong appeal to each and all who believe in democracy' on behalf of himself and the expelled shop stewards asking for the right to be heard at conference. David Johnstone issued a long circular to delegates, protesting against his dismissal 'in such an autocratic manner'. He said he proposed to fight the decision, adding:

'Friends in the Labour Party are prepared to assist me in taking my case to the highest possible courts if necessary, but I realize that if I do so a

---

[1] Executive Minutes, February 1, 1950.
[2] Executive Minutes, March 1, 1950.

great deal of adverse publicity will be directed at our own beloved Association.'

He therefore asked to be heard by conference,

'as I am confident that the rank and file members of our Association will see justice done and will obviate the possibility of affairs of the Association being dragged through the gutter by inevitable newspaper publicity.'

The circular set out a number of allegations. The pre-conference Executive meeting decided 'that certain portions of this were of a libellous character and that Mr Johnstone was not acting in the best interests of the Association': with Allan Hendry dissenting, they expelled him. This step added fuel to the flames. Describing the scenes outside, when giving evidence in the later trial, Brannigan said: 'The precincts of the conference were a seething bed of intrigue.' Within the conference hall, Jock Houston of Paisley attempted to move suspension of standing orders to enable all expelled members to be heard; he failed by thirty-four votes to thirty-three.

For the next eighteen months the Executive had a series of legal cases and negotiations on its hands. Johnstone brought an action in the Court of Session for wrongful dismissal, which was not heard for eighteen months. As for the dismissed Glasgow shop stewards, it was not until the late autumn of 1950 that Sam Brown was allowed again into membership as a new member, and that only after protracted correspondence with lawyers representing him. Gordon Forsyth remained in the wilderness. Negotiations for arbitration proceedings with White, which the Executive had assured the Procurator-fiscal would be carried out, dragged on without reaching an issue. It may be conjectured that that part of his complaints which depended upon the caretaker's torn sheets had been found not to bear the implications originally placed upon them, but that White was reluctant to withdraw from the whole arbitration negotiations until the outcome of the Johnstone case was known. After some months, the Executive withdrew the offer to arbitrate; and, with this out of the way, a special meeting was held on November 26, 1950, at which, after the whole situation had been fully reviewed, James White was dismissed, as was Alex Lamb, the caretaker.

The Glasgow shop stewards and the members and the Co-ordinating Committee reacted strongly. But, fully conscious of what had happened to Forsyth and Brown, they now moved with caution. The General Secretary received a requisition from Glasgow members, bearing 133 signatures, demanding a special meeting of the entire Glasgow membership under Rule 14, Clause 2. The Chairman, Alex Falconer, decided that the requisition did not comply with the rule and declared it out of order. The Officers' Association asked that a deputation should be received, but this was refused by the Executive on the ground that White had consulted solicitors with whom correspondence was proceeding. The Glasgow members, represented by William Wilkie and George Williams claimed a dispute existed on the requisition and demanded arbitration. William Wilkie was a highly respected shop steward in the Scottish Co-operative Wholesale Society; he first went on to the Executive during the war and nearly a decade after this incident became President of the Association. The Executive refused arbitration and asserted that Williams and Wilkie had made defamatory statements about the General Secretary and

'that unless defamatory remarks were withdrawn and an unconditional apology given within one week, they would take whatever disciplinary action considered necessary to prevent abuse of the privilege of membership of the Association.'[1]

The demand to requisition a meeting was dropped. An attempt by the Glasgow ABC Branch to put forward an emergency resolution for the annual conference was ruled out of order by the Executive. All doors seemed locked and barred. Forsyth threatened legal action if his expulsion were not rescinded. White began an action in the Sheriff's Court for £1,000 damages against John Brannigan for allegedly procuring his dismissal. Brannigan told the 1951 Conference at Rothesay that none of the matters could be discussed because, in the light of the pending actions by Johnstone and White, everything would be *sub judice*. An attempt by James White to reverse the chairman's ruling on this same point was lost by forty-five votes to seven. The whole affair, therefore was not discussed directly at this conference, where a resolution was moved by Alex Urquhart of Dunfermline and seconded by Peter McGroarty of Dumbarton 'that no known member of the Communist Party be allowed to hold office in this Association.'[2]

Mr Urquhart argued that 'Little was heard of the Communist Party within the SH & MA because in a well and properly organized machine you found no opposition, but the Communists were ready to grab control of that machine when occasion arose.'

After James Revie of Aberdeen and Andrew Inglis of Kilmarnock had moved its rejection, a debate took place, after which the motion was passed by thirty-two votes to twenty. The incoming Executive moved to implement this at once. Correspondence took place both with the STUC and with the BTUC as to how best to implement the rule effectively. A special Delegate Conference was finally convened on August 4, 1951, at which sixty-five delegates were present from thirty-eight branches, but including only four of the Glasgow branches. The terms of reference were solely to consider a new Rule drafted by the Executive Committee banning members of the Communist Party from office. It stated:

[1] Executive *Minutes*, March 5, 1951.
[2] Report of Annual Conference, 1951.

'Rule 21: No member of the Communist Party shall be eligible to hold any office within the Association either as a lay member, permanent or full-time officer, or act as a delegate to any meetings whatsoever.'[1]

Six delegate speakers were called who spoke in favour of the resolution, which was moved and seconded by Kirkcaldy delegates and supported from Airdrie, Dumbarton, Ayr, and Lanarkshire. A further six delegates spoke for its rejection, which was moved by A. Hutchison and W. Joyce of Glasgow A B and C. They were all Glasgow men, and they argued the merits of the general principle of the resolution which, according to Mr Hutchison, 'would deprive every member from voting for the man they considered to be best fitted for the job'. In his conclusion he insisted that: 'the resolution was not an attack on the Communists but an attack on the personal liberty of every member of the Association.'

In his reply, John Kyle, who had moved its adoption, answered: 'The delegates are present, not to settle the question of the liberty of the members, merely to implement the decision of the Annual Conference.'

It was, in fact, a foregone conclusion, since delegates were already mandated to vote for or against the wording of the Rule, and it was carried fifty-five to nine. It was registered on August 28, 1951, just eight weeks before the hearing began of the Johnstone dismissal case, and when White's case was also pending.

6. THE END OF THE AFFAIR

There was an eight-day hearing which began on October 24, 1951, before Lord Mackintosh in the Court of Session. The gist of Johnstone's case was that he had been wrongfully dismissed since the Executive had been actuated by malice, their motive being to prevent his exposing those who he alleged were engaged in malpractices. The stolen whisky story was in the forefront, a key witness being the ex-caretaker's wife. Judgment was reserved for four weeks; and on November 22, 1951, Lord Mackintosh ruled that Johnstone's case could not succeed, as he had failed to prove that the Executive had acted in bad faith in dismissing him. This left the statements about the stolen whisky, which had been given such wide publicity, neither proved nor disproved; but it should be emphasized that neither Brannigan, Falconer, Callaghan nor Lamb were ever prosecuted in connection with it. It might also perhaps be noted that, during this period, Brannigan was chosen President of the STUC for 1951.

When the 1952 Annual Conference met, the situation was greatly changed: the late Assistant General Secretary was gone, but his insistence on continuing as Labour Councillor in the ward in which the Association considered it had the right to name the candidate caused friction for

[1] Special Delegate Conference Report, August 4, 1951.

several years. James White's case in the Sheriff's court had been lost and his membership lapsed. James Barrie, who had announced his ineligibility to hold office under Rule 21 as a member of the Communist Party, was off the Executive and returned his trades council and shop steward's credential cards.

The Glasgow shop stewards were divided and depressed. Revolt from all quarters seemed to be crushed, as perhaps, to some degree, was lay members' initiative. But there could be no end of the affair until the General Secretary had taken the initiative to come to terms with the lay members, especially those in Glasgow, and to encourage the development of the most extensive possible democratic participation in and control of the Association. This John Brannigan did not do. There were unhappy side effects of the affair. Progressive reforms of union structure were held up and essential organizing work was not delegated to top-ranking executive officers at a time when the Association increasingly required it. Banning members of the Communist Party from holding office had a depressive effect upon organization in depot, garage, and stable. In one garage, where a popular shop steward was obliged to give up office under Rule 21, no one could be found to take over, nor to collect dues. These side effects tended to react upon each other; for not only did the Association temporarily lose the services of valuable officials and potential officials such as Andrew Inglis (Kilmarnock), James Barbour (Perth), and James Barrie (Glasgow), who came within the rule, but also James White, Snr, James White, Jnr, Sam Brown, Gordon Forsyth, George Little, and others who did not. What was more far-reaching was the pervading uneasiness which drove healthy criticism underground and made it less easy than ever to challenge and correct unsuitable courses and practices at an early stage.

Yet in these years the industry was facing new and sometimes un-recognized problems which called for thought and the closest co-operation between a creative leadership and a well-informed membership, quick to react and to display initiative. Perhaps the individual to suffer most in the long run was, after all, John Brannigan. For him it proved a personal disaster; he was never the same man again, for he became the victim of fear which led him to distrust his own members. Because these incidents and dissension were not rapidly overcome, a lack of mutual confidence persisted for years and undoubtedly affected the Association's achievements and reputation. To overcome the after effects quickly would have called for discrimination and qualities of leadership beyond the scope of a man more notable for shrewdness than depth of understanding.

CHAPTER EIGHTEEN

TOWARDS DENATIONALIZATION

I. PROBLEMS OF NATIONALIZATION

THE end of the court cases and of the Johnstone affair coincided with the return of a Conservative Government, when the first hesitant steps towards integration of transport were reversed and such parts of nationalization as conflicted with the interests of the larger road hauliers were dismantled. It also coincided with rising prices, the further distortion of the economy by increasing expenditure on armaments, and the sequence of balance of payment crises with their attendant 'stop-go' financial policies.

Yet compared with the early thirties a new era had opened which presented transport workers with both great opportunities for the future and also considerable problems. If some of these had been foreseen, their complexity had not; and at this stage it was the difficulties which first forced themselves upon the notice of the members of the Association. The young motormen in road haulage were confronted with puzzling and difficult changes from the coming great reorganization; for nationalization did not spring into being at the wave of the pen that signed the Transport Act, 1947.

Although this formally came into operation on January 1, 1948, it was not until three years later that Lord Hurcomb, the Chairman of the British Transport Commission, could say that 'the organization of British Road Services is now broadly complete.'[1] From February 23, 1950, the work of taking over parts of inland transport from the private road hauliers had been carried on under a Labour Government elected with a much reduced majority; by October 1951 there had been a further election and a Conservative Government, pledged to reverse the development towards nationalization, had been returned to power. It is useful to examine the attitude to the problems that arose at various stages in the light of this unstable political background.

To begin with there were three main points of criticism: the limited scope of the Act; all that is implied in the demand for a greater measure of workers' control; and the difficulties which arose during the takeover. There was natural reluctance at first to raise problems which might be

[1] Statement by Lord Hurcomb, CBG, KBE, Chairman of the British Transport Commission, on the progress of British Road Services (February 1951).

thought to embarrass the Labour Government, and criticism was usually couched in restrained terms. But, as time went on, a sense of urgency became apparent. The questions which were arising in the transport worker's mind were: did national ownership mean a real change for him? Could the Labour Government be trusted to be tough with private hauliers? There was a widely held view that the Act in general fell short of the integrated system of transport which the movement had for so long insisted was essential; and in particular that the failure to control C-licensed vehicles provided one of the biggest loopholes of which road hauliers could and did take advantage to escape the Act.

The Association felt extremely strongly on this point and continued their pressure doggedly after other sections had given up. At Hawick on April 5, 1948, the Association's Annual Conference unanimously adopted a resolution moved on behalf of the Executive by John Brannigan which, while congratulating the Government, 'on the steps taken to nationalize the transport industry', went on to raise in moderate terms the two key questions:

'Conference is of the opinion that in order to secure greater co-ordination within the industry, all C-licence operators must be brought within the ambit of the Act.

'Conference also urges the Government to permit of a greater measure of workers' representation, this being a fundamental necessity to ensure the success of a nationalized transport industry.'[1]

Three weeks later at the Scottish TUC meeting in Perth, delegates passed unanimously a resolution moved by the draughtsmen and seconded by the TGWU which, 'whilst expressing its general approval of the Government's nationalization policy, is of the opinion that the success of nationalization depends upon the fullest participation in management by those employed in the industry'.[2] It therefore called upon the Government to apply 'the principle of workers' participation in the direction and management of nationalized industry at all levels'. A Transport & General Workers' Union delegate wanted closer consultation on selecting people for the nationalized boards, which should not 'become jumping grounds for retired admirals, unemployed generals, and people who had consistently opposed the trade union movement'. The point was taken up strongly five months later at the 1948 British Trade Union Congress,[3] in a resolution sponsored by the railwaymen and the miners.

At the Association's 1949 Annual Conference in Aberdeen, the tone of the resolutions on nationalization sharpened; they had three before them.

---

[1] Report of Annual Conference, 1948.
[2] 51st Annual Report of the Scottish Trades Union Congress, 1948.
[3] Jack Stanley, General Secretary of the Constructional Engineering Union, said of the divisional coal board that 'out of forty-six members, eighteen are former company directors, four are high-salaried officers and only nine are trade union leaders.'

One declared that 'the principle of workers' participation' in a nationalized industry 'should be firmly adopted in practice'; and demanded special attention to ensure 'that facilities for training be afforded to acquire the knowledge necessary to the administering of nationalized industry'.[1] An Airdrie resolution demanded

'attention to the salaries which are being paid in certain undertakings and considers these are excessive and create misunderstanding in the minds of the workers as to the efficiency of nationalization.

'It declares that salaries should not exceed £1,500 p.a. It further demands that before appointments are confirmed the authorities should be satisfied that those appointed accept the principle of nationalization.'

Both resolutions were carried unanimously. The third declared that the Act did not go far enough and called for it to be extended to include all A B and C licensed vehicles over 30 cwt carrying capacity. Moving this for the Edinburgh branch, Alex Kitson said:

'It was the opinion of the Edinburgh branch that the employers were exploiting the use of the C-licence and felt that the Government should now consider taking over the whole of the transport industry.'

This was referred back to the Standing Orders Committee. A Kilmarnock resolution, which was remitted, noting the development towards centralization, called on the Executive Committee 'to explore the possibility of unification with other unions in the transport industry'. Dundee called for a new agreement with the TGWU to give the Association the right to organize all commercial transport workers in Scotland. This was rejected when John Brannigan argued that, if the present agreement were broken, it 'would result in a war with another union which would benefit neither'.

There were frequent meetings between transport unions and the Road Transport Executive during the summer of 1949. By early autumn negotiating machinery was set up, with a National Joint Staff Council of twelve trade union members, including one from the Association; three National Joint Negotiating Committees covered (1) operating and ancillary grades, (2) maintenance and repair, and (3) administrative, professional, technical, supervisory and clerical.

When the General Council of the TUC complained to the Minister of Transport about the exceptional increase in C-licensed vehicles, especially in 1948, Alfred Barnes remained unmoved; his view was that it was due to accumulated demand owing to war-time pooling of delivery vehicles, and that the rate of increase would soon drop off. When the Scottish TUC met three weeks later, at the end of September 1949, the Association delegates showed that they were far from sharing the Minister's optimism.

[1] Report of the Annual Conference, 1949.

In moving a resolution their delegate, Sandy Falconer, while categorically denying that C-licence control was dropped from the Act under pressure of the Co-operative movement, said 'that in the first months of 1949 there had been an increase of 3,465 operatives with 7,128 new C-licences'.

The Association's expectation proved more realistic than the Minister's, as these figures of vehicle licences from *Basic Road Statistics* show:

Year	Total Goods Licences	C-licences
1948	757,300	591,400
1953	956,000	798,500
1958	1,222,700	1,049,100
1963	1,476,100	1,278,300

At the Association's 1950 Annual Conference at Oban, new points were made. Markinch branch deplored that A-licences were granted to hauliers 'whose business had been taken over by the Road Transport Executive, thus allowing them to operate in opposition'. Glasgow A B and C branch was alarmed that 'since nationalization, units are overloading vehicles' and called for vehicles to be plated with their carrying capacity. This relatively simple checking device was a demand which David Strachan, shop steward of British Road Services in Edinburgh, especially fought for year after year when he became a delegate to annual conference; when it was finally achieved after a decade of persistent effort, it was one of the great gains.

David Strachan was one who, looking back years later, held the view that nationalization was the beginning of every improvement in the union, and, indeed, of the revival of the Association, not least in Edinburgh. In his view the greatest single step was the machinery of consultative committees and grade representation. Much time was spent first in working out the machinery and then in trying it out, as the undertakings began to be taken over, and the problems which arose in the course of reorganization had to be dealt with. Some of these were reflected in resolutions at Annual Conference and at the Scottish TUC. There had been at first a difference of opinion with the Transport & General Workers as to how the trade union side should be made up on the Divisional Committee. It took some months to reach agreement but, early in 1950, the Association was represented on the Divisional Co-ordinating Committee for the three grades, and held six seats to the T & GWU's three on the Divisional Committee of the operating and ancillary grades. In the Scottish Division, covering 8,288 people in twenty-six groups, ten Joint Negotiating Committees were formed:

'Glasgow would have four such committees and early meetings would be called to explain the structure of the machinery and an opportunity would be taken at all the meetings throughout the country to keep our members posted with information. Adequate representation should be secured from this union on all the committees.'[1]

Important as was representation on the National Staff Council and on the National and Divisional Joint Committees, the test of how nationalization would work depended on the success of the elected Local Joint Committees. These had been elected and had held their first meetings by August 1950. Disciplinary policy and procedure had been laid down, but this was not all plain sailing. Shop stewards were accustoming themselves to new methods of work, and there were many problems still awaiting settlement. There was difficulty over road–rail integration. The former railway cartage contracting staff were being taken over by the Railway Executive; agreement had to be reached with the National Union of Railwaymen, giving transferred workers the option to go on to less favourable railway conditions or to remain on road haulage wages without benefiting from promotion and redundancy agreements. There was difficulty about new grouping and new schedules: through reorganization some men lost the long distance traffic, yet hesitated to transfer to the group of British Road Services which was to handle it. Strong objection was taken to a proposal to introduce road patrols.

The problem which bore most hardly upon the members was the redundancy which followed reorganization when firms were taken over. Although this was a temporary feature, it hit the individual none the less hardly. Because nationalization meant rationalization, with the loss of drivers' jobs, while not enough attention was being given to alternative employment or adequate redundancy agreements, to some men nationalization was even seen at first as a disaster. Again, when some managers were taken over with their local firms on nationalization, there was a tendency for men to feel that there was little change. As early as October 31, 1950, when branches were drafting preliminary resolutions for annual conference, the wording shows the anxiety which was felt. Glasgow A B and C was especially concerned about compensation.[2]

The same branch also viewed 'with grave concern the present method of administration' and asked the Government to review it 'and endeavour to eliminate the present unrest among employees'. This outlook came not only from Glasgow, but also from the East Coast and Fife. Edinburgh stressed that 'full advantage should be taken of the knowledge, skill and experience of workers as well as those who held executive or administrative posts under private enterprise'. Kirkcaldy demanded that there should be

[1] Executive Committee *Minutes*, March 1, 1950.

[2] Their resolution, after supporting the principle of transport nationalization, was 'deeply conscious of the failure of nationalization to secure any tangible improvement in the conditions of the operatives or any reasonable concessions to the consumers, demand an investigation into the millstone of compensation paid to former owners and the tendency to run the industry by former owners.' (*The Highway*, November 1950)

a graduated scale of promotions which took into consideration 'rules governing seniority and redundancy'.

Much had been done. The uneasiness amongst the transport workers was largely due to the slowness of the pace and suspicion that this might be due to the influence of the former owners exercised through their former managers; for many on the managerial side of the nationalized industry were the same 'well kent' faces of the days of private enterprise. But there was also dislocation, redundancy, and some serious grievances. Inevitably with a partial scheme of this character, providing so many loopholes, escape clauses and debatable points, the tempo was unlikely to be that of a military operation. But early in 1951 some 2,900 road haulage concerns had been taken over, employing 75,000 people and controlling 40,000 vehicles and 1,000 depots. The prospect was that another 5,000 hauliers' permits would not be renewed during 1951 as the Road Haulage Executive was expecting to be able to take them over. They had been re-grouped into territorial units of fleets of between one and two hundred vehicles. But the British Transport Commission had also to pay for stores, some of which were fit only for scrap, and all of which had to be sorted out, and premises modified, adapted or abandoned. The scale of the financial transactions in which the British Transport Commission had been engaged was formidable.[1] The total number of vehicles operated fell during 1950; the monthly tonnage rose and so did the loaded mileage, whilst empty running was reduced to seventeen per cent. But the transport workers felt the brunt of the consequent redundancy and transfers.

In his Presidential address at the 1951 Annual Conference in Rothesay, Sandy Falconer brought to light other troubles of British Road Services, which had 'started off in the competitive field with an extreme handicap'. Many traders, he said, who were 'opposed to nationalization on political grounds were giving preference to the private haulier or alternatively providing their own transport if they could get the vehicles under C-licences'.[2] He thought the Government 'should have power to prevent those people who sold their businesses to the State, presumably with the

---

[1] Before nationalization the Scottish Motor Traction had £1,000,000 capital in preference stock and a little over a million ordinary stock. They received £8,400,000 compensation stock. As successor to the railway companies, the Transport Commission owned about half the ordinary SMT stock; and in addition to the compensation stock, agreed to pay half of any repayment to the preference stockholders. That was finally agreed at 25s for each £1, and meant a further financial obligation of £625,000. But this was not all. The ordinary stockholders enjoyed other advantages: 'The company has distributed £4 of British Transport Stock to its ordinary stockholders for every £1 SMT stock they hold. It still retains some assets which have not been transferred to the Commission and these will now belong entirely to the ordinary stockholders. The average dividends received by the SMT ordinary stockholders (excluding the railway companies) in 1945–7 were £403,519. Interest on the compensation stock will be £252,906 and dividend on the non-transferred assets in 1949 was £62,873.'

(From 'Finance of Nationalized Industries', *Labour Research*, December 1950)

[2] Report of Annual Conference, 1951.

goodwill thrown in, from starting up again in competition for traffic which should rightfully be the sphere of the State'. He also thought that if the Government continued 'to allow the development and extension of C-licence operation to proceed unchecked, their own scheme of road transport nationalization under the Act is heading for certain failure'.

The outlook of the rank and file was reflected in a number of remarks by delegates. Andrew Inglis of Kilmarnock said that 'the amount of compensation being paid to former owners was one of the causes of frustration among the people employed in that industry'.

C. Reid of Glasgow A B and C thought 'the question of former owners holding key jobs within the nationalized industry required investigation . . . opportunity should be afforded to workers to train and fit themselves for such situations, so that when the time arose they would be able to take their place in the running of industry'.

A resolution was carried to include C-licences, 'thereby eliminating the exploiting type of employer who has been compensated for his business from starting up again'. Speaking to it, Robert Lowe, Edinburgh, pointed out that, out of 800,000 vehicles, only 40,000 were nationalized: 'There would never be a properly integrated and balanced transport system in the country if the present set-up was allowed to continue.'

Immediately after the 1951 Conference, the Road Haulage Executive decided that road patrols should be begun, despite the objections raised. John Brannigan told the Executive that

'the Unions generally had opposed the introduction of road patrols, but that the Road Haulage Executive had conceded all points made, and the unions had no further practical points to make in support of the abolition of patrols'.

But the feeling was so strong that the Executive could not accept the General Secretary's view:

'Lengthy discussion took place on the matter when various points were made, but it was finally agreed on the motion of Messrs Falconer and McKay that the union was not in favour of road patrols, as they were of the opinion some better form of management on the roads was available.'[1]

But, before the Executive next met, a strike against the road patrol system had broken out in England, and in Scotland the Association called together the grade representatives in the ten local joint negotiating committees.[2] They met on Saturday, June 9, 1951, with Tom Berrey, the Association's chairman, presiding. The questions they asked John Brannigan quickly

---

[1] Executive *Minutes*, May 30, 1951.
[2] These were: Glasgow No. 1 and Glasgow No. 2; Borders; Aberdeen; Ayrshire; Dundee, Perth and Angus; Edinburgh & Lothians; Fife, Inverness and Buckie; and Pickfords.

showed what was troubling the transport workers in British Road Services. These included the length of time for settling complaints, that local joint committees had no power to reach settlements, 'and the general feeling of frustration' among grade representatives about their function.[1] When it came down to detail, representatives pressed that the disciplinary code should cover both managers and men; that Pickfords should not receive special treatment but should come under the name of Road Services; about redundancy and how drivers should be selected for special jobs; and the need for observance of Section 19 of the Road Traffic Act.

Regarding road patrols, the Edinburgh representative, David Strachan, said that these should be operated by the police, not the employer: 'If this were done, there could also be a more thorough check on operators of C-licence vehicles.' The long tradition in Scotland of the rights and duties of shop stewards left some unprepared for the limitations imposed on grade representatives. At the end of the meeting the General Secretary promised that a resolution would be submitted to the TUC which would 'have regard to their discussions'.

At the 1951 British Trades Union Congress in Blackpool, John Brannigan, gave some illustrations[2] of the consequences of the limited form of nationalization, when moving a resolution demanding 'a rigorous check on C-licensed vehicles'.

There had been many teething problems for the new nationalized

[1] A summary of the three organizers' reports given to the Executive that summer, on the eve of the third General Election since the war ended, shows vividly the day-to-day difficulties which were arising.

John Connell reported in his laconic style a strike at the Taylor Group of British Road Services over the operation of the five-day week which caused loss of earnings; about a shop steward dismissed; another member sent home; retrospective payment for a third; and with shop stewards at two other depots meeting the management 're various complaints'.

In Aberdeen, Robert McIntyre's district, the main problem with hand-over again was promotion, and to a less degree, redundancy. He also had to deal with 'vehicles based at Peterhead coming to Fraserburgh and uplifting traffic whilst Fraserburgh vehicles had been standing in the garage'.

Willie Campbell from the East Coast reported redundancy and transfer problems from Peebles and elsewhere; over-long hours, excessive waiting time and extra duties in market work from Galashiels and Haddington; and other cases, ranging from deliberate overloading to claims for 'dirty money' and complaints of lack of consultation on changes which were being introduced.

[2] 'The British Road Haulage Executive took over certain business in this country, and one in particular I should mention, because it is important, the firm of Charles Alexander in Aberdeen, which grew up from a half share in a vehicle to over 100 vehicles taken over by the British Road Services. After he was taken over—and I think he would be adequately paid—he started up in business again against British Road Services by purchasing another contractor's business and he has been successful. He was so successful that he took from British Road Services another semi-Government contract from the Milk Marketing Board.'

'Yet the nationalized industry was short of vehicles', he said, describing how other contractors had had to be hired to enable British Road Services to carry out its contract to transfer the Royal Highland Show 200 miles south from Aberdeen.

transport industry, especially in road haulage. These were gradually being met. The doubts of the transport workers were being removed as concentration on the inevitable growing pains of reorganization and re-grouping began to give place to taking advantage of the immense potential improvements in service, wages and conditions. The prospect of ultimate extension of the scope of the nationalized industry to cover the bulk of road haulage as public acquisitions were increased and licences to private hauliers were reduced, together with pressing ahead with promotion schemes, was soothing the men's suspicions. But whilst nationalized road haulage was still on trial the hopeful outlook for its future was destroyed in one stroke. As a result of the General Election on October 25, 1951, a Conservative Government was returned with a sufficient majority, pledged to denationalize the road haulage industry.

2. THE TRANSPORT ACT, 1953

The Executive Committee drafted a resolution at their first meeting which followed the General Election in November 1951 deploring 'the intimation by the government that they intend to implement their pledges in allowing greater freedom to private hauliers in the road transport industry'. It was for consideration at the annual conference in April 1952, nearly six months ahead. At this time there was intense preoccupation at Head Office with the aftermath of the court cases and with putting into effect Rule 21, which continued for some months; and the Executive did not take the question of denationalization further at their meetings; it was left to the Edinburgh Branch to move a resolution on denationalization. This somewhat slow reaction was to become one of the key points of criticism of the Executive which reached considerable proportions at the annual conferences of 1953 and 1954. At the Annual Conference of 1952 at North Berwick, veteran Tom Berrey of Renfrew, who had joined the Association over thirty years earlier, said, in his Presidential Address, that the Government's intentions 'revealed a vicious vindictiveness which brings back memories of the introduction of the Trade Disputes and Trade Unions Act of 1927. To return road haulage to unrestricted competition which was experienced in the inter-war years would be a most retrograde step . . . to attempt to return any part of the nationalized undertaking to former owners would result in utter confusion.'[1]

Resolutions from three branches were designed to strengthen the nationalized sector or to eliminate some inadequacy. Kirkcaldy branch was 'concerned with the expressed feelings of frustration emanating from the workers' representatives on the local joint committees. . . . By ex-panding the sphere of negotiations of the local joint committees a greater contribution towards the success of the nationalized industry can be made

[1] Report of Annual Conference, 1952.

by the workers'. In moving, John Kyle said that they believed workers had been 'badly let down with regard to what at the outset they thought could be accomplished' at that level. The seconder was David Strachan for Edinburgh, who also moved that the Pickford's division should come under the direct control of the Road Haulage Executive 'and its vehicles be painted with British Road Service colours'; Edinburgh had been concerned about 'the extending ramifications' of this undertaking which still bore its private enterprise name and 'its seemingly independent means of operating'. Another Edinburgh resolution protested against anomalies in working a five-day week. Despite appeals from the General Secretary, this 'was carried by an overwhelming majority'. Then came the Executive's resolution on denationalization, which recalled the effect of private competition and that only by successive Acts since 1930 'has some semblance of order been brought into road transport'.

Three weeks later, the Scottish TUC met at Perth and carried unanimously a resolution moved by the National Union of Railwaymen, and seconded by Sandy Falconer for the Association.[1] In his Presidential Address to the Scottish Trades Union Congress at the conclusion of his year of office, John Brannigan recalled their past record, including the resolution moved by Emanuel Shinwell in 1916, which had declared 'the time now opportune for the State assuming control of all the means of production, distribution and exchange'. In his peroration he concluded:

'Finally, I would say to the Government, do not tamper with the trade union conception of public control of industry. When you start to take back from the public parts of industry which we think should be operated in the public good, you then have to deal with the whole trade union movement; and I warn you if you touch nationalized road transport or steel you will incur the emphatic condemnation of our fellow trade unionists in every other industry in this country. Hands off nationalization!'

This was to be John Brannigan's last speech from the Congress platform.

Two weeks after the STUC on May 8, 1952, the Government issued a white paper[2] setting out its proposals. It declared its purpose to be 'to re-establish a measure of competition between road and rail'; and asserted that the proposals would lead to cheaper transport. It expressed opposition to integration:

'Even if integration in its fullest sense were practicable, it would result in

[1] It deprecated 'the intention of the Government to sacrifice the industry and the people employed therein by a transference of its revenue-earning sections to the satisfaction of private enterprise, knowing that the railways will have to be maintained out of public funds if unbridled competition is allowed to operate.' (55th Annual Report of the STUC, 1952)

[2] British Transport Commission. Annual Report for 1952.

a huge unwieldy machine, ill-adapted to meet with promptitude the varying and instant demands of industry.'

The proposals were to regroup the nationalized undertaking into units to be offered for disposal by open tender. A loss was anticipated, and a levy was to be imposed on road vehicles to meet it. The railways were to be decentralized. The draft Bill published two months later, on July 9, 1952, provided for the lorries to be sold through a Road Haulage Disposals Board, on which there were to be representatives of A, B and C licence-holders, but not of labour. Grouped into transport units for sale, each vehicle would be entitled to an A licence with no twenty-five mile limit for five years. One feature which met with sharp criticism was that the Government had not consulted with the British Transport Commission about the effects of the proposals before the white paper was issued. Yet the Commission had submitted to the new Minister of Transport, A. T. Lennox-Boyd, plans for a simpler form of organization. These had included some 'devolution of authority' to the regions, without 'sacrificing the advantages and economies only to be secured by central control of certain essential matters'. This it combined with the development of road and rail service and freight traffic under a single commercial management. The British Transport Commission stated that:

'Proposals designed to secure these ends were submitted to the then Minister of Transport at the end of 1951, but no consultations took place upon them; when on May 8, 1952 a White Paper was issued, forecasting legislation which would impose upon the Commission a duty to dispose of their road haulage undertakings and would require decentralization of the railway organization.'

The BTC's Annual Report continued that, when the Transport Bill was published,

'The Commission made it clear to the government that they were completely opposed to these provisions. The Commission had also emphasized to the Minister the gravely disturbing effect which in their view the proposals were likely to have upon the efficiency of their services, upon their finances and upon their staff.'

When the trade union conferences met in May their reaction to the white paper was vehement. Some of them immediately called upon the Labour Party to declare that when next in power it would nationalize without compensation. These included the Locomotive engineers, the Foundry workers, and the Amalgamated Engineering Union, whilst railwaymen called for renationalization 'without loss to the community'. The Edinburgh branch of the Association took the initiative at their monthly meeting, and submitted to the Executive Council a resolution 'criticizing the White Paper issued on Denationalization of Transport, and requesting that letter be sent to Mr Attlee and the Parliamentary Labour Party indicating that the transport workers are behind them in opposing the White Paper proposals.

'It was thereafter agreed that a letter expressing Association policy and support be sent to the appropriate persons.'[1]

The Labour Party published a leaflet *Stop The Sell-Out* in support of a joint campaign which was organized together with the TUC which set up a special committee of the transport unions to help. John Brannigan wrote in *The Highway* for August 1952 that in the previous issue he had warned members 'no matter how enthusiastic they may become' not to be 'stampeded into hasty and irresponsible action'. He continued that it was hoped that conferences and demonstrations would arouse public opinion to deter the Government from carrying through 'this vicious proposal':

'At a later stage the members will be timeously advised of the time and place of such conferences, and it is to be hoped they will respond to the lead which will be given.'

Finally, a conference was arranged in Edinburgh on September 20, 1952, and a demonstration in Glasgow on September 21st, ten months after the Conservative Government had confirmed its intention to denationalize. Some sections of the Scottish trade union movement had not waited. In the counties of Clackmannan, Stirling, and West Lothian district committees of the Confederation of Shipbuilding and Engineering Unions had taken the initiative to approach trades councils and start a campaign. Some controversy arose when the STUC informed the local trades councils that they should not co-operate, as it was usurping the function of the STUC.

The road haulage members of the Association had their difficulties; there was no little upheaval and confusion going on, as British Road Services continued regrouping and concentration. Particularly affected were the Edinburgh Parcels and General Group, while work was transferred from East Lothian and Border depots to Hawick. Members had to shift with their vehicles. The 1953 Annual Report of the STUC records that there were conferences and public meetings held in Aberdeen, Kilmarnock, Motherwell, Kirkcaldy, and Ayr. But the big Scottish conference was at the Music Hall, Edinburgh, when the principal speakers were the Rt Hon Emanuel Shinwell, MP and John Brannigan: it was jointly organized by the Scottish Council and the STUC, which provided the chairman, A. D. Mackellar, of the Draughtsmen. A long resolution was passed, insisting that denationalization would make a unified national transport system

[1] Executive *Minutes*, June 11, 1952.

impossible.[1] As well as opposing the whole principle, the resolution also noted objectionable features, such as selling the road haulage undertakings at a loss; and ended by declaring that 'this petty measure' was unnecessary, and 'irrelevant to the economic needs of the nation, especially to the current serious balance of payments crisis. The drive for higher production and more exports cannot succeed without the help of an efficient transport system'. The terms of the Transport Bill itself, in the view of the British TUC were 'nothing more than a series of expedients to alleviate the worst of the inevitable consequences of the denationalization of road haulage'.[2] J. B. Figgins of the NUR moved the composite resolution at the 1952 Margate Congress, which condemned the Bill on two grounds:

(a) that the proposals are based on class interests and are, in fact, against the findings of Royal Commissions and Investigation Committees set up by previous Conservative governments;
(b) that no consultation took place before publication of the White Paper with the British Transport Commission as to their effect.

During the debate, the only difference of opinion was when the vehicle builders' delegate criticized the resolution for recommending that the next Labour Government should renationalize 'without compensation for cessation of business': it should be without compensation at all, he said. A similar resolution was passed four weeks later at the 51st Annual Conference of the Labour Party at Morecambe; here an attempt to introduce the principle of no compensation and expropriation of interim profits in renationalized industries was defeated by 1,652,000 to 2,386,000 after Harry Douglass of the Iron and Steel Trades Confederation, speaking for the National Executive Committee, had opposed it on the grounds that 'Confiscation is the tool of the dictators'. The TUC called a further demonstration at the Albert Hall on October 13, 1952, to which the Association sent its General Secretary and its chairman, John McQuade, himself a road haulage driver.

In the autumn a revised Bill was produced, but its modifications were unimportant. It was debated in November and December and, by February 16, 1953, had reached the Third Reading; it received the Royal Assent on May 6, 1953. The publicly-owned road haulage service, although it was not quite completed, had already made a substantial profit. Now dismantling it began.

---

[1] 'The changes which the Government envisage are being made at the very moment when, as the recent Report of the British Transport Commission shows, substantial progress towards the integration of transport and the raising of efficiency in the industry is being achieved. Denationalization of road haulage will make such integration impossible and will inflict serious financial losses upon the railways.' (56th Annual Report to the STUC, 1953)
[2] 84th Annual Report of the TUC, 1952.

3. DENATIONALIZATION BEGINS

Minor modifications, including some discussion on the question of compensation to British Road Services personnel, had been achieved in what John McQuade, the Association's Chairman, described as 'a calamity in the history of transport'. He was speaking, a month after the Third Reading, at the Association's Annual Conference at Ayr. When the executive council's report came before Conference for approval, Alex Kitson rose to ask delegates to remit back the section on denationalization. He was one of a strong delegation of six members elected by Edinburgh, all of whom were prominent in the debates. They included J. Carabine, who was elected to the Executive that year for the first time, Robert Lowe, David Strachan, J. Brown, and E. Wilson. Kitson criticized the transport unions for 'their meagre efforts' against denationalization. It had to be examined more particularly with regard to the men's future. The rank and file members always suffered; at the end of 1951, 43,294 drivers and mates were employed in the nationalized industry, but in August 1952 they had been reduced to 39,237, or nearly 4,000 in nine months. Yet, on the supervisory side in the same period, the numbers had been reduced by only seven, from 1,283 to 1,276. 'He then called upon the Executive to be more explicit as far as the compensation and the future of the industry was concerned, and added that when the Labour Government came back to power, transport should be nationalized on an all-in principle.'[1] He was supported by Carabine and Strachan (Edinburgh), J. Craig (Airdrie), and John Kyle (Kirkcaldy), who was particularly concerned about protecting 'the men who had served on the various committees set up since the inception of the nationalized industry'. Although the General Secretary twice appealed for Conference to support the report, the decision to remit back was carried by a large majority, forty-seven to seven. A resolution by Aberdeen deploring denationalization was carried unanimously; whilst one from Airdrie called for 'a greater volume of public ownership of industries' from the next Labour Government, with more workers' representatives than hitherto.

In *The Highway* for May 1953, there was a long article on renationalization by J. O'Gormley, written after the Annual Conference. Himself a BRS driver in Glasgow, he discussed the benefits of nationalization and what should be looked for in future measures. Foremost he put security of employment, and contrasted it with the days when there was 'a multiplicity of less reputable small firms running long distance transport, cutting rates and each others' throats at the same time'. It was the driver who suffered most: 'To many of these drivers then the steering wheel became almost like the old-fashioned albert on a watch-chain continually draped in their middle.'

[1] Report of Annual Conference, 1953.

They endured long hours, driving 'very questionable vehicles': yet anyone protesting was never long in a job. His second point was that, before nationalization, accidents which came within the *Construction and Use* regulations would arise because, if a driver failed to take out of the garage an unfit vehicle, he would either lose wages or get the sack. Under nationalization there had been security of tenure and better maintained vehicles: 'We are proud to say that in State transport the threat of loss of wages or sacking through having an accident ceased to exist.' Thirdly, he praised the work of the local joint committees, educational and promotion schemes and improved welfare conditions. He criticized, however, the hardening of attitude of some in managerial positions who were lukewarm to nationalization, in their present attitude to the workers: 'In some cases we are perilously close to conditions prevailing under private enterprise, so much has this attitude developed on the part of those group managers who were heads of private concerns before the take-over.' He ended by admitting that there had been some mistakes:

'Some of my fellow-workers, no doubt embittered by perhaps some lowering of earning capacity or conditions of work caused by centralization, or the economics of running the biggest transport firm ever (British Road Services), may have lost faith in the principle of nationalization; but let us consider the scope and enormity of the project, a feat of organization which could never have come to full growth without some teething troubles.'

An awareness of criticism, expressed or unexpressed, of the shortcomings of the partial measures of nationalization was also apparent in the remarks of the Association's spokesman at the STUC at Rothesay that year. Adam Anderson said that:

'Despite the mistakes made he was confident that nationalized transport had proved a success. An organized transport service was absolutely essential to the economic stability and well-being of the nation.

'The Tories, tongue in cheek, had long championed the cause of the small man, yet prior to 1946 the small man was well on his way out, through pressure from large operators. The future in front of the small man was nationalization or absorption.'[1]

On May 21, 1953, two weeks after the Bill had received the Royal Assent, six members of the Road Haulage Disposals Board were appointed.[2] The same day the members of the board which was to supervise

---

[1] 56th Annual Report of the STUC, 1953.
[2] Sir Malcolm Trustram Eve, QC, as part-time chairman (director of the Yorkshire Insurance Co, chairman of the Cement Makers' Federation); F. J. Orchin, as full-time deputy chairman (formerly chief financial officer of the Road Haulage Executive); Lord Rusholme, of the British Transport Commission; R. H. Farmer (managing director of Atlas Express Company and formerly vice-chairman of the Road Haulage Association); J. W. Greenwood (formerly transport manager of Thomas Firth and John Brown); and W. Gordon Graham (formerly managing director of Morris Commercial Cars).

denationalizing steel was announced; these included two members of the General Council of the TUC and one other trade union general secretary; this caused some controversy. The Edinburgh branch of the Association reacted at once:

'Resolution from this branch condemning the action of leading trade unionists in accepting positions on denationalization boards, submitted and considered, after which it was agreed on the notion of Messrs Berrey and Sheridan no action be taken in the matter.'[1]

That June the Labour Party published a policy document called *Challenge to Britain*,[2] which was to be presented to their annual conference: it gave this specified pledge:

'Labour will take back into public ownership such road haulage units as are needed to provide a co-ordinated transport system, on such terms as will prevent private owners from profiting at the expense of the nation.'

A pamphlet entitled *Labour's Plan for Britain* which summarized these proposals, putting the transport policy in much the same words, was published in *The Highway* for August 1953.

By the end of 1952 the Road Haulage Executive had taken over some 4,000 undertakings, comprising 46,000 vehicles. But 19,000 of these vehicles had had to be sold as scrap.[3] It had had to buy new vehicles to replace these. Now the Disposals Board began to regroup these in order to sell them off. It was not uncommon for private hauliers to buy them up in order to gain the benefit of the A-licence covering them; they were being sold to them at a loss. But the end of 1953 there were lists of establishments put up for sale and the dismantling of the nationalized industry was in full swing. But, although the great sell-out had begun, it was long before it was complete. In Scotland, British Road Services had owned 3,550 vehicles; at the end of September 1954 it was expected that of these some 3,125 were to be offered for public tender, leaving the truncated British Road Services 425 with which to carry on a skeleton service of that traffic for which the private hauliers did not wish to compete. But the process of denationalization ran into difficulties; an Act modifying the scheme had to be introduced in 1956 and it was not until the autumn of that year that some degree of stabilization was reached and the full degree of redundancy was known, three and a half years after the Transport Act, 1953 had become law. The arguments and resolutions passed at conferences of the trade union movement about the degree of compensation in any future renationalization did not pass unnoticed, nor without effect. Some hauliers appeared to have second thoughts.

[1] Executive *Minutes*, August 4, 1953.
[2] Report of the 52nd Annual Conference of the Labour Party.
[3] Para 55, 'Interim Report on Public Ownership', Supplement to paragraph 341 of the General Council's Report to the 1953 Trades Union Congress.

Members of the Association stuck to their guns, and the problems were reflected in the Annual Conferences. In 1954, for the second year running, the Executive Council's report on denationalization came under fire. John Kyle of Kirkcaldy, said that, in his opinion, 'the report did not go far enough in explaining the position in regard to redundancy, compensation for loss of earnings and the position of those workers in the operating and ancillary grades who were over 65 years of age'.[1] Alex Kitson added that 'the Executive Council never came out with any hard and fast policy', and that it appeared that suggestions were not treated with the respect to which they were entitled:

'Some stand should be taken, if not on denationalization, some new policy should be formed by the Executive Council so that when renationalization comes along there should be better protection for the workers.'

John Brannigan replied that the Act was an accomplished fact, and most could be done by getting a new Government:

'He hoped that if and when the men were declared redundant, they would retain their union membership and keep in contact with the union in order that they may be advised of the happenings under the Transport Act.'

He must have regarded it as a severe defeat when the remit back was carried by forty-three to eight, especially as it was immediately followed by another remit being carried in the section on wages; any remit back of the Executive Council's report was unusual at the Association's conferences.

For the next twelve months, uncertainty, dislocation, and some redundancy continued in the nationalized section. By the autumn of 1954, the Disposals Board had found the going slower than had been expected; offers to purchase had not been coming in fast, and many had had to be rejected, being below a reasonable sum.[2] Staffs had been reduced; there had been redundancy. The Association's 1955 Annual Conference met at Rothesay on the eve of the General Election, which took place on May 26, 1955; it coloured the speeches on nationalization of those who confidently expected a new Labour Government to be returned. Peter McGarry in his presidential address noted that 'quite a number' of members in road haulage 'have been enticed to change their occupation in the free-for-all already started in competition for traffic, and this would continue until the new adventurers in the industry started cutting the wages and conditions of the men'. The Executive Council put forward an emergency resolution

---

[1] Report of Annual Conference, 1954.
[2] Noted that up to January 1, 1955, 26,000 offers for purchase of vehicles, etc., had been received, but that a great number of these had been rejected, and only 12,218 vehicles had so far been sold.' (Executive *Minutes*, February 26, 1955)

'referring to the havoc that has been created in the transport industry through the disintegration caused by the dismantling Act'. It called upon 'all transport workers to do all in their power to secure the return of a Labour Government who are prepared to co-ordinate and integrate the inland transport system of this country'.[1]

After this had been carried unanimously, John Kyle of Kirkcaldy, who was elected to the Executive Council for the first time that year, once again moved the remit back of that part of the report dealing with denationalization. He said it contained practically nothing answering the questions that were being asked; few members in BRS knew what was happening. 'Among other things, the members want to know where the Executive Council stood in the event of renationalization; whether in the event of renationalization the Association would allow the ex-employer to retain management in the transport industry; what the Association policy was in regard to redundancy and also with regard to C-licences.' Conference went on to pass unanimously two further resolutions from the Executive, one calling for speedy renationalization 'without further loss to the nation'; and for 'some form of statutory control' to be imposed on C-licences to confine them 'to local operation'.

A fortnight after the Conference had ended, a Conservative Government was returned with an increased majority. The new government, however, soon announced that they would introduce a Bill to allow the BRS to keep such road haulage vehicles as were necessary to continue the trunk service network. By the new year the text of the amending Bill was out; it allowed British Road Services to retain 7,750 vehicles, of which about 1,000 would be in Scotland. Redundancy remained a problem; and British Road Services lost traffic to private hauliers, not because of better services, but because of undercutting—sometimes by as much as twenty-three per cent.

But active resistance to denationalization could make no further headway at the time under a firmly entrenched Conservative Government. The need to prepare for renationalization was nevertheless kept before members through articles by Alex Kitson, published in *The Highway*. In May 1958 he wrote a critical review of transport which he believed 'should be regarded as an essential service to the community', and described the 'chaotic scramble for traffic', with rates slashed to uneconomic levels and some drivers overworked. He raised a number of points on which the Labour Party in opposition would need to adopt a policy ready for the time when they could once more form a government: What would be done about the C-licence holders? What controls would be necessary for co-ordination? Would 'purely commercial considerations' limit their expansion? He thought that checks on the fitness of vehicles and control of licensing were essential: and he argued that while the British Road

[1] Report of Annual Conference, 1955.

351

Services had done 'a wonderful job', they could have done more if the problems had been given more thought before 1945. These were some of the reasons which led him to recommend that the transport unions should set up a panel of their own members at once to work out what would be the ideal integrated inland transport system. It was not until Alex Kitson became the fifth General Secretary that the Association directed much attention to the problems of renationalization and the need for a campaign for it. But that was not until 1959. Problems in many other spheres of activity throughout the fifties increasingly needed a new and vigorous approach.

[*photo: Alex C. Cowper*

13. The platform party at the Association's Annual Conference at Perth, 1963. *Left to right:* James Barrie (Assistant General Secretary); Nanette Thomson (stenographer), Mrs Joyce Smith (cashier), A. H. Kitson (General Secretary), William Frew (President), David Lauder of the NUR (representing the STUC), and John Welch (1964 President).

14. A line-up at the annual parade in the Cattle Market, Glasgow, 1950. From left to right, the carters are: Robert Graham (Central), William Downie and David Waugh (South), William Towell (Western), James Muir (South) and William Collins (Eastern).

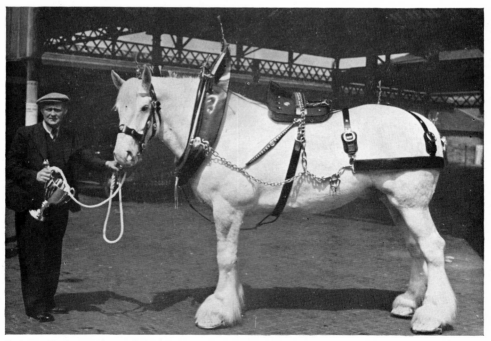

Robert Graham (Central Stables) is holding the Glasgow Agricultural Society Cup for the best groomed horse and best kept harness, which he won in 1951, 1952 and 1953. He is leading the 1952 champion, the Clydesdale 'Iain'.

CHAPTER NINETEEN

AWAY FROM THE OLD
'FRIENDLY SOCIETY'

I. PROBLEMS OF THE FIFTIES

By the time it was facing the problems of nationalization and denationalization, road haulage increasingly dominated the other sections of the transport industry; but these also had their own difficulties. A new era had opened since the days when the Association had grown up, protecting its very strong financial position in a 'friendly society' atmosphere and just about weathering the early thirties, until national recognition had coincided with, and seemed guaranteed by, the establishment of national negotiating machinery. The new era presented transport workers both with greater opportunities for the future, but also with four main problems. Firstly, although in 1940, Road Haulage Wages Order No. 1, with the principle established of statutory enforcement of minimum rates, had looked like the beginning of real advance in wages and conditions of the ill-rewarded transport worker, progress had been arrested. Despite his much increased responsibilities, he was no longer climbing up the relative ladder of wage scales. The weekly average earnings of those engaged in transport and communications in 1948, at 136s 6d, showed them to be in the tenth place: by 1953 they had dropped to sixteenth place, with earnings of 174s 7d. At the same time, the average hours worked per week had risen from 48·8 hours to 49·1 hours, and rose another two hours by 1955.[1] John Brannigan often claimed that at first the Road Haulage Orders had not much more weight with certain types of employer than the old 'Fair Wages Clause'. It depended at least as much as ever upon local vigilance and organization and on-the-spot determination. That called for harmonious and confident relations between the man in the garage and leadership at all levels. Yet this had not received encouragement.

If all was left to be centrally determined through cumbrous and long drawn out machinery, with the apparent deliberate inevitability of the progress of the sun across the sky, where was the room for members' initiative? Moreover, in the workers' side of the various negotiating bodies, at the level of power, the negotiator for the Association was only one among representatives from much stronger bodies. To make headway

[1] Annual Abstract of Statistics, 1959–62.

called for a dynamic approach in the Association's top negotiators, and not only in road haulage but also in other fields of negotiation which were influenced by it. It began slowly to be seen that this vast negotiating machinery, which was thought to be designed to offer protection against the rapacity of the multiplicity of hauliers in the chaos of competition with which the industry had been beset, could become instead a brake on the improvement of wages and conditions. Was it possible that more could be got by voluntary negotiation with the big hauliers as their dominance in the industry, even more marked after denationalization, continually increased?

Secondly, denationalization brought with it many difficulties in the road haulage sector, and not in the British Road Services alone, where the transport workers needed vigilant protection from its effects and from the effects of the retreat from integration. This came at a time when the inevitable upheavals caused by regrouping under nationalization were still in progress and before the system had been allowed to demonstrate its superiority in every direction. If ever a General Secretary needed an ear to the ground, to be quick to act and ever ready with explanation for members, it was in such a situation. Upon occasion, John Brannigan gives the impression of confining himself to urging members to keep in touch with their branch to find out how they would be affected.

Thirdly, there was need to prepare to campaign for renationalization on improved lines and for full integration. For that, systematic education and development of political action and discussion at all levels was crucial. But a criticism made by members was that the Association had not even a policy, either with regard to future compensation if any, nor about the scope of renationalization and what attitude should be taken to C-licences, nor a critical review of the former machinery. Here again it looked as though John Brannigan's view, and perhaps that of the majority of the Executive, was to wait upon events; to look for a lead from the British TUC and from the other transport unions. Once again the impression is gained that John Brannigan was ready to 'wait for the moment when the iron was hot, instead of making it hot by striking'.

Finally, considerable development was obligatory in the Association's internal affairs. There was an urgent need to arrest the post-1951 decline in members, in finance, and in influence. It was, for example, a serious matter that for year after year from 1953 onwards, until Alex Kitson became General Secretary in 1960, the Association lacked a representative amongst the Scottish TUC office-bearers. The situation required an immediate impetus to recruitment; reconstruction of administration, a review of staff and methods; a strengthening of democracy, with stress upon improved relations at all levels; and the development and modernization of the constitution. This meant shaking off the old 'Friendly Society' atmosphere which still clung to the Association—and to which some of its members still clung—and to replace this by the spirit of the new unionism, which would look forward to the twenty-first century rather than backward to the nineteenth.

The test of leadership both in the Executive Council and among full-time, part-time, and voluntary officials at all levels was whether they could and did set about consciously pursuing these objects in this difficult decade. It would mean a break with the past to form a new and harmonious relationship between leaders and members, especially with the new young motormen. But although at annual conferences progressive resolutions were adopted on trade questions and other matters, they were not pursued vigorously. Members of the Executive have asserted that if John Brannigan did not like a resolution he would allow it to run into the sand: a formal acknowledgement from a Ministry or official would be accepted as final. Sometimes months would pass until a resolution became out of date and was dropped on those grounds; progress was often not reported. At times, some sectional interest would be over-represented on the Executive. Only one issue during the fifties was of deep concern to all members of the Association equally; that was the increased demand for speed and ever more speed, legal and illegal, which affected every transport worker in commercial transport, whatever his sector. One of the main problems of the fifties, therefore, with which the Association was obliged to deal was what culminated in the Motor Vehicles (Variation of Speed) Regulations, 1956, which came into operation on May 1, 1957. What led up to this and what flowed from it requires a separate account. First, however, we must look at the work, much of it of high standard, in the day-to-day service provided to members.

2. THE ASSOCIATION'S BENEFITS AND SERVICE

There was, of course, the never-ending flow of sick benefits, compensation and accident cases, retirement grants, the Benevolent Fund, and the Convalescent Home service. For the most part these were handled with such practised efficiency that, during the fifties, they only rarely received more than routine mention in the Executive Minutes. After war-time difficulties and damage, and despite all the post-war problems of re-equipment and re-staffing, St Andrews House at Ayr was well established and functioning well. If the old decorated Horse Shows were fading out, which some of the oldest members remembered as being great days in their childhood, at least the 'Driver of the Year Competition' was instituted in 1956, to which the Association members supplied almost all the winning entrants; there were also the road safety awards, which came to be much prized.

With road congestion ever increasing and further Acts of Parliament creating new legal offences for the harassed driver, very great pressure developed upon the Defence Fund. For some twenty years the supervision of the bulk of this work was in the hands of 'Norrie' MacPherson. This was the old rebel who had built the breakaway from the Transport & General Workers' Union in the late thirties on the individual grievances of the Glasgow bus and tramwaymen and those whom he called affectionately 'the utter scoundrels' of the Empire Exhibition drivers. Scrutinizing new legislation; seeing how it would harass the men, and how it could be made to harass employers; explaining it in popular terms in *The Highway*; taking up individual cases: the old buccaneer came to find himself in his element in such work. He gained a hearing in the Glasgow courts and represented many an Association member there. Legal fees and fines became increasingly costly. A new set of offences and penalties was introduced by the Motor Vehicles (Construction and Use) Regulations, 1951. A whole variety of defects was covered, both in 'the construction and use' of a vehicle, including faulty speedometer, brakes, and windscreen wipers, insecurely fastened loads, and so on. Sometimes the driver alone and sometimes the owner jointly with the driver were charged in connection with the regulations. Anomalies and difficulties arose, which put an added burden on the Defence Fund. So serious did this become[1] that in the autumn of 1951 the Association was obliged to modify the benefits. Yet by 1956 the Defence Fund was insolvent; and they had to decide that each case should be considered on its merits. Under the Road Traffic Act of 1956, the charges of speeding, careless driving, and failing to stop at halt signs increased the difficulties even further.

When the Government announced their intention of bringing in the new Bill to promote road safety, the Association submitted a memorandum on Road Safety. It first made the point that the roads were quite unfit for modern traffic, not least those in Scotland, a subject on which the Association had passed and sponsored many resolutions over the years. But it sharply criticized the increased penalties for reckless, careless, and drunken driving which were proposed. There were disparities between English and Scottish law. An example was that in England, by a High Court decision, a driver could be convicted of speeding on the evidence of only one constable, corroborated by the record of a mechanical device. Eventually, the Road Traffic Act of 1956, introduced not only compulsory inspection and testing of vehicles over ten years old, but also the loss of licence for second offences. There were other new offences and increased penalties which lead to a yet further drain on the Defence Fund. As from July 1, 1957 it was decided that legal fees for Road Traffic offences should be met out of the trade union fund. The Association submitted a resolution

---

[1] The Defence Fund's total which had reached a peak of £12,120 at the end of 1949 had been falling ever since, although income from the contributions was still rising. The General Secretary reported to the Finance Committee that expenditure on fees had trebled since 1945, and fines for 1950 exceeded those for 1946 by £1,874.

to the British TUC, and John Brannigan moved it at Southport on September 9, 1955. He said that road transport workers 'do not believe the uncorroborated evidence of a single policeman'. In contrast to the present position in England, he continued: 'The law in Scotland says that no person can be convicted of a crime or of a statutory offence, except where the legislation otherwise directs, unless there is evidence of at least two witnesses implicating the person accused of the crime or offence with which he is charged.'[1] The present time was opportune for bringing the English law into line, he said, because of the amending Act which was at that time going through the House of Commons.[2]

3. NEGOTIATION AND ARBITRATION

When the war began, national negotiation machinery was still in its infancy; apart from the Road Haulage Wages Board and the Joint Industrial Council for Local Authorities, which took three and four years respectively to arrive at their first Agreement, and the co-operative movement, the great majority of agreements arrived at by the Association were with individual employers. War-time conditions encouraged the wide extension of joint industrial councils, trade boards, wages boards and councils. By the early fifties, the individual agreement was the exception. Many such negotiation boards admittedly or tacitly abided by the outcome of the Road Haulage Wages Council; as time went on they might indeed be said to 'wait for it'. The strong point of the road haulage award was that it was legally enforceable against an employer; the weak points were that many months passed between submitting a claim and the coming into operation of a favourable award, whilst the sums awarded tended increasingly to become minima, with little relation to earnings. The routine submission of a claim and its automatic and deliberate progress through the pipe-line gives the impression of a certain mechanical effect; at the same time, when the government of the day was exercising a credit squeeze, operating capital cuts, flashing a guiding light, or in other ways interposing between parties in negotiation, reactions were sharp and bewildering to

[1] 87th Annual Report of the TUC, 1955.
[2] Exactly a month later he had cause himself to be glad that the principle held in Scotland. After he had visited Ibrox Park on the afternoon of Saturday, October 8, 1955, to see a football match, the Coatbridge police on receiving a wireless message that a car was being driven erratically, sent out road patrol police, who after just avoiding a collision, stopped him and charged him with driving under the influence of drink or drugs. It was exactly six years after the disastrous accident when he had lost his licence for a year on a similar charge. When the case came up for hearing four months later, he was represented by Queen's Counsel at Airdrie Sheriff Court. After a two-day hearing, the sergeant passenger gave evidence which failed to corroborate that of the constable driving the patrol car. Sheriff Thomas Young found the case *Not Proven*, and was reported to have remarked: 'A charge like this is a very serious one, but there is sufficient doubt in my mind to give you the benefit.' (*Daily Record*, February 2, 1956)
It was a narrow escape; he could have been disqualified for life if convicted.

the members. In the road transport industry, where national negotiating machinery was new and still promising, such developments must have been very perplexing for some of those who, like John Brannigan, had been in at the start of the creation of road haulage machinery, watching, in company with Robert Taylor, the experienced Ernest Bevin's deft handling of it. If peaceful though competitive co-existence with the employers in national negotiating machinery were not to run smoothly and solve all ills, what then was the outlook to be? His views on wage restraint underwent modification.

But these difficulties did not become plain for all to see until the middle fifties. Early in the decade, negotiations were in progress, usually without undue difficulty, with a very large number of bodies, on some of which, such as for example, the Scottish Co-operative Wholesale Society, the Association were sole negotiators. In others, such as for members in the Retail Co-operative Societies under the Scottish National Co-operative Wages Board, the Association led for three unions on the workers' side. Co-negotiators in other bodies included the TGWU, the NUR, USDAW, NUM & GW, and others. A black spot was the taxicab trade, where wages were heavily depressed by the tipping system. There had been a strike in 1938 in Edinburgh, where the taxi-drivers were well organized, and there was considerable pressure from here for quick progress, which it was felt it would take a Wages Council to achieve. They had a long tradition, following the amalgamation in 1912 with the Edinburgh & Leith Cab-drivers, which went back to 1885. In 1949, the General Secretary was conducting correspondence with the Ministry of Labour and at the Annual Conference that year he appealed to those in the taxi trade in Edinburgh to provide facts and figures about the tipping system to strengthen his hand. By the 1950 conference, he still had little progress to report. All owners had been asked to meet the Association to discuss a 'very substantial increase' in wages and a reduction of hours to forty-four, with appropriate holidays; in short, the object was to put these drivers on terms similar to those of other transport workers. Yet some of the most recalcitrant taxi-owners had opposed an application to the Edinburgh magistrates for increased fares. In late summer that year, the dispute was referred to arbitration, which was not heard until January 9, 1951. The award was given in the Association's favour and an increase of £1 a week secured. This was regarded as a big step forward, as a taxi-driver shop steward wrote in *The Highway*, in which he commented that, since the end of the year, they had got what they had never had before—a forty-eight-hour week.

Another section of the membership—the horsemen—were far advanced in decline in the post-war years. Early in 1949, one of the oldest contracting firms decided that the horse had outlived its usefulness, being no longer 'economic'; and the two-score carters were given a week's notice. In

The Highway for May 1949, the General Secretary wrote his regret at witnessing 'the fate of many old carters who helped to build up this great organization'. Whilst work had been found for general carters, the railway cartage men had reason to doubt their future. With nationalization the British Transport Commission had taken over the bulk of the men. By 1949 some 2,753 horse-drawn vehicles and 990 animals had come under the Commission: by 1951 only half of the vehicles and a third of the horses were left in the service. Yet in the summer of 1951 there was still occasion for a 'Fancy Cairter's Turn-oot', and not only at the Royal Highland Show. On June 9, 1951, in Aberdeen seventeen of British Railways eighty-nine cart horses paraded, ribbons, tassels, polished brasses and all.[1] But as time went on, the Railway and General Carters Branch in Glasgow grew smaller and smaller, and experienced great difficulty in getting a quorum at branch meetings; and by the late summer of 1956 it had become merged in the Glasgow A B & C branch. When the delegates met next spring at North Berwick, there were some sorrowful speeches of farewell to the horsemen's famous branch:

'It was thereafter unanimously agreed by Conference on the motion of Mr G. Smart (Kirkcaldy) and J. Brown (Edinburgh) to formally record appreciation of the work done by the early pioneers of this great organization who gave birth to the great organization, the Horse & Motormen's Association, and which was today probably one of the soundest and certainly most independent trade unions in the country.'[2]

There still continued negotiating machinery for carters in 1961; and when, at the Annual Conference that year, the Dumfries branch proposed a change of name which would drop 'Horse' from the Association's title, no seconder could be found.

There was a steady trickle of conciliation cases and occasions when the Association had to go to arbitration, but not beyond, which did not attract the limelight, but was part of the essential day-to-day work. The organization of the funeral trade employers in 1949, for example, could not guarantee that their members would observe a tentative agreement reached; and in the same year there were references to arbitration on behalf of members employed by local authorities and in the Aberdeen coal trade, amongst others. But in this respect the main struggles were on

---

[1] As the then District Secretary, Adam Anderson remarked: 'Dobbin's nae deid yet'. It inspired him to relate the story of Auld Charlie and his driver, Airchie: 'It was just on opening time when Airchie drew Auld Charlie to a halt outside the "Coach and Horses". He nipped in and ordered a "glass", which he carried out saying: "here's yer mornin', Charlie". Upon which Charlie throws it down. Returning the empty glass, Airchie jumps on the cart, when the horse says "What aboot yersel', man?" "Na, Na," says Airchie, "Nae fur me, I'm drivin".' (*The Highway*, August 1951.)

There is no recorded instance of a ten-tonner enjoying such fraternal relations with his motorman.

[2] Report of the Annual Conference, 1957.

behalf of co-operative members. In 1951 workers in the retail co-operative societies had to go to arbitration to gain an award. In 1949 and again in 1954 and 1955, there were prolonged differences with the Scottish Co-operative Wholesale Society. The troubles here were at least not due to misunderstanding; the president of the scws was Robert Taylor, former General Secretary of the Association, John Brannigan's immediate predecessor. Perhaps the most difficult case was that of the co-operative private funeral and coach drivers, who had to work excessive hours. It came to a head in 1954, after a number of preliminary skirmishes. An application for an improved working agreement for private and funeral hiring workers having been turned down, the Executive decided to refer it to conciliation in February 1954. But the Board failed to reach an agreement when it met in June 1954, and the decision was left in the hands of the independent chairman. It was the second time that a claim for these men had failed when referred to conciliation. When the men were told, some demanded that token strikes of protest should be undertaken. The Executive Council met and decided unanimously: 'to support the men employed in the private, funeral and coach departments, financially and otherwise, in furtherance of these demands. They deprecated the threat of any unofficial action, but they decided unanimously to take a ballot vote of the members concerned in accordance with the constitution of the union on the question of taking strike action.'[1]

The industrial relations department of the Ministry of Labour urged John Brannigan to reopen negotiations with the scws; but meanwhile ballot papers were returned and a special meeting of the Executive Council was not unanimous as to what next steps should be taken. Finally, it was moved by John Murphy and seconded by Geoffrey Sheridan that 'the ballot should meantime be frozen'.[2] An agreement was reached that the Society would later consider cutting the hours from forty-eight to forty-six a week, but when the time came the scws decided they could not do so. Negotiations continued throughout the summer; and finally, they went once more to conciliation on September 30, 1955 just a year after the first agreement. When the board disagreed again, John Brannigan this time refused to leave the matter in the hands of the independent chairman. The Executive recommended to the members that they should take strike action to enforce their claim.[3] This led the scws to make a new offer of 3s 6d, retrospective to January 1, 1955, which the Executive unanimously decided to accept. While this long-drawn-out tourney was going on, John Brannigan had been contributing his reminiscences to each number of

[1] Executive *Minutes*, August 4, 1954.
[2] The factor which influenced the Executive at the time was that negotiating machinery had not been fully exhausted. But many years later it came to light that, contrary to the resolution and without its being reported to the Executive, the ballot was opened and counted and proved to be against strike action.
[3] Executive *Minutes*, October 5, 1955.

The Highway, under the general title of 'Twenty-Five Years of Service', in some of which he had very sharp criticisms to make of some actions of his predecessor in office of a dozen years earlier. Certainly he had given these negotiations his fullest personal attention, and displayed a high degree of energy.

4. STRIKES AND STRIKE POLICY

This dispute had not come to a stoppage. On other occasions, strikes did take place. From 1951 to 1959 the Association's members were affected by some nineteen work stoppages; of these, six strikes only were initiated by them. Two may be described in some detail, one called by members of the Association, the second declared by members of other unions. They will usefully cast light on the general approach to disputes at this time. Of the remainder, those in which Association members were directly concerned were usually short and small. Typical were the Motherwell local authority employees, who came out briefly in April 1951 when they received only 6d a week increase instead of the 5s 6d to which they were entitled under a Joint Industrial Council award. There were other protests against the same award.

A strike on a larger scale, but for a similar reason, took place at Aberdeen in the coal trade early in 1956. In the spring of 1955 the National Joint Industrial Council for the coal trade agreed a 10s wage increase, as from April 4, 1955. This was paid by most employers. But some firms in Aberdeen refused to pay. Noting that two were under contract with the Aberdeen Town Council, the General Secretary reported them under the Fair Wages Clause, but without success. The Executive Council thereupon decided to refer it to the Industrial Disputes Tribunal. There was no alternative:

'Other coal firms in Aberdeen had made the point that on failure to have these firms recognize the 10s increase they would reduce their wages accordingly, when it was unanimously agreed on the motion of Messrs McGarry and Murphy, that should any attempt be made to carry this out, strike action be taken.'[1]

This was delayed, while the Ministry of Labour attempted conciliation; a meeting was arranged on the regional Joint Industrial Council for the Coal Trade. But months dragged by and, as late as February 1956, no meeting had taken place. It was too much; the men had waited eleven months since the agreement. They went on strike. John Brannigan went to Aberdeen and declared the strike official. The employers finally gave in. This is a good illustration of the impatience which can arise with negotiating machinery; it had taken over a year to enforce an award.

[1] Executive Council *Minutes*, August 3, 1955.

Amongst the other stoppages where Association members had not taken the initiative, was the one-day strike called by the Confederation of Shipbuilding and Engineering Unions in December 1953; and another in June 1955, called by the Associated Society of Locomotive Engineers & Firemen: in both of which the Association paid strike benefit. Again, when the Transport and General Workers Union declared a strike at British Motors Corporation over mass dismissals in August 1956, the Association decided to inform the members through the district secretaries that 'the cargoes regarded as "black" should not be handled either for supply or distribution'.[1] In another strike later that year for which the Association's help was asked, a different view was taken. Draughtsmen employed by Massey Harris-Ferguson Ltd, at Kirkcaldy had gone on strike; but the firm was still producing vehicles, and the engineers were working. The General Secretary told the draughtsmen's divisional organizer, who asked for help, that

'The Association would be prepared to give assistance in the strike, but would not take unilateral action in same and this was unanimously approved by the Executive Council on the motion of Mr J. Murphy seconded by Mr J. Dyce.'[2]

Early the next year, the Association's members were affected by a major strike called in the shipbuilding and engineering trades in March 1957; the total amount paid out by the Association in strike benefit was £1,573.

Transport workers cannot fail to be concerned in strikes in other industries, more particularly the road transport workers who bring raw materials in and take the finished products out of the factory gates. Where the worker finds himself confronted with a lightning strike, and there is no time to seek official advice, he is obliged to use his own initiative to make an equally lightning decision first and consult afterwards. But, when it is public knowledge that a strike is going to take place at long notice, he looks to be relieved of the burden of decision and to have the instructions and guidance of his union. Where these are not promptly given or are not absolutely clear, serious consequences are almost inevitable. This lesson was learned the hard way in the course of events arising out of the strike in 1952 at D. C. Thomson.

The famous case of this Scottish-based press monopoly, which sought to impose a 'document' upon employees, binding them not to join a union, occupied the attention of the whole British trade union movement during 1952 and 1953. The National Society of Operative Printers and Assistants challenged the 'document' and called their members out on strike at the Glasgow works of the firm in April 1952. The Scottish Trades Union Congress was gathering at Perth for its annual meeting, over which

[1] Executive *Minutes*, August 8, 1956.
[2] Executive *Minutes*, November 7, 1956.

John Brannigan was presiding. An emergency resolution was moved approving this action:

'The printing trade unions have, therefore, justifiably declared Messrs D. C. Thomson and Co., Ltd., to be a "black" shop and they appeal to all the unions affiliated to Congress to show their solidarity in any way whatsoever.'[1]

It was passed unanimously. In the struggle which followed, it was essential that supplies of paper, ink and the like should not reach D. C. Thomson. In this the action and vigilance of transport workers would be decisive, whether directly employed in the transport department of firms manufacturing the supplies or by haulage contractors on delivery. On May 6, 1952, the Scottish TUC sent a circular to all affiliated unions with the suggestion that it would be 'most useful if the decision were brought to the notice of all trade union members'. The Printing and Kindred Trades Federation sent a letter also, and later provided copies of it for widespread distribution. Meeting the following day, the Executive Council of the Association gave 'lengthy consideration' to the question:

'After discussion, and in view of the decision of the STUC in the matter, agreed where Association members were compelled to stop work in support of the printing trades, they would, on this occasion only, be paid their basic rates for the time lost.'[2]

Association members employed by many firms loyally refused to handle supplies for D. C. Thomson products, without any incident which required financial aid to be given. The General Secretary issued a circular 'giving guidance to the officials'; but there was a fatal interval, during which a number of Association members became involved in a difficult situation.

A sympathetic strike arose at the Clyde Paper Mills in Rutherglen, where 750 of the National Union of Printing, Bookbinding and Paper Workers refused to produce paper destined for D. C. Thomson. At the firm there were twenty-six transport workers who were members of the Association. The General Secretary later saw the management and it was 'agreed that in respect of the 26 transport workers connected with the firm, these men would not require to go on strike, but that if they became redundant they would be laid off work and thereby entitled to insurance benefit. Following this, however, the men were asked to do strikers' work and consequently came out on strike.'[3] They were out for nine days, at the end of which 'the General Secretary had met the management when it was agreed to reinstate the men with the guarantee that they would not be employed in any way as strike-breakers'.[4] The Association's own records

[1] 55th Annual Report of the STUC, 1952.
[2] Executive *Minutes*, May 7, 1952.
[3] Executive *Minutes*, May 28, 1952.
[4] Executive *Minutes*, June 11, 1952.

take the matter no further. But there were in fact other developments of an unhappy character.

When the Rutherglen Clyde Paper Mills workers went on strike, the Scottish Transport & General Workers' Union put an embargo on all goods from the mills, yet their docker members were confronted with loads being driven to the Glasgow docks by members of the Association. The Scottish Transport & General Workers' Union therefore lodged a complaint with the STUC against the Association; and officials of both the transport unions and of the paper-workers met at Congress office on Thursday, May 29, 1952. The records of the STUC stated:

'While giving consideration to the complaint it was learnt that the NU of Printing and Paper Workers had decided to call off the strike as from Monday, June 2nd, on the assurance from the management that production of newsprint for D. C. Thomson would cease and the employees in dispute would be taken back into employment as speedily as production would permit. There would be no victimization of any worker on strike.

'In view of the above information it was agreed that the difference between the two transport unions was now resolved and that the Scottish Transport and General Workers' Union would lift the embargo on goods received at docks from Clyde Paper Mills.'[1]

This dispute was not included in the General Council's report to Congress eleven months later; it was presented when the General Secretary of the STUC, George Middleton, had to intervene to bring to an end an acrimonious debate. When a delegate challenged John Brannigan about the incident, he replied:

'The Scottish Horse & Motormen's Association brought their members out on strike and gave them full wages for three weeks. When it was decided such action was useless their members returned to work with the full knowledge of the Paper Workers' Union. Throughout the country the Scottish Horse & Motormen had placed a ban on the handling of D. C. Thomson's commodities.'

P. Barrett of the Scottish Transport & General Workers' Union retorted that 'wholehearted support' had not been given to the paper mills strikers and said:

'An example should be made of Mr Brannigan for ordering his men to uplift goods from Rutherglen Paper Mill.

'Mr R. G. Dick (National Union of Printing, Bookbinding & Paper Workers) said it was rather unfortunate that Mr Brannigan should have made false statements from the rostrum. The Scottish Horse & Motormen stopped work only after all the stocks had been taken out of Rutherglen Paper Mills to the D. C. Thomson organization.

[1] 56th Annual Report of the STUC, 1953.

'In Rutherglen they were suffering from the D. C. Thomson dispute and sixty men were still receiving benefit from his union.'

The incident illustrates what an immensely important position is occupied by the transport worker; the need for early and clear-cut instructions; and close understanding between official and members at all stages of disputes of every kind.

5. PRINCIPLES AND POLITICS: SUEZ

John Brannigan lost his seat on the General Council that year. Those in the trade union movement who had backed his candidature and had ensured, indeed, that he should hold the post of President whilst the law cases in which he was involved were still proceeding, now withdrew their support. He never regained his seat; and the Association was not represented on the governing body of the Scottish trade union movement until John Brannigan ceased to be the Association's secretary. It was the only Scottish union of any size in this unhappy position. Yet, during the fifties, the experiences of the Association and its members were largely those of the rest of the trade union movement. There were the recurrent economic difficulties taking the form characteristic in the post-1945 period of balance of payment crises. This was followed by alternate bouts of inflation and deflation, of 'spending sprees' and capital cuts. At the same time the decade was remarkable for considerable distortion of the economy. Major pit closures and railway line closures bore heavily on the industrial north. Unemployment, the shift of population, and reduced prospects for the young people all signalized a very grave situation for Scottish economy in particular. At the same time, increased arms expenditure continued. In the early fifties the cold war fluctuated in intensity; while it eased with the termination of the wars in Korea and Indo-China, a new flash-point threatened in Formosa. Fresh winds were blowing from Africa and from the Middle East. On some occasions these events had an immediate and direct effect on the Association's members. Fuel rationing followed Egypt's decision to nationalize the Suez Canal and the consequent invasion of Egypt by Britain, France and Israel. In broad terms it may be said that whenever military, political or financial events affect the economy, the transport worker is by no means the last to feel it.

In many of these affairs, as well as others where the Association had a particular interest, the annual conferences of the fifties reflect the Association's concern. The decisions were sometimes far from unanimous; in some cases they were reversed over the years.

Two instances arose at the 1952 Annual Conference at North Berwick. In the previous August, the United Nations Economic Committee had produced a report which was not very optimistic about the prospects for the British economy. The Glasgow A B & C Branch put down a resolution referring to this and calling for 'a great volume of trade with the Soviet Union and Eastern Europe, free from the dictates of Wall Street, thus creating a more favourable balance of payments which would be reflected in a higher standard of living for the British people.'[1] The reference was to the US list of commodities which recipients of dollar aid were forbidden from selling to the USSR. But it met with opposition; and, when the fifty-six votes were found to be equally divided, the chairman, Tom Berrey, cast his vote against the resolution. At the 1954 conference the same branch put down a resolution in somewhat similar terms, saying that 'the end of restrictive trade practices imposed by America would bring increasing economic prosperity'. It was supported by Edinburgh, and opposed from Airdrie and Dundee and by the General Secretary, being finally rejected by thirty votes to twenty-two. It was some years before a contrary decision was taken.

An interesting point of principle arose as a consequence of the expulsion of David Johnstone. While he was Assistant General Secretary, the Association had sponsored and supported his successful candidature as Labour Party councillor in the Cowcadden ward of Glasgow. When he had been expelled from membership, the case was altered. When his name came up for renomination on the list of approved Glasgow City candidates, the Executive Council decided to nominate Geoffrey Sheridan instead. The Political Committee of the Association decided 'that the City Labour Party should be pressed with a view to having his name removed from the official panel'. A deputation to meet them was appointed, consisting of the General Secretary and Messrs Falconer, Kitson, and Urquhart; but the deputation never got that far. A selection conference of the City Labour Party had five new nominations before them, including both Sheridan and Johnstone. The expelled Assistant General Secretary was again adopted:

'The General Secretary reported that he had been informed that Mr Johnstone had intimated to the selection conference that anything he had done (presumably court action, etc.) had been done in consultation with the Leader of the Labour Group in Glasgow Corporation, Mr Andrew Hood.'[2]

At the Association's Annual Conference a month later, Alex Kitson introduced an emergency resolution which deplored 'the fact that it is possible within the constitution of the Labour Party for an expelled trade unionist to be recognized as an official candidate in any election to any authority'.[3] Seconded by Alex Urquhart, of Dunfermline, it called on

[1] Report of Annual Conference, 1952.
[2] Executive *Minutes*, March 5, 1952.
[3] Report of the Annual Conference, 1952.

the Executive Council to examine the constitution with a view to putting forward changes, and was carried by forty-three to ten. Six months later Alex Kitson once more raised the question at the Political Committee on October 9, 1952, which decided to take it up formally with Morgan Phillips, the Secretary of the Labour Party. Accordingly, on November 6, 1952, Morgan Phillips came to the Association's office, together with William Marshall, Secretary of the Scottish Labour Party, and A. Dowling, Secretary of the Glasgow City Labour Party, and they discussed the principle whether an expelled trade unionist might hold office in the Labour Party:

'Noted the Secretary of the Labour Party was of the opinion that the matter should have been referred to the National Executive, by the Glasgow City Labour Party, who would have dealt with same through the appropriate machinery.'[1]

At the 1953 Annual Conference, Alex Kitson once more moved, and Bob Lowe seconded, that the Executive Council should submit an alteration of rule to the Labour Party Constitution, to which conference agreed. The Executive Council, defying conference decisions, decided not to do so:

'Should a similar case arise in the future there was sufficient domestic machinery within the Labour Party to deal with the position. Noted this view also expressed by Mr Morgan Phillips, Secretary of the Labour Party.'[2]

Johnstone remained councillor for Glasgow's fourteenth ward until he left the city.

A further move away from a policy of wage restraint was recorded at the 1953 Conference, when the delegates carried unanimously a resolution, put down by the Executive Council, which viewed with concern the steady increase in the cost of living, and therefore declared that 'this union should not be a party to any form of wage restraint until a more equitable standard of living has been established for the workers'. At this time transport workers were near the bottom of the ladder in average weekly earnings, although at the top of it in average hours worked. By and large, this remained Association policy, reversing their original attitude to wage restraint.

The 1953 conference also rejected by forty-one votes to eleven a resolution from Methil, which 'deplored' rearming Germany. Lanarkshire opposed the resolution, as did the Executive, and on this occasion the Edinburgh delegates were divided, with J. Carabine speaking against it and Alex Kitson for it. Soon afterwards the Edinburgh branch became much concerned about the subject and found themselves at variance with the

[1] Executive *Minutes*, December 3, 1952.
[2] Executive *Minutes*, May 6, 1953.

Executive Council. It provides an interesting illustration of relations between Executive, organizer, and branch at this time. At an Edinburgh quarterly meeting in July 1954, a resolution protesting against German rearmament was moved by Robert Lowe. The organizer, Willie Campbell, however, intervened:

'On the insistence of the organizer that we were already committed to support German rearmament, the Chairman rules resolution out of order.'[1]

Robert Lowe appealed against this ruling to the Executive Council, who did not consider it until their September meeting, on the eve of the British TUC, at which the topic was to be the main item. They decided finally that Lowe had not in the first place adopted the right procedure, because 'no notice had been made in connection with such a matter'. As to the intervention of the organizer, they recorded:

'While not necessarily agreeing with the advice given by Mr Campbell to the chairman, that he had been trying to protect what he thought was the policy of the Association and had been actuated in the guidance given by a decision of the 1953 Annual Conference which rejected a resolution, dealing with some aspects of German rearmament.'[2]

This was a significant illustration of an important principle which was due for debate in the Association; for it raised such questions as what a branch could deal with, and when and in what circumstances, especially on political matters; whether resolutions passed or defeated at annual conferences could prevent further discussion; what powers a full-time official should have to invervene in branch affairs. It had considerable importance; for the scope of the Political Conference and of political committees was far from settled six years after the first conference had been set up in 1948. Moreover, the Political Conference was biennial; and this decade was one in which there were swift developments in the international sphere, when new issues were arising, calling for the rapid formulation of policy, which could have far-reaching effects on domestic and trade affairs. How could the membership be adequately consulted? Was it sufficient for them to endorse decisions retrospectively? To what degree ought they to be permitted, or indeed encouraged, to initiate policy? None of this was clear. While the existing machinery was perhaps adequate to carry on the long-term work of running political selection panels for approving municipal candidates to be sponsored by the Association, or in general propaganda work to deal with issues at Parliamentary elections at five-yearly intervals, crises arising from international events were another matter. The case of Suez in 1956, which had a direct and

[1] Edinburgh Branch *Minutes*, July 4, 1954.
[2] Executive *Minutes*, September 1, 1954.

serious effect on the transport worker, was outstanding; but before then matters were arising which led to considerable confusion and doubt.

Shortly after the difficulty over German rearmament between the Executive Council and the Edinburgh branch, the fourth biennial Political Conference took place on November 28, 1954. Here the main discussion was on 'branch participation and recommendation on Political issues, and on the powers of the Political Committee and Political Conference'. After a long discussion the conference made a recommendation to the Executive Council 'to consider the advisability of placing in the hands of the Political Committee and the Biennial Conference the formation of political policy within the union, and they request, if the Executive Council are agreeable, speediest possible steps are taken to bring this about'.[1] The Executive Council, when they considered this on December 1, 1954, decided 'it was a matter which could be more adequately dealt with at a later date when the matter had been more carefully examined'. The new Political Committee returned to the question at their first meeting, on January 16, 1955, when there was 'lengthy discussion' about proposals for 'formation of political policy within the Union'. However, at all branch quarterly meetings in future there was to be an item, 'Political Matters', on the Agenda; and a decision was also taken 'that on important political issues notice of motion should be submitted to the branch'. Apart from this, the General Secretary said, there were so many problems that the recommendation 'would necessitate careful deliberation and it was deferred until adequate time was 'available to examine the implications'.

But within less than three weeks an urgent question arose on foreign policy. The international flash-point was the Chinese island of Taiwan, better known in the West as Formosa. The Leader of the Opposition, Clement Atlee, made a statement in the House of Commons in which he described US actions there as 'an intervention in a civil war'. He called for the exile of Chiang Kai-Shek who, after being defeated on the mainland, was established on Taiwan with US troops and fleet. He also urged that China should be admitted to the United Nations in place of Chiang Kai-Shek's representatives; and that there should be a United Nations plebiscite in the island. The question was discussed at the Edinburgh Trades Council where a resolution on much the same lines was passed unanimously. When the monthly meeting of the Edinburgh branch of the Association received the report from their trades council delegate, Alex Kitson, they themselves took the same position. But when their resolution came before the Executive Council three days later, it was returned to the branch with the advice that 'it should be submitted at their Quarterly Meeting, under the heading on the agenda Political Matters, after which if approved by the Branch it would be carefully examined by the Executive

[1] Report of the Fourth Political Conference, 1954.

Council'.[1] This would mean a delay of two months. At their next monthly meeting, Edinburgh discussed it further:

'Several members feel that as the branch had acted in accordance with the constitution, resolution was in order, and it was finally agreed that protest should be made on Executive Council ruling.'[2]

The Executive Council did not hold a meeting in March; so before they could discuss this protest, Edinburgh's quarterly meeting had taken place, when John Brannigan was present. Robert Lowe moved their resolution on China:

'General Secretary gave Executive Council position that on such matters of international importance they felt that such resolutions should only be submitted at quarterly meetings for discussion and approval. After discussion this recommendation was approved.'[3]

Nevertheless, they passed their resolution, with Alex Falconer moving 'that his dissent be recorded, as chairman would not give him the right to move against the resolution'. Both points came before the Executive Council at their April meeting. But the situation had changed from two months before. The General Council of the Scottish TUC had already sent a resolution to the Prime Minister on February 6th in the same terms, which had been followed by a similar one on February 23rd by the National Executive Committee of the Labour Party itself. So when Edinburgh's decision and protests came to be considered, the Executive first discussed the STUC's declaration and agreed to support it. Next, they considered Falconer's protest about the procedure adopted by Edinburgh's Chairman. They agreed 'that this member be advised that the Executive Council had never seen fit to interfere with the ruling of the chairman of a branch meeting, as he was entitled to exercise his own discretion, but that it was always open to the members themselves to challenge the chairman's ruling.'[4] Then they discussed Edinburgh's request for 'clarification concerning matters to be discussed at monthly meetings', together with the Political Committee's recommendation that they should be ready to consider matters referred from a branch regardless of whether it was a monthly or a quarterly meeting. Finally on this vexed question, they got as far as deciding, 'on the motion of Messrs Carabine and Gowans that they are prepared to co-operate with any branch under the terms set out under Rule 14 and they will give consideration to any matter referred to them by any duly constituted branch meeting'.[5] There the matter

[1] Executive *Minutes*, February 9, 1955.
[2] Edinburgh Branch *Minutes*, March 6, 1955.
[3] Edinburgh Branch *Minutes*, April 3, 1955.
[4] Executive *Minutes*, April 6, 1955.
[5] Executive *Minutes*, April 6, 1955.

rested. It was not until eighteen months later, at the next biennial Political Conference, that there was a decision to prepare a set of model rules for the political section of the Association.

A month after this modest victory for the branch, Robert Lowe and Alex Kitson moved at the 1955 Annual Conference a resolution which Edinburgh had formulated in October 1954, after the brush with the Executive on the German question:

'That the opinion of Conference is that in all matters of major political and industrial importance the Executive Council should consult the branches.'[1]

It was rejected by an overwhelming majority on the ground that they had an Executive Council and a Political Committee to deal with industrial and political matters; and, as the branches met only quarterly, there were many matters on which it would be impossible to consult them. At that time, both Glasgow and Edinburgh, of course, held not only monthly meetings, but also co-ordinating committee meetings as well as their quarterlies; but they were the exception. Perhaps the Edinburgh branch felt a certain consolation when the same four delegates were opposed to each other over the next resolution, in which Edinburgh triumphed, despite the opposition also from the platform. Edinburgh asked that a three-man delegation be sent 'to the Far East, particularly China'. In moving it, with Robert Lowe's assistance, Alex Kitson said that 'the only way to unite the people is for the workers of the world to meet and hear each other's point of view'. After the Lanarkshire delegates and the General Secretary opposed it, conference carried it 'by a large majority'. It was Kitson's last conference as delegate; in the following year he was on the organizing staff.

But 1956 brought a new and grave crisis in international political affairs which directly affected every member of the Association. In June 1956, the last British occupation troops left Egypt; the next month the Egyptian Government announced their intention of nationalizing the Suez Canal. On August 2, 1956, as parliament adjourned for nearly twelve weeks, the army reserve was called out and three days later the parachute brigade sailed for the Mediterranean. The first stage of the Suez crisis had begun. Quite a number of Association members were, of course, reservists, particularly those in British Road Services. The Executive Council made no statement at their meetings of August, September or October. Kilmarnock branch had sent in a resolution calling for 'all possible assistance to the Labour Party in the solution of the Suez Canal crisis'. The Executive Council considered this at its September meeting, when 'it was agreed that desires of the resolution were covered by the recall of Parliament'. The recall took place on September 12th with a

[1] Report of 42nd Annual Conference, 1955.

background of mass demonstrations calling for 'No War Over Suez'. On October 29th, Israel invaded Egypt, and, on October 31st, an Anglo-French bombing offensive was opened. The war was on. It lasted a week before the invading forces were obliged to make a humiliating withdrawal and suffer what was an unprecedented diplomatic rout for two great Powers. The fifth biennial Political Conference opened in Glasgow, when the crisis was at its height, under the chairmanship of J. Carabine of Edinburgh, who described the Government's action as 'bordering on the verge of political and diplomatic delinquency'. Moved by Kitson and seconded by W. Cunningham of Markinch the resolution condemned,

'the action of the Government in their handling of the international situation, particularly Egypt, and their failure to conform to the recommendation of the United Nations Organization. Conference contends that the Government actions are contrary to the will of the people and demands the immediate resignation of the Government.[1]

It was carried unanimously.

Now the bill began to come in. The war had cut off petrol supplies and a fuel crisis had resulted, with petrol rationed, which led to an emergency in transport. All road transport was severely affected and traffic was diverted to railways where possible. Many meetings of British Road Services were held in London which the General Secretary had to attend. He reported to the December Executive Council on short-time working and redundancy which might lead to dismissals. At this stage he was taken ill, and Alex Kitson was appointed to take charge until his return. It was therefore Kitson who reported to the January 1957 Executive Council on the machinery which had been set up. Every effort was being made in British Road Services to avoid anyone being declared redundant. In private industry, the Road Haulage Association had secured from the Ministry of Transport an allocation of seventy-five per cent of their October fuel consumption, and priorities would go to those on essential goods. Some hauliers therefore would have a severely reduced allocation. There was also the question of co-operation between unions and employers:

'Mr Kitson stated that he had raised this aspect with the secretary of the Road Haulage Association and had been advised that a consultative committee had been set up in London between RHA the Transport Road Traders Association and the trade unions.

'To date the Association had not been approached in this connection, but the assurance had been given that this position would be investigated and if possible the union brought into consultation.'[2]

[1] Minute of Fifth Political Conference, November 4, 1956.
[2] Executive *Minutes*, January 2, 1957.

Retail co-operative societies were also rationed. The effects were still being felt three months later, when David Strachan of Edinburgh questioned the General Secretary at the 1957 Annual Conference about the continuance of the rail-heads which had been set up to meet the Suez fuel crisis.

The incident had shown the vulnerability of road transport given an international crisis; it strengthened the long-term case for a policy of integrated transport. That was no immediate comfort to the road transport worker. It also underlined that international political affairs were a bread and butter question for Association members; and that branches and political committees needed a political 'early warning system'.

6. THE INCREASE OF THE SPEED LIMIT

One of the first struggles on which the older carters had fought was for recognition of a normal day's work, the carter's darg. Once this was won, there came the steady battle to reduce the working-day and the working-week. Hugh Lyon had great satisfaction in recording the acceptance of employers of the forty-eight-hour week in 1919, at a time when the rest of the Clyde workers were fighting for the forty-hour week. Thirty years later, in 1949, the average hours worked weekly were 48·8 and they rose well above that in the following decade. Yet road conditions in the interval had changed beyond all recognition. As always, the road haulage employers were less interested in rates of wages than they were in the hours worked; with the coming of the motor vehicle it became possible in transport to increase greatly the intensity of the day's work. The interest of the employers increasingly became centred on speed. Their drive for this, with the ensuing road chaos, had resulted in the statutory limitation of the hours a motor-driver was permitted to drive in a day, the compulsory break in continuous driving, and rest times. These, as we have seen, were fixed by Section 19 of the Road Traffic Act of 1930. Under this section, the limit was eleven hours in twenty-four, with compulsory rest breaks after five and a half hours continuous driving; keeping log books of journeys was made compulsory to provide a check. At the same time, there was a scale of speed limits for commercial and heavy vehicles. That had been the system since 1930; and, although breaches of it and so-called 'illegal running' were notorious, it imposed at least some restriction.

But once the abnormal conditions of war-time were over and the flood of vehicles increased, the situation was transformed. In 1938 there were 513,100 goods vehicles alone licensed. This increased to 757,300 in 1948 and, ten years later, rose to 1,222,700 in 1958. Pressure came from the employers for increased speed. In the autumn of 1948, the Labour Government announced that, as from January 1, 1948, the speed limit for commercial vehicles would be increased to thirty miles per hour. There was widespread opposition in the industry, and the increase was postponed. At the 1949 Annual Conference at Aberdeen, a resolution was moved from Glasgow A B and C and carried unanimously that:

'This Conference deplores the idea that the speed limit be uplifted and further that all vehicles be plated for weight-carrying.'[1]

The purpose of plating to show the permitted capacity of load was to make checking easier and more effective. The Labour Government dropped the proposal to increase the limit; but following denationalization the pressure for more speed came up again. In the meantime, there had been attempts by Association branches, notably in Kilmarnock and Edinburgh, to check offences under Section 19. But the evidence against employers which could only be provided by the men was not forthcoming. Some Scottish drivers at that time were known to be doing three journeys to and from London in a week; reckoned at some 2,300 miles, that meant that men were either working vastly longer than the permitted hours, or driving at excessive speed—or both. Moreover illegal running of that kind meant that vehicles could not be properly maintained nor repaired. Yet it was again proposed to increase the speed limit from twenty miles per hour. At the Arbroath conference in 1954 two demands were voiced. Edinburgh branch, through David Strachan, moved that all vehicles should 'carry a certificate of roadworthiness' and 'be examined once monthly by reputable engineers'. A resolution from Blairgowrie declared 'that in the interests of the general public and our members, the existing limits of 20 m.p.h. on heavy vehicles should not be interfered with or abolished.'[2]

The following year an Edinburgh branch made the case for revising the time limits of eleven hours and five and a half hour's rest in Section 19 of the Road Traffic Act, 1930, which became an important development of Association policy in the next years, when even greater speeds were introduced. The time limits, it was argued, were outmoded and should be reduced to five hours of continuous driving with an aggregate of not more than ten hours in the twenty-four. In moving this, Robert Lowe argued that in the thirties there were 3,000,000 vehicles on the roads, but in the fifties over 5,000,000; in comparison a driver's job fifteen years earlier had been much easier. When this was opposed by A. Herd of Methil and John Kyle of Kirkcaldy, both arguing that it would mean loss of earnings, they were answered by Alex Kitson: 'In some industries there was already established a 35-hour week and 40-hour week, with decent earnings for the workers as well, and there was nothing wrong in the transport industry being brought into line with these people.'[3] The

[1] Report of Annual Conference, 1949.
[2] Report of Annual Conference, 1954.
[3] Report of the 42nd Annual Conference, 1955.

resolution was carried by an overwhelming majority, but at the next Conference an Edinburgh delegate complained that nothing further had been done in the meantime. John Brannigan answered by saying that they 'had not lost sight of the principles involved'.

There were in fact three sides to the question, and a great deal of attention had to be paid for the next three or four years, at first with little success. First, there was continued resistance to raising the speed limit which was effected by the Motor Vehicles (Variation of Speed Limit) Regulations, 1956, introduced in December of that year and becoming operative on May 1, 1957. Secondly, the Association sought to have section 19 of the Road Traffic Act altered to reduce the permitted hours of driving and tighten up on the log sheet provisions. Thirdly the Association argued that there should be a special increase in wages to compensate for the increased strain and responsibility due to the raised speed limit. One of the points which the Association stressed was that the speed limit should not be increased until the roads were capable of carrying traffic at increased speed; not only the road haulage men but every road transport worker was affected.

When John Brannigan had met Alfred Barnes, the Labour Minister of Transport, in 1949, he had been answered with evidence from a number of sources that it would be safe to let heavy goods vehicles travel at 30 mph, given the improvement in efficiency of modern braking and the like. In 1956, Harold Watkinson, the Conservative Minister of Transport, advanced the same arguments. John Brannigan commented in the journal:

'We did not accept the advice of the experts then, nor are we prepared to accept such expert advice today.'[1]

They had met the employers represented in the Road Haulage Association and the British Road Services and, he continued,

'We have always had the same polite reply since ever increasing the speed was first mooted, that was: that no one would suffer in their employment as a result of the increased speed. We have never been able to work out with the employers a formula to administer their glib promises.'

All parties must have had in mind, whilst stopping short of mentioning it explicitly, that illegal running was far from ended. Yet the new Road Traffic Act, 1956 was in operation from November 1, 1956, and the occasion had not been taken to reduce the permitted driving hours of Section 19 of the Old Act. Accordingly, at the 1957 conference at North Berwick, the Aberdeen branch moved a resolution instructing the Executive Council to draw the traffic commissioners' attention 'to the urgent need to see that Section 19 of the Road Traffic Act is strictly enforced

_____
[1] *The Highway*, February, 1957.

and thus put a stop to employers insisting that drivers drive and work more than the maximum 11 hours as laid down by the Act'.

There were loopholes which were being used besides downright evasion, as the mover R. Lindsay pointed out, criticizing Executive Council and officers for giving no guidance to members. He spoke of men being permitted to do work which was not actual driving from 7 a.m. to 5 p.m. 'and then take over driving from 7 p.m. and do 11 hours'. All time, he said, should be counted as driving time. Edinburgh put forward a resolution designed to prevent the abuse of log sheets. The 1957 Conference also passed three resolutions on the speed limit, the most important being one from Edinburgh, moved by George Wilson, calling on the Government to rescind the speed regulations. It was seconded by Glasgow but opposed by the Airdrie delegates, who argued that 'it would be better if the union were to go ahead and negotiate for an increase in wages in relation to the increase in production resulting from the increased speed'. Joe Brown of Edinburgh replied that 'instead of talking about monetary values, the proper approach to it was from the aspect of the extra fatigue imposed on the long-distance driver'. The resolution was carried by forty-three votes to two. In his presidential address, John Carabine argued:

'If, however, certain vehicles were to be authorized to do 50 per cent more operation per hour, as a union we claim as a result the entire operation of transport will be speeded up, and that the wages structure which came into operation resulting from the 1933 Road Traffic Act and which was given statutory enforcement by the 1938 Road Haulage Wages Act, is outmoded and should be replaced by a new structure which takes into consideration substantial wage improvements with longer hours of real rest, and sufficient time to permit of a transport worker having his right to real periods of recreation along with other citizens of this country.'[1]

This was the standpoint of the Association in the next few years. They put it in a resolution, passed on May 1, 1957, viewing 'with very great alarm' the Regulations which took effect that day.

The Association put in their claim for compensatory payment to the Road Haulage Wages Council, to the British Road Services, and to the Scottish Co-operative Wholesale Society. Other employers were approached; the Edinburgh Breweries agreed to give an increase on basic rates to men affected by the speed limits at the end of the year. There had been consultation but differences over the new schedules in British Road Services. But the prospects of compensatory increases were much reduced when the Government imposed a new 'credit squeeze' and called for further measures of wage restraint. This seriously affected current collective bargaining for a proposed fifteen per cent on basic rates for people

[1] Report of 44th Annual Conference 1957.

affected by the speed limit. John Brannigan had argued that 'the whole industry is in some way affected by the increased tempo of operation which must result from the increase of speed from 20 to 30 miles per hour, and as such the whole industry should be rewarded for any increased turnover that is taking place'. In the journal he wrote:

'A claim of this description in my opinion does not come under the category of wage claims that the Government has already pronounced itself on.

'In the meantime our advice to our members is that they should continue to operate at the limit of 20 miles per hour until the employers concede the reward we have asked for.'[1]

But the months passed without gain; unemployment had increased in Scotland and there was little to cheer the delegates when they met at Ayr in March 1958. The Executive Council put forward a strongly-worded resolution which now proposed that Section 19 should be amended to make the maximum permitted hours not exceed ten, with a thirteen hours' rest period in every twenty-four. It declared that 'the practice of employing drivers to the legally permitted maximum of 77 hours in one week at the increased tempo is adversely affecting the health of our members and in the long run will shorten their driving life.'[2] As the General Secretary said: 'While an eleven-hour day was perhaps something a man could do between the age of twenty-five and forty-five, after that age the man could not keep up such a tempo of speed.' A similar resolution was put forward jointly with the Transport & General Workers' Union at the Scottish TUC a month later; and, in September 1958, a resolution put down on the British TUC agenda was referred to the General Council.

Far from improving as the months passed the situation became worse. On November 19, 1958, the Minister of Transport announced in the House of Commons that he was proposing to increase the speed limit further still from thirty miles per hour to forty miles per hour for light goods and public service vehicles. With this went another rebuff to the demand for Section 19 to be revised. The Minister's case was that it 'was specifically directed to considerations of safety and that the provisions of Section 19 could only properly be amended if a sufficient case for doing so had been established on the grounds of safety, which case he did not consider had been established'. This was reported to the December Executive Council meeting. The sixth biennial Political Conference, when it had met on November 16th, had passed the same resolution on Section 19 which had been sent to the Minister of Transport. He had replied that accidents happening in 1957 had shown that ·2 per cent only were assessed by the research experts as being due to fatigue. 'The Minister pointed

---

[1] *The Highway*, November 1957.
[2] Report of the 45th Annual Conference, 1958.

out that on this basis there seemed to be no justification for an amendment requiring a shortening of the limit of time during which a driver may be permitted to work.'[1] The Executive Council regarded this as an excuse, and returned to the attack. With the Economic Committee of the British TUC and the Transport & General Workers' Union, John Brannigan saw the Minister, this time on the resolution which had been submitted to the TUC. The Minister replied that 'he would require to satisfy himself through wider consultation, but would at a later stage meet with the unions before reaching any final decision.'[2] The Annual Conference were not impressed. They repeated their previous year's resolution and added two new ones, dealing with the abuses under Section 19 and the keeping of log sheets, and also on the limited amount of road building.

But John Brannigan did not meet the Minister again; in July of that year he died suddenly.[3]

7. TRYING TO APPOINT A DEPUTY

This was a severe shock. It was the first time that the Association had lost its chief officer through death during his term of office. Throughout the history of the Association to a very great extent the direction of affairs had been in the hands of the General Secretary. His influence was extremely important whenever an organizer sought guidance; it was also indirectly of some importance on occasions where an organizer of highly independent mind avoided doing so. Few would be in doubt as to what 'line Johnny will take' on most topics. After his own differences with Robert Taylor and the breach with David Johnstone, he was in no mood to delegate his authority. Yet there were great demands, a vast increase of new business and difficult problems; many of the organizing staff were approaching superannuation. Brannigan himself was frequently away from Scotland, whether in London, or, for example, in Vienna, the USA, or Helsinki for the International Transport Workers' Federation and other bodies, in Yugoslavia, or at conferences in Britain. He was not always fit to attend to business; yet appearances could be misleading. For one of the characteristics of this quick-minded man was his ability to absorb facts, figures, and statistics at unusual speed; he could grasp the contents of a document while giving the impression of having scarcely glanced at it. Those who might attempt to prompt or correct him in such circumstances, might be justified; on the other hand they might be just as liable to earn for themselves a well-informed rebuff. Again, with his temperament, he was capable of working with speed and brilliance on negotiations in which he was particularly interested; on others, his undoubted capacity for

---

[1] Executive *Minutes*, January 10, 1959.
[2] Executive Council *Minutes*, March 17, 1959.
[3] David Johnstone, the expelled Assistant General Secretary, died in similar circumstances within a short time.

hard work often failed him. He was no lover of the *longueurs* of routine in his later years. Central direction of routine collection and even of essential organizing work were inevitably weakened.

There were four warning signals. Firstly, membership was declining instead of rising. In the second place there was all too frequently poor attendance, and even the lack of a quorum, at quarterly meetings, other than in the bigger branches, such as Glasgow and Edinburgh, where there were also monthly and co-ordinating committee meetings. Thirdly, there was little life and small interest in the Political Committee and its work. Finally, there was an exceptional number of cases of shortages in the collectors' books, even in those of district secretaries. Their supervision, after all, was the direct responsibility of the General Secretary. If he took lightly or failed to follow up the routine reports of the clerical staff, no one else could do it. Between 1951 and 1955 there were no less than eight seriously in arrears, mostly in Glasgow and Lanarkshire. Some shortages were due only to men getting in a muddle through wrong methods of book-keeping or not following instructions; but those were no less an indication of faulty supervision. In two cases, the sums of money were large, and the offender was up for the second time. In 1954 the representative from Edinburgh raised the question of appointing an Assistant General Secretary. It was the second year John Carabine had been on the Executive Council:

'Mr Carabine having noted that various organizers were attending wages councils, etc., made the observation that perhaps the question of appointing an Assistant Secretary to attend these councils should be considered at this time, in order to relieve the General Secretary for other duties.

'After a full discussion however it was generally felt that the time for such action was not opportune.'[1]

Nine months later, when the shortages of two district secretaries were being discussed, the persistent Edinburgh member raised the question of an additional organizer:

'At this point Mr J. Carabine desired the Executive Council to give consideration to the question of the appointment of a further organizer.

'The Chairman ruled that at this meeting the question was out of order; but if he so desired Mr Carabine could give notice of motion to have the matter discussed at the next meeting of the Executive Council. Mr Carabine moved accordingly.'[2]

Only nine days before, Arthur Deakin, the General Secretary of the Transport & General Workers' Union, had died suddenly. This was still

[1] Executive *Minutes*, August 4, 1954. It may be an indication of John Brannigan's dislike of the suggestion that this passage was, surprisingly, not included in the synopsis of minutes submitted to quarterly meetings.
[2] Executive *Minutes*, May 10, 1955.

much in the mind of the members of the incoming executive next month, when John Carabine was elected vice-chairman. When he moved the proposal to appoint a further organizer, Carabine argued that it would give ample opportunity for a person to be adequately trained. 'Although it would be ten years before the General Secretary retired, most of the present organizing staff would retire before him.'[1] This motion was seconded by John Murphy. John Brannigan resisted vigorously; an appointment now would be 'precipitate' and would mean an extra financial burden. Peter McGarry, the outgoing chairman, remarked 'that it may prove to be well spent money'. Tom Berrey and William Wilkie moved for a delay; but the motion was carried by eight votes to two, and the General Secretary was to circularize the district secretaries, from whose applications the Executive Council would select a short leet. A special Executive was called three months later, when nine candidates were interviewed from amongst whom a short leet of three was selected.

'A final vote was then taken on the short leet, when voting was as follows:

A Kitson	8 votes
W. Lang	3 votes
W. Cunningham	0 votes

The Chairman then declared Mr A. Kitson, Edinburgh, appointed to the position of Organizer.'[2]

The appointment took effect from January 2, 1956. From 1940 to 1955 there had been five organizing staff to assist the General Secretary, except in 1942 and 1943 when there had also been an assistant general secretary. With Kitson's appointment the number was at least back to that of 1942 and 1943.

But how strongly this went against the wishes of John Brannigan became clearer at the 1956 annual conference, in April 1956, during a debate at which the Glasgow A B and C put forward a resolution calling for the appointment of an assistant General Secretary in his absence. Edinburgh delegates moved the remit, since the recent appointment of a further organizer showed that 'the Executive Council were already facing up to the contingencies raised by the mover'. Rejection was moved by Aberdeen and Perth. John Brannigan intervened with some vehemence. He declared: 'I opposed the appointment of an additional organizer and gave the reasons why, but the Executive Council reached the decision in spite of that advice.'[3] He added that in his opinion 'the person who is to be given assistance should be consulted in connection with that assistance'; and he warned delegates that 'they were in extreme danger in the stuff they were dabbling with'. In a close vote the remit was carried by fifteen votes

[1] Executive *Minutes*, June 8, 1955.
[2] Special Executive *Minutes*, September 21, 1955.
[3] Report of the 43rd Annual Conference, 1956.

against fourteen for rejection. When the new Executive, which had no less than four members new to office in Jack Cosgrove of Perth, John Dyce of Aberdeen, John Houston of Paisley and T. Irvine of Kilmarnock, met on June 6, 1956 under the chairmanship of John Carabine, it was decided to 'note' the terms of the resolution.

But although the General Secretary had stopped discussion for some time, it did not end the problem. At the end of that year he was taken ill and ordered to have three weeks' complete rest. This was in the midst of the many problems arising from the Suez crisis. The Executive Council met and decided that 'in the best interests of the Association and the General Secretary someone should be put in charge of head office and the affairs of the Association during Mr Brannigan's absence.'[1] It was then unanimously agreed on the motion of John Murphy and W. Wilkie that it should be Alex. Kitson. Just a year later John Brannigan was taken ill again. Once more Carabine returned to the attack and asked the Executive 'to review the matter of having the assurance of the Association should anything happen to the General Secretary'. John Brannigan again resisted strongly. They had appointed an extra organizer 'without regard to cost and were in serious financial difficulty without appointing any more supernumeraries,' he argued. 'He did not know where Mr Carabine got his idea that the work would stop if he was not there. If something should happen to him any one of them could carry on. And also, that he considered the Executive Council would need more time to deal with such a matter.'[2] When the Chairman, John Kyle, accepted a notice of motion for it to be discussed at the next meeting, John Brannigan challenged his ruling:

'The General Secretary pointed out that the chairman had accepted a notice of motion on something that had been already before the annual conference and decided upon by the annual conference and the Executive Council.

'A long discussion ensued during which the General Secretary made many points against the suggestion, and when it was also pointed out that notice of motion should have been submitted in writing.'

There was a passage between them, not minuted; Brannigan said that if the notice of motion were not ruled out of order, he would bring an interdict. 'I told him that if he did so, the legal costs would have to come from his pocket; they would not come out of the Association's funds', John Kyle recalled some years later.

John Carabine duly submitted a notice of motion in writing: 'having in mind the best interest of the SH & MA and its continued success that an Assistant General Secretary should be appointed'. This came up at the

[1] Executive *Minutes*, January 12, 1957.
[2] Executive *Minutes*, February 26, 1958.

next meeting, when John Brannigan argued strongly, on procedure, that the Executive members 'had not had equal time, along with the mover of the motion to study the wording'. The Chairman therefore postponed discussion until the May meeting. John Brannigan changed his tactics; he now said that 'he had given careful consideration to the whole matter and felt that rather than take a decision on the matter now and perhaps create extra unnecessary expense to the Association, he believed it would be in the best interest of the Association if the matter were held in abeyance until 1959 when one of the present organizers would be retiring.'[1] He assured them he would bring it up then for discussion. He had his way and no further move was made until the 1959 pre-conference meeting at Rothesay. On that occasion he said: 'He had given careful consideration to the question and in the light of present circumstances would raise no objection if the Executive Council wished to consider the matter further.'[2] Thereupon John Carabine and John Murphy moved that an Assistant General Secretary be appointed, which was agreed. Brannigan was invited to make a recommendation and he proposed Alex Kitson. 'It was thereafter unanimously agreed by the Executive Council that Mr Alexander H. Kitson be promoted to the position of Assistant General Secretary within the Association, to be in charge of all the organizational work of the Association.'

No announcement was made at the annual conference, nor did the General Secretary refer to it in his editorial notes in the next issue of the journal, in which the new Assistant General Secretary's name appears on the cover. It was decided in May that Kitson be admitted to future meetings and on June 3, 1959 he attended the first Executive Council meeting in his new capacity. It was John Brannigan's last. He died suddenly on July 18th and was buried at Rochsolles Cemetery, Airdrie, after a service in St Andrew's Roman Catholic Church.

It was a great shock to the Executive and officers. It had come near to a tragic fulfilment of John Carabine's apprehensions when he had started five years before to press for the appointment of an Assistant General Secretary lest precisely what did happen should occur. A special Executive Council meeting was held on July 21, 1959 at which Alex Kitson was appointed Acting General Secretary and elaborate arrangements made for the election under rule of a new General Secretary. But at the special branch meetings to take nominations, Kitson received twenty-five nominations from the forty-one branches; fifteen were without a quorum; one put forward no nomination. It was unique; he was unopposed. On September 2, 1959, therefore John Houston, as chairman of the Executive Committee, declared him duly elected and welcomed him to office.

It was the height of the General Election campaign; but the first

---

[1] Executive *Minutes*, March 7, 1958.
[2] Executive *Minutes*, March 17, 1959.

quarterly meeting which the new General Secretary attended thereafter was his own branch of Edinburgh. Their minutes record that 'Chairman Brother Gormley welcomed Brother Kitson to the branch and on behalf of the members congratulated him on his appointment as General Secretary of the Association. Also intimating that the new General Secretary could be sure of having the full co-operation of the Edinburgh Branch in all his activities in furthering the interests of the SHMA.'[1] Thanking them, Alex Kitson told his fellow branch members that it gave him great confidence to find that the members had appointed him to the position unopposed. He thanked them for their display of solidarity and would endeavour to make greater strides for the benefit of the members of the Association. It must have been quite a night in Edinburgh.

[1] Edinburgh Branch *Minutes*, October 4, 1959.

CHAPTER TWENTY

THE LAST RAKE

I. THE FIFTH GENERAL SECRETARY

WHEN Alex Kitson so suddenly found the job of the chief executive officer fallen upon his shoulders at the age of thirty-eight, he had no easy situation to face; yet, at the same time, he enjoyed exceptional advantages. For the past ten years, despite its long history and a loyal membership, the Association had been gradually suffering a slow decline in numbers, in influence, and in activity. Speaking of that time an official with many years' experience commented: 'We were in the doldrums, trailing behind the big battalions. In national negotiations we were accepting what was handed down, and if a claim was refused, well, that was it. If we did initiate any move and it failed to win favour on the Workers' Side of the negotiating machinery, that was usually the end of it. The days were long by when you would see any flashes of the old Johnny Brannigan, with his bursts of energy and quick wit. For several years before his death, he was often not himself. His health failed, his memory was impaired: we officials were often doubtful what his attitude would be to a dispute; it was quite a temptation to take a line of least resistance. It was difficult, for it led to lack of confidence in the members, whether they were right or wrong.'

The new General Secretary was very far from seeking a quiet life, and he had certain advantages which no previous chief executive officer had enjoyed. Kitson had spent his whole working life in the industry, the first ten years at the wheel, and on an extremely wide range of work. No union official and probably few, if any, members had his wide experience of driving practically every kind of vehicle. During most of that time he was a shop steward and active at depot and branch, and at all levels of the union, except the Executive Council, whilst becoming widely known in the Labour movement especially in Edinburgh, Leith, and that area.

Alexander H. Kitson was born in October 1921, at Kirknewton, Edinburgh. His father, a life-long trade unionist, had been a shale miner until that year, when he was victimized after the lock-out. It happened again after the 1926 miners' lock-out. His mother's father, David Greig, was a railwayman, active in the National Union of Railwaymen until he retired in 1937. Branch secretary and NUR District delegate, he would often take his little grandson to union meetings at Mid Calder station on the back of

384

[*photo: Robert L. Nicholson*

15. Five veteran Drivers, who all retired at the end of 1964, with 136 years service with the same firm between them. All have driven the four different types of vehicle: Horse, steam wagon, petrol and diesel lorries. *Left to right:* Jock Shields, George Wylie, Colin Clark, John Forrester and Hugh Brown.

16. Alexander Brown, of Glasgow, driver of an Albion Chieftain 22-ft. platform vehicle, won four trophies in 1957. They were:

1. Champion Scottish Commercial Driver of the Year
2. Trophy presented by the Road Haulage Association
3. Best Driver from the Glasgow area—*Evening Citizen* Trophy
4. Best Driver Holding a Trade Union Card—T and GWO Trophy.

The Association's Banner and the staff and executive members, May Day, 1953.

his bicycle. In the past he had been a Liberal candidate against a Tory, a local publican. Alex Kitson was born in hard times, in the days of mass unemployment, low pay, and economy cuts in everything from tax relief to education. Young Alex took it all in; he missed nothing. When he was ten he took part in his first election campaign in support of a Labour candidate. 'I ran with the figures from polling station to committee rooms,' he relates; and, from the glint in his eye, it would seem that he ran fast and did some thinking as he ran. He won a bursary, but he could not take it up in those days of small grants and cut-backs, when the family was hard put to it. He had to earn quickly; so his schooldays ended in 1935, and, at the age of fourteen, he became a vanboy with St Cuthbert's Co-operative Society, Edinburgh. He had to cycle fifteen miles to work. Two years later he went on to milk delivery, which at that time was organized by the old Shop Assistants' Union, which he joined and in which he became a shop steward. Later he was taught to drive by an old St Cuthbert's stalwart, George Thorburn, with whom he lodged; then he joined the Association, and again rapidly became a shop steward. He was always a motorman; but much of his trade union grounding in the transport industry came from the 'auld cairters', not least those in Leith, like Angus Annal, Jack Dewar, Andrew Wilson, and Big Jim Anderson of Wordie's, Wattie Lamb, an old cabby, Tam Souness of Mutter Howey's Eddie Dishington of Saddlers, and Jimmy Proudfoot of Central Carting Co.[1]

As soon as he became a driver for St Cuthbert's, he began to gain a wide experience, from funeral driving to working from the docks and markets. When he was called up in January 1940, and was found unfit for military service, he was seconded to the Ministry of Labour, under industrial conscription; and for the next five and a half years he drove every possible type of vehicle from eight-tonners to light vans. Sometimes he was on long distance haulage, particularly between Glasgow and Liverpool; occasionally he was sent out of Scotland for weeks and months at a time. By the time the war ended he had a rich experience of working in the industry and as an active trade unionist. As soon as the war was over he was pressed to apply for the position of full-time collector in Leith. He was accepted and began his duties as a full-time official in May 1945.

From 1945 to 1955 he was a district secretary in his home area, where

[1] In the Diamond Jubilee number of *The Highway*, August 1958, A. H. Kitson contributed an article in which he wrote with great warmth of the old 'worthies' then still to be met with at the foot of Leith Walk. 'I think it would only be right to mention some of the old worthies that were still working in the industry owing to the war, and who were better known around the streets of Leith than the local councillors. Such names as Sparrie Broon, Jockie Paterson, Bluey Johnston, Fiery Muir, Tiger Lyon and Reddie Ogilvie. Their names will always be remembered whenever horse transport is talked about in Leith.'

he had close experience of all the problems both of the beginning of nationalization and denationalization and all the questions of post-war reconstruction. He witnessed the troubled times in the Association's internal affairs, with litigation brought by the ex-Assistant General Secretary; in his daily work he was acutely aware of the discouraging effect upon members in garage and depot of the loss of some of the leading shop stewards when Rule 21, banning members of the Communist Party from office, was imposed in 1951. He never got over an incident where, when a highly respected shop steward had to give up his credentials under Rule 21, some 300 men in one depot left the Association in anger, despite every effort of persuasion. Kitson was active on the Edinburgh Trades Council from the time he first became a delegate at the age of twenty; in the early fifties he served on its Executive, and there must have been few trade union officials with whom he was not closely acquainted. He began to be well known at Annual Conferences after the war, where he was elected to the Standing Orders Committee year after year. In 1956 he was appointed organizer.

For twenty-five years the new General Secretary had worked side by side with transport drivers, or had been in closest touch with them, knowing their characteristics, strengths and weaknesses as well as he knew his own. Not only could he talk to the average commercial motorman in his own language; he liked him and had confidence in him, a feeling which was reciprocated. At the same time, Alec Kitson thoroughly understood the point of view of the officials of the union; he had been on the committee of the Officers' Staff Association. He had shared their sense of frustration in recent years, when they knew that if they took up with vigour the case of some victimized member, they might unexpectedly find that John Brannigan would express the view that it was in the best interests of the Association that harmonious relations with that employer should not be jeopardized. Yet caution on the officials' part could well lead to anger, disillusionment, and apathy in the depot. A leading British Road Services shop steward contrasted the approach of the two general secretaries in this way: 'When you had a depot dispute you were always afraid Johnny Brannigan would back out. We would sometimes taunt him by saying: "You're a man of peace." He would get very angry, but it was true; he was a weak man. He was old-fashioned, too. He had come to think that the Association had become his own; he wanted no change at all. When Kitson came, it was different at once; he brought in a dynamic punch. The men knew where they were with him. The information came up from below, and the officials could, and did, make use of it.' Another shop steward said: 'You were fairly sure of *not* getting support from Brannigan. I was making a push to get the shop 100 per cent organized. There were two Nons who wouldn't join up. One was a stubborn fellow but straightforward: the other played about and made excuses. So I went to the

Manager and said: "I'll stand one Non, but not more." He rang up Brannigan, and fetched me to the telephone. Brannigan wouldn't listen: he just told me to lay off. After Kitson took over there was none of that: the Association soon had a fine record.' An appreciable number of full-time officials were nearing retirement; not all were able to find the way to steer a course which did full justice to the members whilst giving loyal support to the chief executive. Again, through his work in the broader movement, Kitson was acquainted with the officers of other unions with which the Association's relations had fallen away in the past years. He was fully conscious, not only of the eight years' loss of representation of the Association on the Executive of the Scottish TUC, but also that, in relations with other unions, there had come to be little disposition to look to the Association for fraternal help in their disputes. Finally, he was of the opinion that it was time that the employers should learn that negotiations would not be left in a rut, but that a vigorous progressive policy would be adopted to take the initiative in improving the position of the road transport workers.

The Association's funds had risen, being thirteen per cent above the level of 1951, representing £20·2 per member. But in other respects the prospect was disturbing. Since 1951 the membership, falling each year, had dropped by fifteen per cent by the time Kitson became General Secretary, 1,000 members having been lost in the first six months of 1959. Branch meetings all too frequently failed to find a quorum. Political committees were quiescent despite the approach of a general election. To arrest the decline, would the newcomer begin to introduce changes slowly and cautiously? On the contrary, the fifth General Secretary brought in changes just as fast as time could be found for full discussion and to win the approval of the Executive Council for such steps as went beyond administrative matters. In fact the Executive responded very quickly indeed to the new initiatives. By the time of the annual conference eight months later, a new climate was to be remarked. At the end of that year the membership figure was only eight per cent below that of 1951, which was surpassed the following year.

2. THE FIRST EIGHT MONTHS

What was needed was that there should be a change in relations between the leadership of the Association and three other groups: the members themselves, the employers, and the other organizations within the trade union and Labour movement. To achieve this, it was necessary that a progressive policy should be apparent in three main spheres: in negotiations, in internal affairs, and in political and social questions. Actions can be more eloquent than policy declarations and manifestoes. There follow a number of events recorded in the minutes, some small in themselves, none of which would be likely to have happened, or to have had the same outcome, under the previous General Secretary. All went to show that a wind of change was blowing.

In Edinburgh, five members were dismissed for refusing to handle 'black' traffic on the instructions of the Association during a printing dispute. They were supported and paid strike benefit. When the then Acting General Secretary gave 'a very full report' to the Executive Council, it was recorded:

'The payment of strike benefit at the rate of 15s per shift was homologated on the motion of Messrs Craig and Montgomery, who congratulated Mr Kitson on the handling of the strike and the Edinburgh members for their fine display of loyalty to the union. . . . Letters of thanks for support given by the union received from the National Union of Printing, Bookbinding and Paper Workers and the Scottish Typographical Association were read and noted with appreciation.'[1]

Immediately he was declared General Secretary, Alex Kitson made some administrative changes and put in hand new organization. He met district secretaries and pressed for the appointment of a Head Office Organizer, which resulted in James Barrie being appointed to that post. The structure for district secretaries and organizers was reviewed, pockets of membership were redistributed, books redivided and tightened up. Reporting to the Organization Committee five weeks after his appointment, Kitson said: 'this was the beginning only of a reorganization which he felt should spread all over the country. It was his intention to send organizers into all the outside areas with a view to covering pockets which appeared to have been overlooked and obtain reports on the further organization'.[2] An agreement was reached with the Scottish Transport Workers' Union not to unload non-trade unionist drivers in Glasgow docks and fruit market: 'and that our members would not load or discharge vehicles at the docks which should be dockers' work'.[3] This amicable arrangement with a brother union was followed up by a check on pence cards at the Glasgow docks, resulting in the enrolling of one hundred new members.

Some stoppages had occurred, notably in British Road Services, where at first members were slow to realize that in future there would be speedy support in negotiations, and no longer any need for a stoppage to gain the fullest attention from Head Office. It was perhaps not surprising that members were slow to note this. As soon as possible, old practices which had long been suspended were reintroduced. During war-time many valuable practices stopped; they were not all resumed after the war, and, during the fifties, John Brannigan had seemed to keep members at arms'

[1] Executive *Minutes*, August 25, 1959.
[2] Organization Committee *Minutes*, October 9, 1959.
[3] Executive *Minutes*, October 17, 1959.

length rather than to seek opportunities to consult with them. Now, however, Alec Kitson made a point of summoning sectional conferences of shop stewards and grade representatives. While negotiation for an agreement with British Road Services on compensation for the new speed limit was in progress, he called together all British Road Service shop stewards and grade representatives; he kept them abreast of events and himself in touch with their feeling.

Any constitutional changes for consideration at the 1960 annual conference would have to be discussed by the Executive Council in the autumn of 1959. The Aberfeldy branch put forward a resolution calling for the deletion of Rule 21, which banned members of the Communist Party from holding any office in the Association. When discussing resolutions for Annual Conference at the October Executive, Jacky Carabine and Alex Paton moved that Rule 21 should be deleted, a motion that was defeated by six votes to three. The Executive then carried by the same margin an amendment moved by John Cosgrove and J. Dyce, which had the effect of confining the ban to official full-time positions. Another rule recommended to the Annual Conference would make paid officials or former employees on superannuation ineligible as delegates to the annual conference. Kitson had strongly argued the case for this change both with the Officers' Association and on the Executive Council, and had tried his best to persuade officials voluntarily to decline nomination, pending a change in the constitution. The thinking behind both these changes of rule was to encourage initiative in the branches and depots and the greatest attendance at conference of the most active lay members working in the industry. There had been a growing tendency for delegates to be chosen from present officials and even former employees of the Association on superannuation. Kitson met the opposition of the officials themselves with the proposal that all should attend conference on a rota system as observers. His view was that it was essential to enhance the standing and authority of the annual conference.

In less than a month after becoming General Secretary, Kitson had to deal with an unusual case which attracted a very great deal of attention throughout the movement in Scotland. The Association of Engineering & Shipbuilding Draughtsmen was in dispute at the firm of A. Findlay & Company of Motherwell, and declared an official strike. Twenty-one weeks passed by without a settlement and finally the draughtsmen appealed for support to other unions, and posted pickets. Kitson instructed members of the Association delivering goods for British Oxygen Gases not to pass the picket line; this immediately brought matters to a head. Complications, however, arose because the Constructional Engineering Union complained that this would affect some 400 of their members within the works. Immediately Kitson referred the matter to the Disputes Committee of the Scottish Trades Union Congress, who called in both unions, together with the draughtsmen, the Amalgamated Engineering Union, and the Transport & General Workers' Union.

'There was a very full exchange of views on the situation facing each union as a result of the strike, and, particularly, the requests for certain forms of assistance addressed by the Association of Engineering and Shipbuilding Draughtsmen to the Constructional Engineering Union with members employed within the affected works and the Scottish Horse & Motormen's Association and the Transport & General Workers' Union, whose members delivered to or collected from the works.'[1]

But while this was in progress the draughtsmen got a very satisfactory settlement of their demand. That year at the STUC their divisional Organizer placed on record 'their appreciation of the assistance rendered to them by the Scottish Horse & Motormen's Association in this particular dispute; it played no small part in helping the union to obtain a satisfactory conclusion. It is difficult to imagine circumstances under which the Association of Engineering and Shipbuilding Draughtsmen could be of similar assistance to the Scottish Horse & Motormen's Association, but, nevertheless, if that occasion did arise in the future the latter union could have no fear about the direct response they would receive from the draughtsmen.'[2] The settlement came close to the New Year's holiday; there were some motormen's children who would long remember their party that year, thanks to the substantial support which the draughtsmen gave to the social committee's fund. During these early months members were never left in doubt as to what attitude the Association was taking henceforth to support members of other unions which were undergoing disputes; picket lines were not to be crossed by Association members.

While Kitson spoke bluntly in condemnation of unnecessary strikes undertaken without prior consultation with the Association, he never lost sight of the men's grievances and showed considerable resource in guiding them out of untenable positions. When he first took office he started from the assumption that the members were in the right. Before members had regained confidence that grievances would be promptly and decisively taken up by officials at all levels, the first Kitson often heard of a dispute was to be telephoned by an employer and brusquely told to order his men back 'forthwith'. He remarked drily to an organizer about an employer on one occasion: 'He's got delusions; he seems to think he pays our wages.' Sometimes there had been a long history of uneasy relations and grievances not righted until some final spark 'set the heather on fire'. In one such case, when a stoppage took place in breach of an agreement and without prior consultation, Kitson found himself in the all too familiar position of a trade union official confronted with angry men for whom

[1] 63rd Annual Report of the STUC, 1960.
[2] idem.

this was the last straw, and a management which refused to negotiate whilst the men were out. Kitson knew that it was an issue on which a co-operative management could have come to terms; and that the men were exasperated by long delay and evasion. He therefore proposed that the men should return to work for one day only, during which the management could demonstrate its willingness to negotiate with the Association. The men accepted; the management refused, and it was now they who were in the untenable position. Many examples of a similar approach, which gave a new and much welcomed lead to the officials, soon greatly improved relations with the members.

A new agreement with British Road Services, with compensatory payment for the increased speed limit, came into force in January 1960. Kitson held many meetings and conferences of members, shop stewards, and grade representatives, being fully aware that without the fullest co-operation considerable difficulties would arise in each depot over the new schedules and changed starting times. Despite the Association's best efforts at all levels of the machinery, negotiations were unsatisfactory and long-drawn out. Finally, things came to a head and a week's strike took place from March 22nd to March 28th. Mass meetings of British Road Service members, and conferences of shop stewards were held, and finally an interim arrangement was made with the Scottish divisional manager of British Road Services pending a final decision on starting times on the National Joint Negotiating Committee. Kitson reported the outcome to a special meeting of the Executive:

'The General Secretary explained that although the strike was unofficial, he had been in sympathy with it and had done nothing to dissuade the men. He felt it had achieved something that would not have been gained in any other way. As there had been some hardship he suggested that grants should be made from the Benevolent Fund to those who had lost wages, and it was agreed unanimously on the motion of Messrs Houston and Montgomery that they receive benevolent grants at the rate of 12s per day.

'It was noted that money collected in other British Road Service depots had been handed over for relief of the men on strike.

'The General Secretary was congratulated by members of the Executive Council on his very fine handling of the whole affair.'[1]

Within the eight months which had passed, this difference of approach by officials, together with the backing of the Executive, gave members an enhanced sense of confidence in the new leadership. The climate had changed; meetings began to be better attended and recruitment increased.

In this period, progress on political and social questions was also to be noted. The Political Committee was strengthened and a course of week-end

[1] Executive *Minutes*, April 1, 1960.

schools began to be worked out which later developed into a most important educational feature for the members, especially benefiting the shop stewards and the younger members. It was decided at a special meeting of the Executive on September 29, 1959 that a donation of £2,500 should be made to the Scottish Council of the Labour Party for the General Election, and a call was made to the membership to work for the return of a Labour Government. Serious attention was paid to policy documents received from the Labour Party. At the Executive meeting in August 1959, the declaration by the Labour Party and the Trades Union Congress on disarmament and nuclear war entitled *The Next Step* was distributed to Executive members prior to discussion at their next meeting: 'After a very lengthy discussion Messrs Craig and Murphy moved that the document be supported. Mr Carabine seconded by Mr Paton moved that the document should not be supported. On a vote the motion was carried by five votes to four votes.'[1] In the past it had come to be the practice for the agenda for the conferences of the Labour Party or the British Trades Union Congress to receive only cursory consideration on the Executive, the responsibility of how the Association's vote should be cast being left to the delegates, usually the General Secretary and the President.

Perceptible progress was made in all these spheres of work in the eight months culminating in the Annual Conference in March 1960, at the conclusion of which the Leith delegate, George Wilson, remarked: 'It was one of the best conferences he himself had ever attended, and the Executive Council report had surpassed anything he had seen in the past.'[2] Two weeks later, at the Scottish Trades Union Congress, Alex Kitson was elected to the General Council. After eight years the Association had regained their seat in the leadership of the Scottish trade union movement.

3. A NEW APPROACH TO NEGOTIATIONS

One of the most marked changes which came over the Association's practice as the sixties opened was in negotiations on wages and conditions. It was not that, for the most part, there was appreciable change in policy; but there *was* a review of methods and a new determination that progress should be made in carrying out policy. Negotiations had frozen into a certain pattern well before the 'pay pause' policy imposed in July 1961 by the Chancellor of the Exchequer, Selwyn Lloyd, or later the 'guiding light' limitation on claims introduced in connection with the National Economic Development Corporation, the National Incomes Commission, and later the Prices and Incomes Board.

Already it was noticeable that, in collective bargaining, events waited

---

[1] Executive *Minutes*, September 2, 1959.
[2] Report of 47th Annual Conference, 1960.

upon the findings of wages councils or national joint negotiating committees; many negotiations, which were supposed to be voluntary, in practice proved to be geared into the awards and orders, or waited to follow their pattern. When at last the findings became operative—and the delay was often very considerable indeed—the latest Road Haulage Order was taken as establishing maxima. It sometimes reached ridiculous lengths: basic rates began to fall out of all proportion to what was being obtained by local negotiations. Instead of being a standard statutorily enforceable against rate-cutting employers, as the Orders had first been regarded, they began to be recognized as a brake on wages. The Executive Council report to the 1960 conference of the Association remarks in regard to those working in milk distribution:

'Difficulty is experienced in this trade because of local negotiations that have improved the basics beyond those laid down in the Wages Council Order.

'We are of the opinion that attempts should be made in the near future to have a voluntary machine set up to negotiate the wages and conditions in the milk distributive industry.'[1]

This was already a straw in the wind. The move away from compulsory negotiation towards voluntary machinery became one of the most marked features of this period. When the question of wage restraint and the policy to be adopted towards it became acute in mid-1961, it gave a further great impetus towards voluntary collective bargaining. The Association was most alert on this subject: and indeed, in some respects gave the lead to other sections of the movement, because its policy was formed on the basis of members' experience in an industry which was particularly susceptible to such pressures.

A second feature of no little importance was that in the previous decade road transport workers had slipped down the basic wage scale: 'We were getting so low in the wages tables, that we looked like being due for relegation', as one British Road Services shop steward remarked. More and more, overtime was felt to be necessary if earnings were to be adequate in comparison with other industries. Basic rates and overtime rates were low; yet the pressure for more speed intensified, whilst traffic density and hazards increased all the time. Raising the legally permitted speed limit for commercial vehicles and removing all speed limit on the motorways which were beginning to appear, gave employers opportunities for speed-up through new running schedules, without paying any compensation for the extra strain to health and greater effort, to their considerable profit.

The Association therefore had to frame and vigorously carry out a policy which would meet four problems: (1) to raise the wages and earnings of the road transport worker; (2) to resist dangerous speed-up; (3) to

[1] Report of the Executive Council, 1960.

reduce the maximum hours of driving permitted under the Road Traffic Act 1930 from eleven to ten in any twenty-four to offset the increased intensity of work; and (4) to achieve a negotiating structure which would be quickly responsive to their members' needs.

Throughout the years that followed, the policy of the Association towards 'pay pause', wage restraint, national incomes policy, or any measures whether fiscal or through planning or development authorities, either governmental or sponsored by the Labour and trade union movements themselves, remained strictly referable to these clearly defined needs of the membership. The Executive Council and the General Secretary paid particular attention to the need for the membership to be fully informed. Great stress was laid on the importance of holding sectional meetings from time to time as well as conferences of shop stewards and grade representatives. Encouragement was also given to a serious expansion of educational work, by week-end schools for young members and shop stewards, in which basic policy was thrashed out, and also in the Political Committee, the biennial Political Conference, and local political committees which functioned at ward level. We shall take a brief look at some of this work in greater detail in later sections.

When Alex Kitson became General Secretary in the autumn of 1959, many of these problems had been with the Association for years; some indeed could be said to be almost in a permanent state of deadlock. Now the leadership saw the central task as being to break the deadlock. This was first observable in two closely related subjects: compensation for the increase in the speed limit to 30 m.p.h., under the Motor Vehicles (Variations of Speed) Regulations 1956, and pressure on the Government to reduce, by legislation, the permitted maximum hours of work for a driver. Although the Association had protested against the increased speed limit as long ago as 1955, they had got nowhere. Moreover, the Road Haulage Wages Council had rejected claims for a compensatory payment. The Road Haulage Association insisted that it was a matter for agreement with individual firms. Pressure had at last succeeded in getting a voluntary agreement with British Road Services for a cut in hours to ten and a compensatory increase in pay of fifteen per cent on basic rates. It was time to move against the private hauliers. The Scottish Brewers came to terms; tenacious negotiation began to produce separate agreements with other firms. The deadlock was finally broken, the campaign gathering impetus all through 1960 and 1961, especially where the membership on the spot showed initiative and militancy. The opponents with whom the Association had to grapple in the struggle for a reduction in the legal maximum hours was first one Conservative Minister of Transport (Harold Watkinson) and then another (Ernest Marples). The Association called for the support of the economic committees of the Scottish Trades Union Congress and of the British Trades Union Congress. The Ministry's line of defence by-passed the Association's case against the increased tempo, the inadequate roads, the enormously increased number of vehicles, 'the adverse effect on the health of road haulage workers', and the fear that 'working life of drivers operating under such conditions will be greatly shortened'. First, the Ministry claimed that there had been some compensating changes through improved roads and vehicles; next, the Ministry insisted that only safety reasons could be considered against changed speed limits. The Ministry was therefore giving consideration 'in consultation with the Road Research Laboratory to the feasibility of undertaking a study of fatigue conditions amongst road transport drivers under present-day conditions'. In July 1959, the Minister wrote to the British Trades Union Congress that he 'did not think there is sufficient evidence at present' to support the condition that increased fatigue was likely to reflect on road safety. Alex Kitson spoke strongly on the subject at the British Trades Union Congress at Blackpool on Thursday, September 10, 1959. It was the first Trades Union Congress which he had attended. He pointed out that the Minister had

'decided not to take the advice of the people who know something about the industry, but has referred the matter to the Road Research Laboratory for investigation.

'The Resolution told him that the introduction of the Variation of Speed Regulations was not in the best interest of the health of drivers or the safety of the general public, the reasons being that the roads in the country were incapable, with the enormous increase in vehicles to carry this burden.'

In support of this he quoted Sir Ewart Smith, addressing the Engineering Section of the British Association, in August 1959:

'He said: "No less than 60 per cent of British trunk roads now carry traffic in excess of their designed capacity and the load is growing at about 7 per cent per annum." I am sure that that is evidence enough, in the first place, that the Increased Speed Regulations should never have been introduced.'

Taking up the Minister's recommendation that the reduction of drivers' hours should be done through industrial negotiation, Kitson retorted:

'If that had been possible there would have been no resolution on the agenda of Congress last year. The road hauliers of this country are not interested in a reduction in hours, and the only people who have shown any concern regarding a reduction in hours are the nationalized section of British Road Services. We are at the moment in negotiation with British Road Services in an attempt to reduce the legal working day from eleven hours to ten. How can we get private employers to discuss a reduction in maximum working hours when they treat eleven hours in 24 as the minimum ?'

Then he turned to the question of bad employers who were forcing drivers to evade Section 19:

'Moreover, the bad employers—and there are large numbers of them in the industry—are more concerned with breaking the law than observing it. I would ask any delegate who has driven to the Congress from London or Glasgow how he would like to undertake that task every evening in the week, in a vehicle weighing from 20 to 25 tons? There are hundreds of drivers in this country midway through their working lives who are obliged to seek light and less remunerative jobs because of the long hours spent in cabins of long-distance wagons. The instances of gastric ulcers, coronary thrombosis and nervous debility is high among drivers.'

The TUC at that time were to discuss the need for a forty-hour week. Alex Kitson ended by pointing out what was happening in fact in the transport industry:

'We were able to establish a 44-hour week many years ago, but we are struggling to have employers in the transport industry observe a 77-hour week. All the statistics that are available relating to road transport since the introduction of the Road Traffic Act, 1930, make apparent that some revision is now necessary.

'The volume of increase in tonnage carried by road in the past 20 years, together with the increased speed and traffic congestion on practically the same roads, is now taking toll of the health of the industry's greatest asset—its human structure; and we feel that more pressure should be brought to bear on the Government to introduce legislation.'[1]

To the Association's conference the following spring, the General Secretary stressed the urgency of reducing hours.[2] One of the problems was that some employers took advantage of a driver's failure to keep strict log sheets. Others put their drivers in fear of dismissal if they insisted upon observing the regulations. The leadership's approach to the problem, at this stage, was first that there should be more investigation officers and a better system. As to the members who feared victimization: 'Mr Kitson said that members should observe rigidly Section 19 and if anything happens, they can rest assured that the Executive Council will support them in every way.'[3] Although constant pressure was kept up, the Association got no satisfaction on the reduction of maximum hours,

[1] Report of Proceedings at the 91st Trades Union Congress, 1959.
[2] Mr Kitson said that the average age of the drivers in the industry today was now 35 to 40 as against 1930 which was 50 to 55; and that was one of the reasons that we suggested the hours should be reduced from 11 to 10. (Report of Annual Conference, 1960)
[3] Report of Annual Conference, 1960.

despite demands from the British Trades Union Congress and the Scottish Trades Union Congress for a committee of inquiry. It became one of the many subjects on which the Association looked for a change of government to achieve the union's policy.

But during 1960 and 1961 great advances were made in negotiating agreements with individual employers for compensatory payments in respect of the increased speed limit. The Executive Report to the 1961 Annual Conference at Aberdeen stated that, of the many important questions which had been pursued during the year,

'The one that has had most material effect is that relating to compensation for the increased speed limit. . . . A campaign was initiated to bring private hauliers into line, and after long and protracted negotiations with several employers we are pleased to report that progress has been made and benefits are being derived amongst large sections of our membership in road haulage. . . . We would like to record our appreciation of the great assistance that was given by the membership to establish the gains that have been made.'[1]

The reduction in the maximum permitted hours was still resisted by the Government; and before negotiations for compensation for the thirty-mile speed limit had been completed with all employers, Ernest Marples, the Minister of Transport, announced changes for the worse. He was introducing new legislation to increase the speed limit of motor coaches and also setting up a committee to inquire into further increasing the speed of commercial vehicles. The Executive Council promptly took the following decision:

'It was agreed on the motion of Messrs Murphy and Kyle that a statement be issued deploring the suggestion to increase the speed limit on commercial vehicles, which would be a danger to the public and to the health of our members, who would be advised not to drive any faster than the present speed limit.'[2]

The Association opposed the new 40 m.p.h. for passenger vehicles but without success; and, as from February 9, 1963, the speed limit for commercial vehicles was increased to 40 m.p.h. The Executive Council said bluntly: 'There is no doubt in our minds that this is another part of the compensation the government had to pay to employers in the road haulage industry for the assistance given in returning a Tory Government at the last election.'[3] The Association was fully conscious of the bearing on road safety of long hours of driving, the strain of intensity of work involved in the speed-up, and, above all, the inadequate roads for which

[1] Executive Report to Annual Conference, 1961.
[2] Executive *Minutes*, May 8, 1961.
[3] Executive Council Report to Annual Conference, 1963.

Scotland was notorious. Indeed, the stand taken by the Association about the state of the roads was an important factor in the campaign to arrest the run-down of the Scottish economy. At the same time, the Executive Council could not be unmindful of the extent to which there were breaches of safety regulations by drivers who succumbed to pressure from employers for ever more speed. A series of steps was taken to meet the problem. Basic rates were low, and so were overtime rates, producing on legitimate running far less than the earnings to be got in some other occupations. Inspection was negligible. A high degree of self-respect, self-discipline, trade union consciousness, and loyalty to their fellow members was called for to set against the provocation and temptations of illegal running. But a responsible approach could be fostered by a trade union only where the leadership and members enjoyed the fullest mutual confidence. Above all, it had to be patent to all that there would be no complacency about the level of wages nor fatalistic acceptance of deadlock in negotiations.

The members were quick to take note of new possibilities in the first few months of the new General Secretary's taking office. In his presidential address to the 1960 Annual Conference, John Houston of Paisley anticipated their mood. 'One of the biggest problems facing the trade union movement today is the question of wages and working conditions and their improvement,' he said:

'Transport is the lifeline of this country, whether it be road or rail, but it is not given its rightful place in the responsibility table in so far as wages are concerned. This has been borne out recently by the unrest that exists on the railways, and the state of affairs in road haulage is no happier.

'It is not right that a road transport worker in charge of a 15 ton truck carrying a cargo that is valued at many thousands of pounds, should be receiving the small pittance of £9 1s 0d per week.'[1]

He went on to warn transport operators:

'If they are not going to face up to this very serious problem of the rate for the job, the industry is heading for industrial disaster, and that was not a threat but a plain fact.'

The next day, George Wilson moved a resolution for Edinburgh Branch which, after stating that the basic rates of pay 'are well below subsistence level on the present-day cost of living level', pledged conference 'to diligently keep before the responsible bodies the necessity for a speedy review of said rates and importance of implementing basic rates on which members of our industry can subsist without recourse to or the necessity for working overtime to make a reasonable living wage'. Alex Kitson replied that 'with the present machinery' it was 'almost impossible' to win adequate advances. In asking for wholehearted support for the

[1] Report of Annual Conference, 1960.

resolution, he added with emphasis: 'More militancy would need to be shown by the members before the Wages Council would agree.'

By the following year, at the 1961 Annual Conference in Aberdeen, the new President, Jack Cosgrove of Perth, was able to report that 'progress made in wages and conditions in all sections of membership has been unsurpassed since the end of the war'. The big change had been the success in negotiating with individual hauliers agreements for compensatory payments for the increased speed limit:

'The achievements attained took long and hard bargaining and were not easy come by, and while we appreciated the assistance given by the membership, more militancy is called for amongst the membership if the progress desired has to be won.'[1]

It would be hard to over-emphasize the significance and consequences of the speed limit agreements at just that stage in the history of the Association; they transformed the situation. Firstly, after years of relative stagnation, the campaign demonstrated to employers and men alike that 'No' would not be taken for an answer to demands to raise the basic wage in the industry from the low levels to which they had fallen in comparison with other industries. Next, it speedily became clear to members that to gain an individual agreement put a premium on a high level of workshop organization and understanding. At the same time, from a tactical point of view, it enabled the leadership to choose the battle ground where organization was strongest. Next, the gains were not sectional; all classes of members, in whatever part of Scotland, could benefit. The first two agreements were reached where organization could be expected to be strongest, in British Road Services and in the Scottish Co-operative Wholesale Society, but the next agreement was won from a big haulier, Charles Alexander of Aberdeen. By the time that fifty per cent of the private hauliers had come to terms, every member was in a stronger position and feeling the advantages of the campaign directly or indirectly.

There quickly followed a great improvement in the relations between the leadership and the members as the conception began to develop that wage negotiation was a matter of interdependence between strong workshop organization and skilful negotiation. For Alex Kitson a cardinal principle was that not only was it not impossible to keep in touch with shop stewards whilst negotiations were in progress, but that indeed it was essential. Principles of modern democratic unionism were a new experience for the members; in a surprisingly short time the consequences began to show. For example, the most active and vigorous members began to offer to take on the arduous jobs of shop stewards and other offices in branch and depot; younger members developed quickly and there was eager response to schools, support for political committees, increased attendance

[1] Executive Council Report to Annual Conference, 1961.

at branches. These things are difficult in the conditions of the transport industry; but they ceased to look insoluble. By the end of 1960, interest in the quarterly meetings had developed to the point where only one out of fourteen failed to find a quorum. The days were long gone by when a Hugh Lyon could take a paternal attitude to 'the auld cairters', whom most regarded as the lowest of the low, who would look up with admiring gratitude at any leader who might be able to speak as sharply to the employer as he did to his own members. The days were also gone by when there was a wide gap, and members were expected to leave it all to officials and accept the results of intricate and sometimes incomprehensible negotiations without further question. The appreciation of the members sometimes found expression in words as well as in deeds. Commenting upon the speed compensation agreements: 'It was unanimously agreed on the motion of Messrs Murphy and Morrison to congratulate the General Secretary and Organizers on the work they had put into the drive for the ten per cent compensation.'[1] Again, there was naturally a quick reduction in the number of strikes unauthorized by the union; and, where stoppages did take place, they were of short duration. In British Road Services there had at first been impatience and a number of strikes without prior consultation, which the General Secretary had firmly criticized. But a year later the situation was changed:

'Mr Kyle said as a member of the Divisional Committee for some years now that he felt he would like the Executive Council to appreciate just what Mr Kitson had done for the union on the Divisional Committee. He said the management had been made aware of the fact that the union were greatly concerned about what was going on in British Road Services and that Mr Kitson would fiercely uphold the men's point of view, with the result that we were now treated with great respect, and an entirely new atmosphere had been created at the meetings.'[2]

This new close-knit relationship between the leadership and the members gave the Association a hitting power disproportionate to its numbers. Employers quickly became aware that a statement by the Association had the massive authority of its members behind it. A further consequence was that the Association's standing was enhanced in the broader Labour and trade union movements. More and more frequently, on wages councils and national joint negotiating committees, the impact of this small union was such that it frequently gave the lead on the workers' side to unions many times its size.

In the course of the campaign to achieve individual agreements on the speed limit the weaknesses and disadvantages of wages councils became clear; not only did awards and orders act all too often as maxima, but

[1] Executive *Minutes*, May 8, 1961.
[2] Executive *Minutes*, January 7, 1961.

there were also many opportunities for delay, and much ingenuity displayed in taking advantage of or of stopping up loopholes. It was becoming clear that wages councils were a drag on the wheel, and that more could be got, and more quickly got, from the employers by voluntary machinery.

The Association was particularly concerned with delays in wages councils. An example was a claim for double-time payment on statutory holidays, with a day off in lieu, which was first considered by the Road Haulage Wages Council on April 9, 1959. Six months later on October 1, 1959 it was agreed in principle; but it was not until May 13, 1960, that final agreement was reached, an interval of thirteen months. At this moment, when the experiences during the campaign to win individual agreements for the speed limit had underlined their disenchantment with the wage-fixing machinery, the Chancellor of the Exchequer, Selwyn Lloyd, introduced the 'pay pause', on July 25, 1961. In the events that followed the Association played a significant part; at the same time their attitude to 'wage restraint' and any planning which involved a national incomes policy in current social conditions became finally and decisively established. As one Government after another put forward proposals about economic development, all of which started from the premise that wage increases should be controlled, it had the effect of intervening more and more in negotiating bodies and all joint machinery. It quickly became apparent to the Association that those who came into the category of the independent members or the independent chairman, could not be expected to ignore a governmental pronouncement and apply themselves solely to the merits of the case made before them. In the Association's view, this role could not be regarded as one independent of government and employers. When such external factors came into play, compulsory arbitration was no longer round the corner; it was in sight. When arbitration had to be embarked upon, the Association adopted the practice of refusing to go to the independent chairman for a decision in the event of failure to agree. This policy was not adopted until a series of cases and events had convinced them from their own experience that it was advantageous.

The events which followed the introduction of the 'pay pause' in July 1961 made history from the point of view of the members of the Association.

4. THE 'PAY PAUSE' STRIKE

Fifteen months earlier, in March 1960, when the Guillebaud Committee's report, establishing the principle of comparability, had been rushed out at the time of the railway strike, the Association's then president had reacted sharply. Jock Houston told the delegates to the Association's Annual Conference at Edinburgh that

'as far as wage restraint is concerned we will have no part of it, but demand that the lot of the commercial motor driver in this country should be examined by an independent authority with a view to the niggardly treatment he has suffered being put right, by giving him a standard that is decent and something he can live on without having to work long hours of overtime'.[1]

He added: 'The railwaymen's fight yesterday is the road transport workers' fight today.'

Fourteen months later in May 1961, a claim was put in to the Road Haulage Wages Council for a substantial increase in wages and a reduction of the working-week. This was considered on July 6, 1961 when the Wages Council agreed to draw up proposals for a three per cent increase and a reduction of the working-week from forty-four hours to forty-two. This decision then went into the lengthy and somewhat contorted pipe-line, from whence it could be expected to emerge by early autumn. But just three weeks after the Wages Council decision, Selwyn Lloyd, the Chancellor of the Exchequer, made a statement in the House of Commons on behalf of the Conservative Government, which had run into an economic crisis. He said that increases in real wages and salaries were desirable 'but only provided that national productivity increases sufficiently'. He called for 'a pause' in pay increases, on the ground that 'we are heavily over-drawing on our productivity account'. In his view:

'There must be a pause until productivity has caught up and there is room for further advances.

'It is not possible in any general statement to cover every particular case. Where commitments have already been entered into they should be met. Subject to this, however, a pause is essential as a basis for continued prosperity and growth.'[2]

The Government would act on those lines with their own employees: 'The government ask that the same lines should be followed elsewhere, both in the private sector and in those parts of the public sector outside the immediate control of the government.' He then went on to foreshadow a permanent national incomes policy, which was in fact adopted by successive administrations, of which the pay pause was to be the first phase:

'In itself however such a pause is certainly not a lasting solution to the problem of rising costs and prices. A pause must mark the beginning of a long-term policy.

'That policy is that increases in incomes must follow and not precede or outstrip increases in national productivity. During the pause we must work out methods of securing a sensible long-term relationship between increases of incomes of all sorts and increases in productivity.'

[1] Report of Annual Conference, 1960.
[2] *Hansard*, July 25, 1961.

Other measures he announced were a two per cent increase in the bank rate and a ten per cent surcharge on all customs and excise duties. When the Executive Council met a week later, they passed a resolution strongly condemning the tax increase, which they regarded as 'a further attack on the standards of the workers, and in no way solves the long term economic difficulties'. On the 'pay pause' they stated: 'They also inform the government that they have no intention of accepting the call for a wage freeze or wage restraint as long as the burden of sacrifice is not equally shared.' The resolution concluded: 'The union will continue to press for increases in wages for all its members, some of whom are still receiving under £9 per week to maintain a family.'[1] If there were any who thought that the claim accepted by the Road Haulage Wages Council was one of the commitments 'already entered into' which would avoid this net, they were quickly disillusioned. The General Secretary warned that the Wages Council when it met to consider objections to the proposals might well follow the line of the Chancellor's statement:

'It was agreed on the motion of Messrs Murphy and Hendry that if this be the case, the General Secretary call meetings of the membership involved with a view to obtaining the improvements proposed from the individual employers through organization.'[2]

Next day the Road Haulage Wages Council met. They had before them a recommendation from the Minister of Labour that the Chancellor's statement be acted upon; there were objections from the employers that no increase or improvement were necessary, and from Association members that the improvements were insufficient. The Wages Council submitted the proposals to the Minister of Labour for approval. On October 9, 1961 the Minister replied that 'in view of the economic circumstances' Road Haulage Order 72 should not operate until January 1, 1962; that was seven weeks later than would be normal. The workers' side approached the Road Haulage Association to convene a meeting of the old National Joint Industrial Council—last in prominence fourteen years before at the time of the great strike in road haulage on the eve of nationalization under the Labour Government; it had been called upon only once since then, in 1955. The employers declined. The Association then approached the Scottish section of the Road Haulage Association asking them to recommend an earlier date to their members; they declined. Thereupon the Association took two steps. They wrote to every employer in Scotland who followed the Road Haulage Wages Council asking that the improvements in RH 72 should be operated by November 13, 1961. Next, mass meetings of members in the main centres were called; they were told that the Executive was prepared to take action if an employer refused the demand.

[1] Executive *Minutes*, August 2, 1961.
[2] Executive *Minutes*, September 20, 1961.

The members approved unanimously. All British Road Service shop stewards were called together also, because the National Joint Negotiating Committee had offered the same terms as those of RH 72.

It was private hauliers outside the Road Haulage Association who first agreed to terms. When private negotiations broke down, the Road Haulage Association attacked the Association and published press advertisements calling on employers to refuse to agree to earlier operation. Over a period of three weeks, 1,000 members took strike action, some £1,260 was paid in strike benefit, and, in addition, those not affected contributed to a strike fund. In Glasgow men were on strike for four days; when the firms began to give in, those which had not already come to terms speedily did so. In a short time it was all over; the Association had won; RH 72 was operated almost universally in Scotland from November 13, 1961. When the Executive met at the end of the month they agreed 'that this had been one of the finest and most successful stands ever made in the trade union movement, and had given great heart to the membership'. The Association had also made recruits:

'The actions of the General Secretary in the conduct of the strike and payment of strike benefit were unanimously approved on the motion of Messrs Houston and Frew and all members joined in congratulating the General Secretary, Organizers and other staff concerned on the work that was put in to bring about this success.'[1]

The Executive also 'noted with satisfaction' that the union had beaten the 'pay pause'.

A senior member of the Executive, himself a past president when John Brannigan was in charge, expressed emphatic views about these events: 'The Association's decision to strike against the delay in implementing this Road Haulage award was as important as the most militant carters in the old days ever achieved. It was time to make a stand; the employers took advantage of Selwyn Lloyd's "pay pause". Kitson gave full support to going it alone. In the past, divide and rule had been the employers' policy; now they got a taste of it. The men greeted it with enthusiasm and it was one of the most momentous decisions. John Brannigan could not have done it; he had fallen away in his last ten years. The Association made great strides since he went; it advanced beyond all description. This struggle was a great achievement.'

One of the results was that the Association approached the Road Haulage Association with a view to setting up voluntary machinery. The Executive Council reported to the next annual conference that 'the impression has got abroad that trade unions have no right to attempt to negotiate outwith the Road Haulage Wages Council'.

[1] Executive *Minutes*, November 29, 1961.

'During the course of the year the leaders of the Employers' Side attempted at the Wages Council to have this union chastised for the approaches it made to individual employers regarding compensation for the increase in the speed limit.

'He was advised by the chairman of the Council that this was a question for the individual trade unions and not the Wages council.

'In view of this we intend in the future to attempt to have the standards of our members employed in this section improve through whichever channels are left open to us.'[1]

Jack Carabine, in his presidential report, praised the members for not accepting any pay pause, and for demonstrating 'that if there was going to be political interference in free negotiation, there was a great danger of encouraging industrial action against political decisions'.[2] He remarked that it 'was with great suspicions that he viewed the entry of the Trades Union Congress into Selwyn Lloyd's National Economic Development Council':

'He was strongly convinced that it was only a prop for a crumbling capitalist system and trusted that the Trades Union Congress representatives would remember that they were representing the interests of the workers. The slogan should be: no wage pause, economic planning that would ensure direction of industry to underdeveloped areas and greater restraint on dividends and profits.'

The following day, conference passed two resolutions which clearly laid down the Association's policy on two subjects: wage restraint and negotiating machinery. The first resolution congratulated

'the Executive Council on its determination to resist by all means any attempt made by Her Majesty's Government to impose a wage freeze policy upon our members while refusing to balance such measures with controls over profits, capital gains and company dividends.'[3]

It was moved by J. Caulfield for Dumbarton Branch and seconded by C. Clark of Clydebank. The next was moved by J. Reid for Edinburgh:

'Believing the Road Haulage Wages Council to be an outdated piece of negotiating machinery which no longer serves the best interests of the transport industry, calls for its dissolution and urges the setting up of a National Joint Industrial Council as a more modern and efficient method, giving a greater coverage to the industry of negotiating wages and conditions.'

[1] Executive Council Report to Annual Conference, 1962.
[2] Report of Annual Conference, 1962.
[3] Report of Annual Conference, 1962.

The Association had been one of the first unions to be affected by the pay pause. Speaking to the first resolution, the General Secretary traced the history of the pay pause and the second phase of the national incomes policy, the National Economic Development Council which was then just coming into operation. He said it looked as though 'unless there was an improved increased production then the workers would not need to expect any increase in wages at all'. He commented:

'We should make it clear to the employers that we want a share of the massive profits in the transport trade and that as far as the Road Haulage Wages Council was concerned, we were not going to stand for it much longer, but would demand that there should be voluntary negotiations on behalf of the transport workers.'

Next year at Perth, the 1963 Annual Conference condemned basic wages in road haulage as 'unrealistic', and demanded a campaign for 'a wages structure more in keeping with the responsibilities and skill of the driver'.[1] Delegates also called for a 'long overdue' improvement in overtime rates. Next year Conference declared its 'complete opposition' to the report of the National Economic Development Council, just introduced; and to 'any form of wage restraint being imposed on workers, unless it is accompanied by a similar restriction on prices, profits and dividends'. When Kitson supported a Beith motion demanding a campaign for the abolition of the Road Haulage Wages Council, he described this body as 'a retarding influence'.

He was speaking of a major action which had just taken place, which had followed upon the 1963 resolution on overtime rates. When, in October 1963, the Road Haulage Wages Council had rejected this claim, the Executive of the Association, after long consideration, decided to apply to 176 firms individually. When there was no response from the employers, most of whom replied that in their opinion it was a matter for the Wages Council, it was decided that a test case should be made. Alex Kitson held a number of meetings with the men and their shop stewards employed by the Tayforth Transport Group, a firm which used 800 vehicles based mostly on Dumfries and Falkirk. The Executive decided 'that intimation be sent to this company that an official stoppage would take place on February 1st if our claim was not conceded'. It would be the first of a series of guerilla strikes. The Road Haulage Association appealed for the strike notices to be withdrawn; but the General Secretary would agree to recommend this only if employers were prepared to negotiate on this and other questions. The employers agreed to set up a committee of six to meet six union representatives, whereupon the strike notices were withdrawn. Discussions were in progress in March 1964 when Alex Kitson told the Annual Conference about these events:

[1] Report of Annual Conference, 1963.

'We were living in the hope, of course, that a Labour Government, when it came back, would solve the problem by nationalizing the road haulage industry and then we would have negotiations on a voluntary basis. . . . But at least we had now reached the stage . . . for the first time in its history in the 34 years since the first Road Traffic Act, the employers in the industry had been forced through the actions of the Scottish Horse & Motormen's Association to come to the negotiating table.'[1]

This, he hoped, would provide the 'roots of a new machine of voluntary negotiation'. Within the year, a National Negotiating Committee of twenty-four members had been set up, half appointed by the employers and half by the unions, free to negotiate on all subjects. The Road Haulage Wages Council remained in being, because its decisions once approved by the Minister, were legally enforceable. Voluntary and direct negotiation had at last been achieved, without losing the advantage of legal enforcement of key decisions. In this, without doubt, the Association had been the pace-makers on the workers' side of the Road Haulage Wages Council.

5. POLITICS AND SOCIAL QUESTIONS

In the six years between the Annual Conference of 1959 and that of 1964, there was considerable development in this sphere of the Association's work; and a growth of the influence and standing of the Political Committee, and, with it, in the number and strength of the local Political Committees. In addition there was vigorous development of the schools held at the Convalescent Home at Ayr where shop stewards, the younger members, and potential leaders of the future Association got valuable help. Many difficult problems were thrashed out at the week-end and summer schools and Political Committees long before they came before the annual or biennial conferences. Students at the schools were expected to take the benefit back into the garages, the work places, and the branches. The fact that thorough and informed discussion had been carried on by so many of the most active members of the Association may account for the surprising degree of unanimity which is observable at the Association's conference during these years, even on difficult international and foreign policy questions. By this time, the Association always made a point of seeing that their delegates to the Labour Party Conference and to the Scottish Advisory Council of the Labour Party were well briefed and fully aware of the majority opinion of members on all main issues.

A topic which took up a great deal of time and attention was the state of the Scottish economy over these years; the relatively high degree of unemployment and the general decline in Scottish heavy industry, and the problems of attracting or directing new industry to Scotland. The

[1] Report of Annual Conference, 1964.

Association's policy was clear-cut. Transport thrives when industry develops, and contracts when it declines; at the same time the existence of an adequate transport system is one of the essential pre-requisites for attracting new industry. A second prerequisite, closely linked to transport, is an adequate fuel supply. The Association therefore viewed with considerable anxiety the run-down of both the mining industry and the railway system in Scotland. Both these industries, basic to Scottish economic development, were nationalized; both bore the heavy financial burdens of compensation to private owners and the cost of modernization from top to bottom. The Association at one and the same time supported resistance to mine and line closures and pressed very strongly indeed that road- and bridge-building in Scotland should be pushed ahead. The roads were worse and the need was greater in Scotland, they claimed, than in any other part of Britain. The case for a fully integrated, publicly-owned transport system, with a far-reaching programme for modernization was self-evident in Scotland; her future, if not her present, clearly depended upon it.

Growing unemployment in Scotland was already noted by John Kyle in his presidential address to the 45th Annual Conference at Ayr in March 1958, recording that at the end of 1957 nearly 62,800 were registered as unemployed in Scotland. By the time of the sixth biennial Political Conference in November 1958, the figure had risen to 80,000. A resolution was passed stressing the 'extreme urgency for the stimulation of old industries and the introduction of new industries'. By 1959 Scottish unemployment had reached 116,510, representing 5·4 per cent of the working population, which was nearly twice the figure for Britain as a whole. In repeating the previous year's resolution, conference added a warning about 'the number of unemployed at present on the Juvenile Register in Scotland'. A sharply worded resolution was submitted to the Scottish Trades Union Congress of 1960, which was taking place immediately after the Association's own conference. This resolution condemned the Conservative Government's Local Employment Bill, designed merely to increase financial inducements to employers opening new factories in areas such as Scotland, which would 'not solve Scotland's unemployment or economic problems', and instead called for 'legislation to direct industry to areas that have been severely affected by their economic policies'. At the seventh biennial Political Conference in October 1960, the Association once more condemned 'the economic policy of the present government which is creating high unemployment in Scotland', and called on the administration 'to provide some new industry within the Lothians', where the shale oil industry had been closed down altogether. The Association went on pressing the question through resolutions to the Scottish Trades Union Congress and the Scottish Advisory Council of the Labour Party. At the eighth biennial Political Conference, in November 1962, a very strongly worded resolution[1] was passed unanimously which again insisted on the need for direction and opposed the policy of mine and pit closures.

In November 1962, the Executive Council decided that the General Secretary should represent them upon a Scottish Project Committee which was set up following conversations that autumn with a group of Scottish Members of Parliament. The proposal was to attempt to draw up some short-term and long-term projects for Scotland; the Scottish Area of the National Union of Mineworkers added their support, and other bodies did the same. At that time, the unemployment figure in Scotland had reached 125,000; emigration was increasing and the prospects of fruitful employment for young people were bleak. The General Secretary gave an account of the formation of the Scottish Project Committee, when speaking at the 1963 Annual Conference at Perth. He spoke of the need for increasing unemployment benefit and pensions, and stopping pit and rail closures 'until such time as the economy was on an even keel':

'There would also have to be some call for new industries. He stated that if the Labour Party got back to power, we would have the planning, but long term planning was not the solution to our problem; we want something immediately.'[2]

It was not the older men but the youngsters who were signing on at the labour exchanges; direction of industry was necessary at once; the Project Committee would survey Fife and set targets for employment and new industries; and he hoped that, when the long-term policy was produced, 'it would be something worthwhile which could be recommended to a Labour Party'. There was some difference of opinion about the policy of direction; an Ayr resolution which asked 'that companies willing to be

[1] 'This Conference declares emphatically that there must be an assured and expanding economy for Scotland. We feel that this can be achieved by encouragement of existing traditional industries, and by direction of enough newer industries to offset declining job opportunities in our present traditional industries. We feel that the present attack in so far as the railway is concerned in Scotland does in no way help the colossal unemployment problem affecting Scotland.

'We further recognize that the Tory Government solution to the problem created by them within the mining industry in this country is in itself a further step by them to bring a nationalized industry to its knees.

'We feel that the only solution to solving the fuel needs of the country as a whole is a national co-ordinated and integrated fuel policy.

'Conference welcomes particularly the action taken by the Scottish Trades Union Congress to alert the government and public opinion about the steadily worsening employment problem with which Scotland is faced. It is convinced that unless there is a radical change in the Government's approach to the Scottish situation by seeing it as a special problem calling for extraordinary consideration, the economic outlook must be one of continuing deterioration.'

This resolution was moved by W. Caulfield (Dumbarton) and seconded by S. Woods (West Calder) at the 8th Biennial Political Conference, Ayr, November 1962.

[2] Report of Annual Conference, 1963.

redirected should be fully reimbursed by the Government' was rejected. A Kirkcaldy resolution demanding direction into areas scheduled under the Local Employment Act was carried unanimously, as were others calling for government-sponsored programmes of public works and 'adequate compensation' to all workers made redundant by rail and pit closures, until they were 'retrained and settled in other jobs'.

By the autumn of 1963 a broadsheet[1] by Mr George McRobie, putting forward the views of the Scottish Project Committee, was published. It concluded that the objective of planning for Scotland should be a 'holding operation', to maintain the present proportion of population.[2] The plan stressed that 'adequate supplies of fuel and transport services are *pre-conditions* of economic development, and in the Scottish economy these two industries have a paramount importance'. As national policies in the two essential services were not 'geared to the potential expansion of economic activity in Scotland', which required a five per cent increase for the next seven or eight years', certain steps needed to be taken at once:

'For transport, the conclusion is inescapable; no curtailment of facilities must be permitted until the needs of all localities have been assessed in the light of employment and trade targets.'

The plan recalled that the Scottish Council (Development and Industry) had reckoned that as against the net total payment by the Government of £60 million to provide an additional 100,000 jobs, the financial benefit to the Exchequer would amount to £80 million.

When the plan was presented to the Annual Conference in 1964, the Executive Council expressed the view that it met the Association's previous resolutions and that 'it will be our policy to pursue such plans with the appropriate authority'. Delegates underlined their endorsement by carrying a resolution demanding immediate steps 'to set up a Development Council for Scotland to produce a plan that will provide for the shifting population and the siting of new industries to relieve the ever declining industry'.[3] Throughout 1963 and 1964, the Scottish Trades Union Congress had held half a score of 'Jobs for Scotland' conferences. At these the Associa-

[1] *A Development Plan for Scotland.* Political and Economic Planning. Vol. XXIX. No. 476. London. 32 pp.

[2] 'To achieve this with a fully employed population would require a net increase in the number of jobs in Scotland of 150,000 over the next six years, of which 100,000 jobs will have to be created by the expansion of manufacturing industry in Scotland.' (*A Development Plan for Scotland*)

To effect this it proposed that widely representative district councils should be set up to assess needs and resources and 'marshal public opinion in support' of district development plans with pilot districts.

'It is suggested, too, that both the interests and the structure of the trade unions equip them to take the initiative in creating District Councils, drawing up employment targets and securing the active co-operation of industry, commerce and local and national authorities.'

[3] Report of Annual Conference, 1964.

tion's General Secretary, who was vice-president of the STUC and took office as president in 1965, was much to the fore. He was insistent on the importance of local initiative, on which the *Development Plan* had also laid stress; and at the Association's 1964 Annual Conference he took occasion to make the point again in the context of the expected General Election:

'Harold Wilson had given assurances that there would be regional planning but we were asking for some autonomy so far as regional planning was concerned; and the control should be taken away from Westminster and placed at St Andrews House, Edinburgh, and this could only be done with a fiscal policy.'

He thought the direction of industry was still needed:

'There was no possibility whatsoever of the economy growing unless pressures were brought to bear on the industrialists of this country to send industry to Scotland.'

The Scottish Project Committee, he explained, had a proposal to meet the case if firms were unwilling:

'The Government should take the responsibility and set up industries in opposition to the firms who were refusing to come to the areas where it was most needed.'[1]

What was done about Scotland's economy, unemployment, and the pit and line closures illustrates the marked change which had come over the Association's political activities. In the past, conference had also considered and passed important branch resolutions, but not a great deal had come of most of them. Now each resolution was strictly pursued; and if the result were not satisfactory, the branch had a report from the General Secretary with recommendations. The main part of the reports of the Executive Council to annual conference was the account in considerable detail of what action had been taken on the previous year's resolutions, with the full text of correspondence. Very few political resolutions were lost in the sand.

Another important, and allied, issue was the improvement of Scotland's roads and bridges. The Association in the past had frequently gone on record for road safety; examples during the fifties were demands that local authorities should call 'safety first' meetings (1952); for dual-carriage roads (1953): and trunk roads (1955). But nothing further happened. From 1960 onward, however, the Association kept up determined pressure and began to see results. In November 1960 the biennial Political Conference expressed not only its general 'dissatisfaction with the progress being made about roads in Scotland', but stressed that a dual-carriageway on the main road between Edinburgh and Glasgow, the notorious A8,

[1] Report of Annual Conference, 1964.

should be given top priority. No less than 1,000 accidents had happened on it in three years. A motor-car manufacturing firm, which had newly opened a factory, demanded, and got, a mile of dual-carriage road laid down on either side of its gates. This added fuel to the anger of commercial drivers who considered that they were daily risking their lives on the remainder of the stretch, leading westwards out of Scotland's capital. The General Secretary began by taking up the resolution with the Secretary of State for Scotland, and pressed for a deputation to be received, at first without result. The branches most concerned were kept informed of the progress of the correspondence. When it became known that commercial drivers were proposing to boycott certain roads, including the dangerous A8 between Edinburgh and Glasgow, the Secretary of State for Scotland agreed to receive a deputation on March 3, 1960.

The longest-serving Executive member, John Murphy, who was first elected to the Executive in 1942 and served until 1964, described other features of the progress made in later years. Since 1959, in his view, the Association had become transformed, and was second to none, with a high reputation. Executive members were conscious that the fifth General Secretary never kept them in the dark; he put before them the facts and the case on which they were able to make an informed judgment. Thus he knew that he had their full support in initiating new policy or new methods. John Murphy said that this was as true on domestic and trade questions as in national and international affairs of high politics, where opinion would sometimes begin by being widely divergent.

There was some anxiety lest a clash of interest might develop in certain circumstances as the Association's political activities matured. Lay members and, sometimes, officials of the union, both part-time and full-time, came increasingly to be elected to town councils, where they found themselves conveners of committees with direct responsibility for the employment of Association members. Similarly, members were elected to boards of management of retail co-operative societies, where the same problem might arise. Where a man became a director of the Scottish Co-operative Wholesale Society or received a managerial appointment in British Road Services, it was another matter; these were full-time appointments. In 1961 the Executive was asked to give their attention to a difficult case. It came up when the East of Scotland organizer, Willie Campbell, went to argue a member's case with the Perth Co-operative Society. Facing him on 'the other side' of the table was the Association's District Secretary, who had been given permission by the Association to become part-time minutes' secretary for the Perth Co-operative Society; later he was elected to the District and Scottish Sectional Boards of the Co-operative Union, about which he neither informed the Association nor sought permission. He did not regard it as his duty to represent members when disputes arose between them and the Perth Co-operative Society.

The Executive were therefore called upon to consider on March 14, 1961, the 'split loyalties' of the District Secretary. It was admittedly an extreme case. Letters between the General Secretary and the District Secretary were reported to the Executive for several months and he was given a hearing before the Executive. His standpoint was that the Association had benefited from his membership of the Perth Co-operative Society Board of Management. The Executive's attitude was that this could not absolve him 'from his responsibilities to the union members when they became involved in disputes with the society, nor would they agree that this allowed an official to take up positions on sectional boards of the Co-operative movement'.[1] He was instructed to relinquish posts in the co-operative movement other than the retail society's board of management, and also to give an assurance that, when questions affecting the union came up he would make the case, or accompany the officer who was responsible.

During these years, the Association considerably extended their international connections, and found the experience both informative and educative. It had become customary for the General Secretary, usually together with the President, to go to the conferences of the International Transport Workers' Federation. In later years, head office staff also went to international summer schools, held by the International Transport Workers' Federation, the International Confederation of Free Trade Unions, and other international organizations. But, with the exception of the delegation to the United States in 1948, there were none exchanged by the Association on its own behalf with other countries. At the 1955 Annual Conference, a resolution was moved that a delegation should be sent to China and other Far Eastern countries: but except for a brief reference the Minutes are silent; the visit did not take place. In the summer of 1957, John Brannigan went on a delegation to the First Congress of Workers' Councils of Yugoslavia, after which the Yugoslav Transport Workers' Union suggest a reciprocal exchange of full delegations. This again, however, was not pursued. Three years later, in 1960, an invitation was received from the Motor Transport Highway and Communication Workers' Union to visit the Soviet Union. John Cosgrove, then chairman, Jack Carabine and James Dyce went with the General Secretary. On their return they reported back to Political Committees and schools, and the Executive decided to send an invitation for a return visit. This took place in the spring of 1961; at the same time a two-man delegation of Jack Carabine and John Cosgrove went to Czechoslovakia, in response to an invitation from the transport workers' union there. Their reports were published[2] as pamphlets. Also in 1961 there were delegations or visits to

[1] Executive *Minutes*, May 8, 1961.

[2] *Scottish Horse and Motormen's Association Delegation Report on Visit to the Soviet Union*, May 1960. *Scottish Horse and Motormen's Association Delegation Report on Czechoslovakia Visit*, May 1961.

the Federal German Republic and to East and West Berlin. Delegations were sent to the German Democratic Republic, to Hungary, and to the International Transport Workers' Federation conferences held in Stockholm, Berne, Vienna, Helsinki, and Copenhagen. In addition, the General Secretary was selected to go to the Duke of Edinburgh's Human Study Conference in Canada in 1962; whilst in 1963 Association members extended their range of international connections by receiving a visit from Commonwealth trade unionists of Malaya, Nigeria, and Pakistan. For several years running, members were sent to schools held by the transport trade union in the German Federal Republic.

The attitude of the Association towards questions of peace and war gradually crystallized over a decade; and it may be noted that this development ran parallel in some degree with the increasing international connections illustrated by the exchange of delegations. The controversy about rearming Germany in 1954 was followed at the fourth biennial Political Conference by a debate on an Edinburgh motion which condemned

'the statement of Winston Churchill regarding his instruction to Montgomery on the stacking of arms for use by the Nazis against the Russians.

'It is detrimental to world peace and is a statement that can only create a situation that could lead to a third world war.'

An amendment that action be left in the hands of the Executive, and deferred, was carried by twenty votes to ten; no action was taken. The 1956 Annual Conference unanimously carried a resolution which was the beginning of a long series, continuing for years, on nuclear weapons. Moved for Edinburgh branch by George Wilson it expressed concern at 'the continued manufacture of atomic, hydrogen and other nuclear weapons and calls on the Government to divert the monies and energies thus being used to more constructive and social problems'.[1] The sixth biennial Political Conference in 1958 passed unanimously a resolution, sponsored by Glasgow A B and C branch, condemning 'the continued testing of H-bombs by all countries'; and the 1959 Annual Conference unanimously passed a resolution, proposed by the Glasgow Local Authority branch, which deplored 'the continuance of the making of atomic and hydrogen bombs and urges the Government to use all nuclear power for peaceful purposes'.[2] By the following year, however, events in Scotland were changing the direction of such resolutions and intensifying concern with them. An emergency resolution in 1960 condemning the opening of bases in Scotland, with facilities for training German military personnel, was carried unanimously. When, during that summer, the atomic submarine base was opened at Holy Loch the seventh biennial Political Con-

[1] Report of Annual Conference, 1956.
[2] Report of Annual Conference, 1959.

ference in October debated three resolutions. An emergency resolution, passed with only one dissentient, urged the British Government 'to abandon nuclear weapons'; no longer to permit 'America or any other foreign power to maintain military bases in this country'; and called for the 'revision of defence agreements with foreign powers and, if necessary, the withdrawal from NATO'. Two other resolutions were carried unanimously. The first opposed the plan to base US Polaris submarines on the Clyde Coast as 'a step that will endanger the lives of the Scottish people and the peace of the world'; the second protested against the 'training of Germans in the use of rockets on Scottish soil'.

Next April, at the 1961 Annual Conference, the Association debated a four-point defence resolution. This reaffirmed the previous year's points and went on to set out a defence policy which the future Labour Government should adopt.[1] This remained the Association's policy, being reaffirmed in general terms by a large majority at the 1962 Annual Conference and again at the eighth biennial Political Conference later that year and in subsequent years. In the years 1962 and 1963, the Association also took up its stand deploring the 'policy and programme of Apartheid' in South Africa and calling for 'a joint programme of non-co-operation': the Association also opposed entry into the European Common Market.

But the biggest single political and industrial issue on which the Association was concerned to arrive at a matured policy was the future of the industry itself.

6. TOWARDS AN INTEGRATED TRANSPORT POLICY

The debate in the movement in 1954 over Clause 4 of the Labour Party Constitution,[2] initiated by the Leader of the Labour Party, Hugh Gaitskell, was regarded by most as a controversy between Left and Right, between those who advocated a Socialist system of society based on the public ownership of the means of production and the planning of the economy for social service instead of private profit, and those who proposed to introduce safeguards and reforms without taking the means of production out of private hands. In popular terms it was sometimes put as being

[1] It called on the future Labour Government to base its policy on:
1. Unilateral renunciation of the manufacturing and testing of nuclear weapons.
2. The cessation of nuclear bases and nuclear submarine bases in the United Kingdom.
3. The continuance to press for universal complete disarmament through the United Nations.
4. Support for the admission of the Chinese Peoples Republic representatives to the United Nations. (Report of the Annual Conference, 1961)
[2] Clause IV PARTY OBJECTS . . . (4) To secure for workers by hand or brain the full fruits of their industry and the most equitable distribution thereof that may be possible on the basis of the common ownership of the means of production, distribution, and exchange, and the best obtainable system of popular administration and control of each industry or service.

between those who wanted 'a socialist transformation of society' and those who wanted 'to make capitalism work'. In its political aspect, most of the first group wanted to see the Labour Party more firmly based on and representing the trade union movement, whilst some of the second group looked to a modification of the Labour Party to enable it to become a non-Socialist 'Radical' Party.

But to the road transport worker, whatever the shade of his political opinion, the debate on Clause 4 inevitably raised the question of the re-nationalization of road haulage in the first place, as an essential stage of an integrated transport policy. For them it was beyond question that a policy in which all forms of transport were integrated and planned was long overdue and was the only solution to otherwise insuperable problems; that integration of privately-owned transport with publicly-owned transport was impossible; and that therefore public ownership of all forms of transport was indispensable.

For many years the Association had been aware of the disasters ahead if all means of transport were not integrated, and that dominance by one private interest was no substitute for integration planned as a public service. This was apparent in the twenties when the private hauliers began to come into conflict with the privately-owned railway companies. The Royal Commission in the twenties showed itself fully aware of the need for integration, but, precisely owing to the diverse conflicting interests of the private owners, unable to recommend the public ownership which would make it possible. During the Second World War, a single control had to be established because integrated running was essential to the war effort. After the war, taking over the railways from the largely derelict privately-owned companies into public ownership together with civil aviation and the partial nationalization of sections of road haulage, was regarded as a move towards laying the basis for an integrated transport policy. Amongst the shortcomings were the financial terms of nationalization; the limitation on control of docks and large parts of road transport; and inadequate measures to meet redundancy arising from nationalization. But before the measures had got under way, came the denationalization of road transport by the Conservative Administration which gained power in 1951. This was followed by the dismembering of the nationalized railway system. Thus the situation was once again not of integration but of the dominance of one type of privately-owned transport over the rest. It was a step in the totally opposite direction from integration.

Parallel to those events was the situation of the fuel industry, one with which transport is interdependent and closely linked. Here coal, gas, and electricity were nationalized, although without some of their profitable sidelines, but oil was left in private monopoly ownership. Instead of an integrated fuel policy which was as essential as integrated transport to an expansion of Britain's economy, there developed a conflict with oil

THE LAST RAKE

interests seeking dominance of the profitable sectors. The mines were run down, electrification of the railways was first delayed and then largely sidestepped. In each case, what British economy appeared to need with great urgency was integration; in neither case could it be achieved without overall control; in both industries this proved impossible without public ownership. In neither case would the private interests submit; in transport, where they were less firmly established, they had been forced to yield temporarily, but had carried through a successful 'fight back'. Such was the viewpoint of the Association.

In the sixties, therefore, the Association looked for the return of a Labour Government which would be expected to reverse these tendencies; it must be pledged to carry through the integration of transport on the basis of public ownership but without its former weaknesses, and pledged also to a fuel policy to match. Any trend to write off, to play down, or, indeed, to delay public ownership, to create a climate in which support of nationalization in general was decried, was naturally viewed with the utmost concern by the Association.[1]

The conclusion which the Association drew from the lost election of 1959 was certainly not that Clause 4 should be dropped from the Labour Party's constitution. Addressing the annual conference at Edinburgh four months later, the president, Jock Houston gave the opinion that 'the reason we lost the Election was not because the word nationalization was "dirty", but because the fruits of it had never been given the publicity that it deserved'. What otherwise would have happened to the coal mines, the railways and road haulage, where the only real improvements had been the direct result of nationalization? He concluded:

'No one rattles the big drum about the big profits made from British Road Services. What about the airlines which we own—they are the greatest and best in the world.

'No, I would say to our people, let us shout from the roof-tops about the benefits that can be derived from public ownership, and re-educate our society in its beliefs.

'To the waverers I would say: if you carry on with this academic approach to Socialism, you will have to take the responsibility of doing serious damage to our great movement.'[2]

That the delegates shared his view was apparent when they passed unanimously an Executive Council resolution reaffirming 'its policy that the Labour Party should continue to support the policy of nationalization of the basic industries and any other industry that is failing in its duty to the state'. In speaking to the resolution, the General Secretary said:

[1] It was certainly in the minds of members when they gave £2,500 to the Labour Party's funds for the 1959 General Election, and when they decided to give £4,000 for the General Election which was due to take place in 1964.
[2] Report of Annual Conference, 1960.

O   417

'We always have maintained in this industry that not only can we have more fruit from nationalization, but an economic service can be given to the people of this country, if we have an integrated system of transport.

'The traders in the West Coast of Scotland would be in a difficult position if it was not for the nationalized section of British Road Services, because irrespective of the cost this is a service to the community, and no private haulier would be interested.'

The following month, Alex Kitson moved a similar resolution, which also called on the Labour Party 'to publicize and popularize this fundamental principle in every way', at the 1960 Scottish Trades Union Congress, where it was carried unanimously. At the annual gatherings of the British Trades Union Congress and the Labour Party that year the Association's delegates pursued the same policy. The following year, at the 1961 Annual Conference at Aberdeen, a resolution sponsored by Glasgow A, B and C branch was carried declaring the Association 'opposed to any alteration in the Labour Party constitution as regards Clause 4'.

Three months earlier the Conservative Government had published a white paper with proposals for reorganizing the nationalized transport undertakings, including the sections surviving in British Road Services. The British Transport Commission was to be abolished, each section to be transferred to separate Boards, with a national advisory council, the railways separated into regions, each with its own profit and loss account. It was the beginning of the era of line closures, which were to have a grave effect on Scottish economy. At the Association's 1961 Annual Conference at Aberdeen, the president, Jack Cosgrove, described it as 'a preliminary step to the breaking up of the lucrative parts of the industry'.[1]

The British Trades Union Congress called a conference of all transport unions early in January 1961, and discussions followed with the Minister of Transport, in which Alex Kitson took a leading part. He spoke in the debate in the following April at the Scottish Trades Union Congress, where the white paper was condemned unanimously, the Government's policy being regarded as 'completely inimical to the co-ordination and integration of the transport services which are essential to the economy of Scotland'. Kitson described the recommendations of the white paper as 'the final act of sabotage to the structure which was built up in 1948 to give us a co-ordinated system of transport in this country.'[2] He gave full support to the railway trade unions which moved the resolution and continued:

[1] 'The object of the break up of the British Transport Commission would appear to be that the government can offer the most profitable parts to the hungry financiers.

'Should this be an attempt to let British Road Services be returned to private enterprise, with which we as a union entirely disagree, it will be fought with every means at our disposal, including direct action if necessary.' (Report of Annual Conference, 1961)

[2] 64th Report of the Scottish Trades Union Congress, 1961.

'There was a strong feeling in the minds of the road transport workers that the more lucrative part of this co-ordinated system, which was the British Road Services, was now being built up to hand back to the financiers because of the profits that could be obtained from road haulage.'

He recalled how in 1948 some 43,000 vehicles were taken over and 'virtually scrapped', with £1,600,000 written off in the first six months. In the next five years, £14,500,000 was spent on new wagons to replace the fleets taken over, and £2,000,000 on rebuilding depots and stores. He added:

'Nothing had been said about that and nothing had been said about the compensations that were paid to the hauliers who had been bleeding the transport workers in this country for nearly 30 years.'

Then he put the Association's policy in defence of the remaining nationalized sector in very strong terms:

'The Minister of Transport had to be warned that if there was ever any attempt to sell out that nationalized section of British Road Services to private enterprise the unions were determined to fight in every way possible and nothing short of industrial action would satisfy them.'

The same year the Association submitted a resolution to the British Trades Union Congress, and supported a composite resolution which deplored the white paper as 'precluding the possibility of an integrated and co-ordinated transport system which is essential to the economy of the country'. In 1962, too, the Association condemned the Government's policy and called on 'the future Labour Government to undertake the policy of a co-ordinated transport system that will be efficient and effective.'[1]

During 1962 some uneasiness began to be felt amongst members because the Labour Party had not published a detailed plan of what they meant to do about road transport when they next formed a government. Accordingly, the Association decided to put down a resolution calling on the British Trades Union Congress, together with the National Executive Committee of the Labour Party 'to appoint a committee to formulate the future policy for commercial road transport'. While this point became lost in a composite resolution, the General Secretary did, however, have an opportunity of speaking on it when the British Trades Union Congress met at Blackpool that year. He pointed out that although the Labour Party had given the assurance that road haulage would be renationalized when the next Labour Government was returned, 'it has not made any reference to the great problem of C-licence operation'. After regretting that the Labour Minister of Transport, Alfred Barnes, whom he described

[1] Report of Annual Conference, 1962.

as 'the architect' of the 1947 Act, had left C-licence operators out of the national reconstruction 'because of pressure from the Co-operative movement', he gave some figures about their rapid growth since 1948. The figures of the expansion which he quoted did not cover retail distribution which, he said, 'has been used so often as a red herring why we should not include C-licence operation in any integrated system'. Between 1948 and 1961 the number of C-licence vehicles had grown greatly, more than doubling.[1] The number of 3-ton licence vehicles was greater than the A- or B-licence haulage vehicles; yet it was a problem which had never been examined closely by Labour Party nor British Trades Union Congress, which was why his Association had asked for policy to be formulated. 'It is regrettable,' he said, 'that we are on the eve of a General Election and no policy has been produced to ensure that a co-ordinated system is introduced.' Next month, at the 1962 Labour Party Conference, the Association had tabled a resolution calling for 'a propaganda campaign amongst the commercial road transport workers'; and also 'for a full examination into C-contract hiring licence operation, with a view to their integration into the transport system'. The Political Committee returned to the same point, bringing a similar resolution before the Association's eighth biennial Political Conference in November 1962. The General Secretary developed the argument in speaking to the resolution. He said that at one time, when there were between 250,000 and 300,000 C-licence vehicles in the country, there were very few which were not working in retail distribution and none were working on long-distance transport. Within three years the figure had gone up to 575,000, and 'the bulk of this transport was taking the place of the road hauliers'. He said that the expansion had taken place before the end of the Labour Government, and that the Labour Party 'must take responsibility that they allowed this to expand'. It made road problems and increased cost. The Association's policy was that an integrated system was necessary for the economy and co-ordination to save costs, though they would 'never accept on integration a policy for redundancy payment as in the mines and the railways'. He concluded:

'We should try and bring pressure on the Labour Party to get a committee into operation whereby we can start formulating the build-up of something that we feel will be worth while for the transport industry.'[2]

Correspondence continued with the Labour Party; and the Political

---

[1] 'What is more important for the haulage and railway industries is that the number of C-licence vehicles of three tons and over has gone up to $5\frac{1}{4}$ times, from 27,307 vehicles to 144,145 in the same period. In terms of tonnage these increases represent over one million tons being carried daily by C-licence operators.' (94th Report of the Trades Union Congress, 1962)

[2] Report of the 8th biennial Political Conference, 1962.

Committee, meeting on February 20, 1963, expressed 'dissatisfaction at their slowness in issuing a more detailed statement of policy. The 'view was expressed that the unions should get together and draw up a policy, if this was not forthcoming from the Labour Party in the near future'. In the Executive Report to the 1963 Annual Conference, an account was given of the correspondence on the future and on rail closures, which was described as 'disturbing, as it gave no assurance as to the future policy envisaged by a future Labour Government'. The report continued about the representations made on road haulage renationalization, stressing their concern during the past thirteen years, about 'the ever-increasing growth of C-licensed operations and its intrusion into the field of long distance haulage'. It concluded:

'We feel that if the Labour Party are to be assured of the support of the road transport workers at the next General Election, they must publicize their intentions on this very serious question. We are still bringing pressure to bear in an attempt to have the intentions made known.'[1]

It was perhaps a reflection of this anxiety which caused the Glasgow A, B and C branch to put forward a resolution that year demanding that when road transport was renationalized 'no compensation should be paid to the owner of any transport undertaking taken over'. This point, too, was pursued; and the Executive Committee decided to put down for agenda of the British Trades Union Congress, to be held at Brighton that September, a resolution which included the following phrase: 'It also calls upon the next Labour Government to refuse any compensation for the renationalization of road haulage.' This could not fail to attract attention. It was put down as an amendment to a composite motion and finally withdrawn; but Alex Kitson spoke about it in forthright terms. He regretted that they were considering merely a motion on a co-ordinated transport system 'instead of giving consideration to the policy that I feel should have been produced by Congress for the consideration of the trade union movement'. Since 1947, he pointed out, they had had an Act which had given the basis for a co-ordinated system until this was ruined by the denationalization Act of 1953:

'It is actually ten years since that happened, and today, both in Congress and the Labour Party, we are still awaiting a policy for a co-ordinated transport system.

'In fact, in Congress we have only started to discuss it. I think we are in a sorry state when we have, just over the hill, the signs of a Labour Government coming back, and we have no policy so far as transport is concerned.'[2]

[1] Report to Annual Conference, 1963.
[2] 95th Report of the Trades Union Congress, 1963.

He recalled that, in 1953, Herbert Morrison had warned the Conservative administration that the next Labour Government would renationalize road haulage and that 'he would not be paying twice for doing so'. Kitson then drew the important distinction between 'co-ordination' and 'integration'.

'Do not let us forget that the Tories believe in a co-ordinated system of transport. Marples has told the transport unions that. What they do not believe in is integration. Dr Beeching and the big haulage companies are talking of co-ordination. Indeed, they are negotiating it. The shareholders of one of the biggest haulage companies in this country, the Transport Development Group, with over 2,000 wagons, have been told about the negotiations by their chairman.

'In fact he has made it quite clear that his company is all in favour of road–rail co-ordination and co-operation, but are bitterly opposed to renationalization.'

That kind of co-ordination would not give the co-ordinated and integrated system they believed in; the private hauliers were only interested in the best-paying traffic, he said:

'When we talk about a co-ordinated system we include in that some regard for the social needs, and we hope that when the Labour Party discuss this, it will be from the viewpoint of social needs that they will examine it.'

When Frank Cousins replied for the General Council, he said that 'the Trades Union Congress endorses the view that compensation should be proper compensation and not improper compensation'. But, he concluded, 'we could not, and have not been asked now to endorse the principle of no compensation at all'.

The Association returned to their struggle with some stubbornness. At the Labour Party Conference in October 1963, they put in a motion which called for renationalization without compensation; for an inquiry into C-licence operation; and for a full survey of the nation's transport requirements 'following which a national transport plan designed to make the maximum contribution to the expansion of the economy and the needs of the community be instituted'. But when there appeared to be little response, and all were aware that a General Election would have to take place within twelve months, uneasiness increased amongst members. This was shown by the appearance of no less than five resolutions on the agenda of the 1964 Annual Conference.

The future of the industry was one of the major preoccupations of the most important 1964 Annual Conference at Dunoon. There were two factors which account for this. In the first place, throughout 1963, the Association had been seriously concerned with the state of the Scottish economy as one of the sponsors of the Scottish Project Committee. They were associated with the National Council of Inland Transport which had been opposing the Conservative Government's policy of reorganizing the publicly-owned railways in accordance with the lines of the white paper of 1960. It was popularly known as the Beeching Report, after the man whom the Government had employed to put it into effect. To carry it out meant that the criterion was what steps could be taken to make any given stretch of line pay its way, and not whether the railways should be run as a public service and whether this service could be improved. The main argument of the National Council of Inland Transport was that no rail closures should take place until a full examination of the whole of transport was made, together with a costing of the national road system and its maintenance. The Association's attitude, being far from sectional, was to give active support to this policy. But meanwhile closures were continuing not least in Scotland; and unless these were quickly brought to a halt, irreversible steps would have been taken and the policy of integration of all forms of transport would be made very much more difficult.

Here the second factor came into play. It was widely felt that only a change of government could stop the closures. A General Election was due during 1964 which could result in the return at last of another Labour Government, after thirteen years. Association members were therefore deeply concerned to know the Labour Party's plans in full detail. Would the former weaknesses of nationalization be avoided? Would the scope of renationalization be wider and take into account the great expansion of the recent years, and the intrusion of C-licence operators into long distance haulage? Would there be redundancy amongst drivers, as there had been for a time upon nationalization, and how would this be met? And, above all, how was renationalization of road haulage to lead into a comprehensive integration which was so long overdue? Nobody doubted there would be many problems and the strongest opposition from powerful interests. But transport workers, especially those in Scotland, regarded the subject as one requiring top priority. In their report to the 1964 conference, therefore, the Executive Council stressed their conviction 'that the integration of transport is the only means of solving this ever-increasing problem', and regretted that the Labour Party had not produced their plan nor 'given any indication of their intentions' in road haulage. About C-licence operation the Report declared: 'the uncontrolled issuing of this type of licence has created, and will continue to create, chaos in the industry and on the roads.'[1] As a contribution to a basic plan, the Report went on to outline five main objectives.

Firstly, the transport problem should be 'divorced from political doctrine' and immediate steps taken to integrate the existing forms of transport. Secondly, that while there was room for all forms of transport, they should be provided where they were most needed; and the aim should

[1] Executive Report to Annual Conference, 1964.

be an efficient system at low cost. Thirdly, transport users should be encouraged to guide the traffic to the most suitable form, with direction, if persuasion were unsuccessful. Fourthly, since extensive capital investment would be so great that it could be provided only by the state, immediate steps should be taken by the Government to finance the road and rail systems. Fifthly, assurances should be given that where a community needed services these should be maintained even if uneconomic. The report then faced squarely the question of sectional differences:

'For too long road and rail interests have been in conflict over types of traffic and have failed miserably to establish an economic co-existence. There is no doubt that both have a very important part to play in any transport system that may be established.

'There is no argument but that railways are most suitable for long distance passenger and goods traffic.

'To ensure that customers are using the most economic method, charges should be fixed taking into consideration all the direct and indirect costs.'

To protect the haulier against the competition of C-licences, there should be 'proof of need' before any further such licences were granted; in the course of time that would gradually confine C-licence vehicles to retail distribution. All contract licensing should be abolished and long term contracts made with the hauliers. The report concluded: 'A policy such as we have outlined is one of a long-term nature and is being pursued by the union through the Trades Union Congress and the Labour Party. In his presidential address, John Welsh added that he trusted that when the Labour Party were returned to power 'immediate steps would be taken to renationalize road haulage, without the liberal compensations that were lavished out in 1949'. He added that it would be 'their duty to ensure that the conditions which had been prevailing in the industry for thirty years and more were rectified'.

The four resolutions[1] on different aspects of transport policy were

[1] *Resolution 39.* 'This Conference of the Scottish Horse & Motormen's Association again reiterates the policy of its Executive Council on the question of an integration and co-ordination of all forms of transport essential to the needs of the country and criticizes the National Executive of the Labour Party for not putting forward details of its plans in this important aspect of policy'—Glasgow Scottish Co-operative Wholesale Society and Retail Branch.
Resolution 41. 'Conference condemns the present conditions of workers in the road haulage industry; and recognizing the fact that only nationalization of transport can resolve these conditions, Conference therefore demands that the Labour Party should declare its policy on transport now.'—Kilmarnock Branch.
Resolution 42. 'That this Conference calls on the next Labour Government to renationalize road haulage immediately it returns to power and where practical, without compensation. It also demands that an inquiry be embarked upon in connection with the operation of C-licences with a view to taking over all C-licences that are outwith retail distribution.'—Executive Council.

discussed on Wednesday, March 18, 1964. During the debate, there was some difference of degree and direction of emphasis. The Dumbarton delegate, Peter McGroarty, in moving resolution 39, said: 'It was the result of a conversation at a week-end school at Ayr, when an MP had been speaking on this subject and informed them so far as he knew the National Executive had no policy.' The Kilmarnock resolution No. 41 led to discussion on responsibility for overloading. The mover, Andrew Inglis, had noted the rapid changes in the industry, with large take-overs of transport firms, with nationalization under capitalist conditions, where 'smaller companies were now only able to exist by cutting rates at the expense of the workers within the industry'; thus vehicles were being 'grossly overloaded'. When McGroarty made the point that employees themselves sometimes overloaded the vehicles, and that some drivers 'did not care what union rules they broke', Inglis replied: 'We all know there are people who are not as trade union conscious as we are, but I do not think it fair to lay the blame on the people within the industry, as there are very few drivers who can tell their employers they are not going to do as instructed.' William Frew, the previous year's president, moved the Executive Council's Resolution No. 42, reminding conference that nationalization of road transport had always been the policy of the union irrespective of what party was in power. 'We should be fighting against the monopoly of capitalism,' he said, 'and we should have an integrated transport system.' In 1948, when the Labour Party were in power, they took over about 14,000 vehicles, but the figures of what was then paid to the hauliers could never be found: 'I have no hesitation in saying that no compensation should be paid to road hauliers when again they are nationalized.' When Ronald Kemp moved Edinburgh's Resolution No. 43, he said he thought it a failure by the Labour Party to put to the electorate that they intended to plan the economy and yet not have control of all forms of transport. The General Secretary wound up the debate, which he welcomed as 'one of the most important parts of the conference'. He said 'If we are going to have integration of transport, we must have some understanding on the workers' side of what integration means'. He concluded with these words: 'It was a disgrace that after twelve years, since denationalization took place, that we still had not formulated a policy within the trade union movement amongst the transport unions as to what we

---

Resolution 43. 'This Conference aware of the vital part all forms of transport play in assuring an efficient and expanding economy in this country (Britain) consider, to achieve or to attempt to achieve under socialist planning a productive growth in the economy without taking into public ownership the forms of transport which are ancillary to the national economy, namely rail, road, sea, air waterways and pipelines is unrealistic. Conference calls on the next Labour Government to take into public ownership all transport connected with or ancillary to the Labour Party's national plan for economic growth.'—Edinburgh Branch.

wanted in this industry and until we got this we would not get the integrated transport system which was so necessary to the economy'. All four resolutions were carried unanimously; the Association's policy on the future of transport in Britain had been stated beyond all doubt.

7. THE END OF A LONG RAKE

For many years the Association had had many of the characteristics of an old-fashioned friendly society type or organization, already becoming an anachronism with the development of 'the Welfare State', which had been demanded as part of the 'war aims' of the British working class during the Second World War. To transform it into a modern union, with a national and international outlook and policy, and, whilst keeping the old local links, and indeed strengthening them, never allowing them to become a chain or brake upon further advance, was a task which could not be accomplished by the chief officers and Executive merely conceiving this as a clear aim; but that was the first step. When the aim was seen as urgent and realizable as the sixties opened, practical steps began to be taken at once, as we have seen; remarkably rapid progress was made in effecting what many Executive members who had experience of the past described as 'a transformation'. Relations with the rest of the trade union movement in Scotland and elsewhere were vastly improved; the approach to and conduct of negotiations received a dynamic overhaul; the future of the industry was brought into focus, and the current problems related to policy in that respect. But most important of all, if the Association was to become a modern, streamlined, and progressive union with clear future aims as well as immediate steady achievement, was the task of establishing new relations between the leadership and the members. If negotiations were to become national in scale, then this called for more, not less, active participation in forming, adapting, and developing policy from the garage and depot upwards. To match a leadership sensitive to the need of every member in changing conditions, in an industry developing in uncontrolled leaps and bounds with complex new problems, there was needed a membership ready to show initiative, to keep a constant flow of information coming up to the leadership, self-disciplined and alert. The old attitude of 'Sit back and leave it to the leaders' was as useless if adopted by members as it was injurious in their leaders.

In the early sixties a useful start was made in restoring confidence in the Association from top to bottom. This was a necessary first step, but it could not alone solve the problems of creating a new and dynamic relationship. The considerable progress in negotiations brought members closer together and yet at the same time divided them. As members in British Road Services, for example, drew closer together in enthusiastic pursuit of the immediate needs and interests of this section, there could be a tendency for them to draw away from their fellow members in the local authority or co-operative sections. The needs of each of the many sections of transport workers clearly called for some degree of sectional organization; yet the government of the association and the determination of policy was in the hands of delegates to annual conference drawn from general branches of members on a geographical basis, in areas of uneven size and uneven distribution of sectional interests. This often resulted in an Executive Council where some sections of members were over-represented and others grossly under-represented. Such a situation militated against quick understanding and reaction to the needs of members; there could arise conflict of interests pursued by different sections overlooking the overriding needs of the members as a whole. Again, exclusive preoccupation with the affairs of garage, section or even commercial transport in itself could become a barrier to members playing their full part in problems affecting transport as a whole, or questions of general concern to the labour and trade union movement and to the British people. On such questions the Association must both inform and consult, at the same time both give and take a lead from all members. To illustrate how the Association was feeling its way forward in its seventh decade, we turn attention to three subjects: amalgamation and closer working with other unions; the development of schools and education in the Association; and finally, the new constitution which came into force in 1964.

At the British Trades Union Congress at Portsmouth in 1962, a resolution was passed about reorganizing the structure of trade unions. In principle the Association supported an examination of such a kind and in 1962 there were informal talks with the Transport & General Workers' Union. Finally, their General Secretary, Frank Cousins, Assistant General Secretary, and Scottish Regional Secretary met the Association's Executive at St Andrew's House in Ayr on February 16, 1963. It was exactly eighteen years after a former General Secretary, Ernest Bevin, had visited Scotland to try and persuade Hugh Lyon's Executive that they should amalgamate with the Transport and General Workers' Union:

'Mr Cousins put forward suggestions on closer unity and after lengthy discussions and questions on the subject, the T & GWU officials left the meeting.

'It was agreed by the Executive Committee to leave further discussion on the subject till a later meeting.'[1]

The view was that, although closer unity was possible and desirable between the two unions, any question of integration would need more study. Fourteen months later, when they reported to annual conference there was not much to add:

[1] Executive *Minutes*, February 16, 1963.

427

'We are of the opinion that an integrated trade union structure in this country should be achieved through a form of industrial unionism which would be in the best interest of the membership that we serve. However, it was decided that we should await the findings of the TUC proposals due to be discussed at the 1964 conference.'[1]

For months there had been discussions, conjectures and exchange of views throughout the trade unions and a number of amalgamations were in progress. In Scotland, opinions differed. It seemed to many that the advantage of the added strength of a large union to confront the employers, with road haulage becoming increasingly centralized with further development towards monopoly, was self-evident. Furthermore, it seemed to them that if the Association's policy was to insist that the future of the industry itself lay in integration under public ownership, then it was a logical step for the Association to favour integration of the trade unions' side. To others it seemed that the apparent strength of greater size might be offset by cumbersome machinery, slowness to understand and react quickly to local needs, lack of a high degree of organization and the compact punch of a progressive policy, which the Association by then enjoyed. Those who held this view instanced the Association's lead in the 'pay pause' strike of 1961, its insistence on voluntary machinery, its democratic policy and procedures. Others, again, were doubtful of the advantages of any general union, however large, over a union specializing in commercial road transport; they pointed to a lower level of organizing amongst their fellow English drivers. Some took a frankly Scottish point of view, that a driver's needs would be lost sight of once his organization crossed the Border. In his presidential address, John Welsh said:

'There had been rumblings in the movement regarding amalgamation, and he was not against closer unity, within the movement, but was not prepared to bury our identity unless the assurances were there to protect the members of this union. Personally he was a believer in industrial unionism, that is, an all transport union for transport workers, and had no doubt many of his fellow Executive Council members would agree with him.'[2]

Finally, the conference unanimously passed a resolution which was put forward by Glasgow Local Authority, giving the Executive authority to continue talks on closer unity:

'This conference of Scottish Horse & Motormen's Association, recognizing the need of the trade union movement to be co-ordinated and efficient in the rapidly changing conditions of modern industry, calls on the Executive Council of the SHMA to pursue a policy of examining every

[1] Executive Report to Annual Conference, 1964.
[2] Report of Annual Conference, 1964.

possibility of closer relationship with other unions in the transport industry particularly where integration or amalgamation may be in the best interests of our membership.'[1]

But although the door was opened for talks which followed in June 1964 between the Transport & General Workers' Union, the General & Municipal Workers, the United Road Transport Workers, and the Watermen and Lightermen, the Association's viewpoint on industrial unionism in the fullest sense was not accepted. Yet the Association remained willing, whenever occasion should arise, to seek ways of closer working with any grouping organizing all transport workers, whether by rail, road, inland and coastal waters, or air, both passenger and freight alike.

The Association in the past had not been slow to take up places offered in summer schools by the British and Scottish Trades Union Congresses, the Labour Party, the International Transport Workers' Federation, the National Council of Labour Colleges, and the like. Indeed, to be selected to go to these was to some extent regarded as a fruit of office. But whilst some were keenly sought after, and it was rare for a rank and file member to attend, others were less popular. Such vacancies were left to the Political Committee to fill. In 1957 it noted:

'provision of Labour Party Scholarship to attend 1957 Summer Schools had been advertised in the Association magazine, but that no applications received.

'Arising from this a lengthy discussion ensued in connection with ways and means to eradicate the apathy existing on political matters within the membership.'[2]

At the same meeting, finding the assets of the Political Fund had much increased, the question of representation in Parliament was raised. On this, John Brannigan minuted: 'It was felt that this was a matter that would require a great deal of organization, investigation, etc., before any action whatsoever taken with regard to same.' But, arising out of that discussion and about 'the education of the members politically, it was agreed that as an encouragement in the education of the members, a day or week-end school be organized by the Association to be held at St Andrews House'. After more than half a year had passed a week-end school was held in November 1957, at which the lecturer was Tom Fraser, MP, later to become Minister of Transport for a short term in the next Labour administration. Fifteen months later a second week-end school was held, on February 14, 1959 addressed by Ernest Davies, MP, another Labour Party spokesman on transport. Only those members who paid the political levy were eligible to attend these schools. They had become

[1] *Idem.*
[2] Political Committee *Minutes,* April 28, 1957.

stamped as schools confined to political questions, which limited their usefulness. The Executive decided in September 1959 to change the pattern gradually. In February 1960 a week-end school was addressed by Tom Oswald, MP, a member of the Transport & General Workers' Union, for whom, years before, Alex Kitson had served as election agent. The subject was 'The Trade Unions and the Labour Party and the work of a Member of Parliament.' All members of the Association were invited to apply for selection and the school was a great success. A month later the Executive Council's Report to the Annual Conference drew attention to the benefit which could be gained from week-end and day schools and made a recommendation:

'The Executive Council feel that this is a field that should be explored within our own organization and attempts made to run industrial week-end schools for our own members.'[1]

Considerable interest at once began to be shown in the idea of the Association running its own educational courses in addition to sending members to outside schools. Some branches began to organize their own; Aberdeen, Edinburgh, and Glasgow were early in the field. In Edinburgh, at their Political Committee which preceded the monthly branch meeting, they started holding talks on 'Why Trade Unionists should be members of the Labour Party'. This led up to a day school on May 22, 1960, attended by twenty-five delegates from four East of Scotland branches on 'Are Trade Unions Dependent on Political Action?' This school was taken by Jim McGrandle, the Scottish organizer of the Labour Party. Edinburgh then started a similar plan on the subject of local government. Glasgow followed the same course of action; and by the autumn they were running a course of fortnightly schools on 'The Shop Steward and His Duties'. A residential school was held in October at the Convalescent Home at Ayr on the subject of 'The Visit of the Union Delegation to Russia'. There were many more schools during 1961 and 1962, following up the resolution put forward first by Markinch branch in 1960:

'With a view to encouraging the younger members of the Association to become fully conversant with the working of our organization and equipping themselves for the purpose of advancing trade unionism generally, Conference suggests that week-end schools should be held periodically at St Andrew's House, Ayr, for this specific purpose.'[2]

Interspersed with week-end and day schools on shop stewards' duties, others were held on the European Common Market, economic planning, and an integrated transport system, as well as other topics, usually being led by Members of Parliament. These were so successful that the Executive

[1] Report of Annual Conference, 1960.
[2] Report of Annual Conference, 1961.

decided to hold a week's summer school in June 1963, at which scholarships for further education were offered for essays written after the school. These were won by Dan Duffy (Glasgow) and Ronnie Kemp (Edinburgh). The following year tutors at the week's school included Ministry and employers' representatives, whilst week-end schools were held on such subjects as nationalization, the Scottish economy, and the history of the trade union movement. This became the pattern of educational policy within the Association which was soon showing important effects. It was already 'paying dividends', the Executive noted in its report to the 1963 Annual Conference:

'The shop stewards' schools have stirred interest in many depots and garages that is assisting in making the membership more active. . . . The benefit derived from the schools is evident in the participation that students now play in discussion within the branches. It is most pleasing to see the reaction of the members who wish to gain more knowledge of the selected subjects.'[1]

The Association soon began to find lively and active young new recruits for officials and officers, full-time and part-time, at all levels. The schools policy was an important factor in establishing a new relationship between the leadership and the members.

It was becoming time for a new constitution in which the emphasis should be on a greater measure of democratic control, and for streamlining and modernizing the organization. The Executive Council decided that, at the 1964 Annual Conference, extra time would be allowed to discuss change of rules:

'As there had been no great changes to the Constitution for over 20 years, it was agreed on the motion of Messrs Murphy & Christie that a Rules Revision Committee be set up consisting of the chairman, the General Secretary and four others to recommend alterations to the rules, which would bring them into line with present day structures and conditions.'[2]

The committee, consisting of John Welsh, Alex Kitson, John Murphy, John Kyle, Willie Frew, and Alex Christie, met five times and finally presented their draft new Constitution to the Executive, which adopted it on October 23, 1963.

When the new constitution came before the 1964 Annual Conference the resolution adopting it was moved by Ronnie Kemp of Edinburgh, seconded by J. Shearer from the Executive Council, and was carried by fifty-four votes to two. The new constitution was registered on July 22, 1964, although not all its provisions came into effect before the following year. Six months later, in November 1964, the ninth biennial Political

---

[1] Report of Annual Conference, 1963.
[2] Executive Council *Minutes*, August 7, 1963.

Conference adopted change of rules which brought its administration fully into harmony.

The objects were altered to confine recruitment to 'the whole of the commercial road transport industry in Scotland and those connected with that industry'. The areas of the union were reduced from seven to five, equalizing the membership to about 3,000 in each area, from each of which one Executive Council member would come, except in the Glasgow City Area which would be entitled to two members. This would reduce the Executive Council from twelve to six members, each holding office for three years, two retiring each year; all would be nominated and elected in the branches. A major change was that instead of the Executive Council appointing one of its own number as President, in future he was to be elected by the branches, as would also the delegates to the Scottish Trades Union Congress. Even the smallest branch was entitled to one delegate, whilst larger branches could send an additional delegate for every 300 members to conference, which was in future to be biennial, alternating with the Political Conference. Benefits were reviewed and subscription rates adjusted.

These changes tended considerably to increase the measure of democratic control by members. One aim was to give a member in a sparsely inhabited area as effective equal rights as members in the great cities. At the other end of the scale the rearrangement of the Executive Council areas reduced the predominance of Glasgow and gave a fairer representation geographically. But one problem remained; the Executive Council was still not representative of all sections. Speaking on this point, the General Secretary said:

'The Executive was not truly representative of the membership we had at the moment. We had three British Road Services men, three from Local Authority, and three Scottish Co-operative Wholesale Society and Retail men on the Executive, amounting to 75% of the whole, and yet no representative from the brewery industry, or bakery trade, so it was not a truly representative body.'[1]

He had tried to encourage sectional meetings, which he felt had to come. The new constitution left the door open for this; the intention was to form trade sectional committees, which would allow of the fullest consultation with members. Each section would meet at least once a year to discuss their problems nationally; it was hoped that this would lead to national agreements where these did not then exist, as in road haulage and in bakery. Such a system of continuous consultation would be of great help to the officers in charge of sections, which it was thought would be likely to fall into such groupings as: Road Haulage and British Road Services; Local

[1] Report of Annual Conference, 1964.

Authorities; Retail co-operative societies and the Scottish Co-operative Wholesale Society; Bakery; Brewery; and Miscellaneous, which would include all under C-licence operation. The Executive was alert to the need to overcome the danger of sectional grouping having the effect of by-passing normal branch organization. The intention was to move towards sectional representation, step by step, judging from experience what would be most fruitful rather than to plunge in at once with a hard and fast scheme. Much stress was laid on quarterly meetings being used fully to discuss the union's national affairs and finance, and monthly branch meetings to continue to deal with local matters.

One change was made 'with deep regret'; no doubt it was especially a source of grief to 300 members in Edinburgh, who as horsemen were still delivering milk by cart. This was the change of name to the Scottish Commercial Motormen's Union. For when the President, John Welsh, 'declared Conference closed at 12 o'clock on Friday, March 20, 1964', the direct connection with the 'auld cairters' was broken at last, and the Scottish Horse & Motormen's Association came to the end of its last rake.

INDEX OF NAMES

GENERAL INDEX